# BEFORE MY HELPLESS SIGHT

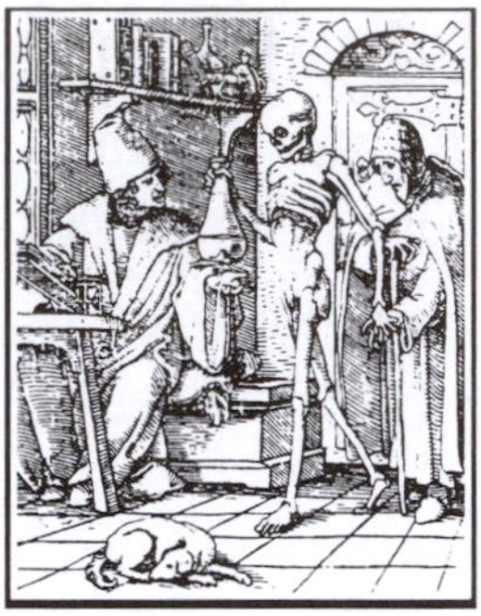

The History of Medicine in Context

Series Editors: Andrew Cunningham and Ole Peter Grell

Department of History and Philosophy of Science
University of Cambridge

Department of History
The Open University

Titles in this series include:

*Negotiating the French Pox in Early Modern Germany*
Claudia Stein

*Contraception, Colonialism and Commerce*
*Birth Control in South India, 1920–1940*
Sarah Hodges

*Crafting Immunity*
*Working Histories of Clinical Immunology*
Edited by Kenton Kroker, Jennifer Keelan and Pauline M.H. Mazumdar

*Maritime Quarantine*
*The British Experience, c.1650–1900*
John Booker

*The Great Nation in Decline*
*Sex, Modernity and Health Crises in Revolutionary France* c.*1750–1850*
Sean M. Quinlan

# Before My Helpless Sight

## Suffering, Dying and Military Medicine on the Western Front, 1914–1918

LEO VAN BERGEN
*Vrije Universiteit (Medical Centre) Amsterdam, The Netherlands*

*Translated by*
LIZ WATERS

ASHGATE

Originally published in Dutch as *Zacht en Eervol: Lijden en Sterven in een Grote Oorlog*, Antwerp/The Hague 1999. The translation of a completely updated version of this book from Dutch into English was undertaken by Liz Waters.

Published by
Ashgate Publishing Limited
Wey Court East
Union Road
Farnham
Surrey, GU9 7PT
England

Ashgate Publishing Company
Suite 420
101 Cherry Street
Burlington
VT 05401-4405
USA

www.ashgate.com

**British Library Cataloguing in Publication Data**
Bergen, Leo van
Before my helpless sight : suffering, dying and military medicine on the Western Front, 1914–1918. – (The history of medicine in context)
1. World War, 1914–1918 – Medical care 2. World War, 1914–1918 – Campaigns – Western Front
I. Title
940.4'75

**Library of Congress Cataloging-in-Publication Data**
Bergen, Leo van
Before my helpless sight : suffering, dying and military medicine on the Western Front, 1914–1918 / by Leo van Bergen.
p. cm. – (The history of medicine in context)
Includes bibliographical references and index.
ISBN 978-0-7546-5853-5 (alk. paper)
1. World War, 1914–1918–Casualties. 2. World War, 1914–1918–Campaigns–Western Front. 3. World War, 1914–1918–Moral and ethical aspects. 4. World War, 1914–1918–Medical care. 5. War casualties–Psychological aspects. I. Title.

D609.A2B47 2009
940.4'75–dc22

2008037954

ISBN 978 0 7546 5853 5

Mixed Sources
Product group from well-managed forests and other controlled sources
www.fsc.org Cert no. SA-COC-1565
© 1996 Forest Stewardship Council
FSC

Printed and bound in Great Britain by
MPG Books Ltd, Bodmin, Cornwall.

# Contents

# List of Illustrations

Whilst every care has been taken to ensure that each illustration has been reproduced to as high a standard as possible, the poor condition of many of the original items means that a number are less than perfect.

# Acknowledgements

I want to thank all those who have contributed to the writing, translation and publication of this book. Aside from all my current and former colleagues at the Department of Medical Humanities (Metamedica) of the VU Medical Centre in Amsterdam, there are several people who should be mentioned by name. They are, in alphabetical order: Hans Andriessen, Hans Binneveld, Joanna Bourke, Chrisje Brants, Kees Brants, Dominiek Dendooven, Tom Gray, Chris Grayson, Petra Groen, Mark Harrison, Onno van der Hart, Maureen Healy, J.M. Hollander, Bert Keers, Jaap van der Linden, Anthea Lockley, Marieke van Loon, Anniek Meinders, Rob Ruggenberg, Emily Ruskell, Jan Schoeman, Herman Simissen, Hubert van Tuyll, Dick Visser, Leon Wecke, Menno Wielinga and Jay Winter. Of course Liz Waters deserves special mention for the beautiful translation. Marleen and Charlotte I thank just for being there. They are my stillness and certainty in this wonderful chaos called life.

The Publishers would like to acknowledge the support of the Nederlands Literair Productie-en Vertalingenfonds (NLPVF), the Stichting Studiefonds Medische Polemologie (Researchfund Foundation Medical Polemology), Leersum, The Netherlands and the Van Coeverden Stichting, Vrije Universiteit Amsterdam, for generous contributions towards the translation costs of this book.

# Introduction

The following work is not the result of weeks or months spent in dark bunkers and damp cellars, leafing through old documents page by mildewed page in the hope of coming upon a remark that will throw an entirely new light on the subject and supersede all previous knowledge in an instant. In that sense it is not an original work. So what exactly is it? This book is an attempt to bring together in a single readable volume all the diffuse knowledge available in primary and secondary literature on the subject of war, and more specifically the military casualties that result from it and the medical treatment they may or may not receive. At the root of the book lies the question of what can happen to a soldier between the moment he steps onto a train or ship bound for the theatre of battle and the point at which he is evacuated wounded or, whether dead or alive, buried in the ground. I have attempted to provide an answer in five chapters – Battle, Body, Mind, Aid and Death – drawing on experiences from the Western Front of a vast conflict that the French, British and Belgians still today refer to as the Great War.

### The photo book *Krieg dem Kriege!*

In 1917–18 Wilfred Owen, the most famous of all British war poets, collected photographs of the dead and maimed, intending to publish them when the war was over. By telling the truth about the war he was fighting, he aimed to warn against any possible repeat.[1] Owen had quickly come to see war as an absolute evil, but he was convinced that only as a fellow combatant could he give voice to the sufferings of the soldiers.[2] He was prevented from fulfilling his self-imposed task by his death shortly before the armistice, and it was left to the German anti-militarist Ernst Friedrich to publish a collection of the type Owen had been planning. Friedrich's book, *Krieg dem Kriege!* (*War against War!*) appeared in the 1920s. The photographs portray the dead and wounded of a disastrous conflict that remains even now the archetype of modern, total war. People responded by saying the photographs were repulsive, but that only proved they were good photographs;[3] Friedrich had chosen them precisely because they were repulsive, and in any case the entire 1914–18 war had been repulsive.

Many people, including the historian Jay Winter, have argued that since the photographs in Friedrich's book were 'almost unbearable to look at' they

1 Verdoorn, *Arts en Oorlog*, 377
2 Day Lewis, *Collected Poems*, 27
3 Holmes, *Firing Line*, 59

inevitably missed their target to some degree. They were unlikely to convince anyone of the horrors of war; at best they might reinforce the views of those who no longer needed any convincing.[4] There is undoubtedly some truth in this, but *Krieg dem Kriege!* prompts us to contemplate how terrible the reality must have been if even its portrayal was unbearable. Reprinted at regular intervals, most recently in 2004, the book unquestionably helped to foster the peace movement, or perhaps more accurately the anti-war mood, of the 1920s and early 1930s. Between the wars many pacifists were convinced – wrongly, as soon became clear – that if people were shown the horrific side to war often enough, humanity would instinctively abandon it as a means of resolving conflict.[5] In the inter-war years in the Netherlands, which had been neutral in 1914–18 yet whose peace movement was the largest in Europe relative to its population, the organization *Jongeren Vredesactie*, or 'youth action for peace', made regular use of the photographs in *Krieg dem Kriege!*, along with a 1929 book derived from it called *Nie Wieder Krieg* (No More War), to underline the revulsion its members felt. The editors of a British counterpart to Friedrich's book, *Covenants with Death*, published in the early 1930s, likewise reasoned that revulsion would translate into aversion. Against the background of a decomposed corpse, T.A. Innes and Ivor Castle wrote on the front cover:

> The purpose of this book is to reveal the horror, suffering and essential bestiality of modern war, and with that revelation, to warn the nation against the peril of foreign entanglements that must lead Britain to a new Armageddon.[6]

The peace activists of the inter-war period endorsed Friedrich's view that his photographs showed people the truth about war. But was that in fact the case? Do photographs of men maimed in battle give the lie to all our stories about the heroism of military combat and the eternal comradeship born out of it? Simply showing the gruesome results of warfare, concentrating our attention solely on its victims, gives a distorted view. Indeed war has so many faces that any single image is a distortion. It is perfectly possible to select war photographs in which nothing is happening, with no sign of conflict at all. Behind such pictures, however, lies another story: an abandoned, totally empty battlefield – so typical of modern warfare but especially of the First World War, in which many men killed or were killed without ever seeing an enemy combatant[7] – is a horrifying sight to a fighting man, a contributory factor in the psychiatric problems suffered by soldiers.[8] The mental suffering and physical pain of men in battle, which come to the fore in this

4 Winter, *Sites of Memory*, 161; Liddle & Cecil, *Facing Armageddon*, 861

5 Addison & Calder, *Time to Kill*, 32

6 Innes & Castle, *Covenants with Death*, front cover; Van Bergen, *De Zwaargewonden Eerst?*, 353–5

7 Holmes, *Firing Line*, 146, 149–50

8 Holmes, *Firing Line*, 66

book, are only one aspect of modern warfare, but it is an important aspect, and one that has received less attention than it is due.

## Heroism alone

Owen and Friedrich were reacting against the time-honoured story portrayed in battle paintings, with occasional exceptions such as Goya's *Desastros de la Guerra*. It is a story told in our own time by the vast majority of war films,[9] in which the heroism of war is magnified while the horrors are deliberately veiled. Should anyone die – a film's leading characters are rarely killed – and should he afterwards appear on screen, he is likely to be fully intact in death. Headless or castrated corpses, burned or putrefying bodies, intestines hanging out of stomachs and severed arms or legs are notably absent from war films. The single leg suspended high in a tree in Mametz Wood, 'with its torn flesh hanging down over a spray of leaf', which Wyn Griffith saw before him for the rest of his life,[10] will not be encountered in most war films. Neither will the putrefying corpses prostrate in a trench in a First World War photograph with which, to the great displeasure of his sergeant, a friend of mine decorated his locker during his military service in the 1960s. The same goes for boots with feet still in them, described by both the Englishman Edmund Blunden and the German Hans Schetter.[11] Although categorized as war films, war is not their subject. A wounded character is likely to have suffered nothing worse than a bullet in the shoulder or leg. Apply a sling or a splint and the action can continue.

To a second, less numerous category belong films like *Saving Private Ryan* (1998). Full of extremely realistic images, they nevertheless help to revive the myth that wars are fought to combat tyranny and oppression, and that those who go into battle – in this case Americans to a man – sacrifice themselves willingly on the altar of freedom. Spielberg's film belongs to the same disagreeable tradition as, for example, *Stoßtrupp 1917* (Germany, 1934): realistically filmed; mythological in content.

This intermediary form brings us to a third category of films, those that present a far more realistic image of war, showing the filth, the destruction, the madness, the lies, the overblown pathos. They are called anti-war films, although some deliberately leave open the possibility that other wars may have been largely heroic or humane and so might more accurately be described as 'anti-this-particular-war films'. After listening to their parents' stories and watching successful movies like *All Quiet on the Western Front*, soldiers of the Second World War were able to anticipate the technological horrors that awaited them, yet most were convinced

9 Holmes, *Firing Line*, 62–3, 67

10 Holmes, *War Walks*, 141; Winter, *Death's Men*, 249; Holmes & De Vos, *Langs de Velden van Eer*, 141

11 Blunden, *Undertones of War*, 71; Macdonald, *To the Last Man*, 142

– perhaps in a defensive reflex – that 'their' war would not, indeed could not be anything like as bad as the war of 1914–18.[12] They refused to acknowledge that since the advent of mass conscription, since the collapse of the distinction between combatant and non-combatant, since appeal was first made to nationalism and other '-isms', since the military deployment of the industrial complex, in other words since the end of the eighteenth century, no war had been either heroic or humane. All modern wars are horrific, both to those with a duty to fight them and to anyone else directly affected. The horrors may be different in each case, but death and destruction have been the main feature of war from Austerlitz to Iraq.[13]

We may be prompted to ask why the young men of the 1930s once more, en masse, rushed to join their national armies.[14] Aside from the fact that conscription left them with no other option, part of the explanation no doubt lies in the fact that they, like the generation before them, felt a duty to fight the 'Great Evil'. Yet we should remember too that just as stories of comradeship and adventure are hard to resist, the stories of horror that evoked such dread and disgust had their own power of attraction. War fascinates. The children of veterans of Passchendaele dreamed of heroic roles in a battle their fathers told them had made any kind of heroism impossible. Take Philip Toynbee, a former peace activist who fought in the Second World War. In *Friends Apart*, published in 1954, he wrote:

> Even in our Anti-War campaigns of the early thirties we were half in love with the horrors which we cried out against, and, as a boy, I can remember murmuring the name 'Passchendaele' in an ecstasy of excitement and regret.[15]

Among a surfeit of wartime horrors from the late eighteenth century onwards, the First World War is unique only in that it was the first in which great industrial powers fought on both sides. The individual was lost in a maelstrom of modern, industrialized warfare. The war of 1914–18 was the first in which machine-guns, tanks, gas, aircraft and flame-throwers were deployed on a massive scale. It was also the first in which the telephone, although it often failed at crucial moments, allowed senior officers to operate from safety behind the lines. The proverbial bond

---

12 Addison & Calder, *Time to Kill*, 36; Hynes, *Soldiers' Tale*, 108; Kester, 'Het (on)gewapend oog', 5–25, 6

13 Whether it is possible to speak of humane or even heroic military exploits before the revolutionary and Napoleonic wars of the nineteenth century depends of course on how we define these terms. But with the possible exception of religious conflicts, the misery inflicted by the wars of the nineteenth and twentieth centuries was vastly greater.

14 An army is the largest unit of the armed forces. It is composed as follows: a section consists of 15 men; a platoon of 60; a company, led by a captain, of 250–300; a battalion (major) of 1,000; a regiment (colonel) of 2,000; a brigade (brigadier-general) of 4,000; a division (major-general) of 12,000; an army corps (lieutenant-general) of 50,000; and an army (general) of 200,000. In theory, that is. In practice, and especially if a conflict is lengthy, the numbers may well be smaller.

15 Hynes, *Soldiers' Tale*, 110

between the foot soldier and the high command was broken, indeed transformed into something close to animosity.[16] For this reason too, and despite the availability of a range of new, mechanized equipment, the First World War and the industrial wars that followed placed even greater demands upon soldiers than previous conflicts, especially in a psychological sense.[17] A 1918 issue of the French trench newspaper *Le Filon* described the soldier's lot:

> Fighting in a modern war means digging yourself into a hole full of water for ten days at a time without moving, it means watching, listening, gripping a grenade in your hand, it means eating cold food, sinking in the mud up to your knees, carrying your rations through the black night, going round and round the same spot for hours without ever finding it, it means being hit by shells coming from heaven knows where – *in a word, it means suffering.*[18]

## War and the individual

One slogan that has caught on in the more radical wing of the peace movement is that every war is a crime against humanity. Whether this can possibly hold true for all wars ever fought is doubtful at best; in some societies war, far from a crime, was a way of life. But when the First World War began it soon became clear that modern warfare in the West involved the dissolution of the individual human being. This began with drill, the tough, regimented exercise that preceded front-line duty, which army leaders regarded as essential for effective performance in battle. The deliberate attempt to strip soldiers of their individuality was to a great degree successful. In his novel *The Middle Parts of Fortune* (reissued only many years later but quickly published in a bowdlerized form as *Her Privates We*), British soldier Frederic Manning observed that soldiers no longer possessed anything, 'not even their own bodies, which had become mere implements of warfare'.[19] Manning's account deals with his own adventures during the First World War, and in writing about that war, fought mainly by very young men, historian Robert Weldon Whalen goes so far as to describe soldiers as children rather than adults. 'Like children, soldiers were totally subordinate to the will of their superiors, and took a childish delight in simple physical pleasures, like warmth and food. The soldier-child was not an autonomous, responsible adult, but a passive and helpless waif.'[20]

It is striking that in the years 1914–18 the disciplining of Commonwealth troops – Canadians, Australians and New Zealanders – did not assume anything

16 Fussell, *Bloody Game*, 29
17 Addison & Calder, *Time to Kill*, 378
18 Audoin-Rouzeau, *14–18. Les combattants*, 46
19 Manning, *Her Privates We*, 205
20 Whalen, *Bitter Wounds*, 188

like the drastic forms devised by the British. Yet soldiers of the Dominion forces were no less effective, in fact they are famed for their courageous, not to say reckless and daredevil performance.[21] If Julius Caesar had been born two thousand years later he would have proclaimed them, rather than the Belgians as in his *Commentarii De Bello Gallico*, the bravest men of all. Their armed forces were in fact more modern and democratic than the British army, whose roots lay deep in the nineteenth century, although their excellent record of service did not prevent the British from looking down on them to some degree.[22] We could be forgiven for wondering why these countries joined the war at all. They were no longer colonies. Only Newfoundland, now a province of Canada, was still technically a British colony in those years, and it had been granted self-government. Canada, Australia and New Zealand nevertheless decided to enter the war as soon as their former motherland, whose king was also their king, declared war on Germany.

The dissolution of the individual reaches its ultimate extreme during battle, as mental and physical catastrophe descend upon the soldier and increasingly upon the civilian. The First World War still provides the starkest examples of this kind of catastrophe. Even today it is used as a reference point, alongside the Second World War, in any discussion of contemporary conflict. In his book *First World War*, historian Martin Gilbert quotes a British journalist's description of the trenches in Bosnia in late 1993. They were reminiscent of the First World War, 'complete with mud'. The accompanying photograph shows a trench with very little mud, but ever since 1918 all trenches have been reminiscent of the First World War, and all trenches are supposed to be muddy.[23]

This book focuses on the individual soldier, so strategy and tactics receive less attention than in most accounts. The names of prominent generals and field-marshals like Von Falkenhayn, Von Hindenburg, Ludendorff, Haig, Plumer, Joffre, Nivelle and Pétain are conspicuous by their absence. Heated debates have arisen about their strategic and tactical thinking. Were they butchers who deliberately sacrificed human lives? Or did they feel genuine compassion for the men who died as a result of the tactics their leaders were forced to adopt? Some regard the generals as fools responsible for an endless series of blunders, men who refused to have any empathy for, or did not even bother to inform themselves about, the circumstances in which men had to carry out their orders. Others regard them as capable military leaders who, from a military point of view, made proper use of the means at their disposal and took decisions which, for all the consequent bloodshed, were necessary for the achievement of final victory.[24] These questions are of little importance to the subject under discussion here. Neither the generals, nor ordinary soldiers, nor 'the circumstances' were primarily responsible for the debacle. The blame lies with war, a more or less autonomous process that never

21 Winter, *Death's Men*, 48, 118
22 Brants & Brants, *Velden van weleer*, 125–6
23 Gilbert, *First World War*, XXI
24 Murray, 'West at war', 266–97, esp. 286–7

submits to human decision-making but forces decisions upon us. Human beings cause wars, people declare war, but at some point war itself becomes an active participant in its own drama, I am tempted to say the main participant. War does not allow those engaged in it to change its nature or direction as they see fit, let alone to make it stop. In the First World War this meant that the circumstances of the time – the massive firepower on both sides and the huge armies, impossible to protect during an advance – inevitably led to butchery. The mass slaughter would have taken place no matter which generals were in charge and no matter what decisions they made (and they made a great many different decisions).[25]

This book focuses primarily on the sick and wounded, but it also tells of the stretcher-bearers, nurses and doctors whose fascinating stories about the men they struggled to help have been indispensable sources. I hope it will become clear that no matter how admirable their efforts, their contribution often seems like the proverbial drop in the ocean. Indeed it often amounted to medical aid in name only. Men who survived artillery fire all too frequently fell victim to the scalpel.

## Who was the enemy?

Most ordinary soldiers had firm opinions as to whether senior officers were butchers or competent military leaders. Books like *Voyage au Bout de la Nuit* (*Journey to the End of the Night*) by Louis Ferdinand Céline and the war diaries of Corporal Louis Barthas make plain that not all officers were held in fond regard and staff officers behind the lines were often profoundly hated.[26] As time went on the average soldier began to wonder who his real enemies were. The men facing him from beyond no man's land? The well-fed generals in their spacious accommodation miles from the front? The politicians who allowed the war to continue? The industrialists, lining their pockets with the profits of war? Or civilians, who seemed incapable of understanding what war actually meant?[27]

There was undoubtedly much hostility towards senior officers, but as Peter Simkins points out in his *World War I: The Western Front 1914–1918*, anyone who blames Haig and Foch for the bloodletting of their 1916 campaigns must give them credit for the advance of autumn 1918 (although it too cost hundreds of thousands of lives). Aside from the fact that the reverse also holds true – Trevor Wilson remarks in his *The Myriad Faces of War*[28] that those who rightly give Haig some credit for the successful offensive of 1918 cannot excuse him his share of the discredit that attaches to the calamities of the Somme and Ypres – there are two further aspects that cast doubt on Simkins' assertion: the remarkably long-delayed

25 Keegan, *First World War*, 315–16, 337–42

26 Barthas, *Carnets*, 360; Ellis, *Eye-Deep*, 197–8; Wilson, *Myriad Faces*, 358; Bourke, *Dismembering the Male*, 146

27 Brants, *Plasje bloed*, 9

28 Wilson, *Myriad Faces*, 483

economic collapse of Germany and the collapse in morale that accompanied it,[29] and the deployment of fresh and well-nourished American troops, even if their initial effect was psychological rather than purely military. These factors were far more important than any brilliant incursions devised by the Allied military leadership, and plans for the advance were in any case modelled to a great degree on the German spring offensive of 1918. This was not just a war between two armies. It was also, some renowned commentators would say primarily, a battle between two economies. The Allies had taken the lead economically and once the United States entered the war it was impossible for the Germans and Austro-Hungarians to catch up. In his *History of Warfare*, British war historian John Keegan claims that the *Materialschlacht* (battle of munitions) known as the Great War could just as easily have ended in a German victory had the United States remained on the sidelines.[30]

Simkins goes on to say that those who look only at the horrors do an injustice to those who fought, endured great hardship, and ultimately gave their lives.[31] I would question this, but as I have said I am fully conscious that the war was characterized not just by suffering but by comradeship and courage. I am conscious too that by concentrating on death and destruction I am not presenting a definitive picture of war in general, not even of the 1914–18 war. If we concentrate exclusively on the horrors of any war, our general impression will be no less distorted than if we focus disproportionately on comradeship, for example, which Joanna Bourke, incidentally, in her excellent book *Dismembering the Male* unmasks as an illusory idealized image, the product of hindsight.[32] There was much heroism in the First World War and, of course, importantly, humour.[33] Charles Edmund Carrington, writing under the pseudonym Charles Edmonds, quite deliberately ended his *A Subaltern's War* with the words:

> It is important ... to remember that not only unpleasant emotions have thus been shared. If we have known fear and discomfort we have also felt courage and comfort well up in our hearts, springing from the crowd-emotion of our company, for even Active Service brings moments of intense happiness.[34]

---

29 Murray, 'West at war', 266

30 Winter & Baggett, *1914–18*, 210; Keegan, *History of Warfare*, 313, 365

31 Simkins, *World War I*, 219

32 Bourke, *Dismembering the Male*, 151–3; Also relevant here is Sebastian Haffner's tirade against comradeship, even though he wrote it in connection with the experiences of 1933. Comradeship does not merely mean that soldiers fight on, it is needed to get them to fight in the first place; it is fatal to any form of individualism and has nothing to do with friendship, is perhaps even incompatible with it. Haffner, *Geschichte eines Deutschen*, 265–72

33 Holmes, *Firing Line*, 74–5; Eksteins, *Rites of Spring*, 105–7; Hynes, *Soldiers' Tale*, 53–4

34 Hynes, *Soldiers' Tale*, 280; Liddle & Cecil, *Facing Armageddon*, 824–5

There were some sectors of the front where, although life may not have been pleasant, it was a good deal quieter than at Verdun in 1916, the Somme in the summer and autumn of that year, or Ypres at any time during the war. Sometimes there was even what was known as a 'live and let live system'.[35] Barthas gives a number of examples, with obvious approval, and according to Blunden it was one of the few sensible things about the war. Their soldierly satisfaction should not disguise the fact that this system, understandably, was a thorn in the flesh of the army leadership, which put an end to it despite the inevitable physical and psychological consequences for the troops.[36] Burial truces, and ceasefires for the retrieval of the dead and wounded, were held fairly regularly until unilaterally banned by the British high command in the spring of 1917 on the grounds that the enemy was treacherous by nature. The army leadership's success in enforcing the ban suggests that the live and let live system was not based on empathy for the opposing side. Hatred of the enemy, which arose soon after the outbreak of war, was strong and vibrant in these sectors too. The importance of the system, if it was ever truly that, should not be exaggerated. Before 1914 it was more the rule than the exception for the enemy to be given an opportunity to collect its wounded, but in the First World War casualties were deliberately shot at, and stretcher-bearers who tried to save them were by no means always spared. The truces that occurred from time to time were therefore less a sign of fraternization between men on opposing sides than the consequence of a shared wish to reduce, for a while at least, the generally astonishing level of violence.

The often cited fraternization between German and Allied front-line troops should be seen as a generalization based on isolated instances. There was certainly respect for the skill and courage of the enemy, along with recognition of and empathy for his sufferings and privations, which were similar on both sides. But respect, recognition and empathy are not the same as friendship. Enmity that often grew into frank hatred was the norm; fraternization was the exception that proved the rule, and however often friendly contact occurred, the dominant feelings towards the enemy remained abhorrence and fear. Most truces seem to have arisen in the absence of any direct threat. A reduction in danger meant a reduction in hatred. When the threat level rose, the dying and killing resumed, with just as much physical and psychological ferocity as before.[37]

The much vaunted Christmas and other truces should not distract us from the main feature of the First World War: its level of violence. In his generally excellent *The Soldiers' Tale*, Samuel Hynes writes that books full of endless suffering, the works of Robert Graves and Siegfried Sassoon for example, do not describe the war. Rather they are personal attempts to come to terms with a conflict the authors

35 Ashworth, *Trench Warfare*, passim; Keegan, *First World War*, 357–8; Glover, *Humanity*, 159–60

36 Barthas, *Carnets*, 355–7, 361; Blunden, *Undertones of War*, 154; Binneveld, *Om de geest*, 69–70

37 Ellis, *Eye-Deep*, 171; Audoin-Rouzeau & Becker, *'14–'18*, 47, 77, 151–2

had experienced at a personal level, so they describe the hangover after the war rather than the war itself. Although he is of course right to point out that not all soldiers were victims who suffered endlessly and passively before returning home bitter and disillusioned,[38] this is a slightly unfortunate remark, not least because a hangover is usually the consequence of an enjoyable, perhaps somewhat too enjoyable evening. Nevertheless, a hangover does not arrive without warning, however much fun went into getting it, and Graves and others describe suffering that undoubtedly originated in the realities of war. Graves certainly did not come to hate war. He was always proud of his years with the Royal Welch Fusiliers and extremely surprised to find his book, *Goodbye to All That*, categorized as 'anti-war literature'. A similar ambivalence emerges when we look at other supposedly anti-war writers: they criticized the war, but at the same time they were part of it and would not have had it any other way.[39]

Personal accounts by Graves and others did not prevent the thousands of anonymous soldiers who implemented the generals' strategy and tactics, the men who suffered as a result of the plans of the high command, all too often being forgotten amid a wealth of detail about the machinations of named staff officers, just as in many war documentaries the features of a weapon are treated as if they were an end in themselves, its qualities extolled at the expense of any consideration of its effects on the human body. To overstate the importance of strategy and tactics, comradeship and courage, and understate the horrors by giving a quick summary of the numbers of dead and wounded in a few final paragraphs, quite often leaving the sick out of account altogether, is likewise to do an injustice to those who fought and died.

No wonder Simkins' belief that to look only at the horrors is to fall prey to distortion is not shared by all historians. John Ellis, for example, wrote in a book to which he gave the expressive title *Eye-Deep in Hell* that we must never forget that this war was unparalleled in its cruelty and suffering, no matter how heart-warming its comradeship, how admirable its deeds of courage and self-sacrifice, how impressive its literary testimony. Books must indeed be written about these uplifting qualities, he says, but the soldiers will have died for nothing if we fail to emphasize that the Western Front was a four-year nightmare 'of filth, decay, noise, blood and death' such as had never been seen before. It was a war in which men fought 'for reasons they hardly understood, for a future they almost ceased to believe in, and which offered nothing when it came'.[40] Dutch battlefield expert Chrisje Brants writes in the introduction to her *Een plasje bloed in het zand* (A Pool of Blood in the Sand), 'They were years in which hope and idealism turned to despair and disillusionment, in which tens of millions of civilians were to discover for themselves what modern war meant and among soldiers alone tens of millions

38 Hynes, *Soldiers' Tale*, 105

39 Liddle & Cecil, *Facing Armageddon*, 821, 829

40 Ellis, *Eye-Deep*, 204

lost their lives.'[41] Perhaps influenced by Dalton Trumbo's novel *Johnny Got His Gun*,[42] she calls into question words that are often used without any real thought: 'honour', 'courage' and 'glory':

> What is honourable about drowning in mud or choking on your own saliva after a gas attack? What is courage and what is cowardice if modern artillery bombardments can reduce healthy young men to incontinent nervous wrecks? Where is the glory in being torn to unrecognisable shreds without ever laying eyes on the enemy?[43]

Jay Winter and Blaine Baggett, in their *1914–18: The Great War and the Shaping of the 20th Century*, wholeheartedly agree. 'There was nothing sacred about asphyxiating after a gas attack at Ypres, or being buried alive at Verdun, or being riddled with machine gun bullets on the Somme.'[44] Roger Chickering writes that the word 'hero' does not properly characterize the men. Soldiers 'were more aptly portrayed as the proletarians of industrial war, or as animals that burrowed into muddy labyrinths for shelter until they emerged – in what were called offensives'.[45]

Some commentators have gone so far as to compare the First World War with the Shoah: the same endless lines of people plodding towards almost certain death; men confined to a small stretch of ground surrounded by barbed wire, plagued by lice and disease. Keegan points out that accounts of the Somme produce much the same range of emotions as descriptions of how Auschwitz was run, and historian Omer Bartov said in his lecture 'Industrial Killing: World War I, the Holocaust, and Representation' that the Shoah, the foremost example of 'militarized killing', cannot be explained without examining the 'industrial killing' of 1914–18 that preceded it, 'the mechanized, impersonal, and sustained mass destruction of human beings, organized by states, legitimized and set into motion by scientists and jurists, sanctioned and popularized by academics and intellectuals'.[46] Perhaps these writers have in mind the words of one British poet on the eve of the Somme: 'It's going to be a bloody holocaust.' But this merely demonstrates that the word Shoah is a better term for the murder of six million Jews in the Second World War. There are even those who, consciously or unconsciously, regard the First World War as the more terrifying of the two, since those transported to the slaughterhouses were

---

41 Brants, *Plasje bloed*, 8

42 Trumbo, *Johnny Got His Gun*, 109–10

43 Brants, *Plasje bloed*, 9

44 Winter & Baggett, *1914–18*, 382

45 Chickering, *Imperial Germany*, 96

46 Keegan, *Face of Battle*, 255–6; Bartov, 'Industrial killing', 1; World War I, the Holocaust, and representation', http://www.anti-rev.org/textes/Bartov97a/index.html, 'Jahrhundert der Kriege', 112, 114, 115; Addison & Calder, *Time to Kill*, 353

not 'the enemy' but the nation's own sons.[47] The latter commentators in particular are clearly wrong. From any perspective, the soldiers of the First World War died in battle, the victims of the Shoah were murdered.

## The soldier as 'Hero'

During the war, of course, courage and honour were generally treated with great respect, at least when spoken of in public. The Battle of Langemarck on 22 and 23 October 1914, in which thousands of German boys with hardly any military training were mown down by rifle fire from highly skilled British professional soldiers, became the subject of mass propaganda in Germany. The students' deaths were proof of the noble, self-sacrificial, heroic character of the German people. They were said to have marched to their deaths singing '*Deutschland, Deutschland über alles*', later to become the German national anthem, which seems unlikely on account of its tempo and rhythm alone. They may have sung some other German song, if only, as George Mosse suggests in his book *Fallen Soldiers*, to avoid coming under fire from their own troops. The fervour was not universally shared, however. With their sceptical attitudes towards courage and honour, Brants, Winter and Baggett are in fact following a line taken at the time by an ordinary German soldier, Herbert Weißer, who in March 1915, two months before his death, wrote that the impression given in history lessons, in stories told by parents and in books was thoroughly misleading. Every soldier was given the honorary title 'Hero'; soldiers stopped being ordinary people, they were Heroes who performed Heroic deeds, spilled Heroic blood, died Heroic deaths and were buried in Heroes' graves.[48] A Hero's death should not be mourned, he had been told, since the *Volk* lived on through the death of each individual soldier, and the community was more important than the individual. A man died in a bodily sense, but his spirit, his courage, his deeds remained to inspire future generations. This was the soldier cult, the cult of the warrior who, even when wounded, looks fiercely into the distance, firmly clasping his rifle, determined to resist the enemy that threatens his home, his wife and children. The cult gave a man's demise on the battlefield a significance above and beyond mere death, an attitude that can also be seen, for example, among Flemish men whose comrades fell at the Yser. Their deaths would give new life to the battle to make Flanders a nation equal in status to Wallonia (the French-speaking part of Belgium), perhaps even an independent state. 'Through your death we are great! Through our struggle you shall live', wrote a fellow villager after the death of stretcher-bearer Lode de Boninge in May 1918.[49]

---

47 Koch, *Het begin van de barbarij*, 7 (column 4); De Schaepdrijver, *Taferelen uit het Burgerleven*, p. 70

48 Whalen, *Bitter Wounds*, 24; Mosse, *Fallen Soldiers*, 70–71

49 De Schaepdrijver, *Taferelen uit het Burgerleven*, 97

But, asks Weißer, were heroic deeds really the hallmark of warfare, were they truly its most prominent and characteristic feature?

> How much of a contribution is made to these heroic deeds by momentary, instinctive excitement, perhaps lust for blood and unjustified hatred? ... There are also very quiet, unrecognized acts of heroism. (Really so much more rare in times of peace??). And there are alcoholism, aesthetic and ethical brutalization, spiritual and physical laziness. When do people ever write about those in their war reporting?[50]

As already noted, hatred soon became a central feature of the war. It may even have been one of the main reasons why the vast majority of soldiers, despite the privations later accorded so much prominence, continued to approve of the war and doggedly fought on. Their hatred resulted in brutalization in battle, which developed no less quickly, fuelled in part by the increasingly ferocious written commentary published in all the belligerent countries, even prior to 1914. It was a process of brutalization completely at odds with a process far more frequently emphasized as characteristic of modern times: civilization.[51]

Anything that creates an impression can later lose its effectiveness. The hollow nature of war propaganda would be a constant theme of pacifist-tinted war literature, or rather literature labelled pacifist, after the conflict was over. Ernst Johannsen, author of *Vier von der Infanterie* (*Four Infantrymen on the Western Front*), on which the film *Westfront 1918* was based, claimed that during the war many soldiers regarded the term 'hero's death' as a mockery. In *Der Mensch ist Gut* (Man is Good) by Leonhard Frank, a woman tries to imagine what the 'altar of the fatherland' must be, on which she is told her son has been sacrificed. She cannot.[52]

Protest was naturally forbidden during the war, but how could the soldiers fail to speak out against all this, in some way or other? They had every right to protest, as they saw it, because it was they who had to endure the privations, they who were forced to kill or be killed. No amount of censorship and regulation could quash their protests, any more than it was possible to prevent 'sheep bleating at the gates to the abattoir', in the eternal words of the trench newspaper *Le Bochofage* on 25 June 1917.[53]

Nevertheless, there was no mass revolt in all ranks, at least not in the form of open protest. There were men who thrived on war and would always regard it as the best of times; some enjoyed it from the start,[54] while others were so deformed

50 Witkop, *Kriegsbriefe*, 82

51 Mosse, *Fallen Soldiers*, 162–33; Audoin-Rouzeau & Becker, *'14–'18*, 49–56, 139; Meire, *De Stilte van de Salient*, 32–3

52 Johannsen, *Vier von der Infanterie*, 36–7; Whalen, *Bitter Wounds*, 30

53 Audoin-Rouzeau, *14–18. Les combattants*, 71

54 Wilson, *Myriad Faces*, 755–6

by the war that they adapted to circumstances and began to find it pleasurable. Niall Ferguson, author *The Pity of War*, claims that this sense of pleasure may in fact have been the most important reason the war, despite all its misery, lasted so long.[55]

None of this should surprise us. War does not involve acts alien to human nature, and the aggression, the tendency to violence, which we probably all have in us to some degree, becomes, as Manning put it, an impersonal and incalculable force, a blind and irrational movement of the collective will, which cannot be controlled or understood. It can only be endured. War is a product of the characters of individuals. It distorts and exploits their personalities until eventually individuals no longer recognize themselves in the deeds they have performed, at the same time knowing that the war is part of them. As Manning wrote, 'a man might rave against war; but war, from among its myriad faces, could always turn towards him one, which was his own'.[56]

This does not alter the fact that only a few had fun, just as only a relatively small group hated the war with a passion. It has often been said that the vast majority felt neither joy nor rancour. Historian Denis Winter, author of *Death's Men*, says we should attribute this in part to the fact that most recruits were so young. They were not mature enough to assimilate their thoughts into a clear opinion about something as complex as war, with its endless torrent of sharply contrasting impressions. Bourke regards this middle group as the normal group, but she adds her own gloss. Most men felt guilty about killing one moment and intense pleasure in it the next. It was not 'normal' neither to hate the war nor to be having the time of your life. The normal reaction was both. A normal man both enjoyed the war and hated it; the two feelings existed side by side within him.[57]

## Victims and perpetrators

It will be clear by now that discussion of the dead, sick and wounded of the Great War has not been entirely lacking. The casualties appear in a number of books, some extremely perceptive, although in the bulk of accounts they are mere statistics, numbers that cannot speak.[58] There are only a handful of exceptions[59] to the general rule that where historians write about the victims of war they do so in a fragmentary way,[60] or briefly in a separate chapter,[61] or as one aspect of a

55 Ferguson, *The Pity of War*, 360

56 Manning, *Her Privates We*, 182; Wilson, *Myriad Faces*, 681

57 Bourke, *Intimate History*, 373; Winter, *Death's Men*, 226; Liddle & Cecil, *Facing Armageddon*, 823, 826–7

58 Verdoorn, *Arts en Oorlog*, 375

59 Whalen, *Bitter Wounds*

60 Winter, *Death's Men*; Brants & Brants, *Velden van weleer*

61 Ellis, *Eye-Deep*; Keegan, *Face of Battle*

study of the work of doctors and nurses.[62] They deserve better. The dead, sick and wounded are an integral part of any war, although not always to the same degree, if only because some wars are too short to produce the huge number of casualties seen in 1914–18. In the First World War, with its vast armies marching in serried ranks towards the machine-guns, military men, politicians, even ordinary men and women learned to see soldiers as units of calculation, as numbers rather than as human beings. This led to the notion, which soon found practical application, that whichever side proved able to take the highest losses would emerge victorious. This was to give the concept of 'victory' a meaning impossible to capture, even with reference to Pyrrhus.

At the same time we should not think of soldiers purely as victims. People occasionally speak of the 'innocent' army, but this is a reference to the generally non-belligerent middle class, the social stratum that produced the writers. Middle-class men joined up in their hundreds of thousands and had absolutely no idea what they were letting themselves in for. They learned very quickly, losing their innocence for ever, and in this sense it is right to describe them as a 'lost generation'. The twentieth century was the first in which soldiers could see themselves as victims rather than as agents or perpetrators. This was a consequence of the total helplessness of the individual in modern warfare.[63] In that sense they were indeed victims. But innocent, unwitting victims or not, the soldiers were also, indeed primarily, the active party. The shot precedes the wound. Although men caught in gunfire and shelling are central to this book, not dying but killing, sanctioned killing, is the main feature of war.

Most of the soldiers of 1914–18 went to the trenches voluntarily and those who recovered from physical or mental wounds often returned to front-line service, mainly out of solidarity with their comrades. After returning to the front in 1918, Owen wrote to his mother that he had gone 'to help these boys – directly by leading them as well as an officer can; indirectly, by watching their sufferings that I may speak of them as well as a pleader can'.[64] It was solidarity like this which caused men to follow orders that meant almost certain death, rather than fear of punishment, patriotism, or loyalty to commanding officers. The vast majority obeyed, aware that refusing orders meant betraying fellow soldiers by making their task even harder, and firmly confident of their own immortality.[65] Nevertheless, when faced with a chance to save their own skins, 'every man for himself' was an even higher command.

Solidarity with other men was not the only reason. Soldiers also fought out of a vague sense of duty, or simply because they had said they would fight, for

---

62 Van Bergen, *Waarde generaal*; Van Bergen, *De Zwaargewonden Eerst?;* Binneveld, *Om de geest*; Eckart & Gradmann, *Die Medizin*; Gabriel & Metz, *A History of Military Medicine*; MacDonald, *Roses of No Man's Land*; Verdoorn, *Arts en Ooorlog*

63 Hynes, *Soldiers' Tale*, 128

64 Howorth, Shell-Shock, 8

65 Wilson, *Myriad Faces*, 681

fear of the consequences if they stopped and, despite everything, faith in the military leadership.[66] Understandable as this kind of loyalty may be, we cannot ignore the fact that without it the slaughter would have been impossible to sustain, and therefore that they called it down upon themselves to some extent. Whatever happened, they were willing to carry on fighting, and that willingness kept the war going.[67] Men were not merely wounded and killed, they wounded and killed in their turn and, as will already be clear, not always with a heavy heart.

## The dead of the Eastern Front and the civilian victims

This book deals only with soldiers who died as a direct result of military violence. The dead on all fronts, for the full duration of the war, are estimated at between eight and ten million. In his book *Heeresbericht* (*Higher Command*), published in 1930, Edlef Köppen wrote out in full the number he reached by adding up the final totals per army: 'eight-million-two-hundred-and-fifty-five-thousand-five-hundred-and-thirty-four'.[68] A further limitation of this study is that I look only at the Western Front. One of several reasons for this is the entirely practical consideration that more facts are available about medical aspects of the war in the West. Furthermore, as medical historian Mark Harrison writes in 'The Medicalization of War – The Militarization of Medicine', since the nineteenth century, military doctors had gradually extended 'their influence within the armed forces by promising to improve morale and manpower efficiency', and it was on the Western Front in particular that 'medicine became an integral feature of military planning'. The French, British and German armies all 'developed sophisticated systems for the evacuation and treatment of the wounded' and 'severe manpower shortages and fear of a public backlash meant that governments and military commanders gave a much higher priority to the medical care of their troops' than in previous wars or at other battlegrounds.[69]

I also needed to consider whether research into the theatres of war in the Dardanelles and the East, in Italy and Africa, would produce much that was really new about sickness, death and injury to add to what could be gathered from the Western Front, apart from a huge increase in the bare statistics and a few relatively rare diseases specific to the East. It is important to add that at no stage did the war in the East reach the absolute impasse that characterized the Western Front for so long. The artillery played a smaller role and the cavalry a larger one, the use of gas was more significant in both military and human terms, and because of the racial

66 De Schaepdrijver, *Taferelen uit het Burgerleven*, 72

67 Andriessen, *De oorlogsbrieven van Unteroffizier Carl Heller*, 105–6; Eksteins, *Rites of Spring*, 176; Wilson, *Myriad Faces*, 361

68 Köppen, *Heeresbericht*, 462; Vondung, *Kriegserlebnis*, 264; Whalen, *Bitter Wounds*, 15

69 Harrison, 'The Medicalization of War – The Militarization of Medicine', 272

aspect the battles were often even more merciless and barbaric than in France and Belgium. Although in the war as a whole there were more deaths in the West than in the East – leaving aside other theatres of conflict – the Eastern Front was the most lethal in percentage terms, certainly in the first year of fighting.

Disease in particular took a heavy toll in the East. Epidemics, including malaria and typhoid (blamed, incidentally, on working-class Polish Jews) wreaked far more havoc than in the West. They were the main reason why deaths in the Serbian army reached 40 per cent and in the Romanian army around 30 per cent. Prisoners of war were not immune: 70,000 Austrian soldiers died in camps that lacked sanitation of any kind. The sufferings of prisoners continued long after the armistice. Spanish influenza tore through the camps like a scythe through dry grass and in early 1919 an epidemic of typhoid followed. Prisoners of war in the East were appallingly underfed, especially in Russian camps and – partly because of the blockade – those of the Central Powers. French and British prisoners received food parcels that alleviated the worst of their hunger, while the Romanians and Italians starved in their thousands.

In the armies of the Western Front, the mortality rate was considerably lower, at around fifteen per cent, but in the East the number of deaths fell after the first year, in absolute as well as percentage terms, whereas in the West the trend was upwards, until ultimately more blood flowed in the West than in the East. By the end of the war, more than half the men who had fought in France and Belgium were dead, wounded or missing.[70]

The desert war of T.E. Lawrence and the Arabs, the only First World War battle on land that is at all reminiscent of nineteenth-century warfare, with hand-to-hand combat and the cavalry as the deciding factor, is simply too small in numerical and geographical terms to be of any real significance to an investigation of this kind, and the same goes for the jungle warfare of the colonies.

All these are factors that would not apply were a book such as this to be written about the Second World War, for example. The differences between the Yser and Gallipoli in climatic, geographical and other conditions, and therefore in the nature of the fighting and the sickness and injury it produced, although considerable, are insignificant compared to the contrasts between Normandy and Iwo Jima, Leningrad and Hiroshima, Kursk and Midway, Arnhem and Stalingrad, El Alamein and Grebbeberg. A book along the same lines as this one but focusing on the Second World War might be impossible to write. The huge diversity of experiences of combat in the 1939–45 war makes it impossible to settle upon a single image, just as there is no single theatre that could be described as decisive. In part this may be a result of the fact that no arena of battle produced books

---

70 Holmes, *Firing Line*, 371; Winter & Baggett, *1914–18*, 77, 362–3; Whalen, *Bitter Wounds*, 40; Townshend, *Modern War*, 104; Vondung, *Kriegserlebnis*, 122, 129; Eckart & Gradmann, *Die Medizin*, 228, 234–5; Eckart & Gradmann, 'Medizin' in *Enzyklopädie Erster Weltkrieg*, 213; Moorehead, *Dunant's Dream*, 224, 270; Keegan, *First World War*, 215; Audoin-Rouzeau & Becker, *'14–'18*, 112

and poems like those of Ernst Jünger, Erich Maria Remarque, Ernst Toller, Henri Barbusse, Louis Barthas, Robert Graves, Siegfried Sassoon or Wilfred Owen. The portrayal of the Western Front by these writers has become fixed in our minds as an image of the 1914–18 war as a whole. But maybe it is simply the truth. Perhaps the First World War was a trench war above all and the Second World War has no Tollers or Owens because it was too large for them, too varied and complex, possibly also because it was the *Second* World War. This is not to say that we have no single established impression of 1939–45, only that it is cinematographic and photographic in nature rather than literary, and what we recall most powerfully are images not of the conflict itself but of the death and destruction it caused, and the racial murder that was integral to it.

This is one more powerful factor that persuaded me to limit my study to the Western Front. Even had the various theatres of war differed substantially in the type and quantity of sickness, wounding and death, it would still remain the case that our image of the First World War is defined by the Western Front. For many, myself included, the First World War means the front in Belgium and France. It means Ypres, the Somme and Verdun, not Tannenberg. It was in the West that the war began, was won and lost, and came to an end. The First World War is Versailles, not Brest–Litovsk.

One of the major differences between the two world wars is that it is perfectly possible to write a book about the victims of the First World War without considering civilian casualties. For the last time, far fewer civilians than soldiers were killed as a direct result of military operations. Leaving the Spanish 'flu out of account, one in five of the dead were civilians. If we look solely at the direct casualties of the violence, the proportion is one in twenty.[71] Were we to ignore civilian victims in any study of the Second World War, essential aspects of the story would be missing, even should we decide to exclude the Shoah on the grounds that it was not an act of war.

Nevertheless, millions of civilians became casualties of the 1914–18 conflict, some directly, most indirectly.[72] Among those directly killed were some 15,000 civilians lost at sea when their ships were torpedoed.[73] Belgian civilians were executed in revenge for the alleged activities of *francs-tireurs*. I say alleged, because it was frustration in the face of unexpected military resistance that led the German high command to terrorize the Belgian population in the early days of the conflict, rather than outrage at sniping by civilians, which was merely an excuse. Civilian snipers were rare and in many places unknown. Every stray shot, every instance of 'friendly fire' between German companies – which occurred quite regularly in the confusion – was attributed to *franc-tireurs*, and many people came to believe in their existence as a result. Perhaps the '*franc-tireur*-psychosis', as Luc Schepens calls it in his *België in de Eerste Wereldoorlog* (Belgium in the First

71 Bleker & Schmiedebach, *Medizin und Krieg*, 261

72 Gilbert, *First World War*, XV

73 Vondung, *Kriegserlebnis*, 122

World War),[74] was fostered by the fact that the Belgian army was inadequately equipped and aided by a uniformed militia – which was quickly stripped of its uniforms for this very reason. Yet the terror did have its *raison d'être*; it was intended to enable the Germans to adhere to their strategic plan. The German high command wanted to avoid a recurrence of the armed civilian resistance seen in the Franco-Prussian War. Many of the atrocities attributed to the Germans may have been exaggerated, but the stories had some basis in fact. Villages were burned to the ground, hundreds of local people were deported, and dozens, sometimes hundreds at a time, were summarily executed or killed by other means. This resulted in at least 5,500 civilian deaths in Flanders, fifteen hundred more than that in northern France. Tens of thousands were forcibly evacuated. The *furor teutonicus*, which would make itself felt so much more violently twenty-five years later, became a familiar concept.[75] It was not only German military action that cost Belgian lives; Belgian civilians were among the casualties of a British gas attack at Nieuport in early October 1916. Nor should we assume that the Germans had a monopoly on furor, which arises from a lethal combination of power and fear that can take hold of soldiers from any country in the world, making them thirst for blood.[76]

The Belgians suffered civilian casualties in the bombardments of Liège and Antwerp, as did the French during the bombardment of Reims in mid-September 1914.[77] Dutch journalist Alexander Cohen wrote of that bombardment, 'It was terrible and overwhelming. I watched as a poor man, a labourer, was mortally wounded before my eyes. His thigh was torn off, half his skull blasted away. Appalling.'[78] For the first time in history, bombardment was not limited to the maximum range of artillery. In the aerial bombing of London, for instance, a nursery school was hit and twenty children killed.[79] In Germany 768 civilians died as a result of Allied air strikes.[80] In the autumn of 1914, hundreds of citizens of Ypres were killed by German artillery fire, including one young girl whose leg was found several metres distant. Her other leg was smashed. Treatment at a French first-aid post could not save her and she bled to death, while a priest tried to keep her mother away to prevent her from seeing the condition in which her child was dying.[81] Injured civilians who were lucky enough to receive some kind

---

74 Schepens, 'België in de Eerste Wereldoorlog', 19

75 De Schaepdrijver, *De Groote Oorlog*, 78–85, 90–91; De Schaepdrijver, *Taferelen uit het Burgerleven*, 64–5; *Kriegsbriefe gefallener Deutsche Juden*, 105; Riemann, *Schwester der Vierten Armee*, 128–9; Townshend, *Modern War*, 17; De Vos, *De Eerste Wereldoorlog*, 35, 38; Heijster, *Ieper*, 57–61; Keegan, *First World War*, 91–3; Tuchman, *Guns of August* 173–4, 314–32; Audoin-Rouzeau & Becker, *'14–'18*, 82–6; Billstein, 'Gashölle Ypern', 105–8; Kammelar, Sicking & Wielinga, *De Eerste Wereldoorlog*, 47–57, 120

76 Richter, *Chemical Soldiers*, 145; Audoin-Rouzeau & Becker, *'14–'18*, 70–71

77 Winter & Baggett, *1914–18*, 64–6; De Schaepdrijver, *De Groote Oorlog*, 93

78 Spoor, *Tegen de Hollandse kleingeestigheid*, 31

79 Winter & Baggett, *1914–18*, 130–32

80 Chickering, *Imperial Germany*, 100

81 Macdonald, *1914*, 374–5

of help and found themselves in military ambulances were often taken not to the most appropriate hospitals but to the closest, whether or not the doctors there had the time or inclination to treat them. They simply had to be got out of the way as quickly as possible. Civilians could not expect much empathy or compassion from soldiers either. The British tended to regard the Flemings as pro-German, while local people saw their allies' stubborn determination to hold on to Ypres as the cause of the destruction of the city and region they loved.

In 1914 American nurse Ellen La Motte began to write a book about her experiences nursing tuberculosis patients. She had moved to Paris in 1913, so she was one of the first American nurses to care for the war wounded. She joined a front-line surgical unit near Ypres run by Mary Borden, under French command. Borden was another of the thousands of American volunteers, but unlike La Motte she was not a professional nurse. Borden published an account of her war experiences in 1929 under the title *The Forbidden Zone*, but La Motte's book, no less dark and certainly no less valuable and well-written, appeared in the thick of it all, in 1916, as *The Backwash of War: The human wreckage of the battlefield as witnessed by an American hospital nurse*. She described the case of a Belgian boy taken by a British ambulance to a Belgian hospital, so that he would not take up valuable space in a British military infirmary, and in doing so she makes clear that the relationship between the people of Flanders and their British allies was not always particularly warm.

> As soon as he came out of ether, he began to bawl for his mother. Being ten years of age, he was unreasonable, and bawled for her incessantly and could not be pacified. The patients were greatly annoyed by this disturbance, and there was indignation that the welfare and comfort of useful soldiers should be interfered with by the whims of a futile and useless civilian, a Belgian child at that.[82]

Bombardment was not the only danger faced by people in towns along the front such as Ypres, those who had not already fled. The local population near the front line suffered repeated epidemics of diseases including typhoid, the result of poor sanitation and the shortage of clean drinking water, made worse by the presence of masses of refugees. Medical aid was scarce and often reserved exclusively for soldiers.[83]

We should remember too that violent deaths occurred even when there was no fighting. Working parties had to be sent out to collect weapons left behind after a battle and to clear unexploded munitions from the territory that had been gained. About a thousand men a month died this way.[84]

---

82 La Motte, *Backwash of War*, 63–4, 67; Cardinal et al., *Women's Writing*, 159; Higonnet, *Nurses at the Front*, Introduction, ix, xiii; Meire, *De Stilte van de Salient*, 63, 66

83 Macdonald, *1915*, 177–8; Macdonald, *Passchendaele*, 86–7

84 Macdonald, *Somme*, 193

There were casualties on the home front too, where women performed war work. Explosions in munitions factories – for example at Fürth in the spring of 1917 and shortly thereafter in Cologne – killed dozens.[85] Many women suffered the physical consequences of extremely unhealthy working conditions. Some became infertile. Graves saw the corpse of a man who had gone down to inspect the sewers near a weapons factory and was gassed by accidentally released chemical vapour.[86] Women in weapons factories should not be seen purely as victims, however. The remarkably perceptive Wilfred Owen wrote several days before his death, at the time of the British and American advance that would finally lead to the armistice, that at that very moment, shells made by women in Birmingham were burying small children alive not far from where he stood.[87]

The fact that work in munitions factories and other tasks were performed by women, who replaced men as they left for the front, was one reason why many of them welcomed the war despite the death toll among husbands, sons, brothers and friends. At last they could put their talents to use. They finally had a chance to play a full part in what they called an 'All man's land', a place that during the war they sometimes seemed happy to experience as a 'No man's land' or 'Herland', populated entirely by women.[88]

The majority of civilian casualties were caused indirectly. Some thirty million European civilians died of starvation and disease in 1914–18.[89] It is important to bear in mind that not all deaths from hunger or sickness in wartime were a result of the fighting, but many were. The privations suffered by German and Austrian civilians were partly caused by the Allied sea blockade. In Vienna the poorer segments of the population began dying of hunger in 1917. Towards the end of the war, state support for families left without an income by the absence of a breadwinner amounted to less than two slices of bread per day. In Germany few died from starvation as such – most who did were hospital patients not expected to recover, who were therefore of no further use to the war effort – but within about a year of the start of hostilities, German civilians began to succumb to illnesses linked to malnutrition, among them more than 140,000 psychiatric patients. The impact steadily increased. In the last winter of the war, around three-quarters of a million German civilians died as a result of wartime privations, barely fewer than would be killed by Allied bombing in the Second World War.[90]

---

85 Winter & Baggett, *1914–18*, 130; Chickering, *Imperial Germany*, 116

86 Graves, *Goodbye*, 217

87 Day Lewis, *Collected Poems*, 177

88 Higonnet, *Behind the Lines*, 204, 214, 216, 225

89 Winter, *Death's Men*, 204

90 Gilbert, *First World War*, 256, note 2; Barham, *Forgotten Lunatics*, 145; Horne, *Price of Glory*, 190–91; Toller, *Jugend in Deutschland*, 75; Townshend, *Modern War*, 13–14; Keegan, *First World War*, 344; Glover, *Humanity*, 65–6; Weindling, *Health, Race and German Politics*, 281; Hofman, 'Oorlog aan het thuisfront', passim; Lerner, *Hysterical Men* (2003), 129

Pre-war Germany imported a large proportion of its food. Much came by ship, so a blockade was an extremely effective weapon. Food supplies immediately fell by a quarter. The quantity and quality of the food available were drastically reduced and the prices of staple foods rose dramatically. Harvests failed when artificial fertilizers could no longer be supplied and livestock numbers fell for lack of concentrates. Then there was the fatal *Schweinemord*, a huge reduction in pig stocks by mass slaughter, based on the argument that pigs were consuming all the grain. Pigs in fact ate hardly any of the grains intended for human consumption, and they did produce manure. For a short time there were plentiful supplies of pork, but in the longer term food production was reduced to even lower levels. The amount of food reserved for front-line soldiers was disproportionate, which indicates that the blockade, regarded by the Germans as a war crime and proof of the inhumanity of the French and British, was not solely responsible for the misery that cost an estimated 1,000,000 Germans their lives. The German war economy too, devoted to an even larger extent than the British and French to the production of munitions, played an important part in their deaths.

The German government concluded in 1917 that each citizen needed an absolute minimum of 45 marks a month to buy sufficient food. Many incomes were already falling short, and the war would last another year. In 1918 the average German adult lived on only 1,000 calories a day, half the basic requirement. Female mortality in 1914 was 11.2 per thousand per year; by 1918 it had risen to 17.8. For French males aged 59 or under in the years 1914–17 (which excludes the year of the Spanish 'flu), what are known as 'excess deaths' – in other words the actual number of people who died in a given year minus the number of deaths that would have been expected – were 6.5 per cent, 7.5 per cent, 0.5 per cent and 1 per cent respectively. For German males they were 3; 0.5; 8 and 21. The figures for French females were 5; 8; 3 and 2.5, whereas in Germany they rose relentlessly: 2.5; 4.5; 11.5 and 30.5. Pneumonia, tuberculosis and other illnesses associated with cold and hunger took a massive toll.

It is striking that mortality among babies did not rise in the war years. Perhaps the falling birth rate made it possible to reserve just enough for infants to eat and drink. Children aged between 5 and 15, however, became chronically sick and died in droves, perhaps partly because in a war economy the health of children was regarded as the responsibility not of government but of private charity. If we set the rate of childhood deaths in Germany in 1914 at 100, then by 1918 it had risen to 190 for boys aged 5 to 10 and 215 for boys aged 10 to 15. For girls aged 5 to 10 it was a little over 207 in 1918 and for girls aged 10 to 15 almost 240. This demonstrates that the shortages hit some harder than others. A similar imbalance can be seen between rich and poor, and between urban and rural populations. Those who had money or lived on the land did not go hungry, but the women and children of the poorer urban classes, with husbands or fathers at the front, were unable to cope. Towards the end of the war the problem became so acute that soldiers at the front saved food, from their own extremely meagre rations or from captured Allied stockpiles, for relatives at home. The armistice brought no respite. The Germans had made the lifting of the sea blockade a condition of their capitulation, but the Allies refused to comply.[91]

This kind of suffering among the civilian population was not confined to Germany. In the final months of the war especially, when the German high command regarded Belgium purely as conquered land to be exploited for the war effort, the privations of the Belgians became acute. Hunger and cold claimed many lives in the last two winters of the war, largely because it became almost impossible to import food. This was partly the result of unlimited submarine warfare – several ships were sunk despite flying flags reading 'Relief for Belgium' – and partly because the British refused to lift their blockade even to help the Belgians. Hunger marches were common. The periodic famines of the nineteenth century had returned. The deportation of men who met minimal medical criteria – and even those who did not – caused further suffering. Many would return with wrecked constitutions, if at all.[92]

In the Balkans there was a huge exodus of Serbian refugees in 1914 and again in late 1915. Many died. Dutch doctor A. van Tienhoven, who would later serve on a committee set up to investigate Austrian war crimes, wrote an account of his medical work for the Serbs. He included photographs that would not have been out of place in *Krieg dem Kriege!*, published ten years later.

> The starving wretches trudged on day and night, and fell to the ground exhausted. How many children must have died on this *via dolorosa*? The parents would dig a little pit and mark the grave of their loved one with a cross of two tree branches. I've seen hundreds and hundreds of them, those simple twig crosses, like so many indictments of the horror of war.[93]

Within six months of the outbreak of war, more than 200,000 Serb civilians succumbed to typhus. And of course we should not forget the Armenians, victims of the first genocide of the twentieth century. The massacre may not actually have been caused by the war, but the war was the impetus for it and made it possible. Up to a million and a half Armenians are thought to have been killed.[94]

---

91 Whalen, *Bitter Wounds*, 71–3, 77–8, 97; Chickering, *Imperial Germany*, 40–43, 102; 140–46; Heijster, *Ieper*, 100; Keegan, *First World War*, 344, 448; Macdonald, *To the Last Man*, xxiii; Holmes & De Vos, *Langs de Velden van Eer*, 118; Weindling, *Health, Race and German Politics*, 288–9; Audoin-Rouzeau & Becker, *'14–'18*, 88

92 De Schaepdrijver, *De Groote Oorlog*, 219–22, 228–30, 233; De Schaepdrijver, *Taferelen uit het Burgerleven*, 84–5

93 Tienhoven, *Gruwelen van den Oorlog*, 98

94 Winter & Baggett, *1914–18*, 144–53; Verdoorn, *Arts en Oorlog*, 364; Tienhoven, *Gruwelen van den Oorlog*, 98–107; Heijster, *Ieper*, 157; Eckart & Gradmann, *Die Medizin*, 228

Then there were the millions who lost their struggle with Spanish influenza, an epidemic that cost more lives worldwide than the war itself.[95] The Spanish 'flu meant that for many soldiers who had survived the conflict both physically and mentally, the suffering did not end on 11 November 1918. They arrived home to find that people they had been forced to leave – wives, girlfriends, children, parents, brothers, sisters, friends – had died of influenza. Corporal O.W. Flowers said later: 'To think I'd gone the four years without a scratch except a bit of gas, and got to the end of the war and then to lose her. ... By the time I got home she'd been buried three days.'[96] This raises questions about the connection between the influenza epidemic and the war, which we shall deal with later.

The voracious requirements of the medical services responsible for treating wounded and sick soldiers had a disastrous effect on civilian health care. Many civilians died of diseases they could just as easily have contracted in more prosperous times but which they might have survived had adequate help been available. To take Germany as an example: of the 33,000 doctors available on the eve of war, 26,000 (1,300 of whom would not live to see the end of the conflict) were sent to serve in military hospitals, along with some 12,000 dentists and pharmacists. Of those 26,000, only about 2,000 were serving as army doctors when war broke out. Even if we leave aside those who were medical officers in the reserve, 17,000 doctors were removed from the general health care system – or in many cases removed themselves from it, since doctors believed that in wartime their place was at the front and in military hospitals. This resulted in a ratio of one doctor per 5,800 civilians, whereas before the war there had been roughly one per 1,500.[97]

The same picture emerges with regard to the more than 200,000 nurses who came to the aid of the German armed forces. Some were volunteers, men and women who had not been active in the medical sector before the war, but many others came from civilian hospitals and medical institutions. This assumes even greater significance when we consider that they all focused their attention on men aged eighteen to forty, a social group least likely to visit a hospital in normal times. Perhaps this helps to explain why many medical practitioners have such vivid memories of their time in war hospitals. Not only were the wounds new to them, they were dealing with patients of a quite different type.[98]

Germany was not alone in this. In Britain the problem was less urgent, since 'only' 45 per cent of doctors joined up, resulting in a ratio of one doctor to 2,350 inhabitants where the norm had been 1,300, but in France no fewer than eighty per

---

95 Macdonald, *Roses of No Man's Land*, 287

96 Macdonald, *1914–18*, 316–17

97 Eckart & Gradmann, *Die Medizin*, 11–21 (article: Ingo Tamm, 'Ein Stand im Dienst der nationalen Sache'); Weindling, *Health, Race and German Politics*, 283; Jenssen, *Medicine Against War*, 16

98 Bleker & Schmiedebach, *Medizin und Krieg*, 15, 262; Winter, *Death's Men*, 200–201

cent of doctors went to the front or to military hospitals, so that of a total of 22,000 only 2,500 were left to serve 35.5 million civilians, an average of one to 14,000. Naturally they were not evenly spread, so whole regions had to manage throughout the war without any professional medical care at all. Where medical services were available they were often useless. The pharmacies were empty. Medicines had been removed along with the doctors. The health of the civilian population was clearly less important than that of the troops, as illustrated by the battle against tuberculosis. From the outbreak of war almost the entire bed capacity of France's TB clinics (desperately inadequate to begin with) was reserved for soldiers. No beds at all were available for women and children.[99] In 1917 America too began to deplete its civilian medical services, and those doctors and nurses who neither volunteered nor were forced to join the army tended to be the least competent.

This left a final total of around forty million deaths among soldiers and civilians, and many millions more suffered permanent physical or psychological damage.[100] To this day there are occasional fatalities as a result of explosions caused by First World War munitions, with dud shells, bombs, mortars and grenades still hidden in fields and woods all along the front.[101] It is even possible that without the First World War the war of 1939–45 might never have taken place, if only because the peace negotiations at Versailles were a triumph of hatred over reason, retribution over reconciliation, and power politics over idealism. No one studying the causes of the Second World War can afford to ignore Versailles. The treaty was not really a peace treaty at all. It was the prelude to a new, terrible and even more spectacular symphony of death,[102] although in recognizing the legitimacy of German resentment at the *Versailler Diktat* we should not forget that the treaty made by Germany with Russia in March 1918 could hardly be described as any more fair and just.[103]

### Animal suffering

The sufferings of cavalry horses, for example, were almost indescribable. The pain caused to animals is not the subject of this book, but it undoubtedly contributed to the mental sufferings of soldiers. The sight of a wounded horse, and perhaps even worse the *sound* of a wounded horse, was harrowing in the extreme. Alan Hanbury-Sparrow described the order received during the retreat from Mons to give wounded horses the *coup de grâce* as 'perhaps the most senselessly savage order ever issued by the staff'. Graves grew used to the sight of human corpses,

99 Eckart & Gradmann, *Die Medizin*, 343–64 (article: Lion Murard & Patrick Zylberman, 'The Nation Sacrificed for the Army?'); Barry, *The Great Influenza*, 143

100 Keegan, *History of Warfare*, 50; Winter, *Death's Men*, 204

101 Keegan, *Face of Battle*, 205

102 Winter & Baggett, *1914–18*, 321, 338–41, 347–8

103 Murray, 'West at war', 288

but he was shocked every time he saw a dead horse or donkey. For Lieutenant J.W. Naylor the most depressing image of the war was of six horses, startled by an explosion, veering off the road and down into the mud of the Ypres Salient, that bulge in the front line where the British faced German troops on three sides. They sank faster and faster, wagon and horses disappearing within minutes. Norman Gladden heard one horse bellow horribly with pain as it ran across the battlefield with its entrails hanging out of its gashed stomach. He was more shocked by that sight, by that 'protest against man's inhumanity', than by all the other images of that afternoon's nightmare that burned themselves into his memory.

Martin Gilbert calculates that in the years 1914 to 1918 more than half a million horses died violent deaths, drowned, or succumbed to sickness and exhaustion. This may be a conservative estimate. At St Jude on the Hill in Hampstead stands a monument to the 375,000 horses that died in the war on the British side alone.[104]

Horses were even killed by biological warfare. Germany sent glass vials of plague bacilli, packed in soap, to Argentina, Spain, Romania and the US to infect the horses and mules intended for sale to the Allies for war service. This was a perilous business in terms of international law, since Spain and Argentina were neutral countries throughout the war, and Romania and the US for a good part of it. On the Eastern Front biological warfare against animals was waged directly. But although Russian units were depleted by drinking water contaminated with cholera, in 1914–18 human beings were spared deliberate bacterial infection. The head of the section involved in attempting to infect animals advised against it, and a certain Dr Winter, who suggested to the German war ministry in 1916 that plague bacilli should be scattered across London, was reprimanded. 'With all due respect for your patriotism, if we take such a step we will no longer deserve to exist as a nation.'[105] The question will always remain: might the chemical horrors have been accompanied by their biological counterparts if someone had been able to convince political or military institutions that biological weapons could be aimed solely at the enemy, without infecting friendly soldiers and civilians, and lead to final victory?

## Atrocity propaganda

The British, for example, felt no particular hostility towards Germany, indeed rather more towards France, and the effort to change this gave rise to what became known as atrocity propaganda. This is another aspect of the war that will not be dealt with here, at least not explicitly. Crucified Canadians and Germans, children

104 Macdonald, *Passchendaele*, 188; Graves, *Goodbye*, 173; Dearden, *Medicine and Duty*, 153; Holmes, *Firing Line*, 106; Gilbert, *First World War*, XX; Dyer, *The Missing*, 44–5; Frey, *Pflasterkästen*, 249–50

105 'Rotz und Milzbrand', 55; De Vos, *Van Gifgas tot Penicilline*, 19; De Vos, *De Eerste Wereldoorlog*, 107

with their hands chopped off, raped nuns or impaled pregnant women have no place in this book. Nor do such documents as a letter published in the British periodical *Comic Cuts*, supposedly written by a German soldier, in which he writes to his wife Greta that he has 'bayoneted seven women and four young girls' in the space of five minutes.[106] It is important to add that there was not in fact any 'propaganda' in the strict sense of the word. No fabricated stories were distributed by the military and political authorities with the aim of fuelling hatred for the enemy and thereby strengthening the will to fight. Propaganda consisted of stories that arose among the ranks of soldiers and civilians, and were sincerely believed by them. Perhaps such tales had a greater and more subtle impact for this very reason, but although neither distributed from above nor deliberately invented, their effect was nevertheless to deepen the gulf between the two sides, increasing the hatred and making the fighting even more horrific.[107] In other words, the victims featured in propaganda were mythical, but the victims of propaganda were all too real.

## The war at sea and in the air

One final lacuna in this book concerns the casualties of the naval and air wars. In some ways the dilemma here is similar to that already discussed in the context of the many different theatres of the Second World War and the focus on trench warfare that characterizes so many accounts of the 1914–18 conflict. In contrast to the Second World War there were relatively few dead and wounded at sea and in the air. Of the more than two million German men in the armed forces who died, only about 35,000 were sailors. This is of course partly due to the fact that the navies of the First World War were tiny in comparison to the land armies, but sailors were also fighting a totally different kind of war and had a comparatively good chance of surviving. Whereas around one in eight soldiers died and one in four were wounded, in the navies the mortality rate was one in sixteen and in the air forces one in fifty. The proportion of sick and wounded was a tenth that of the ground forces.[108] This last statistic is easy to explain. The lives of sailors and airmen were not particularly unhealthy, and where should we look for the wounded? If a ship was torpedoed and sank, the passengers and crew were drowned, save for a few extremely fortunate individuals; if a plane was hit, the pilot died.[109]

Aerial battles and desert warfare provided the First World War with its handful of individual heroes. In the post-war years the cult of the hero underwent a transition. It no longer applied to every soldier, the anonymous soldier, the unknown soldier,

106 Winter, *Death's Men*, 209; Heijster, *Ieper*, 59; Holmes, *Firing Line*, 389; De Schaepdrijver, *Taferelen uit het Burgerleven*, 66

107 March, *Company K*, 115–16; Winter, *Death's Men*, 211–13; Liddle & Cecil, *Facing Armageddon*, 226–7, 326; Guéno & Laplume, *Paroles de poilus*, 46

108 Whalen, *Bitter Wounds*, 41; Vondung, *Kriegserlebnis*, 122

109 Winter & Baggett, *1914–18*, 134–8

but to a few famous characters whose names were known to all, like Canada's Billy Bishop and Germany's Manfred von Richthofen, the Red Baron. These were names that made hearts beat faster and after the war men longed to emulate them. The anachronistic nature of the desert war and the futuristic nature of the air war, in which the enemy was known by name and honoured in death by friend and foe alike, meant that even after 1918 warfare was still bathed in an aura of romanticism. An airman could look his opponent in the eye. If he won, it was down to his own courage and skill. If he lost, it was because his opponent had outclassed him. Air 'ace' Cecil Lewis writes about the ground war with a sense of horror. At least he did not have to sit in a muddy trench 'while someone who had no personal enmity against you loosed off a gun, five miles away, and blew you to smithereens – and did not know he had done it!'[110] Lewis, and many others like him, believed that because modern warfare did not fit the myth of the personal, heroic battle, bound by rules and dominated by horses and bayonets, it was not war at all, it was murder.[111]

Just how far removed the world of the airman seemed from that of trenches and battlefields was illustrated by Billy Bishop, who sat in his plane watching an attack on Arras in early 1917, across territory covered in virgin snow.

> No-man's-land, so often a filthy litter, was this morning clean and white. Suddenly over the top of our parapet a thin line of infantry crawled up and commenced to stroll casually towards the enemy. To me it seemed they must soon wake up and run; that they could not realize the danger they were in. Here and there a shell would burst as the line advanced and halted for a minute. Three or four men near the burst would topple over like so many tin soldiers. Two or three other men would come running up to the spot from the rear carrying stretchers, pick up the wounded or dying and slowly walk back with them. I could not get the idea out of my head that it was just a game they were playing at. It all seemed so unreal. … It seemed that I was in an entirely different world looking down from another sphere on this strange, uncanny puppet show.[112]

## The misery was universal

Another point that may occur to the reader is that this book places a slightly disproportionate emphasis on British suffering. This has nothing to do with any personal bias on my part; it is a straightforward consequence of the material available. More has been published about the British and their Great War than

---

110 Hynes, *Soldiers' Tale*, 87; Keegan, *First World War*, 386–7, 435; Bourke, *Dismembering the Male*, 25; Bourke, *An Intimate History*, 59; Meire, *De Stilte van de Salient*, 75

111 Bourke, *An Intimate History*, 67

112 Winter, *Death's Men*, 185

about the French, Belgians or Germans. It was not at all my intention to make British suffering more apparent than any other. I focus on all those who suffered in the war, irrespective of nationality. Moreover, the surplus of British material means not only that the British dead and wounded appear slightly more frequently than others, but that the less attractive side of the British war effort receives additional emphasis, its 'friendly horrors', to paraphrase one of the euphemisms with which military jargon is replete. I am thinking, for example, of the much more frequent occurrence in the British army than the German, or even Britain's 'own' Dominion forces, of death sentences passed for actual or supposed cowardice.

Ultimately the imbalance in the quantity of material available seems of little importance. When Remarque's *Im Westen nichts Neues* (*All Quiet on the Western Front*) was published, many British soldiers exclaimed, 'That's what it was like!' (although a few unimpeachable individuals such as Edmund Blunden fiercely disputed this).[113] The experiences of British subjects described in the following must surely have closely matched those of soldiers in other armies, no matter in which section of the front they were fighting: French or Austrian, Russian or Turk. After the war, contrasting political, social and economic circumstances led to sharply contrasting reactions, but that is a separate issue. While admitting that he could never fully explain, even to his own satisfaction, why it was so, Bartov wrote that although they may have fought similar wars on the Western Front in 1914–18, French and German responses to it in the post-war period were vastly different.

> At the risk of somewhat over-generalising a highly complex phenomenon, I would suggest that for large sectors of the French population, coping with the traumatic memory of the First World War was only bearable as long as it remained in the past, never to be re-enacted; while for a growing number of Germans, the unbearable memory of defeat and socio-political upheaval could be overcome only by re-enacting, and thereby 'correcting' it in a future confrontation. ... In Germany, we might say, the dead increasingly *scolded* the living for giving up the fight, while in France they constantly *warned* the living against thinking of ever repeating it.[114]

In this book I describe a small part of the total, horrific experience of soldiers who served on the front line between 1 August 1914 and 11 November 1918, voluntarily or not. I see their sufferings as illustrative of the horrors confronted by all those exposed to war. To paraphrase Owen: my subject is war, and the horrors of war. All a historian can do is describe, and yet, as Paul Fussell remarks in his book *The Great War and Modern Memory*, the suffering of the trenches and battlefields of 1914–18 was more horrible than any description provided then or in

113 Liddle & Cecil, *Facing Armageddon*, 814

114 Addison & Calder, *Time to Kill*, 353–4

the decades that followed could suggest.[115] Private Daniel J. Sweeney wrote to his fiancé Ivy: 'I cannot tell you the horrors of this war.'[116] German Lance-Corporal Gotthold von Rohden noted in mid-1915, two months before his death, that attempts to enumerate the losses suffered by various battalions amounted merely to a naked depictions of events, 'and what terrible perceptions of the human soul they contain! Things all the books in the world have not the power to convey.'[117] They are right. I am fully aware that I have not succeeded in conveying even a small part of the horror.

Leo van Bergen

115 Fussell, *Great War*, 174
116 Fussell, *Bloody Game*, 49; also: *J'accuse*, 297
117 Witkop, *Kriegsbriefe*, 121

# Chapter 1
# Battle

## Introduction

### *Changes on the eve of war*

The years leading up to the First World War saw huge change in a wide variety of fields, many of them crucial to the business of war. The European nation states built extensive rail networks, enabling them to move large bodies of troops up to a battle-front quickly. Military offensives became easier to organize, as did defensive consolidations, even though the more traditional means of transport that took soldiers from the rail-head up to the line remained vital and often caused delay.[1] The numbers involved were huge. In the second half of the nineteenth century conscription was reintroduced in almost all European countries, most of which had abandoned it after the Napoleonic Wars. The ease of mobilization and the growth of armies made management essential, requiring the introduction of general staffs.[2] The disadvantages of this would become apparent in wartime; the absence of commanding officers fighting alongside their men and inspiring them widened the gulf between the ordinary soldier and his general.

Armies were equipped with more and better weaponry. During the Napoleonic Wars one artillery piece had been fielded for every hundred soldiers; by 1914 the number had risen to six, each capable of twenty times the rate of fire, while infantry weapons had eight times the rate of fire and ten times the range. By 1914 a company of 300 men could deploy firepower equivalent to that of the entire 60,000 strong army commanded by the Duke of Wellington at the Battle of Waterloo.[3] Wilhelm Lamszus, author of *Menschenschlachthaus. Visionen des Krieges* (*The Human Slaughterhouse: Scenes from the War That Is Sure to Come*), published in 1912, realized after watching a military exercise that a future war would bear no resemblance to 1870–71. ‘It is as if death’, he wrote, ‘had thrown his scythe onto the scrap-metal heap and become a machine operator.’[4]

This kind of firepower was of course very expensive, but money was available. Military expenditure had remained fairly stable for many years, but it rose dramatically in 1912–14, actually doubling in Germany’s case. This is not to say

---

1 Binneveld, *Om de geest*, 25–6; Strachan, ‘Military Modernization’, 80–81; Preston, ‘Great Civil War’, 150

2 Strachan, ‘Military Modernization’, 81–2, 87

3 Binneveld, *Om de geest*, 30, 42–3; Strachan, ‘Military Modernization’, 69–71

4 Vondung, *Kriegserlebnis*, 101

that the Germans were spending more per head of population on their armed forces than any other nation. That honour went to Great Britain, but British expenditure was concentrated on the navy, which would play a relatively minor role in the coming war.[5]

Bigger armies with improved firepower expanded the battlefield enormously. Paradoxically, despite being part of a larger force, an individual soldier's view of a battle, limited at the best of times, became even more restricted. He could see nothing but emptiness or chaos. When war came, millions of soldiers would be killed by an enemy they had never laid eyes on, even though he was sometimes extremely close.[6] Battles were longer, too, lasting several months rather than a few days, and they followed each other in quick succession, since seasonal factors were becoming less important in deciding when to fight or cease fighting, and the necessary reserves could be brought up promptly and in ever greater numbers.[7] Breaks between battles were quiet in name only. Every lull in the fighting involved elements of combat and therefore fear. There was never a complete respite. To say all was quiet on the front could mean that a day had passed on which only a couple of thousand men were killed instead of ten thousand.[8]

At the same time, the battlefield became deeper. In earlier wars a man could often observe the fighting without too much risk to himself; now he was safe only several miles from the front. Ernst Jünger described a group of soldiers killed by a shell as they swam in a stream a long way behind the lines.[9] In this sense too the First World War was a new type of conflict. In all ages men have been forced out of hearth and home and onto the Procrustean bed of a disciplined army, had their wills channelled by rigid restrictions, been compelled to eat whatever was served up to them and to sleep wherever they were ordered to lie down, taught to kill and destroy in ways strictly forbidden to them as civilians. But the entirely realistic fear that they could be killed at any moment made the First World War a much harsher test than any conflict before it, even for men enjoying excellent physical and mental health.[10]

All this led to a huge increase in death and destruction in battle. In the nineteenth and twentieth centuries as a whole, wartime casualties fell steadily in percentage terms as tactics were adapted to changing circumstances, but there were cyclical exceptions to the structural trend, and practically all the battles of 1914–18 were among the exceptions.[11]

The main problem was that while the advantage lay with the defending armies, only offensive action could bring victory. As a result, two weapons and

5 Strachan, 'Military Modernization', 73; Herrman, *The Arming of Europe*, 237
6 Keegan, *Face of Battle*, 258
7 Binneveld, *Om de geest*, 55
8 Addison & Calder, *Time to Kill*, 374
9 Jünger, *In Stahlgewittern*, 123
10 Winter, *Death's Men*, 130–31
11 Binneveld, *Om de geest*, 47, 52

one instrument came to typify the Great War: the heavy guns deployed by the artillery, the machine-guns carried by the infantry, and the surgeons' scalpels. In many ways the war of movement of the first few months had more in common with Napoleonic battles of a century before than with the butchery that occurred a short time later at Ypres. People came out to watch the troops going off to war. Bringing up the rear of each battalion as it marched through Belgium and France in August 1914 were a handful of machine-guns and a couple of medical officers. They would soon demonstrate how much war had moved on. The machine-gun quickly became a dominant battlefield weapon – each German or British battalion had one or two in August 1914 and between twenty and thirty by 1918[12] – while medical services grew to unprecedented levels. War and medicine, destruction and repair, barbarism and progress were soon discovered to be opposite sides of the same coin. The machine-gun and the scalpel exemplified the fact that all those developments that had been such a boon to humanity in the preceding century – advances in transport, production, communications, technology and health care – could be used in pursuit of total destruction. French doctor and writer Georges Duhamel provided an apt description of the field hospital he worked in by calling it 'the first great repair-shop the wounded man encounters after he leaves the workshop of trituration and destruction that operates at the front'. A highly technical civilization was restoring what it had itself destroyed. In Duhamel's view the Great War was a consequence of the use of science and technology without compassion or humanity. On an unprecedented scale, science, previously regarded as neutral, objective and self-consciously international, had placed itself at the service of national war efforts, both in the laboratory and in the mechanisms by which propaganda was disseminated. Philosopher of history R.G. Collingwood was a wartime member of Admiralty Intelligence and after the war ended he was one of the men put in charge of preparations that led up to the Treaty of Versailles (an outcome that he regarded as a failure). He fulminated against the way the word 'civilization' was interpreted predominantly in terms of natural science:

> The War was an unprecedented triumph for natural science. Bacon had promised that knowledge would be power, and power it was: power to destroy the bodies and souls of men more rapidly than had ever been done by human agency before. This triumph paved the way to other triumphs: improvements in transport, in sanitation, in surgery, medicine, and psychiatry, in commerce and industry, and, above all, in preparations for the next war.[13]

12 Ellis, *Social History*, 113–16; Bastier, 'België tijdens de Eerste Wereldoorlog', 24

13 Collingwood, *An Autobiography*, 89–90; Duhamel, *Civilisation*, 266; Van Raamsdonk, 'Nawoord', 200; Eckart & Gradmann, *Die Medizin*, 109; Winter & Baggett, *1914–18*, 348; Otterspeer, 'Wetenschap', 100–101

The sheer number of shells that flew across the skies of France and Belgium between 1914 and 1918 was immense, and artillery became the paradigmatic weapon of modern warfare. The British alone fired some 170 million shells. Shortly before his death at Frianville in March 1915, German soldier August Hopp reacted to the almost constant torrent of explosives by saying that you could no longer tell one explosion from another. The entire hill before him was like a mountain spewing fire.[14]

The artillery seemed perfectly suited to support an attacking force. Heavy guns could destroy enemy positions from far behind the lines and the lighter field guns could knock out machine-gun posts and individual riflemen. It quickly emerged that this was merely an appealing theory. The many rolls of barbed wire laid in front of enemy positions could be fired upon, certainly, but even when blasted to pieces they remained a serious obstacle. The trenches themselves were narrow and dug in a crenellated or zigzag pattern, so shells that did not land precisely on target had almost no effect at all. Methods of determining the exact position of a target had grave limitations. Aerial photography was in its infancy, and although it improved greatly as the war went on, it remained a makeshift business, aside from the fact that the weather was by no means always favourable for taking pictures. Even if artillerymen had good photographs, weather conditions were often too poor for any use to be made of them.

Artillery fire, were it to have the effect the army leadership was hoping for, would have to be extremely accurate and the gunners properly trained. Neither was the case. Although they had a devastating impact at Liège, Verdun, the Somme and Passchendaele, the masses of shells fired before every battle repeatedly failed in their allotted task: the destruction of enemy positions before troops started to advance. Ahead of their attack along the Menin Road during the Third Battle of Ypres in 1917, the British managed to deploy 300 artillery pieces and 500 field guns, with stocks of 3.5 million shells available. They consumed almost half the ammunition before battle commenced, but German artillery was left largely intact.

Even had this been otherwise, even had the targets been visible and the shells fired with precision, a still more colossal quantity of shells would have been needed to knock out enemy troops and destroy their defences. Despite the huge industrial muscle mobilized to bring immense quantities of shells to the front, supplies of ammunition were never sufficient. The front line was simply too long. The number of heavy guns and shells on each side was tiny in relation to the miles and miles of trenches that would have to be destroyed.

There were attempts to resolve this by having troops advance while a protective torrent of shells fell ahead of them: the creeping barrage. Here the problems of lack of precision and inadequate communications came into play. Many shells fell short, exploding amid the troops rather than ahead of them, so that men were

14 Witkop, *Kriegsbriefe*, 36

killed by their own side. They called it being hit by 'a friendly', a characteristically ironic expression that gave rise to the term 'friendly fire'.

Everyone hoped that the industries that produced such formidable defensive weapons would find solutions to meet the needs of attacking forces, but in the end neither gas nor primitive tanks proved the answer to the problems the generals faced; they were helpful additions to existing weaponry but not the key to unlocking the stalemate. Only in the final few months of the war, during the Allied advance, would technical advances in tank design lead to the manufacture of armoured fighting vehicles of military importance.[15]

*The dominant military ideology*

All this was compounded by the fact that the prevailing mind-set was not defensive. Before the war there was an overwhelming faith in attacking manoeuvres, particularly among the French, although the Germans and British were almost equally convinced. The French army had suffered a crushing defeat in 1870 and the strategy the army adopted to boost its image – dented afresh by the Dreyfus affair – was called *l'attaque à outrance*, the 'total offensive' or 'infantry assault to the utmost', a strategy that was to cost hundreds of thousands of lives. What the enemy did was immaterial, the thinking went; it was his location that mattered. The army must not cede an inch of ground. The bayonet was of greater importance than the machine-gun. Heavy artillery would only get in the way. The last remnants of caution in the British *Field Service Regulations* of 1905 were omitted from the 1909 edition. A battle could be decided only by a ruthless and uncompromising attack.[16] Any officer who recognized the disadvantages of this strategy and expressed his misgivings had little chance of promotion.[17]

This emphasis on the infantry assault is understandable up to a point. Although the American Civil War had demonstrated the impact of technological warfare on body and mind, brilliantly described by Eric Dean in his *Shook Over Hell*, it had been a conflict between two relatively unprofessional armies. No one studying the American Civil War could have predicted what would be achieved by putting new technology in the hands of trained soldiers. Any lessons that might have been learned from the subsequent rapid victories of Prussia over Austria and the German States over France were quickly and substantially downplayed. In the years that followed there were no battles, aside from a few colonial wars, from which a more realistic picture could have been derived. The majority of commentators felt that the most recent major conflict, the Russo-Japanese war of 1904–1905, had proven

---

15 Prior & Wilson, *Passchendaele*, 8–9, 11–13, 15, 17, 82, 117, 174; Macdonald, *Somme*, 217; Eksteins, *Rites of Spring*, 144–5; Ellis, *Eye-Deep*, 62; Keegan, *History of Warfare*, 309; Keegan, *First World War*, 439

16 Holmes, *Riding the Retreat*, 48

17 Brants & Brants, *Velden van weleer*, 172–3

yet again just what morale and manpower combined could accomplish.[18] We are left to wonder whether they merely saw what they wished to see.

There were some dissenting voices. The enormous increase in firepower in the decades before the war led one German general to warn in 1912 that even minor success in a modern conflict would inevitably cost a great many lives. Almost twenty years earlier, Polish banker Ivan Bloch had warned that the prevailing faith in the frontal assault was extremely dangerous. Firepower was now so fearsome that the advantage would lie with the defending side, as the American Civil War had taught. It was a lesson reinforced by the Boer War a couple of years after the publication of Bloch's six-volume work *Der Krieg* (*The Future of War*). He nevertheless agreed with those who believed the next war would be short, not because victory or defeat would be rapid but because no country could possibly bear such enormous losses of men and *matériel* for long. In this respect he too was wrong.

Such voices were too few to convince a majority of the military leadership in any country. The 1907 edition of *Cavalry Training* states that although the rifle is an extremely effective weapon, it counts for little against the speed of the horse, the power of the charge, and the terrifying effect of good old cold steel. This type of attack would of course cost lives, but it would be decisive, and a short, bloody war was preferable to a conflict that dragged on for years. Although surely defensive firepower had sometimes decided the outcome of engagements in the recent past, there had as well been occasions in recent military history when battles were won by the cavalry. It was not true that the American Civil War had proven otherwise, the manual claimed, since its cavalrymen lacked proper training, and the Boer War had been an abnormal war in a far off country that offered no lessons for a European conflict. Besides, the next war was certain to begin with a large-scale confrontation between cavalrymen, so they would need to be extremely well trained. Questions about the effectiveness of a cavalry charge in future warfare, however justified, were therefore theoretical.[19]

### *The war*

Even had more realistic conclusions been drawn from previous wars as to the ultimate effectiveness of successful defensive fighting, it is doubtful whether the tacticians and strategists of the First World War would have seen them as relevant. In contrast to all previous conflicts, both sides on the Western Front were highly industrialized. It was perfectly reasonable to argue that although in the past infantry assaults had been unnecessary, since all either side had to do was to wait for a chance to mow the other side down, there could now be no victory without an attack. If both sides remained in their trenches, the war would last until the end of time.

18 Strachan, 'Military Modernization', 76–7, 82; Townshend, *Modern War*, 112

19 Holmes, *Riding the Retreat*, 46–7; Townshend, *Modern War*, 107

The army leaderships did not resign themselves to the stalemate that quickly developed, which they regarded all along as a temporary state of affairs. By some means or other, the natural balance between attack and defence would have to be restored. In retrospect we are forced to conclude that far too often they looked to the lessons of a previous era. The old-style infantry assault remained the favoured tactic, although in reality it was hopeless in the face of modern weapons. None of the large-scale assaults mounted between the time when the German advance of autumn 1914 stalled and the great German spring offensive of 1918 produced any meaningful result. For over three years soldiers were worn down by the three main instruments of defence: bullets, entrenching tools and barbed wire. Of course many soldiers defending their positions met the same fate as their attackers, but the longed-for breakthrough which the repeated offensives were designed to achieve remained elusive until the spring of 1918.[20]

Some historians regard the Battle of Verdun as the opening of a second phase in the long period of trench warfare, in which a war of attrition became one of total exhaustion, of bleeding to death.[21] Historians disagree about whether this 'bleeding white' or '*Verbluten*' of the French army was actually what German generals were planning at Verdun or simply what they felt they had achieved when they looked back on it afterwards.[22] Either way, it was this phase that created our image of the war as a whole: artillery barrages, long lines of soldiers advancing towards machine-guns, and barbed wire coiled across a cratered landscape, empty but for the occasional charred stump of a tree.[23] Attacks on a grand scale gave some dynamism to the otherwise static trench fighting, which the Germans referred to as *der Sitzkrieg*, the sitting war, but they were accompanied by a relentless succession of small, tactical campaigns, aimed at sustaining the fighting spirit and achieving minor adjustments to the front line. A strategically important hill had to be taken, a salient flattened out or reduced in size. It was the big offensives above all, however, that gave a chronological structure to the conflict and produced massive casualties.

The losses were shocking, and not only in numerical terms. The impact of their apparent futility was no less powerful. Campaigns that lasted for months produced negligible permanent gains, so that for every metre of ground an extraordinarily high price was paid in human lives.[24] German poet Ivan Goll scoffed that whole regiments had forfeited their souls for ten metres of wasteland.[25]

So the war of 1914–18 was neither the brief, bloody battle the cavalry had anticipated nor the lengthy but literally bloodless stalemate some had feared. It

20 Ellis, *Eye-Deep*, 80; Prior & Wilson, *Passchendaele*, 6; Townshend, *Modern War*, 12

21 Eksteins, *Rites of Spring*, 143

22 Prior & Wilson, *Passchendaele*, 7–8

23 Eksteins, *Rites of Spring*, 145

24 Binneveld, *Om de geest*, 68–9

25 Eksteins, *Rites of Spring*, 144

was the worst of both worlds, an extremely bloody trench war that lasted more than four years, drawing upon all the achievements of preceding decades in social, technical and medical fields, not for the benefit of humanity but in pursuit of destruction.[26] Before long the opposing nations and their armies found they had no idea why they had taken up arms. They could not say why the war had broken out and wondered whether that had ever really been clear. The political aims were forgotten and political caution abandoned; anti-war voices fell silent or were easily silenced. John Keegan writes: 'Politics even in the liberal democracies was rapidly reduced to a mere justification of bigger battles, longer casualty lists, costlier budgets, overflowing human misery.'[27] The question posed about Verdun by historian Alistair Horne in his *Price of Glory* could easily be asked of the whole war: 'Have so many ever died for so little gain?'[28]

### *Shared affliction*

Those who fought came from all walks of life and all social classes shared in the suffering. There can be no doubt, however, that in percentage terms the upper classes gave more than their due. They produced the officers who served at the front, and it was those officers, leading their men into battle, who left the trenches first and were most likely to be hit. Twenty-seven per cent of British officers died, whereas the figure for ordinary soldiers was twelve per cent. On the first day of the Battle of the Somme, seventy-five per cent of officers who took part in the advance were killed or wounded, compared with fifty per cent of their men. The upper classes even lost out because of their own good health. Whereas abominable living conditions meant that the sons of factory workers quite often failed their medical examinations and therefore gained an advantage, for once, from their low social standing, the sons of the well-to-do were rarely rejected. Add to this the fact that they were more likely to volunteer, and we begin to see why the higher social classes were hardest hit.[29] So many French officers were killed during the Battle of Verdun that Lieutenant-Colonel W.D. Henderson claims many saw it as 'a prime example of officer failure to recognise the changing nature of warfare, thus resulting in massive and unnecessary loss of life'.[30]

Of course this is not to deny that the vast majority of soldiers, and therefore of the dead, wounded and sick, were workers or farm labourers. Over ninety per cent of casualties came from the lower social orders. These were mainly men who before the war had felt little respect for their armies. Urban workforces in particular had encountered their nations' armed forces up to that point primarily as bloody

26 Winter, *Death's Men*, 128

27 Keegan, *History of Warfare*, 21

28 Horne, *Price of Glory*, 215

29 Holmes, *Firing Line*, 349; Wilson, *Myriad Faces*, 759; Winter & Baggett, *1914–18*, 363–4; Frey, *Pflasterkästen*, 302

30 Holmes, *Firing Line*, 350

repressors of social protest, run by the propertied classes. There was therefore a considerable difference between the mores of the traditional armies and those of the men who joined them for the duration of the 1914–18 war. The majority of high-ranking officers came from the countryside, while the vast expansion of European armies made it essential to recruit soldiers from the cities. Many officers regarded urban populations as largely composed of leftwing radicals or, even worse, enfeebled drunkards. For the army staffs this presented one advantage: the blame for any offensive that ended in bloody failure could be placed on the men. There had been nothing wrong with their plans for a great breakthrough, but those responsible for executing them were not up to the task.[31] The most obvious response to this is surely that the quality of available troops is a crucial factor that must always be considered at the planning stage.

The huge losses among Oxbridge boys otherwise destined to become the political, scientific and cultural leaders of the British nation led to talk of a 'lost generation'. There is undoubtedly some truth in this, but it should be seen as a socially determined truth. First of all a generation does not consist purely of the children of the upper classes, and second it was the officers at the front who died in vast numbers. Generally speaking only the relatively wealthy could become officers, and therefore it was the well-to-do who suffered the greatest losses in percentage terms. The deaths mourned and cursed in retrospect by the upper classes were the outcome of social prejudices arising from traditions centuries old.[32]

### *The Great War was too great*

The huge death toll can be blamed in part on the fact that none of the countries involved was prepared for war on such a scale, nor could have been. The influx of recruits in the early months of the fighting caused army leaderships severe problems, especially in Great Britain, where conscription had not yet been introduced. Britain's professional army was far too small for the task at hand. It began by bringing fewer than 100,000 men to the continent and they represented the bulk of the troops available. By the end of 1915, 3.5 million men were serving in the British armed forces. Most countries that became involved put some fifty percent of males born between 1870 and 1900 into uniform, in the case of France and Germany an astonishing 80 and 85 per cent respectively. At the outbreak of war, France managed to arm as many men as the far more populous Germany.[33] In July 1914 there were four million men under arms, by the end of August twenty

---

31 Whalen, *Bitter Wounds*, 42; Dallas & Gill, *The Unknown Army*, 13–25, 30–32, 35, 37; Holmes, *Firing Line*, 132; Strachan, 'Military Modernization', 87

32 Vondung, *Kriegserlebnis*, 115–45 (article: Jay M. Winter, 'Die Legende der "verlorenen Generation" in Großbritannien')

33 Winter & Baggett, *1914–18*, 362; Whalen, *Bitter Wounds*, 39; De Vos, *De Eerste Wereldoorlog*, 16

million.[34] Thousands had died by then. It proved virtually impossible to dress, arm and train all the new recruits, many of whom were very young. They exercised in civilian clothes, with broomsticks for rifles. There was a serious shortage of capable instructors.[35]

After being put through their basic exercises the men were brought up as close to the front as possible by train before covering the final few miles on foot. Denis Winter writes:

> One must imagine men unused to prolonged exercise, constipated and suffering from boils, the flat-footed and the sick, sedentary office workers and clerks, all fitted into army boots of standard sizes, all moving slowly and wearily to the sound of the guns. Experience thus far had been of anxiety and pain, fatigue and companionship. Fear was still to come.[36]

These men had yet to engage in battle after sitting in trenches under shellfire for days on end. In many ways life was actually harder during the short periods of mobile warfare in the first few months and the final half year. In 1918 men had to march again, at a time when fear was familiar and most strongly felt.

Graves recalled the diverse fortunes of his Royal Welch Fusiliers as a coming and going of troops, fresh men replacing the dead and wounded. The first battalion, around a hundred strong, was all but wiped out within two months. By the First Battle of Ypres, in the autumn of 1914, it was down to about forty men. Along with the remnants of the second battalion of the Queen's Regiment – in normal times a thousand strong, by this point reduced to thirty, with two officers – they seized a number of trenches and suffered further severe losses. The battalion was then brought back to full strength to fight at Bois Grenier in December but almost destroyed at Aubers Ridge and Festubert in May 1915 and again at Loos in September 1915, where only one of the officers who led it into battle survived. It was a similar story at Fricourt and at various places during the Battle of the Somme, 'and again, and again, until the Armistice. In the course of the war, at least fifteen or twenty thousand men must have passed through each of the two line battalions, whose fighting strength never stood at more than eight hundred.' The factual accuracy of this statement is questionable, but that such an idea could occur to anyone says enough.[37]

Despite the continuing slaughter, most soldiers simply did what was asked of them. When told to stand their ground they did their best to stand their ground; when ordered to advance they advanced, even in the face of almost certain death. Aside from the obvious reasons – patriotism, a sense of duty, honour and obedience, all of which weighed much more heavily then than now – we should remember

34 Ellis, *Social History*, 113; Keegan, *History of Warfare*, 22

35 Brants & Brants, *Velden van weleer*, 156

36 Winter, *Death's Men*, 79

37 Graves, *Goodbye*, 78

that although many soldiers were not used to the circumstances they now found themselves in, they were accustomed to hard, often extremely hard lives. Working men who passed their medical examinations swapped one difficult, dangerous, sleepless, filthy and exhausting life for another.[38] Perhaps even more importantly, soldiers found themselves in a situation that had a logic of its own, with its own ways of pressuring soldiers to carry on to the bitter end. John Ellis writes:

> The men were cut off from the world they had known, and plunged into an utterly alien environment. The Western Front became a self-contained nightmare whose rules and traditions became ends in themselves, the only thing a man could cling on to in the midst of chaos. This sense of isolation generated the collective pride that helped them endure because it drew the soldiers so closely together.[39]

## 1914

### *The overture*

In late June 1914 in Sarajevo, Serbian nationalist Gavrilo Princip shot and killed the Austrian Archduke Franz Ferdinand and his wife. Austria issued Serbia with an ultimatum. The Serbs were prepared to meet most of the demands, but not to the satisfaction of Austria. Russia came to Serbia's aid. One country after another declared war, compelled to do so by a network of treaties which committed Germany to Austria, for instance, and France to Russia. So when hostilities started on 3 August, Germany was faced with a war on two fronts, as it had expected. The plan, drawn up several years earlier by the since deceased General von Schlieffen, was that France would be defeated first, with Russia held back by a minimal garrison. The consensus was that Russia would be unable to move its entire army up to the East Prussian border immediately. After victory in the West, battle would be joined in the East. In south-eastern France the French army would be held at bay while in the north, via neutral Belgium, the bulk of the German army would move around Paris in an outflanking manoeuvre to attack the French army from the rear. Unfortunately for the Germans, there was a considerable difference between theory and practice. Little went as planned, but until early September it nevertheless seemed as if nothing and no one could halt the German war machine. Every ten minutes a troop train thundered over the Hohenzollern Bridge in Cologne. Within less than a week the Germans had moved a million and a half men up to the Western Front. The French deployed almost as many.[40]

The story captured in the photographs and innumerable written accounts of those opening weeks suggests that millions went to their doom full of enthusiasm,

38 Holmes, *Firing Line*, 133

39 Ellis, *Eye-Deep*, 190

40 Eksteins, *Rites of Spring*, 98–9; Keegan, *First World War*, 55–6

singing and laughing. Did they? Some caution is needed here. When we examine the personal motives that prompted men to join up, it is striking how few of the official reasons for joining the war effort can be found in their memoirs. A sense of duty to the fatherland and, in Britain's case, outrage at the fate of Poor Little Belgium are of course significant, but these are not the feelings the memoirs reflect. To judge by what individuals wrote at the time, the major political causes, the Big Words, were rarely the crucial motivating factors. We should remember that war memoirs were mostly written by a certain type of soldier and the majority were not committed to paper until the 1920s. Perhaps in hindsight the privations the soldiers had suffered made those big words seem ridiculous, so that writers tended to omit them from their accounts. Or perhaps the grander considerations were taken for granted and no longer needed to be stated explicitly. Did grand moral and political causes go unmentioned because they were obviously valid or because they were plainly absurd? The books of the period and most of the diaries and letters suggest that a lust for adventure, social pressures, or oppressive conditions at home were the commonest reasons for going. Taking part in a war meant a chance to be present while history was written. It seems reasonable to ask whether the war was the main attraction. In *Some Desperate Glory*, Edward Campion Vaughan writes of adventure, excitement, death or gladioli. This suggests it was not war that enthused him so much as his image of war, an image of a sable, a horse and great personal glory. Although all these things belong to 'the attraction of war', it is clear that Campion Vaughan did not so much want to go to war as to lead an exciting life.

We may wonder whether the enthusiasm taken for granted and widely felt at the outbreak of war has been exaggerated in retrospect. How many joined up simply because the war was there, just as people tend to climb mountains because they are there? How many men went to war because society expected it of them? Did they go because reporting for duty seemed the right thing to do? To put it another way: was it the war that attracted them, or the fact of living in wartime that propelled them?[41]

Many historians believe people welcomed the war with all the enthusiasm described by the politicians, soldiers and journalists of the day. The evidence suggests that the story is more myth than reality. The monotony and boredom said to characterize the lives of ordinary citizens, from which the war promised escape, were to a large extent figments of the imaginations of a small intellectual elite.[42] In Europe's major cities the declaration of war seems to have been applauded by large sectors of the population, although even in their case it would be wrong to imagine a single shared emotion. In the countryside, however, where the majority of people lived, astonishment and fear were probably the dominant emotions. Many city dwellers will have had similar feelings, but their concerns were drowned out by expressions of enthusiasm. Our retrospective image is determined not so much by

41 Hynes, *Soldiers' Tale*, 44–51, 106; Liddle & Cecil, *Facing Armageddon*, 323

42 Vondung, *Kriegserlebnis*, 243

the majority as by the loudest and most visible.[43] Later many widows would say they could still remember the fear they felt when war broke out. Their memories are hard to reconcile with the photographs of women smiling broadly, cheering their husbands as they leave for the front in August 1914, photographs widely used as propaganda. Perhaps the feelings that overcame these women when their husbands were killed coloured their view of the war, or perhaps the photographs do not tell the whole story. They are after all pictures of groups. They say little about the feelings of individuals. In any case, Jay Winter says the enthusiasm expressed in the streets of Germany lasted no more than a few days and involved only certain limited segments of the population, not even a very large proportion of the country as a whole. Niall Ferguson questions whether the atmosphere among the crowds that undoubtedly formed is best described as enthusiasm. Fear and panic were part of it too. Frenchman Roland Lécavelé, writing under the pseudonym Roland Dorgelès, describes Jacques Larcher, the central character and narrator of his book *Les Croix de Bois* (*Wooden Crosses*), as seeing mainly downcast faces among the crowds immediately after mobilization, although their despondency was quickly transformed into bravura: They want war? Then they shall have war![44]

Even in August 1914 it was obvious that not everyone shared this general eagerness. In Germany, the powerful Social Democratic Party saw its MPs and most of its ordinary members vote in favour of war credits, but this is not to say they all stood and cheered. The party's left wing, which would later emerge as the *Spartakusbund*, was and remained fiercely opposed to the war. In August, fourteen of the SDP's parliamentarians declined to vote in favour of war loans until an urgent appeal for party discipline brought them into line, and in December 1914 Karl Liebknecht became the first among them to announce publicly that he was withdrawing his support for the war programme. A year later there were twenty dissenters.[45] By then Liebknecht was in jail, stripped of his parliamentary immunity. Stefan Zweig too had a deep aversion to militarism and nationalism before war broke out. In late July he found himself on a Belgian beach near Ostend. He travelled home on the last train bound for Germany. He briefly came under the spell of the new martial atmosphere, marvelling at a people that seemed suddenly unified. 'I must confess there was something majestic, marvellous, even seductive in this first euphoric outburst of the crowds, from which one could escape only with difficulty', he wrote, but he could not bring himself to surrender to the surge of patriotism once he reached Vienna. Reason retained the upper hand, and he remained faithful to his old, pacifist, cosmopolitan convictions. To his horror he realized that he was practically alone in this. Many pacifists emerged in Europe

43 Winter & Baggett, *1914–18*, 52–6, 60; Chickering, *Imperial Germany*, 16; Verhey, *The Spirit of 1914*, passim

44 Whalen, *Bitter Wounds*, 71; Winter, Sivan, *War and Remembrance*, 56; Ferguson, *The Pity of War*, 177; Koch, 'Einde aan de onschuld', 1; Dorgelès, *Les croix de bois*, 1; Audoin-Rouzeau & Becker, *'14–'18*, 132

45 Chickering, *Imperial Germany*, 16, 154–5; Ferguson, *The Pity of War*, 178

after the war, but during the war they were rare. Zweig's former friends had been seduced by patriotism and were starting to produce their own variations on Ernst Lissauer's *Haßgesang gegen England* (Hate Song Against England). The 'betrayal by the intelligentsia' that he witnessed arose from a sense of guilt. Fathers living in safety longed to support their sons, who were leaving for the front. With the work of their intellects they too could contribute to the defence of the fatherland.[46]

Another illustration of the fact that the enthusiasm was not universally shared was the suicide along with his girlfriend on 8 August 1914 of a friend of the German philosopher Walter Benjamin, who would follow the same course in September 1940. It was clearly intended as a protest against the war. Then there were the parting words of writer Alfred Lichtenstein, ordered to leave for the front with the first of the troops. '*Am Himmel brennt das brave Abendrot. / Vielleicht bin ich in vierzehn Tagen tot.*' (In the sky sunset burns sweetly red. / In fourteen days from now I may be dead.) He lived another eight.[47]

A Swiss doctor, Otto Lanz, had been intending to visit a German friend in late July 1914. He let the man know a week before his planned visit that he would not be able to come because of the threat of war. He received the reply that there was nothing to fear. The situation had been far more threatening in 1911 and this time too, Lanz's friend said, 'the diplomats will avert the threat. No one wants war.' By the time Lanz arrived, his friend, an officer, had already left for the front. Lanz wrote: 'Events followed each other with such unbelievable speed that an army commander-in-chief of the country accused of starting the conflict was still dreaming about his holiday plans on the eve of war!'[48] And feelings in other countries were little different. In the region everyone feared would become a battlefield, Alsace-Lorraine, there was no enthusiasm for the war at all. Perhaps we should regard Louis Barthas' experience as apposite and accept that there were many like him for whom news of the mobilization came as a fearful shock and who, looking about them, could not find a single likeminded soul among the enthusiastic crowds.[49]

But even if we accept the image of enthusiastic crowds as typical, it was a phenomenon largely confined to Germany and France. Belgium was granted no time to look forward to war. Princip's deed (he was to die of TB in an Austrian prison hospital in 1918)[50] had caused great commotion elsewhere, but Walloons and Flemings read in their newspapers that in late June, somewhere in the Balkans, the Archduke of Austria had been murdered and they turned the page, confident in their internationally guaranteed neutrality. A sex scandal in France was more

46 Zweig, *Die Welt von Gestern*, 162–6, 169–74; Heyman, *World War I*, 82, 178–80; Audoin-Rouzeau & Becker, *'14–'18*, 189, 283

47 Zuckmayer, *Als wär's ein Stück von mir*, 202–3; Winter & Sivan, *War and Remembrance*, 222

48 Lanz, *De oorlogswinst*, 21 (note)

49 Barthas, *Carnets*, 13–14; Ferguson, *The Pity of War*, 176

50 Gilbert, *First World War*, 418

interesting and the second triumph of Belgian cyclist Philippe Thys in the Tour de France was more important. Mobilization came as a shock and was greeted with tears. In the middle of harvest time it was nothing short of disastrous. Many families were left without an income from one day to the next, although the local authorities offered some financial support. The enthusiasm that developed over subsequent days must have been a manifestation of the Belgians' love of their country, and their dismay at the violation of its neutrality, rather than any deeply rooted passion for war. Enthusiasm is not the right word. They were motivated by outrage and hatred.[51]

Nevertheless, within some groups and in certain parts of Germany and France, there was undoubtedly great eagerness to fight, factory workers being one example. It is remarkable, not to say bewildering, to see how willingly and in what numbers the workers, who had so recently expressed trenchant anti-militarism and international solidarity, made their way to the barracks. The national interest, in the form in which was presented to them, was enough to persuade the Germans and French to set aside all their internal differences. Enthusiasm became infectious and the workers, like everyone else, became convinced that the outbreak of war meant a fresh wind would blow through their stuffy societies, and that only in battle could a man ever become truly a man.

The life of future German novelist Carl Zuckmayer changed direction in those last days of July and early days of August. His experience serves as an example both of the pressures on young men and of the attractions of the war. Seventeen-year-old Zuckmayer was on holiday in Domburg on the Dutch coast. Five years later he committed his memories to paper. People heard the news of the murder of Franz Ferdinand and shrugged. In the month that followed, as the international situation increasingly got out of hand, they felt more and more confident, against their own better judgement. Zuckmayer agreed with his father that this war was madness, the ultimate atavism that would bring the whole world to rack and ruin. When it became obvious that they were indeed witnessing a resurgence of primitive instincts, Zuckmayer wrote several poems on the subject, replete with pacifist emotion, fully aware that this meant the end of his youth. 'We did not feel moved in any way, no sense of patriotism, only horror and repugnance at the incomprehensible, senseless automatic slide of a rational world into madness.'[52] When the hotel-keeper's wife asked whether he too would have to serve in this terrible war he cried out, 'Never. ... I'll never go to war, to shoot at other people. I'd rather they lock me up.'[53]

His return to Germany was unavoidable, however, and as he travelled through his native country, a rapid and radical transformation took place, turning him from

51 De Schaepdrijver, *De Groote Oorlog*, 50, 54, 60–62, 64; Chickering, *Imperial Germany*, 10; De Launoy, *Oorlogsverpleegster*, 20; *Van den Grooten oorlog*, 17

52 Zuckmayer, *Als wär's ein Stück von mir*, 189–90

53 Zuckmayer, *Als wär's ein Stück von mir*, 191; De Roodt, *Onsterfelijke fronten*, 320–22

a pacifist into a man who greeted the war with joy. It was a transformation he compared to an electric current driving out all doubt and abhorrence. It sent him into a trance; it determined everything he thought and did. He wanted only one thing: to take part; to be there.

> Suddenly, like a loud drum roll, [everyday life] was drowned out by the outbreak of war. Now there were no questions any longer. Dreaming and youth were over. Fate had spoken – and we greeted it with unbridled jubilation, as if it had freed us from doubt and decision-making. We – a long train crammed with volunteers – sang the *Wacht am Rhein* as we crossed the old bridge of Mainz one sun-drenched morning to travel up to the front as reserve troops. ... To become a soldier, the obligation to serve for a year; it had always seemed an awkward and threatening idea to me as a *Gymnasium* pupil. It had meant conformity, standing still, keeping your mouth shut, obedience, subordination – the loss of all freedom. Now it meant precisely the opposite: liberation! Liberation from the narrowness and pettiness of civilian life, from school and swotting, from having to choose a career and, above all, from everything that we felt – consciously or unconsciously – to be the saturation, suffocation, ossification of our world.[54]

Anyhow, the war would be short and decisive. Everybody would be home by Christmas. It was not at all the kind of war they expected, and Zuckmayer would soon discover that the *Wehrdienst* did not mean liberation but a reinforcement of old norms and values, not liberation from suffocation, from subordination, but those things taken to their ultimate extremes. The army, war – it would be a bitter disappointment, a hell, not even so much because of the horrors as because it was all so different from what he had imagined in his youthful naiveté. Zuckmayer felt this was also true of that much-vaunted phenomenon called comradeship, which was confined, as he saw it, to a few, and ought certainly not to be confused with friendship. Joining an army in wartime had nothing to do with making friends or being self-effacing for the benefit of others. You were forced to be an 'ordinary man', someone 'who neither condoned nor alleviated anything anyone did and who had to get on with his dull, anonymous, dirty work rather than performing "heroic deeds"'. It was above all a matter of survival, at others' expense if necessary. Once at the front, the volunteer, still singing his stirring marches, was met by men who longed for their old lives, to whom there was nothing sacrosanct about the notion of a 'war volunteer'. The newcomers were rechristened 'war-wantons' and their enthusiasm was not regarded as touching and patriotic as it had been at home but instead as stupid and pointless; the idealistic motives behind it were openly and sincerely questioned. If these men, regarded as old-stagers after so few months,

54 Zuckmayer, *Als wär's ein Stück von mir*, 182, 198; De Roodt, *Onsterfelijke fronten*, 322–4

had ever gone into battle cheering, then like Zuckmayer himself they had quickly been cured of all that.[55]

If we accept that the prevailing image of enthusiasm at the start of the war is not the full picture, then early expressions of doubt about the war, which arose surprisingly quickly, are easier to explain. In mid-September, Walter Heymann, who would be dead by early 1915, wrote home that he was feeling the effects of innumerable reports of death and horror. Behind every victory he could sense the destruction. He was afraid for everyone he knew and for himself. True, out of all those bullets zipping through the air only a tiny percentage found their targets, but 'how many have not already been hit'. As early as the bombardment of Liège, even Rudolf Binding, a soldier and writer who regarded war as the ultimate test of manhood, was moved to note in his diary:

> If one sees the devastation, the burning villages and towns, plundered cellars and storerooms where the troops have grubbed about with their foolish instinct for self-preservation, the dead or half-starved animals, the cattle bellowing in the sugar-beet fields, and the corpses, corpses and yet more corpses, the processions of wounded, one after the other – then everything becomes senseless, insane, a horrible folly of nations and their histories, an endless reproach to humanity, a refutation of all culture, an invalidation of faith in the capacity of people and peoples for progress, a desecration of what is holy, so that one feels every human initiative is doomed.[56]

### *The invasion of Belgium*

The Belgian army was no match for the German invasion. It did not lack courage or volunteers, indeed there was great eagerness to defend the country. The Belgian armed forces, composed of a field army and a fortress army, were 200,000 men strong at the time of general mobilization on 31 July 1914 and in August almost 40,000 men joined them.[57] But their weaponry was thoroughly outdated and their commanding officers not up to the task. Field officers were put out of action almost immediately by German artillery.[58]

Medical services were poorly organized. Before the war it had been assumed that the intensity of firepower would prevent any movement of the wounded during a battle, so hardly any stretcher-bearers had been trained. For the same reason no motorized vehicles were provided as ambulances, only horses and carts – after all, once a battle was over it would no longer be necessary to move

---

55 Zuckmayer, *Als wär's ein Stück von mir*, 189, 217, 219; Vondung, *Kriegserlebnis*, 242; Bourke, *Dismembering the Male*, 27

56 *Kriegsbriefe gefallener Deutscher Juden*, 21; Winter & Baggett, *1914–18*, 66; Binding, *Aus dem Kriege*, 21–2; Conzelmann, *Der andere Dix*, 67

57 De Vos, *De Eerste Wereldoorlog*, 21

58 Brants & Brants, *Velden van weleer*, 54

casualties particularly quickly. There were thirty-three SSA trains (*Service de Santé de l'Armée*), whose 300 carriages had room for 3,840 prostrate wounded and seats for another 3,600, but there were insufficient Red Cross staff to man them. Nevertheless the wounded were moved back behind the lines train-loads at a time. They had to be transported from railway stations to hospitals on open stretchers. There were not enough army doctors to treat those who made it that far.[59]

Whatever the deficiencies of the Belgian army, in those early days of August it ensured that at places like Liège – with forts, fortifications and machine-gun posts – the German advance was delayed, even though there was no hope of actually stopping the German armies. The forts around Liège were ultimately outdated, but they proved too robust for German artillery until the Big Berthas were brought in, and the Belgian defenders greeted attackers with hails of bullets. It is not hard to imagine the result. It gave rise to a comment that would be heard again and again in the years that followed, from all sides, and always in tones of utter amazement. A Belgian officer said: '[They] came line after line, almost shoulder to shoulder, until, as we shot them down, the fallen were heaped on top of each other in an awful barricade of dead and wounded.'[60]

Indeed, for all its successes in the first month of the war, the German advance was no simple matter. A stretcher-bearer would later write that every German soldier advancing towards Liège seemed to feel he was approaching death on giant strides. Again and again men were ordered by their commanding officers, frustrated by setbacks that, however insignificant in themselves, were delaying the advance, to march towards Belgian machine-guns. The same stretcher-bearer was moved to remark that the sky around Liège seemed as if 'full of shattered, shredded, stinking lead, sometimes flying back and forth, sometimes whirling up like dust'.[61] It was now that Jünger, the archetype of Prussian soldiery, saw his first wounded.

> I stared, with a queasy feeling of unreality, at a blood-spattered form with a strangely contorted leg hanging loosely down, wailing 'Help! Help!' as if sudden death still had him by the throat. He was carried into a building with a Red Cross flag draped over the doorway. What was that about? War had shown its claws, and stripped off its mask of cosiness.[62]

German soldiers who had left for the front full of enthusiasm only a few days before were now encountering an industrial killing machine. Many of the wounded, along with deserters, crossed the nearby border into the Dutch province of Limburg, or were carried over it. The first to die there of his wounds, two days after the

59 De Schaepdrijver, *De Groote Oorlog*, 73; Evrard & Mathieu, *Asklepios*, 233–5
60 Winter & Baggett, *1914–18*, 64; Heijster, *Ieper*, 53; Tuchman, *The Guns*, 174–80
61 De Schaepdrijver, *De Groote Oorlog*, 69
62 Jünger, *In Stahlgewittern*, 2–3; *Storm of Steel*, 6–7

invasion, was twenty-year-old Adolf Heinrich Graf von Arnim.[63] By the end of August German casualties stood at 12.4 per cent dead and wounded. In September they were 16.8 per cent. The Germans would not suffer such losses again, not even during the Battle of Verdun or the great spring offensive of 1918.[64]

After the introduction of the famous Krupp howitzers the tide rapidly turned. One by one the forts around Liège were knocked out. The bombardment of Fort Loncin, where the Belgian high command had ensconced itself, had a particularly dramatic dénouement. A shell penetrated the fort's magazine. Only a few of its defending troops, among them the general in command, survived the explosion.[65]

Belgian troops, known as *jassen* or *piotten*, were driven further and further back. After the Germans advanced into France in early September, attempts were made to secure the most favourable military-strategic positions, a struggle known, not entirely accurately, as the 'race to the sea'. The Belgian army burst out of its encirclement several times to fulfil obligations towards the Allied troops that had come to its aid (suffering losses of some 8,000 dead and wounded in the process), but Antwerp, considered impossible to capture, fell to the Germans. Tens of thousands of soldiers who remained there disobeyed orders by fleeing to the Netherlands, where most were interned.[66] A small number managed to get to Britain, from where they were able to rejoin the Belgian army. Their experiences in Antwerp had filled them with loathing for the officers they felt had abandoned them to their fate. One of the soldiers interned in the Netherlands, Alfons van Hove, described the situation in Antwerp shortly before it fell:

> No orders reached us any more, no food came any more, soldiers were wandering about, one this way, another that. Whole regiments were without officers and the lads were so frightened they barely knew what they were doing. Thousands of rifles were deliberately destroyed. The artillerymen disabled their own guns and threw the ammunition into the water.[67]

Marie van Gastel worked for the Red Cross at a hospital set up in a school, one of twenty-two quickly fitted out as auxiliary hospitals in Antwerp that August. There were a thousand beds in total. The shortage of space was acute, as she remembered half a century later:

---

63 Leclerq, *Het informatiebureau*, 40

64 Whalen, *Bitter Wounds*, 40

65 De Vos, *De Eerste Wereldoorlog*, 33; Heijster, *Ieper*, 57; Keegan, *First World War*, 97

66 Leclerq, *Het informatiebureau*, 45–7; Holmes & De Vos, *Langs de Velden van Eer*, 87; Bastier, 'België tijdens de Eerste Wereldoorlog', 18; Schepens, 'België in de Eerste Wereldoorlog', 19, 29

67 *Vluchten voor de Groote Oorlog*, 30

> The wounded lay everywhere, on the floor and in the corridors. Meanwhile civilians were fleeing to the Netherlands and to Great Britain. We can hear the roar of the guns getting closer. The Zeppelins fly over Antwerp and drop bombs, while the doctors operate on wounded boys, often without anaesthetic, and we bury the amputated arms and legs in the garden.[68]

By the time Antwerp fell, the Belgian army had been reduced to fewer than 75,000 men, and they were now incapable of fighting. Tired and sick from the August heat and September rains, Belgian soldiers retreated in tattered clothing, many wearing clogs stuffed with straw. Most had diarrhoea, since they had been forced to drink from ditches. They were in no fit state to make any contribution to the great offensive the French army leadership continued to press for. Stretcher-bearer Franz de Backer remembered those 'grotesque first weeks'.

> No one knew what to do with us, food was scarce or unavailable, within a few days we were begging at the roadsides for a meal or a piece of bread. I was unable to eat the first meal we begged. Self-pity, that was, in a spoilt, proud boy from a well-to-do family. With our holdalls, our suits, our civilian clothes or priests' soutanes, crumpled, dusty and torn from sleeping in barns or on cobble-stones, or during the long marches forward and back behind antique Red Cross vehicles, we became dirtier, meaner, more ridiculous by the day. I was hugely disappointed ... when I realized that eating and sleeping were our primary concern.[69]

Historian Sophie de Schaepdrijver wrote with indignation and incredulity:

> As was the case throughout the war, and in all the warring parties, the desire to attack 'to the utmost' was at its most impressive among those men least familiar with the exhausting daily hardships of the war; those who did not know what it was like to fall asleep standing up and to go cross-eyed with hunger, those who had not felt the misery of worn out feet in worn out boots – nor, come to that, the terrors of battle itself.[70]

Dr Harold Dearden of the Royal Army Medical Corps observed Belgian troops at Dunkirk.

> It's impossible to tell officers from men except by the fact that the former spit rather less dexterously and have longer cigarette holders. No one salutes anyone

68 De Munck, *De Grote Moeder*, passim; De Weerdt, *De Vrouwen van de Eerste Wereldoorlog*, 100

69 De Backer, 'Longinus', 14–15, see also: 22; De Schaepdrijver, *De Groote Oorlog*, 95; Heijster, *Ieper*, 70; De Vos, *De Eerste Wereldoorlog*, 54

70 De Schaepdrijver, *De Groote Oorlog*, 98

> else, and on the whole one's pity for King Albert increases every time you pass one of his gallant troops.[71]

The retreat came to a halt at the coast. The German offensive on the Yser in the second half of October cost the lives of thousands of Frenchmen, Belgians and Germans. The Belgian army lost twenty per cent of its men in a single week. Some towns, like Beerst and Vladslo, were captured and recaptured several times over.[72] Kurt Peterson, a German soldier who died a year later, wrote of the Battle of the Yser:

> Assault on Dixmude. Terrible! A repeat of the first attack. Slaughtered once more by the dreadful machine-gun fire. The cries of hoorah that had started were silenced. Everything lay on the ground like lead and around us death wailed and hissed. You could grow old in a night like that.[73]

Belgian soldiers dug in. Or rather, they heaped up some mud, since the ground was so saturated that any hole, however shallow, instantly turned into a puddle. After a few weeks the Belgians began to see the advantage of this. The lowlands around the Noordvaart were deliberately inundated. Until the summer of 1918 there were only occasional skirmishes in this region, certainly compared to the storm that raged for four years at Ypres a little further south. As a British officer wrote shortly after the start of the Third Battle of Ypres, for all the talk of First, Second and Third Ypres, one great long battle was fought around that town from autumn 1914 onwards. The Yser front was relatively quiet by comparison, but total war, even in places of relative inactivity, kills wholesale, lacerates horribly and buries alive. Water provided some protection, but the entire Western Front became an unhealthy place and the Yser even more so than anywhere. There was an acute shortage of food. Malaria, which had at last been driven out of Western Europe a short time earlier, re-emerged as the rotting, swollen corpses of men and animals floated in filthy water. In summer swarms of mosquitoes darkened the sky. There were no latrines. Crammed together in one small area, the Westhoek, 150,000 men had to relieve themselves in their trenches. Water was everywhere but undrinkable, and those who could not resist the torments of Tantalus fell prey to stomach typhus, with intestinal cramps and inflammation of the abdominal mucous membrane. Drinkable water was brought by truck from Dunkirk, or obtained by drilling down to aquifers at a depth of 125 metres. Almost a third of the 20,000 men who would die on the Yser were felled by sickness, partly as a result of the lamentable, antiquated medical services, organizational failures by the Red Cross – which had made clear in early August 1914 that with precisely five ambulances it would be

71 Dearden, *Medicine and Duty*, 27

72 De Schaepdrijver, *De Groote Oorlog*, 100; Brants & Brants, *Velden van weleer*, 54; Heijster, *Ieper*, 70–74; Holmes & De Vos, *Langs de Velden van Eer*, 90–92

73 Witkop, *Kriegsbriefe*, 108

incapable of fulfilling its duty – and the lack of coordination between the military hospitals at the front and the more modern Red Cross hospitals back behind the lines. Of all the Belgian dead, around 40,000 in total, more than 10,000 died of disease – one in four where one in six was the average for other armies. This was not purely a consequence of the poor conditions and lack of treatment options; it was caused in large part by a disregard for instructions on how to follow basic rules of hygiene. Barracks built in the quieter sectors of the front had no washing facilities or urinals.[74] Volunteer medical officer Maurice Duwez wrote about the Yser trenches in his *La Boue des Flandres* (The Mud of Flanders), published under the pseudonym Max Deauville, a work described by De Schaepdrijver with some irony as the 'most malicious book ever to come out of the Westhoek'.

> During those four days' service at the front line, everyone was on watch all night, some in the trench, others at the outposts. The sentries are at their posts there for eight hours at a time, standing in the cold mud. When they are relieved they often have to be carried back because their feet are frozen.[75]

The Belgians were not alone in their suffering. A report by a senior German medical officer reads:

> In recent fights on the Yser, on the canals as well as round about Ypres, the most of the wounds, often even those wounds caused by rifle-fire, are infected. The soldiers lie in wet trenches, and in consequence of the violent artillery fire they can in many cases be picked up only after days have elapsed; *some have lain five or six days in turnip-fields or in deserted trenches* before it was possible to bring them to the field hospital. Serious infections are then not uncommon, such as phlegmon and tetanus.[76]

As the battle went on the remaining 50,000 Belgian soldiers were joined by around 32,000 young men from occupied territory. The march to the front was risky in itself; the route via the Netherlands was effectively blocked, since the Germans had built a border fence with 2,000-volt high tension cables. How many victims it claimed is unknown, but their number probably exceeded the voltage; there were almost certainly German deserters among them as well as refugees. Men living outside Belgium reported for duty too. Over the years, some 100,000 Belgians

---

74 De Schaepdrijver, *De Groote Oorlog*, 101, 175, 177–9, 182; Evrard & Mathieu, *Asklepios*, 237, 247, 267; Heijster, *Ieper*, 71; De Vos, *De Eerste Wereldoorlog*, 55–8, 60, 63; Hendryckx, 'In het spoor', 2; Holmes & De Vos, *Langs de Velden van Eer*, 93–4, 98; Bastier, 'België tijdens de Eerste Wereldoorlog', 23, 25; Schepens, 'België in de Eerste Wereldoorlog', 29; De Munck, *De Grote Moeder*, 5; Meire, *De Stilte van de Salient*, 58

75 De Schaepdrijver, *De Groote Oorlog*, 184; De Schaepdrijver, *Taferelen uit het Burgerleven*, p. 93

76 *J'accuse*, 297

resident abroad would come to reinforce the army on the Yser. They joined troops who lacked everything: officers, food, clothes, boots, morale. With the help of the Anglo-Belgian Committee a Belgian Field Ambulance Service Committee was set up, which set about substantially increasing the number of Red Cross ambulances available to the Belgian army, but medical aid was inadequate and remained so.[77]

An important observation should be made at this point. Although the Belgian high command was largely monolingual, the notion that many men died because the mainly Flemish rank and file were unable to understand orders issued by their French-speaking superiors is a myth. All orders were translated by Flemish-speaking NCOs and in any case few Flemish soldiers were unable to muster the small amount of French needed to comprehend simple commands. The warning '*danger de mort*' will have confused no one. Nor is there any substance to the allegation that many sick or wounded Flemish soldiers died because they were unable to explain to their French-speaking doctors and nurses what was wrong with them.[78] Nevertheless it is true that more Flemings were killed than Walloons (French-speaking Belgians), the ratio in 1917 being a remarkable 70–30. Fifty-seven per cent of the Belgian population was Flemish and fifty-nine per cent of soldiers were Flemings, but because the Walloons were generally better educated, far fewer of them were simple infantrymen. Walloons were mostly placed in the less hazardous artillery and engineering sections.[79]

### *The Germans against the French*

The German advance through Belgium was hard going, and terrible losses were inflicted on both sides, but it was the French who suffered most in the opening months of the war. On 2 August, the day before battle began in earnest, several German patrols crossed the French frontier at Joncherey, close to the Swiss border. In the skirmishes that resulted, a French corporal called André Peugeot was killed. He was the first of the French dead.[80]

As already mentioned, the initial fighting often resembled the old familiar wars of the nineteenth century. Men still regularly fought with sable and lance.[81] So it is intriguing to discover that a young French sub-lieutenant called Charles de Gaulle was already noting in his diary:

> The mannered calm of the officers, who allow themselves to be shot dead standing upright; the bayonets on the rifles of several obstinate platoons; the

---

77 De Schaepdrijver, *De Groote Oorlog*, 123, 173; Moeyes, *Buiten schot*, 126–9; De Munck, *De Grote Moeder*, 11; Hirschfeld, 'Let op, Levensgevaar', 64

78 De Schaepdrijver, *De Groote Oorlog*, 189–90; Holmes & De Vos, *Langs de Velden van Eer*, 99; De Schaepdrijver & Charpentier, *Vlaanderens weezang*, 3

79 De Vos, *De Eerste Wereldoorlog*, 58–9, 102

80 Gilbert, *First World War*, 31

81 Holmes, *Riding the Retreat*, 2

> blowing of bugles calling on men to advance; the wonderful heroic courage of individuals... It is all for nought. In the blink of an eye it becomes clear that no virtue in the world is proof against the fire of the enemy.[82]

French reservists and volunteers, in their traditional and highly visible red trousers, fell to German gunfire in their tens of thousands, in the Vosges Mountains and in Champagne, at Reims, St Quentin and Chateau-Thierry, on the Aisne and the Marne. They advanced in formation, without cover of any kind. Within two weeks their losses had reached 300,000 and five thousand officers were dead. At Roselies near Charleroi on 22 August, the 74th Infantry Brigade lost 1,100 men. On that one day alone, 27,000 Frenchmen died on various battlefields, making it the bloodiest day in French history. In setbacks such as the Battle of Haute Meurthe a month later, an average of 800 men died for every attacking regiment.[83] As a result of the policy of *l'attaque à outrance* the ratio of dead to wounded, which for centuries had stood at one to four or five in most circumstances, was remarkably high: one to three. At officer level it was even higher. Martin Gilbert, writing about the first months of the war, goes so far as to say that the ratio of dead to wounded in the French army was one to two. By the end of August, twenty per cent of French troops and forty per cent of French officers were out of action. Personal courage was valued more highly than caution, so officers always went ahead of their men. Their white gloves and red trousers made them easy targets for German riflemen.[84] A year later their uniforms were changed, but by then it was too late. The armies had dug themselves in.[85]

*The British and their 'Great Retreat'*

Britain declared war on Germany as soon as the German army crossed the Belgian border. Many British men spontaneously reported for service with the British Expeditionary Force (BEF). Their enthusiasm only increased when the BEF suffered defeat at Mons. The battle was costly for the Germans and in accordance with an old British custom the defeat was celebrated as a moral victory. Volunteers would not see the continent for some time. The force that landed in mid-August was a professional army, disciplined and thoroughly trained, and the men regarded war less as a matter of patriotism than simply their job, as their young German opponents would soon find out to their cost. Despite its professionalism, however, the BEF proved no match for massive German numerical superiority.

---

82 Kielich, 'De grote schande', 23

83 Ellis, *Eye-Deep*, 91; Brants & Brants, *Velden van weleer*, 170, 173

84 Brants & Brants, *Velden van weleer*, 173–4; see also: Winter & Baggett, *1914–18*, 71; Ellis, *Eye-Deep*, 91; Holmes, *Riding the Retreat*, 201; Macdonald, *1914*, 230–31; Eksteins, *Rites of Spring*, 100; Gilbert, *First World War*, 123

85 The famous German *Pickelhaube* helmet would be replaced after a while as well. It too was highly visible and offered little protection against modern weaponry.

The British opened fire on 23 August. Their commander, Major Abell, was shot in the head. He was the first British officer to die. His second-in-command was killed too, as was the man who took over from him, and after heavy casualties on both sides the British withdrew, forced to fall back partly because of the French withdrawal that followed defeat on the Sambre. They retreated for weeks, sometimes in a state of utter chaos.[86]

The officers and senior NCOs of the BEF were upper-class chaps, brought up on foxhunting and polo. They were astonished by what they saw. This was not the war they had prepared for and looked forward to, a war that would bring either a glorious death or a life of pride and renown. Professional soldiers, whose horses had almost become extensions of their own bodies, found themselves up against barbed wire and unprecedented firepower. One of them, Francis Grenfell, who like his brother Riversdale and his cousins Julian and Gerald would be dead within a year, described an advance with his company. 'We had simply galloped about like rabbits in front of a line of guns, men and horses falling in all directions.' This did not, incidentally, prevent the Grenfell family historian from extolling Francis' heroic death, any more than it dissuaded the painter of his memorial canvas from presenting the attack as a triumph, with British cavalrymen, sabres drawn, making mincemeat out of German soldiers carrying modern firearms.[87]

Both the British and the Germans reported in detail on the horrors of Mons. Like the Boer War and the Russo-Japanese War, Mons demonstrated the capacities of massed firepower, even though little use had been made as yet of the machine-gun.[88] Lieutenant K.F.B. Tower wrote firstly of the successes. 'Shortly after this the enemy started to advance in mass. … Maurice Dease fired his two machine-guns into them and absolutely mowed them down. I should judge without exaggeration that he killed at least 500 in the two minutes.' Soon, however, he turns his attention to the dead.

> Ashburn had been wounded in the head, and Steele took over command of the Company, which by now was seriously reduced in numbers and the dead and dying were lying all over the place. Colonel McMahon sent up about 100 men under Captain Bowden Smith and Lieutenant Mead to support us, but most of them were killed by shrapnel fire on the way up. Poor little Jo Mead reached where I was when he was immediately shot in the head and died instantly. Captain Bowden Smith was hit with shrapnel in the stomach and lay at my feet in fearful agony. One could do nothing for the wounded.[89]

---

86 Binneveld, *Om de geest*, 41; Gilbert, *First World War*, 56; Keegan, *First World War*, 110, 144

87 Hynes, *Soldiers' Tale*, 35–8

88 Holmes, *Firing Line*, 169

89 Macdonald, *1914–1918*, 18–19

When the order to retreat was issued, British casualties stood at 1,600. German losses were significantly higher, with at least five thousand dead, wounded and missing, possibly ten thousand. Infantrymen in the British army were capable of firing fifteen rounds a minute, which made the Germans think they must all be equipped with machine-guns. In fact they had only a few. German forces were nevertheless depleted by a wall of steel. Forty-six-year-old author Walter Bloem, who had been called up as a reserve officer and was made a captain in the 12th Brandenburg Grenadiers, was the only German company commander to survive action at Mons. In his battalion alone, five officers and half the men were killed. Everywhere he looked, to left and right, lay the dead and wounded, shaking with death spasms, groaning terribly, blood gushing from fresh wounds.

> 'I'm hit, sir! O God! Oh, mother! I'm done for!' 'I'm dying, sir!' said another one near me. 'I can't help you, my young man – come, give me your hand' … Behind us the whole meadow was dotted with little grey heaps. The hundred and sixty men that had left the wood with me had shrunk to fewer than a hundred.[90]

Although the German advance did not go the way the German generals had imagined or hoped,[91] the British were defeated at Mons, and they were defeated in every subsequent battle that autumn. Attempting an attack on the German flank near Valenciennes, the 9th Lancers and the 18th Hussars were mown down by machine-gun fire.[92] A day after the start of the retreat they fought the Battle of Elogues, an encounter given minimal attention in the British *Official History of the Great War* but which claimed more casualties than the Battle of Mons, described at such length. One battalion lost eight hundred of its one thousand men.[93] At Le Cateau two days later, the British lost close to 8,000 men, the Germans 5,000.[94] Private John Stiles wrote in a letter published in the press: 'People who say that the German artillery is no good simply don't know what they are talking about. I can only figure it out as being something worse than the mouth of hell.'[95]

Orders from on high often had disastrous consequences in the British army's dark days between Mons and the Marne. Clarrie Hodgson told how in the middle of a fire-fight, which was already going badly,

> the order came down – *Save the guns*! And the gun teams came dashing down over the hill, right through the middle of all this carnage. And then the Hun opened

90 Holmes, *Firing Line*, 169; Holmes, *War Walks*, 105–6; Holmes & De Vos, *Langs de Velden van Eer*, 70; Gilbert, *First World War*, 58; Keegan, *First World War*, 110

91 Keegan, *First World War*, 108

92 Ellis, *Social History*, 128–9

93 Holmes, *Riding the Retreat*, 146

94 Holmes, *Riding the Retreat*, 195; see also: Gilbert, *First World War*, 96; Macdonald, *1914*, 236 (note)

95 Terraine, 'The Inferno: 1914–18', 177

> up on them – artillery, machine-guns, everything! The horses were silhouetted against the skyline and made a perfect target. It was *absolute slaughter*! Men and horses were just blown to pieces.[96]

The order was quickly followed by another, to everyone's great relief: every man for himself. Officially designated a 'withdrawal', this was a matter of simple flight. Deathly exhausting flight at that. Men marched day and night, covering 140 miles in thirteen days. Many lay in a comatose sleep by the side of the road, in the pouring rain, without coats or anything else to cover them.[97] The roads were packed with British and French troops, civilian refugees, and long columns of primitive farm carts, without either nurses or blankets but piled high with the wounded.[98] Captain Wilfrid Dugmore of the Cheshires wrote:

> I was dead beat not having touched a mouthful of food for over 24 hours, nor had I had a drink, less than 2 hours sleep; we had been marching in a sort of trance, receiving orders which were promptly countermanded … I think I would have welcomed a bullet through a vital spot.[99]

Alan Hanbury-Sparrow described a battalion of infantry in retreat.

> Behind him creeps the battalion at the slow, lumbering pace of an agricultural labourer. Half the packs are missing, three-quarters of the greatcoats gone. … Altogether it's a distressing and alarming sight, this column where no four are abreast and no two in step.[100]

Corporal John Lucy of the 2nd Royal Irish Rifles confirmed what Hanbury-Sparrow had seen.

> Our minds and bodies shrieked for sleep. ... In a short time our singing army was stricken dumb. Every cell in our bodies craved rest, and that one thought was the most persistent in the minds of the marching men… Men slept while they marched, and they dreamed as they walked.[101]

---

96 Holmes, *Riding the Retreat*, 188

97 Holmes, *Riding the Retreat*, 203; Dunn, *The War*, 23, 29, 30

98 Holmes, *Riding the Retreat*, 168

99 Holmes, *Riding the Retreat*, 137; Holmes, *War Walks*, 107; Holmes & De Vos, *Langs de Velden van Eer*, 71

100 Holmes, *Riding the Retreat*, 245–6

101 Winter & Baggett, *1914–18*, 79, 83

The condition of the cavalry was little better. Major Archibald 'Sally' Home described men who 'slept in saddles – they had been going for three days – little or no food, little or no sleep'.[102]

On average men slept for about three hours out of every twenty-four. One officer could not imagine anyone could be so tired and hungry and yet go on living. After each of the short rest stops, it took the men a huge effort to struggle to their feet. Some refused to get up. Others were unable to stand.[103]

This exhaustion is sometimes given as the reason why many soldiers swore they had seen angels covering their retreat, as in the myths and legends. Frank Richards remembered a soldier who pointed to the side of the road and said to him, 'There's a fine castle there, see?' There was no castle anywhere near.[104] Hunger and exhaustion are not required to explain these visions, however. Jay Winter correctly points out in his *Sites of Memory, Sites of Mourning* that even in peacetime many people clung to supernatural beliefs, and they now found themselves in the perfect environment for the spread of such tales.[105]

The machine-gun gradually became a familiar sight in the open landscape of France and Flanders. Even at this early stage in the war, the 1st King's Own of 12th Brigade was caught in machine-gun fire and then shelled. Four hundred soldiers and officers were killed or badly wounded. Lieutenant C.L. Brereton wrote dejectedly: 'Wounded were being hastily dressed by the side of the road, but it was obvious that there were no ambulances, and practically no medical arrangements.'[106]

The British retreated steadily, but on several occasions they managed to turn their fire on the Germans, who were advancing en masse in their field grey. The results make the later use of the same tactic by the British, most famously on the Somme, seem even stranger, and a remark made by Corporal John Lucy in these opening days of the war strikes home. 'Such tactics amazed us, and after the first shock of seeing men slowly and helplessly falling down as they were hit, gave us a great sense of power and pleasure. It was all so easy.'[107]

The Germans retained the upper hand, while the British, utterly exhausted, continued to flee.[108] Captain E. Balfour remembered fighting and marching practically non-stop for six days. 'The Colonel [Ansell] reckoned that he and I had only 10 hours sleep in 8 days. … In addition for 5 or 6 days we got practically

102 Holmes, *Riding the Retreat*, 246

103 Holmes, *Riding the Retreat*, 282; Macdonald, *1914*, 196–7, 237, 368, 371

104 Holmes, *Riding the Retreat*, 196; Terraine, 'Inferno', 178; Bourke, *Dismembering the Male*, 231–5

105 Winter, *Sites of Memory*, 65–7

106 Holmes, *Riding the Retreat*, 185–6

107 Holmes, *Riding the Retreat*, 124, 128; Holmes, *War Walks*, 88; Holmes & De Vos, *Langs de Velden van Eer*, 51; Gilbert, *First World War*, 57

108 Macdonald, *1914*, 236

no supplies.'[109] An eye-witness spoke of cavalrymen asleep in their saddles and infantry marching 'under the miraculous power of discipline' with their eyes shut, 'every man stiff with cold and weak with hunger'.[110]

In such hazardous circumstances, this degree of exhaustion could be fatal. Anyone too tired to walk is too tired to fight, so the retreating troops were largely defenceless. They were barely able to counter enemy rifle fire and few had enough energy left to fire mortars or shells. Gunner Darbyshire could work for no more than twenty minutes amid the earth tremors caused by his own gun. The blood pouring from his ears and nose made it impossible to continue. The lieutenant who took over from him was blown metres into the air only a few seconds later and mortally wounded. Immediately after that, both Darbyshire and Captain E.K. Bradbury, who was standing next to him, were hit. Darbyshire was thrown to the ground unharmed, but Bradbury lost both legs and died a short time later in great pain.[111] Sergeant E.M. Lyons was there:

> In the village [Néry] I assisted the RAMC men to load up the ambulances. After the last one went off I was still scouting around to make sure there were no more wounded. There was one we couldn't put in the ambulance he was so badly wounded so we borrowed a farm cart and packed it with straw and made him as comfortable as possible. He was the battery commander Capt Bradbury who I'm sorry to say died soon.[112]

### *Towards the stalemate*

The Germans could not keep up the pace they had set. They too became exhausted, especially the men who were expected to march right across Belgium, then when they got well inside France to take a more southerly route and finally, once level with Paris, to turn inland. They were required to cover twenty-five to thirty miles a day, for weeks at a time, carrying loads weighing dozens of pounds, onwards and onwards in the hope and expectation of final victory. The British and French meanwhile found there was one advantage to being on the retreating side: their supply lines to their own ration dumps were becoming easier to manage while the Germans were finding it increasingly difficult to feed themselves.[113] Stephan Westman, a doctor who was serving as a young conscript with the 113th Infantry Regiment wrote: 'We slogged on, living, as it were, in a coma, often sleeping whilst we marched, and when the column came to a sudden halt we ran with our noses against the billycans of the men in front of us.'[114] Towards evening on

109 Holmes, *Riding the Retreat*, 284
110 Gilbert, *First World War*, 60
111 Holmes, *Riding the Retreat*, 254
112 Holmes, *Riding the Retreat*, 257
113 Keegan, *First World War*, 118
114 Holmes, *Firing Line*, 116

3 September, a French eye-witness watched a German soldier drop to the ground groggy with exhaustion. All the German could say was 'forty kilometres! forty kilometres!'[115]

On the Eastern Front the Russian enemy turned out to be ready for battle much sooner than expected, and despite the crucial German victory at Tannenberg it was felt necessary to move German troops across from the Western Front to the East. The original plan had taken into account that Russian troops would invade German soil, but when the enemy actually started to threaten their eastern border, the Germans began to see an invasion as a deadly threat to morale at home. They tried to compensate for the resulting shortage of men in the West by having their most westerly troops turn away from the coast sooner than planned. They wheeled round to pass north of Paris rather than to the city's west and south, which meant they were approaching the French not from the rear as intended but on the flank. In early September the British and French, again at great cost,[116] managed to drive a wedge between the German First and Second Armies, throwing them back across the Marne and the Aisne, where they began to dig in. This marked the start of trench warfare. The Battle of the Marne was decisive, determining the course of the rest of the war, and it was a precursor to the *Materialschlacht* that would follow. The Germans used more ammunition on each day of the battle than in the whole of the Franco-Prussian war.[117]

After the Battle of the Marne a transition phase began in which movement and entrenchment went hand in hand as both sides tried to secure the optimum strategic and tactical positions. At Neuve Chapelle, about twelve miles south of the Belgian border near Ypres, the German armies deployed the huge mortars that had destroyed the Belgian forts at the start of the war. The ground shook as if from an earthquake. John Lucy and his men could do nothing but take shelter and wait it out: '[We were] half-blinded and half-choked by poisonous vapors, waiting for the enemy infantry, while our overworked stretcherbearers busied themselves with new dead and wounded.' Towards evening they at last received word that the Germans were approaching. The guns fell silent. 'Thank Christ. Thank Christ. The relief was unspeakable. We stood up, stretching wide and loose, men once more and no longer cannon fodder.' What they witnessed next had already become a familiar sight.

> We let them have it. We blasted and blew them to death. They fell in scores, in hundreds, the marching column wilting under our rapid fire. ... The few survivors panicked, and tried to keep their feet in retreat. We shot them down through the back. A red five minutes. ... We had cancelled out our shell-tortured day with a vengeance.[118]

---

115 Keegan, *First World War*, 118

116 Macdonald, *1914*, 310

117 Chickering, *Imperial Germany*, 35; Audoin-Rouzeau & Becker, *'14–'18*, 44

118 Wilson, *Myriad Faces*, 63–4

Ernst Stadler may have been among the German soldiers Lucy saw die that day. But what made a man a German? Stadler was a Shakespeare specialist, born in Alsace, who had studied at Oxford, taught in Brussels, and was a friend of French authors including Romain Rolland and Charles Péguy (Péguy died at around the same time). When war broke out he had been on the point of taking up a professorship in Canada.[119]

*The First Battle of Ypres*

The largest battle fought in the months between the German advance and the advent of total trench warfare was at Ypres, the small Belgian town that would never be out of the war news from that moment on. A German infantry officer compared the Battle of Ypres to the epidemic of bubonic plague that had reduced the population of the town by ninety per cent in the Middle Ages.[120] In October the Germans concentrated their heavy guns here, throwing several fresh battalions into the battle in the hope of forcing a way through to the sea and capturing Calais. The fresh battalions were partly composed of students, who although enthusiastic were very young and barely trained. Exhorted to join the army by their nationalistic professors, they had volunteered in large numbers. They inflicted further heavy losses, but although they outnumbered the BEF they were no match for it. 'First Ypres' lasted from 22 October to 22 November and cost the British almost 60,000 men, more than 20,000 of whom died. Lucy calculated that by the time the battle was over, sixty-nine out of every hundred soldiers who had landed on the continent in August had been killed or wounded.[121] The 7th Division, which landed at Zeebrugge that October, went into battle with 400 officers and 12,000 men; after ten days of fighting only forty-four officers and 2,336 men were left.[122] Corporal George Matheson wrote from First Ypres, 'We were complaining about the Aisne being bad, but it was a king to the fighting we have done since we came to Belgium. This is pure murder, not war.'[123] During the battle, on 29 October, an order to retreat failed to reach one British squadron. Not a single man in the squadron survived.[124] After the battle the British withdrew completely to build up reinforcements, constructing a new army around the remnants of the BEF by absorbing volunteers, who had now been training for several months. Some had already crossed the channel. The French army, which had also fought hard and suffered greatly at Ypres, took over the entire sector for the winter.[125]

---

119 'Jahrhundert der Kriege', 118

120 *J'accuse*, 299

121 Wilson, *Myriad Faces*, 67–8; Babington, *Shell-Shock*, 43; Holmes & De Vos, *Langs de Velden van Eer*, 108–9

122 Eksteins, *Rites of Spring*, 101

123 Macdonald, *1914*, 418

124 Macdonald, *1914*, 380–81

125 Holmes & De Vos, *Langs de Velden van Eer*, 110

It was the young Germans and the small number of Austrian troops with them who were hardest hit during the First Battle of Ypres. 'We have been forced to endure not only frightful and horrendous things ... here in Flanders, but unspeakable and inhuman things, such that one shuts ones eyes and forgets that one is a Christian', wrote Austrian soldier George Leinhos to his parents. Shortly before Christmas he added, 'How will I receive Christ here, where all the demons of hell have been unleashed?' A well-known Dutch theologian, writing a popular Christian-pacifist work, quoted what Leinhos had said and commented, 'Thank God this pious young man was killed before Christmas 1914 at Dixmude. His conscience is no longer troubled.'[126]

The notion that most of the German troops at First Ypres were young students is a myth. Students were certainly present in greater numbers than before, or on other battlefields, but the German army was as ever largely composed of farm labourers, working-class men and servants. They were certainly young, and many of them were killed. The battle has been known ever since as 'the massacre of the innocents' (*Kindermord*). At Steenakkermolen they met a particularly miserable fate. The village, whose name translates as 'Stonefield Mill', was dubbed *Totenmühle* by the Germans: Mill of the Dead. In the first two days of the battle there was a costly engagement at Bikschote, some way to the north, later known as the Battle of Langemarck. In the war cemetery at Langemarck lie the thousands of German dead of that battle, alongside more than 30,000 Germans who died subsequently or elsewhere. Eighty per cent of the victims of the First World War were no older than thirty, and the First Battle of Ypres and the Battle of Langemarck contributed significantly to this statistic.[127] After the war, in his book *Erlebnisse im Weltkrieg* (Experiences in the World War), *Reichsfinanzminister* and head of propaganda Mathias Erzberger would write of the spilling of 'young German blood in vain at Ypres'.[128] During the war, the early years in particular, he had sung to a very different tune.[129]

The German armies were not alone in being composed of young untrained soldiers. As we have seen, the volunteers of Kitchener's Army – named after the elderly general whose face stared out from posters, his pointed finger urging British youth to join up – began to reinforce the BEF from late 1914 onwards. They too had hardly any training and many had barely reached the minimum age for military service, or had lied. They were surrounded by trained professionals at first, but not for long. Older officers were killed and new officers were fewer in

126 Heering, *Zondeval*, 207; Haas, *Oorlogsjammer*, 27

127 Prior & Wilson, *Passchendaele*, 5; Brants & Brants, *Velden van weleer*, 101; Keegan, *History of Warfare*, 358–9; Holmes, *Firing Line*, 197; Gilbert, *First World War*, 98; Macdonald, *1914*, 367; De Vos, *De Eerste Wereldoorlog*, 81

128 Erzberger, *Erlebnisse*, 58

129 Tuchman, *The Guns*, 322–3; Tucker, *European Powers*, 241–2

number and mostly inferior in quality.[130] By the final days of 1914, half of Graves' platoon was made up of underage boys.

> William Bumford, collier, for instance, who gave his age as eighteen, was really only fifteen. He used to get into trouble for falling asleep on sentry duty, an offence punishable with death, but could not help it. I had seen him suddenly go to sleep, on his feet, while holding a sandbag open for another fellow to fill.[131]

After a while the men's ages were checked and everyone older than fifty or younger than eighteen was pulled back from the front line, including William Bumford. He came of age in 1917, returned to the battalion and was killed almost immediately.

To make joining up as easy as possible, the British had opted for a system in which brothers, friends and acquaintances could be assigned to the same units. These were the Pals' or Chums' Battalions. The policy had the adverse effect that when these battalions were caught in heavy fighting, families, even whole communities mourned devastating losses. The rejoicing was great when things went well, but so was the suffering when things went wrong. Blunden for one was convinced that, particularly because brothers served together, the system led to 'a culmination of suffering'. The army eventually abandoned the system and new recruits were distributed among different army units.[132]

Exhaustion was not confined to the young. The retreat had been tiring, but this waiting day and night for the roar of the guns to subside, with heavy fighting in between, was utterly gruelling. Lyn Macdonald writes that after ten days of fighting at Ypres there was hardly a man, even an officer, who was not thoroughly done in, none 'whose clothing was not stiff with grime, who had not been soaked to the skin a dozen times, who had not slept standing up (if he had slept at all), who had not forgotten what it is like to have a square meal or a night's peaceful rest'.[133]

The retreat, from 23 August to 5 September, cost the British around 15,000 of their initial force of 100,000 men. A horrendous number, people thought then, but before long they would look back with nostalgia to a time when losses were as low as fifteen per cent in two weeks. The British total for 1914 came to 90,000 dead and wounded.[134] It was already getting hard to find either officers or men who had been out since August. After the new offensives of early 1915 – Neuve Chapelle again, Festubert, Aubers Ridge – it would be rare to come upon a soldier, of whatever rank, in one of those rare quiet hours who could tell of the Battle

---

130 Keegan, *Face of Battle*, 219–20; Macdonald, *1914*, 366

131 Graves, *Goodbye*, 81

132 Blunden, *Undertones of War*, 45; Heijster, *Ieper*, 51; Keegan, *First World War*, 298

133 Macdonald, *1914*, 381

134 Macdonald, *1914*, 425

of Mons or the bloody withdrawal from Le Cateau. Assuming he was willing to speak of such things.[135]

For the British, Ypres would ultimately come to symbolize the entire war. At first it was no more than a bulge in the front line that had to be held for tactical reasons. Later it became a matter of prestige to hold the town where so many British soldiers had lost their lives, and later still it would become a symbol of the futility of the war, the endlessness of the struggle, the harsh life of the soldier at the front, surrounded by mud, and the obtuseness of the generals.[136] Later in this chapter, when we reach 1917, we will return to look in detail at the battle that gave rise to this powerful symbolism, known simply as Passchendaele.

The Battle of Ypres was the last major engagement of that first year of the war. For the British it had been a disastrous time, but for the French and Germans those first five months were truly catastrophic. They suffered higher losses in 1914 than in any of the years that followed, even the year of Verdun and the Somme, or the German spring offensive of 1918. Around 750,000 German troops had been put out of action. When France counted its dead alone at the end of 1914 they came to about 300,000 – 50,000 more than the British death toll in the whole of the Second World War. Of those 300,000, 45,000 were under twenty years old and over 90,000 were aged twenty to twenty-four. Another 600,000 Frenchmen were wounded, captured or missing. This is a cautious estimate. Several highly respected commentators give significantly higher figures.[137]

## 1915

### *The spring offensives*

The weeks around New Year's Day 1915, by which time the war as planned should already have been over, several Allied offensives were mounted against strongly defended German positions. The British attacked at Neuve Chapelle and Fromelles on 18 December and lost thirty-seven officers and 784 men. Out of one platoon of fifty-seven men, only four emerged from the battle unscathed.[138]

The rain poured down, turning the ground to sucking mud; rifles jammed and artillery observers were seriously hindered by fog. The weather was the main reason the French offensive in Artois some miles to the south was halted in early

135 Holmes, *Riding the Retreat*, 285; Macdonald, *1914*, 421

136 Brants & Brants, *Velden van weleer*, 70–71

137 Horne, *Price of Glory*, 19; Hynes, *Soldiers' Tale*, 75; Keegan, *First World War*, 6, 146, 343

138 Eksteins, *Rites of Spring*, 107

January. The result: a small gain in ground to the north of Notre Dame de Lorette and to the south of Carency, at a cost of almost 8,000 dead.[139]

The French were able to maintain the offensive begun in Champagne on 20 December for a little longer, until mid-March, although without any significant territorial gains and with losses of almost a quarter of a million dead and wounded. There was heavy fighting around Hartmannswillerkopf too, a strategically important peak in the Vosges Mountains. The French managed to hold it until April, a defensive action that cost 20,000 lives.

The same unhappy result awaited the British when they attacked again at Neuve Chapelle from 10 to 12 March. The remnant of the BEF that had survived First Ypres was wiped out. The old British professional army no longer existed. Although their offensive was doomed from the start because battle was joined with too few men, who were poorly equipped, it is doubtful whether the outcome would have been any different if their numbers and equipment had been appropriate. The preparatory bombardment had cost many German lives, but German positions were still largely intact, so the advancing troops – their officers wearing monocles and wielding sabres – were at the receiving end of a devastating artillery barrage accompanied by machine-gun fire. Two machine-gun posts, or twelve men in total, succeeded in almost completely knocking out two British battalions of around 1,500 men each. A three-day battle produced no result, aside from 13,000 British and 12,000 German dead. The lesson the high command on both sides drew from this was that they needed more men.[140]

It was a lesson they were unable to act upon in time for the Second Battle of Ypres, once more a German offensive, although this time intended mainly as a diversionary tactic to coincide with the offensive at Gorlice and Tarnow in Galicia.[141] Given the enormous number of dead the British might be forgiven for feeling relieved that the forces engaged there were limited. Entire British brigades were wiped out by machine-gun fire. The diary of the German 57th Regiment reads: 'There could never before in war have been a more perfect target than this solid wall of khaki men… There was only one possible order to give: "Fire until the barrels burst."'[142] The Second Battle of Ypres claimed the life of probably the youngest soldier to die in the war. On 24 May fourteen-year-old J. Condon was killed. He is not the reason the battle is remembered. Second Ypres was the first engagement in which gas was used.

Towards the end of the afternoon of 22 April, on the northern side of the front near Langemarck, immediately after a short but heavy barrage, the valves of thousands of cylinders were unscrewed and 168 tons of yellow-green chlorine gas drifted from German positions towards the French in the northern sector, in

139 Simkins, *World War I*, 58–9

140 Brants & Brants, *Velden van weleer*, 104; Ellis, *Eye-Deep*, 93; Ellis, *Machine Gun*, 131–2; Simkins, *World War I*, 62–3

141 Chickering, *Imperial Germany*, 57

142 Ellis, *Eye-Deep*, 93

clouds that gradually turned into a bluish-white haze. French troops without any protective equipment, many of them from the colonies, panicked and left a gap in the front almost eight kilometres wide. The Germans were surprised by the success of their own gas attack and had not arranged for sufficient reserves to follow up, so reinforcements were soon able to close the gap.

Two days later the Germans staged a second gas attack, this time on Canadian positions at St Julien a short way to the south, but the Canadians, using handkerchiefs and hand-towels drenched in water or urine as emergency gas masks, prevented another collapse in the front. Of the 18,000 Canadians holding the sector, 2,000 were killed by the poisonous fumes. The next day, during an Allied attack, the Germans released a cloud of gas that hit mainly French colonial troops from Senegal. Out of sheer terror they killed their own officers, who had been told to shoot them should they turn and run. A British cavalry brigade 'restored order'.

Second Ypres would be one of the few battles of the Great War in which the attacking side suffered fewer casualties than defending forces. The Germans had huge numerical superiority in artillery and an advantageous geographical position, since in the salient the Allies could be fired on from three sides. Maintaining control of Ypres cost the British around 16,000 lives. Some 12,000 French soldiers were killed. The German death toll came to no more than 5,000.[143]

In an effort to relieve the British, the French resumed their offensive at Notre Dame de Lorette in the spring. Over a period of five weeks they gained a few kilometres of terrain here and there. The *attaque à outrance* had degenerated into *grignotage*, or a nibbling away at enemy territory. By the time the offensive was halted more than 100,000 Frenchmen and 60,000 Germans had been killed. Around the same time the French launched an unsuccessful attempt to capture St Mihiel, south of Verdun, at a cost of 64,000 dead.[144] The British supported this offensive with an attack at Aubers Ridge, again close to Neuve Chapelle. The attack began on 9 May and was abandoned the same day. Three British brigades were held back by 15 German companies with 22 machine-guns. One battalion managed to get just 50 men as far as the German trench. A British general complained that he could not see his soldiers, to which his brigadier-general responded that they were lying out in no man's land, and that most of them would never stand again. A single day at Aubers Ridge had cost the British 11,500 men.[145]

In June the French tried again, this time in the Argonne, near Verdun, resulting in 32,000 French dead in less than a month. One battalion was reduced to 200 men.

---

143 Simkins, *World War I*, 63; Gilbert, *First World War*, 145, 164; Dyer, *Missing*, 89; Wilson, *Myriad Faces*, 129; Keegan, *First World War*, 214–15; Holmes & De Vos, *Langs de Velden van Eer*, 111

144 Brants & Brants, *Velden van weleer*, 104; Simkins, *World War I*, 59–60, 69, 73; Horne, *Price of Glory*, 24; Barthas, *Oorlogsdagboeken*, Introduction, 14–15

145 Ellis, *Eye-Deep*, 93; Gilbert, *First World War*, 164; Macdonald, *1915*, 311; Simkins, *World War I*, 71

It belonged to the French Third Army, which had lost 1,200 officers and 82,000 other ranks at Argonne since January, almost half its effective strength.[146]

*Loos*

1915 continued as it had begun: small offensives, many since forgotten, with few results from a military perspective but losses that were made all the worse in human terms by their ultimate futility. The renewed French offensives in Champagne in September and October cost another 85,000 Germans and 144,000 Frenchmen their lives.[147] The archetypal example of this kind of fighting, and the best remembered, was the Battle of Loos in Artois that took place at the same time. Thousands of recruits to the new British volunteer army had their first experience of battle here, and in many cases their last. Within two hours, on the British side alone, more soldiers died than were lost on all sides on D-Day, 6 June 1944. The conviction that success depended solely on deploying more and more men had claimed its first victims.[148]

For the first time too, a British attack took place from behind a cloud of gas. When the moment came to release it, however, the wind had dropped and in places was actually blowing towards their own side. Although a message was sent from the forward trench to divisional headquarters, explaining that the lack of wind made it impossible to release the gas from the cylinders, the order was not changed: they were to deploy 'the accessory', as the British army insisted on referring to gas. 150 tons of chlorine were released. Although in places the gas did reach German positions, taking the men by surprise and suffocating some 600 to death, most of the casualties were British. The gas formed a cloud several metres deep that hung over no man's land before drifting back. At that point the Germans compounded the problem by throwing tear-gas grenades. British trenches were littered with crying, coughing and choking soldiers.

The attack itself was not called off, despite the fact that German positions along most of the opposing front line were little affected by the gas. Some regiments even went 'over the top' more or less voluntarily, because their commanding officers felt they would probably be safer in no man's land than in the trenches. They were in for a rude awakening, the officers especially. Where the gas had reached German positions they made small territorial gains, but British troops as a whole formed an unmissable target. The machine-guns swept across them time and again, and the soldiers kept coming, until barbed wire made it impossible for them to advance any further. Many divisions lost more than half their men, and some

146 Simkins, *World War I*, 73; Ellis, *Eye-Deep*, 91–3; Keegan, *History of Warfare*, 361

147 Simkins, *World War I*, 75; for the battle of Loos and the use of gas see also: Dunn, *The War*, 153–7

148 Brants & Brants, *Velden van weleer*, 104; Ellis, *Eye-Deep*, 93; Babington, *Shell-Shock*, 61

battalions were never heard of again. W.H. Nixon could only describe them as having been annihilated. 'There was nobody left.'[149] Captain W.G. Bagot Chester saw his men fall around him, and when he reached the German wire he realized he was practically alone. He and the few men left around him ran backwards and forwards along the barbed wire in the hope of finding a way through. He and another man took cover in a shell-hole barely large enough to protect their torsos. Their legs stuck out over the edge and were hit several times.[150]

The next day twelve fresh battalions, almost 10,000 men in total, mounted a renewed assault. After three and a half hours of fighting, just under 400 officers and nearly 8,000 men were dead, wounded or missing. Their German opponents knew why. 'Never had the machine gunners such straightforward work to do nor done it so effectively. They traversed to and fro along the enemy's ranks unceasingly.'[151] Harry Fellowes remembered that the Germans abruptly stopped firing and did not even attempt to resume when the wounded struggled to their feet and started stumbling back to their own positions. A short time later he heard a rumour that German soldiers, 'filled with bitter remorse and guilt' had refused to fire another shot. 'I do believe this.'[152]

It was true. The Germans were so appalled by the effects of their own machine-guns that they ignored retreating troops. They would speak not of the Battle of Loos but of the *Leichenfeld von Loos* or 'corpse field' of Loos.[153] Never before in any war had a battle cost the British so many men: more than 50,000 in the space of 3 weeks, of whom almost 16,000 were dead or missing. German losses were negligible by comparison.[154]

The day the British began their attack at Loos, the French mounted a new offensive in Champagne. They too used gas. This time the poison did not affect primarily their own men but the outcome was comparable to Loos. German positions remained intact and by late October, when the offensive was halted, 140,000 Frenchmen were dead or wounded.[155] The painter Otto Dix had volunteered back in August 1914, because war was a thing you simply had to experience. This was the first battle in which he saw active service. Even before he reached the front, the nature of the fighting became clear to him as he watched the returning wounded and was struck by the jaundiced appearance of men who had been gassed. He produced hundreds of sketches, engravings and paintings dating

---

149 Macdonald, *1914–1918*, 105

150 Macdonald, *1914–1918*, 104–5; see also: Brants & Brants, *Velden van weleer*, 114–15; Winter, *Death's Men*, 60; Graves, *Goodbye*, 128, 130–31, 134; Gilbert, *First World War*, 197–8; Wilson, *Myriad Faces*, 257 (incl. note 15); Keegan, *First World War*, 218

151 Ellis, *Eye-Deep*, 93

152 Macdonald, *1914–1918*, 106

153 Gilbert, *First World War*, 199; Keegan, *First World War*, 218

154 Macdonald, *1914–1918*, 107; Wilson, *Myriad Faces*, 263; Brants & Brants, *Velden van weleer*, 105

155 Keegan, *First World War*, 219

from his first experience of battle through to the mid-1930s, works of art on a par with Goya's impressions of the Napoleonic War in Spain. Particularly well known is a brilliant and appalling series of works called 'Der Krieg' (The War). Drawing became a means of escape from the 'tedious bestiality', as he called it. Dix used his pen as well as his pencil and brush. Roland Dorgelès would describe the war as 'ruins, mud, long files of men foundered and fordone, taverns where they fight desperately for litres of wine, gendarmes on the watch, trunks of trees splintered into matchwood, and wooden crosses, crosses, crosses.' Dix quickly noted in his diary: 'Lice, rats, barbed wire, fleas, shells, bombs, caves, corpses, blood, Schnapps, mice, cats, gas, artillery, filth, bullets, mortars, fire, steel, that is war! The devil's work, all of it.' If he had ever felt any enthusiasm – by his own account it was more a matter of curiosity – then it had vanished in no time at all. This did not awaken any pacifist convictions in Dix, even though his drawings might seem to suggest it did. Dix was a devotee of Nietzsche, and he simply sketched and noted what he saw. He soberly ascertained that the war was a pandemonium of violence. He saw what war meant and refused to make it seem any more attractive than it was, but neither did he oppose it. War was an aspect of humanity, and no anti-war campaign could change that. Nevertheless, in the post-war years his demythologized, unheroic impressions were warmly welcomed in anti-war circles and regarded by nationalist Germany as an abomination.[156]

Shortly before Christmas, the Germans released phosgene gas in the Ypres salient. It was ten times stronger than chlorine and a thousand British soldiers were poisoned, of whom 120 died. The strong wind blew the gas right across the curve of the salient and British troops and on as far as another German trench on the Wytschaete Ridge.[157] Like the British at Loos, the Germans had now fallen victim to 'friendly poison'.

For the soldiers in the trenches, the winter of 1915–16 was hard, certainly as hard as the year whose end it marked, the year Macdonald designates as 'the death of innocence'. 1915 was also the year in which the proportion of French officers killed or put out of action for the rest of the war reached 50 per cent, and the number of French soldiers who had lost their lives came close to matching the total British death toll. The French had now suffered casualties of between 1 and 1.5 million dead and wounded, the British 300,000 and the Germans 875,000.[158] But neither that year nor that winter were as hard as the year that came next.

---

156 Conzelmann, *Der andere Dix*, 67, 76, 78, 132–3; Löffler, *Otto Dix*, 13; Winter & Baggett, *1914–18*, 99–101, 257; Liddle & Cecil, *Facing Armageddon*, 859–60; Dorgelès, *Croix de bois*, 101

157 Gilbert, *First World War*, 217

158 Brants & Brants, *Velden van weleer*, 173; Preston, 'Great Civil War', 150; Murray, 'West at war', 273

## 1916

### *Verdun*

The Battle of Verdun – Operation Judgment – began in late February and lasted a full ten months. It still qualifies as the greatest battle of attrition in history. The town on the Meuse was defended against a million German soldiers by 500,000 Frenchmen, who controlled several forts of which Douamont and Vaux are the best known. The fort at Douamont was the scene of particularly bitter fighting, and to this day the bones of more than 100,000 unidentified French and German dead can be seen in the Douamont Ossuary, one of four bone-vaults that France established after the war, the others being at Lorette, Dormans and Hartmannswillerkopf. Fort Douamont fell to the Germans at the end of February without any resistance, and the French then lost 100,000 soldiers in their efforts to recapture this one fort alone, an objective they achieved nine months later. This is enough to indicate the kind of battle it was. Paul Valéry had every reason to describe the Battle of Verdun as a war within a war. Henri Barbusse had every reason to write, with Verdun in mind, that 'two armies engaged in battle are one great army committing suicide'. Jünger had every reason to conclude that Verdun was not a battle but a massacre,[159] a bloody massacre on a few square kilometres that brought no visible benefit or advantage to either side. Many would argue it brought no invisible gains either.

The Germans correctly assumed that the French would give everything to defend Verdun. The forts around the town had been established after a humiliating defeat by the German States in 1870, in a war in which Verdun itself had been held, as it had been throughout 1914. After French capitulation in 1871, Verdun was the last town to be returned to France. The original citadel was built by Vauban, military architect to Sun King Louis XIV and a national hero to many even after the French Revolution. During the Revolution it was at Verdun that Danton cried out before the republican armies that they must not lose heart in their battle with the monarchists. All this had given Verdun great symbolic importance. In military terms it seems reasonable to question the enormous effort devoted to the defence of Verdun, especially since Liège had demonstrated that great military fortresses had had their day. But from a political point of view, giving up the town was unthinkable.[160]

Some claim this was exactly what the German high command was banking on. Before the battle, senior officers hinted to the Kaiser, without saying as much even to their direct subordinates, that they were aiming to bleed the French army white

159 Winter & Baggett, *1914–18*, 164; Brants & Brants, *Velden van weleer*, 205–6; Werth, *Verdun*, 2; Barbusse, *Le Feu*, 362; *Under Fire*, 4; De Vos, *De Eerste Wereldoorlog*, 95; Hendryckx, 'In het spoor', 4

160 Chickering, *Imperial Germany*, 67; Runia, *Waterloo Verdun Auschwitz*, 140; Audoin-Rouzeau & Becker, *'14–'18*, 259

rather than to capture the town.[161] Nevertheless, the question remains: were the Germans correct in claiming they had never intended to seize Verdun? Perhaps the German high command wanted to cover itself against possible failure, to ensure it could publicly justify its actions in retrospect, by putting on record a strategy of *Verbluten* or 'bleeding to death'. Those who support the *Verbluten* theory can point to the fact that the German armies were at no stage deployed at full strength simultaneously. On the other hand, it had long been known that mass deployment in itself would not bring victory. Whatever the case may be, German troops believed the intention was to capture Verdun, and the end result was the steady and relentless spilling of French blood. Not only French blood. The Germans bled too, a prospect that Lance-Corporal Alfred E. Vaeth, who was killed in October 1916, considered before the battle in relation to the war as a whole. Germany would not be defeated, he wrote in late January 1916, but it might well bleed to death, and therefore the Mort Homme, a hill that was particularly fiercely fought over, might equally well be named *Toter Mann*.[162] In late April a French captain wrote of the fighting on and around the Mort Homme:

> I have returned from the toughest trial I have ever seen… four days and four nights – ninety-six hours – the last two days soaked in icy mud – under terrible bombardment, without any shelter other than the narrowness of the trench, which even seemed to be too wide. … I arrived there with 175 men, I returned with thirty-four, several half mad.[163]

The artillery barrage that preceded and accompanied the German assault was overwhelming, and throughout the ten months that followed a torrent of shells fell on the land around Verdun, initially from the Germans side, later from French positions as well. Villages were wiped off the map for ever. Agricultural land was impossible to farm for decades. Forests disappeared from the face of the earth. Even under cloudless skies the sun was barely visible through the multicoloured fumes and clouds of smoke that drifted across the battlefield for months.[164]

The initial barrage was more intense than any bombardment ever seen before. On the first day alone, around a million shells were fired. French writer Jules Romain wrote of that day:

> Over the whole of the front … to a depth of several kilometres, the same dance of dust, smoke, and debris went on, to a thunderous accompaniment of noise. Thousands of men, in groups of two, three, of ten, sometimes of twenty, bent their backs to the storm, clinging together at the bottom of holes, most of which

161 Murray, 'West at war', 276; Marix Evans, *Battles of the Somme*, 8

162 Brants & Brants, *Velden van weleer*, 207–9; Witkop, *Kriegsbriefe*, 124; Horne, *Price of Glory*, 161–2

163 Murray, 'West at war', 277

164 Brants & Brants, *Velden van weleer*, 208–9

> were no better than scratches in the ground, while many scarcely deserved the name of shelter at all. To their ears came the sound of solid earth rent and disembowelled by bursting shells.[165]

Flora and fauna that survived the shelling succumbed to the repeated use of gas. Martin Gilbert wrote that because of a German gas attack on 30 April – in which nearly 600 British soldiers were poisoned, 89 of them fatally – the grass shrivelled and 11 cows, 23 calves, 1 horse, 1 pig and 15 hens died.[166] The Germans tried out an 'improved' version of phosgene for the first time and even the doctors and nurses who treated the casualties were overcome by the fumes.[167]

In the early weeks of the battle, one German died on average every forty-five seconds. At Beaumont the French defenders had a feeling that the tight German formations were approaching death by machine-gun fire at such a rate that they must be being pushed forward by the regiments behind them. Like the British on the Somme, they were 'dying in front and pushing forward behind', as F. Scott Fitzgerald put it in *Tender is the Night*. Fitzgerald described the Germans on the Somme as walking slowly backwards a few inches a day, forced to leave their dead behind like 'a million bloody rugs'.[168] At Verdun the rugs were not left behind; the Germans had to advance over them in their heavy, muddy boots. One German soldier remarked after only a week that at this rate there would be no Germans left after the war. Nowhere were they safe. In early March a German regiment lost more soldiers in the reserve trenches than during the attack on Bois D'Haumont on the first day of the offensive.[169] In the end around 150,000 German soldiers died conquering an area half the size of Berlin. The sight of the wounded streaming back was described by a German general as 'a glimpse of hell', and a French lieutenant observed the French wounded.

> First came the skeletons of companies occasionally led by a wounded officer, leaning on a stick. All marched or rather advanced in small steps, zigzagging as if intoxicated. … It seemed as if these mute faces were crying something terrible, the unbelievable horror of their martyrdom.[170]

Up to this point, German painter Franz Marc, a front-line soldier since September 1914, had believed there was no difference in principle between war and peace. He did not welcome the war, far from it, but civilian life in peacetime held equally little appeal. Both war and peace were times of struggle, one physical, the other

---

165 Winter & Baggett, *1914–18*, 159–60

166 Gilbert, *First World War*, 240

167 Gilbert, *First World War*, 255

168 Horne, *Price of Glory*, 96; Fitzgerald, *Tender is the Night*, 67; Dyer, *The Missing*, 104–6

169 Horne, *Price of Glory*, 153

170 Murray, 'West at war', 277–8

psychological and economic; war was not even the cause of human suffering, it was a consequence of it, a bodily manifestation. Verdun seems to have changed his mind. The days of Verdun were 'the most colossal of all war days. ... No one who did not experience it can imagine the insane frenzy and force of the German incursion.' He suddenly started writing in his letters home about 'this deeply shaming, scandalous war'. On 2 March 1916 he wrote to his wife that for days he had seen nothing but 'the most appalling things human brains can imagine'. He was killed two days later.[171]

Within six weeks of the start of the battle the French army lost almost 100,000 men, dead and wounded. Some French and German army leaders who witnessed it wanted to end the slaughter. But war has rules of its own. By late May, losses had reached 200,000, almost as many as the Germans lost at Stalingrad nearly thirty years later, and the battle would go on for another six months. It was around this time that a French soldier called Alfred Joubaire confided in his diary that humanity had gone mad. 'It must be mad to do what it is doing. What a massacre. What scenes of horror and carnage! I cannot find words to translate my impressions. Hell cannot be so terrible. Men are mad!'[172] It was his final entry.

By early summer the battlefield had become a ghastly abattoir. Mutilated corpses were everywhere and visible to all. Wherever you looked you saw bits of them, not only in no man's land but in the walls of the trenches, shoved aside by soldiers ordered to keep the line free of obstructions. A head, a hand, a foot, a leg, each decomposing and stinking in proportion to the length of time that had passed since it was detached from its torso. One soldier noted: 'We all had on us the stench of dead bodies. The bread we ate, the stagnant water we drank, everything we touched had a rotten smell.'[173]

In high summer the German advance stalled. Summer turned to autumn and the French pressed forward. Autumn turned to winter and battle stopped, along lines not appreciably different from those of ten months before. More than 300,000 French and German soldiers had lost their lives and around 700,000 had been wounded. As a result of the system of rotation used by its high command, almost eighty per cent of the French army had experienced the horrors of Verdun, and the first signs of the mutiny that would break out the following spring were emerging. Written on the road to Verdun were the words *Chemin de l'abattoir* (Abattoir Road). One whole division started bleating like sheep when it was given the order to advance. Neither the Germans nor the French would ever fully recover from the 'massacre of Verdun'.[174]

---

171 Marc, *Brieven*, 72, 73, 89, 123, 125, 127, 131, 132, 134; Brants & Brants, *Velden van weleer*, 163

172 Gilbert, *First World War*, 250; De Vos, *De Eerste Wereldoorlog*, 89

173 Eksteins, *Rites of Spring*, 152

174 Gilbert, *First World War*, 232–3; Horne, *Price of Glory*, 97, 152, 176, 215, 300, 318; Binneveld, *Om de geest*, 47; Simkins, *World War I*, 99, 104; Winter & Baggett, *1914–18*, 157;

In a letter home, German soldier Anton Steiger described a scene in mid-July 1916 that demonstrates the entire madness of Verdun, despite the fact that no one was killed during the action he describes. He and his regiment had occupied an underground shelter 150 metres from Fort Thiaumont. Seen from above it was little more than a pile of earth, with a hole not much larger than the entrance to a fox's den.

> Behind it ruined steps led to the room where we would stay for four days. Under the rubble lay bodies; the legs of one stuck out as far as the knees. Below were three spaces, one of them full of French tracer shells and flares. The room we stayed in, as big as our kitchen, contained French ammunition, and the third space was packed with French explosives. It was pitch dark the whole time, since we had only a few candles. It stank terribly down there, the stench of death. All those four days I could barely eat anything. On the third day the French artillery shot their 28s so accurately at our hiding place that we thought it would collapse completely. On the fourth day, a Friday, they started firing their heavy guns early in the morning and went on until nine-thirty in the evening. That meant ten hours in a shelter under shellfire, ten hours facing death by being buried alive or the prospect of getting blown sky high should a shell hit the store of explosives. That was not to be the outcome. One exit was completely shot to pieces, the other so badly damaged that only with great difficulty could one man crawl through, without his equipment. So because our cellar lay six metres behind that gap and two metres lower, we got hardly any air. Then the French shot what were probably gas shells at the exit. Suddenly the sergeant-major stood up. He felt sick. A few others stand up and fall over. At that point the sergeant-major shouts, 'Out, out, whoever still can!' I and the others are lying on top of our packs. We stand up but the whole lot of us fall down again in a heap. Total chaos follows. Everyone gasps for air. Everyone wants out. Some fall, blocking the rest. Many don't have the strength to wriggle out. I did, thank God, and even managed to help someone else. Outside, straight to the nearest shell-hole! Everybody was white as chalk. We lay there, no longer moving, despite the shells bursting right and left. A few recovered their strength more quickly and fetched others who'd been unable to get out. All were saved. We had to resuscitate three or four of them. After half an hour, at ten in the evening, we set off back, or rather we staggered back. No one could walk properly; we stopped every five minutes.[175]

What is known as the Battle of Verdun actually accounts only for the ten months of heaviest fighting. Even before the battle started there was a series of engagements, and after it had officially ended many more men were killed and wounded. During the war as a whole, a total of around 420,000 German and French troops would die

---

Brants & Brants, *Velden van weleer*, 175, 205–6; Keegan, *History of Warfare*, 361; Preston, 'Great Civil War', 150

175 Witkop, *Kriegsbriefe*, 234–6

at Verdun, and 800,000 were wounded there, many by gas. After the war another 150,000 unidentified corpses – or scatterings of body parts – were collected and interred. To this day human remains are still being found.[176] A German soldier called Paul Boehlicke wrote in March 1918 at Verdun, seven months before he died there: 'Verdun, a terrible word! Countless men, young and full of hope, have lost their lives here – their bodies are now decomposing somewhere, between trenches, in mass graves, in cemeteries.'[177]

### *The colonial troops*

Like Neuve Chapelle in March 1915, and later Loos, the Battle of Verdun demonstrated the problems faced by colonial troops, as distinct from Dominion troops, citizens of Australia, Canada or New Zealand who, despite coming from so far away in geographical terms, had European origins and were familiar with European history, culture and warfare. The problems were particularly acute among French troops from Senegal, although the men of the Indian Army faced similar difficulties if only because, as Mark Harrison describes, their medical services were paltry, especially at the start of the war, even worse in fact than those of the French colonial forces. As the war went on their medical support was improved, partly to bolster the morale of Indian troops, which had declined considerably after rumours circulated about a deliberate British policy of letting them die. Like the Australians, the Indians were regarded as elite troops who – up to and including Neuve Chapelle – were deployed at the toughest places and died in their thousands as a result. They had been encouraged to participate in the war by, among others, the advocate of non-violent action Mohandas K. Gandhi, in the vain hope that afterwards the British would adopt a more compliant attitude towards Indian Home Rule.

Soldiers from the colonies fought in a war whose rationale they were even less able to fathom than men of the European armies, a war that bore absolutely no resemblance to what they knew of combat. They must have felt like Eskimos in a tropical rainforest. Many of their individual deeds, such as the beheading or literal 'de-facing' of German soldiers,[178] were regarded with horror by Europeans. In September 1918, in response to a rare Red Cross protest against the use of poison gas by both sides, the German army high command accused the Allies, not for the first time, of inhumane methods of warfare in the sense that they had deployed 'primitive peoples', under which heading they included not only colonial troops but the Russians and Serbs. Soldiers from the colonies, after all, had been known to commit horrific acts and did not spare the elderly, or women and children.

---

176 Horne, *Price of Glory*, 327–8; Murray, 'West at war', 278

177 Witkop, *Kriegsbriefe*, 345–6

178 Graves, *Goodbye*, 155; Macdonald, *1914–1918*, 66; Brants & Brants, *Velden van weleer*, 113; Van Bergen, *Zo bezien*, 11; Cooter, Harrison & Sturdy, *Medicine and Modern Warfare*, 185, 192

The Germans therefore believed the French and British were in no position to set themselves up as defenders of European civilization.[179] But the mechanical, mass, impersonal slaughter inflicted by men who had never seen their opponents, with torrents of mortars and shells fired from miles behind the lines,[180] must have evoked similar feelings in these so-called primitive peoples. One Indian soldier wrote home that he found himself not in the midst of a war but at the ending of the world. Nor could they understand why a wound did not exempt them from any further fighting. A Sikh wrote to his father in amazement that they were like baked grain flung into the oven a second time, 'and life does not come out of it'.[181]

It was partly because of this inability of soldiers from Asian and African colonies to understand the war they were fighting that the price they paid was so high. Around 250,000 French colonial soldiers were killed. No one doubted their courage. It was one of the reasons they were always in the first wave of an assault, although racist arguments also played a part.[182] To take one example, of the 5,000 Moroccan soldiers deployed at the Battle of the Marne, led by 103 French officers, 4,250 were killed, or 85 per cent. Of their French officers 'only' 50 per cent lost their lives.[183]

Horror at occasional acts by individual soldiers from the colonies is understandable, but grateful use was made of them. Their so-called barbarity was one reason for setting them unusually difficult tasks. German soldiers knew they could expect no mercy from colonial troops, and this made them even more fearful of an attack. At the time of the occupation of the Rhineland in the interwar years, Zuckmayer remarked that such fears had been unfounded and that the Senegalese, like all soldiers in those days, acted out of sheer terror. He wrote:

> They were very close, you could clearly hear them talking and calling to each other as they dragged their machine-guns forward, and those were strange, oppressive sounds, different from what one was accustomed to from the *poilus*. They were the Senegalese, the black auxiliary forces, of whom it was said that they took no prisoners, but slit their captives' stomachs open with long knives.[184]

It was the colonial soldiers themselves who paid the higher price. Senegalese troops were deployed during one of the battles around Fort Douamont in late June 1916. Impossible to control, they immediately occupied several German

179 Riesenberger, *Für Humanität*, 78; Frey, *Pflasterkästen*, 224; Sandstrom, *Comrades-in-Arms*, 77; Andriessen, *De oorlogsbrieven van Unteroffizier Carl Heller*, 23–4; Audoin-Rouzeau & Becker, *'14–'18*, 204–6

180 Whalen, *Bitter Wounds*, 43

181 Keegan, *First World War*, 213

182 Barbusse, *Le Feu*, 48

183 Gilbert, *First World War*, 71

184 Zuckmayer, *Als wär's ein Stück von mir*, 232

positions and made short work of the soldiers manning them. When the Germans in nearby trenches recovered from their shock, a machine-gun was brought into position. What happened next was a consequence of cultural differences combined with the fact that the troops had been sent to the front almost totally unprepared. Horne writes of 'the wretched Africans, never having been under such fire before, incapable of understanding where all the bullets were coming from'. Instead of spreading out, they bunched together in their confusion. Those who survived the slaughter 'were quickly pulled out of the line for further intensive training'.[185] Yet such scenes occurred repeatedly even after Verdun.

### *Somme*

Somme. One of those rare words that has taken on an entirely new meaning. On hearing it few will think principally of a river flowing gently through the French countryside. For many the word has become a synonym for the horrors of the First World War. Although the area saw heavy fighting in 1914 and again in 1918, its reputation is due above all to the five-month battle that took place near the river in 1916, between Amiens and Péronne, and especially the terrible first day, 1 July 1916, the blackest day in British military history, with almost 40,000 British soldiers wounded, 25,000 of them gravely, and around 20,000 killed. The plans drawn up beforehand took into account that 10,000 might be killed or wounded. Even that estimate had been adjusted upwards from calculations based on an earlier plan. Only half the men who went over the top that day were still in one piece by evening. Of the 60,000 soldiers who were first to leave the trenches, hoping to break through German lines, half had been wounded or killed within half an hour. Neither before nor since have so many men of a single army died on one day in such a limited area. During the famously bloody Battle of El Alamein in the Second World War, the British lost 13,500 men in twelve days: dead, wounded and missing. During the Black Week of the Boer War, 3,000 were killed or wounded, and the Boer War as a whole cost the lives of only slightly more than 20,000 British soldiers as a result of enemy fire and disease. If we leave sickness out of account, then the number of British dead on that one July day exceeds that of the Crimean War, the Boer War and the Korean War put together. The army of volunteers, Kitchener's men, was born during the hard labours of Loos and buried less than a year later. Siegfried Sassoon, whose platoon was not among the first to advance, took a quick look at the battlefield after he had finished shaving – a fleeting glance, since merely looking put him in deadly danger. It was as if he had seen 'a sunlit picture of hell'.

With approximately 6,000 dead and wounded, that first day brought the Germans few losses, at least in comparison to the British attacking force. But the Germans too, mainly because they did not want to limit themselves to defensive action, would chalk up heavy losses as the months went by, numbers already familiar

185 Horne, *Price of Glory*, 309

from Verdun. Jünger asked one of the soldiers returning from the front about his experiences. The man told of endless offensives, fields covered in bodies, thirst, the imploring cries of the wounded. 'If a man falls, he's left to lie. No one can help. No one knows if he'll return alive.'[186] When the battle ended the Germans decided to withdraw to the reinforced Hindenburg Line.[187]

In many stories about the First World War, rain is a prominent feature, but the Battle of the Somme began in glorious weather. It did not last. After the war soldiers asked themselves which mud-pool had been worse, the Somme or Passchendaele, but in that sun-drenched July of 1916 the weather made killing and being killed seem all the more unreal. Sergeant Norman Carmichael remembered shells dropping incessantly on the Bois Delville. The explosions tossed the dead into the air.

> In a strange sort of way it was fascinating to watch these bodies rising into the air above the tree stumps and circulating almost in slow motion and coming down again. Horrible, but fascinating. It seemed so strange to be lying there on that lovely warm summer's day watching these bodies going up and down[188]

There was some rain on 2 July, incidentally, and men wounded the day before drowned in flooded shell-holes.[189]

The Battle of the Somme was not originally intended as a lightning conductor to draw fire away from Verdun – the Allied offensive had been planned before the Battle of Verdun began – but it soon became part of an effort to reduce pressure on the French fortress town. Since the French had suffered far more casualties on the Meuse than expected, one result of Verdun was that the British had to mount the attack of 1 July and follow it through largely on their own. Although 50,000 Frenchmen went over the top that first day along with 100,000 British troops, the hardened veterans of France were absent, so the full weight of the battle fell upon the young soldiers of Kitchener's Army. Fewer than a quarter of the British officers and men who took part in the attack had been in uniform before 1914. To take account of this, and perhaps also in view of the fact that they outnumbered their German opponents seven to one, the chosen strategy required no military expertise or personal initiative from the men. Blind obedience would suffice. But

---

186 Sassoon, *Complete Memoirs*, 333; Brants, *Plasje bloed*, 99; Jünger, *Storm of Steel*, 92

187 Middlebrook, *First Day*, 84, 153, 228, 266; Brants & Brants, *Velden van weleer*, 134–6, 146; Fussell, *Bloody Game*, 33, 60; Simkins, *World War I*, 113; Gilbert, *First World War*, 260; Horne, *Price of Glory*, 294; Brown, *Somme*, 255; Macdonald, *Somme*, XIII; Winter & Baggett, *1914–18*, 187, 195; Wilson, *Myriad Faces*, 323, 326; Winter, *Death's Men*, 203; Keegan, *History of Warfare*, 361; Marix Evans, *Battles of the Somme*, 14–15, 33

188 Macdonald, *Somme*, 283; Brants & Brants, *Velden van weleer*, 136

189 Wilson, *Myriad Faces*, 326–7

as usual blind obedience turned out to be disastrous. The German strategy that had so astonished the soldiers of the British Expeditionary Force in 1914 had been adopted as their own. They were ordered to walk straight ahead, en masse, erect, towards German trenches. The preparatory barrage, which lasted seven days and consisted of one and a half million shells, tens of thousands of tons of steel and explosives fired from 1,500 barrels by 50,000 gunners, and which could be heard as far off as London, would undoubtedly have stripped those trenches of barbed wire and no German soldiers would be left alive or in any condition to offer resistance. Indeed, many Germans were killed or wounded in the endless series of bombardments, and a good deal of their defensive workings were demolished. But the barrage was ultimately counterproductive. Not enough German soldiers were put out of the running and not enough of the forward defences destroyed. The main effect was that the enemy knew an attack was coming. There was absolutely no element of surprise.[190]

When the barrage stopped horns sounded, calling the Germans out of their bunkers to man the machine-gun posts. Racked by sleeplessness, they were hungry, thirsty, sick, groggy, deafened, half mad and spattered with the blood of less fortunate comrades, but most were not dead and certainly not defeated.[191] They sprang up and donned their steel helmets. They ran up the steps, many coming upon 'something white and bloody' or 'in the trench a headless body' as they went,[192] and took their places at the machine-guns. A German artilleryman described what he saw.

> We were very surprised to see them walking, we had never seen that before. … The officers went in front. I noticed one of them walking calmly, carrying a walking stick. When we started firing we just had to load and reload. They went down in their hundreds. You didn't have to aim, we just fired into them.[193]

A lieutenant of the 4th Tyneside Scottish turned round when he reached the enemy trench and cried out, 'Oh my God, where's the rest of the boys?'[194] Only two others had made it across with him. A sergeant of the 3rd Tyneside Irish wrote that as he left his trench he could see long lines of men to his left and right. 'Then I heard the "patter, patter" of machine guns in the distance. By the time I'd gone another ten

190 Murray, 'West at war', 273; Van de Hulst & Koch, *Ooggetuigen*, 119

191 Brants & Brants, *Velden van weleer*, 139–42; Fussell, *Bloody Game*, 33; Keegan, *Face of Battle*, 225–6, 231–3, 236–7; Brown, *Somme*, 67; Winter & Baggett, *1914–18*, 180; Wilson, *Myriad Faces*, 323; Whalen, *Bitter Wounds*, 42–3

192 Brown, *Somme*, 66–7; Keegan, *First World War*, 317

193 Ellis, *Eye-Deep*, 94; Fussell, *Bloody Game*, 33; Eksteins, *Rites of Spring*, 145–6; Ellis, *Social History*, 135; see also: Babington, *Shell-Shock*, 73

194 Winter & Baggett, *1914–18*, 183; Wilson, *Myriad Faces*, 323

yards there seemed to be only a few men left around me; by the time I had gone twenty yards, I seemed to be on my own. Then I was hit myself.'[195]

Arthur Agius was not physically wounded but he was left with severe shell shock after that first July day.

> The whole of the valley was being swept with machine-gun fire and hammered with shells. We got the men organised as best we could – those of us who were left. So many gone, and we'd never even got past our own front-line trench! And then we found we couldn't get back. The trenches were indescribable! We were simply treading on the dead. Eventually my Sergeant and I got out on top – we were at the back of the Company. I heard a shell coming. I remember thinking, 'Imagine! Just imagine hearing a single shell in the middle of all this din!' It burst just above my head. The Sergeant was blown one way and I was blown the other. He was killed. I don't know how I got back. I simply don't know how I got back. It was murder.[196]

Thirteen years later Henry Williamson wrote about the first of July:

> I see men arising and walking forward; and I go forward with them, in a glassy delirium wherein some seem to pause, with bowed heads, and sink carefully to their knees, and roll slowly over, and lie still. Others roll and roll, and scream and grip my legs in uttermost fear, and I have to struggle to break away, while the dust and earth on my tunic changes from grey to red.
>
> And I go on with aching feet … and my wave melts away, and the second wave comes up, and also melts away, and then the third wave merges into the ruins of the first and second, and after a while the fourth blunders into the remnants of the others, and we begin to run forward to catch up with the barrage, gasping and sweating, … every bit of months of drill and rehearsal forgotten, for who could have imagined that the 'Big Push' was going to be this?[197]

The disastrous results become graphically clear when the losses of the different regiments and divisions are added up. Almost all found barbed wire in their way, if they got that far. In the Newfoundland Battalion, 658 out of 726 men died, along with all 26 officers. Two whole brigades of the Eighth Division were mown down; in less than 2 hours they lost 218 of their 300 officers and 5,274 of their 8,500 men, while the Germans facing the Eighth Division suffered losses of fewer than 300 dead and wounded. Of the London Scottish, 266 men reported back on the evening of 1 July. They had left that morning 856 men strong. The Inniskilling Fusiliers had fought at Waterloo, losing 427 men there compared to 568 on 1 July 1916,

195 Keegan, *Face of Battle*, 245; Keegan, *First World War*, 317

196 Macdonald, *Somme*, 67

197 Fussell, *Great War*, 29–30; Young, *Harmony of Illusions*, 41

or 61 per cent as against 70 per cent. But the dead at Waterloo fell in the space of three hours, those on the Somme in less than thirty minutes.[198]

Even in places where it was impossible to advance in close formation, such as the wood near Thiepval – or what was left of it – nothing was achieved but death and destruction. J. Wilson of the West Yorkshires told of an attack in which the only way the men could move forward was by crawling through a gap in a hedge.

> The Germans had a machine-gun trained on the gap and when my turn came I paused. The machine-gun stopped and, thinking his belt had run out, or he had jammed, I moved through, but what I saw when I got to the other side shook me to pieces. There was a trench running parallel with the hedge which was full to the top with the men who had gone before me. They were all dead or dying.[199]

The butchery went on. In the first three days the British lost an average of 101 officers and 3,320 men per day, per division (a division consisted ideally of 12,000 men). During the second week, losses for the army as a whole were 10,000 a day. Agnes Savill, a doctor at the Royaumont Scottish Women's Hospital, noted that on 2 July the flood of wounded began to arrive. They continued to pour in for another ten days. Then the rate fell until it was almost bearable by contrast: 2,500 men per day. Even when autumn rains made the ground virtually impassable, the attack was not halted.[200]

The bloodbath was not purely the fault of the chosen strategy. At Serre two units were accidentally given a double rum ration. The legless troops were even easier prey to German machine-gun fire than they would otherwise have been. In September a British tank crew made a mistake at the same spot and began slaughtering its own troops.[201]

It was at the Somme that tanks had their baptism of fire. 'We heard strange throbbing noises,' wrote Bert Chaney in *A Lad goes to War*, 'and lumbering slowly towards us came three huge mechanical monsters such as we had never seen before.' Like gas and flame-throwers, they initially prompted panic and deathly fear, but after a while it became clear that the tank was not the miracle weapon that would break the stalemate. It was too unwieldy, too heavy, too subject to mechanical failure, too vulnerable to shelling and too voracious a consumer of oil to achieve more than a short-term impact. The first time tanks were used, though, on 11 September 1916, their deployment was a success. The British high command had

---

198 Brants & Brants, *Velden van weleer*, 144; Ellis, *Eye-Deep*, 95; Keegan, *Face of Battle*, 244–6, 248, 254–5, 305; Ellis, *Social History*, 135–8; Macdonald, *1914–1918*, 155–6; Macdonald, *Somme*, 69; Gilbert, *First World War*, 260–62; Winter & Baggett, *1914–18*, 183; Winter, *Death's Men*, 203

199 Marix Evans, *Battles of the Somme*, 29

200 Ellis, *Eye-Deep*, 95; Crofton, *Royaumont*, 69

201 Brants & Brants, *Velden van weleer*, 154

wanted to deploy a hundred tanks on the first of July, but even by early September fewer than fifty were available. Seven failed to start and seventeen were put out of action before they could have any effect, but the rest scared the living daylights out of the Germans. 'A supernatural force', one of them said. 'The Devil is coming', another concluded.[202] Official War Office Cinematographer Geoffry Malins wrote: 'It slowly advanced, it breathed and belched forth tongues of flame; its nostrils seemed to breathe death and destruction, and the Huns, terrified by its appearance, were mown down like corn falling to the reaper's sickle.'[203] Lance-Corporal Lee Lovell advanced behind a tank. 'The tank just shot them down and the machine-guns, the post itself, the dead and the wounded who hadn't been able to run, just disappeared. The tank went right over them.'[204]

The Battle of the Somme was accompanied by Allied offensives elsewhere. In the Neuve Chapelle sector, near the small village of Fromelles, the Australians went over the top on 19 July 1916 in support of the already stalled offensive on the Somme, for their own baptism of fire. The fiasco cost the lives of 5,000 Aussies. No man's land was scattered with the groaning wounded. British generals refused to take up the offer of a ceasefire, which made for much bad blood between them and the Australians under their command. Terrible scenes were played out in no man's land. There was a wounded and blinded man who was put out of his misery by a German bullet after stumbling in circles for several days.[205] An Australian survivor jotted down: '& every move they make the German puts the Machine guns on them some are calling for him to do it to end their misery & this only 50 yards from us & there are hundreds there.'[206]

Since their first deployment, in the Dardanelles in 1915, the Australians had been regarded as hardened fighters, unafraid of the devil himself. But Fromelles taught that everyone has his limits. One Australian noted in his diary: 'we thought we knew something about the horrors of war, but we were mere recruits, and have had our full education in one day'.[207] Many of the bodies were not recovered until after the armistice more than two years later.[208]

After less than two weeks the Australians were deployed again, this time near the Somme, at Pozières, to the north of Fricourt and Mametz. Almost 23,000 Australians were dead within a few weeks; only a small minority survived. An Australian historian would later write about Pozières that along with all those soldiers, all romantic ideas about war were buried there, to be dug up again only occasionally, by a very few. 'After Pozières many soldiers looked back to their

202 Moynihan, *People at War*, 115; Holmes, *War Walks*, 143; Holmes & De Vos, *Langs de Velden van Eer*, 143

203 Marix Evans, *Battles of the Somme*, 48–9

204 Marix Evans, *Battles of the Somme*, 49

205 Gammage, *The Broken Years*, 161

206 Gammage, *The Broken Years*, 161

207 Gammage, *The Broken Years*, 161

208 Macdonald, *Somme*, 164–6

boyhood, and saw an unfamiliar world.'[209] Pozières would never be forgotten in Australia, nor would anyone ever forget who had been in command of Australian soldiers there. It is sometimes said that the aversion many Australians seem to feel towards the British had its origins at Pozières in July and August 1916.[210]

The forested areas in particular terrified soldiers on both sides. To the British, Bois Delville, quickly renamed Devil's Wood, and Bois des Fourcaux, High Wood, were synonymous with death and destruction.[211] To the Germans, Bois St Pierre Vaast, near Sailly-Saillisel between Péronne and Bapaume, was a place of terror. Rudolf Binding wrote of his own experience, in his otherwise fairly restrained *Aus dem Kriege* (*A Fatalist at War*):

> Bodies of humans and animals, weapons and equipment covered in earth and liquid mud, spraying up into the sky, trodden into the ground, flung into the air once more, torn, formless. Whole batteries of men and artillery, coagulated, impossible to disentangle, in the crucible of a monstrous pounding-machine.[212]

Sergeant Billy Hay wrote of a strategically important intersection in High Wood:

> There were men everywhere, heaps of men, not one or two men, but heaps of men everywhere, all dead. … They just seemed to be pushing men in to be killed and no reason. There didn't seem to be any reason. They couldn't possibly take the position, not on a frontal attack. Not at High Wood.[213]

The fighting in the Bois des Fourcaux was costly for the other side as well. German NCO Gottfried Kreibohm wrote: 'The artillery fire there was absolutely frantic. Nearly every shell landed in the trench. Some men were buried alive while others were blown into the air.'[214]

The battle for the Bois Delville was if anything even more ghastly. Of 3,000 troops deployed by the South African Brigade, only a little over 750 came back, 600 of them wounded. The rest were left behind in the wood, not wounded or captured but dead. All 2,250 of them. According to Macdonald this was probably the heaviest sacrifice of the whole war by a single brigade in a single battle. As we saw in relation to the horribly costly *attaque à outrance*, the ratio between dead and wounded is normally around one to four. Even among the British on their black first of July, the ratio was one to two. Here four South Africans were killed for every one wounded.[215]

---

209 Brown, *Somme*, 144; Eksteins, *Rites of Spring*, 214
210 Holmes, *War Walks*, 142; Holmes & De Vos, *Langs de Velden van Eer*, 144
211 Macdonald, *1914–1918*, 161
212 Binding, *Aus dem Krieg*, 204
213 Macdonald, *1914–1918*, 161; Macdonald, *Somme*, 150
214 Macdonald, *1914–1918*, 161
215 Macdonald, *Somme*, 151; Marix Evans, *Battles of the Somme*, 39

By late July, the British had lost more than 160,000 men, almost double the entire complement of the British Expeditionary Force at Mons in 1914. Forty thousand were dead. By late September the number of dead had risen to 90,000 and 230,000 wounded had been taken to base hospitals, only slightly fewer in those three months than in the whole of the previous sixteen months of the war. British attacks were, however, producing more and more German casualties. Student Karl Gorzel described one British advance, at Thiepval, between the Schwaben Redoubt and the Leipzig Redoubt. The date: 12 September.

> The English attack began. … At dawn I looked around me: what a wretched scene! Not a trace of a trench left; only shell-holes as far as the eye could see. … The wounded lie helplessly groaning, the supply of water runs out. … The firing increases to such a bewildering intensity that it is no longer possible to distinguish between the crumps. Our mouths and ears are full of earth; three times buried alive and three times dug out again, we wait – wait for the night or the enemy. ... And the bursting shells' dance of death grows ever wilder – one can see nothing for smoke, fire and spurting earth. ...
>
> Suddenly the barrage lifts … and there, close before us, is the first wave of the enemy. Release at last! Everyone who is not wounded, everyone who can raise an arm, is up. And like a shower of hailstones our hand grenades pelt down upon the attacking foe!

To no avail. The British reached the trench. Bitter man-to-man fighting ensued. Eventually the British were beaten back and few of the attackers survived the retreat, but the German trench was littered with dead and wounded.

> We sink down, dazed, upon the tortured earth, bind up the wounded as well as we can and wait for either the next attack or the night. … Reinforcements arrive. Things are quickly cleared up and the dead buried, and a new day breaks, more terrible than the last. Such is the battle of the Somme – Germany's bloody struggle for victory. These eight days represent the utmost limits of human endurance. It was hell![216]

Because of the Battle of the Somme, Thiepval is one of the places only ever mentioned in the context of the First World War. Thousands of soldiers killed there now lie buried in the shadow of a vast monument. The first victim of the war at Thiepval was a civilian, however. In late September 1914 French soldiers had mistaken a French farmer fencing his land for a German setting up a barbed-wire entanglement and killed him.[217]

A cautious estimate suggests that by late November more than 400,000 British soldiers, some 200,000 Frenchmen (who were slowly but surely taking

---

216 Winter & Baggett, *1914–18*, 193

217 Marix Evans, *Battles of the Somme*, 13

on their share of the fighting and therefore of the slaughter) and around 600,000 Germans had lost either their lives – 100,000 British, 50,000 French and 165,000 German – or their minds or some part of their bodies. All this in an area around forty kilometres long and ten kilometres wide. The battle was finally halted after Beaumont-Hamel, one of the objectives of 1 July, was taken on 13 November. The weather was making it simply impossible to fight on. Allied troops were still six kilometres from Bapaume, another of the places they had intended to take on the first day.

Like Verdun, the Somme was not a battle but a mutual, wholesale massacre, a result of the terrible logic of total war.[218] The Somme demonstrated to both sides the insanity of war, of this war at any rate. Edmund Blunden wrote: 'Neither race had won, nor could win, the War. The War had won, and would go on winning.'[219] German soldier Georg Steinbrecher, who was killed in April the following year, declared in November 1916 that 'Death is the only conqueror.'[220]

## 1917

> Ich habe sieben Tage nichts gegessen
> Und einem Manne in die Stirn geknallt
> Mein Schienbein ist vom Läusebiß zerfressen
> Bald werde ich einundzwanzig Jahre alt.[221]

Carl Zuckmayer, *1917*

### *Chemin des Dames*

The extremely harsh winter of 1916–17 – parts of the North Sea froze over – claimed many victims through sickness and 'minor skirmishes', but the elements also forced a break in the ferocious fighting. In the spring battle recommenced in earnest. The French especially, whose death toll had now passed the one million mark, were convinced they could make a definitive breakthrough. Victory would be quick, total and ultimately simple if they could only, one more time, with might and main, with an élan never before displayed... It was not to be. After a disastrous offensive at the Chemin des Dames near the River Aisne northwest of Reims – the

218 Macdonald, *Somme*, 179, 305; Binneveld, *Om de geest*, 47; Keegan, *Face of Battle*, 280; Ellis, *Social History*, 139; Simkins, *World War I*, 122; Gilbert, *First World War*, 199; Brown, *Somme*, 252; Winter & Baggett, *1914–18*, 178–9; Terraine, 'Inferno', 185; Eksteins, *Rites of Spring*, 144; Preston, 'Great Civil War', 151; Keegan, *First World War*, 321

219 Fussell, *Bloody Game*, 34

220 Winter & Baggett, *1914–18*, 186

221 I've eaten nothing for seven days / And I've cracked a man across the brow / My shinbone's been eaten up by lice / Soon I'll be twenty-one years old.

only attack in 1914–18, perhaps in history, unanimously condemned by military historians – protest broke out at the way the war was being conducted, and it was on an unprecedented scale.

One British component of the French offensive was a preparatory battle at Arras that began on Easter Monday, 9 April. Within three days, 13,000 British soldiers were dead. Following on from the professional soldiers of August 1914 and Kitchener's volunteers, it was now the turn of the conscripts. The thirty-nine days the battle lasted before Bullecourt was taken cost the lives of around 160,000 British and Australian troops. This was probably the battle in which the highest British daily death toll was reached.[222]

To the north of Arras lay Vimy. The battle there has gone down as a great feat of arms by the Canadians, who left over 60,000 of their number dead in France in 1914–18. Of the threefold plan – consisting of offensives at the Chemin des Dames, Arras and Vimy in turn – the Canadians alone would achieve their objective. In April 1917 they captured Vimy Ridge and held it through a furious blizzard. At first sight the landscape today contains nothing to suggest that countless Germans and 20,000 Canadians were killed or gravely wounded there, until the observer realizes that the many dips and hillocks have no natural origin. Countless shells and mortars left not a tree standing and every lump of earth was churned over many times. According to an army doctor named MacPhail, after the battle the area looked more like a rough sea suddenly frozen than a French hill. The land was given to Canada after the war, and for each of the more than 10,000 missing soldiers the nation planted a maple tree or a pine.[223]

Nine days later, on 16 April, the attack on the Chemin des Dames Ridge began. The Germans were lying low in their extensive chalk tunnels inside a hill, the Caverne du Dragon. After a preparatory barrage they emerged from several tunnel exits to inflict a bloodbath on the French troops clambering up towards them. In heavy rain and sleet, the French and Senegalese soldiers had to work their way up through a hail of hand grenades and machine-gun bullets. They gained less than a tenth of the six kilometres of terrain they were intending to capture, at a cost of tens of thousands of dead and wounded. They did not seize the promised thousands and thousands of German prisoners.

The French had been assured beforehand that the attack would be halted if it did not go well, but the soldiers, known as *poilus* or 'hairy ones', were repeatedly ordered to advance. Soon 30,000 were dead. The Senegalese, who had already been fighting for two weeks in the forward line without a break, struggled with frostbite in their hands and feet. For the first time, desertion became a problem. The units initially deployed would soon be joined in their protests by virtually

222 Brants & Brants, *Velden van weleer*, 104–5; Macdonald, *1914–1918*, 197; Simkins, *World War I*, 155; Prior & Wilson, *Passchendaele*, 70; Winter, *Death's Men*, 203; Terraine, 'Inferno', 185; Keegan, *History of Warfare*, 361; Smith, Audoin & Becker, *France and the Great War*, 117

223 Brants & Brants, *Velden van weleer*, 125–7; Hendryckx, 'In het spoor', 4

the whole of the French army. The mutiny – in fact it was more like a strike – was not even a direct result of the casualty figures. By the standards of 1914–18, the eventual losses of 187,000 *bonhommes*, as the French soldiers liked to call themselves, as against 163,000 Germans, were not even particularly high. It was the discrepancy between what had been promised, a 'battle to end all battles', and the final result that proved the last straw for the sorely tried French troops.[224] There are two versions, incidentally, of the origin of the word *poilu*. The better known is that the French were unable to shave. The alternative theory goes back to the Napoleonic era and concerns claims by French soldiers that their pubic hair was thick and abundant. It is intriguing to note that the first story refers to the horrible living conditions of the trench soldier, the other to the alleged masculinity and virility of the French soldier.

### *Messines*

The French mutiny – which we shall examine further in the chapter entitled 'Mind' – was resolved by a combination of severe sanctions and compliance with soldiers' demands, but another year would pass before the French were capable of fresh initiatives. They did seize part of the Caverne du Dragon in late June, in fierce, underground engagements so tightly confined that there could be no distinction between battleground and burial ground. Frenchmen and Germans fought at close quarters, inside the hill as well as on it.[225]

Inactivity on the French side as a result of the mutiny meant that the entire weight of the Allied war effort rested on British shoulders. The United States had declared war on Germany in early April, but not for another year could American troops be deployed on the ground. The British had set their sights on the Ypres salient. After two offensives there by Germans forces, it was now the turn of Britain to show its teeth. It has to be said: the first bite was deadly.

Earlier in the war, at Festubert in December 1914, for example, as well as during preparations for the Second Battle of Ypres and on the morning of 1 July 1916, tunnels filled with explosives had been detonated. They were as nothing compared to the Big Bang felt and heard around the little village of Messines in the early morning of 7 June 1917. Nineteen out of twenty-four mines dug over the preceding months blasted the earth into the sky. One had been disabled by the Germans back in 1916. Four others were judged by the British high command to be too far from the objective, so they were not detonated. Their precise location

224 Brants & Brants, *Velden van weleer*, 180–81; Simkins, *World War I*, 152; Horne, *Price of Glory*, 232 (note 1); Murray, 'West at war', 284; Keegan, *First World War*, 355; Liddle & Cecil, *Facing Armageddon*, 385

225 Brants & Brants, *Velden van weleer*, 186

was lost. On 17 June 1955 one of the four exploded in a thunder storm. The others have yet to be found.[226]

The mines that went up dug immense craters in the landscape that instantly served as mass graves for German soldiers, many buried alive. Over twenty kilometres away, in the town of Lille, people thought there had been an earthquake. It is telling that of the 23,000 Germans who did not survive the explosion and the attack that followed, ten thousand were officially listed as missing.[227] Eye-witness accounts are vivid. Captain W. Grant reports that the waiting infantry felt the shocks and heard a growl like an earthquake. 'It seemed as if the Messines Ridge got up and shook itself.'[228] Lieutenant J. Todd remembered that 'the ground on which I was lying started to go up and down just like an earthquake. It lasted for seconds and then, suddenly in front of us, the Hill 60 mine went up.'[229] J.W. Naylor remembered the earth being torn apart, and then 'this enormous explosion right in front of us. It was an extraordinary sight. The whole ground went up and came back down again. It was like a huge mushroom.'[230] Captain M. Greener witnessed destruction beyond imagining.

> The damage of a mine of that size on the surrounding trenches has to be seen to be believed. It was terrific. Everything had gone, certainly within a hundred yards of the lip of the crater. It was an absolute shambles. Some of these concrete pillboxes had been turned right over. Scores of tons they weighed and they'd been tossed up in the air, foundations and all, and turned upside down.[231]

One of the few Germans who lived to tell the tale wrote:

> The ground trembled as in a natural earthquake, heavy concrete shelters rocked, a hurricane of hot air from the explosion swept back for many kilometres, dropping fragments of wood, iron and earth, and gigantic black clouds of smoke and dust spread over the country. … The trenches were now the graves of our infantry.[232]

In the attack that followed, most Germans who had survived the explosion surrendered meekly as sheep. Who could blame them? Their faces were distorted

---

226 Heijster, *Ieper*, 128–9; Marix Evans, *Battles of the Somme*, 18; De Vos, *De Eerste Wereldoorlog*, 108; *Van den Grooten oorlog*, 193–5

227 Simkins, *World War I*, 162; Gilbert, *First World War*, 336; Prior & Wilson, *Passchendaele*, 61

228 Macdonald, *1914–1918*, 213

229 Macdonald, *Passchendaele*, 41

230 Macdonald, *Passchendaele*, 42

231 Macdonald, *Passchendaele*, 51

232 Prior & Wilson, *Passchendaele*, 61

with fear, wild and pale as death. If the term 'shell shock' was ever appropriate then it was here, south of the Ypres salient on 7 June 1917.[233]

Months of digging had created tunnels that varied in length from 65 to 700 metres and contained a total of around 500,000 kilos of explosives. Men had to lie on their backs on planks, which were set into the mines at an angle of 45 degrees. They wrenched and grubbed their way under the German front line. It was extraordinarily exhausting and unhealthy work. The roof might cave in at any moment and many British soldiers still lie buried in the sand. From time to time a tunnel was discovered. The Germans would then try to reach the British mine via one of their own, and this led to some dismal underground fighting in which neither side shrank from using gas.[234]

The enormous blast was preceded by a week-long barrage, in which almost 150,000 tons of shells were fired. The shelling stopped at two thirty in the morning. At ten past three an electrical switch was used to detonate the explosives. Some of the craters were sixty metres across and ten metres deep. Clay and concrete rained down across the entire area.[235]

Although successful, the attack inevitably cost British lives. One of the mines did not explode until the Irish soldiers close to it had begun their advance, and many of them were buried under falling rubble. It says a great deal about the First World War that even after such a heavy blow, those few Germans who went on fighting were able to cause 25,000 British casualties, dead and wounded. Out of eight officers of the 11th Battalion of the Prince of Wales' Own West Yorkshire Regiment, only one returned unscathed. Six were killed and another, Lieutenant S.A.J. Levey, had a leg blown off. He eventually died of complications.[236] The third Australian division to go into action fell prey to a severe German gas attack. Some battalions lost around 10 per cent of their strength, and all in all between 500 and 1,000 men were poisoned. Nevertheless, because of the relatively low British casualty rate and the relatively large amount of territory gained, the mining of the Messines Ridge and the battle that followed it are regarded as the greatest single British success of the war.[237]

233 Macdonald, *Passchendaele*, 45; For the fear caused simply by the knowledge that mines were being dug, see: Dorgelès, *Croix de bois*, 164–74

234 Heijster, *Ieper*, 124–5

235 Heijster, *Ieper*, 126–7

236 Prior & Wilson, *Passchendaele*, 65; Macdonald, *Passchendaele*, 27, 46; Winter, *Death's Men*, 203; Heijster, *Ieper*, 127

237 Prior & Wilson, *Passchendaele*, 61; Talk by Frank Bostyn, 'Dugouts in the Ypres Salient. De vergeten oorlog onder de salient', First World War Symposium, 20–5–2005, Erasmus University Rotterdam

### *Passchendaele (Third Ypres)*

The Third Battle of Ypres as such would not begin for another two months, during which enormous quantities of men and *matériel* were brought into the area, in the expectation that the breakthrough really could be pulled off this time. At this point Ypres symbolized British perseverance. By mid-November, when the battle was declared over with the capture of the village of Passchendaele a few kilometres beyond Ypres, the British would have come to see it as a symbol of the insanity of war.[238]

One of the men who fought the battle through to its end was Edmund Blunden. The Ypres salient had already become synonymous with death and when Blunden heard that he was about to be transferred there he was pleased in a sense. He would be able to confirm that soldiers always exaggerated in depicting the horrors of a specific battlefield. He was mistaken. He soon had to admit that Ypres had been painted in colours no blacker than it deserved.[239] Lieutenant H.L. Birks felt his skin crawl as he crossed the Ypres-Yser canal, as if every gleam of hope was leaving him. The closer he came to Ypres the stronger this feeling became, in direct proportion to the increasing stench of death. 'You could literally smell it. It was just a complete abomination of desolation. I wept when I came into the salient.'[240] On the other side of the front, Hans Schetter would have agreed with Blunden and Birks.

> The whole earth is ploughed by the exploding shells and the holes are filled with water, and if you do not get killed by the shells you may drown in the craters. Broken wagons and dead horses are moved to the sides of the road; also, many dead soldiers are here. Seriously wounded who died in the ambulance wagon have been unloaded and their eyes stare at you. Sometimes an arm or a leg is missing. Everybody is rushing, running, trying to escape almost certain death in this hail of enemy shells on the highway, which is the only passage since the fields are flooded shell holes. I breathe easier when we reach our kitchen wagon. Today I have seen the real face of war.[241]

Canadian doctor Frederick W. Noyes experienced only the final two weeks of the battle, but looking back he wrote:

> One long, weird, and terrible nightmare of water-filled-trenches, zigzagging duck-walks, foul slime-filled shell-holes, half-buried bodies and dead men, horses and mules, cement pillboxes, twisted wire, shrieking shells, flying

---

238 Babington, *Shell-Shock*, 100
239 Blunden, *Undertones of War*, 157
240 Macdonald, *Passchendaele*, 186
241 Macdonald, *1914–1918*, 242–3

> humming metal, crashing aerial bombs, stinking mud, water-logged and blood-soaked trenches – a slough of Despond even Bunyan couldn't conceive of.

He had served in the Battle of the Somme, but Passchendaele 'was the Somme multiplied and intensified ten times over'.[242]

The Third Battle of Ypres is known to the British simply as Passchendaele, after a village that featured only in the final stages of the fighting. It makes little sense in fact to speak of a Third Battle of Ypres, since in reality there were several localized battles, beginning on 31 July with fighting at Pilckem and Frezenberg and ending with the second battle for Passchendaele. This alone is enough to indicate that the offensive did not result in a quick British breakthrough to Antwerp or the harbours at Zeebrugge and Ostend that sheltered German submarines. Instead there were months of plodding through an ocean of mud. The final outcome was the seizure of around seven kilometres of terrain, or seventy metres for each day of the battle, whereas the plans drawn up in October involved gains of a hundred metres every ten minutes.[243] Passchendaele made clear once again that there was not so much a difference in insight between the front-line soldier and the general staff about the tactical realities of the war as a difference of opinion about how those realities should be tackled. For a soldier at the front, the defensive strength of the enemy's artillery determined what the options were. For the general staff this was a problem that had to be solved if the war was ever to be won. The solution they came up with over and over again caused immense suffering and loss of life on the front line.[244]

The British government had decided that the Third Battle of Ypres could only go ahead on condition that if it began to degenerate into another pointless bloodbath it would be halted immediately. This did not happen, which proves, like Verdun and the Chemin des Dames, that a battle once started cannot easily be stopped. Neither the politicians nor the generals are in charge. War takes charge of itself.[245]

Despite the almost constant rain (with the exception of September) and despite serious misgivings among some of the British high command, there were renewed attacks every day, led by officers barely twenty years old, often over the corpses left by the previous sortie, if murderous German machine-gun fire allowed them to get even that far. The preliminary barrage, which lasted more than two weeks and put the Somme bombardment very much in the shade – consisting of four million bombs and shells (or 321 train-loads, the annual output of 55,000 workers), ten per cent of which were filled with gas – had ploughed up the soil many times over. What remained of the drainage system in the lowlands of Ypres after the deliberate flooding of the land around the Yser had now been completely destroyed. Guns sank into the ground and were abandoned. Horses and mules became stuck in

242 Noyes, *Stretcher-Bearers*, 177

243 Liddle, *Passchendaele in Perspective*, 140

244 Leed, *No Man's Land*, 99

245 Brants & Brants, *Velden van weleer*, 70–71; Simkins, *World War I*, 168; Macdonald, *Passchendaele*, 89

the mud, could not be pulled free and had to be put out of their misery. The creeping barrage, designed to land just ahead of advancing troops, either moved forward too quickly for the soldiers wading through liquid sand, leaving them unprotected, or was not fired at all. Attempts to avoid the worst of the terrain made it impossible to move straight ahead, let alone to remain in formation. Men soaked to the skin, who could not be relieved or supplied because of the state of the ground, had to shelter for days in no man's land. They kept themselves alive with rations from the haversacks of the dead and with filthy water from shell-holes. The wounded could not be rescued; the dead could not be buried. If a wounded man was picked up, it would take eight stretcher-bearers fourteen hours to get him to a dressing station. Many drowned in the sucking mud, too tired to resist, and resistance might in any case prove futile. Most fell forwards, wounded, into the mud, which gradually closed over them. Or they slipped and got their feet stuck and then sank agonizingly slowly. Twenty to twenty-five per cent of the British dead at Passchendaele are said to have drowned.[246] Stuck fast, those who did not go under were an easy target for the machine-guns. Some even tried to advance on all fours, but were exhausted within minutes.[247] As a direct result of the battle and the conditions in which it was fought, morale plummeted, with a dramatic increase in drunkenness, desertion, and the number of psychiatric cases, whether or not they were recognized as such.[248]

The rain and the mud had one other daunting effect. Since most of the landscape was more or less flat, concrete pillboxes were the only relatively safe shelters against bullets and shells. But the soaked ground might fail to support their foundations. More than once a pillbox full of soldiers was undermined by nearby shelling so that the entrance sank below ground level. All that awaited the trapped soldiers then was slow death by suffocation.[249]

The battle began on the last day of July. Whether or not many men died or were wounded in the initial attack is a matter of definition. The bald figures are high, but compared to the first days of other offensives and to what was 'normal' between 1914 and 1918, they could have been worse. In total the day's losses were similar to the Somme, but on 31 July 1917 the ratio between British dead and wounded and German casualties was not ten to one but around one to one. Numbers tell only part of the story, and a small part at that. The story told by Lieutenant W.B. St Leger gives the rest of the picture. During the attack his batman, the help and stay of any British officer, was hit in the neck. His sergeant, a man called Harris,

---

246 Brants & Brants, *Velden van weleer*, 94, 97; Ellis, *Eye-Deep*, 95; Prior & Wilson, *Passchendaele*, 93, 167; Fussell, *Great War*, 16; Fussell, *Bloody Game*, 160; Weltman, *World Politics*, 93; Holmes, *Firing Line*, 170; Macdonald, *1914–1918*, 229; Macdonald, *Passchendaele*, 98, 121, 169; Wilson, *Myriad Faces*, 482; Young, *Harmony of Illusions*, 41; Heijster, *Ieper*, 150; Keegan, *First World War*, 387

247 Prior & Wilson, *Passchendaele*, 177

248 Prior & Wilson, *Passchendaele*, 196

249 Sandstrom, *Comrades-in-Arms*, 77; Liddle, *Passchendaele in Perspective*, 331

lost half his face. Fellow officers Turner and Leggett were killed, six friends were wounded, three of them seriously, and St Leger himself was wounded in the knee and carried from the field. In other words, an action that cannot be called a failure from a military point of view (the objectives were not achieved, but neither were the British entirely dissatisfied with the gains made) resulted in the wounding of St Leger and six others and the deaths of four of his friends. His formation was not even part of the first wave, so his account prompts us to contemplate what the personal losses suffered further forward must have been like.[250] As the battle went on the men became exhausted: the British, the few French divisions and the Germans. They were rarely relieved on time, so when a battalion was at last ordered to attack it might already have been reduced to less than half its original strength. On 16 August for instance, several Irish divisions advanced with only 330 of the regulation 750 men per battalion; one had lost all but two officers and three other ranks by the time the battle was over.[251]

The Irish occupied a strange place in the British army in those early years of the twentieth century. Ireland at no stage introduced conscription, but despite the struggle for Home Rule, many Irishmen volunteered. All in all, more than 200,000 must have served in the British army. They were extremely welcome, since they were said to be blessed by nature with a warrior spirit. That same warrior spirit, however, meant that in British eyes the Irish were unsuited to self-government, which after all demanded circumspection, not impulsiveness, restraint rather than aggression.

This is not the place to look in any depth at the motives and backgrounds of the Irish in the British army. It is safe to say, however, that the backbone of the Irish divisions was formed by members of the Ulster Volunteer Force, founded in 1912 to fight for the preservation of the Union with Great Britain and against Home Rule. Nevertheless, many advocates of secession from the United Kingdom served at the front. They did not always find themselves, to put it mildly, on an equal footing with the rest of the army. Suspicions grew that the British general staff was indifferent to the fate of Irish soldiers because of Irish rebelliousness, and it seems there was some truth in this.[252] The 16th (Irish) Division sustained heavy losses during Third Ypres as it waited for hours, under fire from the Germans, for the signal to attack. When the advance finally began, there was no artillery support. Whether or not their suspicions are well-founded, it is clear that the Irish regiments were among the worst hit of all units of the British army. This might also perhaps have to do with the supposed capacities of the Irish as fighting men, which led to their being chosen for deployment in the most dangerous places.[253] On top of all this, Irish soldiers and their officers encountered another hostile world when

---

250 Prior & Wilson, *Passchendaele*, 90, 95; Keegan, *First World War*, 388

251 Prior & Wilson, *Passchendaele*, 102–3

252 Prior & Wilson, *Passchendaele*, 103; Vondung, *Kriegserlebnis*, 121; Johnson, 'The Spectacle of Memory', 41–3; Bourke, *Intimate History*, 118–20, 125

253 Dallas & Gill, *The Unknown Army*, 83

they returned to Ireland. They had served in the British army and had therefore collaborated with the enemy.[254]

The Battle of the Menin Road on 20 September was a British success. But again the word seems inappropriate. In a single day, the four central divisions lost 17,000 men and the divisions on the flanks another 4,000. 5.5 square miles of land were seized. So every square mile cost around 3,800 dead and wounded, three times as many as on the first day of the battle, with its 27,000 casualties for 18 square miles of territory gained. An unfortunate combination of circumstances led to one brigade being almost completely wiped off the map that day, sustaining three thousand casualties, partly as a result of German fire, partly at the hands of its own superiors. The troops, having been pushed towards a row of German machine-guns, fled back towards their own lines, where they were fiercely reprimanded. Their forced return across no man's land finished them off.[255]

The attack on Polygon Wood near Zonnebeke was a British success as well, from a military point of view, and once more it was a tragedy on a human level. 15,375 British soldiers were killed or wounded for a mere 3.5-square-mile gain in territory. The victories of September had cost the British a total of 36,000 men. Passchendaele Ridge was still over 4,500 yards away.[256]

So it went on: yard by yard, the Allies won terrain at the expense of huge numbers of British, Canadian, New Zealand and German lives.[257] One attack took place at Broodseinde in early October. Charles Carrington of the Royal Warwickshire Regiment failed to understand how historians could describe the battle as a tactical masterpiece. 'It was just all-in wrestling in the mud.'[258]

Meanwhile the men were forced to adjust their norms. On 26 October a Canadian soldier wrote that the fighting had been heavy and the price high, 'but we did achieve something'. That 'something' was an advance of 500 yards, at a cost of 3,400 dead and wounded.[259]

Others began to oppose the war. Reg Lawrence wrote on 22 September that he could no longer see any point in taking up arms except to defend one's own home and dear ones. Any other form of military action was simply murder on a large scale. 'No one excuses individual murder (which often has just and cogent reasons) while in war you murder a man you have never seen, who has never done you an injury.'[260]

In late October the last great attack of Third Ypres began. It was the second time that the little village of Passchendaele had been the target. Troops from New Zealand and Australia had made the first attempt to seize the remains of

---

254 Bourke, *Dismembering the Male*, 70
255 Prior & Wilson, *Passchendaele*, 119–21
256 Prior & Wilson, *Passchendaele*, 131
257 Prior & Wilson, *Passchendaele*, 137; Macdonald, *1914–1918*, 243, 245
258 Holmes, *Firing Line*, 155
259 Prior & Wilson, *Passchendaele*, 175
260 Macdonald, *1914–1918*, 241

the abandoned village in mid-October. The battle raged for two weeks. On 10 November Canadian troops attacked again, but after a short advance they were stopped by heavy machine-gun fire while the rain, 'as per usual', poured down. Passchendaele was finally taken, but any attempt to force a great breakthrough was abandoned. A Canadian soldier described the entry into the flattened village.

> The shell exploded bodies were so thickly strewn that a fellow couldn't step without stepping on corruption. Our opponents were fighting a rearguard action which resulted in a massacre for both sides. Our boys were falling like ninepins, but it was even worse for them. If they stood up to surrender they were mown down by their own machine gun fire aimed from their rear at us; if they leapfrogged back they were caught in our barrage.[261]

16,000 Canadians were killed in those two weeks. There were no more reserves. The British guns ceased their thunder, but not for long. Already a new battle awaited Allied troops, in late November at Cambrai. The gains of that battle were negligible. The casualties: 44,000 British and Canadian; 57,000 German.[262]

According to some sources, by the time Passchendaele was over, the British, French, Canadian and German losses added up to a total of 650,000. This is little more than an educated guess. Estimates vary by hundreds of thousands.[263] But if we take these numbers as a starting point – and they will tend if anything to be too low – and consider that the British and their allies gained about thirty-eight square miles, then an average of 3,000 soldiers were killed for each piece of land the size of a football pitch. Blunden's description in his poem 'Third Ypres' of the battlefield at Passchendaele as 'amuck with murder' and consisting of 'swamps of flesh and blood' cannot be dismissed as poetic hyperbole.[264]

There were 70,000 British dead at Passchendaele and many more were so seriously wounded that they would never be able to return to the front. All told the Third Battle of Ypres had reduced the size of the British army by nearly twenty per cent. Losses on the German side were probably even greater; after only a month, for example, eighty per cent of the men of the 15th Infantry Division had been killed or wounded. The editors of the satirical magazine *Simplicissimus* clearly had the gift of foresight. More than a month before the battle began they had

261 Prior & Wilson, *Passchendaele*, 178–9

262 Prior & Wilson, *Passchendaele*, 179; Gilbert, *First World War*, 383; Keegan, *First World War*, 393–7

263 Gilbert, *First World War*, 365; Prior & Wilson, *Passchendaele*, 195; Wilson, *Myriad Faces*, 483; Terraine, 'Inferno', 185; Murray, 'West at war', 287; Marix Evans, *Battles of the Somme*, 63

264 Blunden, *Undertones of War*, 260; Fussell, *Bloody Game*, 142

decorated the front page with a drawing of Death, desperately begging for battle to end since he could not keep pace. Its headline read: 'Death of Flanders'.[265]

Any notion of a 'quick, cheerful war' had vanished by late 1917 or early 1918. Johannsen wrote:

> 1914 lies far, far behind us. Then the bursting of shells didn't roar behind the front-line in the trenches at night. We didn't sink into shit, corpses, slime and water, with bombs from above and dried vegetables in our stomachs. We didn't lie for days on end in the ploughed ground of the shells, without contact, without water, yes, even without weapons. Poison gas didn't creep stealthily through the trenches. Ridiculous, what was called heavy fire in those days. We were still soldiers in the war then; today we're merely automata, ditch animals, miserable, dull-witted creatures. We still lived then, now we merely vegetate, crawling from day to day, waiting, waiting. The end must surely come at some point, either death or peace. Really we ought to be mad already – human beings are tough, tougher than lice and rats.[266]

When the Germans undertook their final great offensive in early 1918, the British relinquished the territorial gains of Third Ypres for strategic reasons. In the form it had assumed in November 1917, the Ypres salient was impossible to defend, which proved that its importance had been more symbolic than military all along. The line around Ypres was now shorter than ever before. It was almost identical to the line a British general had proposed in early 1915, because the defence of the salient as it stood would demand too many casualties. His assessment did not bring him renown for his military insightfulness but dismissal for cowardice. It took more than 100,000 British dead to prove him right.[267]

Even today the Belgians live with the consequences of First, Second and Third Ypres, and the much smaller but deadly skirmishes before, in between and afterwards. The land around Ypres is still a mass grave, containing tens of thousands of bodies of soldiers who sank into the mud. Twenty years after the war, only about a thousand had been dug up and interred, and corpses are still being found as farmers plough their fields. Unexploded shells lie around in enormous quantities too. Duds are destroyed in Houthulst Wood near Langemarck. Pending a legal means of disposal, gas shells, which remain deadly, have been stockpiled

265 Prior & Wilson, *Passchendaele*, 195; Brants & Brants, *Velden van weleer*, 71; Weltman, *World Politics*, 93; Gilbert, *First World War*, 365; Liddle, *Passchendaele in Perspective*, 325–6, 329

266 Johannsen, *Vier von der Infanterie*, 29; Haas, *Oorlogsjammer*, 53

267 Macdonald, *Passchendaele*, 233; Wilson, *Myriad Faces*, 482; Heijster, *Ieper*, 154

for the past several years, since international environmental legislation no longer permits their dumping at sea. Everyone hopes there will be no accidents.[268]

One thought in conclusion. Every time a decision is needed in our day, in a democratically governed country, on whether or not to participate in a war – naturally as part of a humanitarian effort – surveys are held which show, among other things, that public support for a war will crumble if participation results in deaths, whether of soldiers from the home country or enemy forces. But would support actually falter in practice? In war, deaths often prompt an increased willingness to fight, to 'teach those damned murderers of our sons a lesson for once'. It seems quite plausible that if anyone had made a reasonably accurate estimate in July 1914 of the number of dead and wounded the approaching war would cost, and if he or she had been believed, a large proportion of the populations of the belligerent nations would have said, 'The moment things threaten to go that way, we'd better stop.' What actually eventuated was something quite different, certainly in Great Britain. Some of the rumours about casualty numbers circulating at the time of Third Ypres were wildly exaggerated. In response the British war cabinet decided for the first time since the beginning of the war to make the true losses known. It did so in order to reassure the public.[269]

## 1918

### *The German advance*

After the winter of 1917–18, which included the coldest December in thirty years, the German high command came to the conclusion that its forces would have to make haste if Germany was to win the war in the West as well as the East. Both sides had suffered terrible losses, but the Allies would soon have fresh American troops at their disposal. The end of the war in the East meant several German armies could be transferred to the West, so they would have a short-lived but substantial numerical advantage. The soldiers of those armies were not pleased at the prospect. They had thought that after victory in the East they would be allowed to go home, and the troop trains travelling westwards bore slogans such as *Schlachtvieh für Flandern* (cattle for slaughter in Flanders).[270] The war at sea had been lost and the effects of naval defeat were beginning to bite. Which makes it all the more remarkable, incidentally, that in those first few months of 1918 the German war industry reached its peak, in fact its output was greater than at any point during

268 Macdonald, *Passchendaele*, 4, 47, 233; Gilbert, *First World War*, 336; Brants & Brants, *Velden van weleer*, 97; Winter, *Death's Men*, 261

269 Graves, *Goodbye*, 211; Prior & Wilson, *Passchendaele*, 186–7

270 Liddle & Cecil, *Facing Armageddon*, 393; Patrick Dassen, 'Radicalisering, polarisatie en totale oorlog', 249–50

the Second World War. But strategic considerations were not the only stimulus to action. The mental resilience of German troops was wearing thin. Moreover, many were under eighteen or over forty and practically all were untrained.[271] There are various reasons why they agreed to go into battle nonetheless. Hatred no longer played much of a role. One might even say, as does Hew Strachan, that the will and determination with which the Germans went on the offensive was 'the positive expression of war weariness'.[272] Lieutenant Rudolf Hartmann, for example, saw it as a final chance 'to bring about a change in our fortunes. Maybe 20 to 30 per cent of our unit were keen because they hoped to find plenty of food and alcohol; they were mostly the young ones. But the rest of us weren't at all enthusiastic; we just wanted to get the war over and get home.'[273]

Binding too suggested that the will to fight had a lot to do with the hope of securing food and drink. The discovery of wine cellars in Albert and Moreuil gave rise to so much chaos and delay that he estimates it cost the lives of at least 50,000 men.[274] Colonel Albrecht von Thaer wrote that 'entire divisions totally gorged themselves on food and liquor' and therefore failed 'to press the vital attack forward'.[275] Paul Fussell claims that the desire to get hold of food and other commodities was one of the main reasons why the offensive became bogged down.[276]

On 21 March the first of a series of operations began, called Michael, an offensive that quickly became known as *Die Kaiserschlacht*. Based on encouraging experiences with similar tactics in the East, the long bombardment was replaced by an intense but brief barrage of assorted gas shells. The armies did not move forward en masse at walking pace but at speed in small groups known as *Sturmbatallionen* or *Stoßtruppen*, in other words storm-troopers. They were given a fair degree of independence. A solution had finally been found to the biggest tactical problem of the war: how to coordinate firepower and movement. It was a success, but the advance did not live up to expectations. Wherever the Germans went on the offensive, the French and British were driven back, and the scenes that unfolded were reminiscent of the Allied retreat after the Sambre and Mons almost four years before, but although the ratio between deaths on the attacking and defending sides was not so greatly to the detriment of the former as in previous years, the German victory was extremely costly. The first day of Michael left around 7,000 British dead, as against 10,000 Germans. The difference was reduced even further as the battle went on, so that by the end of Michael, on 5 April, the total number of casualties, dead, wounded and missing, would be around a quarter of a million on each side. But one death is not equivalent to another, and the German casualties

271 Brants & Brants, *Velden van weleer*, 341
272 Liddle & Cecil, *Facing Armageddon*, 390
273 Holmes, *Firing Line*, 230–31
274 Holmes, *Firing Line*, 250
275 Keegan, *First World War*, 433
276 Fussell, *The Great War*, 17–18

belonged to irreplaceable elite units. It was therefore a victory of a tactical rather than strategic kind. Attacks were staged wherever the opportunity arose, so they did not necessarily coincide with locations of strategic importance.[277] Jay Winter and Blaine Baggett are right to speak of a tactical masterpiece that turned into a strategic defeat.[278] The new, longer front line proved harder to defend. Not enough troops were available.[279] The realization dawned on at least some German soldiers that they could not burst out. Lieutenant Fritz Nagel wrote that the 'slow and bloody progress' did not resemble a breakthrough, nor could he detect anything resembling a British collapse. 'Judging from the many dead and the never-ending stream of our wounded coming back, it was evident the enemy had no intention of quitting.'[280]

It is probable, indeed almost certain, that one of the British dead during Michael was the writer and painter Isaac Rosenberg. He had initially been a conscientious objector and partly as a result gotten into particularly wretched circumstances. Because of the tempting pay, and because American fellow-writer Ezra Pound had talked him into it, he decided to join up after all. He failed to return from a night patrol on 1 April. His body was never found.[281]

After Michael ended, elsewhere fresh German offensives began. Operation Georgette, launched between Ypres and Neuve Chapelle on 9 April, was one of the few occasions on which Portugal, fighting on the Allied side, actually deployed its troops. In late May at the Chemin des Dames, Operation Blücher followed, named after a general who had gone to the aid of Wellington at Waterloo. This attack brought the German armies back to the Marne for the first time in four years. To the north of Compiègne, Operation Gneisenau began and ended on 9 June, followed a month later in Champagne by Operation Marne-Reims, also known as *Friedensturm*. All to no avail. Although the offensives continued, it had been clear as soon as Michael became bogged down after less than three weeks, with 30,000 German and 20,000 Allied dead, that the shock effect had worn off and German infantrymen were no longer capable, either individually or collectively, of carrying out this kind of attack successfully. Although the British and French front line had shifted, it had not been broken.[282] Nonetheless, war historians including Paul Preston are convinced that despite being far more desperately short of food and equipment than the Allies, Germany would have won the war had the United States not been persuaded by unlimited submarine warfare to enter the fighting.[283]

---

277 Strachan, 'Military Modernization', 91–2; Chickering, *Imperial Germany*, 180; Keegan, *First World War*, 427, 430, 433; Marix Evans, *1918*, 63, 105, 152

278 Winter & Baggett, *1914–18*, 287

279 Murray, 'West at war', 291

280 Macdonald, *To the Last Man*, 259

281 'Jahrhundert der Kriege', 118–19

282 Chickering, *Imperial Germany*, 182; Keegan, *First World War*, 426, 434–7

283 Preston, 'Great Civil War', 150–51; De Vos, *De Eerste Wereldoorlog*, 141

The war went on, all the same. In fact it was probably now at its fiercest since 1914. The price paid was huge. In four months the German army lost around a million men, twice as many as the British and French combined. After two months of fighting, Zuckmayer wrote from Flanders to his friend Kurt Grell:

> What have I experienced (since our last letter)? Offensives. '*Kaiserschlacht*'. Blood. Cambrai. Blood. Gas shells. Kemmelberg. Blood. Horror. A brief time in Lille. Schnapps. Whores. Booze. Armentières: Blood. Killing. Blood. Three steps from insanity.[284]

The losses on the Allied side were catastrophic as well. In the first six weeks of the German spring offensive the British lost as many men as in all the three months of Passchendaele.[285] Eric Hiscock wrote about those days in *The Bells of Hell go Ting-a-Ling*:

> I don't know what happened mentally, but physically I occasionally broke down under the sheer weight of equipment that had to be carried, lack of sleep, and the intolerable discipline that was necessary in 1918 to keep tired and bored soldiers up to something like scratch, and away from mutiny.[286]

This kind of fighting called back memories of Mons and the First Battle of Ypres. Except that now the roles were reversed. One battle at the River Lys cost the lives of thousands of young Britons. Captain C.S. Slack (Med.) of the East Yorkshire Regiment, saw 'nearly all new little boys out from England, only been out a few days, only heard rifles fired on the ranges in England. They were annihilated, either bayoneted or shot.'[287] The Second Battle of Ypres was in the minds of many British soldiers when the Germans released 2,000 tons of poison gas in the same area on 20 April. More than 8,000 British troops were gassed and forty-three died.[288]

*The Allied advance*

The French mounted the first counter-offensive at the Marne in mid-July 1918[289] and in August the British too felt capable of striking back. The long-awaited arrival of American troops contributed to this new confidence, as did the poor mental and physical state of German soldiers. At Amiens on 8 August the Allies mounted

284 Zuckmayer, *Als wär's ein Stück von mir*, 249–50

285 Winter, *Death's Men*, 20; Terraine, 'Inferno', 195; Simkins, *World War I*, 194; Gilbert, *First World War*, 418; Fussell, *The Great War*, 17; Winter & Baggett, *1914–18*, 288, 292–4; Murray, 'West at war', 293

286 Fussell, *Bloody Game*, 160

287 Macdonald, *1914–1918*, 276

288 Gilbert, *First World War*, 415

289 Chickering, *Imperial Germany*, 186

an attack that resulted in 'a black day for the German army'. Twenty thousand Germans died or were wounded, 30,000 were taken prisoner. Douglas MacArthur, who would command American forces in the Southwest Pacific more than twenty years later, walked across the battlefield amid the moans and screams of wounded men abandoned there. He estimated he had seen 2,000 German corpses. A machine-gun post was scattered with bodies, 'the lieutenant with shrapnel through his heart, the sergeant with his belly blown into his back, the corporal with his spine where his head should have been'.[290] Yet we should not be misled by sights and body-counts like these. Roles had been reversed, but not completely. Now it was the French, British, Australians, New Zealanders, Canadians and Americans who were advancing, and therefore it was the French, British, Australians, New Zealanders, Canadians and Americans who died. The Battle of the Marne, for example, cost the Germans 25,000 men, the French around 100,000.[291]

In the short months between the final British offensive and the armistice on 11 November, the British lost around 350,000 men. Many inscriptions on British war memorials illustrate the fact that in 1918 more soldiers were killed than in any other year of the war. Yet for this final battle little lamentation is heard. The loss of lives is easier to accept when it results in military success. This had already become clear during the German advance six months earlier. A German NCO called Fiesmann wrote on 5 May 1918 that it had a positive effect on the soldiers' morale; there was a real sense that the war of movement might be decisive, bringing the longed for return to wife and child. A successful advance made life at the front much more bearable.[292]

The Germans looted as they withdrew, but they never fell into a state of total panic. No matter how many surrendered or refused to go on fighting, the line remained more or less intact, and from their side too, the machine-gun continued its deadly work. The disadvantages of a rapid advance were making themselves felt. It became increasingly hard to supply fresh equipment. Contradictory orders were issued, shells no longer reached the guns, ambulances failed to arrive to collect the wounded and food transport stalled.[293]

The Americans were fresh and well-nourished but inexperienced in battle and their greenness cost them dear. Mistakes were frequent. In July 35,000 Americans were lost at Chateau-Thierry during their own version of the 'total assault', partly because they insisted on operating not under British or French command but as a separate entity. They had been trained prior to the battle under British and French supervision, by British and French officers who felt far too much time was being sacrificed to training and were far more quickly convinced than the leaders of

290 Gilbert, *First World War*, 446; Keegan, *First World War*, 440–42; Marix Evans, *1918*, 170

291 Chickering, *Imperial Germany*, 186

292 Liddle & Cecil, *At the Eleventh Hour*, 34; Murray, 'West at war', 293

293 De Schaepdrijver, *De Groote Oorlog*, 251; De Vos, *De Eerste Wereldoorlog*, 141–2

the American Expeditionary Force (AEF) themselves that the Doughboys were ready for combat. The first divisions to arrive were given a short time to prepare; later arrivals were thrown into battle straight away. Many wandered across the countryside in a daze. Of the two million troops of the AEF, 115,000 would soon be dead and around 300,000 wounded. Aside from the fact that this was a ratio of one dead for every three wounded where one to four is normal, the numbers seem even more shocking when we consider that a large proportion of American soldiers never saw action. Of the more than 100,000 fatalities, around 4,000 were the result of accidents, drowning, suicide or murder. It was fortunate that the war ended in mid-November 1918, since the American army would not have been able to go on fighting much longer. Historian James Cooke has calculated that by the last week of October the Americans were finished, partly because of the Spanish 'flu, which was now stalking both Europe and the US.[294]

The Germans again suffered huge losses. Despite victory in the East and successes in the West that were sustained until mid-1918, it was becoming clear they had lost the war. While some divisions were still fighting the Allies, others rebelled against the Kaiser and his generals. The Kaiser fled and the generals began to negotiate. It was agreed that weapons would be laid down on 11 November. At eleven o'clock in the morning the firing stopped all along the front – not a second earlier and in some cases slightly later.[295] At ten thirty a messenger brought T. Grady of the AEF the order to cease firing at eleven. Until then the gunfire continued. '306th Machine-Gun Company on my right lost twelve men at 10.55, when a high explosive landed in their position.'[296]

Mons had been the backdrop to one of the opening scenes of the war and it would provide the closing scene. On 11 November 57 Canadians died there. They included a man called George Price. He was shot at 10.58 am as he stood talking about the armistice with excited civilians. He was not the last, even aside from accidental casualties, as on 19 November at Hamont where a munitions train exploded. Then there are the countless dead and wounded of the wars that were a direct result of the 1914–18 conflict, like the Russo-Polish War of 1919, the Greco-Turkish War of 1919–22 and of course the Russian Civil War that followed the revolution and lasted well into the 1920s.[297]

294 Simkins, *World War I*, 198, 216–17; Macdonald, *1914–1918*, 294–5; Winter & Baggett, *1914–18*, 303; Ellis, *Eye-Deep*, 106 (note); Verdoorn, *Arts en Oorlog*, 338; Gabriel & Metz, *A History of Military Medicine*, 249; Simkins, *World War I*, 217; Liddle & Cecil, *Facing Armageddon*, 249–51; Kolata, *Griep*, 32–3, 71–4

295 Keegan, *History of Warfare*, 363

296 Macdonald, *1914–1918*, 313

297 Gilbert, *First World War*, 58; Documentary 'The Day the Guns Fell Silent. Before 11', BBC 2, 10–11–1998; Leclerq, *Het informatiebureau*, 143; Marix Evans, *1918*, 235; Audoin-Rouzeau & Becker, *'14–'18*, 223

*The armistice*

The war that was supposed to be over by Christmas 1914, and which many soldiers believed would never stop, had finally ended. Many were not convinced. The war over? They refused to believe it. Most celebrations took place back home, among those who knew that friends and family still out in France or Belgium were safe and unhurt. In the trenches the most noticeable effect was silence. No more roaring of guns, no more whistling of bullets, little revelry either, virtually no jubilation. The soldiers had been beaten numb. Relief? Yes. Festivities? Although joy was certainly one element of the numerous different moods that overcame soldiers when they heard of the armistice, many were incapable of responding with enthusiasm. Some had no reason to feel joyful. The end had come too late and they would either die or face life without arms or legs. Graves later quoted a poem by Sassoon about the armistice, including the words 'everybody suddenly burst out singing', only to remark: 'But "everybody" did not include me.'[298] A Belgian Red Cross nurse, Jane de Launoy, who had worked for much of the war at the Hospital Océan in De Panne, a small town to the south of the Yser front that was referred to as the capital of Belgium in those years of occupation, sighed:

> The war is over. Too much grief shrouds the joy. ... Too much mystery remains unexplained, too much uncertainty, too much menace. Trust has gone. Never again will we be certain of anything.

When a soldier asks her to dance she realizes she is not in the mood.

> My memories of the war are too recent, too shocking. ... I am happy, certainly, yes, yes... but I have lost my faith in life. I've buried my illusions for ever. Because I have learned to see the bad side to people.[299]

This explains why many war memoirs do not end on 11 November but at some indeterminate point before or after, as if the writers wanted to make clear that for them the war had not ended on 11 November 1918. There was no victory. The most important questions asked in war memoirs were not about who had won or lost. They were: Who fought? Who suffered? Who survived?[300] Hynes writes that this clearly applies to Campion Vaughan's book *Some Desperate Glory*. It simply stops at Passchendaele. The war would go on for another year, and Campion Vaughan would take part in countless other battles, but why would he want to write about them? His company had been all but wiped out. Of 90 men only 15 were left. He had learned to give leadership, but what was he supposed to lead, and to what purpose? 'So this was the end of "D" Company. Feeling sick and lonely I returned

298 Graves, *Goodbye*, 228; *Van den Grooten oorlog*, 295–6

299 De Launoy, *Oorlogsverpleegster*, 331–3

300 Hynes, *Soldiers' Tale*, 94

to my tent to write my casualty report; but instead I sat on the floor and drank whisky after whisky as I gazed into a black and empty future.'[301]

Others brought their stories to a conclusion only several years after the fighting ended. Only then did the war belong to the past for them personally, and it could only truly belong to the past when their books had been completed.[302] Zuckmayer never wrote specifically about the war at all – it seemed impossible to describe to civilian readers, and for his companions in adversity any description was superfluous – instead he treated the years 1914–18 as a subdivision of his memoirs. He left for the West in 1914 laughing and singing and returned four years later silent, in his mind the names and faces of all the men who had left with him, none of whom returned. Despite this he was full of hope for a better future. It would take a later episode of German history to destroy that hope.[303]

By 1918 the Spanish 'flu was raging across the world, including its armies. Moreover, despite everything they had experienced, many men dreaded the safer yet unexciting, ordinary, more complex and, for young soldiers, totally unfamiliar life awaiting them. Taking all this into account it is understandable that gloom and sadness predominated rather than joy.[304] Some of the men who had escaped the dance of death would form ex-servicemen's organizations such as Germany's National Association of Disabled Soldiers and Veterans, which was to experience its finest hour one month and eleven days after the armistice when around 10,000 people marched through the streets of Berlin from the Zirkus Busch to the War Ministry. In what Weldon Whalen describes as a parody of the triumphal marches of August 1914, row upon row of war casualties paraded through the cold Berlin streets. Carts packed with disabled veterans headed the march. They were followed by blind men with dogs. Widows and orphans rounded off the procession.[305]

### 1914–18: the casualties

Of the eight million Frenchmen aged 18 to 51 who served in the army between 1914 and 1918, four million were active at the front. Most were wounded at least once, commonly several times. Around 1.5 million did not survive the war. Two million French soldiers were left permanently disabled, out of a population of forty million. Charles de Gaulle calculated that every French division had seen action between ten and seventeen times, and had not been relieved until a third of

---

301 Campion Vaughan, *Some Desperate Glory*, 232; Hynes, *Soldiers' Tale*, 95

302 Hynes, *Soldiers' Tale*, 99

303 Zuckmayer, *Als wär's ein Stück von mir*, 182, 196, 213

304 Macdonald, *1914–1918*, 307; Winter & Baggett, *1914–18*, 319; Hynes, *Soldiers' Tale*, 99–100

305 Whalen, *Bitter Wounds*, 124–5

its men were out of action.[306] The British suffered losses of a million dead and over two million wounded. Around half the men who served were wounded, seriously or otherwise; 3.5 million British soldiers became sick, of whom 30,000 died. In France alone, there were 130,000 hospital admissions of British officers and 2.5 million of other ranks.[307] Taking only the bald statistics into account and including both fronts, the Germans suffered most. Almost two million were killed and nearly 4.5 million wounded. Many died after the war as a result of their wounds. Half of all soldiers who served at some point during the war became casualties, or one in ten inhabitants of the German Reich. In four years a total of almost twenty million hospital admissions were recorded. Over 160,000 hospital patients succumbed to their sickness or wounds.[308]

To these figures should be added hundreds of thousands of dead, wounded and sick Australians, Canadians, Indians and Senegalese,[309] not to mention the millions who were killed or wounded or died of disease on one of the other fronts: Italy, the Middle East, the Dardanelles, Africa and especially Russia. As already mentioned, Serbian soldiers paid the highest price, with figures that are almost beyond belief: 40 per cent killed, a figure 25 per cent higher than for most other armies. The American forces, involved in the fighting for only a short time, were the exception with losses among conscripts of only around 5 per cent, although for those who reached the front the figure was a little over 10. All in all, between 1 August 1914 and 11 November 1918, the number of men either shot dead, killed by shells or so severely lacerated by shrapnel that they died of their wounds is probably over nine million.[310]

John Bourne speaks of 8.5 million dead and 21 million wounded out of a total of 65 million men mobilized. In other words, almost half the total number either did not survive the war or did not come through it unscathed. In this context it is worth noting that countries such as Japan and Portugal mobilized large numbers of men but took part in the fighting only to a very limited degree. The statistics show that hospital was as much part of the everyday life of the soldier as the battlefield and the trench. Weldon Whalen, although careful not to commit himself, suggests that the number killed was closer to 9,500,000, or 181,000 per month, 6,302 per day. Gilbert gives a list of 30 officers and soldiers of a single regiment, all killed at

306 Brants & Brants, *Velden van weleer*, 169–70, 344; Winter, *Death's Men*, 144; Keegan, *History of Warfare*, 361, 365; Keegan, *First World War*, 4; Meire, *De Stilte van de Salient*, 22

307 Brants & Brants, *Velden van weleer*, 344; Ellis, *Eye-Deep*, 106; Winter, *Death's Men*, 185; Verdoorn, *Arts en Oorlog*, 338; Garrison, *History of Military Medicine*, 200; Gabriel & Metz, *A History of Military Medicine*, 246–7; Simkins, *World War I*, 156; Graves, *Goodbye*, 54–5; Bourke, *Dismembering the Male*, 15

308 Brants & Brants, *Velden van weleer*, 344; Garrison, *History of Military Medicine*, 200; Keegan, *History of Warfare*, 365; Gabriel & Metz, *A History of Military Medicine*, 244; Bleker, *Medizin und Krieg*, 261; Whalen, *Bitter Wounds*, 42

309 Brants & Brants, *Velden van weleer*, 344

310 Murray, 'West at war', 295; Hynes, *Soldiers' Tale*, 96

Loos on 27 September 1915, and then writes – not entirely accurately – that such a list could be drawn up for every day of the war, and for every front, then multiplied by 200. He arrives at a figure of 5,600 men killed per day, and soberly concludes that the figure of 20,000 British dead on 1 July 1916, often called to mind with such horror, was reached every four days between August 1914 and November 1918. It is officially accepted that more than half of all deaths were caused by mortar bombs and shells, some containing gas, about 40 per cent by bullets, 2 per cent by hand grenades and less that half of one per cent by bayonets.[311]

There are various reasons for caution in estimating casualty numbers for the First World War, or indeed any major war. Firstly we should be careful not to extrapolate simplistically, by multiplication, from the losses of specific regiments or divisions. Figures for different regiments and divisions diverge enormously, depending to a large degree on where and when they were deployed. One regiment faced fiercer and more frequent fighting than another. Based on the statistics, and compared to other wars, the impression left by the First World War is one of continuous mass slaughter. There is no denying the truth of this, but the proportion of fatalities overall was no more than ten to fifteen per cent, depending exactly how many were mobilized and which casualty numbers we choose to believe. Assuming ten per cent died, some commentators point out this was 'only' five per cent more than during the Boer War. But the absolute numbers are staggering. Another way of expressing them is to say that in percentage terms there were twice as many fatal casualties as in that earlier war. Personally I find it more illustrative of the First World War to point out that the percentage of fighting men killed fell back again in the years 1939–45 to four and a half per cent.[312]

What is the value of these percentage figures in any case? Despite all that has been written about the enormous number of dead, wounded and sick in the First World War – and whichever figure we accept, the number remains vast – there are few mysteries greater than the figures themselves. Take the Battle of Verdun. Some sources speak of 100,000 dead and 500,000 wounded on either side. Historian Luc de Vos gives figures of 160,000 dead and missing Frenchmen, and 220,000 French wounded, while Kurt Tucholsky, for example, speaks of 400,000 dead on the French side alone. One French officer had no hesitation in announcing that there had been 1.5 million French casualties. It is perhaps characteristic that Gilbert writes at one point in his *The First World War* of more than a million French dead in the war as a whole and elsewhere of almost 1.4 million. Of course this is not a discrepancy, but it is telling that almost 400,000 dead seem simply to have been rounded down.[313]

311 Whalen, *Bitter Wounds*, 38; Binneveld, *Om de geest*, 47; Holmes, *Firing Line*, 210; Gilbert, *First World War*, 200, 541; Winter & Baggett, *1914–18*, 108, 362; Ellis, *Eye-Deep*, 106; Garrison, *History of Military Medicine*, 198; Gabriel & Metz, *A History of Military Medicine*, 239

312 Winter, *Death's Men*, 204

313 Gilbert, *First World War*, 31, 541

The first and perhaps primary cause of all these mysteries lies in the word 'casualties'. Sometimes it is used to refer to the dead, sometimes the dead and wounded, sometimes the dead, missing, wounded and sick, and it often includes prisoners of war as well. If the word 'casualty' is used in a purely military sense – in other words, if no distinction is made between 'losses' and 'casualties' – prisoners of war may well be included. After all, it makes little difference to the fighting strength of an army *why* a soldier cannot take part in a given action, only *whether* he can take part. On the other hand, if he had first lain wounded in no man's land, a prisoner of war was quite likely to be placed under some heading such as 'survived', and the same applies to the wounded who did not recover sufficiently to return to the battlefield but were not left permanently disabled. Captives might not survive if their prisoner of war camps were visited by epidemics, as was quite common during the First World War, yet most soldiers did not regard prisoners of war as casualties. Men generally saw capture as shameful, but Louis-Ferdinand Céline – who had gone to war with enthusiasm and emerged from it with a medal and a citation[314] – noted a dialogue that was probably fairly typical: '"Did you hear about the First Hussars, taken prisoner in Lille, every last one of them. ... Talk about luck!" ... "The bastards!" "Yeah, wasn't that something!"'[315] Barthas declared that a group of German prisoners who escaped must be insane. Who on earth would want to return to the trenches and battlefields? In short, there is some doubt as to whether all the men listed as casualties were exactly that. Conversely, many soldiers could be regarded as war casualties even if they were not included in the official listings because (for the time being at least) they were able to go on fighting. Many civilians living in areas near the front died of diseases such as typhus that they would probably never have contracted had it not been for the war. They too were 'casualties of war' but not categorized as such.[316]

Another complicating factor is that many countries were not in a position to keep accurate lists of the missing, or for understandable reasons had no interest in doing so. In Germany the publication of 'final scores' was forbidden. With the wounded and sick there is the further problem that although hospitals kept track of whether they were treating a case of 'a bullet wound to the stomach' or 'influenza', they did not record whether one and the same person was affected. In other words, hospital statistics recording 100 wounds might refer to 50 men with an average of 2 wounds each. Then there is the problem of the missing. Were they all drowned in the mud or mutilated beyond recognition, as the vast majority undoubtedly were? Or did some successfully desert? Did they surrender? Faced with the prospect of death or maiming, did they opt for survival at any price?[317] The

314 Liddle & Cecil, *Facing Armageddon*, 835

315 Louis-Ferdinand Céline, *Voyage*, 47

316 Barthas, *Carnets*, 502–3; *Van den Grooten oorlog*, 97

317 Whalen, *Bitter Wounds*, 38, 95; Werth, *Verdun*, 513–14; Audoin-Rouzeau & Becker, *'14–'18*, 38

suffering will never be fully known in numerical terms, and in any case suffering does not manifest itself in numbers. Suffering manifests itself in individuals, and individual suffering speaks tough, extremely tough language. Suffering in this personal sense will take a central place in the pages that follow.

# Chapter 2
# Body

The history of acts of war in '14–'18
is inseparable from a history of corporality.

Stéphane Audoin-Rouzeau & Annette Becker, *'14–'18*

## Conditions in the trenches

### *Clothing*

Much of the suffering that afflicted the troops, whether physical or psychological, arose from conditions in and around the trenches. The most noticeable problem they faced was the inadequacy of their clothing, both in quantity and in quality. In his book *Krieg* (*War*), Arnold Vieth von Golssena, writing as Ludwig Renn, described his one and only pair of underpants as a rag. Only the legs were still in one piece; they had no seat left, nor any buttons. In desperation he sewed laces to the sides and tied them round his waist.[1] In *Mud and Khaki*, H.S. Clapham describes how he walked around for six months with a large hole in the seat of his trousers and was once unable to change his underwear for a month.[2] There were times and places where no one changed a single item of clothing for a week and British rifleman H. MacBride managed to go 42 days without removing his tunic or boots.[3] The clothing shortage was so acute that it was not unusual for the dead to be stripped. Jünger describes undressing French corpses to change into their fresh linen as a peculiar, slightly disturbing experience, although he soberly allows practicality to override emotion. At least everything would serve a useful purpose instead of being left to rot.[4] Decay would set in soon enough in any case, according to Barbusse:

> Everything made for soldiers is ordinary, ugly and of poor quality; from their cardboard boots, with their uppers held on by cats' cradles of bad thread, to their ill-cut, ill-made, ill-sewn, ill-dyed clothes of flimsy, transparent cloth – blotting-paper – that a day's sunshine discolours, an hour's rain soaks through, not to mention their thin leather straps, brittle as wood shavings, torn by the buckles,

---

1 Renn, *Krieg*, 190

2 Winter, *Death's Men*, 19; see also: Dunn, *The War*, 475

3 Winter, *Death's Men*, 83

4 Jünger, *In Stahlgewittern*, 17; Renn, *Krieg*, 213

> their flannel underclothing thinner than cotton and their tobacco which looks like straw.[5]

Improvisation was therefore the key. Anything that might help protect a man against the cold and rain was put to good use, which produced some carnivalesque attire. Barbusse wrote:

> The great drama, in which we are the actors, has lasted too long, and we have ceased to be surprised by the appearance we have taken on or the clothing we have invented to protect ourselves from the rain that falls from above, the mud that comes from below and the cold, that sort of ubiquitous infinity. Animal skins, rolls of blankets, balaclavas, woollen hats, fur hats, scarves, spread out or wound into turbans, paddings of knitwear and darnings, surfacings and roofings, glued, rubber, black or in every (faded) colour of the rainbow, cover the men, disguising their uniforms almost as much as their skin, and expanding them.[6]

Many of the thick winter greatcoats were of reasonable quality, but they could become enormously heavy when wetted by rain.[7] They were often too long and had to be ruthlessly shortened, otherwise the mud they picked up would make it impossible to walk. Getting about was already far from easy given the shortage of decent boots.

A man might occasionally get hold of a good pair, but growing demand encouraged suppliers to put profit before quality. Blisters and calluses resulted. British doctors even invented a special term for this category of foot complaint: footslogger's nodules. They might be up to three quarters of an inch wide and half an inch thick.[8] Wear and tear struck at the cruellest moments. Frank Hawkings, author of *From Ypres to Cambrai*, remembered men being forced to wrap puttees around their feet in late November because their boots had disintegrated.[9]

Naturally there was a widespread belief that the enemy's clothing was far superior. This led to soldiers being specifically ordered to remove clothing from enemy corpses so that it could be sent back behind the lines for examination. Undressing dead men was never a pleasant business and it was sometimes daunting. Blunden wrote: 'We are required to send back specimens of German army underclothing. Paige and Babbage … have to cut the clothing off with jack-knives. The frost has made it particularly difficult.'[10]

5 Barbusse, *Le Feu*, 193; *Under Fire*, 164–5
6 Barbusse, *Le Feu*, 13–14; *Under Fire*, 13
7 Barbusse, *Le Feu*, 355
8 Winter, *Death's Men*, 78–9
9 Winter, *Death's Men*, 19
10 Blunden, *Undertones of War*, 165

*The soldier's burden*

Greatcoats heavy with rainwater bring us to the subject of the soldiers' baggage. During the retreats and advances of 1914 and 1918, their heavy packs made the exhausting marches almost unbearable. A man had to carry a load weighing at least twenty-five kilos and sometimes more than forty. Barbusse described it as 'monumental, crushing', what with flares, periscopes, wire-cutters, spare clothes (if he had any), shaving kit, food, drinking water, tea, cigarettes, matches, a Bible and perhaps other books, family photographs and so on. A Swiss, Ulrich Braker, serving in that famous German regiment whose name, the Itzenplitz, conjures up images of Schweijk rather than serious combat, opened his shirt after a march to feel some fresh air on his chest and 'steam rose up as if from a boiling kettle'. One British soldier, a former choirmaster, sighed that it was no fun having to carry your house on your back.[11]

Under the weight of his vast pack, which Horne says made a soldier look more like a deep-sea diver than an infantryman, even the strongest might eventually collapse. During an advance or a rapid retreat, men commonly fell out and they were not always able to connect up with their units again. A man known to be weak might sometimes carry a note written by a corporal and addressed to the assistant provost martial, so that were he to trail far behind he would not be taken for a deserter as soon as he ran into the military police. Exhausted men were helped by their comrades, who would support them for a few miles, one at each elbow, before collapsing themselves.[12] Frank Richards wrote about the retreat in his book *Old Soldiers Never Die*:

> We marched all night again and all next day, halting a few times to fire at German scouting aeroplanes but not hitting one. … We reservists fetched straight out of civil life were suffering the worst on this non-stop march, which would have been exhausting enough if we had not been carrying fifty pounds or so of stuff on our backs.[13]

John Harris of the 95th Rifles was convinced men had died because of the weight of their loads. After slipping on the muddy roads, they struggled like beetles to get back on their feet.[14]

Apart from the obligatory equipment, a soldier would lug all kinds of personal belongings with him, things to which he was attached because they reminded him

---

11 Holmes, *Firing Line*, 119–20; Holmes, *Riding the Retreat*, 45; Winter, *Death's Men*, 78; Keegan, *History of Warfare*, 302; Keegan, *First World War*, 86; Eksteins, *Rites of Spring*, 141; Tuchman, *The Guns*, 172; Andriessen, *De oorlogsbrieven van Unteroffizier Carl Heller*, 75; Dorgelès, *Croix de bois*, 32–3

12 Winter, *Death's Men*, 78

13 Terraine, 'Inferno', 177

14 Holmes, *Firing Line*, 120; Horne, *Price of Glory*, 62

of home, of his peaceful life in days of order and tranquillity. After listing all the nicknacks a French infantryman needed to carry in addition to his standard equipment, Barbusse wrote:

> Every time he reaches his post after so many kilometres by road and so many through the trenches the *poilu* does swear that next time he will get rid of a mass of stuff and relieve his shoulders from some of the weight. But every time he gets ready to set off he takes up this same exhausting, almost superhuman burden, and never gives it up, though he curses it.[15]

When a soldier arrived at the front line there was no respite from the heaving of loads. Shells had to be moved; the endless transferring of shells from place to place made men feel as if they might die of exhaustion. Many regarded few war duties with such horror as the carrying of gas cylinders, not only because they tended occasionally to leak but because they were so heavy.[16] On 10 August 1917, four days before he was relieved of his Sisyphean task for all time, a Bavarian artilleryman called Gerhardt Gürtler, a theology student from Breslau, wrote:

> The worst part of all of life here is the lugging of shells. In themselves the wicker baskets are not even particularly heavy, seventy to eighty pounds, but a hundred, a hundred and fifty, two hundred of them is no picnic. ... Lugging of shells followed by more lugging of shells.[17]

If the men's packs could so severely slow their marching, we need have no illusions about their effect during an attack. However hard they tried, the loads the men carried – at the Battle of the Somme, for instance, they might weigh over thirty kilos – meant they could rarely move at above walking pace. During every advance, rolls of barbed wire had to be carried forward, a far from simple task, especially under machine-gun fire. On the Somme each man went over the top with a rifle plus ammunition, hand grenades, iron rations, a waterproof cape, empty sandbags, a tin hat, two gas helmets, goggles to protect against tear-gas, a field dressing, a pick or shovel, and a full water bottle.[18] The *Official History* states that the weight

> made it difficult to get out of a trench, impossible to move much quicker than a slow walk, or to rise and lie down quickly. This overloading of the men is by many infantry officers regarded as one of the principal reasons for the

15 Barbusse, *Le Feu*, 194; *Under Fire*, 165

16 Richter, *Chemical Soldiers*, 47–51; Horne, *Price of Glory*, 159

17 Witkop, *Kriegsbriefe*, 326

18 Keegan, *Face of Battle*, 244; Macdonald, *Somme*, 59; Gilbert, *First World War*, 258–9; Marix Evans, *Battles of the Somme*, 15

> heavy losses … for their men could not get through the machine gun zone with sufficient speed.[19]

It is questionable whether major offensives would have succeeded if men had carried less baggage and therefore been able to advance more rapidly. After all, the cavalry fared hardly any better. In fact it is doubtful whether the pace of attacks – massed attacks that is, rather than those of the small, highly trained German *Sturmbatallionen* of the spring of 1918 – could ever have been much faster than they were across the craters and mud pools that covered the sometimes broad, sometimes extremely narrow strip of land between the two sides.[20] This was one more reason why the horse was no longer useful to an attacking force. Unable to take cover, it presented an even easier target to the machine-guns than the men themselves, and it was incapable of making the crossing at a gallop because of the appalling state of the ground. The few horses that reached enemy trenches were caught in row upon row of barbed-wire entanglements and mown down.[21] So although the loads the men carried were undoubtedly a hindrance, the mud and the pockmarked landscape would in any case have greatly limited the speed of attack. Nevertheless, with some cynicism, British historian Peter Liddle pointed out a conceptual error in the *Official History*'s account: 'In the event, many thousands of men offering so bulky and slow-moving a target would crumple to the ground quickly enough but would not rise at all, never mind quickly.'[22]

### *Hunger and thirst*

The weight he had to carry was as nothing compared to the two greatest torments that can afflict a man and which afflicted the troops throughout their time in the trenches: hunger and thirst. Water that was not plainly filthy was almost always scarce, which made washing a luxury. Lieutenant Charles Worsley reported in late 1914 that he had at last been able to shave. It was the first time in ten days that water had touched his face.[23] Corporal Louis Barthas had a splendid New Year's Day 1915. After seventeen days in the trenches he was finally able to wash his face and hands.[24]

That was merely water clean enough to wash with. Drinking water was often extremely scarce, especially in the dry summer months when the heat could be stifling. There were some appalling scenes. At the time of the Somme offensive, in the burning July and August sun, many soldiers could not resist the urge to remove water bottles, even if covered in flies and contaminated by rats, from the

19 Ellis, *Social History*, 133–5; Holmes, *Firing Line*, 121
20 Richter, *Chemical Soldiers*, 44
21 Prior & Wilson, *Passchendaele*, 10
22 Gilbert, *First World War*, 259
23 Macdonald, *1914*, 379
24 Barthas, *Carnets*, 86

often partially decomposed corpses around them, including men they had known. They had long ago drunk all their own water, which came in tins rinsed with petrol and lime chloride – an unappetizing but far from superfluous precaution – and fresh supplies were frequently delayed.[25] Many farmers with wells on their land made the situation worse by charging soldiers a fee to use them. In the British army, drinking without permission during a march was an offence subject to Field Punishment No. 1, a sanction we shall look at in the final chapter when we consider punishments, including 'death by execution'.[26]

If thirst was a torment in dry periods, in times of particularly bad flooding it was hell indeed. Soldiers suffered unquenchable thirst, caused partly by their dry biscuits, while water polluted by corpses lay everywhere they looked. Estimates suggest that by early 1915, in the inundated area around the Yser alone, tens of thousands of bodies floated on the floodwaters or under the murky surface.[27] Men crawled out of their trenches and risked their lives to fill their bottles with water from beneath the greenish-brown slime that coated ponds and flooded shell-holes, despite knowing they were certain to have been polluted by gas or by the decomposing flesh of men and horses. They knew the risks and accepted them.[28] W. Harrison wrote that soldiers drank water from one particular hole for several days until a dead German was dragged out of it,[29] and Second-Lieutenant Roger Campana saw a soldier drinking from a pool covered in green scum at the Mort Homme near Verdun in 1916. A dead man was floating nearby, 'his black face downward in the water … lying on his stomach and swollen as if he had not stopped filling himself with water for days'.[30]

In theory there was no need to go hungry. Daily rations ranged from a little over 4,000 calories in the case of the Germans to 4,700 for the Americans. German soldiers were allocated a thousand more calories a day than civilians – again, in theory – and they needed it, since extreme physical exertion was required of them. The British supplied a total of well over 3,240,000 tons of food during the war, but unfortunately for front-line troops, nothing like this enormous quantity reached the forward trenches. Corporal P.J. Clark started each meal by dividing up bread meant for one person into sixteen or twenty pieces.[31] This was no biblical parable – men went hungry. The quality of the food was indifferent even when initially shipped out and it might not be unloaded until many days or weeks later. As the

25 Macdonald, *Somme*, 206; Renn, *Krieg*, 179, Jünger, *Das Antlitz*, 178; Horne, *Price of Glory*, 182; Dearden, *Medicine and Duty*, 56; Winter, *Death's Men*, 102

26 Winter, *Death's Men*, 79

27 Liddle & Cecil, *Facing Armageddon*, 454

28 Macdonald, *Somme*, 206

29 Winter, *Death's Men*, 102

30 Horne, *Price of Glory*, 183; Brants & Brants, *Velden van weleer*, 237

31 Macdonald, *1914–18*, 265–6

war went on, the size of rations declined and their quality deteriorated. Diarrhoea was the rule rather than the exception.[32]

Examined in isolation, the severity of the distribution problems seems rather strange. A static war like that of 1914–18 ought to have been ideal when it came to feeding the men. The high command knew exactly where they were, not only at any given moment but for some days or weeks to come. In periods of mobile warfare in 1914 and 1918, food supply problems were in fact even greater than in the long years of trench warfare, and frugal meals of little nutritional value had to be thrown down at the side of the road somewhere as close as possible to the advancing or retreating troops. These were consumed by the men who came upon them first and therefore by the fittest, those least in need of sustenance.[33]

The situation was almost as bad during static periods, however, partly because the terrain became more impassable the closer you got to the front. Endless delays were inevitable. Food was lost, or deliberately destroyed as it began to rot. We should remember that food transports were plagued by artillery fire, which not only destroyed vehicles and supplies but often blocked the route. A fair amount of food fell into the filthy and putrefying water, although this did not always mean no one would eat it. Even at the best of times rations arrived garnished with mud and filth.[34] Extremely low temperatures made it even harder to keep the men adequately fed, and the winter months of 1916–17 on the Somme were especially frightful. Soldiers with frostbitten fingers and toes sometimes had to hold out for weeks without a warm meal. Their tea had a layer of ice on it and their bread and canned meat were frozen. When the thaw came the roads turned to muddy ditches overnight and no supplies arrived at all.[35]

Inevitably there was theft along the way. This was not the main problem, although understandably many front-line soldiers felt it was. Much resentment and animosity was directed at those who unloaded food at the ports and at soldiers in the rear, known on the German side as *Etappenschweine*. Soldiers in danger zones will always nurture a profound aversion for those who – in their view at least – are out of danger.[36]

Among the British, the shortage of supplies was caused mainly by a lack of sufficient shipping capacity to get the required amount of food across the Channel, although occasionally a train-load might disappear after arriving on the continent. In 1917 the consequences of unlimited submarine warfare began to bite. This led to an official campaign, initiated in the winter of 1916–17, to persuade soldiers to manage on even smaller rations. The campaign slogan, 'Eat Less and Save

32 Ellis, *Eye-Deep*, 125–7; Barthas, *Carnets*, 295

33 Macdonald, *1914*, 236

34 Binneveld, *Om de geest*, 67; Ellis, *Eye-Deep*, 125; Winter, *Death's Men*, 102, 147; Horne, *Price of Glory*, 62; Macdonald, *Somme*, 314

35 Brants & Brants, *Velden van weleer*, 154–5

36 Fussell, *Bloody Game*, 173; Holmes, *Firing Line*, 77–9

Shipping', proved a slightly unfortunate choice of wording, since soldiers at the front quickly rephrased it as 'Eat less and save shitting'.

The quality of the food declined markedly in the time that elapsed between the baking of bread and preparing of meat in the British Isles and their arrival at the front.[37] Men commented that army biscuits might actually have been quite nourishing if only they had been able to get their teeth into them. All too often they were hard as cement. Fred Darby stuck a stamp to the back of one inedible biscuit and sent it home to his wife, from a civilian post office, with a message on the other side: 'Your King and Country need You, and this is how they feed you.'[38] Denis Winter concluded that 'army rations were like an assault course', which 'could hit the stomach of the most honest soldier'.[39]

British troops largely subsisted on a type of canned food called Maconochie, a mixture of potatoes, meat, beans and vegetables. It was a far from appetizing mush, identified as one of the lesser yet more impressive horrors of the war.[40] It could actually be reasonably nutritious, at least if it came from the Maconochie factory itself, or alternatively from a firm called Moir Wilson. Unfortunately the British government had ordered stocks from other companies too, and many soldiers claimed there was widespread profiteering. Frank Richards said in relation to one of the other manufacturers:

> Before ever we opened the first tins that were supplied by them we smelt a rat. The name of the firm made us suspicious. When we opened them our suspicions were well founded. There was nothing inside but a rotten piece of meat and some boiled rice. The head of the firm should have been put against the wall and shot for they sharked us troops.[41]

Sometimes you got lucky. Someone might manage to shoot a rabbit, occasionally there were even a few chickens. Or men might happen upon a patrol that had come under fire and been left unburied with its rations barely touched. If there were officers among the dead, the men's joy knew no bounds, since there was a considerable difference between officers' rations and those of other ranks.[42] But such moments were drops of bliss in an ocean of misery. Private J. Bowles remarked: 'I am obliged to say that when we left the trenches, we were practically starving.'[43]

The *poilus* were even worse off, despite the fact that in theory they consumed more calories than the British. It was always extremely difficult to get food up to

---

37 Ellis, *Eye-Deep*, 127; Wilson, *Myriad Faces*, 357
38 Macdonald, *Somme*, 98
39 Winter, *Death's Men*, 148
40 Terraine, 'Inferno', 181
41 Fussell, *Bloody Game*, 102
42 Fussell, *Bloody Game*, 111; Winter, *Death's Men*, 19
43 Macdonald, *1914–1918*, 131

the line, because field kitchens – with solid tyres and coal-fired ovens – could not move beyond the reserve trenches. From there on food had to be distributed by individual soldiers known as carriers, who plodded through the mud, under fire all the way. The French distribution system virtually collapsed in December 1915. Of their 300,000 field kitchens, only just over half were still functioning. When French army propaganda of the time, in self-satisfied style, tried to have everyone believe that soldiers at the front were given two meals a day, the high command found itself in receipt of 200,000 angry letters of protest. The French quite often went without food altogether and the little they did get was consistently poor. At dawn Barthas and his men would receive their entire supply of rations for the next twenty-four hours: 'a little cold coffee, a scrap of dried meat and bread spattered with mud'. The bread was rarely 'fresh' (which officially meant no more than eight days old) and French soldiers were able to stave off starvation only thanks to supplementary packages sent by their families. Barbusse summed it all up when he wrote: 'As it is past dinner-time we demand our food. It's there already, because it's the remains of what we had last night.'[44]

But it was the Germans who were worst off. French propagandists were quite right to say that the French were better fed than their German opponents. Distribution was a huge problem for the German army, since meals often had to be carried several miles under artillery fire, but the main hindrances were the blockade and the priority given to the war economy. Meat and bread rations were steadily reduced, and the nutritional value of food supplies fell relentlessly. While the French suffered severe shortages of food, the Germans went without on a regular basis.[45] Jünger wrote:

> Aside from a rather watery soup at lunchtime, there was just a third of a loaf of bread with an offensively small quantity of 'spread', which usually consisted of half-off jam. And half of my portion was invariably stolen by a fat rat, which I often vainly tried to catch.'[46]

Towards the end of the war, German soldiers sometimes had nothing but gherkins to eat, which they referred to as 'gardener's sausage'.[47]

Hunger led to horrifying scenes. The dead were almost torn apart in the search, perhaps fight, for scraps. Even the Americans felt plunder was necessary on occasions, although they were generally well fed compared to the British, French and Germans; it was common practice, and those who did not wish to take

44 Barbusse, *Le Feu*, 253; *Under Fire*, 214; Brants, 'Inleiding', 16; Barthas, *Carnets*, 45; March, *Company K*, 19; Ellis, *Eye-Deep*, 127, 129; Audoin-Rouzeau, *Men at War*, 43, 60; Horne, *Price of Glory*, 62; Binneveld, *Om de geest*, 67–8

45 Ellis, *Eye-Deep*, 127–8; Renn, *Krieg*, 275–6; Johannsen, *Vier von der Infanterie*, 67

46 Jünger, *In Stahlgewittern*, 147, *Storm of Steel*, 182

47 Jünger, *In Stahlgewittern*, 236

part turned a blind eye. The same went for food as for clothing: why let it go to waste if the owner no longer had any use for it?[48] Although dead horses and mules were a ghastly sight, they provided some welcome supplies of meat.[49] Johannsen described what happened when a wounded horse was given the *coup de grâce*.

> The infantrymen immediately throw themselves at it. One man goes to sit at the neck, slices a piece off and shares it out. The NCOs have difficulty driving the men away from the horse.[50]

Soldiers were regularly dispatched to search for food, an occupation not without its hazards. One night in March 1916 at Verdun, Second-Lieutenant Campana sent eight men out to forage. Five came back. Without any food. The next night he sent out another eight. Not one man returned. In the night that followed, no fewer than a hundred men from various companies went out to hunt for anything that might perhaps be edible. They were mown down by machine-gun fire. Horne described the scene: 'After three days without food, Campana's men were reduced to scavenging any remnants they could find upon the bodies lying near their position. Many had been decomposing for several weeks. The experience was more the rule than the exception.'[51] Eduard Offenbächer wrote in May 1915: 'One barely alleviates one's raging hunger with the wonderful white bread that the young Frenchman over there, with that little red speck on his chest, was carrying in his haversack.'[52]

*Rain and mud and cold*

> O German mother dreaming by the fire,
> While you are knitting socks to send your son,
> His face is trodden deeper in the mud.
>
> Siegfried Sassoon, *Glory of Women*

Although there was often little or nothing to drink, soldiers of the Great War could not complain about a lack of water. There was either plenty lying around or great floods of it (Yser, Ypres, the Somme). In January 1915, five days before his death, German soldier Karl Aldag wrote from his Flanders dugout: 'Mud and water fill the trench, water from below and rain from above. Day and night we lie low, moving earth, shovelling water and pumping it. And all the time that sense of futility, knowing it's all completely pointless! The water remains.'[53] Eugen Röcker

48 Holmes, *Firing Line*, 127, 354
49 Renn, *Krieg*, 364; Barthas, *Carnets*, 332–3, 425, 429
50 Johannsen, *Vier von der Infanterie*, 25; Haas, *Oorlogsjammer*, 59
51 Horne, *Price of Glory*, 182–3
52 Witkop, *Kriegsbriefe*, 191
53 Witkop, *Kriegsbriefe*, 31

wrote home that in his shelter it was impossible for him to sleep in his bunk, since it was floating around in deep water.[54]

Along with post from family and friends and deliveries of food, the best thing a trench had to offer a Frenchman was the hole he dug into the side of it. The danger of collapse meant that the British and Germans were officially forbidden to excavate such spaces for themselves, but the *poilu* was always happy to take the risk if it meant he could get a little sleep without feeling the rain and stay, however briefly, relatively dry.[55] Readers of the trench newspaper *L'Horizon* were told in July 1918: 'Here we are caught in the rain. This simple word, rain, which is virtually meaningless for the townsman, the civilized man who has built a house and a roof to shelter him in bad weather, this word contains all the horror of being a soldier on campaign.'[56] Barbusse noted: 'Damp rusts a man as it does a rifle, more slowly, but more profoundly.' And later: 'It is raining – the same rain that, in my memory, attaches to all the tragedies of the Great War.'[57]

It had started more or less straight away. Rain fell at regular intervals from September 1914 onwards, as was perfectly normal in Belgium and France, but in December it began to bucket down. In Flanders, Artois and Picardy, fifteen centimetres fell in a month. That had not happened since 1876. Between 25 October 1914 and 10 March 1915 there were only eighteen dry days. The excessive rainfall did have one healthy outcome for the troops: their rifles jammed when mud got into them. Apart from that it only made life more unpleasant. Rivers burst their banks. On the Somme the men sank so deeply into the water and mud that ropes were sometimes needed to pull them out. At La Bassée a dam gave way and soldiers drowned in their trenches. March 1916 was the wettest month in 35 years, and at Passchendaele in 1917 it rained almost without a break throughout the month of August. The battle with the elements was often harder, and indeed better documented, than the battle with the human enemy.[58] On 13 December 1916, T.D. McCarthy wrote in his Somme diary that the war was more a question of men against the weather than of British troops against Germans. That evening a patrol went out. It was forced to walk back and forth continually to avoid getting stuck in the clay. 'Many men were stuck for hours. A man … whom we relieved was stuck for 43 hrs and died afterwards.'[59]

The battle with the elements was so appalling that it led to a few short-lived instances of fraternization. Front-line hostilities of all kinds stopped now and again because both sides were too busy trying to survive the weather and the ground

54 Witkop, *Kriegsbriefe*, 308

55 Horne, *Price of Glory*, 61

56 Audoin-Rouzeau, *14–18. Les combattants*, 37

57 Barbusse, *Le Feu*, 20, 264; *Under Fire*, 18, 223

58 Eksteins, *Rites of Spring*, 102; Ellis, *Eye-Deep*, 45; Brants & Brants, *Velden van weleer*, 69; Manning, *Her Privates We*, 182–3

59 Brown, *Somme*, 288

conditions.[60] As far as Graves knew, one February day at Ypres when everyone, British and German alike, had to climb out of the trenches to avoid drowning was the only occasion other than Christmas Day 1914 when a truce was silently agreed upon.[61] But Barthas described a similar scene, on 10 December 1915 at Neuville-Saint-Vaast, as did Jünger, this time in the autumn of 1917. There too the trenches had filled with water to such a height that soldiers on both sides had no choice but to get out. The men were completely exposed and not a single shot was fired from either side.[62] This suggests that rain truces, although perhaps not common, are likely to have occurred at fairly regular intervals.[63]

During a battle there was no chance of a rain truce. In the night of 27–8 August 1917 at Passchendaele, Campion Vaughan heard all around him 'the groans and wails of wounded men'. They included 'faint, long sobbing moans of agony, and despairing shrieks'. Later he understood why they had sounded so desperate. Wounded men who thought they had found safety in shell-holes had realized the craters were slowly filling with water, but the muddy sides made it impossible to climb out. The next day, after their cries had ceased, he saw water pouring out over the edges.[64]

Where there is rain there is mud, and persistent heavy rainfall produced immense quantities of the stuff.[65] The trench newspaper *L'Argonnaute* described the mud on 1 June 1916: 'It is everywhere, under your feet, under your hands, under your body when you lie down. It does not blow away with the wind, it sticks to your clothes, it gets right through to your skin, it soils anything that falters and everything that dies.'[66] The different armies came to resemble each other even more than armies naturally do. *Le Bulletin Désarmé* of 1 March 1918 stated: 'The mud camouflages a man from head to foot, burying beneath its sediment all distinctions of age and physiognomy.'[67] In this sense the effects of mud were similar to those of gas masks.

The battlefield was sometimes more lake than field. The same issue of *Le Bulletin Désarmé* described it as follows: 'The greasy tide, of alarming depth, awaits you and draws you in; duty pushes at your back. In one of those foolish decisions which throw you over the parapet on the morning of a big offensive, you take a chance and plunge into the vile bath.'[68] *L'Echo du Boqueteau* of 12 March 1917 told its readers: 'We were living in mud, seeing nothing but mud everywhere,

60 Brown, *Somme*, 287

61 Graves, *Goodbye*, 162

62 Barthas, *Carnets*, 215–16; Werth, *Verdun*, 401

63 Audoin-Rouzeau, *Men at War*, 37; Gilbert, *First World War*, 218

64 Campion Vaughan, *Some Desperate Glory*, 228; Heijster, *Ieper*, 144; Keegan, *First World War*, 390

65 Holmes, *Firing Line*, 131

66 Audoin-Rouzeau, *14–18. Les combattants*, 38

67 Audoin-Rouzeau, *14–18. Les combattants*, 38

68 Audoin-Rouzeau, *14–18. Les combattants*, 38

and bodies, and more bodies! And yet more mud! And yet more bodies!'[69] August Hopp wrote: 'A pile of five bodies lay in front of the barrier [blocking the trench to French troops further along]. We kept having to walk over them, pressing them down into the mud, since artillery fire made it impossible to get them out of the trench.'[70]

A.W. Hancow of the Royal Garrison Artillery described an army camp in France that typified the war years:

> The whole area where the troops lived was a sea of mud. Not the mud you would get on your Sunday boots after a hike in the hills at home, but ankle deep liquid. In this muddy lake, like the minarets in some eastern city, almost floating were hundreds of bell tents. Each tent was the home for twelve men, with all their kit.[71]

The verbs and metaphors used in these quotations suggest that the mud seemed to many soldiers like a living organism, as did death.[72] Captain De Lécluse spoke of mud as a treacherous, frightening substance that clung to you, benumbed you and slowly swallowed you, an image echoed in *Le Bochofage* of 26 March 1917: 'At night, hiding in a shell-hole, which it fills to overflowing, the mud, like an enormous octopus, lies in wait. The victim arrives. It throws its foul slobber out at him, blinds him, closes over him, buries him. One more man gone…'[73]

The soldiers of the Great War often used the word 'hell' to describe what they saw and experienced. As Samuel Hynes writes, this was partly because in the days before 1914 they would have received few if any impressions that could have helped them to clarify in their minds their experiences in the trenches and on the battlefield, but it was also because to soldiers who had grown up with religious concepts, like the devil and damnation, hell was the obvious metaphor for the terrors they witnessed daily. The landscape they found themselves in and the horrors they experienced reminded them of descriptions of the underworld they had heard in the days when they sat at school desks or listened to sermons in church. It was where they would end up when they died, if they did not live virtuous lives. They now discovered that hell was not somewhere far below the ground, and that men did not end up in hell only if they had sinned in life. No, hell was Flanders and France in the here and now,[74] and to many, hell was the mud above all. Not death but mud. Not crumps but mud. Barbusse wrote of men who

69 Audoin-Rouzeau, *14–18. Les combattants*, 88

70 Witkop, *Kriegsbriefe*, 39

71 Holmes, *Firing Line*, 111–12

72 Audoin-Rouzeau, *Men at War*, 76

73 Sandstrom, *Comrades-in-Arms*, 35; Audoin-Rouzeau, *14–18. Les combattants*, 39

74 Winter, *Sites of Memory*, 68–9; Sandstrom, *Comrades-in-Arms*, 81–2, 86; Winter & Sivan, *War and Remembrance*, 210

drowned simply because they were unable to pull themselves free, and he went on to say that hell was made not of fire but of mud.[75] The author of the article quoted above, published in *Le Bochofage* of 26 March 1917, agreed. 'Men die of mud, as they die from bullets, but more horribly. Mud is where men sink and – what is worse – where their soul sinks. … Hell is not fire, that would not be the ultimate in suffering. Hell is mud!'[76]

Men whose corpses lay in the mud might not always have died in the fighting. Thousands were killed not so much in the mud as by it. According to future British Prime Minister J. Boyd Orr, who entitled his war memoir *As I Recall*, no fewer than forty soldiers a day drowned in the slime. He was referring to the British side alone.[77] Jünger wrote:

> From time to time one of us would disappear up to the hips in mire, and would certainly have drowned but for the presence of his comrades and their helpfully extended rifle butts. … The least pleasant aspect of this chase was the prospect that almost any sort of wound was enough to see you to a watery grave. We hurried along the crater rims, as along the narrow walls of a honeycomb. Trickles of blood here and there indicated that some unlucky men must have gone there before us.[78]

Although sometimes, in the summer of 1917 for example, the rain fell in sheets without any appreciable let-up, we should not be deceived into thinking that in 1914–18 substantially more rain fell on France and Flanders than was usual in any given four-year period. The rain and mud were real enough, but they became a myth. The First World War is bound up with images of rain and mud, even though there were periods of beautiful weather and times when dust was far more in evidence than anything approaching a quagmire.[79] Nevertheless, the intensive pounding and churning of the ribbon of land known as the Western Front, mainly by shelling and the endless conveying of men and equipment in both directions, meant that rainfall had a far more destructive effect on the structure of the ground than in normal circumstances. There was no escaping the mud. It was everywhere, not just in places that usually tended to be wet.

In France men had to totter across wet clay. With each step they struggled to tug their feet free of the sucking loam. They could usually muster enough strength to pull their boots out, but many lost their footwear and had to wrap puttees around their feet or even go barefoot. It might take hours to cover the short distance between one trench and the next, and getting about in such conditions was utterly

75 Barbusse, *Le Feu*, 254

76 Audoin-Rouzeau, *Men at War*, 38; Gilbert, *First World War*, 313

77 Winter, *Death's Men*, 96; Hynes, *Soldiers' Tale*, 70

78 Jünger, *In Stahlgewittern*, 165; *Storm of Steel*, 199–200

79 Liddle, *Passchendaele in Perspective*, 140–58; Liddle & Cecil, *Facing Armageddon*, 827; Meire, *De Stilte van de Salient*, 52

exhausting.[80] To César Méléra, Verdun meant above all sinking up to the ankles 'in the fetid mud … disgorging an awful smell and a heavy opaque air'.[81] The always sodden land near the Somme became endlessly boggy. In this sense the Somme was on a par with Ypres.[82] The early weeks of the Battle of the Somme in 1916 were fought in fine dry weather, but when rain came in mid-August it came with a vengeance. The water combined with the clay to create an astonishingly viscous goo. It was not that you would sink to any great depth – except perhaps in periods of extremely heavy rainfall – but it could prove extremely hard to pull free. Often there was no way to get out without help. Horses and mules that became stuck had to be shot. Marching in mud was extraordinarily tiring and took a huge toll on both body and mind. In *The Somme*, A.H. Farrar-Hockley quotes one unnamed soldier who describes suddenly being stuck in a trench, unable to see anything except corpses rotting in water and a few booted feet sticking up out of the clay. 'The mud makes it all but impassable, and now, sunk in it up to the knees, I have the momentary terror of never being able to pull myself out. Such horror gives frenzied energy, and I tear my legs free and go on.'[83]

The writer John Masefield was near the Somme in the summer and autumn of 1916. In a letter he wrote:

> To call it mud would be misleading. It was not like any mud I've ever seen. It was a kind of stagnant river, too thick to flow, yet too wet to stand, and it had a kind of glisten or shine on it like reddish cheese, and it looked as solid as cheese, but it was not solid at all and you left no tracks on it, they all closed over, and you went in over your boots at every step and sometimes up to your calves.[84]

Here Masefield was describing the roads to the front, not no man's land or the trenches and their surroundings, let alone the battlefield.

If France had mud, Flanders was mud. By and large, in France it was a matter of slipping over or getting your boots stuck. In Flanders you sank and were trapped. 'Oh, the mud!' wrote Duwez.

> The terrible mud, the worst thing of all, the mud in which an army crawls about, in which horses, men, guns and carts look like vermin spattered with waste; a bloody, liquid pus that carpets the Flemish soil and eats at it, that eats its way into the landscape, the suffering landscape that only here and there still shows its fresh green, its blue sky and the red roofs of its houses.[85]

80 Witkop, *Kriegsbriefe*, 147
81 Eksteins, *Rites of Spring*, 153
82 Brown, *Somme*, 14, 229
83 Farrar-Hockley, *The Somme*, 206
84 Marix Evans, *Battles of the Somme*, 55
85 De Schaepdrijver, *De Groote Oorlog*, 177

Although soldiers who had fought on the Somme but not in Flanders continued to dispute the matter, the fighting around Ypres, and especially the Third Battle of Ypres, will always be remembered as the muddiest of all. Blunden wrote of 'a dead sea of mud' and Guy Buckeridge writes in *Memoirs of my Army Service in the Great War* that at Third Ypres the conflict could no longer be called a war at all. Were it not for the shooting and the shells flying constantly overhead it would be more accurately compared to working in a sewer.[86] During the battle, Lieutenant Jim Annan and his men laid some of their wounded against the back wall of a pillbox. During a pause in the fighting they heard screams and were just in time to see the mud flowing into the mouths and noses of the wounded and threatening to close over them.[87] Even for the Germans, who were mostly on the defensive at Third Ypres, the battle was a washed-out hell. Gürtler wrote that they were up to their knees in water with shells exploding around them, destroying everything, men, trees, buildings and defences, and covering them in black sludge, so that they looked as if they had been in a mud bath.[88]

Third Ypres also provides the best evidence that the war itself was mainly responsible for the terrible state of the ground, not the rain. The area around Ypres was waterlogged even in dry weather, but thousands upon thousands of mortars and shells fired in the preparatory bombardment, which for various reasons lasted almost a week longer than originally intended, ploughed up the ground, breached the dykes and destroyed every form of natural drainage that allowed water to flow out from the Flemish lowlands. Add to this the high groundwater level that resulted from the inundation of the neighbouring area around the Yser and it will be clear that even without the rain, the land around Ypres would have offered attacking British forces little in the way of a firm footing. With the rain, the outskirts of Passchendaele turned into quicksand, an enormous morass of liquid earth, metres deep in places, in which soldiers could only make progress, if at all, by pulling each other forwards.[89] At Passchendaele Campion Vaughan was held fast by the mud more than once:

> August 16: … I felt my feet sink and though I struggled to get on, I was dragged down to the waist in sticky clay. The others passed on, not noticing my plight until by yelling and firing my revolver into the air I attracted the attention of Sergeant Gunn, who returned and dragged me out. …
>
> August 27: … Exhausted by my efforts, I paused a moment in a shell-hole; in a few seconds I felt myself sinking, and struggle as I might I was sucked down until I was firmly gripped round the waist and still being dragged in. The leg of a corpse was out of the side, and frantically I grabbed it; it wrenched off, and casting it down I pulled in a couple of rifles and yelled to the troops in the gun

86 Blunden, *Undertones of War*, 221; Eksteins, *Rites of Spring*, 147
87 Macdonald, *Passchendaele*, 123–4
88 Witkop, *Kriegsbriefe*, 326
89 Macdonald, *Passchendaele*, 89

> pit to throw me more. Laying them flat I wriggled over them and dropped, half dead, into the wrecked gun position.[90]

Campion Vaughan was lucky to survive. Many others drowned.

The cold the men felt was directly connected to the rain and the mud. Soaked to the bone, Jünger concluded that nothing, not even artillery fire, could break a man's resistance so thoroughly as wet and cold.[91] No clothing could protect a man against the chill of a wet night in a filthy trench, in temperatures that dropped well below freezing in winter. British infantryman H. Drinkwater was of the opinion that 'one who has not stood all night in a muddy trench with sodden clothing cannot know the sheer ecstasy of the first gleam of sunshine'.[92] In early 1915 Campana wrote: 'We don't think of death. But it's the cold, the terrible cold! It seems to me at the moment that my blood is full of blocks of ice. Oh, I wish they'd attack, because that would warm us up a little.'[93] The trench newspaper *Le Crapouillot* put it like this:

> Poor and happy civilian, you have never been cold. You'd have had to be here all this winter, in sectors where cross-fire prevented you from lighting braziers, sitting tight for six days and six nights, your stomach frozen, your arms clumsy, hands inert, feet numb; you'd need to have felt in despair that nothing in the world can warm you again, to have bitten your icy moustache in a rage, unable to sleep for the pain of being cold.[94]

In his poem 'Exposure', Owen described the frost 'shrivelling many hands, puckering foreheads crisp. ... All their eyes are ice.' He was speaking from experience. In the winter of 1916–17 he was up at the line with his 2nd Manchesters. He wrote that the small cookers they had with them were unable to melt the ice, so despite the snow lying everywhere they 'suffered cruelly from thirst'. He felt completely isolated in a frozen desert, with no sign of life and thousands of signs of death – not a single blade of grass, not an insect, only the occasional bird of prey circling like a vulture. 'The marvel is that we did not all die of cold. As a matter of fact, only one of my party actually froze to death before he could be got back, but I am not able to tell how many have ended in hospital.'[95]

The heating available in shelters offered little comfort. It could certainly get warm in a crowded dugout, but the effect of burning coal in a small space without

---

90 Campion Vaughan, *Some Desperate Glory*, 196, 223–4
91 Jünger, *In Stahlgewittern*, 138; Eksteins, *Rites of Spring*, 148
92 Winter, *Death's Men*, 96
93 Eksteins, *Rites of Spring*, 148
94 Audoin-Rouzeau, *14–18. Les combattants*, 39
95 Day Lewis, *Collected Poems*, 161; Eksteins, *Rites of Spring*, 148

a chimney is easy to imagine. From time to time soldiers suffocated in their sleep.[96]

*Vermin*

> Ssh! Boys; what's the noise?
> Do you know what these rats eat?
> Body-meat!
>
> E.W. Tennant, *The Mad Soldier*

The conditions in and around no man's land that made life hell for the soldier made it a heaven for vermin. Mice, cockroaches, fleas, lice and rats of every shape and size teemed above, below and within the trenches and dugouts. Flies and mosquitoes, whose numerous bites could make a man's head swell to a grotesque size, flew across the landscape in giant swarms and carpeted the soldiers, living and dead. Nits established themselves in their hair, so regular visits to the barber were made compulsory. Mites caused unbearable itching and men scratched until they bled. Infection then caused widespread scabies.[97]

The conditions suited rats perfectly. Food lay everywhere in the form of rations or corpses – eyes and livers were their favourite – and there were virtually no natural predators. Each rat was capable of producing several hundred young each year. Raymond Asquith, son of the British Prime Minister and himself a Member of Parliament, wrote about a litter of kittens growing up in his trench. The men hoped they might keep the rats at bay. Asquith had little faith in this idea. The rats would win, but not without fighting a war of attrition first. He attributed human characteristics to rats, unpleasant human characteristics. As they gnawed at the faces of the dead they made 'obscene noises and gestures'. And they were starting to get tremendously big. There are reports of rats the size of rabbits or even cats. Perhaps revulsion at the black or brown creatures made them seem bigger than they were, but they could certainly grow to unusual proportions, and the absence of natural enemies made them extraordinarily bold. One British officer found two rats between his sheets, fighting over a torn off hand. Many soldiers woke up as rats walked over them or started to help themselves to their food. Men might not even be left in peace while eating; Graves and his fellow officers never ate their frugal meals without a revolver next to the plate. Some men hung their food from the ceiling, but even there it was not always safe. A wounded soldier too badly hurt to defend himself had a fair chance of being eaten alive. The only enemy the rats encountered was an unnatural one: gas. A gas attack would result in a huge death toll among rats, but the positive effect was short-lived. As soon as the gas had dissipated, more rats would start arriving from neighbouring trenches. Horne writes that rats seemed to be the only creatures who really profited from the war,

---

96 Winter, *Death's Men*, 95; Ellis, *Eye-Deep*, 51

97 Frey, *Pflasterkästen*, 316–17; Ellis, *Eye-Deep*, 58; Duhamel, *Civilisation*, 46–7

although, he adds cynically, there were few other respects in which the life of a rat differed from that of a soldier.[98]

The men nurtured a profound loathing for rats. A Flemish teacher serving at the front wrote: '[The rats] had their eyes on the remains of the corpses, and infection and disease clung to their whiskers and sticky tongues. ... Where they had passed through, no supplies were left. They ate everything up, and even the dogs were nauseated by the cadaverous smell they gave off.'[99] The presence of rats was one of the few things about the war that Jünger truly detested. 'They are repellent creatures, and I'm always thinking of the secret desecrations they perform on the bodies in the village basements.'[100]

All this indicates one advantage of rats. They helped to remove corpses from the battlefield, which led some to remark that it would be better to control the problem instead of trying to eliminate it. Barbusse reported that you would always find two or three dead rats lying near a corpse, having either been poisoned or eaten themselves to death. Within the body would be two or three more, alive. The following not untypical report is from another French soldier:

> One evening, whilst on patrol, Jacques saw some rats running from under the dead men's greatcoats, enormous rats, fat with human flesh. His heart pounding, he edged towards one of the bodies. Its helmet had rolled off. The man displayed a grimacing face, stripped of flesh; the skull bare, the eyes devoured. A set of false teeth slid down on to his rotting jacket, and from the yawning mouth leapt an unspeakably foul beast.[101]

Rats were a universal plague and like so many of the hardships suffered on both sides, they produced a sense of shared adversity. In his novel *Johnny Got His Gun*, Dalton Trumbo describes the thoughts and dreams of Joe Bonham, a deaf, dumb and blind war invalid without arms or legs. Thinking and dreaming are all he is capable of now.

> He remembered the face of a Prussian officer they discovered one day. ... He was a captain. He was lying with one leg straight up in the air. The leg was swelled so much the pants looked as if they were ready to bust open. His face was swelled too. His moustache was still waxed. Sitting on his neck and chewing away at his face was a fat contented rat.

98 Gilbert, *First World War*, 212; Babington, *Shell-Shock*, 62–3; Frey, *Pflasterkästen*, 227–8; Graves, *Goodbye*, 116–17, 160; Ellis, *Eye-Deep*, 54; Winter, *Death's Men*, 97–8; Holmes, *Firing Line*, 113; Macdonald, *1914–1918*, 137; Eksteins, *Rites of Spring*, 149–50; Horne, *Price of Glory*, 61; Dunn, *The War*, 259; Andriessen, *De oorlogsbrieven van Unteroffizier Carl Heller*, 61

99 Brants & Brants, *Velden van weleer*, 58

100 Jünger, *In Stahlgewittern*, 26; *Storm of Steel*, 43

101 Ellis, *Eye-Deep*, 54; Barry, *The Great Influenza*, 119

The soldiers run after the rat, yelling and screaming, catch it and smash it to a pulp. 'It didn't matter whether the rat was gnawing on your buddy or a damned German it was all the same. Your real enemy was the rat and when you saw it there fat and well fed chewing on something that might be you why you went nuts.'[102]

With so many men in such cramped, unhygienic conditions, lice were the second great plague. Barthas wrote:

> We carried thousands of them on us; they had set up home in the slightest fold, along the seams, in the collars of our tunics; some were white, others black, others grey, with a cross on the back, like the crusaders; some were tiny and others fat like grains of wheat, and the whole brood went forth and multiplied at the expense of our skin.[103]

On average each louse would set its teeth into the skin of a man to drink his blood more than ten times a day, although they needed only one meal in ten days to survive. Campana regarded the lice on the skin of the *poilu* as a greater danger than the 'vampires of Congo or Polynesia'. For the Scots above all, with their kilts, which were the ideal breeding ground for lice, this creature represented a threat to both health and morale. They experimented with their own delousing techniques, some injuring or burning themselves so badly that they ended up visiting hospital, where they were often refused treatment because their wounds were self-inflicted. The Germans were even worse off than the British and French. Shortages back in Germany meant that after a few years the bundles of straw they slept on were replaced with paper mattresses. Not only were these much less comfortable, they turned out to be an even greater paradise for lice.

As they did to rats, soldiers attributed unpleasant human characteristics to lice. The louse lay in wait for its victim, hiding in straw or paper, ready to jump onto his skin at the appropriate moment, and such moments came all too frequently. There was simply nothing you could do about lice. Everyone had them, some more than others. They laid their eggs about five times a day in the seams of clothing and multiplied at a dizzying rate. A. Abrahams once counted 103 lice on his clothes and body. In relatively peaceful periods, men could be seen all along the front inspecting their clothes for lice. But whatever they did to them, squash them flat, burn them in candle flames, drive them off with powders and pomades, nothing really helped. In 1915 the 'Lousoleum' appeared in the German trenches, a mobile de-lousing station. Hundreds of soldiers a day were treated by medical personnel. The previous year a powder called 'Nick-o-louse' (to suggest St Nicholas) had been a popular Christmas present. But the de-lousing of hair and clothes brought only temporary relief. No matter how thoroughly clothing was washed, some eggs always survived in the seams. After a while the Germans, at their wits' end, sought salvation in gas, but even that proved no lasting solution.

---

102 Trumbo, *Johnny Got His Gun*, 84–5

103 Barthas, *Carnets*, 209

Of these efforts, however, not the last was heard. After the war the German poison gas programme, under the leadership of Jewish-German nationalist and chemist Fritz Haber, would continue to function as a vermin-extermination programme. This was merely a cover for renewed attempts to develop chemical weapons. A gas called Zyklon had already been produced to combat lice, and after the war it was further 'improved' and given the name Zyklon B. Haber had therefore been involved in the birth of a gas that would be used in the next war in an attempt to exterminate his own people.

There were really only two things a man could do about lice: forget about them or put up with them. Forgetting about lice was only possible with the aid of either alcohol or fear. No one was troubled by lice in the bars of France and Belgium or during an attack. This suggests that for all the discomfort and disease lice were capable of causing, the damage they did was mainly psychological. Few things were worse for morale than the ubiquitous presence of bloodsucking lice, and they had the annoying habit of becoming active at the very moment a soldier started to fall asleep, just at the point when he finally began to feel slightly warmer.[104] *Le Pépère* of 21 April 1916 said: 'When the time comes for us to move to a new sector, if someone tells us, "the boches are twenty metres away", we feel a chill; but if we are told: "the dugouts are full of lice" – that we find really revolting!'[105] In the absence of drink and fear there was no alternative but to tolerate the unwelcome guests. They were a fact of life, and you just had to try to make the best of things. Arnold Zweig wrote: 'Lice, like superiors and Fate, are beings of a higher order; you may struggle against them, but you must, to a greater or lesser degree, come to terms with them.'[106]

Rats and lice were by far the most irritating vermin, and the most dangerous to physical health, but flies too were a constant threat to a soldier's well-being. The front was carpeted in flies of every shape and size, mainly because of the tons of dung that thousands of horses produced every day. Flies formed clouds around the latrines, so no one needed to ask where those were, and every sniper knew exactly where enemy soldiers would turn up at regular intervals, especially in view of the frequent epidemics of diarrhoea. (We should not form too sophisticated an

---

104 Brants & Brants, *Velden van weleer*, 58; Ellis, *Eye-Deep*, 54–6; Binneveld, *Om de geest*, 67; Fussell, *Bloody Game*, 32; Renn, *Krieg*, 178–9; March, *Company K*, 65–6; Eksteins, *Rites of Spring*, 147–9; Whalen, *Bitter Wounds*, 66; Jünger, *In Stahlgewittern*, 146–7; Winter, *Death's Men*, 96–7; Holmes, *Firing Line*, 112; Macdonald, *Passchendaele*, 75–6; Wilson, *Myriad Faces*, 357, 675; Eckart & Gradmann, *Die Medizin*, 238–9, 301; Liddle & Cecil, *Facing Armageddon*, 317; 'Jahrhundert der Kriege', 121; Andriessen, *De oorlogsbrieven van Unteroffizier Carl Heller*, 26, 55; Dorgelès, *Croix de bois*, 63–4; De Backer, *Longinus*, 25–6; Documentary: Förscher für den Krieg. Fritz Haber, ARTE-television, 24-07-2002

105 Audion-Rouzeau, *14–18. Les combattants*, 42

106 Whalen, *Bitter Wounds*, 66

impression of these latrines, incidentally. Blunden, for example, described one as a shell-hole, with two dead Germans lying in it.)[107]

Flies crawled into the ears, noses and eyes of sleeping men. Millions of flies attacked food and swarmed around the living and especially the dead. The many corpses that could not be recovered after battle were often covered by a thick, crawling, buzzing black layer that, once it began to take off, darkened the sky and spread a smell of death and decomposition across the surrounding area. The swarms made a sound capable of drowning out the noise of shelling. Rain and even gas were sometimes welcomed, since they were the only two scourges capable of driving off the flies, for a short time at least.[108]

### *Noise and stench*

To the squealing of rats and the deafening hum of flies were added the noise of bullets and shells, the bellowing of dying horses, and the screams and moans of wounded men, which were so harrowing that risky rescue operations were undertaken, sometimes more to quieten the wounded than to help them. You could begin to hate men who took too long to die. Their cries produced nothing but fear, despair and sleeplessness.[109] Leonhard Frank wrote: 'The moaning of the wounded ... just wouldn't stop, for three days and three nights it just wouldn't stop.'[110]

This constant racket, which rarely abated and never died away completely, sometimes accompanied by the surreal singing of birds, was one torment among many that the trench soldier had to put up with. It is described in *Johnny Got His Gun*.

> He never wanted to hear the biting little castanet sound of a machine gun or the whistle of a .75 coming down fast or the slow thunder as it hit or the whine of an airplane overhead or the yells of a guy trying to explain to somebody that he's got a bullet in his belly and that his breakfast is coming out through the front of him.[111]

During a bombardment the noise was loud enough to split the eardrums and it quite commonly caused permanent hearing loss, especially among gunners. The sound of one shell bursting nearby is deafening, let alone thousands. Many men said you did not so much hear the noise as feel it. A Canadian soldier even wrote that it had assumed a tangible form; for him the barrage had become a solid, immovable

---

107 Blunden, *Undertones of War*, 128

108 Ellis, *Eye-Deep*, 57–8; Winter, *Death's Men*, 98; Holmes, *Firing Line*, 115; Jünger, *In Stahlgewittern*, 74; Macdonald, *Somme*, 100, 205–6; Marix Evans, *Battles of the Somme*, 42

109 Ellis, *Eye-Deep*, 106; Fussell, *Bloody Game*, 43

110 Frank, *Der Mensch is Gut*, 80–81

111 Trumbo, *Johnny Got His Gun*, 10

ceiling of sound.[112] In *Up to Mametz*, Wyn Griffith described the impression made on soldiers in the forward trenches by the final bombardment before a battle.

> The sound was different from anything known to me. It was not a succession of explosions or a continuous roar. I never heard a gun or a bursting shell. It was not a noise; it was a symphony. It did not move; it hung over us. It seemed as though the air were full of a vast and agonized passion, bursting now with groans and sighs, shuddering beneath terrible blows. And the tumult did not pass in this direction or that. It did not begin, intensify, decline and end. It was poised in the air, a stationary panorama of sound, not the creation of men.[113]

This almost physical presence of sound had a devastating effect on a man's nerves. Sergeant Paul Dubrulle, a Jesuit, described the misery of a barrage at Verdun. He was caught between walls of noise, walls that advanced towards him and slowly knocked him senseless.

> When one heard the whistle in the distance, one's whole body contracted to resist the too excessively potent vibrations of the explosion, and at each repetition it was a new attack, a new fatigue, a new suffering. Under this regime, the most solid nerves cannot resist for long; the moment arrives where the blood rises to the head, where fever burns the body and where the nerves, exhausted, become incapable of reacting. It is as if one were tied tight to a post and threatened by a fellow swinging a sledgehammer. Now the hammer is swung back for the blow, now it whirls forward, till, just missing your skull, it sends the splinters flying from the post once more. This is exactly what it feels like to be exposed to heavy shelling. Perhaps the best comparison is that of seasickness; … finally one abandons oneself to it, one has no longer even the strength to cover oneself with one's pack against splinters, and one scarcely still has left the strength to pray to God.[114]

Although the noise was deafening and solid, it was possible to distinguish different sounds within it. The practised ear could tell precisely what kind of shell was coming.[115] Some, such as the whizz-bang, had nicknames that reflected the noise they made, but the ability to tell one sound from another only helped to make men crazy. Was that second noise an echo or another shell? Will this be a direct hit or not? Some sounds were a tougher test of a man's sanity than others. Gunner George Worsley of the 2nd West Lancashire Regiment, for example, found the

---

112 Ellis, *Eye-Deep*, 63–4; Binneveld, *Om de geest*, 50; Dearden, *Medicine and Duty*, 183–4

113 Winter, *Death's Men*, 175

114 Ellis, *Eye-Deep*, 64–5; Holmes, *Firing Line*, 232–3; Winter & Baggett, *1914–18*, 167–9

115 Barbusse, *Le Feu*, 226–7

sound of his own artillery worse than that of the Germans. The ceaseless racket from behind and above his head worked relentlessly on his nerves.[116]

A similarly stultifying effect was produced by the appalling, constant, unremitting stench. You never got used to it. The smell was intolerable, fouling clothes and food and bodies. You could smell the front before you could see it.[117] *I Remember the Last War* by American Robert C. Hoffman, published in 1940 as a warning against US participation in the Second World War, includes the lines: 'Did you ever smell a dead mouse? This will give you about as much idea of what a group of long dead soldiers smell like as will one grain of sand give you an idea of Atlantic City's beaches.'[118] Siegfried Sassoon wrote in *Aftermath*: 'Do you remember … the stench of corpses rotting in front of the front-line trench?'[119] And a French soldier noted at Verdun: 'We all had on us the stench of dead bodies. The bread we ate, the stagnant water we drank, everything we touched had a rotten smell, owing to the fact that the earth around us was literally stuffed with corpses.'[120]

It was not only corpses that stank. The stench of the battlefield was a mixture of decomposing bodies, the chloride of lime spread to combat infection, creosote used to deter flies, human and animal excrement, smoke from spirit stoves, and human sweat. Charles Carrington wrote of the sharp, acrid scent of burned and poisoned mud.[121] A British officer, swathed in bandages from head to toe, exclaimed when he was passed a handkerchief sprinkled with eau-de-cologne: 'By Jove, it's worth getting hit for this, after the smells of dead horses, dead men and dead everything.'[122]

The stench was ubiquitous, but it was more offensive in some places than others. At Verdun, the Somme and Ypres corpses lay closer together and remained unburied for longer than anywhere else. On one tour of inspection Barbusse and fellow soldiers were forced to wade through an open latrine.

> A disgusting odour rises out of the passage, leaving no doubt about its nature. Those who have gone in stop, protest and refuse to go forward. We pile up on one another, causing a blockage at the entrance to these latrines.
>
> 'I'd rather go out in the open!' yells one man. But there are flashes breaking through the clouds overhead and the landscape is so awesome to look at from the shadows of this teeming pit, with those sprays of resounding flames in the sky above it, that no one takes up the madman's appeal.

116 Macdonald, *Somme*, 208

117 Binneveld, *Om de geest*, 49; Fussell, *Bloody Game*, 32; Macdonald, *1915*, 310; Macdonald, *Passchendaele*, 24; Frey, *Pflasterkästen*, 45–6

118 Fussell, *Bloody Game*, 179

119 Fussell, *Bloody Game*, 199

120 Ellis, *Eye-Deep*, 59; see also: Guéno & Laplume, *Paroles de Poilus*, 51

121 Ellis, *Eye-Deep*, 59; Holmes, *Firing Line*, 177–8

122 Gilbert, *First World War*, 130

> Since we can't go back we must go through, whether we like it or not.
>
> 'Forward through the shit!' shouts the first man in line.
>
> We set off, choking with disgust. The stench becomes intolerable. We are walking through filth and can feel its slithering softness against the earthy mud.
>
> Bullets whistle overhead.
>
> 'Heads down!'
>
> Since the passage is not deep we are obliged to crouch very low if we are not to be killed and have to advance, bent over, through the mire of excrement and paper under our feet.[123]

Corporal Broizat of the French army had to move up to new positions with his men at night and he asked himself what it could be that stank so excessively, even by the standards of the front. When the sun rose he received his answer. The trench had been dug straight across a mass grave.[124]

*The trenches*

> You stand in a trench of vile stinking mud
> And the bitter cold wind freezes your blood
> Then the guns open up and flames light the sky
> And, as you watch, rats go scuttling by.
>
> The men in the dugouts are quiet for a time
> Trying to sleep midst the stench and the slime
> The moon is just showing from over the Hill
> And the dead on the wire hang silent and still
>
> A sniper's bullet wings close to your head
> As you wistfully think of a comfortable bed
> But now a dirty blanket has to suffice
> And more often than not it is crawling with lice.
>
> Sidney Chaplin

It will be clear from all this that life in and around the trenches was filthy, foul, sickening, deafening, dispiriting and extremely unhealthy. It was safer than in no man's land, but that was about all. Anyone who peered over the breastwork out of curiosity, even for a second, stood a fair chance of being shot by a sniper. A man might be buried, alive or dead, in the foxhole where he was hiding. In a trench there was a good chance of being ripped apart by a bursting shell, indeed death in the trenches was rarely quick or clean. Unless they were caught by a sniper's bullet, few of the men killed while still in their trenches were hit in the head or

123 Barbusse, *Le Feu*, 338; *Under Fire*, 286–7

124 Kielich, 'De grote schande', 28

heart by a single shot. Shrapnel and shell splinters made for a long, painful death. Repetitious tasks that offered a short-term distraction might help to ward off the effects of unrelieved tension. These might be voluntary activities like letter writing, or jobs imposed from above such as the cleaning of rifles or repairs to the sides of trenches. Most of these chores were unpleasant and eventually they became part of the daily grind, as men set about them again and again.[125] Safety precautions had to be observed, which meant keeping the trenches in good condition, and physical activity was regarded as extremely important for the health of the men. According to Graves, it was those who let the work get on top of them and sat back sighing about how awful it was to be forced to live like this, in a hole, who were most likely to suffer from frostbite and rheumatism.[126] To keep the trench up to scratch, to ensure the parapet was firm and high, men used literally everything they could lay their hands on. Corpses were there for the taking. Frank Richards wrote of the trenches on the Somme in late July 1916 that some parts of the breastwork were built out of dead bodies, 'and here and there arms and legs were protruding'.

> In one bay only the heads of two men could be seen; their teeth were showing so that they seemed to be grinning horribly down on us. Some of our chaps that had survived the attack on the 20th July told me that when they were digging themselves in, the ground being hardened by the sun and difficult to dig away quickly, if a man was killed near them he was used as head cover and earth was thrown over him. No doubt in many cases this saved the lives of the men that were digging themselves in.[127]

Whether or not it was clever to try to avoid work, those who complained had a point. Life in the trenches was dangerous, extremely harsh and monotonous. Even the constant danger, the unremitting discomfort and the ubiquitous presence of death and destruction eventually only added to the tedium. Artillery and snipers were a perpetual threat, and during an attack there were hand grenades, gas and bayonets to think about. Only attacks and counterattacks did anything to break the deadening routine. In the scheme of things, however, offensives were rare, and men felt little eagerness for them to begin.[128]

None of this alters the fact that trenches differed according to location and nationality. It made a good deal of difference whether the walls were of sand, clay or chalk, whether they had been dug in high or low-lying land, in flat or hilly country – and indeed whether they were inhabited by men called Hermann, Pierre, Tommy or Jan.

---

125 Simkins, *World War I*, 82; Winter & Baggett, *1914–18*, 101; Townshend, *Modern War*, 112; Hynes, *Soldiers' Tale*, 69

126 Graves, *Goodbye*, 85–6

127 Hynes, *Soldiers' Tale*, 69

128 Brants & Brants, *Velden van weleer*, 58; Prior & Wilson, *Passchendaele*, 9–10; Binneveld, *Om de geest*, 63, 65; Fussell, *Bloody Game*, 53; Horne, *Price of Glory*, 61

Although there were of course both good and bad among the results, as a general rule British optimism and conceit made for particularly miserable conditions. Why should time be spent making decent trenches if the men would be in them only for a few weeks?[129] Near Cambrin lay a typically British section of the front line. The trenches there, named after London streets, were so narrow that stretcher-bearers sometimes had to lift the wounded high over their heads, above the edge of the trench.[130] One British soldier said:

> The whole conduct of our trench warfare seemed to be based on the concept that we, the British, were not stopping in the trenches for long, but were tarrying a while on the way to Berlin and that very soon we would be chasing Jerry across country. The result, in the long term, meant that we lived a mean and impoverished sort of existence in lousy scratch holes.[131]

R.A. Scott Macife complained in late 1914 that the trenches were far too shallow and the walls too low, so that you had to lie on the filthy wet ground to get any protection.[132] Two years later there had been little improvement. Captain Alfred Bundy wrote of his trench on the Somme that it was not much more than 'a series of joined-up shell holes, mostly with 12 inches of water above 12 inches of mud'.[133]

French trenches were no better. This was again partly because the high command refused to resign itself to the fact that it was fighting a static trench war.[134] Barbusse described a trench as 'a maze of long ditches in which the last remnants of night linger. ... The bottom of it is carpeted with a viscous layer that clings noisily to the foot at every step and smells foul around each dugout because of the night's urine.'[135] At Verdun many of the French trenches were only about fifty centimetres deep even after the men had spent the whole night digging. By the time evening approached, enemy fire would have virtually destroyed them again. The *poilus* had to lie down all day to hold their positions, which made defecating in the normal manner impossible. The men did what they needed to do as best they could where they lay. Dysentery, spread mainly by flies, became common, the epidemic or bacterial variety in particular, especially when the weather was hot and water in short supply. Between July and September 1916 there was a major epidemic of dysentery, with 126 cases per 100,000 troops by September.[136]

---

129 Fussell, *Bloody Game*, 32; Holmes, *Riding the Retreat*, 241; Liddle & Cecil, *Facing Armageddon*, 318

130 Brants & Brants, *Velden van weleer*, 113;

131 Fussell, *Bloody Game*, 32

132 Fussell, *Bloody Game*, 42

133 Brown, *Somme*, 223

134 Liddle & Cecil, *Facing Armageddon*, 223

135 Barbusse, *Le Feu*, 6–7; *Under Fire*, 7

136 Horne, *Price of Glory*, 176; Dearden, *Medicine and Duty*, 80; Joules, *The Doctor's View*, 32–3

Barbusse estimated the length of the French trenches. They were a total of 6,250 miles long, or just under 10,000 kilometres. Fussell calculates that the British and Belgian trenches were almost as long as the French, and the German trenches must have extended roughly as far as all the Allied trenches put together. If this is correct – by no means all estimates agree – then the trenches dug between the North Sea coast and the Swiss Alps stretched a distance almost equivalent to the circumference of the earth.[137]

Compared to those of the Allies, the German trenches, built as if for eternity, were models of cleanliness, expertise and effectiveness.[138] This must have been the result partly of knowledge and skill, partly of a more defensive mentality, but it is worth remembering that the Germans had retreated and dug themselves in after the Battle of the Marne. They therefore had the choice of terrain, selecting land that was strategically and geographically most suitable for the digging of trenches.[139] Nevertheless, on the German side too, whether under sustained bombardment or not, life was almost unbearable, even for those with a roof over their heads. Paul Melber, an NCO with the Bavarian Ersatz Division, sat in a chalk tunnel near the Somme in November 1916 with his fellow machine-gunners. 'It's full of men – sleeping comrades lying everywhere. The air is horribly foul since most of the ventilation shafts are plugged.'[140] Rüdiger Krüger 'washed' every morning by spitting into his handkerchief and wiping it over his face a few times. 'All quite practical and done in a couple of moves. And yet, how I long for an orderly existence, where you can take the rags off your body and get a night's sleep more often than once in eight days.'[141]

Out of the trench, in the line of fire, it made no difference whether you were German, British or French. Melber again: 'The crater is … full of slime and water at the bottom. … A few feet away a hole has been dug into the side of the crater and is covered with a groundsheet. Here is where one sleeps. If Tommy does not bother us, this will be our home for four days.'[142]

The number of days in a row that a man spent in a trench had a profound effect on his state of mind. Rules from on high about how much time a soldier was allowed to spend in the forward trenches without a break soon turned out to be largely theoretical. The rules were applied whenever possible, but actual practice was often very different. Owen remembered being in the line for twelve days in a row. 'For twelve days I did not wash my face, nor take off my boots, nor sleep a

137 Fussell, *The Great War*, 37; Byerly, for instance, talks of 5,000 miles, and she is probably referring only to the Allied side. Byerly, *Fever of War*, 95

138 Ferguson, *The Pity of War*, 350; Winter & Baggett, *1914–18*, 91

139 Fussell, *The Great War*, 45; Keegan, *First World War*, 194

140 Macdonald, *1914–1918*, 173

141 Witkop, *Kriegsbriefe*, 292

142 Macdonald, *1914–1918*, 174

deep sleep. For twelve days we lay in holes, where at any moment a shell might put us out.'[143]

That was not a record by any means. Men might not get out of the trenches for weeks (except to move towards the enemy), whereas British rules said they should be there for no more than four days per month and a maximum of one week at a time. In late 1914 an army doctor advised that no battalion should spend more than 48 hours on the front line. A Scottish battalion was at that very moment enduring a tour of duty that lasted 38 days. In 1914 a battalion of the West Yorkshires spent 70 out of 90 consecutive days in the trenches. Alfred Vaeth wrote from Miraumont that he had finally been relieved after 7 weeks. 'Finally a chance to wash again! Finally a rest!' In February 1916 a battalion of the 5th Royal Warwickshire Regiment left a forward trench after 28 days, and during the Battle of the Somme 2 to 3 weeks at the front was quite common. Blunden even wrote that they had just broken the world record, after which, before they were finally allowed a break, they had been ordered to take a German position. A battalion of the 13th Yorkshire and Lancashire Regiment was relieved after 7 weeks and 2 days. It would not be hard to add to this list, although these remained exceptions to the rule.[144]

The prescribed time was quite exhausting enough. On 23 December 1914, Percy Jones of the Queen's Westminster Rifles watched a regiment of Royal Fusiliers leave their trench. The soldiers were 'tattered, worn, straggling, footsore, weary and looking generally broken to pieces. Hairy, unshaved, dirty-faced, and dressed in every possible variety of head-dress, the men looked like so many prehistoric savages rather than a crack regiment of the British Army.'[145] In July 1916 choirmaster Peter McGregor wrote to his wife: 'I am all right – just the same as ever – but no – that can never be. The four days we were in the trenches has turned me upside down. No man can experience such things and come out the same.'[146]

Lack of sleep was a soldier's worst enemy, and not only during an advance or retreat. The work at all hours and the noise of every conceivable kind meant he often slept hardly at all during his time in the trenches. Everyone was tired all the time, sometimes deathly tired, never at any stage properly rested. In his diary, Frenchman Charles Delvert described a night in a trench in January 1916:

> Lights out. Now the rats and the lice are the masters of the house. You can hear the rats nibbling, running, jumping, rushing from plank to plank, emitting their little squeals behind the dugout's corrugated metal. It's a noisy swarming activity that just won't stop. At any moment I expect one to land on my nose. And then

---

143 Day Lewis, *Collected Poems*, 164

144 Ellis, *Eye-Deep*, 28; Winter, *Death's Men*, 81; Witkop, *Kriegsbriefe*, 124; Winter & Baggett, *1914–18*, 101; Blunden, *Undertones of War*, 112, 119–20; *Van den Grooten oorlog*, 180

145 Eksteins, *Rites of Spring*, 103

146 Eksteins, *Rites of Spring*, 212

> it's the lice and fleas that begin to devour me. Absolutely impossible to get any shut-eye. Toward midnight I begin to doze off. A terrible racket makes me jump. Artillery fire, the crackling of rifle and machine-gun fire. The Boches must be attacking Mont Têtu again. The charivari seems to quiet down about 1:30. At 2:15 it starts up again, this time with a frightful violence. Everything shakes. Our artillery thunders away without pause. At 3:00 the cannon shots become more spread out and slowly things quiet down. I doze off so as to get up at six. The rats and the lice get up too: waking to life is also waking to misery.[147]

This was a night on which Delvert was at least allowed to try to get some sleep. Often it was between sunset and sunrise that the trenches came to life. All kinds of minor tasks that sniping made too dangerous to perform in daylight had to be done under cover of darkness.[148]

After several days at the front – certainly after several weeks – soldiers of all ranks were capable of falling asleep under more or less any circumstances, even during a battle, and at any time of day or night. They slept, or half-slept, sitting, standing, walking, on horseback, with their heads resting on the butts of their rifles or on their knees, even with their feet in water. Sleep rarely lasted more than an hour. Life in the front line often meant days or weeks of nodding off and jolting awake, nodding off and jolting awake. Jünger wrote:

> Between ten at night and six in the morning, only two men out of each platoon were allowed to sleep at a time, which meant that we got two hours a night each, though they were eaten into by being woken early, having to fetch straw, and other occupations, so that there were only a few minutes left as a rule.[149]

Waking a man might be difficult. One time when Graves was due to relieve another soldier on sentry duty the relief screamed in his ears, threw water over him, thumped his head against the edge of his bed and flung him to the ground. Nothing helped. Graves was asleep and he went on sleeping, understandably so. Horne writes that soldiers at Verdun sometimes went ten or eleven days without sleep. During the Battle of Loos Graves managed only around eight hours' sleep in ten days. He kept himself awake and alive by drinking a bottle of whisky a day.[150] Lack of sleep could be fatal. An officer of the Cameron Highlanders dropped off in a muddy shell-hole and drowned.[151]

In some places the mud made it impossible to lie or even sit down. On one occasion two soldiers reportedly thought of a solution. When they could no longer

147 Eksteins, *Rites of Spring*, 150
148 Winter & Baggett, *1914–18*, 101
149 Jünger, *In Stahlgewittern*, 5; *Storm of Steel*, 10
150 Graves, *Goodbye*, 135–7; Horne, *Price of Glory*, 176
151 Macdonald, *Passchendaele*, 124

fend off sleep, they stood back to back to prop each other up, while a third kept watch in case they started to topple.[152]

Some men with shell shock were executed, and others were no doubt shot for falling asleep on duty. A certain Private Saunders was saved from court martial only by the resolute intervention of his corporal. Not all will have been so lucky.

The effect of lack of sleep on the physical and mental condition of officers and men was disastrous. According to Captain F.C. Hitchcock, author of *Stand To*, it was the main cause of physical and mental exhaustion. Soldiers became suspicious, restless, unpredictable.[153]

The extraordinary fatigue produced by trench life meant that men were extremely irritated to find times officially designated as rest periods made anything but restful. Noyes goes so far as to claim that 'rest' was the most misleading word in the army lexicon. Behind the lines, all sorts of tasks had to be performed to help keep the trenches intact and quite apart from allowing the men no chance to recuperate, the work was dangerous. If the front was hell, said Barthas, then rest was purgatory.[154] Sassoon described a day during a rest period.

> Got up at 9:30 after a miserable hour's sleep – cold as hell – and started off at 10:45 with a fatigue-party to carry up trench-mortar bombs from dump between St. Martin Cojeul and Croisilles. Got back very wet and tired about 4:30. Rained all day – trenches like glue.[155]

Laying barbed-wire entanglements was a particularly unpopular task. Hands and legs could get badly scratched and men became caught on their own wire. During the Battle of the Somme W.J. Coggins and his platoon were sent to help out at a hospital for a week's rest. 'A week's rest! My God! We were carrying the wounded. We were in it day and night! … And this was a week's rest! *What a bloomin' rest!*'[156] Sixty years after the armistice Denis Winter wrote: 'Still today men remember the unfairness of using rest for hard labour, back-breaking labour … which men thought they had been rested from for the time.'[157]

In short, men lived in the midst of death, they walked over corpses, whether buried or not, and everyone knew that he might be killed at any moment. They lived with filth, vermin and indescribable noise, and sleep was as precious as drinking water and food. If they did sleep, or try to sleep, it was often under damp

152 Macdonald, *Roses of No Man's Land*, 185

153 Winter, *Death's Men*, 100–101, 178; Holmes, *Riding the Retreat*, 135; Holmes, *Firing Line*, 115, 123–4; Wilson, *Myriad Faces*, 357

154 Noyes, *Stretcher-Bearers*, 65, 183–4; Barthas, *Carnets*, 133, 151; De Backer, 'Longinus', 25

155 Fussell, *Bloody Game*, 65

156 Macdonald, *1914–1918*, 178

157 Winter, *Death's Men*, 158–9

blankets on soaking wet mattresses. This naturally led to all kinds of physical and mental ailments.[158]

## Disease

### *Introduction*

The First World War was one of the first in which more men were killed by gunfire, whether the enemy's or their own, than by disease. This is usually attributed to improvements in medical services and standards of hygiene, but it was no less the result of the huge death toll achieved by artillery and machine-guns and the high rate of infection that made many wounds fatal. It does not alter the fact that disease was rife. Dirt, urine, faeces and unhygienic surroundings all played their part, and practically every form of illness that accompanies poor living conditions was widespread. Disease was not just a serious problem on a human level, it was a substantial military threat. Even though the mortality rate among soldiers who contracted diseases was far lower (at around one per cent) than that of the wounded (some thirty per cent), sickness was and remained the main cause of loss of manpower. It should be noted here that the word 'disease' had a different meaning in the trenches than in normal life. A large proportion of men who took part in offensives may have had heavy colds or 'flu but they were not regarded as sick. This made it possible to claim that given the circumstances the health of the troops was surprisingly good.[159] If the definition of the word 'ill' had been the same in 1914–18 as it is today, there would have been practically no healthy soldiers left to fight battles. Almost everyone was poorly, although in most cases not seriously enough to report themselves sick, let alone to be recognized as too ill to fight.[160] Nevertheless, the statistics are appalling.

In 1917 one French base hospital compiled a list that shows exactly how many soldiers were brought in and what was wrong with them. Of over 100,000 patients, a quarter had scabies and other skin infections. Another quarter had diseases such as myalgia, rheumatism, or trench fever (an initially mysterious condition that we shall return to shortly). In other words, around half the hospital's patients had become casualties of the wretched conditions in and around the trenches. Among the British the proportion was even higher, with up to 60 per cent falling sick. Of the six million occasions on which British doctors treated soldiers in 1914–18, 3.5 million were for illness rather than injury.[161]

158 Ellis, *Eye-Deep*, 52; Prior & Wilson, *Passchendaele*, 160

159 Liddle & Cecil, *Facing Armageddon*, 454; Eckart & Gradmann, *Medizin*, 210

160 Binneveld, *Om de geest*, 15; Winter, *Death's Men*, 99; Barthas, *Carnets*, 522

161 Ellis, *Eye-Deep*, 58

Life was no better in the German army. German doctors treated over seven million cases of disease, again more than fifty per cent of total troop numbers.[162] Around 166,000 German soldiers died of illness, with lung disease caused by cold, rain and gas the most lethal, resulting in 47,000 deaths. Influenza (14,000 fatalities) and typhus (11,000 fatalities) were feared too. Spanish 'flu struck all the armies like a sledgehammer, but the highest percentages were found among the Americans, even though they were active for only a short time. Around 23 per cent of US troops caught the virus. On 10 October 1918 it was announced that 20,000 American soldiers had died of 'flu or pneumonia in the space of two months. The distinction between the two was vague and many deaths from pneumonia may have been the result of influenza.[163] Bronchitis, measles, tuberculosis, pneumonia and venereal disease were everyday problems in the American Expeditionary Force, but it was Spanish 'flu that pushed its death toll from disease up to seventeen per cent, far higher than the overall wartime average. More Americans were buried in France because of the 'flu epidemic than as a result of enemy fire.[164]

*Sickness in the trenches*

The most common diseases during the war as a whole were various kinds of stomach complaints and skin infections. Of course it is hardly surprising that skin disease became epidemic, given the horribly unhygienic conditions at the front. As often as not the men were unable to wash more than once a fortnight and access to clean underwear was felt to be something close to a miracle.[165] Nevertheless, there is hardly any mention of skin disease in the literature of the war years. In describing his son's experiences, E.E. Cummings' father refers to skin problems, but my researches have not turned up any other examples. Cummings Jr in fact caught his disease in a French military jail after the war was over, while serving time there on false allegations of spying.[166] Skin disease was probably seen as too trivial and banal, compared to all the other things that could happen to a soldier during the war, to be worth writing about.[167]

Similarly, vomiting and diarrhoea were probably regarded as too commonplace to mention, but for some soldiers these everyday afflictions symbolized the horrors of war. Diarrhoea, for example, was not a question of physical discomfort alone but of embarrassment as well. Scott Macife was among the few who wrote about it. On Christmas Eve 1914 he sent a letter to his father saying that none of the men

162 Whalen, *Bitter Wounds*, 53

163 Gilbert, *First World War*, 477; Vugs, *In veel huizen wordt gerouwd*, 23–4

164 Garrison, *History of Military Medicine*, 204; Marix Evans, *Battles of the Somme*, 74

165 Audoin-Rouzeau, *Men at War*, 43

166 Cummings, *Enormous Room*, xvii

167 La Motte, *Backwash of War*, 133

felt well. His whole battalion had been suffering for weeks from an epidemic of diarrhoea.[168]

Enteritis (inflammation of the bowel) was certainly felt worthy of mention and it too was the order of the day. During Third Ypres the regimental historian of the German 74th Infantry Regiment noted that within a period of 11 days, 5 officers and 165 men had been sent to hospital suffering from enteritis. Only 40 men had been admitted during the same period for other sicknesses or wounds.[169]

Soldiers probably regarded themselves as lucky that bubonic plague did not break out, given the immense rat population, but rats were directly responsible for at least one serious illness. Weil's disease, an infectious form of jaundice, became widespread in the last two years of the war. Early cases emerged in the course of 1915 around the Aisne and the Meuse, where the plague of rats had assumed extraordinary proportions. Weil's disease never became truly epidemic, but many men caught it, and although only a tiny percentage died, they were put out of action for long periods.[170]

Lice too caused more than simple itching and discomfort. Doctors were aware that they spread typhoid fever, but they also carried a paratyphoid-like illness that wreaked havoc on a vast scale and became known as trench fever or 'pyrexia of unknown origin'. British doctors distinguished between trench fever and pyrexia (which in the early months of the war was sometimes diagnosed as myalgia or rheumatism), but these were almost certainly one and the same disease. German doctors spread their bets even further by calling it either *Wolhynisches Fieber*, five-day fever, intermittent fever or Meuse fever (while on the Eastern Front German troops often referred to it as Polish or Russian fever). The disease was first described in 1915, but the connection with lice was established only in 1918 and no effective medication was found until after the war. It usually began with acute shooting pains in the shins, followed by a high fever, and although it was not fatal, recovery took six to twelve weeks. On the Allied side alone there were over 200,000 cases of trench fever. In 1917 the disease was responsible for half of all bouts of illness in the British army. It was at this time that American medical officer Bernard Gallagher declared that in his view soldiers with trench fever were having everyone on. When he developed the disease himself a few months later he changed his mind.[171]

Although measles, diphtheria and mumps were hardly any more prevalent than in peacetime, the number of patients with other infectious diseases increased enormously. As the war went on and exposure to poor conditions with it, the

168 Fussell, *Bloody Game*, 41; Liddle, *Passchendaele in Perspective*, 330

169 Liddle, *Passchendaele in Perspective*, 330

170 Ellis, *Eye-Deep*, 55; Eckart & Gradmann, *Die Medizin*, 308–9; Joules, *The Doctor's View*, 35

171 Ellis, *Eye-Deep*, 57; Macdonald, *1914–1918*, 248; Brants & Brants, *Velden van weleer*, 70; Gabriel & Metz, *A History of Military Medicine*, 243; Joules, *The Doctor's View*, 37–8

situation became steadily worse, but the decline set in immediately. Whereas in 1914 only 13 out of every thousand soldiers were troubled by poor teeth, this had risen to 41 by 1915. Hospitals frequently diagnosed a serious form of gingivitis that became known as trench mouth. It was an inflammation of the gums caused by a lack of hygiene and a poor, monotonous diet. In 1914 and 1915 respectively, 24 and 52 out of every 1,000 soldiers had breathing difficulties. In 1914 57 men in every 1,000 had digestive disorders and by 1915 the proportion had doubled. In the first year of the war influenza was practically unknown, whereas in 1915 it laid low 75 in every 1,000 troops. A hospital list from 1917 records 8 cases of anthrax and 6,025 cases of dysentery; 1,275 men were suffering from enteritis, 692 from meningitis and 1,660 from tuberculosis, a disease that was becoming less prominent by 1914 but which flared up again in the early years of the war, especially among young adults.[172] Bowel problems and digestive disorders were common, as always in wartime, although it is not clear exactly what gave rise to individual cases: bad food and drinking water, or fear.[173]

The French army, notorious for its leadership's lack of interest in trivial matters like hygiene and inoculation, was plagued by typhus. In the final months of the war there were 50,000 cases, some 10,000 of them fatal. Between 1914 and 1918 almost 130,000 *poilus* caught typhus. The mortality rate was 9.5 per cent. When American troops arrived at French training camps, they discovered to their horror that virtually all the water supplies were contaminated with typhus. In the German army too the disease wreaked havoc. According to official records, 116,481 men were affected and the mortality rate was half a per cent higher than among the French. The epidemic reached its zenith after the front stabilized, the static nature of the war making it easier for the disease to spread. Vaccination programmes were hastily arranged and they were the main reason, although probably not the only one, that within a year the typhus epidemic had been beaten. In cases where the illness affected soldiers who had been vaccinated, it generally took a milder form. In Germany and perhaps elsewhere (such opinions were censored), some doctors doubted the safety and efficacy of the vaccine, but their alternative explanation for the decline in the number and severity of cases – the implementation of hygiene measures – seems hypothetical at best, given conditions at the front. The absence of a decline in other diseases for which there was no vaccine, such as paratyphoid fever and dysentery, casts further doubt on alternative theories, in fact these two diseases became increasingly prevalent as the war went on. Some German soldiers claimed that the type of typhoid vaccine used was worse than the disease itself for several days afterwards. They felt as if plague was being fought with cholera. But although the side-effects could be unpleasant, raising the body temperature to as high as 40 degrees, it is important to note that most men had far milder reactions,

172 Winter, *Death's Men*, 98–9; Brants & Brants, *Velden van weleer*, 70; Sassoon, *Complete Memoirs*, 326; Langford, 'Age Pattern', 7; Thomas, *Die Katrin wird Soldat*, 291–4; Mierisch, *Kamerad Schwester*, 110–15

173 Whalen, *Bitter Wounds*, 53

and in any case they soon recovered. In the British army everyone was inoculated quite soon after the conflict became bogged down, and the Americans were given their injections immediately on arrival. These two armies had little trouble with typhus. Only 208 British soldiers died of stomach typhus and among American troops the figure was 227. Here too there was a sharp contrast with the French and Germans, who suffered, respectively, 112,500 cases with around 11,500 deaths and 125,000 cases with around 15,000 deaths. Although vast numbers of British soldiers were vaccinated, inoculation was not compulsory by law in the British army, nor would it ever become so. In practice, however, a man had to be extremely determined and resourceful to resist military and medical pressure. The general feeling among doctors was that soldiers, certainly in times of war and in such unhygienic conditions, should not be allowed to evade inoculation.[174]

It is perfectly understandable that at the beginning of the war there was hardly any mention of vaccination, that even during the war it was slow to get off the ground in many armies, and that it was never forced upon British soldiers, however powerful the arguments of doctors and commanding officers. This can all be traced back to a Europe-wide debate that had started just prior to 1914 between advocates and opponents of compulsory vaccination. The question boiled down to whether the interests of the nation should outweigh individual self-determination and bodily integrity. The war had an impact on this debate in the sense that those who favoured compulsion – among them most doctors, partly because they believed medical authority should override the will of the current or future patient – were handed an additional argument: the fighting strength of the army. The prevention of disease through compulsory vaccination was beneficial for the armed forces and should therefore be supported by any good citizen. Opponents of compulsion could be painted as unpatriotic.[175]

Rheumatism was another permanent and unwelcome guest in the trenches. Jünger had never suffered from rheumatism before, but after only a few rainy days he felt pain in his joints.[176] It was one of many sicknesses that were a direct result of the combination of cold and damp. During the winter of 1915–16 a regimental diary noted: 'It is surprising that the whole battalion has not got pneumonia.' Bronchitis and influenza were rampant. The British First Army reported in the second half of January 1915 that the number of sufferers that week added up to seventy officers and 2,886 other ranks. Of them, forty-five officers and 2,320 men were listed as sick. If we leave out the war itself, at the same time a corps commander correctly pointed out that the weather was the most significant factor in the loss of effective

174 Linton, 'Was Typhoid Inoculation Safe and Effective?', passim, esp.: 102, 110, 114–15, 117, 123–4, 129–30, 133; Verdoorn, *Arts en Oorlog*, 363; Gabriel & Metz, *A History of Military Medicine*, 245; Renn, *Krieg*, 166–7; De Vos, *Van Gifgas tot Penicilline*, 20; De Vos, *De Eerste Wereldoorlog*, 83, 107; Eckart & Gradmann, *Die Medizin*, 301; Whitehead, *Doctors*, 222; Hardy, 'Straight Back to Barbarism', 287

175 Hardy, 'Straight Back to Barbarism', passim

176 Jünger, *In Stahlgewittern*, 6–7

troop numbers.[177] This continued to be the case. In the winter of 1916–17 Mary Pollard of the Queen Alexandra's Imperial Military Nursing Service wrote:

> All that winter we took in bronchitis and rheumatism cases. Some of the bronchitis patients were as bad as the men who were gassed, but the rheumatism cases really were the worst. It was pathetic to see these young men absolutely crippled with rheumatism, sometimes doubled up as if they were men of eighty instead of boys in their twenties.[178]

Third Ypres produced similar scenes. The ratio between the sick, the dead and the wounded remained roughly the same, but only because so many more men were killed or gravely wounded between August and November 1917 than in the winter of 1916–17.[179]

Temperatures continually switching between icy cold and thaw, combined with damp and ill-fitting footwear, produced one of the greatest plagues to hit the trenches: trench foot or immersion foot, which the French called *pieds gêlés* and the Germans *Nasserfrierung der Füße* or *Fußbrand*. The latter term was also used for gangrene of the feet, which illustrates how serious the affliction was. Puttees would shrink in water and mud, constricting the flow of blood, and the same effect resulted from standing in icy water for hours on end without being able to move. Plunging boots into water just once and then keeping them on for the next twenty-four hours was enough to produce the condition, which often made walking impossible. Feet first went numb, then started to burn, turned red and blue and swelled up, making the wearing of boots more intolerable than ever. Extreme cases would develop into gas gangrene, a complication we shall look at in the chapter 'Aid'. At that stage amputation of at least one toe and quite often the whole foot was unavoidable. Men who had not been wounded lost limbs. 'Can anyone possibly imagine what this means?' wrote Henriette Riemann in her *Schwester der Vierten Armee* (Nurse in the Fourth Army), a remarkable book that includes the suicide of a wounded soldier and even an abortion performed on one of the nurses.

Among the British alone, some 75,000 soldiers were taken to hospital with trench foot or frostbite. In the feet there was little difference between the two conditions, as the French name *pieds gêlés* and the German *Nasserfrierung* suggest. Indeed in the first winter of the war they were often confused. Frostbite was one of the few afflictions that increased hardly at all as the war went on, partly because it was so common from the start. In 1914, 34 out of every 1,000 soldiers got frostbite; in 1915 the proportion increased by only 4. In the French hospital list from 1917 mentioned earlier, 21,487 cases were recorded, mainly in feet. On the Allied side alone, a total of 115,000 soldiers suffered frostbite, making it and

177 Eksteins, *Rites of Spring*, 103; Macdonald, *Roses of No Man's Land*, 67
178 Macdonald, *Roses of No Man's Land*, 186
179 Wilson, *Myriad Faces*, 482; La Motte, *Backwash of War*, 134

trench foot among the most common of all disorders. It was rarely fatal. In the British army trench foot caused a total of around 40 deaths.[180]

The number of patients with trench foot rose dramatically in the winter of 1914–15. The British army made it compulsory to rub the feet every day with a salve consisting largely of whale oil, and from mid-1917 onwards this was accompanied by the application of talcum powder and camphor. Every soldier had – in theory – three dry pairs of socks with him, and he was ordered to change his socks at least once a day. But although this prevented a repeat of the problem on the same scale, in its most severe form at least, a considerable number of cases occurred the following winter. The army high command was furious. From 1916 onwards soldiers were simply forbidden to develop trench foot. The duty officer was obliged to ensure men took the prescribed precautions, and if there were too many cases of trench foot in a battalion, the officer in charge would be dismissed. Anyone who contracted trench foot, at least if he were an ordinary soldier or junior officer, would be court-martialled.

This was not as unreasonable as it sounds. Like trench fever and trench mouth, trench foot was one way out of a terrible mess, court martial or no court martial. A very painful way, certainly.[181] Kathleen Yardwood of the Voluntary Aid Detachment described the sufferings of patients.

> Some of the trench-feet and frostbite cases were so bad that they had to be sent home. We had a tremendous number of frostbite cases at the beginning of 1917. In fact we had a whole ward of them. … Their feet were absolutely white, swollen up and dead. Some of the toes dropped off with it. … It was very painful for them when the feeling started to come back, and some had to have crutches. They couldn't walk at all, because they simply couldn't feel their feet.[182]

Although mainly intended to combat self-inflicted injury, the new rules were not merely the product of harsh discipline. Graves reported that in one battalion on the Somme in the winter of 1916–17, half the men were put out of action by trench foot. There were several different reasons for this. First of all, both men and officers had fallen prey to apathy, so neither the prescribed preventive measures

---

180 Riemann, *Schwester der Vierten Armee*, 191, 206, 237; Ellis, *Eye-Deep*, 48; Brants & Brants, *Velden van weleer*, 70; Winter, *Death's Men*, 99; Simkins, *World War I*, 42; Gilbert, *First World War*, 219; Macdonald, *Roses of No Man's Land*, 66, 184–5; Gabriel & Metz, *A History of Military Medicine*, 243; Wilson, *Myriad Faces*, 66; Heijster, *Ieper*, 90–91; Dunn, *The War*, 431; *Van den Grooten Oorlog*, 191

181 Brants & Brants, *Velden van weleer*, 70; Ellis, *Eye-Deep*, 48–51; Winter, *Death's Men*, 96; Macdonald, *1914–1918*, 252; Macdonald, *Roses of No Man's Land*, 184–5; Macdonald, *Somme*, 315; Graves, *Goodbye*, 144–5; Gilbert, *First World War*, 219; Brown, *Somme*, 229; Liddle, *Passchendaele in Perspective*, 179; Liddle & Cecil, *Facing Armageddon*, 454; Dunn, *The War*, 99–100, 285

182 Macdonald, *Roses of No Man's Land*, 186

nor compulsory inspections were always carried out properly. There is likely to have been a direct connection between the level of morale in a battalion and the number of cases of trench foot it reported. Making trench foot punishable was one way of ensuring that the necessary precautions were taken.

Unfortunately it was often impossible to perform all the various prescribed measures with sufficient thoroughness – and anyhow there was no guarantee they would be effective. There was often not enough time, or oil, or clean and dry socks. It was far from easy to convince a soldier in a cold and wet trench that he should take off his boots and socks and rub his bare feet with oil, not to mention the physical impossibility of doing so in mud several inches deep. The men seldom if ever had a chance to rest their feet for hours with their boots off. So although they were not permitted to develop trench foot, they got it nonetheless. There was nothing they could do to prevent it. Blunden for one was absolutely outraged by the new sanction.

Another cause of debilitating sickness was pneumonia. Enid Bagnold of the Voluntary Aid Detachment, working in the Royal Herbert Hospital in Woolwich, published her *A Diary Without Dates* against the wishes of the military authorities. She reports on the case of a boy of seventeen. 'Five days ago he was walking on his legs; five days, and he is on the edge of the world – to-night looking over the edge.' Nevertheless, given the circumstances it is astonishing how rarely men contracted pneumonia. In the British army fewer than 8,000 cases were reported, or a little over 0.1 per cent (with peaks among colonial troops of 0.27 per cent). As many as 12 per cent of those who caught it died, however. These numbers should be treated with caution, since the AEF, relatively small and only in France for a short time, recorded no fewer than 20,445 cases, a third of them fatal. The apparent absence of pneumonia from the British army is all the more remarkable, not to say implausible, when we consider that another affliction generally attributable, like trench foot and frostbite, to cold and damp did take a substantial toll. In the French hospital list of 1917, 15,214 men are recorded as suffering from nephritis, an inflammation of the kidneys that was often preceded by a throat infection. This painful condition affected 35,563 British soldiers during the war and around one per cent of cases were fatal. The connection between nephritis and trench life was so obvious that the British called it 'trench nephritis' while the Germans spoke of *Kriegsnephritis* or *Schützengrabennephritis*.[183]

### *Heart problems, venereal disease and Spanish 'flu*

So far we have looked at diseases that were directly attributable to conditions in and around the trenches. There are a further three disorders that put men out of action, one of which caused a huge number of deaths. The origins of the first of the

183 Bagnold, *Diary Without Dates*, 78; Winter, *Death's Men*, 52, 99; Gabriel & Metz, *A History of Military Medicine*, 251; Blunden, *Undertones of War*, 234; Joules, *The Doctor's View*, 45

three were diverse, no doubt sometimes related to the war and sometimes not; the second is inherent to any war, indeed to life in general; and the third did not arise because of the war but had an enormous impact at a human level. They were: heart problems, venereal disease and Spanish 'flu.

Cardiac trouble was a common ailment. Perhaps it would be more accurate to say that it lay at the root of many common ailments. Some commentators even claim it was the largest single cause of debilitating illness. Its origins were often unclear – which is reason enough to explain it to some degree in psychological terms – and this made the results of treatment extremely unpredictable. Doctors working at the front came up with two rather vague diagnoses: 'disordered action of the heart', also known as 'soldier's heart', a psychological disorder that we shall look at more closely later, and 'heart-valve disorders'. Every heart ailment regarded as genuine was assigned to one or other of these categories.

In two cardiac hospitals in Britain, with 950 beds between them, heart specialists carried out research into this specific problem from 1915 onwards. Precise descriptions were produced, but explanations were harder to find. Patients' pre-war medical histories were as varied as their symptoms. They often had no previous history of heart problems, so more rigorous medical examinations for new recruits were unlikely to be of much help. From a military point of view the illness might just as well have been fatal. Aside from the irregular heart rhythm as such, the symptoms – exhaustion, shortness of breath, dizziness – made a man completely unsuitable for front-line duty, and they almost always recurred if a soldier, apparently cured, was sent back up the line.

Of course various possible explanations were found. A British medical officer by the name of Mackenzie pointed out that in 1,600 of the 2,000 cases he had examined, infection was the cause of the heart problems, and that practically all those affected had been through periods of too little rest. Thomas Lewis considered the possibility of an 'effort syndrome', in which the slightest activity was sufficient to produce symptoms. It was not the physically weak alone who seemed vulnerable to the syndrome; even men who had previously enjoyed perfect physical health could contract it after extreme exhaustion at the front. Lewis too identified infection as the direct cause and most likely origin, but he suggested some part might be played by poison gas, or by a latent weakness of the heart that was made manifest by conditions at the front. This spectrum of possible contributory factors had one and the same outcome: an inability to perform physical work. Therapies had little effect. Only one in seven patients had recovered completely by 1925, although half were by then able to work to some extent in physically undemanding occupations.

The Americans were suspicious. The symptoms came and went according to the degree of violence men were subjected to, and in their view almost all cases were attributable to anxiety neurosis. They compared the condition to a well-known disorder that had emerged during the American Civil War known as Da Costa's syndrome, diagnosed by and later named after one Dr Jacob Mendez Da Costa, who referred to it as 'irritable heart'.

We will probably never know who was right, but it is clear that the horrors of war could manifest themselves in either mental or physical symptoms. Heart problems were a recognizable and respectable expression of ill health. From a military point of view it was obvious that sufferers were not suitable for front-line duty, and the diagnosis of a cardiac complaint relieved both the patient's doctor and the army of an unsuitable man in a way that preserved the honour of all concerned.[184]

Although some doctors claimed that war had a positive effect on soldiers who had previously wrestled with sexual neuroses or impotence, it would generally be more accurate to say that wartime experiences stripped men of their sexual desires along with any possibility of satisfying them.[185] As far as actual sex went, the impediments were often physical as well as psychological, although of course amputation of the genitals would see a man sent home. Sheer physical fatigue meant that many soldiers wanted nothing other than to lie on their bunks. They did not even feel like masturbating.[186] Nevertheless, twice as many suffered from venereal disease as from any other complaint. Given that the chances of infection in a single sexual act have been estimated at no more than about three per cent, it is clear that many soldiers in the vicinity of the trenches and on short-term leave must have shared their beds with prostitutes or local women. Leave in Paris was particularly feared by army doctors. This does not alter the fact that, generally speaking, precious little sex is mentioned in war memoirs. The same applies to personal experiences of killing. Individual contributions to the beginning or ending of a life are perhaps part of one and the same taboo. Many men saw others go off to visit prostitutes, and many saw others in the act of killing, but few admitted to taking part in such activities themselves.

Why did sex have such a powerful attraction for those who felt up to it, aside from the obvious reason that it is a pleasurable activity? First of all, the complete absence of women at the front gave an added charge to encounters between the sexes. The subjects of thoughts and dreams that had gone on for weeks suddenly came to life. Some soldiers, consciously or not, may have hoped to extend their own lives in some sense in the form of a son or daughter, since they were to be granted only a short time on earth. Apparently it did not much matter who the mother was. Then there were men who did not want to depart their earthly existence as virgins. The stress of combat and the constant fear of death meant that many soldiers no longer felt bound by the sexual norms and values prevailing in peacetime and in civilian surroundings. Above all, though, sex must have been a means of escape, a fleeting break from a dismal and cutthroat reality.

---

184 Dunning, 'Het soldatenhart', 49–54; Hyams, 'War Syndromes', 398–9; Shepard, *War of Nerves*, 65

185 Hirschfeld, *Sittengeschichte*, 168–70; Leed, *No Man's Land*, 183–4; Higonnet, *Behind the Lines*, 62; Lerner, *Hysterical Men* (2003), 47

186 Bourke, *Dismembering the Male*, 160

How did they get their hands on women? Many prostitutes were actually recruited by the armies. For many French and Belgian women living near the front, sex was the only way to earn enough to eat. Both men and women paid a high price in terms of disease, but soldiers were willing to take the risk, and some even picked up infections deliberately.

Among French troops, with their relatively loose sexual morals, over a million men contracted what other nationalities often called a 'French disease'. There were around 200,000 cases of syphilis. At least two wounded men contracted syphilis in hospital, which proves nowhere was safe. Prostitutes were officially required to be examined for signs of disease twice a week, but checks might be far from thorough. Even so, the French were not the worst affected. According to official statistics, the most sexually active were troops from Dominion countries. The British army – in which an estimated 400,000 cases of sexually transmitted disease occurred during the war as a whole – had an official rate of venereal disease of 3.7 per cent in 1916 (significantly lower, incidentally, than in 1911, in peacetime) whereas more than twenty per cent of Canadian soldiers had some form of venereal disease. In most cases they had contracted it in Britain, which prompted the Canadian government to put considerable pressure on the British to keep their prostitutes away from Canadian troops. In the French army the rate of venereal disease was just over 8 per cent, or 80 per 1,000; in 1917 the British managed to reduce theirs to 32 per 1,000, while the Australians, despite far-reaching preventive measures, continued to record no fewer than 85 cases per 1,000. These statistics too, however, should be treated with some caution. In the early 1900s a German doctor called A. Blatschko had published a study of venereal disease and war, in which he calculated that in the wars of the nineteenth century, over seventeen per cent of British soldiers had been put out of action by sexually transmitted disease. We should remember too that in static warfare (with occupation and trenches) the percentages are usually higher than in a war of movement. The low ratio given in official statistics for infection among British troops may be attributable, at least in part, to the effect on record-keeping of British cultural reticence about sexual matters.

The problem for the British – and to a lesser extent the Germans – was that the norms and values applied in the army were those of the landowning classes. Most infantrymen were young men of the labouring classes, with little education, who regarded regular sex as essential to good health, and this applied to an even greater extent to farmers' sons from Australia and New Zealand, despite the fact that most had been given little opportunity to vent their lusts back home. Up to a point the same went for British working men's sons; they were allowed many more opportunities to avail themselves of women in France than they had enjoyed in Great Britain, or could ever have hoped for at home, and they were not constrained by upper-class attitudes. Lieutenant-Colonel John Baynes went so far as to say that throughout the war the British soldier was prepared to make love to any woman he could lay his hands on, no matter where or when. Yet proper protection, in the form of condoms, was not provided until 1918, and compared to the Australian and New Zealand forces British supplies were scant even then.[187]

Although there was no unambiguous policy – some regarded a strict enforcement of moral norms the only permissible measure while others wanted to regulate sexual intercourse or at least tolerate it – the average British soldier was expected to behave in a gentlemanly manner, which meant among other things a degree of sexual restraint. Although there were brothels behind the lines, the men were kept away from the opposite sex as far as possible. Often the only 'women' a British soldier saw were comrades in drag during cabaret performances, and the majority will not have had sexual experiences with women on anything like a regular basis during the war. Several British soldiers later wrote that the war had not brought them to sexual maturity any more quickly, in fact it had delayed the process. Nevertheless, the number of soldiers who contracted venereal disease – as said, 400,000 in total of whom 150,000 needed hospital treatment – indicates that many British men had encounters with French or Belgian women. Clearly the measures taken by their superiors did not help a great deal. In 1916 there were eight specialist VD hospitals in France for the British alone, and another twenty back in Britain. They had a total of 17,000 beds, and 14 ordinary hospitals made another 15,000 available. Nevertheless, for most of the war, prophylactics were regarded as unnecessary and many even thought them amoral, although there were individual doctors who ignored the rules and distributed contraceptives.

For a long time the only preventive measure recognized by the British army was the short leg or short arm inspection, a weekly examination of the genitals, trousers round the ankles, which the men regarded as extremely embarrassing. This sense of shame in fact indicates the main purpose, so regular inspection should be regarded above all as an attempt at deterrence. More often than not the inspecting officer had no idea what he was supposed to be looking for, but the army gambled that the mere fact they were regularly examined would put soldiers off visiting *les filles*. Embarrassment remained an aspect of the system even after the British started treating infection some years later. Pots of medication – salvarsan, manufactured in 1910, or the traditional pills and ointments containing mercury – were placed near the latrines, so that anyone in need of them would be unable to conceal the fact from everyone else. This will have done nothing to encourage the use of such treatments. At the same time the 'policy of embarrassment' continued

187 Riemann, *Schwester der Vierten Armee*, 189; Ellis, *Eye-Deep*, 153; Brants & Brants, *Velden van weleer*, 70; Winter, *Death's Men*, 99, 150–51; Holmes, *Riding the Retreat*, 34; Holmes, *Firing Line*, 93, 95; Verdoorn, *Arts en Oorlog*, 366; Graves, *Goodbye*, 195; Eksteins, *Rites of Spring*, 213; Macdonald, *Somme*, 160; Toller, *Jugend in Deutschland*, 46; Winter & Baggett, *1914–18*, 104; Hirschfeld, *Sittengeschichte*, 185, 193–4; Heijster, *Ieper*, 101–4; Eckart & Gradmann, *Die Medizin*, 198, 202, 205–7, 212–14, 223; Liddle & Cecil, *Facing Armageddon*, 224–5; Bourke, *Dismembering the Male*, 156; De Schaepdrijver, *Taferelen uit het Burgerleven*, 90; Nys, 'De grote school', 407; Audoin-Rouzeau & Becker, *'14–'18*, 59, 65; Davidson, Hall, *Sex, Sin and Suffering*, 125

in the form of threats that a soldier's parents or wife would be informed. The French and Belgians underwent inspections as well, commonly known as *inspection du verrou*, bolt inspection, or *inspection des culasses mobiles*, a reference to a detachable gun barrel. Whatever afflictions their soldiers may have been subject to, undue modesty was clearly not among them.

Around 30 per cent of sexually transmitted disease had its origins close to the front. All troops, with the exception of the Belgians, had access to officially tolerated, regulated brothels, partly because some commanding officers feared that otherwise soldiers would engage in behaviours they regarded as even more immoral: homosexuality and masturbation. The Americans, for whom the existing French brothels were out of bounds, established their own official whorehouses as soon as they arrived, despite the fact that they had waged a powerful campaign against venereal disease prior to their entry into the war using the slogan 'masturbation is better than prostitution', which indicates an attitude diametrically opposed to that which prevailed in the other armies. They quickly began to distribute contraceptives, both condoms and chemical prophylactics, after it became clear that effective control and regulation were impossible. They took pains to ensure that moral crusader Woodrow Wilson would not find out, since the generals were afraid that if he knew what was going on he might withdraw all American troops from the continent. The AEF therefore made the contracting of a sexually transmitted disease a punishable offence, with the threat of prison for those who failed to seek medical treatment.[188]

The Belgians are the single exception. They had no official brothels. According to De Schaepdrijver this had more to do with frugality than with moral concerns. Unofficial houses of pleasure thrived as a result, one example being a *staminee* (pub) in the village of Beveren called De Veertien Billekens or 'The Fourteen Buttocks', so named because seven women were available there.[189] Another reason why the Belgian army had no brothels of its own had to do with an argument about venereal disease that had arisen among army doctors before the war. As Liesbet Nys explains in her *De grote school van de natie. Legerartsen over drankmisbruik en geslachtsziekten in het Belgisch leger (circa 1850–1950)* (The Nation's Great Educator. Army doctors on alcohol abuse and venereal disease in the Belgian army), many Belgian medical officers regarded the army barracks as a kind of moral hospital in which young Flemings and Walloons would be schooled in the appropriate norms and values. The soldier was to be prepared for a virtuous life as a good citizen of the fatherland, and everything must be done to break him of any bad habits, such as the frequenting of brothels and the abuse of alcohol that often went with it. Convincing a soldier of the frightful consequences of venereal disease was one means by which he could be urged to live a virtuous life.

188 Hirschfeld, *Sittengeschichte*, 178–9; March, *Company K*, 68; Eckart & Gradmann, *Die Medizin*, 205, 224, 362; Bourke, *Dismembering the Male*, 156–7, 161; Barry, *The Great Influenza*, 138–9; Manning, *Her Privates We*, 142; Nys, 'De grote school', 406

189 De Schaepdrijver, *De Groote Oorlog*, 191; Holmes, *Firing Line*, 96

That Belgian army doctors propounded this viewpoint is not as strange as it may seem, since in the eyes of a large segment of the population, including many medical men, army barracks were a source of moral and therefore physical degeneration. The honour and reputation of the armed forces were at stake, but clearly the Belgian battle against venereal disease was motivated not only by the demands of sanitation and military objectives but by the more general social and moral goals of the time. Signs of decline were detected everywhere and it was essential that they be halted and turned around. The barracks must become a citadel against which degeneration would smash itself to pieces and out of which the battle for regeneration could be joined. Although for a long time Belgian army doctors had recognized that soldiers had sexual needs and therefore attempted to guide them in the right direction – by checking the health of prostitutes so that men need not resort to rape or masturbation – shortly before the war they came under the influence of civilian doctors who had been advocating sexual abstinence for some time. Prostitution was no longer seen as a necessity but as an evil that must be combated. The system of 'approved' prostitutes therefore came in for harsh criticism, although when war came many doctors and others reviewed their positions. Health checks for prostitutes would limit the number of men put out of action and therefore improve the effectiveness of the army and with it national security. The Belgian army never went so far as to tolerate brothels close to the front line, however, and this was not purely because it did not wish to pay for their supervision. Army chaplains remained strongly opposed to the idea, despite the new circumstances, and they were not alone. Volunteer army doctor and later Flemish nationalist Frans Daels regarded abstinence as the highest command of all. 'Chivalry' towards women was of enormous importance, he said, since it helped to ensure they would not be cast 'to their doom' or driven to commit immoral acts.

These and other appeals were not sufficient to prevent the Belgian army from encountering problems with sexually transmitted diseases, known as 'lesions of Venus' or 'Venus 'flu'. Army doctors concluded in 1917 that seven per cent of Belgian solders were infected with a venereal disease, twice as many as a year earlier. Sexual contact with female civilians behind the lines was common. 'There are no *jeunes filles* left here,' wrote soldier, author and poet Louis Boumal in a melancholy mood, having spotted the umpteenth pregnant fifteen-year-old, 'a skinny immature little body with a big misshapen belly'. Naturally all contact with prostitutes or local women was seen as undesirable by the Belgian church, by soldiers' parents, and by the army high command, but was it so undesirable as far as the girls themselves were concerned? On at least one occasion it undoubtedly was. On 26 March 1918 a Belgian soldier was convicted of rape and murder – it was the last time the guillotine was ever used in Belgium.[190]

190 Nys, 'De grote school', 392–3, 397, 401–2, 405–6, 413–15, 417, 420–21; Wesseling, *Soldaat en krijger*, 33–4, 125–9; De Schaepdrijver, *De Groote Oorlog*, 194; De Vos, *De Eerste Wereldoorlog*, 63; Holmes & De Vos, *Langs de Velden van Eer*, 101

British brothels at army base camps were open between six and eight in the evening. There were class distinctions, of course. Brothels marked by a red lamp were for other ranks, while officers sought satisfaction in brothels with sober blue lighting. How busy they were is a matter of dispute to this day. Given the limited opening times, base-camp brothels must have been quite packed, despite claims that everyone politely waited his turn, supervised by the military police. But Graves, who was disgusted by what went on in and around them, spoke of lines of soldiers waiting their turn at town and city brothels frequented by men on leave (it was on leave that seventy per cent of cases of syphilis and gonorrhoea were contracted). Graves believed that in off-base brothels three prostitutes served 150 soldiers in a single night and each woman worked through almost the equivalent of an entire battalion every week, until she was literally used up. Prostitutes usually reached that point within a month, he said, and then withdrew to enjoy spending their money, as far as they could with a wrecked constitution.

There is some doubt as to whether this sexual traffic did indeed produce endless queues. Many claimed they had never seen lines of waiting soldiers as described by Graves in his book. There is indeed reason to doubt that such scenes were common. For a year records were kept of the number of soldiers visiting the red-light district in Le Havre. The tally rose steadily, reaching 171,000, which would mean that on average 'only' 80 men a day visited one of the brothels. Maybe this can – or even should – be called a large number but it is nowhere near 150 per evening. Moreover, there is probably some truth in the argument used by Private Surfleet to counter the innumerable stories of unbridled lust. He claimed – and he was not alone – that it was far from easy to find suitable women. Most Frenchwomen were too tired after working in factories all day, in jobs that before the war had been done by their husbands, brothers and sons. On the other hand it is arguable that long queues must have developed if demand outstripped supply to such a degree.[191] Nurse La Motte claimed there was no shortage at all.

> Have you ever watched the village girls when a regiment comes through, or stops for a night or two, *en repos*, on its way to the Front? Have you ever seen the girls make fools of themselves over the men? Well, that's why there are so many accessible for the troops. Of course the professional prostitutes from Paris aren't admitted to the War Zone, but the Belgian girls made such fools of themselves, the others weren't needed.[192]

This did not apply to Belgian women alone. In France too a growing number undoubtedly prostituted themselves, quite apart from those who worked in one

191 Ellis, *Eye-Deep*, 153–4; Brants & Brants, *Velden van weleer*, 70; Holmes, *Firing Line*, 95–6; Graves, *Goodbye*, 103–4, 151; Wilson, *Myriad Faces*, 360–61; Eckart & Gradmann, *Die Medizin*, 198; Bourke, *Dismembering the Male*, 157; Frey, *Pflasterkästen*, 19–20

192 La Motte, *Backwash of War*, 107

of the *maisons des tolérances*.[193] Nevertheless, we may wonder whether it is right to conclude from La Motte's story that war and venereal disease always and everywhere go hand in hand, and her assessment that the primary cause was the local women's lust for the soldiers' bodies seems questionable. Sexologist Hans Magnus Hirschfeld observed that experiences of war, such as the sight of uniformed men, increased the libido of local women, but we should take economic need into account here. Lacking any other source of income, Belgian and French women sold their bodies as their only remaining possessions. Alexander Moritz Frey, for example, wrote in his novel about first-aid posts, *Die Pflasterkästen. Ein Feldsanitätsroman* (*The Cross Bearers. A Story of the Medical Corps*), about a woman who, after sharing her bed with a soldier, asked him to give her a few marks, telling him of a sick mother and a father killed in the war. Largely because of the Great War, a widespread realization began to dawn that prostitution could result not only from debauchery, loose morals or lasciviousness but from simple poverty.[194]

In contrast to the French, who were quite open about the sexual appetites of soldiers, British sexual norms produced a rather ambivalent attitude to brothels. The difference was elucidated by Dr Harold Dearden, who described the contents of a letter he had found on a dead French soldier – although this particular story should not tempt us to exaggerate the virtues of either the average British soldier or his wife left behind in Britain.[195] It was a letter from the dead Frenchman's wife, in which she wrote that she did not mind at all that he visited prostitutes, which she took as a foregone conclusion. She did however ask him to choose women who looked a little like her. After all, she was the one waiting for him, the one who loved him. She enclosed a little money so that he could go to a prostitute who was not harbouring any disease. No British woman, claimed Dearden, would ever have sent such a letter, and no British man would have appreciated receiving it, which is not to say of course that a French soldier would display quite so much empathy were he to find evidence of promiscuity on the part of his wife.[196]

The British high command acknowledged the needs of its soldiers, if only to prevent unnecessary physical and mental suffering and the even greater loss of manpower that would result. Before long the total number of 'non-effective mandays' resulting from venereal disease had reached several million. Sexually transmitted disease illustrated the fact that it made little difference whether a man was put out of action by the enemy or by sickness. To army commanders, syphilis meant a minimum of five weeks and gonorrhoea more than four weeks of inactivity for the man concerned. The home front wanted nothing to do with regulated prostitution, however. So at the same time as brothels were being established,

---

193 Eckart & Gradmann, *Die Medizin*, 214

194 Leed, *No Man's Land*, 47; Cooter, Harrison & Sturdy, *Medicine and Modern Warfare*, 213; Frey, *Pflasterkästen*, 144–5; Nys, 'De grote school', 406–7

195 Bourke, *Dismembering the Male*, 156

196 Dearden, *Medicine and Duty*, 175–6; Dorgelès, *Croix de bois*, 238

the British, taking their lead from the Americans, added venereal disease to their list of military offences, alongside trench foot. 'Healthy activities' on leave were advocated as a means of keeping 'unhealthy activities' in check as far as possible, but in practice the charge of 'sickness as a result of reprehensible behaviour' was the main instrument of policy. If venereal disease was diagnosed, pay would be docked and leave postponed for a year. Prevailing moral norms also dictated that 'prophylactic packets' would be distributed after men returned to barracks rather than when they left, even though disinfection worked best immediately after intercourse.[197]

In 1918 the hypocrisy of all this was resolved, in the sense that moralism was declared the winner and pragmatism abandoned. Venereal disease was now seen by the Allies as no different from any other everyday sickness not caused by the fighting, and it was treated accordingly. At the same time as the distribution of condoms was beginning in earnest, military pressure from Canada and American and primarily religious pressure from across the channel led to brothels being declared off limits, despite the fact that of those who had visited the regulated brothels the previous year, only 243 had become infected.[198]

Official German policy was ambiguous, but the Germans were guided by pragmatism, which was paramount throughout. Like the Dominion forces, the German army based its official line on ethics and morals but had less faith in the efficacy of such attitudes than the British did. In Germany too there was powerful opposition to the pragmatic approach, especially from religious groups, and it was far from easy to arrange for chemical prophylactics and condoms to be distributed, but the German army did teach men how to use them. In practice this meant that soldiers had every opportunity to satisfy their sexual desires without anything to that effect appearing in their medical or service records, despite the fact that abstinence was the official line. As a result, although there were some elements common to both sides, the general picture was very different in the German army than elsewhere. The Germans had neither the puritan morals of the British nor the anarchistic love lives of the French. Theirs was the only army on the Western Front that set up a sophisticated system of prevention, and they made a start on this even before the war began. By around 1900 the pragmatic approach had ensured that soldiers were well informed and aware they had two options: prevention or disinfection. For several years before the war a system of compulsory medical checks had been in place for both prostitutes and soldiers, with compulsory treatment for anyone who tested positive. During the war a national network of hospitals treating venereal disease was established, analogous to tuberculosis testing centres, where free check-ups were available. According to British medical historian Paul Weindling, First World War methods of combating venereal disease

197 Eckart & Gradmann, *Die Medizin*, 222

198 Ellis, *Eye-Deep*, 154–5; Brants & Brants, *Velden van weleer*, 70; Winter, *Death's Men*, 151; Verdoorn, *Arts en Oorlog*, 366; Eckart & Gradmann, *Die Medizin*, 215

in Germany serve as a prime example of the increasing influence of the state on initiatives to promote hygiene during the years of conflict.[199]

In occupied areas too, the German army opened hospitals to treat venereal disease, including one in the Bedelaarsgesticht (Beggars' Institute) in Bruges. It was intended not only for the 'syphilitic women' of Bruges but for women from all over German-occupied western Flanders.[200] Aside from the damage that sexually transmitted diseases could do to the health of the army, the family and the nation, one of the reasons behind the stringency of German measures and their prompt introduction was a fear of venereal disease as a weapon of war. In 1870 the French newspapers had called on women to infect as many German soldiers as they could, and in 1914–18 widespread rumours suggested that a repeat of this subtle form of biological warfare was in prospect.[201]

German doctors made official twice-weekly visits to army brothels (for which the Germans used the words *Feldpuff*, *Offizierspuff* and *Feldfreudenhaus*), so that they could identify infected women as quickly as possible. Streetwalkers were subjected to meticulous checks and sent to work in brothels, where it would be far easier to keep an eye on them. Partly because German army brothels, according to Westman at least, were too few in number and too far from the front to meet demand, doctors performed spot checks on local prostitutes as well. Before they went on leave men were given 'love boxes' containing various forms of antiseptic. One thing these measures had in common with those of the British high command was that they provoked protest from the home front, where people said the army was encouraging adultery. It is ironic, therefore, that in retrospect it seems male passions at the front may have done less to change attitudes to sexuality than adultery by lonely women left behind at home, as described by Johannsen, for example. Much of the venereal disease that became evident during the war was contracted by soldiers on home leave. The governor general of occupied Belgium, Von Bissing, rightly pointed out that sexually transmitted disease was much more common among soldiers who were not living near the front line, in fact only around 30 per cent of cases originated there.[202]

A second similarity with other armies is that the Germans carried out medical inspections en masse. At an early stage Major von Töply (Med.) had described such inspections as 'completely irrelevant'. Nevertheless, soldiers were forced to take part at least two to three times a week in what they called a *Schwanzparade*

199 Hirschfeld, *Sittengeschichte*, 172; Eckart & Gradmann, *Die Medizin*, 215, 218, 226; Sauerteig, 'Ethische Richtlinien', 323; Weindling, *Health, Race and German Politics*, 285–6, 291; Davidson & Hall, *Sex, Sin and Suffering*, 83

200 Gevaert & Hubrechtsen, *Oostende 14–18*, 79, 81 (with acknowledgements to P. Verbeke, Bruges)

201 Hirschfeld, *Sittengeschichte*, 173–4

202 Chickering, *Imperial Germany*, 119–20; Eckart & Gradmann, *Die Medizin*, 211; Johannsen, *Vier von der Infanterie*, 20–21; Davidson & Hall, *Sex, Sin and Suffering*, 85; Weindling, *Health, Race and German Politics*, 285

(prick parade) or *Troddelappel* (tassel muster). Like the British, Germans soldiers found this highly unpleasant, although they could not help laughing at the whole business, especially if a soldier regarded up to then as an annoying stickler for regulations was discovered to have the dreaded drips and sores. Infantryman Perhobstler noted down some of the remarks the men fired at a doctor charged with carrying out such an inspection.

> 'I haven't a drop of juice left for myself and you expect me to have anything left for a whore!' 'You ought to inspect the *Etappenschweine* [men serving behind the lines] who are regular guests in the brothels!' Such were the men's curses, and some very different ones too. The doctor on duty became crude if anyone didn't have his works ready in time. The medical corps NCO sneered: 'Pull your foreskin back further! That usually comes pretty easily to you!'[203]

German officers, although no less likely to be infected, were spared this embarrassing performance. However futile the parades may have been from a medical point of view, the exemption given to officers seems to have had consequences, since in February 1917 a secret army memorandum pressed for junior officers to be included in inspections. This never got beyond the stage of recommendation.[204]

The *Gesellschaft zur Bekämpfung der Geschlechtskrankheiten* (Society for the Combating of Venereal Disease) was called upon for help in control and prevention. It distributed a pamphlet which stated that every soldier had 'a holy duty' to remain healthy 'for his fatherland', especially in times of war 'when the highest demands are made of his capacities'. It gave a series of helpful hints on how to prevent venereal disease and suggested some quick and effective measures to take if prevention failed. The appeal to a man's duty to the fatherland convinced some German doctors that contracting a sexually transmitted disease was indeed a crime that should be harshly punished. In a speech to medical officers, Dr Max Flesch expressed his belief that men who voluntarily reported within six hours of sexual contact should be exempt from prosecution, but that soldiers caught during medical inspections, who must therefore have dodged disinfection treatments, should not escape court martial.[205]

As with trench foot, the dilemma presented by the question of whether or not punishments should be introduced proved impossible to resolve. In practice, as the British had found, the prospect of punishment led to greater alertness among soldiers. Without the fear of punishment, men would have less incentive to adhere to the preventive rules. The rate of infection in the German army fell after the ban came into force – in official statistics at least – and the number of soldiers

203 Hirschfeld, *Sittengeschichte*, 176

204 Hirschfeld, *Sittengeschichte*, 176–8

205 Hirschfeld, *Sittengeschichte*, 174–5; Eckart & Gradmann, *Die Medizin*, 220; This idea, incidentally, closely matches a suggestion by a high-ranking Belgian military doctor in 1842. Nys, 'De grote school', 410–11

deliberately contracting diseases dropped. Venereal disease was of course the perfect self-inflicted wound, since its medical consequences were not great in the short term and the means of contraction – whether through sex or by rubbing the member with pus from an infected person – was a good deal more pleasant than a bullet wound. Nevertheless, no punishment short of execution could be worse than the lives the men were already leading, so the effect of the new measure should not be overstated, and the introduction of penalties meant that disease was hidden or went unreported, which cannot have done much to expedite either prevention or treatment.[206]

German soldiers who became infected were sent to special centres where their Spartan treatment was intended to persuade them to be more careful in future. It was a forlorn hope. The war years saw no decline in the frequenting of brothels, although few prostitutes bore even a passing resemblance to Mata Hari. One of the women inspected by Stephan Westman was well above pensionable age and her hair was full of lice. Nevertheless, meticulous inspections ensured that among the Germans venereal disease was nothing like the problem it was among the Allies. With just under 300,000 cases in the vast German army it was a normal disease in numerical terms and not such an acute threat as it seemed elsewhere. According to Zuckmayer, who like Graves talks of long queues of soldiers, each having to seek satisfaction from a prostitute who could pleasure five men an hour, there was a medical officer in every brothel who counselled the men and ensured maximum possible hygiene.[207]

Erwin Blumenfeld, who after the war would become a world famous photographer, gives a description of a German brothel. He worked as a *Feldfreudenhausbuchhalter* (bookkeeper at a field brothel) in *Feldfreudenhaus* number 209 in Valenciennes. The brothel opened its doors at ten in the morning. Eighteen prostitutes worked there, six of them reserved for officers. A visit cost four marks – no small sum in those days, certainly for an ordinary soldier – of which one mark was for the prostitute, one for the owner and two for the German Red Cross, which was in charge of inspections at this particular brothel. Blumenfeld says that each prostitute had 25 to 30 clients a day, which adds up to a total of around 500.[208] This does not actually prove the existence of endless queues, but the evidence suggests that from time to time there must have been lines of men waiting. Still, it seems reasonable to conclude that reports of overflowing brothels arose more from personal disgust than from objective observation.

If venereal disease as such was not a problem that got out of hand among German soldiers in wartime, one psychological difficulty did arise. When the war began the troops enjoyed the support of the home front, but civilians increasingly came to see returning soldiers as louse-ridden sources of infection, as walking tuberculosis bacilli and oversexed clap-carriers. Men were cheered as they left but

206 Hirschfeld, *Sittengeschichte*, 178; Frey, *Pflasterkästen*, 230–31

207 Zuckmayer, *Als wär's ein Stück von mir*, 239

208 Eckart & Gradmann, *Die Medizin*, 216

far less heartily welcomed on their return, largely because of the stories of sexual misconduct by soldiers that were soon doing the rounds.[209] On home leave, and certainly when they returned after the armistice, many men who had left for the war out of a desire to be of service to society noticed that society was not eager to welcome them back. Their status on their return was lower than when they left.[210]

The fear felt by the German population had some basis in fact. Many of the diseases the soldiers brought home were infectious, and this certainly applied to venereal diseases. Fear had a distorting effect on statistics, so they are less than reliable, especially those that suggest the Germans had a low rate of infection compared to the Allies. Findings like these were tailored to military objectives; a focus on humanitarian concerns might have produced quite different figures. For one thing, the statistics stop abruptly on 11 November 1918. For civilians the problem only began to assume its full magnitude after the war, and given the state Germany found itself in, it certainly seems plausible that the problem of sexually transmitted disease was even greater there than in the Allied nations. Medical provision for returning soldiers and the women they infected will have been far from optimal immediately after the war.[211]

The epidemic of a form of influenza known as Spanish 'flu – because the first reports of a new and virulent strain came from neutral Spain, where there was little censorship – is estimated to have claimed at least twenty million lives, very likely tens of millions more, before vanishing in mid-1919 as suddenly as it had appeared a year earlier. It ranks as one of the three deadliest epidemics in human history, along with the worst outbreak of bubonic plague in the sixth century and the fourteenth-century Black Death. It is telling that every time new figures appear, the estimated death toll rises. The subtitle to a Dutch book published in 1978 speaks of 'over 20,000,000' dead, but the book itself is more cautious, claiming the number was between fifteen and twenty million. The author states that the figure of around twenty million deaths is practically the only aspect of our knowledge about the 'flu epidemic that can be regarded as a solid fact, but a recent article in the *Bulletin of Medical History* suggests fifty million died and the authors state that the margin for error is as high as one hundred per cent. So a figure of 100 million dead is perfectly credible.

The wide diversity of estimates is a result of inadequate and poorly organized statistical data. Cases sometimes went unrecorded, especially in agricultural regions, and much of the data is of debatable quality. Different sets of statistics use different time frames, definitions and population samples, while some even contain internal contradictions. Misdiagnosis must have been common as well. Many people diagnosed as having died of tuberculosis, bronchitis, heart failure,

209 Winter & Baggett, *1914–18*, 104; Whalen, *Bitter Wounds*, 53, 66–7; Eckart & Gradmann, *Die Medizin*, 350

210 Wilbrink, 'Moeder', 7 (column 7)

211 Hirschfeld, *Sittengeschichte*, 186–8

malaria, cholera, dysentery, measles or typhus will in fact have died of the 'flu, whether or not they were already weakened by other health problems. It is also worth noting that once the influenza epidemic became known and much talked about, misdiagnosis will have occurred in the other direction as well. Doctors were far too busy anyhow, with their innumerable patients, or too ill themselves, to fill in all the details that would have been required for the compilation of a reliable statistical database. Recent research suggests the new strain of the virus was of the 'normal' type, and although there are many hypotheses, its remarkably aggressive and deadly character remains mysterious. The first cases of the new and fatal variant were reported well before 1918.

It seems likely that it was at some point in 1915 that humans first became susceptible to a virus initially circulating in birds and later in pigs, but perhaps the crossing of the species barrier occurred even earlier. This would explain the rapid spread of the disease, referred to in Dutch as a *windvlaag des doods* or blast of death. Somehow it managed to emerge simultaneously, or almost simultaneously, in places that had no discernable connection between them, such as troop movements for example. The deadly second wave began in August 1918 in places as diverse as Sierra Leone, France and Massachusetts. In other words the 'flu did not originate in 1918 but surfaced in 1918 with formidable intensity and disappeared a year later after three waves had passed, the first the least deadly, the second the most deadly of all. Some speak incidentally of a fourth wave, since there was also a 'flu epidemic in 1920, but it is unclear whether this was indeed a final flare-up of Spanish 'flu or an attack by a different strain of the virus. It is beyond doubt that in 1916 there were several early outbreaks, each limited both in duration and in geographical extent, one at the British training camp at Étaples in northern France and one a year later at the army base in Aldershot, south-west of London. It was not until 1918, however, that the Spanish 'flu assumed its epidemic form.

The first wave, in the spring of 1918, was not yet lethal, in most cases at least, although it already displayed a curious pattern in that more young adults went down with it than would normally have been expected. From the summer onwards all the armies of the Great War saw a return to the days when disease cost more lives in wartime than enemy action. This was the second wave, in which the disease was 25 times more deadly than normal 'flu, producing lung complications that were often fatal. Once infected, only 20 per cent of people escaped becoming seriously ill. Of the remaining 80 per cent, 1 in 40 died, compared to a normal rate for severe influenza of 1 in 1,000. In November 1918 almost three quarters of the available beds were occupied by 'flu patients. There were even a few who had been affected by the milder version prevalent back in the spring, but generally speaking those who had caught it earlier, to everyone's consternation at the time, were the lucky ones. The 'flu took an enormous toll of well-nourished and fit Americans. In October the base camps in America saw fatalities rise from just over two per thousand to more than two per hundred. This indicates that there is no simple answer to the many questions concerning the relationship between war and influenza, just as general questions about the relationship between war and epidemic disease, or between war and hunger, are often more complex than they seem at first sight. These three horsemen of the Apocalypse do not appear to be quite so automatically linked as is often assumed.

We can be certain that the war did not cause the 'flu. The question that remains is whether the war enabled the epidemic to assume the proportions it did. Until quite recently it was universally assumed that US troops brought the 'flu to Europe, since the American population was showing signs of the epidemic by March 1918, whereas the earliest reports from other countries began to emerge in May. By February and March 1918, dozens of military bases in the US were seriously affected by the disease, which medical officer George E. Sper describes as shooting through army camps 'like a meteorite'. This remains the theory most often subscribed to, but there are those who disagree. Influenza specialist Kennedy F. Shortridge, for example, claims the 'flu was brought to Europe by Chinese workers, employed as work teams on the Allied side. Given the aggressive nature of the virus, it seems likely that even without the war – the element that both these theories have in common – the virus would have found its way to other parts of the world. The disease might perhaps have been less widespread and virulent had it arisen in peacetime. Australian troops took part in the war, but their country was spared the disease for some months, probably because of the strict quarantine policy returning servicemen were subjected to. Quarantine failed to keep the disease out altogether, but it did delay its arrival and by the time it broke out in Australia it had lost much of its virulence. Nevertheless, it was still infectious and deadly enough to prompt Australians to use the word 'plague', the term most commonly used elsewhere to describe the epidemic. Because of the war, many other countries hesitated for a long time before introducing stringent quarantine regulations, and wartime conditions made them difficult to implement in practice. There was also resistance on ideological grounds: too much attention to means of curtailing the 'flu would draw resources away from the war effort and might diminish the morale of both soldiers and civilians. People and equipment that might otherwise have been deployed to tackle the disease by scientific and medical means were in short supply because of the war. Nevertheless, the epidemic was so rampant that even in peacetime, and even if far more medical personnel and resources had been available, saving many more lives, the 'flu would still have developed into a lethal pandemic.

Of course the war meant that many people were in a weakened state and therefore more susceptible to the virus, but the 'flu did not lay low only the elderly, the hungry and the working classes. It felled all types of people who came into contact with it. As already mentioned, this particular strain presented a great danger – even in areas unaffected by the war – to precisely those in the age category usually least threatened, people aged between fifteen and forty, although it is important to remember that the distinction here is a statistical one. The number of deaths in this age category rose most in percentage terms, but in absolute terms it was probably children aged five or under to whom the disease was most fatal. One possible explanation is that while many viruses are more damaging the older the patient is, in this case older people (those over 50) were spared because they tended to have acquired antibodies during previous epidemics of influenza in the mid- to late nineteenth century, unlike those under 40. We do not know, however, whether they had all contracted 'flu viruses of the same sort – clearly these previous strains must for some reason have been far less deadly. There had almost certainly been no earlier pandemics on the scale of 1918–19, lethal or not, so it remains unclear why the same 'young adult' pattern can be detected worldwide. Whatever the reason, the way it affected different age groups explains why soldiers succumbed in such numbers. It was not simply because they were weakened by wartime privations. The 'flu, after all, paid no heed to the war and spread like wildfire in belligerent and neutral countries alike. In the neutral Netherlands, where there was no real famine despite the shortages (certainly compared to Germany) around 17,000 people died in November 1918 alone. In total the Netherlands lost around 50,000 citizens to the pandemic.

In America and Canada, further away from the theatres of war and even less subject to famine among the general population, millions succumbed, including many who had never had any connection, direct or indirect, with the war. Even in one of the most remote places in the world, Western Samoa, one in five of the population died. The arrival of a single steamship spelled the end for 9,000 islanders.[212] So although soldiers leaving for the front and others returning home will certainly have contributed to its spread, the essential explanation probably lies in the aggressive nature of the virus itself.[213] This raises doubts as to whether the fact that the German army was hit first and hardest – in the first wave alone, half a million German soldiers became bedridden – can be attributed to the demoralized and famished state it found itself in, as many commentators believe.[214]

The extent to which the pandemic affected the conduct of hostilities remains a subject of discussion to this day. In due course the 'flu threw a spanner in the works, certainly, and not just because it was deadly. For three weeks in May 1918 the British fleet was unable to sail because so many sailors were in bed. Commanding officers complained that the 'flu was affecting their fighting strength. Planned offensives had to be delayed, and in Germany the ultimate failure of the spring

212 Brusse, 'De grootste plaag', 6; Gabriel & Metz, *A History of Military Medicine*, 243; Gilbert, *First World War*, 437; Winter & Baggett, *1914–18*, 314–17; Eckart & Gradmann, *Die Medizin*, 321–42 (article: Jürgen Müller, 'Die Spanische Influenza 1918/19'); Shortridge, 'The 1918 "Spanish" flu', 384–5; Heyman, *World War I*, 77; Joules, *The Doctor's View*, 40–42; Feenstra, 'Spaanse griep', 1; Barry, *The Great Influenza*, 4–5, 92, 94, 97, 98, 171, 234, 267, 328, 364, 375–6; Kolata, *Griep*, 14–15, 18, 23, 25, 87–8, 111, 294–6, 365–97 (esp. 377–9, 382, 383–5, 387, 389, 396); Moeyes, *Buiten Schot*, 356–9; Langford, 'Age Pattern', 1–5, 11, 16–19; Johnson & Mueller, 'Updating the Accounts', 105, 107–8, 113, 115; De Gooijer, *Spaanse Griep*, 6, 15, 18, 23, 94, 161, 173; Byerly, *Fever of War*, 71–2, 75–7, 98–100; Fabi, 'Der alltägliche Krieg', 78

213 Eckart & Gradmann, *Die Medizin*, 9–10, 321–42

214 Brants & Brants, *Velden van weleer*, 341; Simkins, *World War I*, 198; Keegan, *First World War*, 437–8; Barry, *The Great Influnza*, 171

offensive was attributed in part to the 'Flemish fever', as the Germans called the 'flu. It goes without saying that the disease did little to improve the morale of the men. Nevertheless, its effects in purely military terms were probably minimal, even during the deadly second wave, leaving aside a few local, short-term delays to the Allied offensive that preceded the armistice. This too was a result of the extremely virulent character of the virus. The 'flu came, killed, and moved on. Furthermore, it was a fickle disease. In some regiments the percentage of men who contracted it was less than ten, in other regiments ninety per cent were in hospital. The rapid arrival and departure of the disease and the uneven distribution of its effects, which meant that it terrorized personal and public life at any one place for only a short time, probably also help to explain why it has become a footnote in world history even though the number of deaths alone suggests it deserves extensive coverage. Another explanation may be that the influenza inevitably became identified with the war, which needed to be forgotten about as quickly as possible. Futhermore, as medical men began to study the 'flu they realized that it put paid to the notion, increasingly prevalent at the beginning of the twentieth century, that medical science would soon be able to master bacteria and therefore disease. The influenza epidemic reinforced the point that not all serious diseases were caused by bacteria. They were gradually forced to accept the unpleasant truth that there were some illnesses in the face of which medical men were powerless – a notion they were more keen to keep silent than emphasize.[215]

However we decide to characterize the relationship between the war and the Spanish 'flu, it is clear that given the huge number of deaths it caused among soldiers almost overnight, no book about the First World War, and certainly no book about the victims of that war, can ignore the greatest epidemic that has raged on earth since the Middle Ages. Comparisons with medieval plague were made from the start. One of the very first German reports about the 'flu stated that there had been an outbreak of it in Spain.[216] The influenza may have been of little significance militarily, but from a purely human point of view it was a disaster of enormous magnitude.

As we have seen, the first signs of a true epidemic were present in the spring of 1918. It seems to have been checked with little difficulty, but then the virus suddenly broke out in a much more virulent form.[217] Margaret Ellis, trainee nurse at the General Hospital in Étaples, witnessed the despair of the medical profession.

> The only treatment apparently was to keep an even temperature in the ward, that was the main thing we were told. We just had to give them fluids and keep walking up and down seeing if anybody wanted anything. They were all

215 Eckart & Gradmann, *Die Medizin*, 326, 335, 342; Tucker, *European Powers*, 360; Kolata, *Griep*, 23–4, 74, 76–7; Barry, *The Great Influenza*, 171; Byerly, *Fever of War*, 75, 82–87; Vugs, *In veel huizen wordt gerouwd*, 19

216 De Launoy, *Oorlogsverpleegster*, 286; De Gooijer, *Spaanse griep*, 19

217 Macdonald, *Roses of No Man's Land*, 285

> incontinent so you were continually changing beds and washing. I remember doing one boy from head to foot, and ten minutes later I had to start doing it all over again.[218]

Peggy Marten of the Voluntary Aid Detachment saw whole convoys of sick men arrive at the hospital, 'some of them semi-conscious'.

> We couldn't do much for them. We gave some of them steam inhalations, but mostly it was a case of keeping them warm, keeping them nourished, hoping that they wouldn't get pneumonia. But many of them did. I remember one man. I just happened to peep over the screen and an orderly was starting to wash him. The man's face was dark blue, so I told the orderly to stop, and I went and reported it to Sister. He died in the early evening, and then in the morning, when we came on duty, one of the medical staff came to Sister and said that he wanted her to go down and see this body. It had already started to decompose. They called it influenza but it seemed to us to be some frightful plague. It was very, very serious and it was as hard as any push that we'd had from the fighting, and the proportion of deaths was higher – much higher – than we'd had from wounds at any time. It was very heavy work and very depressing.[219]

Captain Geoffrey Keynes of the Royal Army Medical Corps would never forget the sight of the mortuary tents. 'There were rows of corpses, absolutely *rows* of them, hundreds of them, dying from something quite different. It was a ghastly sight, to see them lying there dead of something I didn't have the treatment for.'[220]

One of the reasons why medical staff were helpless was of course that they themselves were not immune. Doctors, nurses and stretcher-bearers became infected and died.[221] Kitty Kenyon of the Voluntary Aid Detachment wrote in her diary that the previous night she had gone to the front door of the ward and had seen stretcher-bearers coming round the corner.

> I knew it must have been Franklin being carried down the road. He has been one of our orderlies for so long that it must have been hateful knowing all the last

218 Macdonald, *Roses of No Man's Land*, 286

219 Macdonald, *Roses of No Man's Land*, 286–7

220 Macdonald, *Roses of No Man's Land*, 287

221 De Launoy, *Oorlogsverpleegster*, 286, 324; Noyes, *Stretcher-Bearers*, 199; It has been suggested that one of the doctors who died of the 'flu was John McRae, the Canadian author of 'In Flanders Fields', the best known of all WWI poems (Kolata, *Griep*, 37). However, this is unlikely in the extreme, not only because the official cause of death was pneumonia but because he died in January 1918, some months before even the first, least deadly wave. Eijkelboom, *De War Poets*, 122

> details and knowing that he would be carried out on a stretcher under a Union Jack, like so many men that he had accompanied himself.[222]

One sad incidental circumstance was that everyone knew the war might end at any moment. Jünger pointed out that because of the 'flu many men would have to stay at the front even longer than expected, because the reserves had gone down with it.[223] Of course this was not the saddest aspect. The poet Apollinaire had been through many battles, a bad head wound, trepanning and, as a slightly sarcastic Jay Winter put it, had survived various other forms of military medicine, only to die of 'flu two days before the end of the war.[224] Peggy Marten lamented: 'It was so near the end. They'd gone through all that frightful thing, and then they couldn't go home.'[225] Another nurse, Margaret Ellis, wrote: 'On the day the Armistice was declared, there wasn't one man in the ward who knew. They were all delirious, not conscious enough to know, too ill. There wasn't one man who understood. Not *one* man.'[226] Many soldiers died shortly after the armistice, as did many civilians, perhaps infected by the returning husbands, brothers and friends they had welcomed so warmly.[227]

## Wounds

### *Introduction*

In 1911 the *Royal Army Medical Corps Training Manual* estimated that in a future war sick soldiers would outnumber the wounded by twenty-five to one. In reality the ratio in France was roughly two to one.[228] Given the huge number of soldiers who contracted some form of disease, this makes the Western Front the theatre of an astonishingly bloody conflict. For example, of over 6 million British men in uniform, 44 per cent were wounded and 12 per cent killed, a total of almost 3.5 million. If we take into account that only a third of men in the British armed forces actually spent any time at the front, then it is clear that of those who did, few escaped being hit and many were wounded several times. Almost all non-fatal wounds can be attributed to bullets and shells. The relative percentages given in the sources range from 20 per cent suffering bullet wounds as against 80 per cent injured by shellfire (among the French up to 90 per cent) to 40 and 60 per cent

222 Macdonald, *Roses of No Man's Land*, 286; see also: 289, 290

223 Jünger, *In Stahlgewittern*, 226

224 Winter, *Sites of Memory*, 18–20; Winter & Baggett, *1914–18*, 312–14; 'Jahrhundert der Kriege', 118

225 Macdonald, *Roses of No Man's Land*, 287

226 Macdonald, *Roses of No Man's Land*, 293

227 Gilbert, *First World War*, 508

228 Joules, *The Doctor's View*, 30

respectively, whereas in the Franco-Prussian war the percentages had been 90 per cent rifle fire and 10 per cent artillery. Other causes of wounding played a very small part, at least in percentage terms. Of soldiers fortunate enough to reach hospital alive, 21 per cent had been hit in the torso, 51 per cent in the arms or legs and 17 per cent in the head. These figures alone show that wounds to the head and trunk were more likely to be fatal than those to the arms and legs. The low percentage of chest wounds recorded is no doubt attributable to the fact that many soldiers hit in the torso did not make it to hospital. Those who died in the field and never reached treatment centres were not included in the statistics. German surgeon and nationalist Ferdinand Sauerbruch made a study of one battlefield in the Vosges mountains and concluded that between 30 and 40 per cent of fatalities were caused by chest wounds.[229]

Wounds to the abdomen proved even more deadly than wounds to the head. Of one British sample of a thousand soldiers with stomach wounds, 510 died on the battlefield, 460 on their way to hospital and 22 following surgery. Only 8 survived, or 0.8 per cent. In this particular case the circumstances may have been extreme – other studies conclude that the survival rate was 8 per cent – but clearly the survival chances for men with abdominal wounds were small, even compared to chest wounds which, despite proximity to the heart, were survived by 72 per cent (again, if they made it into the statistics). In the light of this it seems easier to understand why one Royal Army Medical Corps officer who had been hit in the stomach spent 48 hours holding everyone at bay with his revolver, so that they would not try to help him by getting him onto a stretcher and taking him to a first-aid post. Only by lying still and allowing the wound to heal by itself could he hope to survive. He believed that anyone with an abdominal wound who was taken to an aid post and arrived there alive was extremely lucky. Once he was moved, he would need to be treated very promptly indeed. It usually took too long to get to an aid post, let alone to a dressing station further back behind the lines. Even if he reached a field hospital quickly, there would always be at least a few men ahead of him waiting for treatment, and it was impossible to treat the majority of abdominal wounds at dressing stations close to the front. According to German statistics, 23 per cent of men with wounds to their arms and 12 per cent of men wounded in the leg died. This is surely almost entirely attributable to infection.[230]

Despite meticulous record-keeping by army units and hospitals, the number of wounded can only be guessed at, since hospitals kept track of wounds, not the people who had received them. In other words, a man admitted to hospital with two different wounds would be entered in the statistics not once but twice.[231]

---

229 Lanz, *De Oorlogswinst*, 14

230 Chickering, *Imperial Germany*, 195; Gilbert, *First World War*, 541; Winter, *Death's Men*, 192–4; Ellis, *Eye-Deep*, 109 (note); Keegan, *Face of Battle*, 264; Simkins, *World War I*, 124; Graves, *Goodbye*, 194; Verdoorn, *Arts en Oorlog*, 354, 360; Whalen, *Bitter Wounds*, 42; Eckart & Gradmann, *Die Medizin*, 137

231 Whalen, *Bitter Wounds*, 40

The percentages given above relate to millions of wounded. Along with the fact that the sheer numbers overwhelmed medical practitioners (a problem we shall examine later), the scale of the suffering contributed to a substantial drop in home-front enthusiasm for the war. In percentage terms few of the wounded crossed the Channel, but they were nevertheless so numerous that the British government was forced to arrange for hospital trains to carry them into London only after dark. In the early weeks of the war large crowds had welcomed the wounded arriving at Victoria Station with flowers and music; now they were taken out through a side entrance to waiting ambulances in the dead of night.[232]

*Bullets and shells*

The essence of warfare, as the First World War makes graphically clear, can be described as the handing over of one's body to the state, giving the government free rein to dispose of it as it sees fit, even if that means it will be grotesquely mutilated by bullets and shells, most, but not all, fired by the enemy. Nevertheless, in theory bullet wounds were relatively clean. If the bullet entered the body undamaged, there was usually little bleeding, only a bluish hole with smears of blood around it. Rotation of the bullet could cause contusions, but even then heavy bleeding was rare, since shock reduced blood pressure and severed blood vessels sealed themselves off.

The amount of pain was not directly related to the seriousness of the wound. It depended mainly on where the bullet hit and had little to do with how life-threatening the damage might be, since the level of pain is determined by the number of nerve endings at the place affected and the presence of certain tissues such as ligaments. Wounds in nerve-rich places like heads, hands, and feet were extremely painful, but hand and foot injuries were rarely fatal. Harold Macmillan suffered more pain from a wound to his hand than from one to his pelvis.[233]

However, if the bullet did not go straight to its target but ricocheted, as was very often the case, then the consequences could be ghastly. The twisting bullet did not enter the flesh point first but made a huge hole and could easily smash a bone. Even in the first month of the war, the *British Medical Journal* recorded bullet holes measuring five by three inches as a result of ricochets.[234] Charles Carrington had the terrible experience of seeing a soldier with a head wound caused by a ricocheting bullet.

> Pratt was hopeless. His head was shattered. Splatterings of brain lay in a pool under him, but he refused to die. Old Corporal Welch looked after him, held his body and arms as they writhed and fought feebly as he lay. It was over two hours before he died, hours of July sunshine in a crowded place where perhaps a dozen

232 Brants & Brants, *Velden van weleer*, 146
233 Bourke, *Dismembering the Male*, 117–18; Winter, *Death's Men*, 194
234 Ellis, *Eye-Deep*, 109; Winter, *Death's Men*, 109, 194

> men sat with the smell of blood while all the time above the soothing voice of the corporal came a gurgling and moaning from his lips, now high and liquid, now low and dry – a death rattle fit for the most bloodthirsty novelist.[235]

The same effect might be produced if a bullet was thrown off course within the body, by contact with a bone for example. In that case it might be made worse by splinters of bone that could fly around inside a man. A bullet moving off course in the flesh might close off blood vessels, stagnating the circulation and creating pressure nearby that overwhelmed vital organs.[236]

The severity and extent of such wounds is far from surprising. However small a bullet may be, the speed at which it hits the body gives it incredible power. Speed multiplied by weight could produce a discharge of energy equivalent to 7,200 horsepower. A single horsepower is defined as the energy required to lift an object weighing 275 kilos thirty centimetres into the air in one second. Barbusse writes that when a man standing next to him was hit by a salvo of bullets, his own body shook as a result.[237] Penetration of the flesh was therefore only the first problem a wounded soldier had to deal with. Part of the body explodes after a bullet hits.[238] The stories of the fifty per cent of men who survived such physical trauma are remarkable, in fact it is quite astonishing that they survived at all. For a while at least, a man might live with even the most terrible wounds from bullets and shell fragments. Jünger witnessed a fire fight in which one of his men was killed, but not instantly. 'Even though his brains were dribbling down past his chin, he was still lucid as we carried him into the nearest shelter.'[239] John Michael Stanhope Walker was chaplain at a casualty clearing station in Corbie that had been set up in a half burned-out factory, and he kept a diary. In late August 1916 he thought he had seen the last word in horror and decided to spare the reader a description. 'Strange to say, he still lives.'[240] Barthas was surprised by a soldier who suddenly jumped forward and fell between him and his comrades:

> We stood there a moment, horrified: the man had almost no face left; a bullet had hit his mouth and exploded, blasting through his cheeks, shattering his jaws, ripping out his tongue, a bit of which was hanging down, and the blood gushed abundantly from these horrible wounds. ... Nevertheless someone recognized the soldier; 'It's Gachet,' he said. 'From Corporal Barthas' squad.' The wounded man confirmed with a nod that he was indeed Gachet. I had failed to recognize

235 Winter, *Death's Men*, 109
236 Keegan, *Face of Battle*, 265
237 Barbusse, *Le Feu*, 132
238 Whalen, *Bitter Wounds*, 50
239 Jünger, *In Stahlgewittern*, 178; *Storm of Steel*, 212
240 Moynihan, *People at War*, 83

> a man in my squad, but would even his own mother have recognized him in a state like that?[241]

The main source of bullets was the machine-gun. Innumerable descriptions make clear that the comparison sometimes drawn between bursts of machine-gun fire and sustained volleys from disciplined nineteenth-century professional army riflemen is ultimately misplaced. Keegan is right to point out that rapid rifle fire did sometimes come close to the effect of the machine-gun, without ever equalling it, but such an effect could be achieved only after long and intensive training. Even in the hands of an amateur the machine-gun was deadly. It had a devastating effect at minimal cost. The invention of the machine-gun meant that killing was no longer an achievement of disciplined human beings but a mechanized, industrialized, non-human, indeed inhuman act. Man was no longer master of the battlefield.[242]

Few accounts have come down to us that describe what it was like to be wounded. Josiah C. Wedgwood remembered the incredible impact, which he compared to a cart-horse kick. J. Bell commented that the sensations that accompanied being hit could be extremely deceptive. He thought he had received a huge knock to the head, only to discover later that his foot had been blown off. Shock instantly deprived him of the power of speech.[243] R.H. Tawney described being struck by a bullet as a visit by all the riders of the Apocalypse at once. He was wounded on that momentous first day of July 1916. He had no idea what most people felt, but:

> What I felt was that I had been hit by a tremendous iron hammer and then twisted with a sickening sort of wrench so that my back banged on the ground, and my feet struggled as though they didn't belong to me. For a second or two my breath wouldn't come. I thought, 'This is death,' and hoped it wouldn't take long.[244]

What bullets did on a small scale, and generally only when they were deflected or deformed, explosives did on a large scale and practically always. The power of a bursting shell or mortar bomb was virtually inconceivable, even in that pre-atomic era. According to Eric Hiscock, a British double-decker bus would fit perfectly into the hole left by the blast of a Monstrous Minnie. It would then sink into the ground until, 'like thousands of once-living English and German fighting men, it would be lost to sight forever'.[245] An explosion could have any number of different effects, and almost all were terrible. Men were mutilated beyond recognition or picked up from the earth like dolls and flung back down. A body could even disappear into thin air; nothing recognizable, perhaps nothing at all, might remain of what

241 Barthas, *Carnets*, 72

242 Keegan, *Face of Battle*, 229–30; Ellis, *Social History*, 113, 142

243 Winter, *Death's Men*, 193–4

244 Hynes, *Soldiers' Tale*, 20–21; Wilson, *Myriad Faces*, 328

245 Fussell, *Bloody Game*, 162

a moment before had been a human being. A medical officer with the 2nd Royal Welch Fusiliers remembered a man who was hit. When the smoke cleared there was no trace of him to be found.[246]

A shell exploding nearby could result in excessive pressures or vacuums within the body, causing damage to the lungs, brain or spinal cord that was sometimes fatal. Three soldiers of the Welch Fusiliers were found sitting in a shell-hole, dead, without a scratch.[247] The opposite was more often the case, of course – far more often. A man might fear mortars most of all, because of their precision and the resultant feeling that they were intended specially for him. The mortar in particular conjured up the image of a cat on one side, grinning with power, and a mouse on the other side, quaking with fear.[248] Graves found a type of German mortar known as a canister the greatest trial of all. When it exploded it was comparable only to the dawning of Judgement Day, he said. The canister was a type of fragmentation bomb. The hollow space inside a two-gallon drum, around a cylinder of explosive, was packed with scrap metal: rusty nails, screws, nuts and bolts, shell fragments, spent bullets and so forth. One unexploded canister, taken apart by Graves and his men, even contained half a set of false teeth. Those that went off threw their contents in all directions, causing horrible injuries to anyone nearby. When Graves and his men found the gun emplacement where the canisters were being fired from they showed no mercy, even though the crew tried to surrender.[249]

Fear is seldom rational or based on anything in the way of objective statistics of death and wounding, but Graves' aversion to this particular explosive device is understandable. Most wounds from shellfire were not the result of the blast itself. Around seventy per cent of injuries were caused by pieces of metal flying through the air, in other words by shell fragments and shrapnel. Their velocity was low compared to bullets, but they were heavy and usually flew in clusters, so they would cause not just one wound but several at the same time. Dirty scraps of clothing were usually driven into the flesh, so it was rare for a man to avoid infection, which could lead to the dreaded gangrene. Only good solid cover could protect a man against shrapnel and shell splinters, which could penetrate steel helmets. The exterior wounds caused were generally not very large, but shards of metal wreaked just as much havoc inside the body as ricocheting bullets.[250] Duhamel worked in an *autochir*, a mobile field hospital just behind the front lines for surgical procedures that had to be carried out immediately. He compared some of the wounds he saw on the operating table to leaky boats letting in water through every seam.[251] Fifty years later Zuckmayer still vividly remembered the first time

246 Keegan, *Face of Battle*, 264

247 Keegan, *Face of Battle*, 264

248 Winter, *Death's Men*, 114; Macdonald, *1914–1918*, 131

249 Graves, *Goodbye*, 161

250 Duhamel, *Vie des Martyrs*, 154; Winter, *Death's Men*, 115; Keegan, *Face of Battle*, 264–5; Gabriel & Metz, *A History of Military Medicine*, 239–40

251 Horne, *Price of Glory*, 65; Van Raamsdonk, 'De secretaris', 125

he saw a man standing next to him hit by a shrapnel shell, his face reduced to a bloody pulp with a long, loud cry issuing from it.[252] Towards the end of the war, incidentally, shrapnel shells were almost entirely replaced by high explosives, since the targets consisted less of people than of earthworks, defensive structures and installations. Shrapnel was a horribly effective anti-personnel weapon but practically useless against serious fortifications.[253]

Shell splinters above all, in other words fragments of shell casing that flew around wildly and with invincible force, instilled terror. They could cause wounds that turned the stomachs of onlookers. Their effects were comparable to those of the traditional cannon ball in the far off days of sixteenth- and seventeenth-century warfare. Legs were hacked off, stomachs gouged open, heads torn from bodies, faces horribly mutilated. Castration was far from rare.[254] It was often astonishing that a man was not killed outright when hit by a splinter. August Hopp wrote: 'Seckinger had got a shell fragment straight through the eyes. Both eyes had been torn out and it had damaged his brain. The poor lad was still alive, even conscious ... He died four hours later.'[255]

The knowledge that some men survived such wounds did nothing to reduce the terror they evoked. Frank Richards wrote:

> I wasn't worrying so much if a shell pitched clean amongst us: we would never know anything about it. It was the large flying pieces of shell bursting a few yards off that I didn't like: they could take arms and legs off or, worse still, rip our bellies open and leave us still living. We would know something about *them all right.*[256]

Sassoon, for one, felt no particular preference. He pointed out that bullets only seemed to be neater than shells that blasted a man off the ground, shook him to pieces and tore him apart, darkening the sky with smoke and contaminating the air with the smell of sulphur. Bullets, however, flew around the battlefield in huge numbers like insane, merciless hornets. 'The big guns roar their challenge and defiance; but the machine-guns rattle with intermittent bursts of mirthless laughter.'[257]

### *The chemical horror*

> As under a green sea, I saw him drowning.
> In all my dreams, before my helpless sight,

---

252 Zuckmayer, *Als wär's ein Stück von mir*, 222
253 Townshend, *Modern War*, 114
254 Keegan, *Face of Battle*, 265; Ellis, *Eye-Deep*, 109; Binneveld, *Om de geest*, 49
255 Witkop, *Kriegsbriefe*, 46
256 Terraine, 'Inferno', 185–6
257 Fussell, *Bloody Game*, 53

He plunges at me, guttering, choking, drowning.
…
If you could hear, at every jolt, the blood
Come gargling from his froth-corrupted lungs,
Obscene as cancer, bitter as the cud
Of vile, incurable sores on innocent tongues,–
My friend, you would not tell with such high zest
To children ardent for some desperate glory,
The Old Lie: Dulce et decorum est
Pro Patria mori.

Wilfred Owen, 'Dulce et Decorum'

The First World War is perhaps remembered most of all for the use of poison gas. But gas was not the only discovery by modern chemists that would ravage the battlefield. The flame-thrower – used mainly against men sheltering in small bunkers and foxholes – was also developed in the laboratory and used first by the Germans. It too gave Ypres, more specifically a place called Hooge, the dubious distinction of being the first spot on earth to witness its effects. It consisted of a cylindrical oil drum and a steel tube from which burning oil was squirted under high pressure. After small-scale tests at Malancourt in February 1915, 'liquid fire' was deployed in anger for the first time on 30 July 1915. It was targeted at the inexperienced British 14th Division. The lines of trenches were close together and the weather was favourable – from the point of view of the German army. It is not hard to imagine the results. In the middle of the night, at a quarter past three, the flame-throwing units left their trenches, followed by regular troops. The new weapon gave a deafening roar and spouted fire dozens of metres, a dazzling flame in the dark of the night. The panic was huge, the fate of the British troops ghastly. Men hit by the flames were burned alive, their bodies never found. Those less seriously burned, or frozen with fear, were bayoneted. From that moment on, the smell of oil, smoke and burning flesh would be added to the already intolerable stink of the trenches, of no man's land and the battlefield.[258] Barthas described an attack with flame-throwers:

> But what is this? Is hell opening up under our feet? Are we standing on the lip of an enraged volcano? The trench fills with flames, sparks, acrid smoke, the air is unbreathable; I hear whistling and crackling noises, and alas screams of pain as well. Sergeant Vergès' eyes are burnt; at my feet two unfortunates roll on the ground, their clothes, their hands, their faces burning, like living torches. ... [*The next day.*] Lying on the ground in front of us, gasping for breath, the two unfortunates I had seen in the flames were so unrecognisable that we could not tell who they were. Their skin had gone completely black. One of them

258 Macdonald, *1915*, 422–3; Heijster, *Ieper*, 113–14; Holmes & De Vos, *Langs de Velden van Eer*, 112

> died in the night, the other, in the grip of delirium, sang little songs from his childhood, conversed with his wife, his mother, spoke about his village. Hearing that brought tears to our eyes.[259]

Fortunately, conditions were never again as ideal for the deployment of flame-throwers as they had been at Hooge during that first attack.[260] The weapon had little effect in a military sense, in the long term at least, partly because the version used in those days had such a short a range and used so much oil. Psychologically it had an enormous impact, however. Once again men were confronted with a new and abominable invention, a piece of technology that would not decide the war but would increase its horrors. The flame-thrower, both the full-sized *Flammenwerfer* and the more convenient, compact model, formed the umpteenth and to many the definitive step away from the kind of war the soldiers had imagined when it began. The war they had expected was based on what their schoolmasters knew, on poems by Rupert Brooke and books by Rudyard Kipling; it was the sort of war in which victory or defeat was decided by personal honour and courage. For Louis Mairet, who called his war diary *Carnet d'un Combattant* (Notebook of a Combatant), the flame-thrower in particular symbolized 'this merciless war' and was a 'glowing vision of this century of madness'.[261]

The way the flame-thrower was perceived is well represented by the description in the closing passage of *Toward the Flame* by First-Lieutenant Hervey Allen of the US 28th Division. His book covers a period of only a few weeks in the summer of 1918, when his unit attacked German fortresses before being practically wiped out. Although he fought on until October and experienced other battles, he ended his book thus:

> Suddenly along the top of the hill there was a puff, a rolling cloud of smoke, and then a great burst of dirty, yellow flame. By its glare I could see Gerald [a fellow officer] standing halfway up the hill with his pistol drawn. It was the *Flammenwerfer*, the flame throwers; the men along the crest curled up like leaves to save themselves as the flame and smoke rolled clear over them. There was another flash between the houses. One of the men stood up, turning around outlined against the flame – 'Oh! My God!' he cried. 'Oh! God!'.
> *Here ends this narrative*.[262]

The psychological effects were comparable to those of gas, and that was not all the two had in common. Just as many soldiers became the victims of their own gas, the flame-thrower gave a new slant to the term 'friendly fire'. Once the initial period of adjustment was over, the full weight of the barrage was targeted at flame-

259 Barthas, *Carnets*, 126, 129

260 Simkins, *World War I*, 73

261 Eksteins, *Rites of Spring*, 165; Weltman, *World Politics*, 98

262 Hynes, *Soldiers' Tale*, 97–8

throwing sections as soon as they were identified, partly because of the anger the weapon aroused. One direct hit would be enough to set a whole crew alight, the fire-spouting men becoming torches themselves.[263] Even a well-aimed rifle shot could put the operator out of action. The weight of the apparatus almost always made him fall backwards and the jet of flame would then point towards his own men.

Despite the fact its impact was short-lived, the weapon extremely hazardous for those using it, and the weather conditions and terrain rarely completely suitable, the flame-thrower did achieve some military successes. It was deployed in the first few days of the Battle of Verdun in late February 1916, for example. French soldiers doused with burning fuel fled in complete disarray, wailing with pain, their clothes and hair on fire. Wherever the *Flammenwerfer* appeared in those early days it caused panic. In the Bois d'Haumont an officer and 63 men surrendered to one flame-throwing section.[264] During the attack on Fort Vaux in late May and early June 1916, the French army held out against a sustained barrage of German mortars and shells for longer than expected. Gas and chemicals were then set alight. Stretcher-bearer Vanier wrote two days later, 'Several grenadiers came back with terrible wounds: hair and eyebrows scorched away, barely human any longer, black, wild-eyed creatures.'[265] A little over a month later, British troops on the Somme were again attacked with flame-throwers and one entire British battalion was eliminated. Thirty-three of its officers and 1,300 men were either killed or captured.[266]

The considerable likelihood of being torched themselves was reason enough for the French and British to use their own flame-throwers more cautiously than the Germans. The British version made its debut on 1 July 1916,[267] and the French used theirs for mopping up operations after successful attacks, but deployment by both armies was relatively limited. If there was any resistance when trenches were stormed, then the man operating the flame-thrower might be hit and catch fire, making him more of a danger than an asset to his own troops; and if there was little resistance to an attack on a trench, the reasoning went, then the flame-thrower was virtually useless.[268]

The Americans did not share the reticence of their allies. In late May 1918, for instance, they used the terror weapon in their attack on the village of Cantigny. One man from Kansas remembered that the Germans caught as they fled from a dugout had made him think of 'rabbits coming out of burning straw sacks'. The living torches ran about fifteen yards, then fell down dead.[269]

---

263 Horne, *Price of Glory*, 81–2; Heijster, *Ieper*, 115
264 Horne, *Price of Glory*, 269
265 Brants & Brants, *Velden van weleer*, 227–9
266 Gilbert, *First World War*, 265
267 Richter, *Chemical Soldiers*, 148, 155
268 Eksteins, *Rites of Spring*, 164–5
269 Gilbert, *First World War*, 426

The flame-thrower was undoubtedly the chemists' most terrifying weapon, but it was gas that came to symbolize the chemical horrors of the First World War. If the flame-thrower emitted the breath of Lucifer, then gas was a blast from Satan. Yet in the final analysis the fear of gas was disproportionate. In contrast to many stories doing the rounds then and since, gas claimed few victims in relation to the vast casualty figures for 1914–18.[270] Norman Gladden was quite justified in stating that gas caused fear 'that was out of all proportion to the damage done'.[271] Both Otto Muntsch, author of *Leitfaden der Pathologie und Therapie der Kampfgaserkrankungen* (Guide to the Pathology and Therapy of Sicknesses caused by Gas Warfare), published in 1932, and Lieutenant-Colonel J.F.C. Fuller, author of *The Army in My Time* (1935), went so far as to claim that gas was a humane weapon. Fuller was even referring to mustard gas, the most deadly of all the gases used. Gas was much more likely to put a man out of action than to kill him, he said, whereupon he could be made a prisoner of war. The long-term effects of gas were slight, and the immediate impact was often psychological rather than physical – namely fear.[272]

There is a good deal of evidence to support the views of Muntsch and Fuller. The percentage of wounded among troops subjected to a gas attack was low in comparison to other weapons and the vast majority were only slightly hurt and able to return to their units after a few days' rest. The number of deaths caused by gas (a weapon of little strictly military significance on the Western Front) seems almost negligible when set beside the overall totals. One might even say that those wounded by gas, compared to those hit by shrapnel or bullets, were the lucky ones.[273]

In the war as a whole, West, East and elsewhere, around 800,000 soldiers are said to have been affected by gas, with a margin of error of an astonishing 200,000 either way, only counting the more or less seriously inflicted. Among them were around 180,000 British soldiers, 190,000 Frenchmen, 70,000 Americans and 80,000 Germans. The number of dead has been estimated at roughly 90,000, or some 1 per cent of the total. Gas casualties who reached hospital spent on average only about half as many days there as men hit by bullets or shellfire, so the resulting number of 'non-effective mandays' was significantly lower. The death rate was only half that of wounds by rifle, machine-gun or artillery fire. Of all the British soldiers wounded by gas – 9.5 per cent of the casualty total for 1915 to 1918 – around 6,000 died. Fewer than 10,000 were permanently disabled. After dramatic improvements to the quality of protective clothing, 70 per cent of gas casualties recovered fairly quickly; across all armies an average of 93 per cent were able to return to the front in due course. Some 3,000 Germans died as

270 Richter, *Chemical Soldiers*, 1

271 Holmes, *Firing Line*, 212

272 Winter, *Death's Men*, 123; Eckart & Gradmann, *Die Medizin*, 136

273 Richter, *Chemical Soldiers*, 218–19

a direct result of gas poisoning. Overall, between two and three per cent of men wounded by gas, seriously or not, died, on the German side a mere 1.66 per cent. This lower percentage is probably due to the more frequent use of gas by the Germans themselves, their more effective protective clothing and their better 'gas discipline', which meant that German troops adhered more strictly to the rules telling them how to behave during a gas attack.

The arguments used by Muntsch and Fuller are fallacious nonetheless. As with the low percentage of chest wounds, we need to take into account that the fatality rate of two per cent relates only to casualties registered as such. As with all other wounds, those who died immediately from gas poisoning and therefore did not reach first-aid posts are not included in the statistics, especially if they were hit by shellfire after they died. And how severe did a man's condition have to be before he was diagnosed as suffering from 'gas poisoning'? Gas in small doses was rarely if ever fatal, and most cases of poisoning were minor. Among serious cases the death rate was as high as twelve per cent.[274] 'Recovered' meant 'returned to the front'. If a poisoned man could walk and swing his arms he was declared healthy; no one asked whether he was really physically and mentally fit to face the horrors of the front once more.[275] Furthermore, it is important to add that Muntsch and Fuller, in constructing their arguments, gave an inaccurate picture of how gas was used, perhaps deliberately. Gas was not deployed because it was more humane than bombs, shells and bullets, as Modris Eksteins correctly points out. It was intended as yet another scourge of front-line troops. Far from being used instead of artillery it was deployed alongside it. Men wounded by gas were not taken prisoner but killed. A British gunner wrote in 1915: 'They bayonet everyone who has been too overcome by the fumes to move and then turn their high explosives onto the wretched crowd of people who remain struggling for breath.'[276] Frankly, the argument that gas was deployed to force the enemy to surrender was a line of reasoning tailored to its own impact on public opinion.

Soldiers were not afraid of gas simply because it killed. There were so many other things that could kill them, although they were undoubtedly convinced gas was far more deadly than reasonably objective studies later showed it to be. Despite the fact that an alert soldier could generally escape gas more easily and effectively than he could dodge mortars and shells, most would have preferred mortars. Gas symbolized the dehumanizing nature of the war even more than the deafening bombing and shelling they were used to. Silent as an assassin, it killed and wounded insidiously, randomly, never quickly and painlessly. *Le Filon* of 20 March 1917 included an article entitled 'Gas: For Those Who Have Seen It'.

---

274 Verdoorn, *Arts en Oorlog*, 365; Simkins, *World War I*, 3; Whalen, *Bitter Wounds*, 42; Koch, *Menschenversuche*, 228–9; De Vos, *Van Gifgas tot Penicilline*, 94; March, *Company K*, 41

275 Winter, *Death's Men*, 125

276 Eksteins, *Rites of Spring*, 162

> With the cloud, death enveloped us, impregnating our clothes and bedding, killing everything living around us, everything that breathed. Little birds fell into the trenches, cats and dogs, our companions in misfortune, lay down at our feet never to awaken. Then we saw our comrades making their way to the first-aid post and we waited long and anxiously for the enemy or for death. My friends, there we spent the most painful long hours of our lives as soldiers. We had seen everything: mines, shells, tear-gas, woodland destroyed, the ghastly rending of mortars falling one after another, the most terrible wounds and the most murderous avalanches of metal, but nothing can compare with this fog which for hours that felt like centuries hid from our eyes the sunlight, the daylight, the white purity of the snow.[277]

Gas meant having to wear protective clothing that transformed men's faces into identical 'pig-snouts'. It had a significant impact as a weapon of war, but as with the flame-thrower the effect should be seen primarily as psychological. Major Billy Congreve remarked that gas added yet another new horror to a war that was horrific already, 'and there is something depressing in gas'.[278]

The pernicious effects of gas on men's minds made gas hysteria, the collective panic during a gas attack, a common phenomenon. Men were all too quick to raise the alarm, sometimes several times in one night. According to Hervey Allen, gas shock was as normal as shell shock. Regimental Medical Officer Captain Charles McMoran Wilson – better known as Lord Moran, later to become Winston Churchill's personal physician – thought that gas was one of the main causes of war neurosis, and he attributed this in part to its tendency to convince a soldier that human beings were unfit by nature for modern warfare.[279] On top of this many men, especially the British, continued to feel repugnance towards the use of gas, which they saw as unsportsmanlike and as contravening the accepted rules of combat. In examining these responses we should take into account that chemistry was more advanced in Germany than in Britain and France,[280] but this sense that the laws of war were being violated may help to explain as well why the Germans were the first to use gas and used it more often than the Allies. In Eksteins' view, the Germans were fighting to destroy the status quo embodied by Great Britain. Existing rules about how to conduct a war were part of that status quo, and the Germans saw them as both alien and outdated.[281] Most British soldiers, even when using gas themselves, continued to regard it as unacceptable, despite the fact that the Germans had used it first. Although many, like Lance-Corporal Ramage of the 1st Battalion Gordon Highlanders, found it odd to protest against gas and not

277 Audoin-Rouzeau, *Men at War*, 72

278 Holmes, *Firing Line*, 212

279 Holmes, *Firing Line*, 212; Winter, *Death's Men*, 121; Binneveld, *Om de geest*, 66; Shepard, *War of Nerves*, 64

280 De Vos, *De Eerste Wereldoorlog*, 108

281 Eksteins, *Rites of Spring*, 160

against bullets,[282] the general feeling among the British was that a soldier was not supposed to use such a weapon. Many were convinced it would bring disaster down upon them. Graves' comrade Captain Thomas said on the eve of Loos, 'We're sure to bungle it.' He was convinced that the trouble stirred up would outweigh any advantage gained. Hanbury-Sparrow was one of those calling gas 'the Devil's breath'. It 'went against God-inspired conscience'.[283]

The fact that the word 'gas' was rarely used is closely bound up with this feeling. While the Germans were relatively forthright in calling it a *Kampfstoff* (battle agent), the British, as we saw in the previous chapter, used an even more euphemistic term, 'the accessory'. This was in a sense an accurate description, and we cannot lightly dismiss the claim that it was used purely to pull the wool over the enemy's eyes should messages be intercepted, rather than to obfuscate its true horror. Use of any other word was a punishable offence. The various different types of gas had code names too. Chlorine gas for example was called red star, and the meaning of this term was kept secret for some time even from 'the Specials' as the British gas sections were called.[284]

It is interesting to note that Barbusse's central character Barque rejects out of hand the British notion that gas attacks were unsportsmanlike. He agrees with Ramage that it is ridiculous to use the world 'unfair' in the context of war.

> 'That's a really unfair move,' says Farfadet. 'What is?' says Barque, jeering. 'Yes, not decent, I mean, gas...' 'Don't make me laugh,' says Barque, 'you and your fair and unfair weapons. When you've seen men cut open, chopped in half or split from top to bottom, spread around in pieces by ordinary shells, their bellies gaping and the contents dug out, skulls driven right into the lungs as if from a blow with a mallet or a little neck in place of the head with a blackcurrant jam of brains dripping all round it, on the chest and back... When you've seen that then come and tell me about clean, decent weapons of war!'[285]

This does not take away, however, that, if stories about the low mortality rate require at least some qualification, the fear of gas was further justified by the fact that its effects, even in small doses, were extremely painful and distressing. Even if they did not prove fatal, the consequences were dreadful, and they could last for years, even for the rest of a man's life. The corrosion of the lungs rarely healed completely and lung damage often caused a thickening of the blood, which might

282 Liddle & Cecil, *Facing Armageddon*, 326

283 Holmes, *Firing Line*, 212

284 Strachan, 'Military Modernization', 71; Dunn, *The War*, 146; Brants & Brants, *Velden van weleer*, 100, 115; Graves, *Goodbye*, 123; Wilson, *Myriad Faces*, 256; Ellis, *Eye-Deep*, 65; Verdoorn, *Arts en Oorlog*, 267; Klee, *Auschwitz*, 269; Richter, *Chemical Soldiers*, 32, 46–7

285 Barbusse, *Le Feu*, 230–31; *Under Fire*, 196; also: Ureel, *De kleine mens*, 72; *Van den Grooten oorlog*, 215

lead to serious heart problems. The eyes by no means always recovered within a few days either, in fact loss of vision often manifested itself as a major injury only later. In 1978 Denis Winter estimated that in 1990 there would still be 400 veterans of the First World War alive who had been blinded by gas. Perhaps, he added, the fear of gas was not so irrational as many observers thought.[286]

The most famous soldier to have been temporarily blinded by gas was German corporal Adolf Hitler. He was wounded in a British gas attack at Wervik on 14 October 1918. He required nursing until after the war ended, but although he describes his eyes as having been turned into glowing coals, the damage proved temporary.[287] This has been suggested as a possible reason why poison gas was not deployed on the battlefields of the Second World War. Hitler is said to have found its use repugnant. This may well be true, but the deduction is – obviously, perhaps – incorrect. Quite apart from the fact that away from the battlefield gas certainly was used in Nazi Germany, and that Germany had a chemical and biological weapons programme led by Hitler's personal physician Karl Brandt, it was not the Germans alone who decided against deploying it. It is important to remember that in the 1939–45 war there were strategic and tactical considerations that adequately explain the decision not to use gas during military offensives. If that war too had been a *Sitzkrieg* rather than a *Blitzkrieg*, gas would probably have corrupted the air over the battlefield once more.

The chlorine gas used at the start of the war could be deadly, but types of gas introduced later were many times stronger. Chlorine could be seen and smelled, so a large cloud was fairly easy to avoid, and a wet handkerchief across the mouth was reasonably effective in neutralizing it. This did little to reduce the terror instilled in the troops. A dose of three parts gas to 100,000 parts 'normal' air provoked a coughing fit that could immobilize a man. In higher doses the effects were much worse, until at a ratio of one part to a hundred, death from extensive damage to the lungs and bronchi was inevitable. The symptoms were comparable to acute bronchitis along with all its known side-effects. The build-up of fluid in the alveoli made it impossible to get sufficient oxygen into the bloodstream. The casualty found himself drowning on dry land. Death from poisoning by chlorine gas often took several days, and the patient became unconscious only a few minutes before he died.[288] Towards the end of the war, Jünger and his men were hit by German gas that drifted back into their own defensive positions, suffering watering eyes, burning mucus membranes, vomiting and intense coughing fits.[289] Of an earlier episode he wrote:

---

286 Eckart & Gradmann, *Die Medizin*, 140; Winter, *Death's Men*, 124

287 Heijster, *Ieper*, 81; Schrep, 'Gebrochen an Leib und Seele', 60

288 Winter, *Death's Men*, 121–2; Holmes, *Firing Line*, 213; Horne, *Price of Glory*, 65; Brants & Brants, *Velden van weleer*, 115–16; Ellis, *Eye-Deep*, 66; Macdonald, *Roses of No Man's Land*, 84–5; Barthas, *Carnets*, 532; Schmidt, *Karl Brandt*, 17

289 Jünger, *In Stahlgewittern*, 195

> Outside the company office in Monchy, we saw a lot of men affected by gas, pressing their hands against their sides and groaning and retching while their eyes watered. It was a bad business, because a few of them went on to die over the next several days, in terrible agony.[290]

Remarque, whose famous novel *Im Westen nichts neues* is generally regarded as saying as much about how the war generation looked back on their experiences as about the conflict itself,[291] has his central character Paul Bäumer express with a sigh the hope that the masks will seal properly, since he is familiar with 'the terrible sights from the field hospital, soldiers who have been gassed, choking for days on end as they spew up their burned-out lungs, bit by bit'.[292]

Another reason, then, why fear of gas was more rational than the mortality statistics might suggest is precisely this sense of horror. It terrified both sides. Men waiting for a favourable wind to allow them to release their gas were fearful their location would be discovered and the full force of enemy artillery targeted on them and their gas cylinders and shells. Some companies were more likely to arouse the hatred of the other side than others, and gas companies were among them.[293] If they did not die in the shelling they might well fall prey to their own gas. The British head of the Specials, Charles Howard Foulkes, said later that in the second half of 1916 around 20,000 gas cylinders had been stored at the front of which only twenty-five were destroyed by shellfire, resulting in thirty-one deaths, and that in 110 attacks around that time there was only one case of a cloud that had been blown back by the wind, killing 'only' nineteen men. Denis Winter commented: 'Even had this been publicized at the time, no doubt it would have been treated with the same suspicion reserved for all divisional news.'[294]

Along with Captain Thomas' reference to bungling, these comments by Foulkes tend if anything to confirm that gas did not affect targeted areas only. We shall return to this point, but it will be clear by now that although most of the gas released did travel towards the enemy, accidents, leakages, enemy shellfire hitting stockpiles of gas and changes in the wind caused deaths among those using or intending to use it. Leakage, for example, was a problem for which no adequate solution was ever found, while enemy shelling produced a perpetual state of fear in soldiers close to the cylinders. There was always a chance that a gas cylinder would be hit even if no one was deliberately aiming at it, and since the men would not be expecting a release, the consequences might well be worse than during a planned attack. Many would have inhaled a significant amount by the time they

---

290 Jünger, *In Stahlgewittern*, 57; *Storm of Steel*, 81

291 Eksteins, *Rites of Spring*, 275–99; Liddle & Cecil, *Facing Armageddon*, 809, 822

292 Remarque, *Im Westen*, 54

293 Richter, *Chemical Soldiers*, 222

294 Winter, *Death's Men*, 125–6

got their masks on, if they were able to do so at all.[295] A further problem was that gas clouds sent out a warning that troops were about to advance. It was this factor that led the Canadians to conclude, after their costly but successful attack on Vimy Ridge of 9 April 1917, that had they not used gas they would ultimately have suffered fewer casualties. Only one German prisoner said he had seen a comrade killed by gas during the attack and not a single Canadian had seen a German wearing a gas mask.[296] Although the Canadians were not directly affected by their own gas, they could nevertheless be said to have fallen victim to it.

All this makes clear first of all that any assessment of the lethal effects of gas needs to take into account the indirect casualties of its use in the field, and secondly that, despite the apparently low mortality rate, it is understandable that many personal accounts of the war emphasize the horror of seeing gas casualties. The two most frequently discussed manifestations of this response are major artistic achievements: the painting *Gassed* by John Singer Sargent, now on display in the Imperial War Museum, and the poem 'Dulce et Decorum' by Wilfred Owen.

After the war, Singer Sargent was commissioned to paint a commemorative canvas and he chose as his subject a line of soldiers blinded by gas, a scene also captured on film in 1918. Each soldier, his eyes bandaged, has his hand on the shoulder of the man in front as they make their way past groups of other gas casualties, left and right, ahead and behind. The man at the centre has turned his head away to vomit. Another lifts his legs high as if climbing stairs. They are led by an orderly, the only representative of the medical profession in a scene full of wounded. A little further on, a second line of men is visible. In the background soldiers are playing football. War artist Henry Tonks was with Singer Sargent when he observed the scene. 'They sat or lay down on the grass, there must have been several hundred, evidently suffering a great deal, chiefly I fancy from their eyes which were covered up by pieces of lint.'[297]

Owen's 'Dulce et Decorum' is about a soldier who dreams that through the green glass of his mask he can see a man dying of gas poisoning. Owen was convinced that if civilians could hear the sound a soldier made as he gargled blood, they would never again serve up to their children, thirsting for honour and glory, Horace's old lie that it is a sweet and honourable thing to die for one's country.[298]

Doctors and nurses were the people who had most contact with gas casualties, however, not painters and poets. In her *Roses of No Man's Land*, Lyn Macdonald describes the astonishment of medical staff at the sight of the first gas casualties.

> Nothing in their experience … had equipped them to deal with wards full of men gasping for breath; with the terrible rasping sound of their struggle; with their

295 Macdonald, *1915*, 526; Richter, *Chemical Soldiers*, 96, 130–31, 184, 221

296 Richter, *Chemical Soldiers*, 175–6

297 Dyer, *Missing*, 90–91; Gilbert, *First World War*, 473–4

298 Winter & Baggett, *1914–18*, 228; Brants & Brants, *Velden van weleer*, 116; Fussell, *Bloody Game*, 166; Gilbert, *First World War*, 352–3

> blue faces and livid skins; and, worst of all, with their terror as the fluid rose higher and higher in the lungs until eventually they drowned in it. The terror was made worse by the fact that most of the men were blinded and trapped in darkness in their suffocating bodies.[299]

Bernard Gallagher was working in Southampton at the time of Passchendaele and he told of the many badly poisoned men who had lost the power of speech and developed chronic coughs. 'But those conditions usually improved after a few weeks. In some of the worst, the face and eyes would be so badly burned and swollen that the patient's eyes were completely shut and one would hardly recognise the face as that of a man.'[300] Duhamel saw a soldier with various wounds caused by gas. 'His eyes had quite disappeared under his swollen lids. His clothing was so impregnated with the poison that we all began to cough and weep.'[301] Medical officer Octave Bueliard wrote of the effects of chlorine.

> The panic is enormous. Whole regiments throw down their weapons and flee the trenches. Many fall to the ground. Their bodies jolt with spastic convulsions. Everyone coughs, vomits, spits blood. Emitting their death rattle, they gasp for breath in their terrible mortal struggle. They are trampled by those fleeing who, blinded by the stinging gas, stagger as they try to escape the deadly cloud.[302]

In hospital Hoffman saw many 'horrible cases of mustard gas'. Some had been temporarily blinded and were forced to lie in bed for what seemed an eternity with their eyes bandaged; others could walk a little after a time, but only with their legs wide apart, because, so Hoffman had heard, 'their testicles had in some cases shrivelled up like dry peas in a pod'.[303]

In his book *All For a Shilling a Day*, William Pressey described his own physical condition after he was gassed.

> [I] was being carried on a stretcher past our officers. … I heard someone ask 'Who's that?' 'Bombardier Pressey, sir.' 'Bloody Hell.'
>
> I was put into an ambulance and taken to the base, where we were placed on the stretchers side by side on the floor of a marquee, with about twelve inches in between. I suppose I resembled a kind of fish with my mouth open gasping for air. It seemed as if my lungs were gradually shutting up and my heart pounded away in my ears like the beat of a drum. On looking at the chap next to me I felt sick, for green stuff was oozing from the side of his mouth.[304]

---

299 Macdonald, *Roses of No Man's Land*, 85
300 Macdonald, *1914–1918*, 248
301 Duhamel, *Vie des Martyrs*, 139
302 Kielich, 'De grote schande', 29
303 Fussell, *Bloody Game*, 175
304 Moynihan, *People at War*, 140

An autopsy report by a British doctor published in the *Official Medical History of the War* reveals the horrific effects of what was probably mustard gas all the more graphically for its tone of objective detachment.

> Case four. Aged 39 years. Gassed 29 July 1917. Admitted to casualty clearing station the same day. Died about ten days later. Brownish pigmentation present over large surfaces of the body. A white ring of skin where the wrist watch was. Marked superficial burning of the face and scrotum. The larynx much congested. The whole of the trachea was covered by a yellow membrane. The bronchi contained abundant gas. The lungs fairly voluminous. The right lung showed extensive collapse at the base. Liver congested and fatty. Stomach showed numerous sub-mucous haemorrhages. The brain substance was unduly wet and very congested.[305]

Whereas doctors were generally able to maintain a degree of detachment in their written accounts, this was too much to ask of nurses, who had the most direct contact with the casualties over extended periods. Nurse C. Macfie who worked at Casualty Clearing Station no. 11 in Godswaerveldt during Passchendaele wrote:

> The mustard gas cases started to come in. It was terrible to see them. … The poor boys were helpless and the nurses had to take off these uniforms, all soaked with gas, and do the best they could for the boys. Next day all the nurses had chest trouble and streaming eyes from the gassing. They were all yellow and dazed. Even their hair turned yellow and they were nearly as bad as the men, just from the fumes from their clothing.[306]

Nurse S. Millard hated gas.

> Gas cases are terrible. They cannot breathe lying down or sitting up. They just struggle for breath, but nothing can be done. Their lungs are gone – literally burnt out. Some have their eyes and faces entirely eaten away by gas and their bodies covered with first-degree burns. We must try to relieve them by pouring oil on them. They cannot be bandaged or touched. We cover them with a tent of propped-up sheets. Gas burns must be agonizing because usually the other cases do not complain even with the worst wounds but gas cases are invariably beyond endurance and they cannot help crying out. One boy today, screaming to die, the entire top layer of his skin burnt from face and body. I gave him an injection of morphine. He was wheeled out just before I came on duty. Where will it end?[307]

---

305 Winter, *Death's Men*, 123

306 Macdonald, *Passchendaele*, 87

307 Winter, *Death's Men*, 123

During the final offensive, in September 1918, De Launoy described a scene the essentials of which come close to Owen's 'Dulce et Decorum'.

> The men lie fully dressed on their beds, unable to breathe, blue, wild and unkempt, with clenched fists: casualties of gas attacks. Some find it impossible to lie still, others are flat on their backs with cuts to their arms where we have to extract 400 grams of blood. Mustard gas, phosgene... Many will never recover their sight. ... Why are those who want and prepare for war not strangled to death with the cruellest torments? ... Those who profit by the annihilation of others while they themselves are safe. I went in with a message and I forgot what I had to say. Really, anyone would walk out of that room![308]

This outpouring recalls a similar response by Vera Brittain, a nurse with the Voluntary Aid Detachment, later to become a feminist, a novelist and, because of her wartime experiences, a pacifist, in a letter she wrote to her mother, which she includes in her moving book *Testament of Youth*.

> I wish those people who write so glibly about this being a holy War, and the orators who talk so much about going on no matter how long the War lasts and what it may mean, could see a case – to say nothing of 10 cases – of mustard gas in its early stages – could see the poor things burnt and blistered all over with great mustard-coloured suppurating blisters, with blind eyes – sometimes temporally [*sic*], sometimes permanently – all sticky and stuck together, and always fighting for breath, with voices a mere whisper, saying that their throats are closing and they know they will choke. The only thing one can say is that such severe cases don't last long; either they die soon or else improve – usually the former; they certainly never reach England in the state we have them here, and yet people persist in saying God made the War, when there are such inventions of the Devil about…[309]

Gas masks were largely responsible for keeping the death rate relatively low and they did make some men feel safe. That is not to say they were popular. The conclusion reached by Rudolf Hanslian in his much reprinted book *Der Chemische Krieg* (*Chemical Warfare*), first published in 1925, that the psychological effects of gas were neutralized once effective respirators became available,[310] needs to be put into perspective if not repudiated altogether. Firstly the masks were never completely effective and secondly there is at least some truth in Richard Holmes' observation: 'Central to the question of fear of a weapon is the soldier's perception

308 De Launoy, *Oorlogsverpleegster*, 289

309 Brittain, *Testament of Youth*, 395; see also: Rompkey & Riggs, *Your Daughter Fanny*, 110, 113; Panke-Kochinke & Schaidhammer-Placke, *Frontschwestern*, 84–138

310 De Vos, *Van Gifgas tot Penicilline*, 106

of his ability to do something about it.'[311] To many men gas remained a terrible weapon against which they could do little, no matter what sort of masks they had with them. According to Graves, no soldier really believed in the effectiveness of respirators, and doubts were only reinforced by the often contradictory instructions on how to use them.[312] Gas continued to inspire fear.

Furthermore, what was often said of steel helmets applied at least as much to gas masks. They saved lives, but at the same time they made a soldier look more 'inhuman' and therefore lowered the barrier to killing a man. Many noted that the introduction of the steel helmet was accompanied by an intensification of the conflict. The tin hat was one of the things Blunden felt had transformed the war from a 'personal crusade into a vast machine of violence' and which Jünger said had marked a new era of bureaucratically-organized violence.[313] The gas mask was another.

Protective clothing soon began arriving at the front in huge quantities. The British alone produced a total of around 27 million gas masks, of which the first 300,000 black gauze prototypes were ready within a week of the start of the gas war. It was not until 1917 that the proper box respirator was introduced. Until then men used fabric gas helmets or hoods, and at first many had to make do with veils delivered at great speed from France and crudely impregnated, or pads of cotton waste wrapped in muslin. In the days of the first gas attacks, preparation consisted of running around with the nose clasped shut, breathing through the teeth.[314] If they could manage it at just the right moment, soldiers covered their mouths with handkerchiefs or socks they had urinated on, which was neither pleasant nor anything like a simple matter. Stuart Cloete, a second-lieutenant at the time, remembered a sergeant using a great deal of strong language to explain to the men that the handkerchiefs must be wetted by pissing on them. Cloete says it was by no means easy to urinate on something you were holding in your hand while, as he writes, the urine steamed in the cold air like water from a hot tap.[315] This measure was not as useless as it may sound, incidentally, since the ammonia neutralized the chlorine to some degree.[316]

The early masks in particular were extremely uncomfortable. Those provided to men on both sides in late 1915 worked for only about half an hour. Masks of any sort – not only the early varieties, although they had the greatest impact since men were not yet used to them – were perhaps even more symbolic of the dehumanization of war than gas itself. They deprived the soldier of his last remnants of individuality.

311 Holmes, *Firing Line*, 211
312 Graves, *Goodbye*, 90–91
313 Blunden, *Undertones of War*, 76; Holmes, *Firing Line*, 380
314 Ellis, *Eye-Deep*, 67–8; Winter, *Death's Men*, 124
315 Brants & Brants, *Velden van weleer*, 100; Macdonald, *1915*, 232–3
316 Ellis, *Eye-Deep*, 67

Masks and other protective clothing had the ironic effect that since everyone looked like everyone else, so that they seemed interchangeable, each soldier became even more a part of the whole yet at the same time more isolated. Eating and drinking were quite a performance, not to mention that which inevitably follows eating or drinking. It was hard to move around. Work was twice as difficult. Hearing was compromised and the glass eye-pieces fogged up almost immediately. The fabric the early gas helmets were made of was impregnated with chemicals, which mingled with sweat, dribbled out and irritated the skin. The box respirator closed off the air supply so effectively that soldiers had a sense they were suffocating. A man could no longer feel his body, only the rapid pounding of his heart. Remarque's Paul Bäumer felt a buzzing and droning sensation in his head inside the gas mask. 'It is nearly bursting. Your lungs get strained, they only have stagnant, overheated, used-up air to breathe, the veins on your temples bulge and you think you are going to suffocate.'[317] Jünger remembered donning a mask only to remove it again immediately 'because I'd been running so fast that the mask didn't give me enough air to breathe; also the goggles misted over in no time, and completely whited out'.[318] Johannsen's *Vier von der Infanterie* features the following scene: '"Gas, Gas!" Everyone grabs the masks, the hated gas masks. They're in enough difficulty as it is and now that sweating inside a mask, that gasping for air, and those fogged-up bits of glass in front of the eyes.'[319] George Worsley wrote of the masks, which sometimes had to be worn for twenty-four hours at a stretch: 'You can't describe how uncomfortable they are, because they make you feel as if you're choking. There's a grip that holds your nose tightly and you have to breathe through the mouth, through a tube you hold between clenched teeth. Your mouth and throat get unbearably dry.'[320]

The desire to be able to see properly and the urge to end the suffocating feeling sometimes led to masks being taken off too quickly. Remarque's Bäumer saw a shelter full of young recruits,

> their faces blue and their lips black. In one of the shell holes some of them have taken their gas-masks off too soon; they didn't realize that the gas lies longest down at the bottom, and when they saw others without their masks they tore theirs off, and swallowed enough to burn their lungs to pieces. There is no hope for them.[321]

Even the earliest masks were effective in the sense that gas was no longer seen as a weapon that would decide the outcome of the war, but the discomfort of wearing them was so great that many soldiers continued to opt for the sock soaked

317 Remarque, *Im Westen*, 55; Noyes, *Stretcher-Bearers*, 111–12
318 Jünger, *In Stahlgewittern*, 55–6; *Storm of Steel*, 79
319 Johannsen, *Vier von der Infanterie*, 30
320 Macdonald, *Somme*, 316
321 Remarque, *Im Westen*, 96–7

in urine.[322] The improved protective clothing that came later was never really accepted, although it offered almost total security when properly used. Ronald Dorgelès called the gas mask 'This pig snout which represented the war's true face.'[323] Hanbury-Sparrow wrote:

> We gaze at one another like goggle-eyed, imbecile frogs. The mask makes you feel only half a man. You can't think. The air you breathe has been filtered of all save a few chemical substances. A man doesn't live on what passes through the filter – he merely exists. He gets the mentality of a wide-awake vegetable. You yourself were always miserable when you couldn't breathe through your nose. The clip on the gas mask prevents that.[324]

In other words, while the often odourless, sometimes invisible and always inaudible gas made the war seem even more inhuman than it already was, the clothing intended to protect men against gas had exactly the same impact.[325] There is a paradox here. Dispersing when under attack is a physically beneficial but psychologically detrimental reaction; similarly, clothing designed to protect against gas was good for the body but bad for the mind. Gas was a major cause of neurosis and so was the clothing designed to protect against it.[326]

As we have seen, the gas war proper started in April 1915, but this was not the first time chemists achieved an effect in the field. Tear-gas, for example, was already familiar. At Neuve Chapelle on 27 October 1914 the Germans had fired several hundred 105 mm howitzer shells filled with a gas called dianisidine. In March 1915 the French were bombarded with tear-gas at Nieuport. These gases were little more than irritants and the Allies barely took account of them. In the first gas attacks on the Eastern Front, futile from a military point of view, xylyl bromide and xylylene bromide were used, and this did not pass without comment. The Dutch periodical *Het Leven* (Life) reported in early 1915 on a German tear-gas attack near the Polish town of Bolimow. The Russians informed their allies about the attack, although it had caused them little difficulty, partly because the low temperatures had transformed the gas into a solid. The British and French paid scant attention.

Despite these incidents, the notion that it was Germany that started the gas war requires some qualification. Both sides had conducted experiments to study the military application of gas and had built up large stockpiles. In August 1914 the

322 Prior & Wilson, *Passchendaele*, 16; Winter, *Death's Men*, 124

323 Eksteins, *Rites of Spring*, 163

324 Winter, *Death's Men*, 124

325 Verdoorn, *Arts en Oorlog*, 367

326 Macdonald, *1915*, 500, 507; Brants & Brants, *Velden van weleer*, 115; Ellis, *Eye-Deep*, 65–9; Babington, *Shell-Shock*, 176; Winter, *Death's Men*, 124; Holmes, *Firing Line*, 213; Eksteins, *Rites of Spring*, 163; Macdonald, *Passchendaele*, 222; Wilson, *Myriad Faces*, 128

French army went to war with around 30,000 shells containing a bromide-based concoction. Shortly after war broke out, the Germans got hold of a letter in which the French high command warned its troops about artillery shells that would release vapours after an explosion, irritating the eyes, nose and throat. They called them turpinite shells, since the gas had been invented by the Paris-based chemist and explosives expert Eugène Turpin, who in 1884 had discovered the explosive picric acid, known as melinite, that gave the world its first explosive shells. During the First World War, melinite was replaced initially by trinitrotoluene (TNT) and later by a mixture of TNT and ammonium nitrate known as amatol.[327]

More and more German soldiers were admitted to hospital with symptoms of poisoning. During the Battle of Argonne, turpinite drove some German troops to despair. In September 1914 both the British and the French had bought up supplies of chlorine gas and the French especially had considerable stocks of gas munitions by the time of the German gas attack in April the following year.[328]

This suggests that the British and French governments should not have been particularly indignant, indeed probably were not, when the Germans deployed their chlorine gas. It also explains why they were able to supply their troops with gas masks so quickly. It was a question of who would be the first to start using 'the real stuff'. The reluctance to do so was probably slightly greater among the British and to a lesser extent the French than among the Germans, however, and none of this alters the fact that it was the Germans who were the first to bring their heavy gas cylinders to bear. They were so heavy that men had to pause repeatedly, taking four hours to carry a single cylinder the mile and a half from the depot to the front line.[329]

Partly in response to France's turpinite shells, or so they claimed, German scientists working for chemicals giants like Bayer, Badische Anilin and IG-Farben were encouraged to put their knowledge to practical military use. A *Kriegschemische Abteilung* (Chemical Warfare Department) was established under the leadership of a prominent chemist at Berlin's Kaiser Wilhelm Institute for Physical Chemistry whom we have already met, Fritz Haber. He introduced the idea that the use of chlorine gas, developed before the war, in large quantities within a small area would enable the Germans to regain the initiative despite inferior manpower and shortages of equipment, bringing them ultimate victory. Experiments on animals had shown it to have a powerful effect on all living beings. Haber was concerned about being prosecuted for war crimes, but in 1918, while the war was still being fought, he was awarded the Nobel Prize for chemistry for his pre-war discovery of a procedure for synthesizing ammonia from nitrogen. This discovery had enabled

327 De Vos, *Van Gifgas tot Penicilline*, 18; De Vos, *De Eerste Wereldoorlog*, 69; Keegan, *First World War*, 214

328 Koch, *Menschenversuche*, 228; Simkins, *World War I*, 66; Wilson, *Myriad Faces*, 126; Brants & Brants, *Velden van weleer*, 99; Macdonald, *Roses of No Man's Land*, 84; Richter, *Chemical Soldiers*, 7; Heijster, *Ieper*, 106–8

329 Eksteins, *Rites of Spring*, 160–61; Macdonald, *1915*, 485

the Germans to make artificial fertilizer, but it also meant that German explosives manufacturers were no longer dependent on imported saltpetre, access to which could be reduced considerably or even cut off altogether in wartime. Haber had therefore proved his worth even before the war. It is quite conceivable that without the new chemical procedure he developed, Germany would not have been able to continue fighting for very long after 1914.

Although he had converted to Protestantism, Haber's Jewish origins would make him *persona non grata* in post-1933 Germany. Around the time Hitler came to power he renounced his nationalistic beliefs to some extent, in protest against Nazi practices, and in May 1933 he resigned his post. But because of his activities and achievements during the Great War, the holding of a commemorative meeting in early 1935 on the first anniversary of Haber's death was not such a courageous act as we might imagine. Although officially forbidden by the regime, the event drew a large number of guests. His closest colleague during the war, Otto Hahn, who later also became a Nobel Prize winner for chemistry and was one of the leading scientists behind the German atomic research programme in the thirties and forties, gave the official commemorative speech. Twenty-one years earlier, Hahn had told Haber that the use of gas went against the laws of war, but Haber had brushed this remark aside, reminding Hahn about the French turpinite shells.

As soon as First Ypres ended in late 1914, the Germans became determined to shorten the line of the salient. Big Berthas were brought up, and the army on the ground was given permission to use gas. Yet it was more or less by chance that Ypres became the place where gas was first deployed. The general in command at Ypres, unlike his colleagues, had no objection to the use of gas on a large scale. That is to say, he did not persist in his initial objection; he too had been disgusted by the idea at first. On 22 April 1915, at half past five in the afternoon, having waited all day for a favourable wind, the Germans released dozens of tons of chlorine gas from their cylinders. It formed a cloud 6 kilometres wide and 900 metres deep that blew towards British and French trenches between Steenstrate and Poelcapelle. That this particular sector was hit was also more or less a matter of chance. The gas cylinders available there were being held in reserve in case the wind was not right in the sectors where the attack was supposed to take place. The Belgians to the north of Steenstrate were barely affected at all, but two unsuspecting and unprepared Algerian divisions got the shock of their lives. Those who could fled in total panic, but men directly hit were unable to move and died a slow and horrific death. Five thousand Algerians are said to have been killed and between 10,000 and 15,000 to have suffered poisoning of varying degrees of severity, although it is conceivable that these figures were exaggerated somewhat by British propaganda.[330] Canadian J.D. Keddie of the 48th Royal Highlanders recalled the first attack.

---

330 Friedländer, *Nazi-Duitsland*, 159–60, 420; Heijster, *Ieper*, 105–6; De Vos, *Van Gifgas tot Penicilline*, 19, 86, 105; Keegan, *First World War*, 214; Eksteins, *Rites of Spring*,

> We did not get the full effect of [the gas], but what we did was enough for me. It makes the eyes smart and run. I became violently sick, but this passed off fairly soon. … The next thing I noticed was a horde of Turcos making for our trenches behind the firing line; some were armed, some unarmed. The poor devils were absolutely paralysed with fear.[331]

The advancing Germans saw nothing but the dead or seriously wounded. There was no resistance at all. Binding noted in his diary on 24 April: 'The consequences of the successful gas attack are ghastly. Poisoning people – I don't know. Of course, first the world will be furious and then it will do likewise. The dead all lie on their backs with their fists clenched. The entire battlefield is yellow.'[332]

Up to a point Binding was right. The world was furious and the world did likewise, but the attack was not really a success. The gap left by the Algerians was quickly closed by Canadian troops, although they too faced gas attacks in the days that followed. Sixty per cent of Canadians affected had to be sent home. When the war ended, many were still unable to work and would remain so for the rest of their lives, which were expected to be short.[333]

The fact that the Allies were unprepared for a gas attack was their own fault, incidentally, even aside from their failure to respond to the Russian warning mentioned earlier. There had been many indications such an attack was coming. Several days earlier the Germans had wrongly accused the British of using gas, which the Allies might have chosen to see, indeed perhaps ought to have seen, as an attempt to justify their own deployment. The British had intercepted a message indicating that the Germans had arranged for 20,000 primitive gas masks to be made in Ghent, and when the British took Hill 60 at Ypres they detected a stinging smell of gas, which was dismissed as tear-gas. The French had even captured a German soldier who told them in detail about cylinders of chemicals. The gas mask he had with him ought to have been enough to persuade them to take his story seriously, but he gave so many details that the British thought it was a trick and that they were dealing with a double agent. The man received a ten year jail sentence from a German court in the early 1930s, incidentally, for leaking so much information. It eventually transpired that he had been carrying a gas mask because

---

161; Macdonald, *1914–1918*, 81; Billstein, 'Gashölle Ypern', 101–4, 110; 'Jahrhundert der Kriege', 120–21; Audoin-Rouzeau & Becker, *'14–'18*, 210

331 Macdonald, *1915*, 194

332 Heering, *Zondeval*, 226; Binding, *Aus dem Kriege*, 89

333 Winter, *Death's Men*, 121; Brants & Brants, *Velden van weleer*, 99; Koch, *Menschenversuche*, 228; Macdonald, *1915*, 192–4; Richter, *Chemical Soldiers*, 8; Heijster, *Ieper*, 109; De Vos, *Van Gifgas tot Penicilline*, 86–7, 93, 105; De Vos, *De Eerste Wereldoorlog*, 83

of a direct hit on German cylinders in March 1915; the first four soldiers killed by German gas were Germans.[334]

Flemish civilians too noticed they were having breathing difficulties on 22 April. In nearby Boezinge they spotted a French officer coming to size up the situation. When he got to a bridge, his horse refused to cross. He proceeded on foot and came face to face with a 'hallucinatory spectacle of stumbling, blood-spitting and dying soldiers. Some jumped into the water of the canal in search of relief for the burning pain in their chests, others rolled on the ground and tore open their clothes, throwing their weapons down at random'.[335]

It should be remembered that despite the enormous panic, despite the large number of dead and wounded and despite the fact that a German soldier in a gas mask would not have to fight as he had assumed but instead could simply walk past or over the dead and dying, this attack was no more than a local success. The same goes for the attempts that followed, on 24 April and 1, 5, 8 and 24 May. It was soon clear that the breakthrough, let alone the final victory that Haber had hoped for or perhaps even expected, would not be brought about by gas.[336] This was a conclusion the soldiers who had been surprised by the early gas attacks found hard to believe at this point. Sergeant Billy Hay, for example, wrote about his first experiences with gas in the spring of 1915:

> Of course, the chaps were all gasping and couldn't breathe, and it was ghastly, especially for chaps that were wounded – terrible for a wounded man to lie there! The gasping, the gasping! And it caused a lot of mucus, phlegm, your eyes were stinging as well. You couldn't stop to help anybody, even if he was your brother, he'd still be lying there badly injured, and you mustn't help, so you'd got to go on with the attack or there'd be nobody to contend with the attack. … There was all the chaps lying about wounded and crying. That was heart-rending, that was, all night long we could hear them.[337]

Most casualties arrived at aid posts only after several hours and by then the effects had reached the next stage. Their eyes still stung, their dry throats still burned, they were still unable to speak, but the nausea and vomiting were over. The masses of yellow foam that had streamed incessantly from their mouths and noses had now turned to mucus, spotted red from the bleeding of their lungs and airways. Lack of oxygen had already exhausted them and their chests were swollen to twice the normal size by the accumulation of fluid. If pneumonia followed, which was often the case, they were past hope and medical intervention was futile.[338] Lieutenant-

334 Brants & Brants, *Velden van weleer*, 99; De Vos, *Van Gifgas tot Penicilline*, 87, 91, 105

335 Brants & Brants, *Velden van weleer*, 101–2

336 Prior & Wilson, *Passchendaele*, 15; De Vos, *De Eerste Wereldoorlog*, 83

337 Macdonald, *1914–1918*, 83–4

338 Macdonald, *1915*, 233

Colonel G.W.G. Hughes of the medical corps would never forget the first gas attacks at Ypres:

> Men lying all along the side of the road between Poperinghe and Ypres, exhausted, gasping, frothing yellow mucus from their mouths, their faces blue and distressed. It was dreadful, and so little could be done for them. I have seen no description in any book or paper that exaggerated or even approached in realization of the horror, the awfulness of these gassed cases. One came away from seeing or treating them longing to be able to go straight away at the Germans and to throttle them, to pay them out in some sort of way for their devilishness. Better for a sudden death than this awful agony.[339]

One person who died as an indirect result of the first gas attack at Ypres was Fritz Haber's wife, the chemist Clara Haber. She was a firm opponent, unlike her husband, of the use of his scientific work to develop weapons of war, regarding it as an abuse of his achievements. In her view it was wrong to use science in the way it was now being used by medical researchers on both sides, whether to support the war effort or to 'prove' the physical and mental inferiority of the enemy. Pure science was becoming applied science and experiments performed in its name – in prisoner-of-war camps, for example – were designed to support conclusions drawn in advance. She believed the military and political use of scientific knowledge was a perversion of that knowledge, which ought to be employed for the benefit of mankind as a whole rather than for its destruction in the name of any one army, people or race. She had already protested to her husband several times, but he paid no attention and went on with his eventually successful attempts to convince the German military leadership of the efficacy of chlorine gas as a weapon of war. The attack at Ypres had made absolutely clear what her husband was doing. After a furious argument between them, Clara shot herself through the heart. Haber had chosen not to halt his work for her sake, so he would have to go on without her. His wife's death did not prevent him from travelling to the Eastern Front a few days later to prepare for the deployment of poison gas there, which illustrates the fact that it was not a particularly happy marriage even aside from this difference of opinion. The gas attack at Ypres almost certainly prompted his wife's suicide, but it was probably not the fundamental cause.[340]

Before long the Allies responded in kind, but with even less military success. When the British tried to direct a cloud of chlorine gas towards enemy lines on 25 September 1915 at Loos in Artois, the wind refused to cooperate. The gas was intended to compensate for inferior artillery firepower, but the outcome was a bitter experience and an abject failure. Since the gas was to be deployed in support of a French attack, the British were unable to wait until the most suitable

---

339 Eksteins, *Rites of Spring*, 162; Richter, *Chemical Soldiers*, 6

340 Documentary: Förscher für den Krieg. Fritz Haber, ARTE-television, 24–07–2002; Audoin-Rouzeau & Becker, *'14–'18*, 144–5, 209, 212–14

moment, as the Germans had done at Ypres. They were forced to release the gas on a specified day at a pre-arranged time. There was a bad omen too. Sixty minutes before zero hour a German trench mortar scored a direct hit at one of their gas emplacements, filling a trench with chlorine. As already indicated, this would not be the last unfortunate incident of its kind.[341]

There was of course no way to control the direction in which gas moved once it had been released from the cylinders. Not until 1916 did the armies develop techniques and stockpiles that allowed them to fire shells containing gas. In some sectors the wind turned easterly, blowing the cloud back towards Allied trenches, and methods of calculating exactly how the air would carry the gas and arranging its release accordingly were in any case far from reliable. On this occasion it was impossible to use anything like the intended amount of gas and great clouds of chlorine hung over the men who released it. Sergeant-Major Morrison was so frustrated that he carried several cylinders towards the German trenches, where he did his best to puncture them by firing at them. He eventually succeeded. A jet of liquid chlorine killed him. Richard C. Gale of the Specials described the walk back as a terrible nightmare of mud, death and destruction, and L.W. White said that he had to walk over corpses. In short, the gas probably worked to some degree as a smokescreen to the British advance, but there can be no doubt that more British soldiers than Germans were killed or wounded by Allied gas that day. Among the dead that day was Rudyard Kipling's only son – although it is doubtful whether gas had anything to do with that. Kipling immediately ceased writing poetry that glorified war.[342]

Most British troops involved escaped alive, but theirs was an unenviable fate all the same. G.O. Mitchell of the Specials was forced to leave the trenches for about twelve hours.

> I was in a very exhausted condition, couldn't breathe properly and had a deuce of a headache. Going down the communication trench and across the fields near Vermelles were streams of wounded of all descriptions, a sight I don't want to see again but will have to I'm afraid.[343]

A doctor remembered the day as a long nightmare in which only one thing was clear: that he would have to treat more and more wounded every minute.[344] All told, the offensive at Loos, which lasted a mere few days, cost the British 50,000

341 Richter, *Chemical Soldiers*, 61–2; Gilbert, *First World War*, 200; Winter, *Death's men*, 256

342 Prior & Wilson, *Passchendaele*, 16; Simkins, *World War I*, 66; Richter, *Chemical Soldiers*, 69, 71, 77, 83, 92

343 Richter, *Chemical Soldiers*, 82

344 Richter, *Chemical Soldiers*, 83

casualties. Not far short of five per cent were victims of gas, quite a high figure compared to other offensives in which gas was used.[345]

Loos left no one in any doubt that a gas arms race had started. Both sides quickly began training special troops, an overall total of some 17,000 men. The French established a new service, to be run by General Ozil, the British had their Special Brigade commanded by Charles Howard Foulkes, whose title was Director of Gas Services, and the Americans developed a Chemical Corps, headed by Amos Fries, who argued more fiercely than anyone that gas was a humane weapon. The Germans had set up Gas Regiment Peterson back in February 1915, named after its commander Otto Peterson, the colonel who was in charge of military preparations for the attack at Ypres. In 1916 they added a second regiment, and the German high command was expanded to include an *Inspekteur der Gasregimente im Großen Hauptquartier* (Inspector of Gas Regiments at General Staff HQ). Competition increased as new gases were concocted to penetrate the latest gas masks. In a fairly disorganized, sometimes chaotic quest, with doctors and pharmacologists playing an increasingly prominent role, thousands of new and diverse agents were discovered and tested in laboratories on both sides. Most were never deployed, some because they were too dangerous even for the lab technicians working with them, others, such as British green star, because they were easily ignited and proved lethal in field tests, and others, such as yellow star, because they corroded the cylinders, causing them to leak. Nevertheless, an average of once a fortnight a new gas was released somewhere along the front, including nerve agents such as prussic acid. Of all the various types, 38 were used on a significant scale: 12 kinds of tear-gas, 15 kinds of suffocating gas, 3 blood-poisoning gases, 4 gases that burned the skin and 4 that affected the stomach. During the war a total of 136,200 tons of chemicals were released into the atmosphere. Even the small Belgian army, which was not subjected to severe gas attacks until mid-1917 and used gas itself only from late October that year, had fired between 190,000 and 260,000 gas shells by the end of the war.[346] Its use still required justification. In *De Legerbode* (Army Messenger) of 1 November 1917 readers were told:

> The wind being favourable, a cloud of suffocating gas was thrown at the enemy bank of the Yser; this is the first time it has been released from Belgian trenches, since until now its use has been repugnant to us, despite the memory of all our comrades who were suffocated to death by it at Steenstrate in 1915.[347]

---

345 Richter, *Chemical Soldiers*, 86

346 Richter, *Chemical Soldiers*, 182; De Vos, *Van Gifgas tot Penicilline*, 86, 93; Koch, *Menschenversuche*, 228–9; Cooter, Harrison & Sturdy, *War, Medicine and Modernity*, 66, 72, 74; Eckart & Gradmann, 'Medizin', 211; Russell, *War and Nature*, 39, 53–4, 60–63, 65–6, 68, 71–2

347 De Vos, *Van Gifgas tot Penicilline*, 106

Although several kinds of gas, especially phosgene, proved effective, experiments continued, since it was believed that the use of a wide diversity of gases would make it harder for the enemy to take defensive measures, even though some products were virtually useless as weapons. All this experimentation is illustrative of the fact that the First World War altered the relationship between military men and scientists. Before 1914 they had occupied separate worlds, but now the distinction was eroding steadily, like the distinction between civilian and military life in general. Pure research, once it became focused on the military situation, increasingly transformed itself into applied research. More and more scientists began to see the laboratory as their battlefield, just as front-line doctors and psychologists increasingly regarded the battlefield as their laboratory.[348]

Gas became more and more powerful. It could be lethal even in small doses. Graves tells of an order frequently issued before mid-1916, telling men simply to continue advancing during a gas attack without stopping to put on their masks. In one company in which Graves served this led to twelve deaths, casualties of one of the stronger types of gas.[349] Constant inventiveness and a steady increase in quantity and deployment brought a growth in the number of gas casualties despite improvements to protective clothing. In 1918 there was a considerable escalation in the gas war. At least one in every five German shells was filled with gas. The British army, for instance, had more gas casualties to deal with that year – over 110,000 – than in the previous 3 years put together. The proportion of German casualties attributable to gas, only 0.85 per cent in mid-1915, reached 4.6 per cent by 1918, firstly because gas discipline in the German army had begun to decline and secondly because in June 1918 the Allies started using mustard gas. Whereas in May a little over 3,000 German gas casualties reached hospital, in June 6,000 were treated and in July no fewer than 12,800. One of the last men to die of gas poisoning was Ludwig Hirsch, a German NCO who succumbed in early October. A week before he had still been in good spirits, at least that was the impression he gave his family.

> Everything lost, life itself saved, that sums up the past two days. My naked self, my uniform, steel helmet, gas mask, that's all I brought back. ... We had to wear our respirators for over ten hours. In our dugout there were four deaths from gas. I got a fair dose of gas myself and I'm having a lot of difficulty breathing. Every twenty metres I have to stop for ten minutes to get my breath back. ... I'll certainly have to go to hospital. Don't be alarmed, in a few weeks everything will be back in balance again. We can't thank our God enough that he has so mercifully spared me for you.[350]

---

348 Richter, *Chemical Soldiers*, 182; Cooter, Harrison & Sturdy, *War, Medicine and Modernity*, 74; Petri, *Eignungsprüfung*, 45–77

349 Graves, *Goodbye*, 176

350 *Kriegsbriefe gefallener Deutscher Juden*, 58–9

The US army, fresh to the war and inexperienced with gas, calculated that 31.5 per cent of its wounded in 1918 were gas casualties. The fact that the American Expeditionary Force had always regarded gas as a major threat now appeared justified also from a military point of view. Nevertheless, or even better: this leads to the conclusion, 1918 was the year in which gas defeated all the previous ones from a humanitarian perspective too. Although the number of deaths from gas declined as a percentage of those affected, absolute numbers steadily increased.[351]

The British had their red star and later blue star, which stayed closer to the ground. These in turn were replaced by white star, British phosgene, which was first used on the Somme. The German counterparts to these red, blue and white stars were *Grünkreuz*, *Blaukreuz* or *Gelbkreuz* (green-, blue- or yellow-cross gases). German gas was transported in containers marked with a cross, the colour of which indicated the type of gas they contained. Blue-cross gases irritated the eyes, nose and throat; green-cross gases, such as chlorine and phosgene, damaged the lungs; and yellow-cross gases like mustard gas burned the skin and, when inhaled, the airways. Some types of gas were simply known as blue cross or green cross.[352] Sometimes two gases were used simultaneously, which led men to talk of motley crosses. Hahn, who attributed the lack of scruples about using gas to the mind-poisoning effects of the substances themselves, took a job at Bayer in Leverkusen:

> [There] I was engaged in the development of a gas that was a mixture of chloromethyl, chloroformate, and phosgene, which was originally merely called an 'admixture'.
>
> Besides this, other new gases, Grünkreuz (green-cross) and Blaukreuz (blue-cross), [...] were being developed. Blaukreuz was a strong irritant that could partially penetrate gasmasks. Grünkreuz was a typical poison gas, resembling phosgene. When the two substances were used simultaneously – the mixture was called Buntkreuz (motley cross) – those attacked were forced to tear off their gasmasks, leaving themselves exposed to the poison gas.[353]

An American cavalryman called George Patton fought at Passchendaele. He wrote to his wife: 'The Germans shoot a gas which makes people vomit and when they

351 Verdoorn, *Arts en Oorlog*, 367; Holmes, *Firing Line*, 212; Winter, *Death's Men*, 125; Eckart & Gradmann, *Die Medizin*, 143, 145, 147, 150

352 Klee, *Auschwitz*, 269; Brants & Brants, *Velden van weleer*, 115; Winter, *Death's Men*, 121; Simkins, *World War I*, 66–8

353 Eckart & Gradmann, *Die Medizin*, 145; Macdonald, *1914–1918*, 222

take off the masks to spit, they shoot the deadly gas at them. It is a smart idea, is it not?' Apparently it was, since the British quickly adopted the same practice.[354]

The 'heavier than air' gases used later in the war, such as blue star, had one major disadvantage. Although they did more damage to the enemy, since they sank into craters and other war-related or natural geographical features, they failed to act as a smokescreen, making advancing troops an easier target for enemy machine-guns.[355] This serves as a reminder that in judging the effectiveness of a specific gas we should look not only at the direct casualties but at those hit by bullets, mortar bombs and shells as a result of its use.

Phosgene (COCL2) was chemically related to the chlorine gas used at Ypres (CL2) but twenty times stronger. It was practically odourless and invisible and when first inhaled it was only a slight irritant, so many men did not realize in time that they were breathing a lethal concentration of gas. This made it greatly feared. It was the strongest of the green-cross gasses and inhalation almost always led to serious lung damage. As it began to take effect, a man would become short of breath and start to belch; the pulse doubled, the face became ashen, and according to Denis Winter two litres of yellow fluid an hour rose in the lungs. Slow death by drowning took about two days. Not without reason, the Germans called phosgene the queen of battle agents.

Phosgene was one of the first gases to be deployed in shells rather than cylinders. This method of delivery was tried out on a small scale at Ypres in late 1915, as a trial run for larger scale deployment at Verdun. The first Frenchmen to confront it there were amazed to see the shells, which made a soft buzzing noise, fail to explode on landing. They thought that for some incomprehensible reason the Germans were firing a large number of duds. They soon realized their mistake. They detected 'a pungent, sickening odour of putrefaction compounded with the mustiness of stale vinegar', as one of the survivors described it. They put on their masks, but the coughing and spluttering only got worse, not only because they had already inhaled a substantial dose but because better masks were needed to filter out this new gas. Their condition was not improved by the fact that wearing a gas mask makes breathing difficult at the best of times. Phosgene killed anything with which it came into contact. The countryside around Verdun was stripped of its last remaining flora and fauna. Cavalry horses writhed on the ground, dying, their mouths coated with foul foam. The doctors who came to help the wounded and priests giving the last rights had to work wearing gas masks, and even so, from time to time one would clutch his throat and fall to the ground. Green cross was appropriately named, since the victims' grey complexions changed after death to a dull green.

---

354 Gilbert, *First World War*, 362; Andriessen, *De oorlogsbrieven van Unteroffizier Carl Heller*, 148

355 Richter, *Chemical Soldiers*, 223

The gas turned against its inventor, incidentally. After sniffing his new invention he was able to enjoy a late-night party before he died.[356]

Phosgene may have been the most feared gas but it was not the most deadly. That was the five times stronger yellow cross, better known to the French and Belgians as *Ypérite*, since it had first been deployed just before Third Ypres. The British called it mustard gas, because although almost odourless it smelled slightly of mustard. Under its German name *Lost* – an abbreviation of the two chemists who had prepared the gas for military use, W. Lommel, working at Bayer, and Wilhelm Steinkopf, who worked under Haber at the Kaiser Wilhelm Institute – it became notorious in the next war, when new applications were tried out at the infamous Nazi 'medical' institute of Alt Rehse.

Mustard gas, dichlorodiethyl sulphide, was discovered in 1860 by the British scientist Frederick Guthrie and later described in detail by a German, Victor Meyer, who developed an 'improved' version. It was not actually a gas at all but a brownish liquid. Shells containing mustard gas delivered it in the form of a mist of fine droplets that would spread far and wide. Generally speaking, in fact, the word 'gas' is slightly misleading. Only a minority of the chemicals used, such as chlorine, were gases in the strict sense of the word, meaning substances that exist in vapour form at ordinary atmospheric temperatures. Many agents were liquids, a few were solids. All, however, were referred to as 'gas'.

Mustard gas penetrated clothing and caused painful, suppurating blisters. The only chance of escaping was to be lucky enough to spot the liquid on the ground and move away in time. Its fluid and corrosive character ought to have put a definitive end to the wearing of the kilt in modern warfare, since the garment offered almost no protection at all. But the authorities would not hear of that. The kilt represented an ancient tradition, and skirted Scots advancing – the Germans called them 'women from hell' – were a daunting sight on the battlefield.[357]

No adequate protection against mustard gas was found until after the war. The first signs would become visible only two to six hours after inhalation: slight swelling and red blotches. Perhaps this explains why it was rejected as useless when British and French chemists first tested it in 1916. They decided it was insufficiently noxious, having failed to wait long enough for it to take effect. Its low toxicity in early tests may also have been due to the less effective method of synthesis used by the Allies. Once this problem had been solved, mustard gas was found to be extremely poisonous, and the Allies deployed it from June 1918 onwards. The danger of retaliation had earlier prompted Haber to warn the German high command not to use *Lost* until absolutely confident that very soon after its deployment the war would end in victory.

356 Macdonald, *Roses of No Man's Land*, 84; Klee, *Auschwitz*, 269; Winter, *Death's Men*, 122; Horne, *Price of Glory*, 285–7; De Vos, *De Eerste Wereldoorlog*, 92

357 Moynihan, *People at War*, 80; Liddle & Cecil, *Facing Armageddon*, 318; Billstein, 'Gashölle Ypern', 119–20

Once contaminated, a soldier first started to sneeze, as if he had caught the 'flu. After about twelve hours the seriousness of his condition became obvious. The skin developed large blisters, the eyes became extremely painful and swollen. Vomiting began. Body temperature rose. Pneumonia developed. The bronchi and mucous membranes corroded away. Before long, jaundice consumed his body from inside and out, and all this after contact with extraordinarily tiny quantities. Men who had absorbed larger amounts sometimes coughed up great chunks of their bronchial tubes, lost their seared genitals, or developed burns that went right through to the bone. The pain was unbearable and the worst affected patients had to be tied to their beds, where they usually spent four or five weeks, many leaving only for burial. Casualties hovered on the verge of death much longer than victims of other gases, who were generally out of danger if they survived the first 48 hours. Death from yellow cross usually occurred between one and three weeks after poisoning, mainly as a result of secondary infections to the airways.[358]

Mustard gas was an enduring weapon of war in the sense that it was quite stable and remained potent for a long time. The British used it less as an offensive weapon than to strengthen their defence by contaminating large stretches of ground, so that the enemy would be forced to withdraw. Nevertheless, because men often realized too late that they had been exposed to it (the slight odour was usually undetectable amid all the other smells of the battlefield), it was found to have offensive uses as well. The innovative Allied strategy of deliberately spreading fear and terror became the main aim of gas deployment from 1918 onwards. Denis Winter claims that in the last year of the war mustard gas was responsible for 90 per cent of gas casualties and fourteen per cent of casualties overall. Soldiers will not have been sorry that the first shipment of an even more effective American version of mustard gas called Lewisite did not reach the coast of Europe until after the armistice had been signed.[359]

Mustard gas was first used near Ypres, between Wieltje and Hooge in mid-July 1917. A.F.P. Christison said the next day:

> C Company under Captain Harry Rowan was on my right. .. [He] heard the gas alarm and his men put on respirators. After wearing them for some time in the heat of the morning and no attack developing they thought the original alarm was false as no gas had been smelt. What they did not know was that this was mustard gas, had no smell, and had delayed action. The C Company trenches were saturated with [the] stuff and the whole Company were struck down. By nightfall every officer and man was either dead or in hospital.[360]

358 Liddle, *Passchendaele in Perspective*, 195; Klee, *Auschwitz*, 264, 269; Ellis, *Eye-Deep*, 66–7; Winter, *Death's Men*, 122; Eksteins, *Rites of Spring*, 163; Heijster, *Ieper*, 146; De Vos, *Van Gifgas tot Penicilline*, 92, 105; Eckart & Gradmann, *Die Medizin*, 145–8

359 Winter, *Death's Men*, 122, 124; De Vos, *Van Gifgas tot Penicilline*, 97

360 Macdonald, *1914–1918*, 222

More than 50,000 shells were fired bearing a yellow cross. Again the number of casualties per shell was negligible, but the sheer quantity meant doctors had to work day and night. Several thousand Allied soldiers were poisoned and 87 died. Over the next 3 weeks a million shells, 500 dead and thousands more wounded followed. Within a month and a half, almost 20,000 British soldiers had been affected by gas; many were blinded, either temporarily or permanently, and around 650 died within a week or 10 days of an attack. Five days after the Germans first deployed *Lost* the British retaliated. A hundred thousand shells containing chloropicrin, also known as 'PS', 'Aquinite' or 'Klop', were fired. Seventy-five Germans died.[361]

The doctors were generally unable to do anything for the most seriously affected. Major J.W. McNee of the British medical services described a typical case.

> Exposed to mustard gas on the morning of 28th July, 1917. Admitted to casualty clearing station on the evening of 29th July, suffering from severe conjunctivitis and superficial burns of face, neck and scrotum. Respiratory symptoms gradually developed and death occurred about one hundred hours after exposure to gas.[362]

In the days after the first mustard gas attack, the CCS at Mendringhem alone received more than a thousand gas casualties. Many were actually victims of the very first attack. They had crawled into shell-holes with yellow cross lying in the bottom where it had failed to evaporate and did not notice as it soaked into their clothes. After several days they emerged from their hiding places. Their uniforms had burned through in patches and their skin was covered in blisters.[363] Corporal H. Bale and his men faced eight hours of shelling with mustard gas in the summer of 1917.

> After about six hours, the masks were no good. They'd been neutralized, and we were starting to choke. … By morning, everyone was round the shell holes vomiting and they had to send quite a lot of people out to bring us in. We needed one on each side of us, we were in such a bad way. … By the time we got to Vlamertinghe we were blind, we couldn't see anything. They led us down into the dressing-station, sat us on a plank and told us, 'Open your mouths'. We waited with our mouths open and suddenly someone shot something like 200 per cent ammonia into your mouth. It nearly knocked the top of your head off. We got bathed and put into bed and I don't remember anything more till I woke up in hospital at the base. … I was there for a long time. Stone blind! I think the worst

361 Gilbert, *First World War*, 346–7, 351; Liddle, *Passchendaele in Perspective*, 195; Ellis, *Eye-Deep*, 65–6

362 Gilbert, *First World War*, 351

363 Macdonald, *Passchendaele*, 87

> part was when they opened your eyes to put droplets in them – it was just like boiling water dropping in! Then every day they bathed all the burned spots, and *that* was no joke. I remember my left thigh was nothing but a mass of matter.[364]

A humane weapon indeed. But Barbusse's Barque was right. Gas proves that despite all the rules of combat agreed at Geneva and The Hague, words like 'fair' and 'humane' are meaningless in total war. What counts is victory, irrespective of the means by which it is achieved.

*The lucky wound*

The lightly wounded stood a good chance of being sent back up to the line before very long. Those with serious wounds risked dying or being disabled for life. But there was an intermediate category: the Blighty, the *Heimatschuss*, the *bonne blessure*. Such a wound was the best of all ways to get out of the war. Being wounded meant there was no need to feel any guilt. A Blighty was serious enough to keep a man out for the duration, but not so serious that he would go through life horribly maimed. Soldiers had little respect for modern medicine, as we shall see, but its ability to heal wounds that would once have been fatal so that a man could set off home and say goodbye to the front for ever was generally welcomed. There were exceptions of course. Charles Ruck of the London Regiment, 63rd Division was hit in the knee during the *Kaiserschlacht* before he had a chance to engage the enemy. 'To end like this, without honour and glory – just a casualty! … I knew I had a Blighty one, but I didn't feel grateful that I'd been spared a worse fate.'[365]

A wound like his was rarely seen as a stroke of misfortune, indeed a man would thank God for his luck. The loss of a finger, a toe, or if necessary a hand or foot was an acceptable price to pay. A man would be called a lucky devil by his colleagues, and they meant it. He had a chance of growing old, perhaps even on a small war pension. Aside from their dislike of enforced idleness, this was one reason why some soldiers preferred to go into battle than to sit waiting in a trench. You could die either way, but the chances of a wound to the arm or leg were much higher during battle than in the trenches, where there was a greater likelihood of a nasty head injury.[366]

In his *Old Soldiers Never Die*, Frank Richards wrote that he was always hoping for 'a beautiful Blighty'.[367] The name comes, incidentally, from the Hindustani word 'bilayati', meaning 'foreign', which was used to refer to Britain. Farfadet,

364 Macdonald, *1914–1918*, 223

365 Macdonald, *To the Last Man*, 354; Latzko, *Menschen im Krieg*, 147; Johannsen, *Vier von der Infanterie*, 36

366 Graves, *Goodbye*, 95; Frey, *Pflasterkästen*, 299; Hynes, *Soldiers' Tale*, 71–2; Holmes, *Firing Line*, 183; Jünger, *Das Antlitz*, 105, 179; Brown, *Somme*, 76; Andriessen, *De oorlogsbrieven van Unteroffizier Carl Heller*, 168, 171, 205, 221–2

367 Fussell, *Bloody Game*, 111

another of the central characters in Barbusse's *Le Feu*, says: 'At the beginning ... I thought it odd when I heard people say they wanted a "good wound". But all the same, whatever you say, I understand now that after all it's the only thing a poor soldier can hope for that isn't totally mad.'[368] An American serving as a private in the Canadian army, one of the first men to go over the top on 1 July 1916, was hit in the wrist almost immediately. He turned round with a contented look and said: 'I've got mine. I'm off.'[369] Corporal A. Gale was wounded and knew immediately that it was a Blighty. It was a serious wound, but not fatal. 'I was thankful! I can remember what I thought before I passed out. … "Oh good! I'm on the way home."'[370] Ernst Toller remembered the case of a soldier who was hit by shrapnel while sitting on the latrine. 'Now he's living like a duke in hospital', was one comment.[371] On 20 September 1914 Walter Limmer wrote a letter to his parents, and what he told them makes clear once again that, among some German soldiers at least, enthusiasm for the war evaporated very soon after it began:

> My sweet, good parents, dear brothers and sisters! Yes, I can hardly believe it myself, but it is true, I'm on my way (wounded) to you and the *Heimat*. Oh, how happy I am to be able to see a less oppressive world again than this world of horror! At last I am released from the miserable thought that keeps ensnaring me of never seeing you and your world again. If no exceptional, appalling event stands in the way, then fate has given me back the hope of being able to look into your dear eyes again.[372]

Four days later Limmer died of tetanus.

Some men went looking for a wound. It was a risky business. Graves wrote about a soldier who stuck his hand in the air. Nothing happened. A whole arm. Again nothing happened. The man asked himself where the Germans had got to, peered over the parapet for an instant and got a bullet in the forehead. Another was more successful. Laughing, he walked back with three fingers missing on his right hand. On the way to the nearest aid post he was killed by a sniper.[373] Graves too was hoping for a wound. He was convinced it was his only chance of surviving the war. He volunteered for night patrols, which were known to be extremely hazardous, since he believed that although night patrols were dangerous, they were less deadly. After dark men shot more or less at random, making the chances of being wounded extremely high but at the same time reducing the likelihood of a vital organ being hit. Moreover, at night the aid posts were less busy.[374]

368 Barbusse, *Le Feu*, 61; *Under Fire*, 52
369 Keegan, *Face of Battle*, 270 (note)
370 Macdonald, *Somme*, 280
371 Toller, *Jugend in Deutschland*, 43
372 Witkop, *Kriegsbriefe*, 9
373 Graves, *Goodbye*, 94–5
374 Graves, *Goodbye*, 111

Graves was not alone. There were of course exceptions, men who chose to go on fighting if only because they did not want to let their comrades down,[375] but after a while many soldiers went looking for places where they had the maximum chance of a lucky wound. Later in the war many came to regard any wound as lucky, even if it was little more than a scratch, since it meant their moral obligation to go on fighting had evaporated. A wound, no matter how slight, made them feel they had done their duty and the army ought to leave them in peace.[376] These attitudes lead us on into the domain of morale, into the realm of the mind.

375 Holmes, *Firing Line*, 183

376 Keegan, *Face of Battle*, 270 (note); Jünger, *Das Antlitz*, 165

# Chapter 3
# Mind

## Introduction

Alongside physical suffering there was the inevitable problem of psychological trauma. It was not so much the nature of the problem as the numbers affected that surprised the medical profession. Mental illness and psychiatric damage, like physical ailments, were sometimes mild but they could be extremely serious, life-threatening or lifelong. They ranged from a degree of numbness in situations that would have been extremely shocking under normal circumstances, through utter brutalization or intense fear all the way to severe neurosis. In his evidence before the War Office Committee of Enquiry into Shell Shock,[1] Fuller said he had seen many men who were in a perfectly healthy frame of mind when they embarked for the continent whose first experience of being under fire caused physical fear, which quickly abated to be replaced by indifference. This mental state might then develop along a path that led to extreme nervousness and finally complete psychological breakdown. In other words, healthy fear degenerated first into indifference and later into obsessive fear, and the chances of this happening were greater than in previous wars because of new military technologies that increasingly depersonalized war. There was far less opportunity, after all, to work off one's emotions in modern conditions of combat than in a face to face battle.[2]

## From health to neurosis

### *Morale*

The constant awareness of death and destruction, the apparent hopelessness of the fighting and the complete lack of information all clearly impacted on morale. Depression, lethargy and drunkenness steadily increased and the number of cases of desertion and neurosis rose.[3] This trend was noticeable even before the conflict became bogged down in trench warfare, particularly among retreating French, Belgian and British troops. A British officer noted: 'We can do no more. The men fall in the ditches and lie there just to breathe. … The order comes to mount.

---

1 Liddle & Cecil, *Facing Armageddon*, 511

2 Leed, *No Man's Land*, 183; Shepard, *War of Nerves*, 57; Bourke, *Fear*, 204–5

3 Winter, *Death's Men*, 100; Wilson, *Myriad Faces*, 483

I ride bent over with my head on the horse's mane. We are thirsty and hungry. Indifference overcomes us.'[4]

Trench warfare accelerated the process. Soldiers asked themselves more and more openly what they were actually doing at the front. In the Belgian army, for example, just over 1,200 men were officially guilty of desertion in 1916, meaning that they had been absent without leave for three days or longer, compared to over 5,600 in 1917,[5] although these remained individual cases. To this day it seems astonishing that for all the talk of 'discipline with a revolver in the back' the refusal to go on fighting never became a major obstacle to the war effort – aside from the French mutiny of 1917, whose significance is sometimes overstated. Nevertheless, although the British at no stage experienced mass mutiny, at least not at the front, their armed forces did collapse in the spring of 1918, during the Germans' great spring offensive. The same happened to the German army to a far greater degree a few months before the end of the war, in fact there are indications that even in 1917 desertion was so widespread in some regiments as to justify the use of the word mutiny.[6] Among French and then British troops, the rot set in two and a half to three years after they first faced slaughter on a massive scale. Taking the number of soldiers who had gone to war in 1914 as a starting point, by the time soldiers rebelled many regiments had suffered losses totalling over a hundred per cent. Keegan claims that the German army took so long to collapse because the Germans had a steady series of victories to celebrate, some of great consequence, like Tannenberg, some comparatively short-lived, like the successful advances of the spring of 1918, so that despite all the traumas they suffered, morale remained high.[7] Hew Strachan qualifies Keegan's explanation rather intriguingly by saying that the collapse of an army can indicate problems of varying degrees of seriousness. The British retreat of spring 1918 was not an affair of anything like the magnitude of the German retreat six months later and there was never any real mutiny in the British armed forces, whereas by 11 o'clock on the morning of 11 November 1918, large parts of the German army had been refusing to fight for some time.[8]

In the French army too morale remained excellent at first, despite massive losses. During the first year of the war, for example, there were only slightly more than 500 cases of desertion. But the *bonhommes* were not professional soldiers. Like the Belgians, many suffered from what they called *le cafard*.[9] French artilleryman Sergeant Paul Lintier described it in his diary, in a passage partly deleted by the censor:

---

4 Murray, 'West at War', 269

5 De Schaepdrijver, *De Groote Oorlog*, 207; De Vos, *De Eerste Wereldoorlog*, 103

6 Liddle & Cecil, *Facing Armageddon*, 387

7 Keegan, *Face of Battle*, 271; Keegan, *First World War*, 421–2, 430–31

8 Macdonald, *Passchendaele*, 26

9 Lemercier, *Lettres*, 36–7; De Bruyne, *We zullen ze krijgen!*, 68, 86, 117

> There are days of uncurable depression. It seizes one suddenly, fetters one … one doesn't know why … and it is this that makes this gloomy feeling the more unsettling … a deep-seated, indefinable, indescribable malaise … waiting for some misfortune. One doesn't know what it will be. It's one more misery amongst so many miseries. One calls that *le cafard.*[10]

It usually stemmed from an irrepressible longing for hearth and home and the resumption of pre-war life. It might be prompted by events that were in themselves quite trivial, at least to anyone looking at them from the fireside, with his feet up, in times of peace and repose; as trivial as the shortening hours of daylight, say, or thoughts of home and family, or images of the past or indeed the future; as trivial as the stench that clung so tenaciously to the *poilu*. *Le Crapouillot* summed it up succinctly: 'We're sad because we smell bad.'[11] The main cause of despondency was not trivial at all, of course. It was the ubiquity of death, destruction and ugliness, and the all too realistic sense of being unable to do anything about it.[12]

After a while the front-line soldier would head off back to the rear. For fresh, untested troops on their way up the line, the sight of the men they were being sent to relieve must have been extremely sobering, rather like encountering creatures from another planet. Their expressions said all there was to say about *le cafard.* Lieutenant Georges Gaudy described his regiment returning from Douamont in May 1916.

> First came the skeletons of companies occasionally led by a wounded officer, leaning on a stick. All marched, or rather advanced in small steps, zigzagging as if intoxicated. … It was hard to tell the colour of their faces from that of their tunics. Mud had covered everything, dried off, and then another layer had been re-applied. … They said nothing. They had even lost the strength to complain. … It seemed as if these mute faces were crying something terrible, the unbelievable horror of their martyrdom. Some Territorials who were standing near me became pensive. They had that air of sadness that comes over one when a funeral passes by, and I overheard one say: 'It's no longer an army! These are corpses!'[13]

Barthas wrote of a distressing sight.

> Seven days of sleeplessness, tiredness, thirst, anxiety had made these healthy men, these splendid, disciplined companies, into a herd of bunched-up stragglers, sick men who seemed at death's door, and yet the joy of feeling alive and out of danger gave them an air of calm contentment.[14]

---

10 Lintier, *Le tube 1233*, 133–4; Ellis, *Eye-Deep*, 190–91
11 Liddle & Cecil, *Facing Armageddon*, 224
12 Audoin-Rouzeau, *Men at War*, 55–6; Winter & Baggett, *1914–18*, 241
13 Horne, *Price of Glory*, 188
14 Barthas, *Carnets*, 310

As we have seen, after the disastrous attack at the Chemin des Dames in April 1917, French conscripts were no longer willing to be used, for ever, without any limit, as cannon-fodder. The millions of deaths their ranks had accepted up to that point had destroyed their will to attack. Defending your country was one thing, but the attack, certainly the total offensive, the *attaque à outrance*, had become profoundly objectionable. Most were fully prepared to go on fighting, but fighting was not the same as being ordered to run – or even walk – blindly towards the enemy and almost certain death by people who had no idea of the practical unfeasibility of their notions about how to win a war. To make matters worse, only the most rudimentary medical facilities were available for the wounded. Barthas in particular emphasized this aspect. He condemned both the shortages of medical staff and the crude indolence of the people available.[15]

In early May 1917, the French 21st Colonial Infantry Regiment refused to follow orders, although it returned to the trenches after the instigators of the protest were arrested. Far from putting an end to the insubordination, this sequence of events marked the start of the mutiny. The high command was faced with unwilling soldiers in unprecedented numbers. In Champagne, for example, only two out of sixteen divisions were prepared to continue fighting. Nevertheless, only about 40,000 of the roughly two million French soldiers stationed at the front at the time were involved in the protests, and in many places there was no real mutiny at all. French troops did not refuse to obey orders while they were in the trenches, they simply refused to go back up the line once they had been moved to the rear. This was not the result of a plot by socialist opponents of the war as the army high command believed. The patriotic desire to defend the fatherland by warlike means was never in doubt or in danger.[16]

Fewer than 3,500 men were court-martialled for mutiny, all selected by their own officers and NCOs with the assent of fellow troops. Some 550 were condemned to death and nearly fifty ringleaders were actually shot. More than twenty thousand men vanished into prisons and punishment camps or were transferred to the African colonies. Several of the most intractable units were sent to the front, where they were deliberately fired on by their own artillery. The term friendly fire does not begin to cover this kind of cleansing of the ranks. In the end the main outcome was that a new high command took charge. Its officers came to take a look for themselves at the lives and sufferings of the French troops. The *attaque à outrance* was abandoned. If the mutiny was more a protest against incompetent leadership than a rebellion against the war, then it was in fact a success. But after the mutiny was over, the *Grande Armée* would never be truly *Grande* again.[17]

---

15 Winter & Baggett, *1914–1918*, 229–33, 241; Keegan, *First World War*, 358

16 Brants & Brants, *Velden van weleer*, 170–71; Babington, *Shell-Shock*, 97–8; Murray, 'West at War', 184; Audoin-Rouzeau & Becker, *'14–'18*, 147–9

17 Winter & Baggett, *1914–1918*, 241; Brants & Brants, *Velden van weleer*, 181–2; Murray, 'West at war', 285; Marix Evans, *Battles of the Somme*, 63; De Vos, *De Eerste*

The British experienced no mass mutiny at the front and the rate of self-wounding, often seen as an indicator of low spirits, was never excessive. This should not be taken to mean that morale in the British army was high. Time and again attacks achieved nothing, and the huge losses had a detrimental impact on the will to fight. The effects were written as clearly on the faces of British troops as on those of the *poilus*. In his book *The War of the Guns* artilleryman Aubrey Wade wrote about the reinforcements that walked past him in the direction of the front line during Third Ypres, wearing the expressions of men walking towards certain death. 'No words of greeting passed as they slouched along; in sullen silence they filed past one by one to the sacrifice.'[18]

On a small scale the British did have a mutiny of their own. At Étaples on the French coast they ran a fiercely hated base camp. On 12 September 1917 a corporal was due to be court-martialled for his part in a fight there. No one had any doubt that the sentence would be 'death by execution', but on the evening of 10 September, 1,500 others decided that they too must appear before the court martial. There was such dissatisfaction about conditions in the camp that this prosecution proved the final straw, although order was restored within a few days. The Étaples training camp, known as the Bull Ring, was notorious for its strict regime and miserable accommodation. Many were happy to be able to leave for the front line and one Scottish soldier described his time there as a fourteen-day sojourn in hell.[19] Owen twice mentioned in his letters the facial expressions of men at Étaples. On the first occasion, in late 1916, he wrote of faces like 'emotionless humps'. In late 1917, shortly after the Étaples mutiny, he described eyes with a look you would never encounter anywhere else; it could not be captured by any actor or painter, 'for it was a blindfold look, without expression, like a dead rabbit's'.[20]

Morale was no better on the other side of the front. In the summer of 1916 it occurred to Wilhelm Hermanns that the Germans had lost the Battle of Verdun.

> We saw a handful of soldiers, led by a captain, emerging slowly, one by one, between the trees. The captain asked what company we were, and then suddenly he started to weep. Was he suffering from *Kriegsneurose*? The captain said: 'When I saw you coming, I thought of how I came six days ago on this same road with one hundred men. Now look at those who are left!' We looked as we passed them. They were about twenty men. They walked like living plaster

*Wereldoorlog*, 130; Ellis, *Eye-Deep*, 183–5; Brants, 'Inleiding', 19; Keegan, *First World War*, 357; Audoin-Rouzeau & Becker, *'14–'18*, 148–9

18 Prior & Wilson, *Passchendaele*, 196; Wilson, *Myriad Faces*, 482

19 Blunden, *Undertones of War*, 17; Dallas & Gill, *Unknown Army*, 66–73, 139; Liddle, *Passchendaele in Perspective*, 361–2; Meire, *De Stilte van de Salient*, 66

20 Day Lewis, *Collected Poems*, 21, 173; Dallas & Gill, *Unknown Army*, 139; Holmes, *Firing Line*, 65; Dyer, *The Missing*, 40

> statues. Their faces stared at us like those of shrunken mummies, and their eyes seemed so huge that one saw nothing but eyes.[21]

In his memoirs, Zuckmayer looked back to a night in September 1916 on the Somme, after a week of bombardment and gas, without food or sleep. It was damp and cold and he was alone.

> When dawn began to break, and in the clear light our fate appeared sealed, I felt completely indifferent. ... I lay face down and raised my carbine from time to time. But the defensive instinct was dying. I wanted only to go on sleeping. To give up. To fade away.[22]

On this occasion he was literally on his own, but he was lonely in a more general sense too. All soldiers lived and died alone. 'In my memory the whole war is to me a single great inhuman loneliness, even when one was surrounded by people and longed for solitude.'[23]

Depression was made worse by homesickness and by the stories told by soldiers who had briefly been back to Germany on home leave, stories that made their comrades fear the worst about the circumstances in which their own families and friends were attempting to survive. For their part, soldiers on leave told people about the conditions in which they were fighting. This suggests that the much discussed wall of incomprehension between life at the front and life behind the lines was not as impermeable as is often imagined. In 1916 these reciprocal outpourings of dejection prompted the head of the German field medical service to warn that such exchanges could create a vicious downward spiral leading to deep depression. His somewhat paradoxical conclusion was that the best solution would not be an even more rigorous separation between soldier and civilian but more leave, more time for the soldier to spend with his family and friends instead of the prolonged absence that had become the general rule.[24]

### *Numbness*

It was not morale alone that suffered in wartime conditions. Individual combatants' personalities underwent changes that were in most cases negative. Vera Brittain's fiancé, Roland Leighton, expressed it by saying: 'I feel like a barbarian, a wild man of the woods, stiff, narrowed, practical, an incipient martinet perhaps.'[25] Feelings that were normal in civilian life, like empathy and grief, soon vanished. The men's *joie de vivre* and erotic fantasies faded and sank 'into the mire that covered

21 Winter & Baggett, *1914–18*, 171 (slightly altered)
22 Zuckmayer, *Als wär's ein Stück von mir*, 232–3
23 Zuckmayer, *Als wär's ein Stück von mir*, 235
24 Liddle & Cecil, *Facing Armageddon*, 387
25 Brittain, *Testament of Youth*, 216

everything', as De Schaepdrijver put it, writing of the Belgian soldiers at the Yser front for whom the impossibility of leave was a further demoralizing factor. Apathy was the men's only weapon against humiliation, discipline, being ordered about, the thoroughly boring routine, wretched living conditions, homesickness, and the ubiquity of death.[26] Barthas felt reduced to the status of a mule. Any sense of humanity and self-worth had gone. He and his men were nothing but beasts of burden, with 'their passivity, their indifference, their lethargy'.[27] Franz Marc wrote in mid-July 1915 that life at the front had absolutely ceased to touch him. 'It is as if it were no longer real and present; an existence of pure externality with which you comply.'[28] One young American soldier, Donald Kyler, had been overseas for a year and he was tired,

> physically and mentally. I had seen mercy killings, both of our hopelessly wounded and those of the enemy. I had seen the murder of prisoners of war, singly and as many as several at one time. I had seen men rob the dead of money and valuables, and had seen men cut off the fingers of corpses to get rings. Those things I had seen, but they did not effect [sic] me much. I was too numb. To me, corpses were nothing but carrion.

Jan-Gom Gheuens would later recall this numbness in his novel *De Miskenden* (The Disrespected): 'The only thing that can save us from insanity is to live without cares! So we allow the horrors of war to smash themselves to pieces against the shield of our callous indifference.'[29]

Insensitivity was actually essential if the soldiers were to carry out the tasks they had been set, and this applied in equal measure to doctors and nurses. Apathy and indifference were a wall a soldier built to avoid going completely crazy, although of course habituation played a significant part as well.[30] This was most obvious in the calm way the men dealt with confrontations with the dead after a while, as long as a corpse did not look too horrific.[31] Doctors were no different. They built a hardened shell around themselves. RAMC surgeon Hayward walked out of a building packed with bodies and body parts and went on a butterfly hunt.[32] John W. Harvey of the Friends' Ambulance Unit, a Quaker and therefore a member of a group not usually thought of as lacking in feeling, referred in a letter from Ypres

---

26 Vondung, *Kriegserlebnis*, 94; Holmes & De Vos, *Langs de Velden van Eer*, 102; Bastier, 'België tijdens de Eerste Wereldoorlog', 25

27 Barthas, *Carnets*, 168

28 Marc, *Brieven*, 75

29 Marix Evans, *1918*, 222; De Schaepdrijver, *De Groote Oorlog*, 206; De Vos, *De Eerste Wereldoorlog*, 63

30 Winter, *Death's Men*, 227; Audoin-Rouzeau, *Men at War*, 51

31 Binneveld, *Om de geest*, 49; Macdonald, *1914–1918*, 305; Eksteins, *Rites of Spring*, 153–4; Babington, *Shell-Shock*, 51

32 Winter, *Death's Men*, 226; Noyes, *Stretcher-Bearers*, 90

to the many ghastly sights he had witnessed 'that would be too full of horrors and pity to bear but for human nature's capacity to get hardened by familiarity to anything'.[33] There were limits, though. Even the far from squeamish Dearden felt upset as he watched a German soldier, both legs blown off, drag himself along the road on his chest and elbows.[34]

According to Ernst Jünger, after only quite a short time dead soldiers were given no more than a passing thought, recognized as if they were stones or trees.[35] This was also mentioned by August Hopp.

> You stood or sat on the dead as if they were rocks or chunks of wood. Whether one had his head blown away or torn off, whether another had his chest ripped open, or a third had bloody pieces of bone sticking out of his tunic – that no longer worried you. ... We sat on corpses, it didn't bother us; as long as we didn't have to sit in the mud.[36]

A French soldier saw one of his oldest friends killed right next to him, but he noticed that his thoughts had soon wandered off onto other things.[37] William Clarke remarked that your feelings came to the fore only if a man with whom you were particularly friendly was killed, and even then they subsided again fairly quickly.[38] Like everyone else, Barthas noticed he was becoming armoured against all forms of emotion. An accident in which three of his friends were killed had little effect on him. Like Zuckmayer he felt that soldiers, himself included, were now only really interested in their own fate. 'War is the best school for egoism.'[39] Charles Carrington saw a man wounded in the throat: dumb, helpless, dying. He walked on.[40] Wilfred Owen realized towards the end of the war that he had been beaten into insensitivity. One sign of this was that he no longer took his cigarette out of his mouth as he wrote 'deceased' across letters that arrived for his men.[41] Frank Richards wrote that he was eating Maconochie when a grenade exploded in his trench. A man standing behind him was killed and sand was sprayed everywhere. 'Our Maconochie was spoilt but I opened another one and we had the luck to eat that one without a clod of earth being thrown over it.'[42] A British general encountered a man with a sandbag slung over his shoulder. To his enquiry as to

33 Eksteins, *Rites of Spring*, 154
34 Dearden, *Medicine and Duty*, 225
35 Jünger, *In Stahlgewittern*, 29; Holmes, *Firing Line*, 180
36 Witkop, *Kriegsbriefe*, 39, 46
37 Audoin-Rouzeau, *Men at War*, 50–51
38 Bourke, *Dismembering the Male*, 77
39 Barthas, *Carnets*, 332
40 Hynes, *Soldiers' Tale*, 70
41 Gilbert, *First World War*, 476
42 Fussell, *Bloody Game*, 107

what was in the bag, the soldier calmly answered, 'Rifleman Grundy, Sir'.[43] Legs sticking out of the sides of trenches were used to hang equipment on.[44] A hand that appeared from a trench wall was shaken to comments like: 'Now then, Jerry, get on wi'it; no bloody skrimshankin' 'ere.'[45] Wounded horses were a sight some would never get used to, but Abbé Thellier de Poncheville, a psychiatric nurse, recalled that troops had passed by without even glancing at a horse fighting for its life in the mud of a crater,[46] and a book by the French writer and soldier Charles Delvert includes a scene in which not one man from a company filing past stops to help a soldier whose leg has been shattered by a shell.[47] There are plenty more stories like these.[48]

According to Duhamel this had to do with the fact that in peacetime death was not part of normal life. If it was spoken of at all, then guarded terms were used, wrapped in thick layers of symbolism. It was different in wartime. 'One eats, one drinks beside the dead, one sleeps in the midst of the dying, one laughs and one sings in the company of corpses.'[49] Barthas watched a shell kill eight soldiers and seriously wound ten others. The dead were laid at the side of the road ready for burial and life went on. 'An accident like that occurring in peacetime would have been covered in the newspapers for days, but at this point it was just a simple, everyday accident.'[50] Surfleet once saw a friend terribly wounded. He had apparently detonated a grenade while urinating in a shell-hole and he was hysterical, begging Surfleet to put him out of his misery. Thinking back to that scene, Surfleet was amazed he had stayed so calm; a much milder sight in civilian life would have driven him to distraction. Later he would thank God for that numbness. In another incident not long afterwards he stood eye to eye with several putrefying corpses. He was convinced that if he had seen them when he was a fresh young soldier he would not have survived the experience mentally.[51]

Fatalism became a normal reaction. If a bullet had a soldier's 'name on it', so men in the trenches believed, then it would hit him no matter what. There was no point running away; after all, a bullet was faster. If there was no such bullet, he would get through unharmed. It was as simple as that. Fleeing or ducking was pointless. One Australian soldier wrote that he had seen hundreds of men walking straight ahead through a heavy barrage without being hit and hundreds more who had been wounded or killed as they tried to dodge shells. To an officer who told

---

43 Winter, *Death's Men*, 205

44 Holmes, *Firing Line*, 181

45 Holmes, *Firing Line*, 243

46 Horne, *Price of Glory*, 186

47 Horne, *Price of Glory*, 187

48 Brants & Brants, *Velden van weleer*, 206

49 Duhamel, *Vie des Martyrs*, 241; Horne, *Price of Glory*, 187; Winter & Baggett, *1914–18*, 165

50 Barthas, *Carnets*, 396

51 Wilson, *Myriad Faces*, 359; see also: Brittain, *Chronicle*, 252

him to pull his head in or it would be hit, Gordon Fisher said, 'Who cares?'[52] Men reasoned: right now I'm alive so I don't have to worry, and if I do get hit then the worrying will be over.[53]

The numbness took its toll, of course. It was expressed not only as indifference to the most ghastly scenes of warfare but in mental exhaustion and an inability to concentrate. After several weeks in the trenches, a man would become stupefied and his face expressionless, his eyes dull. He went into a trance, a narcosis induced by the conditions. German student Hugo Steinthal remarked:

> Whoever has been in these trenches for so long as our infantry, and whoever has not lost his sanity in these hellish attacks, must at least have lost feeling for a lot of things. Too much of the horrific, too much of the incredible has been thrown at our poor chaps. To me it's unbelievable that all that can be tolerated. Our poor little brains simply can't take it all in.[54]

No matter how numb a man became, he continued to see the horrors. He absorbed and suppressed them, yet slowly but surely they did their destructive work. The perpetual tension made even ordinary activities close to the front line, let alone fighting, more exacting than normal. It has been said that for every five minutes of battle the physical organs perform the work of twenty-four hours. A soldier at the front was therefore continually overworked and, as will be clear by now, he had little opportunity to sleep. This inevitably affected his mental state. Bardamu, the central character in Céline's *Voyage au Bout de la Nuit*, sighs, 'Oh, how you long to get away! To sleep! That's the main thing! When it becomes really impossible to get away and sleep, then the will to live evaporates of its own accord.'[55]

Australian historian C.E.W. Bean, who had seen active service at the front, recalled that 'survivors, even after a day's rest, looked like men who had been in hell. Almost without exception, each man looked drawn and haggard and so dazed that the men appeared to be walking in a dream and their eyes looked glassy and starey.'[56] Sassoon noted that the effect of war on morale was perceptible after only a few weeks. Graves wrote that after three weeks a fresh arrival at the front would know enough about the rules of danger and safety to be a good soldier. Next came a period of efficiency after which, about six months later, a steady decline set in. Within a year most were worse than useless. Richard Aldington, author of *Death of a Hero*, commented that after six months most soldiers could no longer function normally. By that point they were 'horribly afraid of seeming afraid'.[57]

52 Holmes, *Firing Line*, 240; Macdonald, *1914–1918*, 255; Barthas, *Carnets*, 438
53 Manning, *Her Privates We*, 150; Wilson, *Myriad Faces*, 359
54 Eksteins, *Rites of Spring*, 172
55 Céline, *Voyage*, 29–30
56 Winter, *Death's Men*, 186–7
57 Winter, *Death's Men*, 133; Graves, *Goodbye*, 143

Of course not all men became numb. For those who did not, life in the trenches was almost unbearable. To Zuckmayer, of all war words 'numbed' was 'the most bestial'. During the spring offensive of 1918 he wrote:

> *I'm not being numbed* – I'm becoming wilder and wilder, and every death that I see, contorted and bloody, grinning fixedly, with a yellowed face, is – *every* one of them is to me: *the first of the dead!* And the terrible thing: alone. Not a single person. Everyone around me is 'going numb'. Only I'm not![58]

*Inhumanity*

Although numbness had its advantages, it could tip over into inhumanity and a complete lack of respect for human life. There are of course countless signs of exactly the opposite, like the tales of suicidal acts performed to cover a unit's retreat.[59] Jünger once spared an enemy soldier who had shown him a photograph of his wife and children.[60] There are many stories of human affection in wartime, although we should be wary of exaggeration. They include tales of officers or men who, as a result of their extreme mutual dependency, entered into lifelong friendships even though in civilian life they would probably not have given each other a second look. Friendship – or rather comradeship, which is actually something quite different from friendship – acquires a deeper significance in wartime, as does hostility. The innumerable stories of sacrifice, empathy and comradeship do nothing to absolve behaviour of the opposite kind. War inevitably brings out the worst in people as well as the best, and when things get tough the motto is often, although not always: every man for himself and the devil take the hindmost.[61]

This is a book about soldiers as victims, but of course we should never forget that soldiers are perpetrators too. War is more about attempting to kill other people than about being killed, and the killing is sanctioned and encouraged by the very authorities responsible for convicting and punishing those who commit acts of violence in peacetime. This paradox, this reversal of norms and values, is one of the main causes of the psychological problems that so often arise among soldiers, and which find such clear expression in the process that robs a man of his humanity, although as we shall see, other causes are no less important.

In wartime people are ordered to do things that are otherwise strictly forbidden. Everything that is valued in peacetime, including human life, is stripped of its value in times of war. Soldiers become alienated from the civil society that produced them, indeed it actively alienates them, until they become strangers to their own world and even to themselves. The fear, lack of sleep, appalling experiences, ubiquitous

---

58 Zuckmayer, *Als wär's ein Stück von mir*, 250

59 Brants & Brants, *Velden van weleer*, 207

60 Jünger, *In Stahlgewittern*, 199

61 Hynes, *Soldiers' Tale*, 10

violence and group pressures of wartime are a lethal combination.[62] They lead to what one historian of the holocaust, Christopher Browning, has called 'battlefield frenzy', which, by the way, should not be confused with war crimes that arise from methodically implemented government policy. They are a different matter again. War leads to degeneracy, which can in turn lead to appalling behaviour by people of whom it would least be expected in peacetime. Many soldiers understandably came to see human life as worthless. Brute force was the answer to every problem. Some would claim that the effects of this brutalization were apparent after the war. In 1914 political murder was a shocking exception to the rule, whereas after 1918 it became the order of the day.

Political violence should not be attributed purely to the psychological effects of the war on front-line soldiers, however. It is extremely hard to say whether and to what extent soldiers were 'dehumanized' by the war, in the sense that they might continue to do what they had learned to do of necessity during their time in the army: kill. Aside from the fact that some soldiers developed an aversion to violence as a result of their wartime experiences, the majority were no more likely to commit violent crimes after the war than before, although they may sometimes have been better able than most to understand fellow ex-servicemen who did resort to violence. The other major wars of the twentieth century did not leave a legacy of political violence, certainly not on the same scale, in fact Bourke suggests that in some cases there was a decline in crime rates. Politically-motivated killing became more normalized in Germany, after all, than in any of the other belligerent nations, and among the perpetrators were not only veterans of the front but men who had not experienced active service, who therefore cannot have been coarsened and dehumanized by it directly. So alongside the influence of the war on the thoughts and actions of individuals in later years, other factors too, political and economic, must have been important in stimulating the use of violence for political ends in the years after 1918.[63]

The fact remains that inhuman acts were observed during the war and understandable fears arose as to what this would mean for post-war society. The post-war regeneration of Europe would depend to a great degree on returned servicemen. Civilians asked themselves whether years of unimaginable violence would have turned soldiers into criminals, revolutionaries or barbarians (for many these amounted to the same thing). Would a *Frontschwein*, a Tommy Atkins or a *poilu* be capable of the self-discipline necessary to function within civil society and help to restore it to full economic and spiritual health? Civilians were not alone in worrying about this. As early as July 1916, Sergeant Marc Boassoan asked the same question when he looked at his French comrades, 'these exhausted creatures, emptied of blood, emptied of thought, crushed by superhuman fatigue'. Ludwig Lewinsohn, chairman of the soldiers' council of the German Fourth Army (the

62 Holmes, *Firing Line*, 392

63 Browning, *Doodgewone mannen*, 198–9; Von der Dunk, *Voorbij de Verboden Drempel*, 123, 133; Bourke, *Intimate History*, 356–8, 363

revolution was beginning to take shape) felt that the problems his country faced would only increase when a great hoard of barbarians returned home.[64]

On the eve of Verdun, a twenty-one-year-old Frenchman, Lieutenant Derville, who was to die on the Aisne in 1918, suggested that in the not too distant future they might all reach 'the degree of brutishness and indifference of the soldiers of the First Empire'.[65] In the face of an immediate threat, hatred and a thirst for blood blotted out all other feelings. During the British retreat in 1914, Lieutenant-Colonel Wormald led one of the few successful attacks. It was one of those rare occasions in the years 1914–18 when the bayonet was used more than the rifle as such. The German regiment they targeted (it happened to be named Queen Victoria's Own) was taken completely by surprise. Paul Maze noticed some Germans hiding in a stook of corn. Bayonets were driven in, producing hideous screams. '[The men] were showing to one another the blood dripping off their sword-blades.' Among the survivors were men with six or seven stab-wounds who had also been hit by bullets.[66] Barthas described the fight for Hill 304 during the Battle of Verdun: 'Woe betide anyone who .. fell into enemy hands alive; any sense of humanity had been banished.' Soldiers, the wounded, stretcher-bearers: by this point no distinction was made between them.[67]

In their memoirs men repeatedly asked themselves whether it could really have been they who acted like savages, who struck and stabbed and killed in cold blood, even when their opponents were defenceless, who killed because it was their duty to kill.[68] Gorch Jachs, who died in the German offensive of March 1918, said that because of his 'steel-hard nerves' he could 'look the dead calmly in their crushed eyes'.

> [I] can hear badly wounded comrades groaning without collapsing and can do much more that I cannot say. In many ways I have become a riddle to myself, and often shudder at myself, am terrified at myself. And then again I feel that I still have the weakest, most pitying heart in the world.[69]

Killing often began to feel pleasurable. No longer considered an act of war, it had become a game. Bean wrote of Australians who seemed to be having the time of their lives 'ratting' at captured Pozières, chasing shrieking Germans with their bayonets and shooting from the hip. They would wait quietly, sitting on doorsteps smoking, until the next German appeared, making a desperate attempt to get away.[70] On another occasion an Australian wrote with great satisfaction about the

64 Dyer, *Missing of the Somme*, 16 n.; Leed, *No Man's Land*, 7
65 Horne, *Price of Glory*, 186
66 Holmes, *Riding the Retreat*, 216–18
67 Barthas, *Carnets*, 298
68 Winter, *Death's Men*, 210
69 Leed, *No Man's Land*, 4
70 Winter, *Death's Men*, 210

fate of a group of German soldiers who tried to surrender. Describing in a letter to his father the pleasure of bayoneting them, he used the words 'good sport'.[71]

Dearden told with barely concealed delight of an Irishman who had come upon a German during a night patrol. The man was half asleep. He asked for a shovel and used it, virtually severing the German's head from his torso. 'It's a fine tool, is a shovel', he said contentedly as he gave it back to its astonished owner.[72]

In his book *A Social History of the Machine Gun*, John Ellis often quotes Lieutenant-Colonel Graham Seton Hutchison, author of *History of the Machine Gun Corps*. Hutchison wrote about his experiences as a member of that corps, telling of his admiration for the beauty of the machine-gun and the magnificent way he had killed Germans with it. He also used it to hurry along British troops he felt were not getting up to the line quickly enough. He sent the stragglers off in the direction of the enemy where, he writes with satisfaction, 'they perished to a man'. In the attack on High Wood during the Battle of the Somme his company was virtually wiped out. Along with just one fellow soldier, he crept forward between the dead and wounded until he reached one of the machine-guns. He fired towards the advancing Germans and watched them fall, 'chuckling with joy at the technical efficiency of the machine'. Hutchison's stories reminded Ellis more of the Vikings he had read about in his youth than of the so-called officers and gentlemen who landed in Belgium in 1914.[73]

There are certain similarities between these stories and an article that appeared in the *Jauer'sche Tageblatt* of 18 October 1914 and was republished in 1915 in *J'accuse. Von einem Deutschen* (*J'accuse. By a German*). The book is both a description and an indictment of 'German atrocities', published anonymously but written by Richard Grelling, a German living in Switzerland. Grelling was accused of being 'unpatriotic' and a Dutch doctor, E. van Dieren, who supported the German side, even referred to him as 'an inferior type'. He relates a story told by an NCO called Klempt and confirmed by Klempt's commanding officer, Lieutenant von Niem. The setting is 24 September 1914, and the officer's report is entitled 'A Day of Honour for our Regiment'. It is a tale of bloodthirsty hatred, of delight in killing, of the effectiveness of propaganda and the deplorable fate of soldiers who chose to surrender at the wrong time, in the wrong place, to the wrong people.

> Already the first Frenchmen are being discovered. They are smashed down out of the trees like squirrels; below they are 'warmly' received with blows of the butt and bayonet, so that they no longer need a doctor; we are no longer fighting honourable enemies but treacherous brigands. ... And we will give them no quarter. We shoot standing up, or at most kneeling; no one thinks any longer about taking cover. We come to a slight depression in the ground, where dead

71 Holmes, *Firing Line*, 389

72 Dearden, *Medicine and Duty*, 134–5

73 Ellis, *Social History*, 142–4

> and wounded red-trousers lie piled in a tangle on top of each other. The wounded are beaten to death or stabbed, since we know that all these scoundrels will shoot us in the back if we pass them by. ... Those of a particularly tender disposition give the French wounded the *coup de grâce*, while others give them as many thrusts and blows as they can. ... They lay groaning and crying for quarter, but whether they are wounded slightly or severely, our brave fusiliers spare their country the cost of caring for many enemies.[74]

Stories like this provoked responses of frank astonishment. Psychiatrist John T. MacCurdy wrote in 1918:

> At the present time there are millions of men, previously sober, humdrum citizens, with no observable traits of recklessness or blood thirstiness in their nature, and with a normal interest in their own comfort and security, not only exposing themselves to extraordinary hazards, but cheerfully putting up with extreme discomforts, and engaged in inflicting injuries on human beings, without the repugnance they would have shown in performing similar operations on the bodies of dogs and cats.[75]

Respect for the dead reached absolute zero at times. 'Sometimes Tommy is not a pleasant animal', wrote Corporal W.H.L. Watson, an Oxford undergraduate, after watching British infantrymen fighting to wrench as many belongings as possible out of the clothes of their German opponents in the early weeks of the war. 'One dead German had his pockets full of chocolate. They scrambled over him, pulling him about, until it was all divided.'[76]

Zuckmayer would not have been surprised by any of this. Referring to the Senegalese, who in Western European eyes were capable of truly abject deeds, he wrote that in certain situations there simply were no innocent, innocuous people.

> One never knows what they are capable of. And it does not help to hear later that they meant no harm by it. This particular night [the night in which he heard Senegalese troops on the other side of no man's land] I may have killed several of them. I too meant no harm by it. I was afraid. Anyone who isn't afraid isn't brave, he's merely stupid. At that time we knew that fear was a habit impossible to break, that it always returns like sweat or digestion. You develop a certain technique that enables you to cope with fear. For that you get a 'medal for bravery'.[77]

74 *J'accuse*, 301; Van Dieren, *Over den Oorlog*, front cover
75 Bourke, *Intimate History*, 248; Bourke, *Moral Economy*, 3–4
76 Holmes, *Riding the Retreat*, 283–4
77 Zuckmayer, *Als wär's ein Stück von mir*, 232

This psychological aspect of the war could be as fatal as any physical wound. It took a strong character to resist those 'assassins of the mind' that the conditions of trench warfare had spawned. Some men, including Toller or Sassoon, discovered that their fierce protests in defence of life itself – protests that naturally found little positive echo – functioned as a safety valve that enabled them to survive the presence of death all around them. Most, however, will have fared as Paul Bäumer did, the central character in Remarque's *Im Westen nichts Neues*. Like Toller, of whom more later, he knows how it feels to kill an enemy soldier in single combat. Like Toller he discovers that his opponent is not the abstract monster of propaganda but a human being like himself. But unlike Toller he resigns himself to the impossibility of avoiding killing in wartime and goes on to become a remorseless and efficient soldier. He is a kind of automaton, dead in the midst of life. His own end will be nothing more than the death of his earthly frame. Like many soldiers who are not actually dead but imagine themselves to be so, his spirit has departed the land of the living long ago.[78]

### *Fear*

The basic source of psychological problems and personality changes was fear: fear of bombardment, of gas, of mutilation, fear of death, fear of fear itself, or of showing fear, and fear of the war in general as the cause of it all. Numbness, indifference and apathy must have run very deep in many cases, but often they were no more than a mask. Whether the numbness was genuine or not, fear almost always lay behind it, and this could lead to decisions that may seem odd. Wounded men refused surgery, even if it might save an arm or a leg, because once they recovered they would have to return to the front.[79]

On 1 July 1916, Private Surfleet watched men stumble back from the front line. They were pale as death, with bloodstained hands and uniforms and makeshift bandages. Each one had a look of indescribable fear in his eyes. 'I know, now, I *hate* this warring business,' he wrote.[80] Private A. Worden remarked that no one should ever think that soldiers got used to war and danger. Nothing could be further from the truth.[81] Fear was ubiquitous and perpetual, even when there was no immediate reason for it.[82] Cigarettes were among the most sought-after articles; chain-smoking was a thoroughly normal activity and in times of danger lighting up was an instinctive reaction,[83] although not without its dangers in the presence of snipers. There were other ways of trying to suppress fear. One officer in the German army was convinced nothing could happen to him as long as his

78 Remarque, *Im Westen*, passim; Whalen, *Bitter Wounds*, 45–7, 188
79 Whalen, *Bitter Wounds*, 113; Brittain, *Chronicle*, 317
80 Wilson, *Myriad Faces*, 354
81 Winter, *Death's Men*, 161
82 Renn, *Krieg*, 182
83 Holmes, *Firing Line*, 129

dog was with him. When the animal disappeared one fateful day, the officer, who had always functioned perfectly well until then, broke down. He knew for certain that he would soon be killed; he could no longer sleep and took to drinking heavily, something he had abhorred in the past and refused to tolerate among his subordinates.[84]

Fear was universal and unrelenting. Hoffman wrote that every soldier was terrified of never getting home to see his loved ones again. Even worse was the fear of ending up like some of the dead they had all seen at some point. 'They lay there face up, usually in the rain, their eyes open, their faces pale and chalk-like, their gold teeth showing. That is in the beginning. After that they are usually too horrible to think about.'[85]

Perhaps even greater than the fear of an atrocious death was the fear of an atrocious life.[86] Many soldiers were more deeply affected by encounters with men who were horribly wounded than by the sight of mutilated corpses. One Australian remembered an explosion at Pozières. He looked towards a shell-burst and saw something dark through the smoke. 'It was a shapeless black thing, flapping. … It was a man, blackened, not a bit of flesh not burnt, rolling around, waving his arm stump with nothing on it.'[87]

Mutilation (which we will look at in more depth in the next chapter) of the kind not followed by death – or not immediately – was Hiscock's greatest and most persistent fear. He had seen so many soldiers with one or more limbs amputated or blasted off, men who had lost their jaws or been blinded or paralysed. Should he become seriously wounded he wanted death to follow. That would be better than spending the rest of your life maimed or disfigured.[88] His opinion was fully shared by Hoffman, who in 1918 found himself in a hospital where most of the patients were only lightly wounded, as was he. Most, but not all. During a walk through the hospital he happened upon a ward where the seriously wounded were treated. Twenty years later he looked back on that moment.

> There were men who had their faces marred almost past recognition as anything human. Some had lost noses, jaws or ears. The records prove that men who lived had been shot through every single part of the body, every organ, even all parts of the brain. Men normally die who are shot through an important internal organ – heart, intestines, or liver. Usually a head shot kills the man instantly; but many have lived when shot through the head.

84 Holmes, *Firing Line*, 266
85 Fussell, *Bloody Game*, 180
86 Holmes, *Firing Line*, 182
87 Holmes, *Firing Line*, 181
88 Fussell, *Bloody Game*, 161

> Few have any idea of the horrible cripples left by the last war. Even in the years which have intervened since the ending of the war, hundreds of thousands of men have been kept in hospitals – some of these men so severely wounded that they are never permitted to be seen by others. While it is no harder to lose a nose than a finger, what a horrible thing it does to a man's face. I could not help but think how I would have looked from the bullet which left its mark on my cheek if I had not turned my head just at the right instant. I might have been here with these men, having only half a face of my own.[89]

Attacks of intense fear, which punctuated the unrelieved latent anxiety, brought men to the point of panic. This was not confined to young and inexperienced recruits. Anyone, even the most hardened old campaigner, could be overwhelmed by terror. Jünger, who suffered from nightmares,[90] fell prey to it after seeing one particularly appalling sight.

> I lost my head completely. Ruthlessly, I barged past everyone on my path, before finally, having fallen back a few times in my haste, climbing out of the hellish crush of the trench, to move more freely above. Like a bolting horse, I rushed through dense undergrowth, across paths and clearings, till I collapsed in a copse by the Grande Tranchée.[91]

Jünger was lucky. It was quite common for panic attacks to be nipped in the bud by shooting the soldier or NCO concerned. Individual panic, after all, could lead to general panic, which even an officer's drawn pistol or revolver could do nothing to curb.[92]

Fear was ever-present, but some events contributed more to it than others. Soldiers' individual sensitivities differed, although naturally the fear of being killed was familiar to all.[93] Night patrols were one source of fear. Men would scout out no man's land at night, facing both the constant danger of coming upon enemy troops and the risk of being mistaken for an enemy patrol and shot by their own side on the way back. Sassoon became a casualty of one such mistake and it spelled the end of his time on active service.[94] An additional factor was that such patrols were not always carried out for reasons that were genuinely important from a military point of view. When the purpose of such activities is not understood, the fear is all the greater. John William Rowarth was once ordered out into no man's land to fetch a piece of German barbed wire. His commanding officer wanted to have something to show his wife when he next went on leave in the hope that,

89 Fussell, *Bloody Game*, 169

90 Boterman, 'Oorlog als bron', 257

91 Jünger, *In Stahlgewittern*, 19; *Storm of Steel*, 31

92 Holmes, *Firing Line*, 227, 229; Macdonald, *1914–1918*, 251

93 Audoin-Rouzeau, *Men at War*, 75

94 Sassoon, *Complete Memoirs*, 649; Winter, *Death's Men*, 87–8

filled with pride in her courageous husband, she would more than fulfil her marital duty. No wonder Rowarth wished upon the officer a sudden, crippling form of impotence.[95]

Mines instilled terror as well. Front-line soldiers could hear any digging that went on beneath them and if the noise stopped there was no sense of relief, since that meant the explosives were in place and it was only a matter of time before they would be electronically detonated. Anyone caught in the blast would at best survive seriously maimed. More likely they would vanish without trace and without any warning, other than a juddering of the soil just before the ground lifted into the air.[96]

There were other specific sources of fear, such as heavy shelling and the individual catastrophe a bursting shell could cause. A barrage confronted the soldier with the enormous violence of which the human race was capable and against which individuals were utterly powerless. Barbusse wrote of one spell in the trenches that was truly frightful. 'The 18th Company was in the vanguard: eighteen killed and some fifty wounded – at least one man out of three in four days. And that was without any attack, just from shelling.'[97] To Paul Dubrulle, dying from a bullet wound seemed a comparatively small matter: 'parts of our being remain intact; but to be dismembered, torn to pieces, reduced to pulp, this is a fear that flesh cannot support and which is fundamentally the great suffering of the bombardment.'[98]

In April 1917 the trench newspaper *La Saucisse* published a story about a man sheltering during a bombardment. It begins: 'There's nothing more horrible in war than being shelled.' Few would have disagreed.

> Soon the noise becomes hellish; several batteries thunder simultaneously. Impossible to make anything out. Shells fall continually, without interruption. He feels that his head is bursting, that his sanity is wavering. This is torture and he can see no end to it. He's suddenly afraid of being buried alive. He sees himself with his back broken, smothered, digging into the earth with his clenched fists. He imagines atrocious agony; he wishes with all his strength that the shelling would stop, that the attack would begin. … What has happened to his friends? Have they gone? Are they dead? Is he the only one left alive in his hole? Then suddenly there's a vision of those who are dear to him: his wife, his mother, his child. … He wants his final thoughts to be of those he loves. … Then comes inner rebellion, a mad impulse to leap up. It's too stupid to stay there, waiting for death! Anything is better than that! Oh! To see danger face to face!

95 Leed, 'Fateful Memories', 94–5

96 Winter, *Death's Men*, 126–7

97 Barbusse, *Le Feu*, 52; *Under Fire*, 44

98 Holmes, *Firing Line*, 232–3; Winter & Baggett, *1914–18*, 167–9

> To fight!!! To act!!! The deluge continues. Blind force is unleashed. And the man remains in his hole, powerless, waiting, hoping for a miracle.[99]

German Vice-Sergeant-Major Arthur Goldstein described shelling that lasted all day.

> It sets in horribly at sunrise: 'Barrage!'... Ceaselessly the earth shakes. Ceaselessly the shots and impacts resound, like a monstrous roll of drums. ... Towards midday the firing increases to become a true frenzy, comparable at the outside to the raging of the sea whipped up by a storm. ... Finally at five o'clock the storm abates.[100]

Gürtler wrote of a barrage during Third Ypres:

> Nothing makes such an impression as a continuous, terrific bombardment such as we have experienced in this battle in Flanders, especially the intense English fire during my second night at the front. ... Darkness alternates with light as bright as day. The earth trembles and shakes like a jelly. ... And those men out there hear drum-fire, the groaning of wounded comrades, the agonized cries of fallen horses, the wild beating of their own hearts, hour after hour – night after night.[101]

Surfleet recorded in his diary that God alone knew how awfully afraid he was during a barrage,[102] but many of his comrades must have known too. In early February 1918 Laurie Rowlands wrote to his girlfriend Alice about low morale among the troops, the loss of any sense of patriotism, the hope that the government would decide to sign a peace treaty no matter what the terms, and his own baptism of fire in the Ypres salient in 1917, at Broodseinde. He divulged to her that if a fellow had ever been afraid it was him. Years after the war, J. Drury remembered an eighteen-year-old soldier who had shaken like an aspen leaf non-stop for twenty-four hours after a dud shell landed less than ten metres from him. Journalist and Coldstream Guardsman Rowland Feilding, author of *War Letters to a Wife*, described a sniping officer who was in the habit of clutching the arm of whoever was next to him every time a shell passed close overhead. Feilding is sometimes accused of having wandered around the battlefield more as a sensation-seeking sightseer than as a man in search of the truth,[103] but the fact remains that even the most self-confident could not keep their lips and eyelids from trembling, or avoid either nightmares or

99 Audoin-Rouseau, *14–18. Les combattants*, 79; Liddle & Cecil, *Facing Armageddon*, 222–3

100 *Kriegsbriefe gefallener Deutscher Juden*, 51

101 Witkop, *Kriegsbriefe*, 327–8; Winter & Baggett, *1914–18*, 202

102 Wilson, *Myriad Faces*, 357

103 Keegan, *Face of Battle*, 259; Winter, *Death's Men*, 117

depression as a result of bombardment. No one could survive days and nights of it without being affected in some way. Jünger wrote that after days under shellfire, a man would march back with a frozen stare, his eyes dead and empty.[104] J. Christie, an officer, woke up when shelling from his own side started. He was shaking from top to toe and barely able to speak. He later wrote that he had not been in the least frightened and that his symptoms were purely outward and not inward. Not long after this attack of nerves, however, he was put on a boat back to England.[105]

Christie had started trembling as soon as the barrage began. The physical symptoms of psychological pressure became more powerful and diverse as the shelling went on. A. Burrage screamed the words that Sassoon used in his poem 'Attack': 'Oh, Christ, make it stop' and Sassoon himself wrote in 1925 in his *Repression of War Experience*: 'I'm going crazy; I'm going stark, staring mad because of the guns.' No one was immune. Some cried, others could not stop telling jokes, almost all shook. If they were not afraid while the barrage lasted, the fear came later, when the real danger had passed.[106]

Moran believed that many soldiers were prepared to die, as long as it was a quick and in some sense beautiful death, but death by shellfire, with its hideous wounds and often agonizing death throes robbed them of all self-respect. According to Moran, shelling made more men flee the trenches than any other aspect of warfare,[107] often with fatal consequences.

It was not just the prospect of being hit that instilled fear. Many men broke into a sweat after receiving even a non-fatal wound. Some initially reacted to wounding with indifference and apathy, others panicked. Amazement was actually the most common response. Fear came next. The screams of the wounded that feature so prominently in war memoirs were caused less by pain than by the fear of dying.[108]

Another cause of fear was the presence of aircraft. Every time he spotted a plane, Cloete wanted to run. The noise and the goggled figures in the cockpit made him extremely nervous. His spirits flagged. Planes could kill. Bombs were not just thrown by men or fired from mortars, they were dropped from aircraft, which made them much more likely to hit their targets. F. Symons described an aerial attack.

> Bombs dropped from aeroplanes do great damage. One was dropped thirty yards from our HQ. Two fellows near by saw the plane coming and one said to the other, 'Wouldn't it be a bugger if they dropped the bomb here.' Drop it they did and he had his leg blown off. I saw it hanging across his chest like a leg of

104 Whalen, *Bitter Wounds*, 44

105 Winter, *Death's Men*, 117–18

106 Winter, *Death's Men*, 118–19; Terraine, 'Inferno', 186

107 Binneveld, *Om de geest*, 65, 80–81; Winter, *Death's Men*, 119; Holmes, *Firing Line*, 199

108 Whalen, *Bitter Wounds*, 52

> beef. All he said was 'Dear me. Dear me,' about a hundred times and said the Lord's Prayer over and over. He died in the night. It then dawned on me what war was.[109]

One thing that gave fear of shelling an extra dimension was the far from remote chance of being buried alive. Everyone had nightmares and one of the most common featured a collapsing dugout or shelter, or heaps of earth pressing down on a man after an explosion. Johannsen described exactly that, the interminable half-hour between the moment a soldier was buried alive and point at which, half insane, he succumbed to his wounds and lack of oxygen. They were thirty minutes of hope and despair, of slowly going under, unable to move.[110] According to psychoanalyst Ernst Simmel, being buried alive as the result of an explosion was the most common cause of war neurosis, since survivors felt as if they had returned from death to the land of the living.[111]

The fear of such an experience could be almost as bad as the experience itself. Private T.C.H. Jacobs of the 1st West Yorkshire Regiment remembered a German barrage on the morning of 21 March 1918 during which he crouched against the wall of a trench, his face distorted with fear. Not for a moment did he fear death, but he was terrified that the walls would cave in and bury him alive.[112] This was no disproportionate or irrational fear. Dearden once walked along a captured German trench in which he saw not only a pile of corpses but two boots sticking up out of the ground, thrashing wildly, and he pondered with horror the fact that beyond that pair of boots a man was fighting a hopeless battle, lasting several minutes, against inevitable death by suffocation.[113]

Shelling was the main cause of death and maiming, and a soldier's total powerlessness during a barrage was an additional factor that caused fear and stress. Bombardment lasting days or even weeks condemned men to inactivity for the same length of time. It was impossible either to attack or to flee. They could only sit, wait, and feel afraid. After several days amid shells flying overhead and bursting around him at Hooge in June 1915, it was inactivity above all that made H.S. Clapham long for that one shell that would put him out of his misery.[114]

We should not take this notion of fear arising from inactivity out of context, since that would suggest men were happy when ordered to attack. They often were, but there can be no doubt at all that they were afraid as they went into battle. The scale of death and destruction on the battlefield was immense. In August 1916, two months before his death, German NCO Friedel Dehme wrote that he had gathered his men around him shortly before they were due to go over the top.

109 Winter, *Death's Men*, 127–8
110 Johannsen, *Vier von der Infanterie*, 83–4; Stuiveling, *Het Vraagstuk*, 38
111 Leed, *No Man's Land*, 22–3
112 Holmes, *Firing Line*, 208; Keegan, *First World War*, 427
113 Dearden, *Medicine and Duty*, 186
114 Holmes, *Firing Line*, 231; Audoin-Rouzeau, *Men at War*, 73–4

He set off along a fairly sheltered route, but when he looked round he saw that no one had followed him. He went back and did his best to convince the men, then ordered them to go with him, across the open field this time, since the sheltered path had been pulverized by shelling. Two men followed his order.[115] Graves tells of a captain who on two occasions had to shoot one of his own men before he could get his company out of the trench.[116]

Graves was more afraid of battle than of shelling. That is to say, bullets terrified him more than artillery fire. Shells were aimed not at men but at positions, whereas a bullet, even if fired at random as was usually the case, always gave the impression that it was intended for whoever it hit. What was more, you could hear a shell coming, whereas a bullet was a silent assassin.[117] This was another of the reasons why soldiers were so terrified of gas.

Real or feigned numbness was a defence against the horrors and a similar mechanism suppressed fear most of the time. Neither men nor officers commonly went mad from one moment to the next, but their muffled dread worked on their minds. There was a paradox here. The soldier was forced to suppress his fear and fellow feeling in order to carry on doing what he had to do in the short term, but this very suppression meant that in the long run his mental state was subjected to even more strain, and with it his ability to function. Practically everyone was afraid. Those who showed their fear might be regarded as cowards, or at best as psychiatric cases, but those who suppressed their feelings stood a greater chance of becoming psychiatric cases in the proper sense of the term. The suppression of fear has been identified as one of the main causes of serious war neurosis.[118]

### *Self-mutilation and suicide*

> In winter trenches, cowed and glum
> With crumps and lice and lack of rum
> He put a bullet through his brain
> No one spoke of him again
>
> Siegfried Sassoon, 'Suicide in the Trenches'

On 1 November 1914 the life of poet Georg Trakl, who had suffered psychiatric problems even before the war, ended with an overdose of cocaine, to which he was addicted. Trakl, a pharmacist by profession, was not the martial type, but he was drafted and became a lieutenant with the Austrian Medical Corps. The horrendous hospital cases he faced every day soon made him severely depressed. When a

115 Witkop, *Kriegsbriefe*, 249
116 Graves, *Goodbye*, 155
117 Graves, *Goodbye*, 83
118 Holmes, *Firing Line*, 207

wounded man shot himself in the head as he watched, Trakl decided life on earth had nothing further to offer him.[119]

Trakl and his unidentified patient were two of the many soldiers who did not succeed in suppressing their fear and staving off *le cafard*. Self-inflicted wounds and suicide may have been fairly rare in percentage terms, but they were a regular occurrence in the trenches of the First World War. If we take wounds caused other than by enemy fire – that is to say friendly fire, accidents and suchlike – then there are indications that as many as a quarter were self-inflicted. Men shot themselves in the hands or feet, swallowed acid, injected paraffin under their skin, anything that might bring an end to the whole show.[120]

There is probably a connection between the number of suicides and self-inflicted wounds and the degree of military success the men were experiencing at the time. This certainly seems a reasonable conclusion to draw from reports in the early months of the war about British soldiers who had killed themselves, or attempted to, and from German suicide figures. While the suicide rate back in Germany fell steadily, the rate among soldiers increased in the final phase of the conflict. In August 1918 there were officially 3,500 cases; 3 months later there were more than 5,100.[121] Few would doubt that the true figure was higher.[122]

In *Dismembering the Male*, Bourke regularly turns her attention to professional malingerer Rowarth, who confessed outright that he would rather be a living coward than a dead hero. When he noticed that doctors quickly became suspicious of feigned neurosis, he put his foot under the wheel of a truck.[123] Ernest Barraclough told a story about two stretcher-bearers, one of whom borrowed a gun and shot the other through the hand, which was held out for the purpose. The scheme was not entirely successful, since the bullet went through the wrist rather than the palm, but despite this and the undoubtedly sickening pain, there was joy all round.[124] Their story serves as a useful reminder that 'self-inflicted wounds' were not always literally that. Sometimes a fellow soldier was prepared to shoot or stab a man in a part of the body not essential to life. (This could happen by accident too, of course, but then it was up to the men concerned to produce evidence that no wilful intent was involved.)[125] Clearly Rowarth was not such a coward as he claimed. Self-injury was closely bound up with the horrors of war, with the destruction, the stench and the filth, but not with cowardice. It took a good deal of courage to point

---

119 'Jahrhundert der Kriege', 118; De Roodt, *Onsterfelijke Fronten*, 75–114

120 Sassoon, *Complete Memoirs*, 421; Bourke, *Dismembering the Male*, 86; Schrep, 'Gebrochen an Leib und Seele', 60

121 Whalen, *Bitter Wounds*, 42; Verdoorn, *Arts en Oorlog*, 362; Holmes, *Riding the Retreat*, 68; Keegan, *Face of Battle*, 270; Brown, *Somme*, 52–3; Vondung, *Kriegserlebnis*, 103; Bourke, *Dismembering the Male*, 38, 77; Köppen, *Heeresbericht*, 256

122 Eckart & Gradmann, *Die Medizin*, 279–80

123 Bourke, *Dismembering the Male*, 83

124 Bamji, *Queens' Hospital*, 2–3; Frey, *Pflasterkästen*, 233–4

125 Liddle, *Passchendaele in Perspective*, 364; Wilson, *Myriad Faces*, 358

a gun at your foot and put a bullet through your own flesh and bone, or to have someone else do it.[126]

Whether the joy of the stretcher-bearers Barraclough saw lasted long with a court martial in prospect is another question, but men shooting themselves in the hands or feet knew they were taking a risk. If discovered to have wounded themselves they would be sent to a special hospital and nursed until well enough to face a court martial. To British soldiers in particular, this was not an attractive prospect.[127]

For the army the problem in such cases lay in proving that the wound was self-inflicted. For the men concerned the problem was precisely the opposite: how could anyone prove he had not deliberately injured himself if senior officers and medical staff suspected he had? Hiscock ran into this problem. His rifle, smeared with mud inside and out, went off as he was cleaning it. The bullet passed through his arm. The wound had only just been bandaged when his lieutenant confronted him, white with rage, revolver drawn. Hiscock was arrested. He faced court martial and possible execution. He was sent off to hospital wearing a stigmatizing green label that made obvious to everyone the crime his superiors believed he had committed. He faced hostile glances and found himself in a ward with around thirty men, including officers, who were to be court-martialled for self-wounding. One had deliberately taken a little too long to throw a hand grenade, another had cut off a toe with a razor blade and a third had held his hand above the parapet until a bullet hit his wrist. Hiscock came away shaken but unharmed,[128] but we are left to wonder how many men were unjustly convicted of wounding themselves, just as we may wonder how many men were wrongfully convicted of desertion when they had simply got lost, or of cowardice when they were suffering from severe neurosis. But more of that later.

A man who survived a suicide attempt would be admitted to hospital, where an ambivalent attitude surrounded his treatment. His fate depended entirely on the attitudes of those in charge of his care. A story told by Hiscock demonstrates that the records of suicide are as unreliable as practically all the other seemingly precise casualty figures. '[The nurses decided that] the man next to me in the ward … had died of wounds. He had, I learned later, put a Mills bomb under his right leg after a bombardment at Ypres that had lasted for most of a day.'[129]

Not all military personnel were capable of empathizing. Peter Riedesser and Axel Verderber, authors of *Aufrüstung der Seelen* (Armament of Souls), regard the fact that one army pathologist by the name of Neste invariably attributed suicide to inherent bodily causes as illustrative of a total lack of empathy among medical officers. Many believed there was no connection between suicide and the war.[130]

---

126 Hynes, *Soldiers' Tale*, 59

127 Macdonald, *Roses of No Man's Land*, 220

128 Fussell, *Bloody Game*, 146–51

129 Fussell, *Bloody Game*, 149

130 Riedesser & Verderber, *Aufrüstung der Seelen*, 112

Those who failed to kill themselves outright but later died might not be exposed and dishonoured, but they were less likely to be spared if a suicide attempt failed altogether. The wounded man would be treated purely so that he was fit to stand trial. He would probably be condemned to death and in that sense get what he wanted. La Motte found this paradoxical situation incomprehensible: 'to nurse back to health a man who was to be court-martialled and shot, truly that seemed a dead-end occupation'. The medical officer at the hospital where she worked felt it was these suicide attempts in wartime that were impossible to understand. Why would anyone choose to kill himself, he reasoned, at a time when it was so much easier than usual to achieve an honourable death? La Motte's supervisor Mary Borden was able to see the ridiculous side to it. The man who needed nursing so that he would be reasonably healthy when he was court-martialled – La Motte and Borden were almost certainly writing about the same patient – had probably decided to end his own life because of disappointment in love. He made further attempts in hospital, by repeatedly removing the bandages from his head. Borden gave a clear hint to the nurse on duty that she should 'forget' to replace the bandages next time, so that he would die of infection.[131]

There were indeed cases that suggested pathologist Neste and his psychiatrist colleagues were right. A man might read bad news from home with a shrug, dismissing it as trivial compared to what he had to endure at the front, but there was always a chance it could lead to suicide. Graves came upon a man who had put the barrel of his rifle to his mouth and pulled the trigger with his toe. His decision had been prompted by a letter in which he was informed that his girlfriend had taken up with another man.[132] It is impossible to say whether the same thing might have happened if he had never left home, but there is every chance he would have lived were it not that the message came as the proverbial last straw after all the miseries he had suffered.

Most suicides that were recorded as such seem to have coincided with major offensives. While the Battle of Verdun raged, several French officers rented hotel rooms where they hanged themselves.[133] But leave might drive a man to suicide as surely as service at the front line. The first and last dead men Graves saw during his time in the trenches were soldiers who had killed themselves. Graves believed one incident had resulted from a combination of miserable weather and news of an impending attack.[134] Men who had seen hell wanted to avoid going back there no matter what. Others who had heard innumerable stories about the front were determined to avoid going there even for the first time. Possibly some responded with suicidal acts because their lives up to then had not been particularly happy.

131 La Motte, *Backwash of War*, 3–4, 5, 7; Borden, 'The Forbidden Zone', in: Higonnet, *Nurses at the Front*, 119–28; Higonnet, *Nurses at the Front*, Introduction, xxi–xxii

132 Graves, *Goodbye*, 88–9, 103

133 De Schaepdrijver, *De Groote Oorlog*, 249;

134 Graves, *Goodbye*, 200; Hynes, *Soldiers' Tale*, 59

Thirty-three-year-old widower Richard Hicks was given home leave in the autumn of 1915 after finishing his training. He was due to embark for the continent shortly. His father wrote: 'I last saw my son alive at bedtime on Tuesday. He was quite cheerful. At 8.15 next morning I found my son dead with a rope around his neck, the other end tied to a bed post.'[135]

It almost goes without saying that suicidal tendencies were relatively common among those who had lost limbs or been maimed in other ways. Hans Korn wrote in late 1917 that he found it truly horrific to be disabled at nineteen. In exchange for his right arm he would happily walk into the barrage again.

> I simply keep asking myself what I have done to deserve it. I have prayed, and apart from that I have always done my duty, and yet our Lord God has allowed me to become a cripple. If only he had let me die a Hero's death straight away. I have reached the stage that I am ready to take my own life. If I think about the end of the war and my comrades coming home to the sound of music, I believe it will make me crazy. I pray every day that our Lord God will allow me to die.

His disability and the shock to his faith, along with a lack of social confidence and unhappiness in love, did indeed lead Korn to make an unsuccessful attempt on his own life.[136]

The methods of assessment used in hospitals do not inspire much confidence in the reliability of the official suicide figures, which appear precise but in fact offer little more than an indication. They tell us only the number of cases in which suicide was said to have been the cause of death, and if suicide verdicts are hard to reach in peacetime, in periods of order and repose, how much more so at a time when death is triumphant and chaos reigns? In the midst of such slaughter there was a good chance of suicide going undetected; on the other hand few would claim with confidence that every suspected suicide was exactly that. Fewer still would hazard a guess as to how many of the dead on the battlefield became desperate enough to use the last of their strength to end their own lives. How many men followed the line of reasoning of the doctor quoted earlier and volunteered for a mission not just knowing that it was equivalent to suicide but hoping it would prove so? How many were so reckless that we might choose to define them as men who killed themselves without being found out, as examples of suicide dressed up as heroism?

---

135 Winter, *Death's Men*, 36

136 Vondung, *Kriegserlebnis*, 104–5

## Neurosis

### *Introduction*

Suicide was the conscious, physical way out; neurosis was the subconscious, psychological way. Sufferers from combat neurosis in the First World War became known as shell-shock cases, and the term is used to this day, but in the early months of the war the Royal Army Medical Corps distinguished between four different types of neurosis: shell shock, a term invented by British soldiers in 1914; hysteria; neurasthenia; and disordered action of the heart (DAH), also known as effort syndrome or, among the Americans, soldier's heart. Often diagnosed in men who had not yet seen front-line service, DAH soon disappeared as a diagnostic option, although it seems to have been on the verge of a come-back among the British towards the end of the war. The diagnosis seemed only to make the symptoms of cardiac arrhythmia worse, with the heart beating yet more unevenly, slowly, or quickly after medical attention was paid to it than before. A diagnosis of DAH therefore seemed to stand in the way of recovery and a return to the front, so before long it was kept from the soldier himself, unless he was thought to have no chance of getting better. Some doctors claimed that DAH was misdiagnosed neurasthenia, or perhaps a pre-existing heart problem that had previously gone unnoticed.[137] Hysteria and neurasthenia were themselves frequently referred to as shell shock, perhaps not by all doctors but certainly in everyday speech.

A diagnosis of hysteria was made on the basis of symptoms, not their presumed cause. The symptoms consisted of partial or total loss of control over bodily functions and might be expressed in convulsions or paralysis. Neurocirculatory asthenia, otherwise known as neurasthenia, was initially a diagnosis regarded as appropriate when the most prominent symptom was nervous exhaustion. As time went on it became an umbrella term covering all sorts of mental ailments originating in fear. Psychologist W.H.R. Rivers and others preferred to speak of fear neurosis, a milder form of mental disorder whose most obvious manifestations were headaches, nausea, dizziness, memory loss and chronic fatigue.[138] Generally speaking, however, neurasthenia was diagnosed whenever there was a suspicion that the cause lay in prolonged exposure to extreme mental and physical strain.[139] In 1916, the year in which it was most prevalent, neurasthenia accounted for more than thirty per cent of all cases in which a man who was suffering no physical illness or injury was dismissed from the British army.[140] Ultimately there was no clear-cut distinction between the four categories of mental illness, and the dividing

137 Young, *Harmony of Illusions*, 52, 60–61; Hyams, 'War Syndromes', 399; Gillespie, *Psychological Effects of War*, 181–5; Shepard, *War of Nerves*, 65–6; Shepard, 'Early Treatment', 451

138 Howorth, *Shell-Shock*, 4; Binneveld, *Om de geest*, 98

139 Young, *Harmony of Illusions*, 52; Joules, *The Doctor's View*, 50

140 Bourke, *Dismembering the Male*, 109

line between neurasthenia and hysteria was particularly vague. If doctors were asked to name the symptoms, they tended to tell an almost identical story in either case, although this did not prevent them from insisting there was a marked difference between the two. The diagnosis seems to have depended to a great degree on time and place and above all on the knowledge of the doctor responsible for treatment, which was by and large chronically inadequate. Soldiers with the same symptoms might be diagnosed quite differently. There is little doubt that epilepsy was sometimes mistaken for neurosis and vice versa.[141]

Clearly there is something odd about the term 'shell shock', officially defined as:

> emotional shock, either acute in men with neuropathic predisposition, or developing slowly as a result of prolonged strain and terrifying experience, the final breakdown being sometimes brought about by some relatively trivial cause. [Or] nervous and mental exhaustion, the result of prolonged strain and hardship.

For one thing, this definition was used only by English speakers. Germans suffered from *Kriegsneurose* (war neurosis), *Granatshock* (shell shock in the original British sense) or *Granatfieber* (shell fever), a peculiar condition that allowed patients to function perfectly normally most of the time, until someone, deliberately or not, let slip the word 'trench' or 'shell'.[142] Frenchmen were affected by *trouble nerveux* (nervous trouble), *choq traumatique* (traumatic shock) or *traumatisme de guerre* (war trauma), and Belgian soldiers on the Yser suffered from *d'n klop* or *la kloppe* (derived from 'beklopt': a Dutch word for 'not quite right in the head' or even 'completely mad'). It was a condition diagnosed in soldiers who kept glancing around in a panic, had a huddled stance as they shuffled along the trenches, or lay stiff with fear on their bunks and could not be roused. In *Maskers op? ... maskers af!* (Masks On? ... Masks Off!) Louis E. De Mey wrote of it as follows:

> Stout lads have felt their minds give way under the violence of war. ... They were destined to play a role in life. ... Now they lie here, and only outwardly do they still seem like people. ... Here lies a boy whose body shakes incessantly with massive nervous shocks. Over there is one with his eyes wide open: he looks into the misty distance ... and simply lies motionless. Then there are those who wander around; suddenly they stop still in the strangest poses, as if

141 Young, *Harmony of Illusions*, 59, 61; Gijswijt-Hofstra & Porter, *Cultures of Neurasthenia*, 265–6; Shepard, 'Early Treatment', 447; Micale & Lerner, *Traumatic Pasts*, 216

142 Babington, *Shell-Shock*, 48; Thomas, *Die Katrin wird Soldat*, 245

> contemplating something extraordinary ... or they come up to you, shyly put out a hand and say the most incoherent things.[143]

The inadequacy of the term shell shock, however, is not a purely linguistic matter. The term was first used after several soldiers who had been near exploding shells died some time later, even though they had no apparent wounds. At the time the British thought about mental disorders largely in biological terms, an attitude that prevailed all over Europe but in Britain more than anywhere else. A physical cause had to be found for every psychiatric profile and sure enough, microscopic bleeding and other vascular changes to the brain were discovered in these particular men. One of the early cases suffered constant trembling, which set in immediately after an explosion, along with depression and fits of weeping. The following day he temporarily lost the power of speech and was unable to do anything. That evening he became manic and screamed incessantly: 'Keep them back, keep them back!' After a night's sleep with the help of morphine and chloroform he seemed better when he woke the next day, but he died a short time later.[144]

After a while it became clear that insanity like this had all kinds of causes; it did not occur only in the near vicinity of bursting shells that might have damaged the nervous system. Some of the men affected had not even been near the turmoil of battle, so efforts were made to find possible emotional as well as biological causes. Partly at the insistence of psychologist Charles S. Myers – the one who had introduced it in the medical world at the beginning of the war –, in 1917 the British authorities, medical and military, began officially using the term Not Yet Diagnosed (Nervous) or NYD(N). Shell shock was to disappear from their vocabulary, they decided, since it was bad for morale. It suggested too direct a connection between mental disorders and the business of war. This may have been an effective strategy as far as the military top brass and the medical elite were concerned, but the term was never successfully marginalized let alone abolished. From late 1915 or early 1916 onwards, every British war neurotic was shell-shocked, and measures introduced in late 1916 aimed at enforcing a ban on the use of the term came too late to have any effect. Shell shock had become a synonym for war neurosis of all kinds, and the use of the term in general parlance would only increase after the war. Any connection with its original meaning had been lost.[145]

A second reason why doctors and others in authority wished to adopt more neutral terminology – a subject we shall examine in the next chapter under the heading of military psychiatry – was that a number of the symptoms exhibited by war neurotics could be seen among psychiatric patients in peacetime. It was for this reason that medical officer Frank Richardson, author of *Fighting Spirit:*

143 De Schaepdrijver, *De Groote Oorlog*, 183; for a definition of shell shock see: Jones & Wessely, 'War Syndromes', 67

144 Young, *Harmony of Illusions*, 51

145 Myers, *Shell Shock*, 92, 97, 101; Jones & Wessely, 'War Syndromes', 67–8; Gersons, 'Posttraumatische stressstoornis', 895

*a Study of Psychological Factors in War*, criticized another term in common use: soldier's heart. He wanted to see it replaced everywhere and in every case by the term DAH, also current in peacetime, because that was a disorder it closely resembled.[146] Yet we should ask ourselves whether terms like soldier's heart or shell shock, or those of later vintage such as combat exhaustion or combat stress, are as objectionable as their detractors claim, even if not perhaps strictly accurate from a medical point of view. The symptoms may have been fairly similar to mental illness in peacetime, although medical historians Edgar Jones and Simon Wessely are quite right to point out that the symptoms of shell shock bear 'little resemblance' to the modern definition of Post Traumatic Stress Disorder. The cause, however, was generally very different. It is virtually certain that many of the men who suffered from neurosis in wartime would never have become mentally ill had they not experienced – or feared – the extreme conditions of front-line service. Older terms for the same psychological response include 'nostalgia', which referred to the problems that afflicted young American soldiers during the Civil War and were thought to stem largely from homesickness, and 'tropical weakness', diagnosed during the Spanish-American War of the late nineteenth century. These names make no reference to war and neither does the current term, PTSD. Similarly, unlike soldier's heart and shell shock, the diagnoses DAH and NYD(N) had no wartime connotations. These acronyms offered a way of avoiding terms that suggested it might not be the fault of the soldier himself that he had collapsed, but rather that his problems were due at least in part to the intolerable pressure his circumstances had placed upon him.[147]

It seems more than credible that this was in fact precisely the reason why the term 'shell shock' became synonymous with war neurosis in general, despite the well-founded medical criticism of it, in the context of the 1914–18 war. Terminology like NYD(N), DAH, hysteria and neurasthenia were meaningless to soldiers and civilians alike. Shell shock on the other hand, like *Granatshock*, *Granatfieber* and so on, contained references not only to war but to artillery and trench warfare in particular. The term says something about the 1914–18 war, just as for example 'combat exhaustion' says something about the Second World War and 'combat stress' about the war in Vietnam. Moreover, to a soldier the term was attractive in that it placed the blame for a mental disorder outside the man himself and even sounded a heroic note. It did not of itself impose the stigma of being labelled either a coward or mentally inferior, whether for reasons of heredity or not.

'Shell shock' has another special feature, one that raises it above its continental equivalents such as *Kriegsneurose* or *choq de guerre* and one that in my view

---

146 Babington, *For the Sake of Example*, 285–6; Liddle, *Passchendaele in Perspective*, 194

147 Jones & Wessely, 'War Syndromes', 67; Jones, Wessely, *From Shell Shock to PTSD*, 2–3; Myers, *Shell Shock*, 66; Winter & Baggett, *1914–18*, 212; Hyams, 'War Syndromes', 399; Busfield, 'Class and Gender', 309

has enabled it to stand the test of time and become a universal term, no longer a strictly British one. It is a feature that explains why shell shock has evolved from a medical diagnosis for nervous collapse under combat stress into a metaphor for almost everything that war – sometimes even ordinary life – can do to the human mind.[148] Shell shock is concise, alliterative, powerful, not only suggestive of a war fought with mortars and shells but sounding like war, like the bursting of mortars and shells. This has helped enable it to grow from a term for the insanity suffered in wartime into a term for the insanity of war itself, the First World War in particular. Shell shock says something not only about the shock that the experience of war inflicted on the individual psyche but about the widespread shock caused by the outbreak of war, the general shock caused by the way it was fought, and the universal shock the war had brought about by the time it ended, a shock that can still be felt to this day.

*Definition*

Determining exactly what should be defined as a war neurosis has always been a difficult and perilous business. The official British definition of a mentally ill or wounded soldier ran as follows: 'the man who becomes ineffective in battle as a direct result of his personality being unable to stand up to the stresses of combat.'[149] This is a broad definition – many would say too broad – embracing anyone whose existing mental disorder was made worse by the conditions of combat, along with anyone whose physical wounds, especially disfigurement and castration, were naturally accompanied by psychiatric problems, and anyone who suffered from purely psychological problems caused exclusively by the circumstances in which he found himself.[150] Such problems could be extremely severe. When he recovered, E. Meddemen said he hoped never to experience such a nervous collapse again. He would rather be hit.[151]

As we have seen, in the British army from around the turn of 1916 onwards, all psychiatric cases came under the heading of shell shock, a term that, although already in use among both officers and men for some time, was introduced into medical science by Myers. He had qualified as a doctor but was working as a psychologist, and he would later admit that the term was ill-chosen, for all the reasons given above. Myers, like his old companion Rivers, had been part of a small group of pre-war British psychiatrists and psychologists who were more interested in possible psychological causes of insanity than in its presumed organic origins.[152] Perhaps it was because of this that Myers quickly realized neurosis

148 Winter, 'Shell-Shock', 3

149 Babington, *For the Sake of Example*, 283–4

150 Holmes, *Firing Line*, 254

151 Macdonald, *Roses of No Man's Land*, 213

152 Myers, *Shell Shock*, 109, 127–8; Howorth, *Shell-Shock*, 1–2; Shepard, *War of Nerves*, 21–2; Binneveld, 'Shell Shock Versus Trouble Nerveux', 56

was by no means always caused by a bursting shell. Even an event that seemed insignificant compared to the things soldiers had to deal with every day could prove the final straw.[153] The War Office Committee on Shell Shock, which carried out research in 1920 and published its report in 1922, concluded that there were three types of psychological wounding. At the top of the list came displacements of atmospheric pressure, carbon monoxide poisoning, and microscopic brain haemorrhages following an explosion. These were the causes that gave shell shock its name. Occasionally the committee made reference to the weight of the excessive loads men carried, or to uniforms that fitted too tightly, pressing in on the chest. In actual fact few soldiers had problems that could be traced back to any of these physical causes. Secondly there was psychological dysfunction as a result of mental and physical exhaustion, which occurred much more frequently and which often cleared up after a few days' rest (although it might be no simple matter to convince the patient of this). Third on the list were the true war neuroses.[154]

Various distinctions had been noted during the war, and it was striking that neurosis expressed itself differently in officers than in other ranks. Ordinary soldiers were usually seen as hysterics, in other words their problems must have lain dormant, perhaps for quite some time, before suddenly worsening into mental confusion, often manifesting itself in physical disability. Men without any discernable sickness or injury became blind, paralysed or unable to speak. Their paralysis was real, and it was not always confined to the legs. Paralysis of the right arm – and therefore the trigger finger – was frequently recorded. Psychoanalyst Simmel believed that muteness and stuttering were the result of internal resistance to officers' orders against which no protest was permitted. A soldier had to be silent and obey, so he became silent. Neurologist Frederick W. Mott agreed. This explained why muteness was rare among officers.[155]

It was Simmel, incidentally, who attempted to explain the prevalence during battle of neurosis rather than psychosis, which was rare among the troops in 1914–18, although problems that developed after the war tended to be psychotic in nature. He concluded that neurosis not only represented a flight from the trenches and from reality in general but formed a buffer against the more serious psychosis. Neurosis could be seen as a transitional stage on the way to a complete and more fundamental break with reality, which normally occurred only after a man arrived home. If it occurred at all. The most 'normal' response by far was to forget about the war and get on with life. Of those soldiers who emerged from the conflict with few mental problems or with only mild neurosis, a small proportion were found to be schizophrenic years later.[156]

---

153 Ellis, *Eye-Deep*, 116–17; Macdonald, *Roses of No Man's Land*, 213–14

154 Holmes, *Firing Line*, 257; Gilbert, *First World War*, 275–6; Howorth, *Shell-Shock*, 2; Dean, *Shook Over Hell*, 30; Shepard, *War of Nerves*, 138–41

155 Leed, *No Man's Land*, 167–8; Joules, *The Doctor's View*, 51

156 Leed, *No Man's Land*, 189–90

Some doctors went so far as to argue there was a direct connection between causes and symptoms. A man who had thrust a bayonet into an enemy soldier's face might develop a tic in his facial muscles. If he had bayoneted the enemy in the stomach he would present with intestinal problems. Blindness was the result of witnessing extraordinarily horrific scenes, while being no longer able to endure the screams of the wounded could lead to deafness. Other doctors refused to accept that any such firm link existed. Instead they pointed to the accumulation of impressions a man had to deal with in a war. If a man dragged his feet, for example, it did not mean he was unable to cope with his memory of being stuck in the mud. Rather, this second group of doctors argued, a conflict had arisen in the soldier's psyche between the desire to move forwards out of a sense of duty, comradeship, fear of people in authority and so forth, and the desire to flee, prompted by a fear of death.[157]

Officers reacted in ways that can usually be explained in the light of the less demanding physical tasks and more demanding mental challenges they faced. Because of their greater responsibility for, and control over, what they did or declined to do, they usually suffered from nightmares, sleeplessness, memory loss, crying fits, or panic attacks, all commonly suppressed by drink. According to Graves, officers who had served for two or more years at the front without spending several weeks either on technical courses or in hospital were alcoholics to a man. Their long-term complaints and the comparatively consistent severity of their mental problems indicated neurasthenia rather than hysteria. In percentage terms, neurasthenia was twice as likely to be diagnosed among officers as among other ranks.[158]

The responsibilities placed on officers made them only half as likely, again in percentage terms, to break down while battle raged but more likely to do so after an offensive was over. Leave, and ultimately the armistice, allowed officers in particular to relax in peace, and sometimes this was exactly what tipped the balance, leading to mental illness or in some cases suicide. This helps to explain why among British men suffering from war neurosis in 1916–17 there was one officer for every six men, whereas the overall ratio of officers to other ranks in the British army was around one in thirty.[159]

In the long run the responsibilities that went with service as an officer made psychological illness more severe and persistent. Like their men, officers and NCOs sometimes developed paralysis without any demonstrable physical cause.[160] Ellis writes of an NCO who had been in France and Flanders without a break from August 1914 to July 1915 and who went on leave in an apparently normal state of mind. Immediately on arrival in London he collapsed. It emerged that

157 Leed, *No Man's Land*, 178–9

158 Winter & Baggett, *1914–18*, 212; Ellis, *Eye-Deep*, 117; Graves, *Goodbye*, 144; Bleker, *Medizin und Krieg*, 193; Hynes, *Soldiers' Tale*, 63

159 Verdoorn, *Arts en Oorlog*, 366; Bourke, *Dismembering the Male*, 112

160 Holmes, *Firing Line*, 269

his breakdown had been prompted by a dread that he would not be able to stand up to his increasing responsibilities when he returned to the continent. In eleven months on active service he had been buried alive once, wounded twice and gassed twice, without suffering any obvious mental problems.[161] Of course the distinction between hysteria and neurasthenia does not explain why British officers received better treatment and were not returned to the front so quickly as their men, let alone why a majority of officers were never sent back at all, while only a minority of ordinary soldiers were allowed to remain in Britain. That was simply one of the differences between officers and men, and many people saw it as a perfectly acceptable policy, stemming from the nature of the military hierarchy and the strict class system that prevailed at the time.[162]

The distinction between officers and men should be borne in mind in examining how their problems were diagnosed. All the available statistics about neurasthenia among officers and hysteria in other ranks are drawn from doctors' records. But were their assessments correct? Diagnosis is always based on a combination of clinical judgement and social and cultural considerations. In the British army, Irishmen and lowland Scots were more likely to be labelled malingerers than men from any other national or regional groupings. In the German army, Jews were regarded with suspicion as being 'innately' less able to cope with the masculine demands of war. Some people believed the Jews were responsible for Germany's failure to win the war, claiming they shirked front-line service. Northern Germans were said to be mentally tougher than southern Germans, and generally speaking an ordinary soldier was more likely than an officer to be regarded as hysterical, simply because he belonged to the lower social classes. The lack of clear-cut categories of mental illness meant that men with identical symptoms were diagnosed differently according to who happened to be treating them. On several occasions Myers quite rightly observed that doctors, whether they worked up near the front line or back in Britain, were called upon to diagnose mental illness without any experience or knowledge of the matter and without ever being sufficiently interested to study such problems in depth. Those who did have the requisite qualities and qualifications often served under those who did not. The sources therefore do little to reinforce the diagnoses of 'neurasthenia' among officers and 'hysteria' among ordinary soldiers. Indeed Allan Young, author of *Harmony of Illusions*, claims that the symptoms displayed by several officers described in the medical literature as neurasthenic are more suggestive of hysteria. One explanation might be that a diagnosis of hysteria was made only when supported by circumstantial factors. Other ranks were expected to develop symptoms of hysteria, since they were physically and mentally weak, and generally inferior to the class from which officers were born. Although neurasthenia, like hysteria, might point to 'congenital' weakness, only neurasthenia could be produced by external factors alone. It was therefore a less stigmatizing diagnosis than hysteria, even if it did

161 Ellis, *Eye-Deep*, 121
162 Ellis, *Eye-Deep*, 121

not always seem so to the officer concerned. Attaching labels to men from the lower social classes was obviously a far simpler matter than defining the problems of the male offspring of the wealthy. Furthermore, in the decades before the war – primarily but not exclusively in Germany – hysteria had been associated with the lower classes and with women in particular, whereas neurasthenia was a disorder of the upper classes, affecting both men and women.[163]

Generally speaking, neurotics could expect little sympathy from the military and political authorities, from doctors, or even from ordinary citizens. Men who suffered psychological problems after a major battle or after shelling lasting for weeks were treated with some understanding, but others were regarded with suspicion or met with a shaming silence.[164] Officers were saved from the same fate, to some degree at least, by the diagnosis of neurasthenia. Another distinction between the two was at least as important: medical theories surrounding hysteria prescribed harsh treatment, designed to restore the will to fight, whereas rest and a good diet were regarded as the best treatments for neurasthenia.[165] It seems reasonable to conclude that doctors were reluctant to diagnose hysteria in officers because they wanted to spare members of their own class the pain and indignity of electrotherapy.

### *Numbers*

It is impossible to know for certain how many men suffered from shell shock, *trouble nerveux*, *d'n klop* or *Kriegsneurose*, since although several doctors had warned before the war about the disastrous effects on the human psyche of massive artillery firepower, for a long time there was resistance to the idea that combat could cause psychological problems. We should take into account the possibility that among soldiers found to be suffering from war neurosis, some were not so much neurotic as retarded. They ought never to have been declared fit for service, but soldiers were needed, so the official standards for mental capacity were minimal.[166] Nonetheless, no one doubts that the number of shell-shock cases was high, so high that it soon became obvious something would have to be done, although the response was half-hearted in comparison to the facilities put in place to treat physical wounds on a similar scale. A handful of specialists were

163 Myers, *Shell Shock*, 51, 90–91, 112, 120–21, 124; Young, *Harmony of Illusions*, 62–3; Mosse, *Shell Shock*, 4; Kaufmann, 'Science as Cultural Practice', 137; Bourke, 'Effeminacy, ethnicity and the end of trauma', 60; Von der Dunk, *Voorbij de Verboden Drempel*, 121–2; Gijswijt-Hofstra & Porter, *Cultures of Neurasthenia*, 10, 16; Busfield, 'Class and Gender', 307

164 Bourke, *Moral Economy*, 8

165 Bourke, *Dismembering the Male*, 116

166 Brants & Brants, *Velden van weleer*, 322; Dean, *Shook Over Hell*, 63; Cooter, Harrison & Sturdy, *War, Medicine and Modernity*, 152–3

recruited, on a temporary basis, and a few specialist hospitals were opened.[167] This is one more reason why official records on the subject of war neurosis are deficient, especially in relation to the early years of the war. In the absence of reliable evidence, the compilers of Britain's *Medical History of the War* settled upon the figure of around 80,000 cases, or two per cent of British men mobilized, a percentage that gave little cause for alarm. In fact it was a misleading extrapolation, greatly underestimating the scale of the problem. We may nevertheless wonder, like John Ellis, at a situation in which around 20,000 men per year on the British side alone were officially driven temporarily or permanently insane.[168]

The American Expeditionary Force, active for only a short time, recorded around 70,000 cases of mental illness – some say the real figure was closer to 100,000 – and more than 40,000 men were dismissed from service prematurely as a result. This is cause enough to doubt the British statistics, and there are other reasons for questioning the British total of 80,000. German psychiatrist Robert Gaupp concluded in 1917 that neurotics formed the largest category of casualties in the German army. The rapid advance of the early weeks of the war appeared to confirm the presumed mental resilience of the German soldier, but once the conflict became bogged down the German army faced a problem of war neurosis on an increasing scale and after a while it was comparable to that of the other armies. Again the figures diverge, but even an official report by the German military medical service for 1914–18 gives a figure of over 600,000, or to be precise: 613,047. Entire German companies were afflicted with repeated bouts of vomiting or unstoppable crying fits. Of course we need to bear in mind that far more Germans than British saw active service, but not seven and a half times as many. A difference in diagnosis played its part too. The 80,000 British men with shell shock were the most serious cases, whereas the German figure of 600,000 included all soldiers who had displayed some form of psychological problem. Recent figures suggest that the German and British armies each had about 200,000 psychiatric patients, despite the fact that the German army was far larger. (So much for the statistically greater resilience of the British soldier.)[169] Even these more recent figures, however, are no more than an educated guess.

Although Britain began the war with a professional army, there is no reason to assume that the German soldier was more likely to suffer nervous collapse. In fact the reverse holds true, not because of any innate psychological disparity but

---

167 Ellis, *Eye-Deep*, 117–18

168 Ellis, *Eye-Deep*, 118; Gilbert, *First World War*, 61; Young, *Harmony of Illusions*, 41–2

169 Van Bergen, '80,000 British Shell Shock Victims', passim; Verdoorn, *Arts en Oorlog*, 367; Binneveld, *Om de geest*, 81; Gibelli, *Schell Shock et Grande Geurre*, 4; Riedesser & Verderber, *Aufrüstung der Seelen*, 12; Chickering, *Imperial Germany*, 99; Eckart & Gradmann, *Die Medizin*, 90, 92–3 (note), 93; Heyman, *World War I*, 77; Kaufmann, 'Science as Cultural Practice', 125; Shepard, 'Shell-Shock', 40; Eckart, 'Eiskalt mit Würgen und Schlucken', 9

because in the early years of the century it was impressed even more strongly upon British youth, especially the middle-class boys who attended British public schools and were later to become officers, that manliness meant not showing any emotion. They must suppress all fear, indeed they were not to feel any fear. Far from making them better able to endure their harsh wartime experiences, this only made them more vulnerable.[170]

The statistics of war neurosis are arbitrary by definition. It will be clear by now that the distinction drawn in many accounts between normality and madness is meaningless. In his book *Shell-Shock*, Anthony Babington writes that given all we know about the war it is no wonder so many collapsed. The miracle is that a much larger number of soldiers 'remained firm and sound in mind'.[171] Was this in fact so? Were those not officially diagnosed as shell-shocked, who had no *Kriegsneurose* and did not suffer from *d'n klop* or *choq traumatique*, stable and psychologically healthy? There is of course no hard and fast distinction between having and not having a neurosis of some kind that bears any comparison to the distinction between having or not having a broken leg, or influenza. Many soldiers who were not officially suffering from neurosis certainly had symptoms of exhaustion, and they were exposed for long periods to extraordinary stress and mortal fear. All soldiers dealt time and again with the loss of comrades, often including family members and good friends.[172] This left its mark, yet most were assumed to be mentally healthy. On a sliding scale from normal to plainly mad, a line had to be drawn somewhere. The two per cent of British soldiers who officially suffered from shell shock must be seen in the context of the seven to ten per cent of British officers who suffered a nervous collapse at some stage and the three to four per cent of other ranks who broke down.[173] In other words, at some point somebody had to say: that man is shell-shocked and that man is not. There was no obvious way of knowing where the line should be drawn. In practice an ordinary soldier would be relatively quick to say he had crossed that line, whereas an officer would be reluctant to agree. There were also significant differences between doctors, whose decisions generally ranged across the middle ground. We can say with certainty that the official boundary lay closer to 'absolute insanity' than to 'functional normality'. It is clear too that as the number of dead, sick, and mentally and physically wounded rose disturbingly, suggesting that human reserves were steadily being used up, the boundary shifted even further in the direction of absolute insanity. More and more soldiers who were not officially diagnosed with war neurosis were suffering from disorders that made it virtually impossible for them to function properly.[174] H. Quigley of the 12th Royal Scots, for example,

170 Withuis, 'Het oplappen van soldaten', 91; Young, *Harmony of Illusions*, 65–6; Hynes, *Soldiers' Tale*, 63–4

171 Babington, *Shell-Shock*, 124

172 Hermans & Schmidt, 'De traumatische neurose', 536

173 Gersons, 'Posttraumatische stressstoornis', 894

174 Ellis, *Eye-Deep*, 118–19

thought of the war as 'that time of emotional stress and unequalled difficulty of retaining mental stability'. Another officer recalled that his nerves had given out in direct proportion to the length of time he spent at the front. Lieutenant J. Tyndale-Biscoe of the Royal Horse Artillery was eighteen and sitting in the officers' mess when he suddenly broke into a sweat. He said that if the Germans started shelling at that moment, he would definitely run away. A German salvo came over and he fled, along with the man sitting next to him, who had apparently been unnerved by what his fellow officer had said. Laughing like madmen, they ran from shell-hole to shell-hole until eventually they came to their senses. Quigley, Tyndale-Biscoe, the man next to him, and many others like them were all officially declared fit for front-line service.[175]

Clearly, medical data on the subject of shell shock should be regarded as unreliable, almost by definition. After Passchendaele, for example, doctors reported that 267 officers and 3,771 men were suffering from neurosis. Even the figure of 5,346 cases given later by the leader of the medical team responsible for treating the condition, neurologist Gordon Holmes, would mean a rate of no more than about one per cent of the total number of British soldiers deployed. But neither of these figures includes those labelled 'shell-shocked (sick)' as opposed to 'shell-shocked (wounded)' – the same goes for the total of 80,000 incidentally, a point we shall look at shortly – and there can be no firm diagnoses for officers and men who had undoubtedly suffered a nervous collapse but had not reported it. Many medical officers tended to do all they could to prove a man was *not* neurotic, and this too must have helped keep the figures to a minimum.[176]

Few of the men who experienced psychological problems ended up in one of the specialist hospitals. If all those with symptoms had been hospitalized, practically no one would have been left to carry out the orders of the general staffs. Mental exhaustion of varying degrees of severity was regarded as normal. It was part of the everyday burden of a fighting man.[177] True madness was something else.

As early as the Battle of Mons, whole British divisions slowly but surely drifted away en masse because they were sick of fighting.[178] A few men were allowed home. By late 1914 more than a hundred British officers and 800 men had been treated for psychiatric problems,[179] even though in the early weeks of the war many doctors refused to acknowledge the existence of such conditions. The numbers began to increase dramatically once the war became bogged down at the end of 1914, when men had to dig themselves in and thousands of bombs and shells began flying incessantly across no man's land. The new specialist hospitals were filled not long after they opened and the additional hospitals set up to take

175 Ellis, *Eye-Deep*, 119

176 Babington, *Shell-Shock*, 100–101, 104–5; Shepard, *War of Nerves*, 53–4

177 Ellis, *Eye-Deep*, 121

178 Holmes, *Firing Line*, 229

179 Gilbert, *First World War*, 61; Babington, *Shell-Shock*, 43

the overspill were soon full to capacity as well.[180] Most such establishments were on the continent, and from 1917 onwards most were close to the front, but the British were forced to open six new mental hospitals back in Britain to add to the six psychiatric institutions already in existence there.[181]

Ambulance nurse Claire Elise Tisdall of the Voluntary Aid Detachment described the arrival of a train-load of mental cases. It was the first time she had encountered psychiatric patients. There was no room for her in the ambulances, so she was left waiting at the station while the 'ordinary' wounded were taken to hospital. She saw a blacked-out ambulance approaching and asked one of the male nurses – at that time female nurses were kept well away from the most severely shell-shocked patients – what it was for. Surely the train must be empty by now. It was not. The ambulance had come to fetch the remaining passengers: psychiatric patients who were regarded as hopeless cases. 'There was nothing you could do and they were going to a special place. They were terrible.'[182]

After about half a year the extent of the problem began to emerge. The main editorial in *The Lancet* of December 1914 pointed to potential difficulties, although understandably with a degree of non-committal caution.[183] A month earlier, in the *British Medical Journal* of November 1914, Dr Albert Wilson had expressed the view that the war would produce only a limited number of psychiatric cases. He added that should problems arise in this area, a good stiff drink would generally prove the best remedy. There were officers who insisted, no matter what happened, that the word 'fear' did not exist in the vocabulary of their companies, and others who sniffed that they would cure any soldier who seemed on the verge of having trouble with his nerves speedily, professionally, and permanently by tying him to the barbed wire for a while.[184] Of course such remarks – which were heard a good deal less often after the Battle of Loos and hardly at all after the Somme[185] – did nothing to relieve the problem; if anything they made it worse. Nothing anyone said could conceal the fact that during the war 30,000 British men suffering psychiatric problems were brought home for good, or that in 1917, 4 out of every 1,000 British men serving overseas became seriously mentally ill, compared to 2 soldiers per 1,000 back in the British Isles and 1 in every 1,000 civilians. Nor could anyone ignore the fact that in 1922 some 50,000 British ex-servicemen were in receipt of war pensions because they were still mentally disturbed.[186]

Martin Gilbert assumes that the percentage of British soldiers suffering from war neurosis was not significantly different from the proportion in the other

180 Soesman, *Oorlogspsychose*, 33–4; Binneveld, *Om de geest*, 81

181 Gilbert, *First World War*, 357–8

182 Macdonald, *Roses of No Man's Land*, 216; Binneveld, *Om de geest*, 15; Thomas, *Die Katrin wird Soldat*, 245

183 Babington, *Shell-Shock*, 45

184 Winter, *Death's Men*, 129

185 Gilbert, *First World War*, 201, 275

186 Winter, *Death's Men*, 130; Holmes, *Firing Line*, 257

armies. He therefore concludes that based on the figure of 50,000 men with war pensions in 1922, in four years of war in the West and East around a quarter of a million soldiers must have suffered a nervous collapse. Aside from the fact that it is unclear why he multiplies the figure of 50,000 by five, there are various reasons for regarding this as an extremely arbitrary calculation. First of all we cannot be certain that the British percentages applied to the other belligerents. Secondly, in 1921 65,000 British veterans were allocated pensions on the same grounds. If Gilbert had made his calculations on that basis – and why pick 1922 rather than 1921? – he would have arrived at 325,000 cases. If he had started out from the figure of 80,000 mentioned earlier, which most people accept (and which was also the number of men qualifying for a pension in 1928), then his extrapolation would have produced a figure of 400,000. Elsewhere in his book, Gilbert does refer to the figure of 80,000 cases at the end of the war, although only in the context of neurosis 'including what came to be known as "shell-shock"'. Elsewhere he talks of 50,000 'genuine cases' in November 1918.[187]

Aside from these discrepancies it is misleading to use the figure for war pensions as a basis for calculation, since it is a minimal figure, certainly in Britain, where soldiers still suffering from psychiatric problems after the war were required to prove these had arisen from their experiences of combat. Many will have been unable to do so. No allowance was made for the fact that in some soldiers the condition assumed problematic proportions only after the armistice.[188] Many ex-servicemen who had suffered from shell shock during the war were refused pensions even though they were seriously mentally ill and had been recognized as such by the authorities. Many others had become ill or made their problems known only after the war. Then there were soldiers who wandered around the battlefield, stunned and vacant-eyed, who in most cases must have been severely traumatized; those who survived will often have been in no position to apply for a pension, successfully or not. Moreover, as already mentioned, a relatively arbitrary distinction was made between soldiers who were 'shell-shocked (sick)' and those who were 'shell-shocked (wounded)'. Only those in the 'wounded' category qualified for decorations and pensions and were included in the total of 80,000. Those categorized as 'sick' were regarded as having psychiatric abnormalities that could be traced back to their pre-war personal and familial circumstances or to 'character defects'. The 'shell-shocked (wounded)' on the other hand were defined as men whose problems originated in organic disturbances caused by the war. It was essential to place a large proportion in the 'sick' category, since only then could the huge loss of troop numbers attributed to shell shock be justified without the authorities having to identify the war as the main villain of the piece.

As soon as the one-sided organic approach had been abandoned, and with good reason, the war could be downplayed as a cause of neurosis. Psychiatrists went in search of traumas in a man's early years, or illnesses presumed to be

187 Gilbert, *First World War*, 61, 275–6, 541–2
188 Leed, *No Man's Land*, 188

hereditary.[189] Psychiatrist E.E. Southard discovered that one of his patients, who had begun having fits, had a family history of epilepsy. He automatically regarded this as more relevant than the fact that the man's first convulsion occurred after he had served two years at the front, been wounded four times, lost his father and five brothers, and survived being buried alive. Many other doctors had the same attitude. Yet in a study of the relationship between inherited disease and neurosis, Douglas Thom concluded that he could find no significant difference between soldiers who had suffered a nervous breakdown and those who had not. Four to five per cent of neurotic patients had a family history of mental illness, compared to three to five per cent of 'normal' soldiers.[190]

It was impossible to distinguish with any certainty between the 'sick' and the 'wounded', and the difference was made even less clear-cut in practice by the lack of psychiatric expertise among doctors charged with the task. Moreover, some doctors shared the notion that the 'sick' were actually cowards, and this must have influenced the diagnostic process. Around forty per cent of psychiatric cases were categorized as 'wounded'. This is actually quite a high percentage. Many doctors, realizing they knew little and wary of the stigma imposed by the word 'sick', opted for 'wounded' if there was any room for doubt, to be on the safe side. In September 1918 the authorities decided that henceforth no man still on active service on the continent could be declared 'shell-shocked (wounded)'.[191]

The figures for 1921, 1922 and 1928 show that a fall in numbers due to natural wastage seemed to set in quickly at the start of the decade but proved short-lived. After a few years the number of shell-shock cases began to increase again, either because psychiatric problems that had arisen during the war were only now being recognized as such, or because neurosis emerged only later in some patients, who then succeeded in demonstrating a connection with the war. By 1939 a total of around 120,000 British ex-servicemen had been granted either a pension or a one-off payment for psychiatric damage stemming from their war experiences. Shortly before the Second World War, 30,000 British men were still receiving pensions for mental problems traceable to the previous conflict. They accounted for fifteen per cent of all war pensions being paid out at that time.[192]

### *Causes*

It does not take long to sum up the causes. Apart from a handful of cases of men who ought to have been declared unfit for duty from the outset on psychiatric grounds, the main cause was simply the war. Even if we examine the matter more

189 Myers, *Shell Shock*, 92–5, 96; Gersons, 'Posttraumatische stressstoornis', 895–6; Shepard, *A War of Nerves*, 29

190 Leed, *No Man's Land*, 172

191 Myers, *Shell Shock*, 97–8, 99, 101 (note); Liddle, *Passchendaele in Perspective*, 192; Babington, *Shell-Shock*, 87–8, 96–7, 120

192 Babington, *Shell-Shock*, 121; Macdonald, *Roses of No Man's Land*, 217 (note)

closely, the conclusion is briefly stated. There were almost as many origins of shell shock as there were patients. Particularly prominent causes were: shock or fear induced by explosions; the incessant noise; seeing horribly mutilated bodies, living or dead; the death of a friend; the sight of a physical wound to the sufferer's own person; and being buried alive.[193] Otto Binswanger, a German professor of psychiatry, wrote in an article published in 1922 that he found it difficult to say anything meaningful about war neurosis, not because few hard facts were available but because he had too many facts and they were too diverse. It was this same Binswanger, incidentally, who observed in the first year of the war that the soldier's psyche had changed. The enthusiasm and patriotic self-sacrifice he seems to have detected early on were quickly transformed into blind hatred and a ruthless urge to destroy.[194]

First among equals was the fear of being killed,[195] which paradoxically could transform itself into a desire to die. F.C. Bartlett wrote in his *Psychology and the Soldier*, published in 1927, that every lengthy stay at the front caused a man's thoughts to wander towards home and death. The unrealistic wish to be allowed home and the realistic fear of being killed could mutate into a longing for death. Once this happened, nervous collapse was not far away.[196] Here too, as with depression and general unease, the main instigator of madness was shellfire. If there was anything that could make a man wish to die, it was shelling, the fear of shelling, the noise of shelling, the helpless wait for a barrage to end. As the American Civil War had demonstrated decades earlier, bombardment was physical and mental torture, even if you were sitting more or less out of danger in an underground shelter. According to one British officer, shelling reduced a human being to a shivering beast. Various factors such as noise, fear, the arbitrariness of death and wounding, compounded by lack of sleep, all came together during a barrage.[197] Those who were not in deep dugouts pressed themselves flat to the ground and might try to dig themselves deeper into the earth with their fingernails.[198]

At Passchendaele, Reg Lawrence came upon two German soldiers who could not have been much older than seventeen. They were clutching each other, crying, frozen to the spot by the barrage that had just ended.[199] It was the last day of the Third Battle of Ypres. On the first day of the battle, Lieutenant Jim Annan had seen a man driven mad by the mortars and shells that flew incessantly overhead and exploded around them.

193 Binneveld, *Om de geest*, 81; Macdonald, *Passchendaele*, 146
194 Kaufmann, 'Science as Cultural Practice', 125; Mosse, *Fallen Soldiers*, 163
195 Gillespie, *Psychological Effects of War*, 180
196 Leed, *No Man's Land*, 22
197 Ellis, *Eye-Deep*, 62–3; Winter & Baggett, *1914–18*, 212
198 Macdonald, *1914–1918*, 84
199 Macdonald, *1914–1918*, 241

> He came running back towards us just like a spectre waving his arms, and shouting and yelling, 'Mother! Mother! Mother!' I left the platoon – I shouldn't have done that, but I went a little towards him and got hold of him and said: 'Come on. Come on over here, till we see to you.' But he was like a mad thing. He just shook me off and ran on yelling, 'Mother! Mother!' completely off his head. That was the last we saw of him.[200]

Aside from shelling, almost any event could push a soldier over the edge. After six men had been on sentry duty for sixteen hours without a break at Beaumont-Hamel in late 1916, 'one tried to bayonet the relief and another had to be forcibly held down'.[201] Barbusse wrote about a man who became distraught almost to the point of madness after coming upon the place where his native village had once stood, a settlement now completely wiped off the map.[202] And Moran described the case of a soldier who finally cracked on receiving a message that the last of his brothers had been killed.[203]

Renn tells of a front-line soldier who went mad after the man next to him was blown to pieces. A shell fragment had detonated a hand grenade on his belt.[204] On their way to the front, British Major C.A. Bill and his men passed a soldier who was struggling to escape the mud, into which he had sunk above his knees. Despite the efforts of four of them it proved impossible to free the man. After a while they had no option but to resume their march up to the line. Two days later they marched back along the same road and found the man still wrestling with the mud. He was now up to his neck in it and completely insane.[205]

During the Battle of the Somme, one German soldier found himself unable to stand up for the umpteenth time to run a few metres forward towards enemy fire. Hans Henning Freiherr Grote watched him suddenly burst into tears: '"My wife, my children! ... I can't do it any more, lieutenant!" It is terrible to see a strong, brave man cry. I feel that every order here is pointless, if the spirit is broken by horrific impressions.'[206] These cases seem entirely understandable. As we shall see, however, there were men whose problems cannot be explained by the things that apparently triggered them, unless we choose to define their cause as the war as a whole. There were some soldiers who went 'mad' without any direct prompting at all.

The mental sufferings of the men were not necessarily eased when they arrived at hospital – assuming of course that they did reach hospital at some stage. Many men suffering only mild trauma were driven completely insane at Casualty

200 Macdonald, *Passchendaele*, 100
201 Winter, *Death's Men*, 87
202 Barbusse, *Le Feu*, 165–7
203 Holmes, *Firing Line*, 198
204 Renn, *Krieg*, 265
205 Wilson, *Myriad Faces*, 473
206 Jünger, *Das Antlitz*, 167

Clearing Station no. 62, behind the lines at Ypres, where a special ward for shell-shocked patients admitted around 5,000 men during the Third Battle of Ypres.[207] Protracted bombardments at the CCS were an even greater test for the mental patients than for the doctors, the nurses, or the physically sick and wounded. Rifleman J.E. Maxwell lay in that ward. He described two patients running back and forth screaming, utterly distraught, as shells flew over and burst nearby.[208] Hoffman described a similar scene at a field hospital in July 1918:

> The wounded that came in now were particularly serious cases – men who had been wounded by tremendous shells. There was such screaming and anguish displayed by these sorely-wounded men. Seldom was it quiet at night. Men whose nerves broke would be screaming at night. There were many cases of shell-shock – men who had their maniacal moments when they felt they were still at the front, being subjected to shell fire. They were out of their minds and there was nothing that could be done about it; but it made it most unpleasant for the other wounded.[209]

This was reason enough for a base hospital that had a wing for shell-shock cases to arrange for its door jambs to be lined with rubber, its window sashes covered with felt and a thick carpet laid on the floors. Every sound was an abomination to the patients.[210] Grace Bignold of the Voluntary Aid Detachment said: 'Anything made them jump, a door banging, any sudden noise.'[211]

Despite the wide variation, there are several general factors that the causes of neurosis in 1914–18 have in common. War neurosis is not synonymous with the Great War to the extent we tend to assume.[212] It was first mentioned by Herodotus in his report on the Battle of Marathon in 490 BC[213] and some even see signs of PTSD – using the term highly anachronistically – in the Gilgamesh epic. Nevertheless, there are a number of reasons why war neurosis and the First World War are so often mentioned in the same breath, the most obvious being the abnormal level of violence. It is no coincidence that the term most commonly employed by the English speaking soldiers was 'shell shock'. In the end, however, the War Office Commission on Shell Shock concluded that five per cent at most of recognized cases of war neurosis could be traced back to physical causes. The remainder had emotional roots, perhaps combined with physical problems such as a general reduction in physical fitness due to the men's enforced sedentary

207 Macdonald, *Roses of No Man's Land*, 219
208 Macdonald, *Passchendaele*, 152
209 Fussell, *Bloody Game*, 175
210 Macdonald, *1914–18*, 250
211 Macdonald, *Roses of No Man's Land*, 215
212 Hynes, *Soldiers' Tale*, 62
213 Babington, *Shell-Shock*, 7

existence.[214] Some of these emotional factors too, however, were more typical of the First World War than of previous wars.

Many believe 'loss' to be a cause of neurosis: loss of family, friends, acquaintances or comrades. The war of 1914–18 brought loss on an unprecedented scale.[215] The number of conscripts too was unprecedented. Ordinary boys, working-class lads, had neither the martial mentality, the tradition of heroism and sacrifice, nor the good health seen in the majority of professional soldiers. In the later years of the war especially, the age and level of fitness required for admission to the armed forces were steadily reduced, while at the same time training declined in duration and quality. Moreover, this was the first war in which several modern inventions – gas, the aeroplane, the tank, the flame-thrower – were deployed on a significant scale. They may not have decided the outcome of the war but they certainly magnified its horrors enormously. Many psychiatrists quickly discerned a relationship between the technological character of modern warfare and the prevalence of neurosis. Machinery became dominant, relegating human beings to a secondary role, and the alienation of the individual soldier from the war he was fighting increased. These were some of the direct causes of neurosis.[216]

As a result of the unprecedentedly harsh experiences soldiers were put through, an already familiar phenomenon presented itself more often than in any previous conflict: fear of death or mutilation provoked a 'fight or flight' response. These two alternatives represented spurious if instinctive resolutions. Putting up a fight could at best lead to the death or mutilation of your opponent; it would not reduce your own chances of suffering. Soldiers could not simply go home if they did not want to fight on, so another way out was sought, whether a self-inflicted or deliberately incurred wound, surrender and captivity, or madness. Given the emphasis placed by the Judeo-Christian tradition on the commandment 'thou shalt not kill', the deliberate killing of an enemy must have been another important cause of serious psychiatric problems. This was often demonstrably the case, as in paralysis of the right arm,[217] but it is important to point out that it was not typical. Most soldiers who suffered psychiatric collapse had never killed anyone, at least so far as they knew. Twenty per cent of British war neurotics had never even personally taken part in a fire-fight. The fear of killing was a far less significant cause of neurosis than the fear of being killed, in fact psychiatrists were amazed at the ease with which a man could bring himself to kill an enemy soldier, often acting as if the opponent were no longer human. Men who were unable to live with the fact of having to kill were seen as exceptions to the rule. As Bourke correctly points out, 'The emphasis on emotional breakdown and psychiatric illness has obscured the fact that most men coped remarkably well with the demands being made upon them in wartime'.

214 Howorth, *Shell-Shock*, 2

215 Wilson, *Myriad Faces*, 752

216 Leed, *No Man's Land*, 164

217 Bourke, *Moral Economy*, 1–3; Leed, *No Man's Land*, 178

Psychiatrists decided that in many cases men were driven insane precisely because the type of war they were fighting made it almost impossible to kill anybody. There was hardly any man-to-man fighting, for instance. The impossibility of taking action that would destroy the enemy, the powerlessness and passivity of trench warfare, the impotent waiting for almost certain death made men mad. Sassoon believed the uncertainty of the war was the main factor in driving soldiers crazy. Certainty of any kind, he felt, even the certainty of death, would have come as a welcome relief.[218] Ordinary soldiers were quite rightly convinced that they could have no influence at all on what might happen to them. All a man had left was his mind, only his thoughts were still free, and so – unless he was wounded or killed – he fled inside himself, since within his own mind he could fight his own battle.[219] Neurosis was inextricably bound up with the enforced immobility of soldiers in the trenches. Illustrative of this is the fact that the number of men suffering from war neurosis fell dramatically when the conflict became a war of movement again, even though there was no reduction in the ferocity of the fighting, in fact quite the reverse. Men were becoming physically fit again and they could see the results of their efforts. They stopped feeling that their presence at the front was pointless.[220] We should be careful, however, not to generalize too much about the positive effect of the resumption of the war of movement on the mental health of the troops. It was an effect that showed itself mainly in those who had the upper hand: the Germans in the spring of 1918; Allied forces in the autumn of that year.

Closely connected to the men's immobilized impotence was the emptiness of the battlefield. A soldier rarely if ever saw the opposing side, except during a few major advances. Many found the invisibility of the enemy unbearable. It was in total contrast to the image with which most had joined up and gone into battle. Robert Michaels, a captain in the Australian army, wrote to his son: 'Modern combat is played out almost entirely invisibly; the new way of fighting demands of the soldier that he … withdraw from the sight of his opponent. He cannot fight upright on the earth but must crawl into and under it.'[221]

Eric Leed, author of *No Man's Land. Combat and Identity in World War I*, writes that the emptiness created when the two sides dug themselves in destroyed any notion of war as a human struggle. The threat was felt, but the sources of that threat, enemy soldiers who could be engaged with as human beings, remained out of sight. Moreover, digging in meant that the earth was both a home and a constant source of danger. Everyone knew the apparently empty landscape was full of enemy soldiers. The German language makes the point rather well: the

218 Bourke, 'Effeminacy, ethnicity and the end of trauma', 58; Winter, *Death's Men*, 141; Young, *Harmony of Illusions*, 63–4; Gillespie, *Psychological Effects of War*, 180; Shepard, *War of Nerves*, 33

219 Bourke, *Moral Economy*, 3

220 Leed, *No Man's Land*, 181

221 Leed, *No Man's Land*, 19

landscape was *Heim* (home), but at the same time *unheimlich* (forbidding).[222] It is worth remembering too that before the war hysteria was seen primarily as a female condition. The trenches made it a man's affliction. A common factor among those who suffered from hysteria seems to have been that they lived sedentary lives over which they could exert no influence, and which they would never have wished upon themselves.[223] We shall look at this in more detail in the section of the next chapter devoted to military psychiatry.

A number of researchers have suggested that neurosis develops as a result of threats to the ego, in other words to the individual in all his physical and mental manifestations. The causes are variable, but clearly war renders up innumerable situations in which the ego is threatened. Soldiers were fearful of physical destruction and some fled towards the escape route that we call neurosis, a way out that was both personally and socially more acceptable than mutiny, desertion or self-harm. It was rarely a matter of deliberate deception. The soldier himself was not conscious of the background to his neurosis.[224]

Another special feature of the First World War was that its purpose remained unclear to many of those who were fighting it. Why had it started? Why was it continuing? Why was it being conducted the way it was? The notion of a battle against ultimate evil, which was characteristic of the Second World War and other conflicts, and which – although we should be careful not to overstate the case – kept many people going, was less evident in the years 1914–18.

### *Symptoms*

As with the causes, so with the symptoms, perhaps to an even greater degree: the many varieties of madness were expressed in many different ways. This is quite logical. It is often possible to identify a connection between symptoms and causes, so the symptoms are likely to be at least as diverse as those who suffer them. The characteristic paralysis of the right arm demonstrates how specific the symptoms could be. There is a famous piece of film footage showing a soldier who no longer reacts to anything – at least according to the accompanying explanation – except the word 'shell!' On hearing it he leaps out of bed to take cover.[225] Babington writes of a man who screamed incessantly: 'He's gone! He's gone!' After a while it became clear that his brother had been killed as he stood next to him in a trench.[226] One of Rivers' patients at his war hospital for mental cases at Craiglockhart had broken down after he bent to pick up what he thought was a ball lying in the bottom of a trench. It was indeed a ball. An eyeball. Insanity had robbed him of his sight. Another had fallen face-first into the stomach of a corpse in an advanced state of

222 Leed, *No Man's Land*, 19–20; Higonnet, *Behind the Lines*, 202
223 Withuis, 'Het oplappen', 87–8, 90; Winter & Baggett, *1914–18*, 212
224 Whalen, *Bitter Wounds*, 62
225 See also: Babington, *Shell-Shock*, 47
226 Babington, *Shell-Shock*, 52

decomposition. The man could no longer keep food down, not only because he knew he had tasted rotting intestines but because the intestines had belonged to a German.[227]

In German hospitals behind the lines, Westman watched men experience over and over again the horrors of an artillery bombardment or gas attack. ‘They covered their faces with their hands, so as to protect them from shell splinters. Others cried out for their gas masks, which they could not find, and still others heard voices under their pillows or under their bed covers, threatening them with death.’ It was said, no doubt accurately, that soldiers in the grip of war neurosis wore the expressions of hunted animals.[228]

The belief that the war would never end, which Paul Fussell examines at length in his *The Great War and Modern Memory*,[229] was another factor that impacted on the mental health of the troops. Otto Dix, often tormented by depression, would find himself crawling through the trenches at night for another decade. Blunden wrote shortly before his death in 1974 that his experiences in the First World War had haunted him for the rest of his life. After the armistice, Sassoon regularly dreamed of having to leave for France again. Charles Carrington thought at first that the war had made him grow up fast. He later realized that it had put his development on hold for more than ten years. It took a new shock – the economic crash of 1929 – before he was able to get on with his life. The reactions of some, like the poet and composer Ivor Gurney, were more extreme still; even during hours of daylight they were unable to absorb the fact that the war had ended. Wounded in 1917, Gurney was admitted to a mental institution for the first time in 1918. Between 1919 and 1922 his condition seemed to improve. Then, after several attempts at suicide, he was sent to an asylum again, this time for good, and up until his death in 1937 he wrote war poetry pervaded by his fear of combat and his sense of guilt at abandoning his comrades. No one could convince him that all sides had laid down their arms in late 1918. It should be noted that Gurney, like Trakl, had experienced psychiatric problems prior to 1914, and at first the war actually seemed to do him good. His mental state was apparently influenced not only by the horrors of the front but by his stay at various hospitals, which included a doomed love affair with a nurse. Gurney was not alone in his fate. In 1998 a former soldier of the Black Watch, David Ireland, was interviewed in Stratheden Hospital in Scotland. He had been there since 1924.[230]

---

227 Young, *Harmony of Illusions*, 76; Leed, *No Man's Land*, 19; Withuis, ‘Het oplappen van soldaten’, 92–3; Shepard, *War of Nerves*, 88

228 Holmes, *Firing Line*, 269; Brants & Brants, *Velden van weleer*, 322; Dean, *Shook Over Hell*, 30

229 Fussell, *Great War*, 71–4

230 Sassoon, *Complete Memoirs*, 555; Fussell, *Great War*, 73–4; 256, 264; Liddle, *Passchendaele in Perspective*, 424; Leed, ‘Fateful Memories’, 87; Conzelmann, *Der andere Dix*, 135; Shepard, *War of Nerves*, 158–60

Some of those who continued to suffer for many years from their war experiences, like Carrington and Sassoon, had a feeling that they had led several different lives – before the war, during the war, and after the war – and had been unable to integrate them into a single whole. Many men, especially those sent to the front when they were very young, had seen the war as a form of higher education. When they returned home they discovered that the knowledge and skills they had gained were of no value at all in civilian life.[231]

None of this alters the fact that, as already suggested, many men presented symptoms that seemed to have little to do with the immediate causes of their psychological wounds. Rifleman Arthur Russell, a stretcher-bearer, had gone with a group of men who had orders to dig a communication trench, in case any of them should be wounded. It was a bitterly cold night. Russell did not have to dig, so he suffered even more from the cold than the others. At some point he took the pick from one of his companions to allow him to rest for a short time. As he worked he gradually became a bit warmer. Then the point of the pick hit 'something hard and unyielding as a block of concrete' and suddenly pins and needles shot through his body like an electric shock. He lost consciousness. There was not a scratch on his body, but he was struck dumb and paralysed, able to move only his eyes.[232]

Bagnold describes a similar case. The man in question would have been perfectly able to cope with the sheltered life he had led in Britain, but he collapsed under the pressure of the fighting around Ypres. He spent his days half asleep and murmuring, then suddenly screaming, high and loud. He would nod and give a friendly smile to anyone who greeted him as he sat in his chair, and for hours at a time he would move his eyebrows up and down and repeatedly fit imaginary gloves to his fingers. The war had created a new world, in which nobody lived except the man himself.[233]

Renn described a soldier who was partially buried when a shelter collapsed. He discovered his foot was stuck. Instead of simply taking off his boot to free himself he removed all his clothes and reported for duty completely naked.[234] Another story features a German soldier who was blown into the air by a shell and although apparently unharmed had been mute ever since. He could hear perfectly well and answer by nodding or shaking his head, but he no longer uttered a word.[235]

Myers described the case of two men who were the only survivors of a shell that hit their dugout. One wandered in the open totally nude. He believed he was going to bed. Within a few days he was able to return to front-line service. The second lay in a coma for over a fortnight, then woke up, said 'Did you see that one,

231 Leed, *No Man's Land*, 3

232 Macdonald, *1914–1918*, 249–50

233 Bagnold, *Diary Without Dates*, 101–24; Winter, *Death's Men*, 135

234 Renn, *Krieg*, 206

235 Winter & Baggett, *1914–18*, 212

Jim?' and fell back into deaf-mute lethargy. Some time later he started screaming battlefield orders in a vehement, hysterical voice. After that he recovered.[236]

There were cases in which it was impossible to discover any direct provocation at all. One of writer and soldier Oskar Maria Graf's fellow patients was called August. He climbed out of the trench one day and walked in what he believed to be the direction of Germany. Finding two bags, he threw them over his shoulders, and every time he saw anyone dead or wounded he cut the buttons off the man's uniform, until the bags were full. When he got close to Strasbourg he was grabbed by the scruff of the neck and delivered to a psychiatric institution.[237] Duhamel remembered a corner of a trench in which a wounded man with severe meningitis sat endlessly repeating '27, 28, 29 ... 27, 28, 29'. No one knew why he had fallen prey to his strange mania for counting.[238]

Neurotics were frightening to look at. Tisdall regularly had to nurse men suffering from war neurosis.

> It was a horrible thing, because they sometimes used to get these attacks, rather like epileptic fits in a way. They became quite unconscious, with violent shivering and shaking, and you had to keep them from banging themselves about too much until they came round again.[239]

Barthas watched a soldier being carried away by four friends. 'Oh, these wild eyes, this contorted face, dreadful, grimacing, having lost all human expression. What horrible scene must those eyes have witnessed before madness invaded his brain?'[240] Journalist Philip Gibbs described a sergeant-major at Thiepval jerking around as if suffering a terrible epileptic fit. He constantly clawed at his mouth – a response quite frequently noted – and uttered the most terrible cries of sheer mortal terror. Gibbs denounced the generals who branded all neurotics cowards. 'They had not seen, as I did, strong, sturdy men shaking with ague, mouthing like madmen, figures of dreadful terror, speechless and uncontrollable'. In the psychiatric ward at a base hospital, Rifleman H.V. Shawyer regularly met a soldier, not yet twenty, whose hair was a shade whiter every time he saw him. In wards like these, some men crept up close together while others wanted nothing to do with their fellow sufferers.[241] Graf gives a terrifying description of such a ward.

> One constantly leaned out of the window, plucking at his hospital dressing-gown. Innumerable others ran around the room in circles at great speed. One

236 Winter, *Death's Men*, 136

237 Graf, *Wir sind Gefangene*, 205

238 Duhamel, *Vie des Martyrs*, 123–4

239 Macdonald, *Roses of No Man's Land*, 216–17

240 Barthas, *Carnets*, 124

241 Ellis, *Eye-Deep*, 118; Macdonald, *1914–1918*, 250; http://www.spartacus.schoolnet.co.uk/FWWshellshock.htm; http://www.bbc.co.uk/religion/programmes/thought/documents/t20060817.shtml.

> suddenly fell down and thrashed about convulsively, screaming and roaring. Out of a corner came a blubbering, whining little voice that said without a pause: 'I'm mad! I'm mad!', then fell into quaking sobs: 'Maria! Maria!' The man in the bed next to me plucked at his entire body from time to time, heaved himself into the air and ground his teeth loudly. In the middle bed across from me lay a young man, half sitting up, who repeatedly pointed into the air with his fingers spread and shouted 'Neu-Ulm! Neu-Ulm! Neu-U-u-ulm! Hey! Neu-Ulm! Neu-Ulm!' And finally there was a man who from time to time leapt from one bed to the next in a kind of St Vitus' dance, tearing off his clothes, grabbing his genitals and gawping at them.[242]

Many of these patients had been through comparable experiences, but the effects differed from person to person. Sometimes a man was a danger to his fellow soldiers. During the Battle of the Somme, Private Reg Parker walked through a dressing station immediately behind the front line. It was overrun with wounded and he saw his sergeant-major among them, but instead of welcoming Parker he almost shot him. 'He was brandishing this revolver. Berserk! Didn't know what he was doing. He was absolutely shell-shocked. They all were!'[243]

Despite this diversity, certain features are mentioned repeatedly when soldiers, doctors or nurses describe the symptoms of psychiatric disorders. There was of course the indescribable fear of returning to the front, but another common phenomenon was a man's inability to remember what had happened immediately before he lost his nerve, sometimes the absence of any memory of the war. Physical manifestations included 'a vagueness of gaze, a loose-lipped, too-ready smile, a vacancy of expression'. Severe headache, the inability to walk, incontinence, constant shaking, nervous twitches to the face known as tics, hallucinations, stuttering, muteness and deafness are symptoms mentioned time and again in written accounts. Many psychiatric patients were utterly apathetic and many more could not sleep or only very badly, terrified of the nightmares that pursued them.[244] Sassoon wrote:

> But by night each man was back in his doomed sector of horror-stricken Front Line, where the panic and stampede of some ghastly experience was re-enacted among the living faces of the dead. No doctor could save him then, when he became the lonely victim of his dream disasters and delusions.[245]

---

242 Graf, *Wir sind Gefangene*, 189–90

243 Macdonald, *Somme*, 69

244 Ellis, *Eye-Deep*, 118; Binneveld, *Om de geest*, 81; Riedesser & Verderber, *Aufrüstung der Seelen*, 11; Graves, *Goodbye*, 164; Macdonald, *Roses of No Man's Land*, 214–16; Macdonald, *Passchendaele*, 146; Babington, *Shell-Shock*, 46–7, 68–9

245 Sassoon, *Complete Memoirs*, 557; Young, *Harmony of Illusions*, 43

Zuckmayer suffered increasingly from visual delusions as the war went on, and after the war he was more troubled by nightmares than ever: under fire, in a juddering bunker, unable to cry out or move until a scream woke him, soaked in sweat. He adds that these were common manifestations of war neurosis, frequently experienced by men who had come to feel at home in the trenches, in a war of gas and bombardment, and they sometimes went on for years.[246] Even worse were the nightmares suffered by men like the young officer who had lain next to him in a hospital in Mainz in 1918, where Zuckmayer spent some time recovering from concussion. The officer leapt out of bed and shouted: 'They're coming! They're coming! They're coming!'

> He saw the shapes of men, as they heaved themselves out of the trench in smoke and mist for the assault. Then he stood pressed into the corner of the room, his face distorted, arms stretched stiffly out in front of him as if he were tightly gripping a bayonet, not recognizing me when I tried to help him, thrashing about wildly; he had to be taken back to bed by two orderlies, where slowly, frequently sobbing, he calmed down.[247]

An article by Dr Robert Gaupp appeared in the *Münchener Medizinische Wochenschrift* (Munich Medical Weekly) of March 1915. He too had discovered that in many cases a sick man would fall into a kind of dream state that might last for hours and could sometimes go on for weeks, and from which he might emerge quite suddenly. The symptoms initially suggested serious concussion, but Gaupp soon realized they were psychogenic in nature. He recorded that symptoms often disappeared relatively quickly, but they almost always returned with full force the moment the doctor uttered the words 'front-line service' or even 'garrison duty'. If an affected man was forced to return to the front under suspicion of faking his symptoms, attacks of rage were quite common, a form of total insanity that might otherwise manifest itself in melancholia.[248] Dutch psychiatrist F.J. Soesman made Gaupp's findings known in the neutral Netherlands that same year.

> Gaupp tells of a young officer who allowed himself to be distracted from his symptoms by conversation but who, if anyone began speaking even with the greatest of caution about his return to the front, burst into loud wails and sobs, exclaiming: 'Professor, as long as the war goes on I cannot become well.' The memory of seeing dead soldiers was enough to make him tremble in every limb.[249]

---

246 Zuckmayer, *Als wär's ein Stück von mir*, 213; De Roodt, *Onsterfelijke Fronten*, 335–6

247 Zuckmayer, *Als wär's ein Stück von mir*, 213–14

248 Soesman, *Oorlogspsychose*, 34–6

249 Soesman, *Oorlogspsychose*, 36

Soesman was one of several Dutch psychiatrists who were quick to seize upon the debate about war neurosis in the belligerent nations. Aside from professional interest, their involvement was based on what they saw as the duty of scientists in neutral countries to oppose the nationalization of science in wartime and to pursue the kind of fundamental, in-depth research for which practitioners of applied science in warring countries no longer had either the time or the inclination.[250]

Alongside psychiatric illness resulting from front-line service, similar problems arose among soldiers who had not yet been to the front. They were tormented by worries about those they had left behind, often including wives and children in indifferent health. These worries could lead to their being declared 'unfit for front-line duty', after endless talk of patriotism and comradeship and threats of harsh punishment had proven ineffective.[251] There were perfectly laudable reasons for appealing to a man's sense of comradeship, incidentally. Although rejection by the army as unfit was a blessing from a physical point of view, it might do nothing to reduce mental suffering, which would be compounded by feelings of guilt about having abandoned fellow soldiers. The case of Ivor Gurney provides a clear example of this effect.

### *The alleged hallmark: cowardice*

> It's better to be a coward for five minutes ... than dead your entire life.
>
> Edlef Köppen, *Heeresbericht*

Although a subconscious flight into insanity was far from unusual, there is no reason to conclude that neurosis was caused by cowardice. Rarely were symptoms found to be less than genuine, and faking was no simple matter. Nevertheless, as Gibbs pointed out, in the early years of the war especially, the neurotic was commonly considered a deserter or a coward.[252] After all, if he was suffering from mental exhaustion as a result of the conditions of war, then why was one soldier affected more than another? Any man who was treated as mentally ill or psychologically wounded rather than as a deserter had his luck to thank more than anything else. Many officers regarded neurosis as extremely convenient for the man concerned. In their view it was simply a new, rather charming euphemism for what had previously been called cowardice or lack of discipline. A number of officers testified before the War Office Committee on Shell Shock that the public acceptance of neurosis had been little short of a disaster. They believed it had given neurotics the kind of legitimacy that ought to be reserved for the physically disabled. E. Macpather, for example, could see no difference between shell shock

250 Overbeek, 'Oorlogspsychosen en verwondingen', passim; Kuiper, 'Voordracht over zenuwverwondingen', passim, esp. 91; Binneveld, 'Nederland en de oorlogsneurosen', 39–40

251 Soesman, *Oorlogspsychose*, 37

252 Babington, *Shell-Shock*, 96

and cowardice. Both were the result of fear.[253] It is telling that the wound stripes British soldiers were allowed to sew onto their uniforms from mid-1916 onwards for every wound they had received were restricted to physical wounds.[254] As we shall see, some of those accused of cowardice, court-martialled and condemned to death were in fact mentally ill at the time of their arrest.[255] Perhaps this was one reason why so many psychological wounds expressed themselves in physical symptoms. Paralysis was not a punishable offence.

In August 1915 Gordon Fisher found a fellow British soldier in a dugout shortly after the order had been given to attack.

> His face was yellow, he was shaking all over, and I said to him, 'What the hell are you doing here? Your battalion is out in front. What are you doing back here?' He said, 'I can't go. I can't do it. I daren't go!' Now, I was pretty ruthless in those days and I said to him, 'Look, I'm going up the line and when I come back if you're still here I'll bloody well shoot you!' … When I came back, thank God, he'd gone. ... He'd got genuine shell-shock. We didn't realise that at the time. We used to think it was cowardice.[256]

Lieutenant-Colonel Frank Maxwell of the 12th Middlesex Regiment wrote in a letter to his wife dated 26 July 1916:

> 'Shell shock' is a complaint which, to my mind, is too prevalent everywhere; and I have told my people that my name for it is fright, or something worse, and I am not going to have it. Of course, the average nerve system of this class is much lower than ours, and sights and sounds affect them much more. It means … that they haven't got our power of self-control, that's all.[257]

Lieutenant-Colonel Jack of the 2nd West Yorkshires noted in his diary in November 1916 that one of his officers, who had been on active service with the battalion in France since 1914, was now clearly suffering from nervous exhaustion. He requested permission to send the man home, so that he could be given time to recover. He was told there was no such thing as a 'worn out' soldier. His application was refused.[258]

As we shall see in the next chapter, even some of the doctors treating mental illness regarded sufferers as malingerers. A typical example comes from Hooge in July 1916. After several days of battle and front-line duty in the trenches,

---

253 Leed, *No Man's Land*, 166, 171; Dunn, *The War*, 250–51

254 Ellis, *Eye-Deep*, 117

255 Brants & Brants, *Velden van weleer*, 321–2; Holmes, *Firing Line*, 256; Macdonald, *1914–1918*, 249; Macdonald, *Roses of No Man's Land*, 213

256 Macdonald, *1915*, 476

257 Liddle & Cecil, *Facing Armageddon*, 305

258 Eksteins, *Rites of Spring*, 172–3

prolonged because the relief had been delayed, a British medical officer held a sick parade. A long queue formed. Men presented with the most diverse ailments: trench foot, fever, sore throats and minor shrapnel wounds. One young fellow was clearly suffering from shell shock, but the doctor, who had a reputation for treating suspected malingerers extremely harshly, believed he was a coward. It is worth bearing in mind that the medical officer had also been hard at it for days on end and was probably too tired to recognize a genuine case of shell shock. When the trembling soldier's turn came to say what was wrong with him, he seemed incapable of describing his symptoms, and the doctor was either unable or unwilling to reassure him. The soldier could only splutter and mumble until, in despair, he cried out: 'I've lost my hat, sir. My hat! I've lost it. It's my hat…' The doctor almost exploded with fury and the man was lucky not to be arrested on the spot.[259]

No one was immune to psychiatric problems. In such circumstances anybody might suffer a nervous collapse.[260] Even hardened, experienced sergeants had their breaking point. In fact there was a specific term for it: old sergeants' syndrome. According to German psychiatrist Max Nonne, who treated some 1,600 patients during the Great War, it was clear that even people with previously healthy nervous systems could develop mental problems.[261] Indeed one man testified before the War Office Committee on Shell Shock that conditions in the French trenches were such that it was impossible not to crack up at some stage or other.[262] Alan Hanbury-Sparrow, a veteran of earlier wars and a physical and mental survivor of three years on active service, broke down at Passchendaele. One night under gas attack finally proved too much, although he must have been through many such nights.[263] During the spring offensive of 1918 even war-horse Jünger temporarily collapsed. A shell exploded in the midst of his company:

> Half stunned I stood up. From the big crater, burning machine-gun belts spilled a coarse pinkish light. It lit the smouldering smoke of the explosion, where a pile of charred bodies were writhing, and the shadows of those still living were fleeing in all directions. Simultaneously, a grisly chorus of pain and cries for help went up. ... I had to leave the unlucky ones to the one surviving stretcher-bearer in order to lead the handful of unhurt men who had gathered around me from that dreadful place. Half an hour ago at the head of a full battle-strength company, I was now wandering around a labyrinth of trenches with a few, completely demoralized men. One baby-faced fellow, who was mocked a few days ago by his comrades, and on exercises had wept under the weight of the big munitions boxes, was now loyally carrying them on our heavy way, having picked them up

259 Macdonald, *1915*, 418–19
260 Howorth, *Shell-Shock*, 1; Busfield, 'Class and Gender', 307–8
261 Gillespie, *Psychological Effects of War*, 167; Shepard, 'Shell-Shock', 36
262 Leed, *No Man's Land*, 181
263 Holmes, *Firing Line*, 217–18, 223

> unasked in the crater. Seeing that did for me. I threw myself to the ground, and sobbed hysterically, while my men stood grimly about.[264]

Clear evidence that anyone could fall prey to psychiatric problems, that they were not confined to those in whom they might have been expected for various reasons, is provided by the extensive psychological tests American soldiers had to pass in 1917 and 1918 before they were declared fit for service at the front. The testing did little to reduce the total number of American cases of mental illness, in fact Thomas W. Salmon, who was in charge of psychiatric work for the American army, never expected it to. Salmon was the most prominent among the advocates of 'forward psychiatry' and its much-lauded formula for treatment: proximity (to the front), immediacy (of treatment), and expectation (of a return to the front), first developed by the French as we shall see in the next chapter. The cynics of the time said this too was pure theory and would not stand the test of hard reality. Sure enough, the proportion of American troops who became war neurotics – as said, there were almost 70,000 of them within a year – was no lower than in the other armies. In *A History of Military Medicine*, Richard A. Gabriel and Karen S. Metz calculate that around 3.5 per cent of US soldiers with the AEF had psychiatric problems, and of those only about 40 per cent were ever able to return to the trenches.[265]

The outstanding war records of several of the best known sufferers from mental illness, or perhaps more accurately of those who were admitted to psychiatric hospitals, such as Toller, Sassoon and Owen, proves there was no essential connection between neurosis and cowardice.[266] Graves claims that Owen, although he does not mention it anywhere himself, had been unjustly accused of cowardice by a superior officer, which finally triggered his collapse.[267]

The fact that the tension and horrors of the front could be too much even for a man such as Owen presented the military high command with a problem. There were many neurotics who, like Owen, had previously won medals for heroism. Some were eager to return to the front. If they were labelled cowards then they would have to be punished as such, and this would be taken as an insult by fellow soldiers and have a seriously detrimental effect on discipline.[268] Toller and Sassoon presented a similar difficulty, although it is important to remember that although both have gone down in history as 'famous psychiatric cases' they were not mad at all. Like the leading character in Edlef Köppen's *Heeresbericht*, Adolf Reisiger, who also was locked up in an asylum, they had protested against a continuation of the war. Toller came from a highly respected Prussian family, and part of the

---

264 Jünger, *In Stahlgewittern*, 190–91; *Storm of steel*, 225–6

265 Gabriel & Metz, *A History of Military Medicine*, 249–52; Shepard, *War of Nerves*, 125; Shepard, 'Shell-Shock', 40

266 Winter, *Death's Men*, 129

267 Graves, *Goodbye*, 217

268 Bourke, *Dismembering the Male*, 111

reason he was sent to a mental hospital was that his mother could not believe her son had turned into a socialist and pacifist. He must therefore be crazy. It almost became a self-fulfilling prophecy; being forced to live among idiots left its mark on him. Hospital staff failed to realize they were dealing with a former front-line soldier who had been decorated for bravery. When he asked for medicine to help him sleep the nurse refused. 'First you betray your country and then you whimper and ask for sleeping draughts!'[269]

Toller was not the only German soldier to engage in political protest against the war.[270] All kinds of strategies were used to force rebels into uniform, including Georg Grosz, Walter Mehring and the medical student Wieland Herzfelde. They responded with a wide range of tactics to avoid having to serve. They might be subjected, like Grosz, to painful medical examinations and confined to mental hospitals, but in the end they usually won and were exempted on the grounds of 'psychopathological defects'. According to Zuckmayer the army did not want to have to deal with 'such people'. 'In the end they did not matter. Their strong minds were regarded de facto as subnormal and they were not seen as a danger that needed to be taken seriously.'[271]

After the publication on 23 July 1917 of his famous 'A Soldier's Declaration', Siegfried Sassoon, who had been decorated several times for bravery (it is tempting to say for recklessness and a murderous death-wish), escaped a court martial almost against his will. His friend Graves had managed to convince highly placed acquaintances that Sassoon – who for obvious reasons chose not to use his first name when he published his protest – should instead be declared insane, since he was suffering, like so many others, from blood-drenched nightmares and daylight visions. Graves 'betrayed' his friend by dismissing his public protest against the war – written by a man very much in his right mind – as the scribblings of a neurotic, in order to save him from court martial and possible execution. The military authorities did not take a great deal of persuading. They were already struggling with their own version of precisely this problem. What were they to do with an officer who had been awarded the Military Cross for bravery and who later denounced the war? Their answer was that anyone who said the war was insane was himself insane. A number of psychiatrists pointed to Sassoon's 'strange first name', which might indicate 'latent family degeneracy'. As in Toller's case, the diagnosis of 'insanity' was the perfect way to take the edge off a protest and silence the agitators without having to call the legitimacy of the war into question.[272]

After treatment, during which it quickly became clear to Dr Rivers that his patient was anything but mentally disturbed, Sassoon returned to the front. The personal safety and literary and sporting recreation that hospital had provided

269 Toller, *Jugend in Deutschland*, 77; Köppen, *Heeresbericht*, 457–60

270 Leed, *No Man's Land*, 168

271 Zuckmayer, *Als wär's ein Stück von mir*, 245

272 Sassoon, *Complete Memoirs*, 496; Leed, *No Man's Land*, 168; Higonnet, *Behind the Lines*, 65

for him were the opposite of what he wanted. His return was therefore largely at his own request. The military authorities would have kept him in hospital until the end of the war if he had continued to protest, and anyhow he believed that after everything he had experienced it was only with his unit at the front line that he could have any sense of moral self-worth. He began to believe that by his protest and subsequent hospital treatment he had betrayed and abandoned his men, a feeling that became unbearable when his battalion suffered heavy losses at Ypres in September 1917. He decided he must go back. Rivers' military duty was to get him to return, and his efforts to achieve this made use of Sassoon's sense of disloyalty and the moral conflict that arose from it. At the same time, however, Rivers had become convinced his patient was not mentally ill, even if a number of commentators did see daredevil Sassoon's pacifist outpourings as a symptom of neurosis: anti-war neurosis. He had recognized that the war was a collective act of insanity and his realization of this indicated he was in perfectly good mental health. There was therefore no longer any reason not to send him back into the insanity. The army declared him insane because he said the war was insane, whereas Rivers regarded him as sane – and therefore as fit for combat – for the same reason, although he had officially confirmed to the army medical authorities that Sassoon was ill.[273]

On 12 January 1917 Wilfred Owen left with several of his men for a stay of four days in a forward dugout in no man's land. When he got back he wrote to his mother.

> I can see no excuse for deceiving you about these last four days. I have suffered seventh hell. I have not been at the front. I have been in front of it. … The Germans knew we were staying there and decided we shouldn't. … I nearly broke down and let myself drown in the water that was now slowly rising over my knees.[274]

Only a sudden reduction in the intensity of German shelling had brought him back to his senses. From that moment on, everything he wrote was dominated by horror, anger and compassion: horror at the nature of life at the front; anger that civil society, the church in particular, did not understand what was happening; and compassion with those who suffered as a result of it all.[275]

Three months later he reached his limit. A barrage had already severely unnerved him when a shell exploded close by, throwing him into the air. He landed near the body of a fellow officer who had been practically blown to pieces. He

273 Sassoon, *Complete Memoirs*, 512–57; Brants, *Plasje bloed*, 15, 199; Graves, *Goodbye*, 211; Winter & Baggett, *1914–18*, 219, 222, 224; Babington, *Shell-Shock*, 110–13; Leed, *No Man's Land*, 210; Higonnet, *Behind the Lines*, 61–9; Moeyes, *Siegfried Sassoon*, 150–53, 227–9; Shepard, *War of Nerves*, 89–90; Koch, 'Einde aan de onschuld', 5–6

274 Gilbert, *First World War*, 307; Winter & Baggett, *1914–18*, 224–5

275 Fussell, *Great War*, 289

returned only several days later, stuttering and trembling from head to foot. This must have been the moment when his commanding officer questioned whether he had enough courage for the job. But the doctors had a different explanation: shell shock. To his sister he wrote: 'You know it was not the Bosche that worked me up, nor the explosives, but it was living so long by poor old Cock Robin (as we used to call 2/Lt. Gaukroger), who lay not only near me, but in various places around and about, if you understand. I hope you don't!'[276]

Back in Britain he was transferred to Craiglockhart, the hospital where Sassoon was staying at the time. It was one of six special institutions for the treatment of officers. He showed some of his poems to Sassoon, who encouraged him to go on writing, and several of Owen's best poems were first published in *Hydra*, the hospital newspaper. He would later write about his fellow patients in the poems 'Dead Beat', which tells of a soldier who dies without having been physically wounded, and 'Mental Cases': 'These are men whose minds the Dead have ravished.'[277] In 1918 Owen returned to the front. A week before the end of the war he was caught in machine-gun fire. News of his death reached his parents while they were listening with relief to the bells of Shrewsbury cathedral, ringing to celebrate the armistice.[278]

All these stories indicate that the fact most soldiers did not break down in the four long hard years of war had little to do with their cool-headedness, strong nerves, courage or character. A human being is apparently able to cope with a huge amount of mental stress and suffering, but an individual's psychological survival is largely a matter of luck. That one event required to snap tense nerves did not occur, or relief arrived just in time, or a minor physical wound intervened. A man might be saved from psychiatric illness by bad luck too, of course. He was quite likely to be seriously wounded or killed before he reached the stage of mental breakdown.

---

276 Fussell, *Great War*, 289; Winter & Baggett, *1914–18*, 226

277 Gilbert, *First World War*, 318; Winter & Baggett, *1914–18*, 226, 229

278 Winter & Baggett, *1914–18*, 19; Holmes, *Riding the Retreat*, 258; Gilbert, *First World War*, 502; Shepard, *War of Nerves*, 90–95; Binneveld, 'Shell Shock Versus Trouble Nerveux', 69

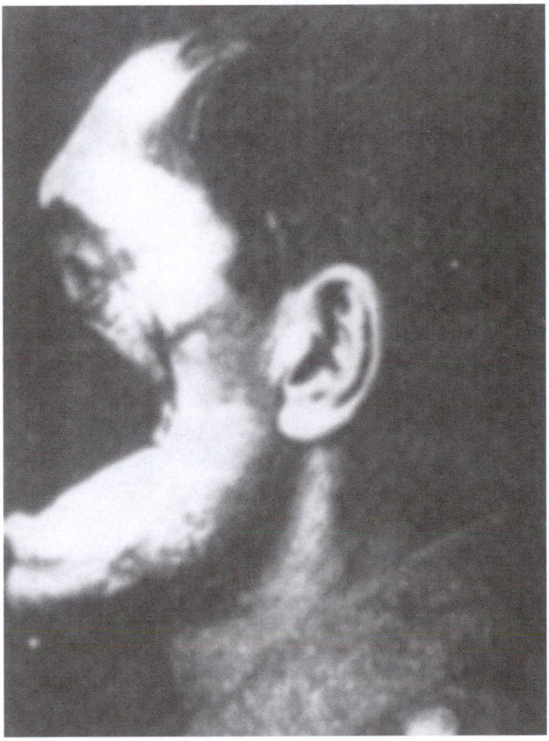

1 One of the most famous pictures from Ernst Friedrich's *Krieg dem Kriege!* (*War against War!*), 1924. The man – perhaps sadly enough – survived his injury. Photo courtesy of the Anti-Kriegs Museum, Berlin

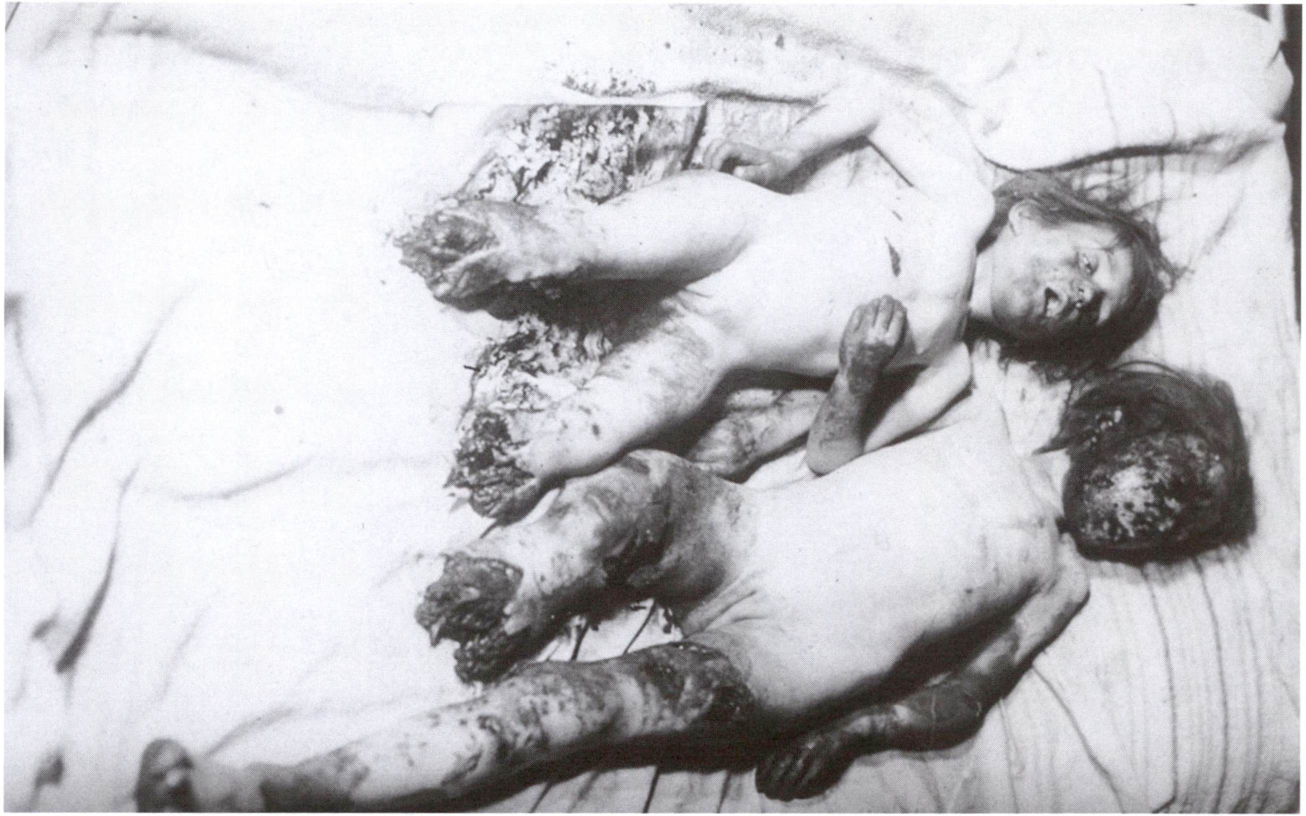

2 Civilian victims: two Belgian girls. Photo courtesy of In Flanders Fields Museum, Ypres

3 Artillery: the big killer. Battle of the Somme: British 8 inch howitzers of 39th Siege Battery, Royal Garrison Artillery in action in the Fricourt Mametz Valley, August 1916. Photo courtesy of the Imperial War Museum, London (Negative Number: Q 5818)

4 Gas and machine gun: two other characteristics of World War I. Photo courtesy of In Flanders Fields Museum, Ypres

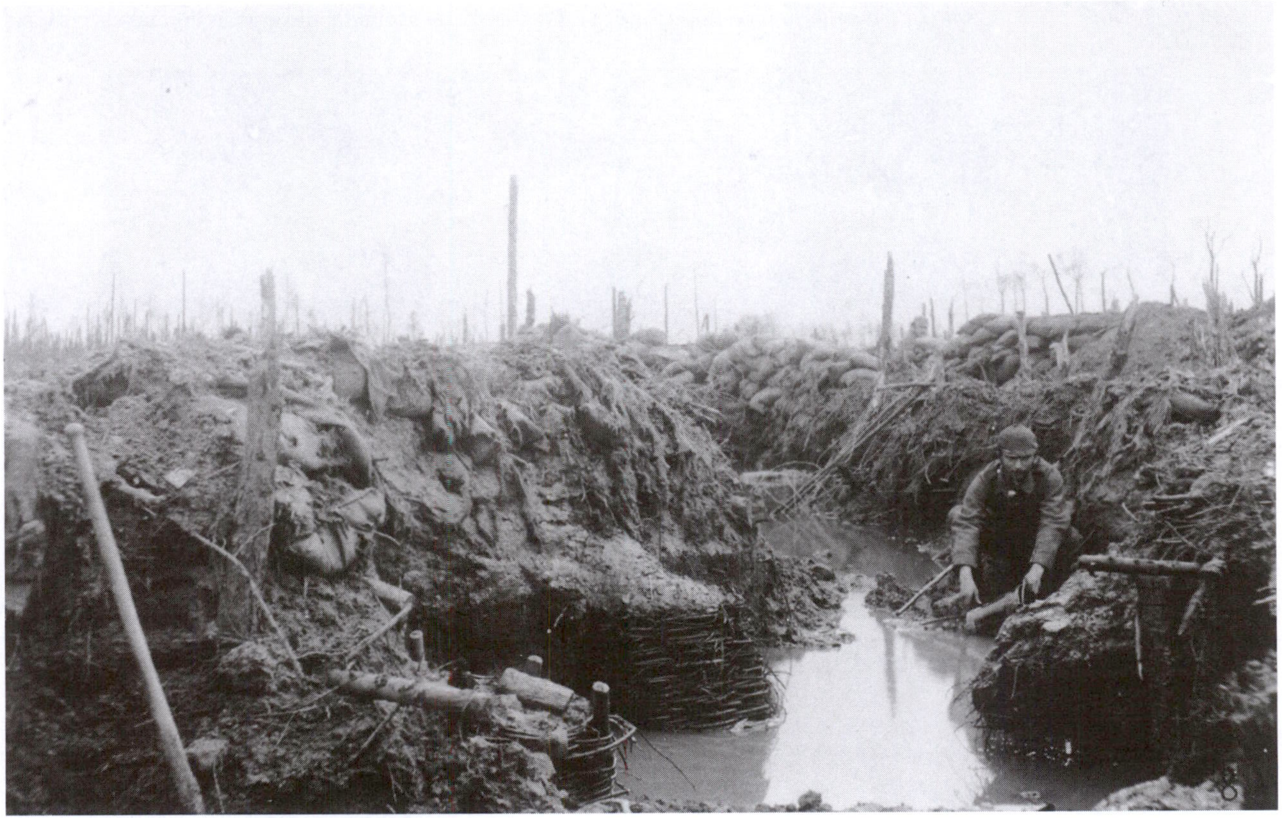

5 Ypres trench, winter 1915. Photo courtesy of In Flanders Fields Museum, Ypres

6 No Man's Land or Dead Man's Land. Photo courtesy of In Flanders Fields Museum, Ypres

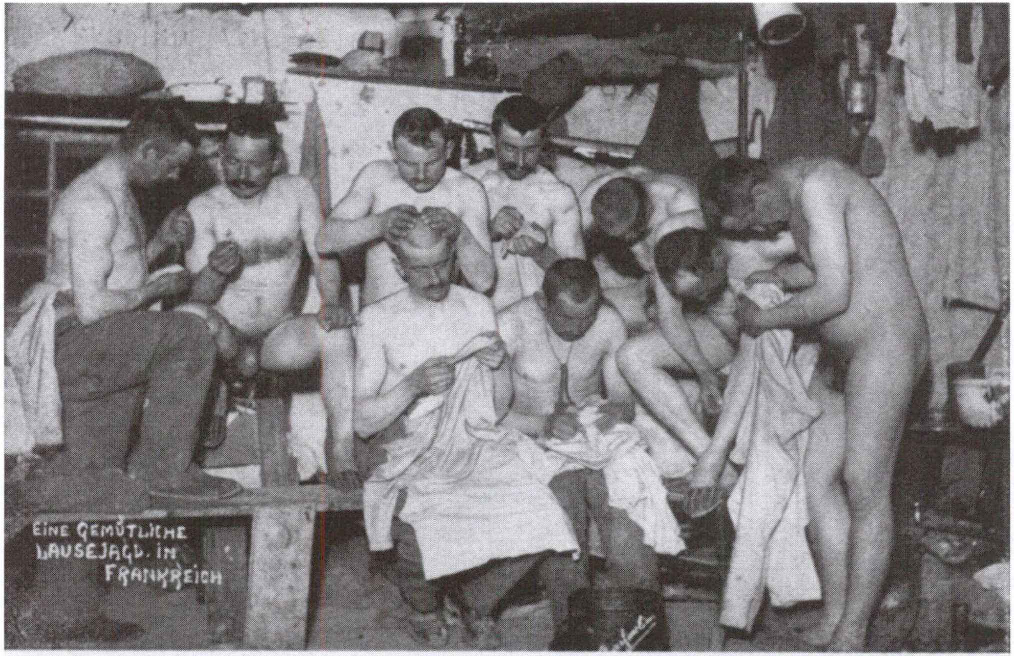


**Lausejagd in den Vogesen im Sommer 1916**
*Photographische Aufnahme*

*Eingesendet von Ing. L. in H.*

7 German Soldiers hunting for lice, Vosges summer 1916. Hans Magnus Hirschfeld, *Sittengeschichte des Weltkrieges. Ergänzungsheft*, 24

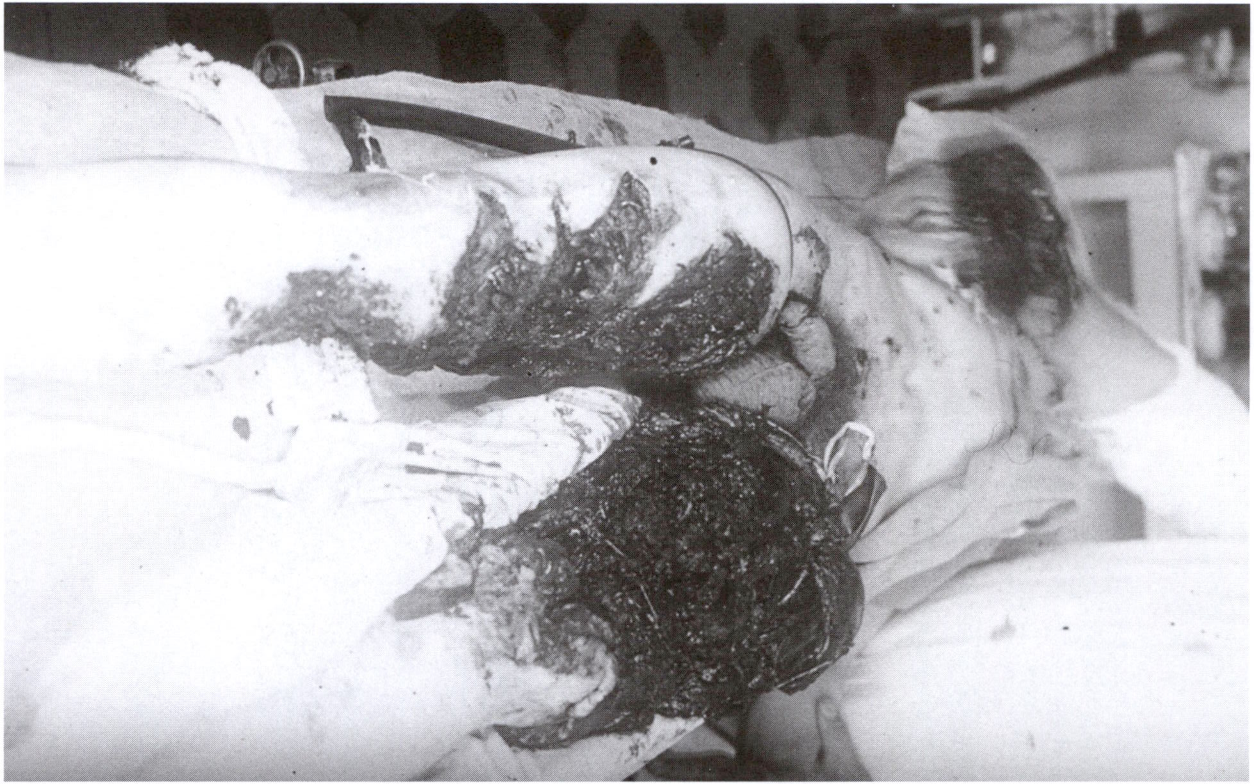

8 Victim of artillery: a man with shattered legs, probably just before amputation. Photo courtesy of In Flanders Fields Museum, Ypres

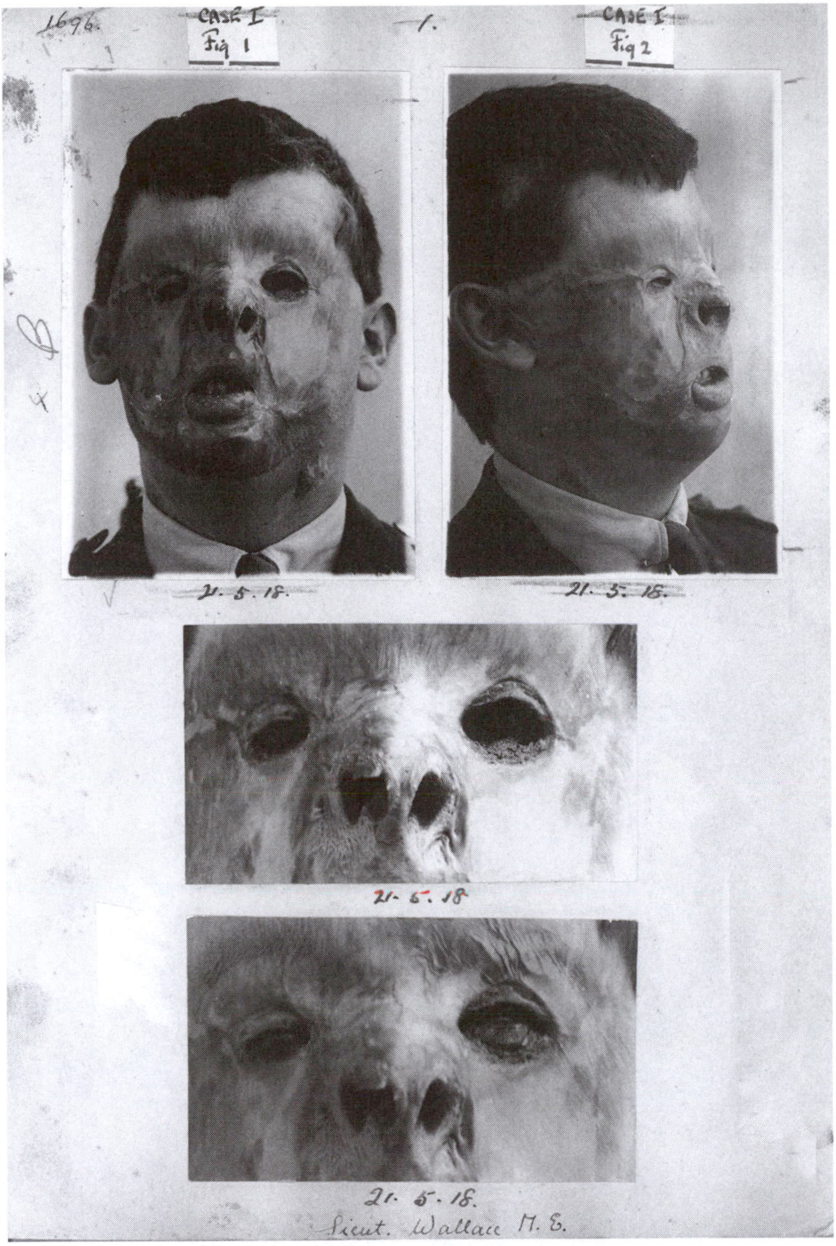


9 Lieutenant Norman E. Wallace, Canadian Field Artillery, attached RFC. Wounded 22 September 1917, aged 22; victim of a flame-thrower. Photographs taken 21 May 1918, 2 weeks after admission to the Queen's Hospital, Sidcup. The annotations are in the hand of Harold Gillies. By permission of the Gillies Archives, Queen Mary's Hospital, Sidcup, UK

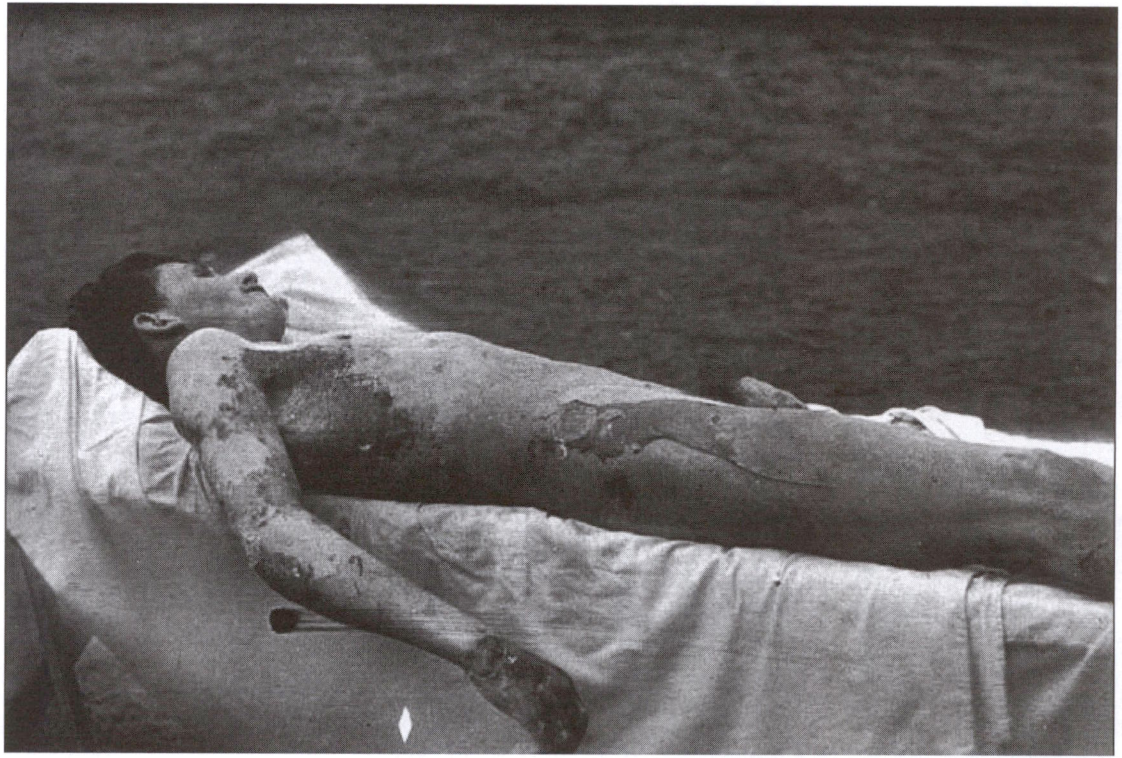

10 French medical picture taken on March 31, 1918. The dead man is a French soldier of the 99th Infantry Regiment, who was killed by German mustard gas. © *Heritage of the Great War*, ed. Rob Ruggenberg. Accessed 10 November 2008 http://greatwar.nl/weekpictures/voorpagina98.html

Gesundheitsvisite im Ausbildungslager Königsberg

*Photographische Aufnahmen*

*Eingesendet von M. S., Mühlhausen i. E.*

11 Looking for VD. Hans Magnus Hirschfeld, *Sittengeschichte des Weltkrieges. Ergänzungsheft*, 36

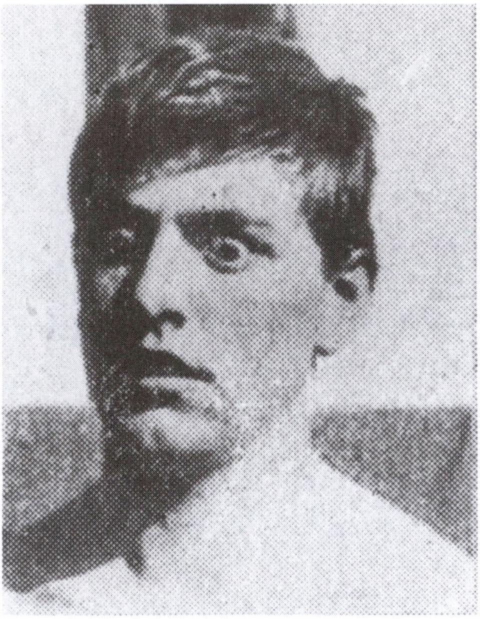

12 Patient suffering from war-neuroses (shell shock). From Arthur Frederick Hurst, *Medical Diseases of the War* (London, 1918). Reproduced with permission of Wellcome Library, London (L0023554)

13 Helping an ambulance through the mud. Photo courtesy of the Imperial War Museum, London (Negative Number: Q 4015)

14 A German hospital soldier with oxygen and primitive gasmask. Photo courtesy of In Flanders Fields Museum, Ypres

15 The interior of an Australian advanced dressing station on the Menin Road during the Third Battle of Ypres (Passchendaele), 20 September 1917. Photo courtesy of the Imperial War Museum, London (Negative Number: E(AUS) 715)

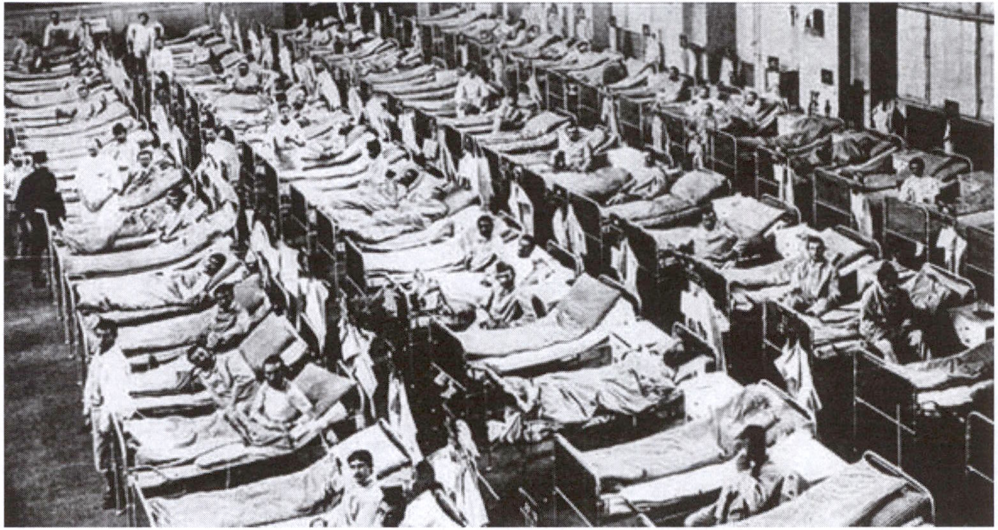

16 German army hospital in Berlin. © *The Great War Primary Document Archive*, Ray Mentzer. Accessed 18 November 2008. http://www.gwpda.org/photos/bin01/imag0045.jpg. Taken from Halsey, Francis Whiting, ed., *The Literary Digest History of the World War*, 10 vols, New York and London 1920

17 A critical view on medicine in wartime. *Oorlog of Vrede* (*War or Peace*), 1931

18 On the beach near the hamlet of Oostduinkerke, Belgian soldier, 2è Grenadiers, Aloïs Walput is tied to a pole and shot by his fellow men. The execution of this 21-year-old war-volunteer took place on 3 June 1918. © *Heritage of the Great War*, ed. Rob Ruggenberg. Accessed 10 November 2008 http://www.greatwar.nl/executions/executiebe.jpg

19 The beginning of an ossuary. Photo courtesy of In Flanders Fields Museum, Ypres

20 Row upon row of crosses. A German war cemetery containing 5,000 graves at Sailly-sur-la-Lys, October 1918. Photo courtesy of the Imperial War Museum, London (Negative Number: Q 9540)

## Chapter 4
# Aid

You can read about war, and the wounded,
but when you are brought face to face with it,
I tell you, it is heart rending.
...
If this war does not soon end there won't be a man living on the face of the earth.
It is brutal; it is cold-blooded murder; it is hell upon earth.

Frances Cluett, VAD nurse

### Introduction

Medical aid for soldiers had been improving steadily since the mid-nineteenth century, not least because of the introduction of conscription in many countries, based on nationalist sentiments, which obliged the state to pay more attention to military medicine. Conscription was also one of the reasons why the Red Cross, established in the 1860s, began to succeed where its forerunners had failed. It was an organization that offered the political and military authorities the possibility of giving a humanitarian gloss to military imperatives, and at minimal cost. The medical profession generally had no objection to being incorporated into the military world, and medical men to make increasing use of military metaphors, just as military men increasingly began to use medical metaphors. With improved health care, wounds overtook disease as the principal cause of death in wartime. The percentage of wounded who died – based on outcomes for those who reached hospital alive – was reduced from fifteen in the nineteenth century to eight in the years 1914–18. Despite increased firepower, the ratio of dead (men who died more or less immediately of their wounds) to wounded, which as we have seen was roughly one to four, remained steady. It seems that around one in five wounds was almost instantly fatal, irrespective of the weapon that caused it. Aside from pure chance, the differences between army units in this respect reflect the regularity with which they were involved in heavy fighting and the ways the armies to which they belonged adjusted their strategies and tactics to the prevailing conditions.

Medical services expanded rapidly. The Royal Army Medical Corps, for example, grew from a total of 20,000 doctors and nurses at the beginning of the war to 13,000 medical officers and 150,000 other staff by 1918. Their medical knowledge and nursing abilities often left much to be desired. In her *Schwester der Vierten Armee* Henriette Riemann gives some graphic examples. Their inadequacies are directly attributable to the situation the war created, in that while it was necessary to reduce entry requirements, there was hardly any time, even where the facilities were available, either for initial training or for refresher courses. British medical officers were required to supervise facilities for more than 600,000 patients, half of them back in Britain, and at first they had no motorized ambulances on the continent. Nor were there any actual beds. The wounded lay on the ground on stretchers and there was a shortage of trolleys and dressing tables.[1] All this improved greatly in the years that followed, in which around 9 million British sick and wounded were treated and 1,088 million doses of drugs administered. Doctors and orderlies applied 1.5 million splints and 108 million bandages, used 7,250 tons of cotton wool and fitted over 20,000 artificial eyes.[2] The German military medical service gave no less than 200 million inoculations, an average of fifteen per soldier. Whenever an epidemic threatened, whole regiments would line up to be immunized or to receive booster injections. The German army had 3,355 hospitals at its disposal, amounting to almost 200,000 beds. A collection for medical aid to soldiers raised 534 million marks, plus donated material worth another 200 million.[3] The American army had 443 medical officers in 1916 and another 146 in reserve. By the end of the war their number had risen to almost 31,000 and the Army Nurse Corps had grown from 400 to 21,500. In addition there were more than 200,000 support staff, both men and women. When the American Expeditionary Force left for France, it estimated that 73,000 beds would be sufficient. This assessment was quickly adjusted to 600,000 and by the end of the war a total of 380,000 were available, 260,000 in France and 120,000 back in the US.[4] Denis Winter comments: 'If the pain represented by these figures could be similarly quantified, then it would be beyond any man to comprehend such grief.'[5]

Yet no matter how hard they worked and how extensive the medical services became, there can be no other conclusion than that the medical profession was powerless. At the end of the nineteenth century Ivan Bloch had predicted that it would be practically impossible to offer substantial medical help to the wounded. La Motte would later concur: 'The science of healing stood baffled before the science of destruction.'[6] For one thing, although there was a huge number of doctors and nurses available, there were never enough staff to treat either the physically wounded or the many psychiatric patients. When Blunden's regimental

1 Ellis, *Eye-Deep*, 111; Riemann, *Schwester der Vierten Armee*, 61–2, 66; Verdoorn, *Arts en Oorlog*, 337; Gabriel & Metz, *A History of Military Medicine*, 247; Van Bergen, *De Zwaargewonden Eerst*, 37–91; Hutchinson, *Champions of Charity*, 57–104; Van Bergen, 'Blijdschap op het slagveld!', passim

2 Winter, *Death's Men*, 197; Lupton, *Medicine as Culture*, 65–8

3 Whalen, *Bitter Wounds*, 61; Lichtenstein, *Angepaßt und treu ergeben*, 19

4 Garrison, *History of Military Medicine*, 196–7; Verdoorn, *Arts en Oorlog*, 338

5 Winter, *Death's Men*, 197

6 Bloch, *Die Unmöglichkeit*, passim; La Motte, *Backwash of War*, 55; Whitehead, *Doctors in the Great War*, 153

doctor was killed, for example, his place had to be taken by a vet. Doctors were sent so many psychiatric cases that they had little time to administer therapies, and as Myers pointed out this had disastrous consequences for individual treatments, for the war effort, and for those who needed to finance war pensions for men who continued to suffer.[7]

There were two main reasons for the shortage of doctors. Firstly, no matter how successfully the percentage of live casualties who died was reduced, the absolute numbers of sick and wounded remained on a steep upward curve in comparison to previous wars.[8] Secondly, although the battle against traditional causes of death was to some extent successful, they were replaced by new horrors. The filthy and desolate conditions in the trenches and on the battlefield meant that most wounds became infected, in an era before the discovery of antibiotics, and it might take hours to move a wounded man to a first-aid post. If we include those not found by stretcher-bearers, or found but not picked up by them, and men who died before they reached an aid post, then the death rate among wounded British and German soldiers was one in six or seven, in the case of the French as high as one in four. The mortality rate of eight per cent mentioned at the start of this chapter applies only to those who reached an aid post alive. Of all the wounded, in other words, no fewer than fifteen to twenty-five per cent died. Combatants on the Western Front were in fact relatively lucky. On the Eastern Front more than half of all Russian and Serbian wounded died.[9]

German, British and French medical units were organized along roughly similar lines, although there were significant differences in practice. Care and evacuation of the sick and wounded took place in a number of stages, according to the nature and severity of the illness or injury. The more serious a man's condition, the further he would be taken from the forward trenches, until he might eventually arrive at a specialist hospital well behind the lines, out of artillery range. To take the British army as an example, each regimental aid post was as close as possible to the front line, usually in the second or third trench, in a dugout or perhaps a cellar. It was manned by a regimental medical orderly and sixteen stretcher-bearers, increased to 32 should that be felt necessary. The aim was to ensure there would be enough stretcher-bearers to bring in 300 wounded, based on the estimate that when it went into battle, 60 per cent of a regiment would be wounded, or around 600 men, of whom half would be able to make their own way back.

It was at the regimental aid post that initial diagnosis took place and field dressings were replaced with fresh bandages. Certain injections might be given at this stage. Surgical operations were carried out only very sparingly, mostly amputations that could not be delayed. Denis Winter writes that nevertheless, because the wounded were allowed to dump their kit on the battlefield, a pile of amputated limbs was practically all an aid post had to show for its work, aside

7 Blunden, *Undertones of War*, 203–4; Myers, *Shell Shock*, 112

8 Verdoorn, *Arts en Oorlog*, 329, 331

9 Brants, *Plasje bloed*, 8–9

from a modicum of equipment.[10] Clearly the purpose of an aid post was little more than to prepare a man for the journey back down the line. Because of their forward position, it was these treatment centres that saw the highest fatalities among medical staff. About 1,000 British and 1,500 German medical officers were killed at first-aid posts. In total more than 6,000 doctors died of wounds or disease in the British army alone and over 17,000 were wounded, according to the official statistics.[11]

Further towards the rear was the advanced dressing station. Here too, minor surgical operations were carried out if the situation demanded it, but the ADS was primarily a temporary resting place en route, a little way back from the firing line. From here the journey continued to the main dressing station or to the better equipped casualty clearing station, both of which were located about ten kilometres behind the lines.[12] This was the final stage for those who were not to be allowed to continue their journey to safety. During an offensive each division would have one forward CCS and two further to the rear, and from 1917 each was equipped to deal with a thousand sick and wounded. It was here that most operations and amputations were carried out. Even doctors found them 'gruesome places indeed' during major battles, partly because many military surgeons, certainly in the early years of the war, did not have the necessary expertise to carry out amputations competently. In general they tried to avoid sending men any further back. A patient who seemed likely to recover within about three weeks would be kept close to the front line. Only amputees and the severely wounded were transported on by hospital train – or, if destined for Britain, by hospital ship – to army or Red Cross base hospitals. These trains were nevertheless regularly seen crossing the French, Belgian and German countryside, just as the carts that carried the wounded from stations to hospitals became a common sight in the cities of the combatant nations.[13]

No amount of organization could resolve all the problems that inevitably arose. Some countries – France above all – were plainly less successful than others, but although the British army's medical service, for example, was much better organized than its French equivalent, it too ran into operational difficulties time and again. During the Somme offensive, because of the continual rotation of different divisions, it became impossible for sanitary detachments to do even a halfway decent job, and a large number of dysentery cases resulted. It was a problem solved only on the eve of Third Ypres when detachments responsible for sanitation

10 Winter, *Death's Men*, 197

11 Verdoorn, *Arts en Oorlog*, 256; Garrison, *History of Military Medicine*, 197, 200; Gabriel & Metz, *A History of Military Medicine*, 249; Barbusse, *Le Feu*, 317–19

12 Liddle, *Passchendaele in Perspective*, 180–81; Brants & Brants, *Velden van weleer*, 146; Ellis, *Eye-Deep*, 109–10; Bleker & Schmiedebach, *Medizin und Krieg*, 218; Simkins, *World War I*, 156–8; Winter, *Death's Men*, 196

13 Liddle, *Passchendaele in Perspective*, 188; Noyes, *Stretcher-Bearers*, 64; De Weerdt, *De Vrouwen van WOI*, 108

were permitted to operate independently of the medical services attached to each division.[14] A second problem, and one that lay at the root of many others, was that absolute priority was given to the machinery of destruction. In the trenches the movement of ammunition was of primary importance, next came reinforcements and only in third place the wounded. In light of this it seems perfectly rational that stretcher-bearers received orders stating that, if overwhelmed by sheer numbers, they must leave the more seriously wounded to wait. What matters in wartime is victory; anything that might contribute to it comes first.[15]

No amount of organization is ever equal to the pressure, chaos and frenzy of a battlefield. During every offensive, doctors worked day and night. They had no way of dealing with the unremitting stream of casualties, even if they chose to disregard 'enemy wounded'. The hospital became an impersonal factory, with no time for individual attention, which made it a bleak place for most soldiers.[16] La Motte wrote that months of quiet, of boredom, could suddenly be replaced by days, weeks or months of intensely hard, apparently endless and largely fruitless medical labour.[17] Army doctors and orderlies were perhaps hardened to this, but civilian medical staff brought in as temporary reinforcements, who were often regarded with suspicion or even contempt,[18] tended to be far less resilient in the face of all they saw and experienced. This was certainly true of non-medical civilian volunteers, like Bagnold and Brittain. Sensitivity to the horrors emerges clearly in the works of Georges Duhamel too, but he was famous even before the war for his internationalist and anti-militarist convictions.[19] American doctor Harvey Cushing, who volunteered for ambulance duty in France before America entered the war, wrote in his diary of 'the dreadful deformities (not so much in the way of amputations but broken jaws and twisted, scarred faces); the tedious healing of infected wounds, with discharging sinuses, tubes, irrigations and repeated dressings'.[20]

The appalling conditions often forced doctors to resort to amputating limbs far sooner than they would have wished. In the British army alone, more than 40,000 soldiers underwent amputation. Around 70 per cent lost a leg, 30 per cent an arm, and almost 3 per cent lost both arms or both legs. There were individuals who lost all their limbs. The frequent need for amputation had to do with the high incidence of wound infection and the types of weapons deployed in 1914–18. Often there was neither the time nor the opportunity to attempt other forms of treatment,

---

14 Liddle, *Passchendaele in Perspective*, 175–8; Liddle & Cecil, *Facing Armageddon*, 457; Busse, *Soldaten ohne Waffen*, 55–6

15 Winter, *Death's Men*, 196

16 Renn, *Krieg*, 125

17 La Motte, *Backwash of War*, v–vi, 82

18 Bourke, *Dismembering the Male*, 147

19 Zweig, *Die Welt von Gestern*, 149

20 Brants & Brants, *Velden van weleer*, 241; Macdonald, *Roses of No Man's Land*, 66; Thomas, *Die Katrin wird Soldat*, 294

especially given the desperate shortage of medical equipment and the poor quality of the available supplies. More often than not, doctors were simply powerless. The head injuries and abdominal wounds they faced were often so severe that surgery would have been little more than a waste of time and equipment.[21]

The task facing medical staff was made even harder by the fact that as the war went on fresh manpower became increasingly scarce and standards of fitness for new recruits steadily fell. Captain James C. Dunn (Med.), a hero to Robert Graves despite his tough methods and his anti-Semitism, noted at the Battle of the Somme that on average the physical condition of new recruits to the Royal Welch Fusiliers was good, but that nevertheless a huge number of men among them had malformations or other ailments that made them quite unsuitable for the kind of work soldiers needed to do. A year later Sassoon wrote of the same regiment: 'a recent draft had added a collection of under-sized half-wits'.[22] There is another factor we should take into account. The steady decline in the health of recruits as the war went on was partly a result of the battle waged by doctors against malingering, and more generally of the rapid pace at which medical examinations were carried out. A British medical officer once said that about twenty to thirty per cent of new recruits had not undergone a medical examination of any kind, let alone a test of mental health. Estimates suggest that under 40 per cent of British soldiers in the First World War were in a good state of physical and mental fitness when they joined up. There are documented instances of Frenchmen called in for medical testing despite being blind. Given that a single French medical team in the Dordogne, for example, examined 150 to 200 people an hour in early 1917, it was inevitable that ailing or invalid recruits would regularly be passed fit for front-line service.[23]

All this led to a situation in which army medicine meant dragging the wounded out from the debris and trudging eight men strong through the mud for hours, risking life and limb to deliver just one casualty to an aid post perhaps only half a mile away, in the hope that he would not die on the way. Army medicine meant having to tell stretcher-bearers to lay the wounded in the mud outside the aid post because there was no room inside, or that they should have saved themselves the trouble, since no more time or effort would be wasted on such a seriously wounded man. It meant amputating limbs without anaesthetic, operating in confined spaces with no lighting, without any form of asepsis, antiseptic or hygiene, head in foul air and feet on slippery wet dirt, because there was no linoleum on the floor, indeed no floor, not even duckboards.[24] It meant working with insufficient equipment, of

21 Keegan, *Face of Battle*, 266; Horne, *Price of Glory*, 185; Bourke, *Dismembering the Male*, 33

22 Liddle, *Passchendaele in Perspective*, 352; Shepard, *War of Nerves*, 139; Macdonald, *1914–1918*, 183

23 Eckart & Gradmann, *Die Medizin*, 349; Shepard, *War of Nerves*, 26, 172

24 Macdonald, *Passchendaele*, 126; Frey, *Pflasterkästen*, 281–2, 301, 319; Van Bergen, 'Met te weinig riemen', passim; Rompkey & Riggs, *Your Daughter Fanny*, 111, 114; Riemann,

dubious quality, repairing wounds and treating sicknesses so specific to this war that most doctors had little or no previous experience of them. It meant breathing the poison gases given off by the clothes and bodies of casualties, which often overwhelmed medical personnel. Army medicine meant pressure of time, a struggle to save any wounded who had a chance of survival so that the voracious demand for manpower could be met. Finally, army medicine meant numbness, insensitivity, because no one would have enough stamina for it otherwise. K.E. Luard, a nurse with the British Red Cross, saw many men die at Ypres in August 1917. Their beds were filled again immediately.

> One has got so used to their dying that it conveys no impression beyond a vague sense of medical failure. You forget entirely that they were once civilians, that they were alive and well yesterday. … All you realize is that they are dead soldiers, and that there are thousands like them. … Pretty beastly, isn't it?[25]

Mary Borden, who suffers a complete breakdown at the end of her *Forbidden Zone*, described the numbness she experienced in her surgical hospital, a numbness that turned her into the mental counterpart of the physical wrecks she faced every day.

> Sometimes arms and legs wrapped in cloths have to be pushed out of the way. We throw them on the floor – they belong to no one and are of no interest to anyone – and drink our cocoa. … There was a man stretched on the table. His brain came off in my hands when I lifted the bandage from his head. When the dresser came back I said: 'His brain came off on the bandage.' 'Where have you put it?' 'I put it in the pail under the table.' 'It's only half of his brain,' he said, looking into the man's skull. 'The rest is here.' I left him to finish the dressing and went about my business. I had much to do.[26]

Some medical staff never got used to the job, never became numb, despite knowing their survival depended on it. In May 1918, De Launoy noted in her diary that 'the terrified death throes of so many, the screams, the despairing hands on my dress, the sufferings of the poor people' were a 'real torment' to her. 'And I must get on with it and pretend I have no feelings at all.' Evadne Price, who wrote under the pseudonym Helen Zenna Smith, based her *Not So Quiet* on the war diaries of ambulance driver Winifred Young. 'I whimpered like a puppy... I couldn't go on... I was a coward... I couldn't face those stretchers of moaning men again... men torn and bleeding and raving.' Bagnold said that the necessity of becoming inured to all this meant it was the observer and not the dying man who was poisoned. On

*Schwester der Vierten Armee*, 62, 98

25 Moorehead, *Dunant's Dream*, 219–20

26 Borden, 'Forbidden Zone', 92, 98, 102, 149–50; see also: Panke-Kochinke & Schaidhammer-Placke, *Frontschwestern*, 102, 112

a more practical level, habituation saddled doctors and nurses with a dilemma. It was impossible to keep feeling the pain of every individual, yet that was precisely what good nursing required. Partly as a result of this particular dilemma, the use of drugs like morphine, so easily available, was not confined to the patients.[27]

Leaving all this aside, it is useful to trace the system of medical help from beginning to end, starting with the wounded on the battlefield.

## From wounding to aid post

On the battlefield the many wounded got in the way. Unlike the dead, they could not be ignored. They would not even serve as cover, as dead men did, and you could not go and sit on them as you could a corpse, for some protection against the mud or rising water. The wounded had a right to be brought back behind the lines, so they had every reason to try to attract attention, preferably from a group of stretcher-bearers, but at least from fellow soldiers. Any man could give them first aid, by sprinkling them with tincture of iodine, before moving on and pointing out to stretcher-bearers the place where they were lying. Often, however, troops were forbidden to help the wounded during an offensive. The instinct to stop and tend a comrade had to be curbed, since it delayed forward movement and reduced fighting strength.[28] Military tasks must always take priority. Sergeant Joseph-Auguste Bernadin remembered arriving at a trench full of exhausted and wounded soldiers during the attack on Hartmannswillerkopf in January 1915: 'Two paces from me sits an unfortunate fellow, his upper body naked in the icy rain. "I'm freezing," he moans, his teeth chattering. "Help me, comrades, lay a coat over me!" Two units have already passed us; no one stopped.'[29] In late 1914 Barthas saw the following scene:

> In the squad in front of us a bullet had gone right through a man's shoulder and he bled profusely, eventually dying for lack of first aid; but goodness knows where the stretcher-bearers had got to and anyhow we couldn't delay our march, having been ordered not to stop to look after anyone, not even to save our own brothers. We passed in front, or rather stepped over, this first wounded man, as he breathed his last.[30]

---

27 De Launoy, *Oorlogsverpleegster*, 264; Bagnold, *Diary Without Dates*, 78, 88; Cardinal, Goldman & Hattaway, *Women's Writing*, 198, 202–3

28 Jünger, *In Stahlgewittern*, 129; Manning, *Her Privates We*, 146, 154; Gabriel & Metz, *A History of Military Medicine*, 248; De Vos, *De Eerste Wereldoorlog*, 63; Holmes & De Vos, *Langs de Velden van Eer*, 101; De Bruyne, *We zullen ze krijgen!*, 201

29 Brants & Brants, *Velden van weleer*, 307

30 Barthas, *Carnets*, 68

Shortly before the Battle of the Somme, all soldiers were reminded that helping the wounded was a task for stretcher-bearers and not for ordinary soldiers. This does not mean, of course, that the order was always obeyed. Near the German wire, a group of Australians heard someone call for a stretcher-bearer. 'It was an appeal no man could stand against; so some of us rushed out and had a hunt; we found a fine haul of wounded and brought them in.'[31]

Generally speaking, even when not explicitly forbidden to do so it was difficult for the men to assist the wounded. Battlefield conditions often made it impossible to stop for a moment to comfort a comrade in distress and bind his wounds, let alone to get him back behind the lines. Even stretcher-bearers might be unable to find or reach casualties. The heaviest of the fighting in the hills around Münster in the Alsace in February and March 1915, for example, took place in appalling conditions. Dogs were relied on to indicate where the snow-covered wounded were lying, while stretcher-bearers moved around on skis. Wounded men often froze to death or succumbed to their wounds before they were found.[32]

Many injured men were forced to treat their wounds as best they could themselves, using the field dressings every soldier carried, then to mark the spot where they lay as clearly as possible and wait for the stretcher-bearers. There was a good chance none would turn up, and if they did they might already be carrying a wounded man. All this time a casualty would be exposed to heat or cold, to extreme thirst, to rainfall, shellfire and sniping. Lieutenant Hornshaw of the West Yorkshires compared the wailing of men in pain to the scraping of big, wet fingers down an enormous window, and it was commonplace, especially at night.[33] Or perhaps it just seemed louder at night.

Being wounded often caused a man to lose all sense of time and place. Half dazed, he lay or sat with gunfire all around, incapable of making effective sounds or gestures.[34] Cloete was able to set off back, but he experienced a sense of dissociation.

> I still felt no pain but I was tired. At this point I became two men. My mind left my body and went on ahead. From there I watched quite objectively and with some amusement the struggles of this body of mine staggering over the duckboards and wading through the mud where the boards were smashed. I watched it duck when a salvo of German shells came over. I saw it converse with gunners who were stripped to the waist, too busy to talk but a corporal gave my body some rum. … I then rejoined my body. The rum may have done it.[35]

---

31 Holmes, *Firing Line*, 195; Manning, *Her Privates We*, 154

32 Brants & Brants, *Velden van weleer*, 305

33 Brants & Brants, *Velden van weleer*, 146

34 Ellis, *Eye-Deep*, 106; Winter, *Death's Men*, 196; Holmes, *Riding the Retreat*, 67–8; Graves, *Goodbye*, 134; Wilson, *Myriad Faces*, 326; Brants & Brants, *Velden van weleer*, 195

35 Winter, *Death's Men*, 196

Men simply waited for death on the battlefield, knowing that with the chaos around them, the shortage of stretcher-bearers, the profusion of wounded and the nature of their wounds, their chances were extremely slim.[36] Some were fortunate enough to be picked up, although it was not unusual to have to wait two or three days. Many more died before they were found, or drowned in the shell-holes they dragged themselves into for cover. Even if they were located and given first aid, they could have no confidence of being saved. American Raymond Austin wrote to his mother about the darker side of the Allied advance in 1918.

> The ambulance service didn't work very well the first day. The road between Croix-le-Fer and Missy-aux-Bois was thickly lined with wounded, tagged (name, injury and first-aid treatment) awaiting transportation. Many died there before they could be got to the dressing stations.[37]

Sometimes the wounded, whether accompanied by stretcher-bearers or not, might imagine themselves safely on their way back but then get hopelessly stuck in the sucking mud.[38] In the fight for Bois Delville during the Battle of the Somme, German Lance-Corporal Heinrich Renzing went so far as to say that anyone wounded was better off dying quickly. No help was possible during the day, 'and who would find him at night?'[39] When the ground was wet and muddy, stretcher-bearers would not even be sent out after darkness fell, since it was impossible for them to operate.[40]

Saddest of all was the fate of those who lay dying or drowning close to their own trenches, even in them, when artillery or machine-gun fire was so intense or the terrain so impassable that no one could be sent out to bring them in. They died as their comrades watched, helpless, perhaps forced to endure their screams and moans.[41] In late August 1917 a young officer at Ypres realized the cries he was hearing had acquired an extra dimension. The wounded had crawled into shell-holes for cover and they were drowning.[42] Sweeney wrote to his girlfriend on 25 July 1916: 'You cannot realize what it is like to see poor lads lying about with such terrible wounds and we cannot help them.'[43] Henri Desagneaux, a *poilu*, lay at Verdun amid a growing heap of wounded, as men stumbled up to him and his comrades with the last of their strength, despite the fact they had absolutely nothing

36 Horne, *Price of Glory*, 183

37 Marix Evans, *1918*, 140

38 Prior & Wilson, *Passchendaele*, 168–9; Binneveld, *Om de geest*, 50; Holmes, *Firing Line*, 186–7

39 Macdonald, *1914–1918*, 167

40 Macdonald, *Passchendaele*, 119

41 Elles, *Eye-Deep*, 106; Fussell, *Bloody Game*, 106; Winter, *Death's Men*, 194; Prior & Wilson, *Passchendaele*, 98; Macdonald, *1914–1918*, 106

42 Prior & Wilson, *Passchendaele*, 98

43 Fussell, *Bloody Game*, 49

to offer them. Screams for help alternated with the cries of men begging to be put out of their misery, but neither demand could be met. It was many hours before they grew quieter.[44] Scenes like this led César Méléra to remark: 'He who has not seen the wounded emitting their death rattle on the field of battle, without care, drinking their urine to appease their thirst … has seen nothing of war.'[45] Proximity was not always the same as visibility, incidentally. Those who made no sound, because their vocal chords had been severed or because they were dead, might not be found for a long time, even if they were lying a stone's throw away.[46]

Gravely wounded men slowly bleeding to death, severely poisoned men coughing up their lungs, soldiers on the point of drowning: any of these were quite likely to beg to be shot, but only rarely was anyone around who had the nerve, and would have been allowed, to kill them.[47] At Passchendaele in October 1917, Sergeant T. Berry watched a man slowly sinking. 'He kept begging us to shoot him. But we couldn't shoot him. Who could shoot him? We stayed with him, watching him go down in the mud. And he died.'[48]

Many felt tormented for years after failing to give the *coup de grâce*, even if it was forbidden by their own religious convictions, indeed even if they had never really had the opportunity,[49] as was the case for Private R. Le Brun in late October at Passchendaele:

> [One of our infantrymen] was sitting on the ground, propped up on his elbow with his tunic open. I nearly vomited. His insides were spilling out of his stomach and he was holding himself and trying to push all this awful stuff back in. When he saw me he said, 'Finish it for me, mate. Put a bullet in me. Go on. I want you to. Finish it!' He had no gun himself. When I did nothing, he started to swear. He cursed and swore at me and kept on shouting even after I turned and ran. I didn't have my revolver. All my life I've never stopped wondering what I would have done if I had.[50]

Not everyone shrank from such acts. In *Kneeshaw Goes to War*, Herbert Read wrote about a man who marched beside Kneeshaw, Read's alter ego in the book. Under the weight of his equipment the man slowly sank into the Passchendaele mire. He kept his grip on the rifles held out to him, but it was no good. Slowly but surely the mud sucked him deeper and deeper. After a while there was only

---

44 Winter, Baggett, *1914–1918*, 169–70

45 Eksteins, *Rites of Spring*, 153

46 Keegan, *Face of Battle*, 260; Barbusse, *Le Feu*, 252–5

47 Brants & Brants, *Velden van weleer*, 97–8; Holmes, *Riding the Retreat*, 208–9; Holmes, *Firing Line*, 188; Witkop, *Kriegsbriefe*, 328; Johannsen, *Vier von der Infanterie*, 104; March, *Company K*, 123

48 Macdonald, *Passchendaele*, 200

49 Brants & Brants, *Velden van weleer*, 97–8

50 Macdonald, *Passchendaele*, 219

one thing his comrades could do for him. 'Not a neat job – the revolver was too close.'[51]

If an ordinary soldier was certain that death was only a matter of time, he was permitted to give a wounded man morphine. It was an alternative to shooting him. He would pass away quietly and other men would not be disturbed by his moans as he died.[52]

A soldier might be carried back only to find that no further effort would be wasted on him. During the fighting in the hills of Alsace-Lorraine in 1915 it was hard to move the wounded out. On the French side it was particularly difficult, since the military hospitals were far away and could only be reached by steep paths down into the Thur Valley. Bernadin wrote:

> Most of the bodies had been covered with tarpaulins. Groans could be heard coming from one of these wretched bundles. 'But he's not dead yet at all,' I said to a soldier who was shooting in the direction of the enemy through an embrasure opposite. 'No, not yet. But the officer here says there's no sense in taking him back. He's been lying there forty-eight hours.'[53]

Some were lucky, if only after a long wait. In late August 1917 at Ypres, Lieutenant G.E. Winterbourne of the Queen's Westminster Rifles heard a man cry out during a pause in the bombardment.

> [We saw] a poor chap about fifty or sixty yards away. He was absolutely up to his arms in it, and he'd been there for days and nights – ever since the last attack – and he was still alive, clinging on to the root of a tree in the side of his shell-hole full of liquid mud. Lieutenant Whitby took three men over to see if they could get him out. But they couldn't get any purchase on the ground because it was all soggy round about. The more they pulled, the more they sank in themselves. Eventually, from somewhere or other, they got a rope, got it under his armpits and were just fixing up a derrick to see if they could hoist him out of it when we had to move on, because there was trouble up in front. All we could do was leave a man behind to look after him. It was another twenty-four hours before he was rescued.[54]

This was no isolated incident. There are many known cases of wounded men who managed to stay alive for days, perhaps by drinking rainwater, and were then brought back to their own lines and eventually recovered completely. The human body seems able to withstand a great deal.[55] The official record for 'surviving

51 Liddle, *Passchendaele in Perspective*, 431–2
52 Holmes, *Firing Line*, 188; Macdonald, *Somme*, 97
53 Brants & Brants, *Velden van weleer*, 308
54 Macdonald, *Passchendaele*, 138–9
55 Ellis, *Eye-Deep*, 106

wounded in battlefield conditions', fourteen days, is held by one Private A. Matthews. He was wounded at Gommecourt on 1 July 1916. On the fourth night several lightly wounded men crawled into the shell-hole alongside him. They had kept themselves alive by eating the rations of the dead, of which there was no shortage, and they gave Matthews some supplies before going on their way. For whatever reason, they were unable to fulfil their promise to send help. After a few hours they became hopelessly lost and ended up back with him, then they made another attempt and disappeared for good. Ten days later Matthews was finally found and carried back. His wounds were serious, but by some miracle not septic. A year later he was declared fully restored to health.[56]

Wounded soldiers might manage to limp or stumble to an aid post, or they might be carried back by comrades when the offensive was over, or by stretcher-bearers, perhaps after waiting several days. Generally speaking, those who made their own way back were relatively lucky. Their wounds would keep them out of combat for the time being, and most were not grossly maimed for life. There were exceptions. Jünger saw a man who had been hit by a bullet that 'had drilled through the top of his helmet, and ploughed a furrow along the top of his skull. I could see the brain rise and fall in the wound with every heartbeat, and yet he was capable of going back on his own.'[57]

When rescuers succeeded in reaching a casualty, it was still touch and go whether he would live. Sassoon found two wounded men in a deep crater, one of whom he knew.

> [Mick O'Brien] is moaning and his right arm is either broken or almost shot off: he's also hit in the leg (body and head also, but I couldn't see that then). Another man … is with him; he is hit in the right arm. Leave them there and get back to our trench for help, shortly afterwards Lance-Corporal Stubbs is brought in (he has had his foot blown off). Two or three other men are being helped down the trench; no one seems to know what to do; those that are there are very excited and uncertain: no sign of any officers – then Compton-Smith comes along (a mine went up on the left as we were coming up at about 11.30 and thirty … men were gassed or buried). I get a rope and two more men and we go back to O'Brien, who is unconscious now. With great difficulty we get him half-way up the face of the crater; it is after one o'clock and the sky beginning to get lighter. I make one more journey to our trench for another strong man and to see to a stretcher being ready. We get him in, and it is found he has died, as I had feared.[58]

Return journeys with wounded men might be extremely arduous. Private W. Lugg picked up a man and struggled to get him to an aid post 400 metres away across the

---

56 Wilson, *Myriad Faces*, 329–30

57 Jünger, *In Stahlgewittern*, 177; *Storm of Steel*, 211

58 Fussell, *Bloody Game*, 57; Gilbert, *First World War*, 251

mud of Third Ypres. They arrived ten hours later. This was not abnormally long.[59] Frenchmen wounded at the Mort Homme sometimes spent thirty hours being carried back on hand carts or tied to donkeys, dragged along by men who all stood a fair chance of being hit.[60] On the hilltop at Le Ligne, to the north of Münster, French commanders who had stayed back on a nearby peak could see nothing of the fighting that began on 20 July 1915, which was fierce despite the persistent freezing fog. They could see only the results of the battle, long lines of wounded who had stumbled back to their own defensive positions. Many others were unable to walk and simply lay where they had fallen. A few were lucky enough to be carried away from the battle on donkeys – a journey that took 24 hours.[61]

Those who got back to their own trenches, with or without help, found their ordeal was far from over. They were more vulnerable than other men to shellfire, since they could not react quickly. There were so many wounded that shelters and dugouts quickly filled and men moving along the trenches often had no choice but to walk over them.[62] Many died after arriving at an aid post, since they had already lost too much blood. Blood transfusions were certainly an option, and the circumstances were such, with a huge amount of supply and demand, that their use gradually increased. In practice, however, the technique was still in its infancy. The Germans made only minimal use of it and the British too were hesitant until 1917, when the arrival of the Americans made transfusions more common. The procedure raised so many unanswered questions that British doctors preferred to administer saline solutions, especially to help men survive shock, although Canadian experts pointed out repeatedly from 1915 onwards that this addressed only the quantity of blood lost, not the quality. Old habits die hard and much depended on whether and to what extent Canadian ideas, published in 1916 in British medical journals, were absorbed by doctors at the front. Moreover, transfusion, because it was new and the circumstances of its use extraordinary, was a far from gentle affair. Donors were often bled so hard they had to be sent home for two weeks to recover, which made the high command all the more wary of using the technique on a regular basis. Transfusion, unlike so many other medical interventions, does not seem to have been used merely to make wounded men fit to return to battle. It was employed to save lives, or in an attempt to ease an inevitable death, so there was no ignoring the fact that it cost the army healthy soldiers. Sometimes the lightly wounded served as donors. All told, bleeding to death was less common than in previous wars, at least among those who managed to reach hospital.[63]

---

59 Macdonald, *Passchendaele*, 118; Gabriel & Metz, *A History of Military Medicine*, 248

60 Brants & Brants, *Velden van weleer*, 236–7

61 Brants & Brants, *Velden van weleer*, 302

62 Wilson, *Myriad Faces*, 378

63 Sassoon, *Complete Memoirs*, 616; Verdoorn, *Arts en Oorlog*, 360; Brants & Brants, *Velden van weleer*, 241–2; Winter, *Death's Men*, 203; Eckart & Gradmann, *Die Medizin*, 7,

Irrespective of how many men were left behind on the 'field of honour' after a battle, the stream of wounded was relentless, and most of those who arrived at aid posts were brought in by stretcher-bearers. Theirs was an extremely tough and wearying existence. Barbusse writes in *Le Feu*: 'Now, through the fog, we can see the bent backs of men who are joined together by something they are carrying. They are stretcher-bearers bringing a new body. They come towards us with their haggard faces, panting, sweating and grimacing with the effort.'[64] Duwez believed that only a man who had carried a stretcher could have any idea 'of the weight that lay on his shoulders'.

> The shoulders become very painful after a while. The wrists too, trying to reduce the burden, soon grow rigid with fatigue and pain. The wood presses on the bones with its full weight. You have to stop a moment, lay down the load and change places with your neighbour to move the burden to the other shoulder.[65]

Their work was extremely strenuous. A stretcher-bearer's equipment often proved almost useless in battle conditions, although these were precisely the circumstances for which it had been designed. The two-wheeled carts available to French stretcher-bearers were useless on the blasted terrain around Verdun. Dogs trained to search for the wounded were driven mad by shellfire. Stretchers were impossible to keep upright and wounded men frequently fell off them.[66]

Their lives were extremely hazardous too. A stretcher-bearer could rarely step onto the battlefield without becoming a target, and he was unable to duck every time he heard a shell coming, as an infantryman or runner could. Many were wounded or killed. Their mortality rate exceeded even that of other units which suffered heavy losses, including cavalry, ordnance and quarter-master corps. Only the infantry, artillery, tank and signals corps had higher casualty rates. They were rarely deliberately shot at, but in the chaos of battle it was hard to distinguish them from everyone else, and nobody was immune to ricochets and shell splinters. The best they could hope for was that very occasionally, when the need for medical aid became critical on both sides, a cease-fire would be silently agreed upon so that stretcher-bearers could do their work. Some stretcher parties were attached to the medical services of their respective armies. They relied on volunteers to make up the numbers, so the physical and psychological hardships of their dangerous existence meant they were chronically short-staffed. In the final analysis few were

---

109–33 (article: Thomas Schlich, 'Welche Macht über Tod und Leben'); Eckart & Gradmann, 'Medizin', 211; Liddle & Cecil, *Facing Armageddon*, 460; Pelis, 'Taking Credit', passim

64 Barbusse, *Le Feu*, 134–5; *Under Fire*, 137; Frey, *Pflasterkästen*, 61–2

65 Evrar & Mathieu, *Asklepios*, 241

66 Horne, *Price of Glory*, 183; Heijster, *Ieper*, 139; *Van den Grooten oorlog*, 158

awarded medals, but all in all it may come as no surprise the most decorated of all British soldiers of the Great War, Private W.H. Coltman, was a stretcher-bearer.[67]

The weather and the resulting state of the ground were no less difficult for stretcher parties to deal with than for the fighting men. As suggested by Lugg's ten hour trek, at Third Ypres it was particularly hard going. Sergeant Robert L. McKay of the 109th Field Ambulance, 36th (Ulster) Division – a mobile medical unit with a strength of ideally around 10 officers and 230 other ranks – wrote that his team could barely put one foot in front of the other. It was the first time he had served as a stretcher-bearer and he hoped – in vain – that it would be the last. He would prefer to go into battle. All this plodding through the mud meant that even during the heaviest fighting it was sometimes rather quiet at the hospitals. No wounded arrived. The stretcher parties were busy battling the elements.[68]

In good weather and on reasonably flat dry ground, a wounded man could be carried by two stretcher-bearers, although four was more usual. During Third Ypres a minimum of six to eight were needed to carry each stretcher case, and they quite often took six hours to get a man to an aid post no more than half a mile from where he had fallen, within sight of enemy guns all the way. It was not unusual for two of the team at any one time to be fully occupied pulling the feet of the other four or six out of the mud.[69] Sometimes stretcher parties had to be expanded to twelve. Sergeant W.J. Collins of the Royal Army Medical Corps explained.

> A stretcher squad consists of four men and you lift the stretcher up and on to your shoulder, and each corner had a man. Now that's the only way you can carry a man properly. But, my God it was hard work, really hard. I mean, the road there was all lumps and bumps. … And of course it's hard on the shoulders. When the conditions got really appalling, it required twelve men to a stretcher, but they couldn't get on the stretcher all at the same time. … You could get six … one in the middle one side, one the other, and then they would stop and another six men would take over. You see, you're dragged down in the mud and of course you're plastered in mud yourself. And not only that, they're not fed up like boxers for a contest, they're living on bully beef and water and dog biscuits. No hot meals! Hot meals? Never heard of them.[70]

Shawyer sighed that during the Battle of the Somme a man would always be picked up sooner or later, but during Third Ypres a stretcher case had no real chance at all.

---

67 Holmes, *Firing Line*, 197; Jünger, *In Stahlgewittern*, 168; Frey, *Pflasterkästen*, 300; Winter, *Death's Men*, 196; Horne, *Price of Glory*, 183; Wilson, *Myriad Faces*, 326; Whalen, *Bitter Wounds*, 53; Levy, 'The Military Medicinemen', 292

68 Liddle, *Passchendaele in Perspective*, 180; Payne, 'British medical casualties', 25

69 Brants & Brants, *Velden van weleer*, 90; Prior & Wilson, *Passchendaele*, 97–8; Macdonald, *Passchendaele*, 119; Macdonald, *Roses of No Man's Land*, 222

70 Macdonald, *1914–1918*, 247

> At one aid post a doctor said to the stretcher-bearers, 'Only bring back men we've got a hope of curing. If you get a seriously injured man, leave him to die quietly. Too often you bring men back here and before we can help them they're gone. You're wasting your time and ours.' I thought it was a terrible thing to say. But that was Passchendaele![71]

Towards the end of the battle, when the quagmire was deeper and the distance between the front and the aid posts longer than ever, two teams of eight – four times the normal number – had to be sent out to collect just one wounded man. This meant that a regiment's thirty-two stretcher-bearers could carry no more than two or three casualties at a time, instead of the usual eight, just when the need was greatest. It was hard enough to find two men to carry a stretcher, let alone four, or eight, or so Noyes says of the Somme and the same must surely hold true for Third Ypres, indeed the shortage there may have been even more acute.[72]

Noyes' remark suggests that conditions during the Battle of the Somme were a torment to all stretcher-bearers. Surfleet acted as a temporary stretcher-bearer, helping another man to carry a casualty back behind the lines on 13 November 1916. The further they went, the deeper and stickier the mud became. At each step they slowly sank up to their knees, since they had to push down with all their weight on one foot to pull the other foot out of the mud. Their boots tore at their heels until they bled. The wounded man slid back and forth on the stretcher, becoming more fearful with every step. All this with shells bursting to left and right, in front and behind. Somehow both men managed to duck every time they heard a shell falling, so low that their faces touched the mud. 'The horror of that passage remains indelibly stamped on my mind', Surfleet wrote.[73]

When the conflict became a war of movement again in 1918, the difficulty of bringing in the wounded increased. The distance between the front and the medical teams became significantly longer for advancing troops, especially if a man had to be taken all the way to a field hospital, while the means of transport and the state of the ground had barely improved at all.[74]

Most unpleasant of all for a stretcher-bearer was having to carry a man across a battlefield, but the trenches were little better. As we have seen, some were so narrow that the stretcher had to be held above the bearers' heads. This was particularly dangerous for the wounded, but conditions in the trenches did not exactly suit the bearers either. McKay, serving on the Somme in the spring of 1916, tells of a trench seven feet deep and three to three-and-a-half feet wide. There were planks along the bottom, but weather, wind and intensive use meant they were no longer lying where they had been placed. Some had even turned edge-upwards, making it extremely difficult to walk along them with a load.

71 Macdonald, *1914–1918*, 247
72 Gilbert, *First World War*, 364; Noyes, *Stretcher-Bearers*, 124
73 Wilson, *Myriad Faces*, 355–6
74 Gabriel & Metz, *A History of Military Medicine*, 251

> Imagine what it was to carry a patient down this at night; the entire length of the trench would be about half a mile, but only ten or twelve yards in any one part of it straight. In some places there were shell-holes too – three feet deep and filled with water, and the only plan of passing them was to walk right through them, because if a person stepped on the side of the hole, the soil gave way and they generally came down. Trench boots were served out to us but they only made matters worse; the soles being rubber, a person could obtain no grip in the mud at all. On one particular night a stretcher party was taking a patient down, and one man named Jackson, from Dublin, took his trench boots off and walked it in his stockinged feet, and this was through six or seven inches of snow and mud.[75]

An already difficult task was made even harder by the fact that not all soldiers appreciated what bearers did. Although many men showed profound respect for them – in stark contrast to the repugnance evoked by nursing staff, which was presumably due in part to their supposed safety behind the lines – there were soldiers like Barthas who considered stretcher-bearers to be 'front-dodgers' and 'profiteers', like telephonists, secretaries and gendarmes. He regarded them as shirkers, prepared to do their job only if threatened with violence.[76] La Motte mentions one soldier who had a similar feeling. Lying in a hospital bed he yelled at two stretcher-bearers:

> '*Sales embrusqués*! (Dirty cowards)' he cried angrily. 'How long is it since I have been wounded? Ten hours! For ten hours have I laid there, waiting for you! And then you come to fetch me, only when it is safe! Safe for you! Safe to risk your precious, filthy skins! Safe to come where I have stood for months! Safe to come where ten hours I have laid, my belly opened by a German shell! Safe! Safe! How brave you are when night has fallen, when it is dark, when it is safe to come for me, ten hours late!'[77]

Surfleet was one of a group of men who picked up a soldier wounded in both legs and one elbow and did their best to carry him back. After many diversions they abandoned the attempt. There was no option but for Surfleet to go on ahead and ask a group of real stretcher-bearers for help. He found it a sobering experience. They said they could not leave their aid post, which led Surfleet to conclude they were far too comfortable in their safe place. He returned to his comrades in the forward trench.

> After a few moments of profound and prolonged profanity, we picked up the stretcher and, spurred by the very anger in our hearts, hurried along to that

75 Brown, *Somme*, 28

76 Barthas, *Carnets* 148, 194, 533; Frey, *Pflasterkästen*, 17–18

77 La Motte, *Backwash of War*, 17–18

> R.A.M.C. Post. We handed our burden over to them; I can still see those swine sitting there, smoking and drinking tea while that lad lay there on the stretcher; I can still feel my blood boil (and I am not easily roused to anger) and still hear, without the slightest blush, the flow of abuse we poured out to them until, eventually, they did put the lad on a trolley and set off with him to the Dressing Station.[78]

Of course there were stretcher-bearers who tried to cut corners, but in general this kind of anger was unwarranted. It seems understandable, all the same, quite apart from the fact that many of the wounded were in such a wretched state that they no longer knew what they were saying. After waiting for hours on the battlefield, they had to endure a long journey to the forward trench and from there along the communication trenches to an aid post, a journey that would stick in a man's mind for many years. In Flanders in the winter of 1914, Captain Maurice Mascall experienced a night in which an endless stream of wounded arrived at an aid post. 'It was a horrible sight seeing these poor fellows brought in covered from head to toe with mud. Some could walk with help and they all had to go down these horrible plank roads in the dark, tripping and stumbling and often falling into the mud.'[79]

H. Baverstock of the New Zealand Division was wounded on the Somme in late September 1916.

> I suppose the time was about 2 o'clock on the Saturday afternoon. After a few hours, two stretcher-bearers of the Harauki Regiment found me and dragged me quite a distance on the sunken road. … All the while, they were being sniped at, for we were pretty well exposed. Having done all they possibly could for me, they told me they would have to return to Flers to get their stretcher. Whether those two brave Medical Corps chaps were killed I could not say, for I never saw them again. The chances of their reaching Flers were poor, for the sunken road was a complete death-trap. There I lay for about two days. To the best of my judgement, a slight retirement took place that night, so I assumed that I was lying in No Man's Land. … The back of my clothes was soaked in blood. … The hardest sound I had to try to bear was the shrieking and groaning of some poor chap a few yards away. That went on for an hour or two and then suddenly stopped. During the afternoon of the Sunday the weather broke and heavy rain came down. … At long last, early on the Monday morning, two other stretcher-bearers found me and lifted me on to their stretcher. They took me to Bogle's Post, an advanced aid-post somewhere near Flers. … I saw some poor fellows who had died on the stretchers on the way from Flers being lowered into graves already dug and waiting for them.[80]

---

78 Wilson, *Myriad Faces*, 357
79 Macdonald, *1914–1918*, 44–5
80 Macdonald, *1914–1918*, 170–71

All this with a ligature in place, which was risky in itself, especially if the journey took a particularly long time. There was a fair chance a limb would die or become infected.[81] Others had no use for ligatures. During the Battle of the Somme, Sergeant J.E. Yates saw a man whose right arm and right leg had been blasted off.

> His mind was quite clear as I laid him on the fire-step. His left hand wandered over his chest to the pulp where his right shoulder had been. 'My God,' he said, 'I've lost my arm.' The hand crept down to the stump of the right thigh. 'Is that off too?' I nodded. It was impossible to move him at the time. For five hours he lay there fully conscious and smoking cigarettes. When at last we tried to carry him out the stretcher stuck in the first traverse. We put him on a groundsheet and struggled on. But our strength was gone: we could not hold his weight. 'Drag me,' he suggested then, and we dragged him along the floor of the trench to the medical dugout.[82]

Scott Macife reported on an earlier case in a letter to his father in late 1914. There were no stretchers left in the trench and it was impossible to carry a wounded man who had arrived there. He had to be dragged along the ground. 'You can imagine the condition in which he arrived.'[83] Nineteen-year-old Lieutenant Alistair Crerar, wounded in the leg, spent several nights in a shell-hole, being shot at from both sides, before arriving back in his trench. The trench proved too narrow for a stretcher and he was lugged back with his arms round a stretcher-bearer's neck. By horse, ambulance and train he reached hospital in Le Touquet five days after he was wounded.[84] Scott Macife was right to point out that even a trip with stretcher-bearers and without being held above the parapet of the trench did nothing to help the healing process. August Hopp wrote of soldiers who died during 'the agonizing, laborious transport through the narrow trenches'.[85]

Martin Müller and a fellow German soldier, a man called Tschoppe, were scouting out no man's land in the winter of 1916, less than six months before Müller's death on 20 July, when Tschoppe was wounded in the stomach. It was early evening, so they were unable to get back. The wait for help began.

> After an endlessly long wait, something suddenly rustled ahead of us. I immediately thought the English were coming; a soft voice called my name. Strauß and another soldier crawled into our hole. It was ten to twelve. They had got lost and had found their way back to the right area only by following the moans of the wounded. But now, quickly to work! With our combined strength

81 Verdoorn, *Arts en Oorlog*, 360
82 Macdonald, *1914–1918*, 157
83 Fussell, *Bloody Game*, 42
84 Brown, *Somme*, 217–18
85 Witkop, *Kriegsbriefe*, 45–6

> we freed my legs, which had sunk almost completely into the tenacious slime, and made them flexible again. Then we laid Tschoppe as comfortably as possible on a tarpaulin and then, like lightning, out of the hole and off towards our own lines. Even for three of us the load was heavy, but we managed. Just as we finally reached our own wire entanglement, the tarpaulin tore. We quickly unfolded a new one and moved on. Carrying him over the barbed wire was particularly difficult and dangerous, all the more so because the lads on the other side were shooting at us again spiritedly. But eventually, towards one o'clock, we arrived in the trench with our poor mortally wounded load. He was bandaged and carried back behind the lines. He was still fully conscious. On the way to the hospital Tschoppe succumbed to his terrible wounds.[86]

As will be clear by now, and as Müller's story confirms, helping the wounded was a hazardous business. Here is a handful of examples out of thousands.[87] During First Ypres Sergeant-Major Frederick Hall twice left his own trench to take wounded men to safety through a hail of German bullets. The second time it cost him his life.[88] On 1 July 1916 Company Sergeant John Streets, wounded and on his way to an aid post, turned back towards the firing trench to help a member of his platoon who had not been able to move back down the line under his own steam. He was never seen again.[89] A little over two weeks later a wounded German managed to make his own way back to the trenches. Four stretcher-bearers carried him on from there. A shell hit and killed all five of them.[90] A British gunner told of a rescue operation at Passchendaele on 10 November 1917 in which five of the soldiers who had gone forward to help a wounded man were killed.[91] Frank Richards wrote about a route to a casualty clearing station, also at Passchendaele, that was littered with corpses. Some were wounded men who had died along the way, or been hit a second time, but there were stretcher-bearers among them.[92] Perhaps they included Captain Noel Chavasse, who was twice awarded the Victoria Cross for bravery in fetching the wounded, the second time posthumously.[93] At the end of one battle, six Canadian stretcher-bearers were discovered to be missing. Private F. Hodgson, another Canadian stretcher-bearer, came upon their scattered remains the next day as he made his way to an aid post, where he delivered a wounded man who had died en route.[94] A wounded Jünger – who lived until 1998, reaching the age of 102 – was carried on a stretcher-bearer's back and later by one of his own men. Both

86 Witkop, *Kriegsbriefe*, 184–6
87 Macdonald, *1915*, 117; Macdonald, *Somme*, 102–3; Jünger, *Das Antlitz*, 180
88 Gilbert, *First World War*, 144
89 Gilbert, *First World War*, 261
90 Witkop, *Kriegsbriefe*, 234
91 Prior & Wilson, *Passchendaele*, 55
92 Fussell, *Bloody Game*, 112
93 Gilbert, *First World War*, 354
94 Macdonald, *Passchendaele*, 221–2

were shot dead under him.[95] Saving one wounded man often cost several lives. It was perfectly rational for officers to forbid rescue attempts, as they did quite regularly, in an attempt to minimize casualties.[96]

Civilians too sometimes attempted to rescue wounded soldiers. The results were little different. Duhamel writes of a man named Deracourt.

> [He] never talked of himself, much less of his misfortune. I knew from his comrades that he had fought near Longwy, his native town, and that he had lain grievously wounded for nine days on the battlefield. He had seen his father, who had come to succour him, killed at his side; then he had lain beside the corpse, tortured by a delirious dream in which nine days and nine nights had followed one upon the other, like a dizziness of alternate darkness and dazzling light. In the mornings, he sucked the wet grass he clutched when he stretched out his hands.[97]

The wounded knew that efforts might sometimes be made to rescue them even if they were beyond hope. Many had probably devised similar attempts themselves, even carried them out, when they were battle-fit. Graves describes one such incident at the start of the Battle of Loos. The battlefield was littered with dead and wounded, and the sounds of pain and distress were terrible. One man, a popular company commander called Samson, was only about twenty yards from the trench, so his cries were particularly agonizing. Three men were killed trying to rescue him and four were wounded. When his own orderly finally reached him, Samson sent him back with the message that he was no longer worth saving. When at last it became possible to bring in the wounded, Graves found him dead. He had been hit in no less than seventeen places and had stuck his fist in his mouth so that his groans would not prompt any more men to try to rescue him.[98]

## From first aid to hospital

Initial treatment took place at an aid post, often little more than a table and a supply of dressings in one of the dugouts. It was these aid posts especially, often within range of the guns, who were responsible for the image of wartime medical care painted in this chapter's introduction. They were dimly-lit places, sometimes even pitch dark, damp, often with no fresh air and poorly heated in cold weather. The swarms of flies that blanketed the battlefields and trenches did not stop at the doors to the aid posts, in fact flies were attracted to them by the smell of blood.

95 Jünger, *In Stahlgewittern*, 246–7

96 Sandstrom, *Comrades-in-Arms*, 171; Fussell, *Bloody Game*, 43

97 Duhamel, *Vie des Martyrs*, 72

98 Graves, *Goodbye*, 133; Holmes, *Firing Line*, 196; for tragedies that occurred as the wounded were transported, see also: Lefebvre, *Die Hölle*, 234–7

This was one of several reasons why it was fanciful to think that dressings and instruments could be kept free of germs. In his book *Arts en Oorlog* (Physician and War), Dutch doctor and pacifist J.A. Verdoorn points out that mortal danger was ever-present, since 'the aid posts were within range of enemy artillery, so a direct hit could blow to bits all the casualties who had converged on them, along with all the staff'.

> In this environment of death and suffering, of blood and sweat, the front-line medical officer in charge, physically and mentally exhausted after working day and night, had to ensure the reliable functioning of this part of the chain of medical aid and at the same time more or less decide the fate of each of the countless wounded who passed through the aid post.[99]

Battalion doctor Duwez described his job:

> Our aid post is located in a small café, in a street perpendicular to the firing line. Straw has been hastily laid on the blue tiles. The dressings, the brown bottles with red labels, the nickel instruments from our opened bags are piled high on the bar. Two men, wounded by falling bricks, sit on the ground dazed, leaning back on the wall, their bleeding heads bandaged with field dressings. Ambulances come all the way to our post. Stretcher-bearers are available to us. As I am talking with two of them, one is suddenly hit in the leg by a projectile. A snapping sound reverberates, as if someone has broken a thin plank of wood, and the man falls to the ground howling.[100]

Surfleet finally reached an aid post after a wearying journey, only to discover that it could offer their casualty little relief. The doctor, sleeves rolled up, was clearly exhausted. Bleeding men lay everywhere, jammed against and on top of one another. Over, under and between them were bloodstained bandages. He felt suffocated by the sickly, penetrating smell of blood, disinfectant and anaesthetic.[101] Dearden too, in his *Medicine and Duty* (a book named after the most common diagnosis by British war doctors and, according to Shepard's *A War of Nerves*, the one most hated by soldiers, roughly translating as: a good dose of medicine and then back to the front), described an aid post as a combination of mud, rain and blood, where it was impossible to offer any shelter to the wounded. Greatcoats taken from prisoners of war were used as blankets and many of the wounded who had been saved at great risk to others were killed by shellfire.[102] Hayward, an RAMC surgeon, wrote:

---

99 Verdoorn, *Arts en Oorlog*, 342–3; Jünger, *Das Antlitz*, 178
100 Evrard & Mathieu, *Asklepios*, 240
101 Wilson, *Myriad Faces*, 356
102 Dearden, *Medicine and Duty*, 189; Shepard, *War of Nerves*, 26

> At about 1 am the ambulances began to arrive. It is impossible to convey an adequate picture of the scene. Into the tent are borne on stretchers or come wearily stumbling, figures in khaki wrapped in blankets or coats, bandaged or splinted. All of them are caked in mud or stiff with blood and dust and sweat. Labels of their injuries are attached. Many are white and cold and lie still. Those who make response are laconic or point to their label. I have never seen such dreadful wounds.[103]

Scenes like this were described time and again, by non-medical men like Dorgelès and by doctors like Louis Baros, who worked at Verdun. He described the place where he was expected to treat his patients as a cross between a pig-sty and an abattoir, complete with rotting food scraps and heaps of amputated limbs, crawling with maggots and swarming with flies.[104] But it was Barbusse who gave the most penetrating description of the disconcerting sight of a deeply filthy, stinking, overcrowded, understaffed airless hole. After walking for several hours with a wounded man, making his way through a network of communication trenches and waiting in a queue of casualties, Barbusse reached the aid post.

> In the hubbub of groans and lamentations, in the strong smell given off by innumerable wounds, in the flickering light of this cavern, teeming with confused and incomprehensible life, the first thing I try to do is find my bearings. Weak candle-flames shine along the walls of the shelter, only piercing its darkness in their immediate surroundings. At the back, far away, as in the far corner of a dungeon, there is a vague hint of daylight; by this clouded window one can make out the main objects stationed along the corridor: stretchers as low as coffins. Then moving around and above them broken and leaning shadows, while lines and clusters of ghosts swarm against the walls.
>
> I turn round. Next to the wall opposite the one through which the distant light is filtering a crowd has gathered, in front of a canvas stretched from the roof to the ground. This tenting forms a compartment with a lamp inside it, which can be seen through the brown, oily-looking canvas. Inside the compartment, by the light of an acetylene lamp, injections are being given against tetanus. When the canvas is raised, to let someone in or out, the light floods crudely over the scruffy, tattered clothing of the wounded who are stationed in front, waiting for their injections, and who, bent over beneath the low ceiling, sitting, kneeling or crawling, push so as not to lose their turns or to take someone else's, with shouts of: 'Me!' 'Me!' 'Me!', like barking dogs. In this corner, with this constant struggle going on, the warm stench of acetylene and of bleeding men is frightful to endure.

---

103 Winter, *Death's Men*, 198

104 Sassoon, *Complete Memoirs*, 447, 448; Macdonald, *To the Last Man*, 353; Lefebvre, *Die Hölle*, 232–3; Dorgelès, *Croix de bois*, 315–21

Several shells hit the aid post and a number of casualties are killed along with their doctors and nurses, creating even more chaos than before. Then the stream of wounded starts to flow again. It goes on and on.

> Just as I am plunging into the depths I see the trenches, in the distance, still moving and dark, still filled by the crowd that, overflowing from the ground, pours endlessly towards the first-aid post. For days and nights you can see long streams of men flowing and mingling, men torn from the battlefields, from the plain with its entrails bleeding and rotting down there, to infinity.[105]

He describes the state in which medical staff found some of the casualties who arrived at the aid post:

> There are several of them around a wounded man, lit by a candle, and they are shaking as they try to keep him down on his stretcher. The man has no feet. He has horrific dressings on his legs with tourniquets to stop the bleeding. His stumps have bled into the cloth bandages wound around them and it looks as though he is wearing red breeches. His face is devilish, glowing and dark, and he is in a delirium. They are pushing down on his shoulders and knees: this man, whose legs have been cut off, wants to get up off the stretcher and go away.[106]

Even the doctors and nurses at the aid posts sometimes found it hard to believe the wounds they were seeing. At Passchendaele a man who had come from the trenches at Hooge reported to Sergeant Collins.

> I saw a wound there which exceeds the bounds of credibility. A man came in from Hooge trenches. He walked up to me and said, 'Sergeant, there's a doctor here, isn't there? I've got terrible trouble here. I've been wounded here.' So I looked, and I said, 'Oh, Gor blimey' so I got him in my ambulance and I took him back to Captain Rogers. I said, 'This man's got a rather uncomfortable wound, Sir.' He said, 'What's the matter with him?' I said, 'He's got a shrapnel bullet right in the top of his penis, split it open as if it had been cut equally and *there it's lodged*.' Can you imagine that![107]

The wounded sometimes poured in at such a rate that all kinds of non-medical considerations had to be taken into account in making the initial selection, known as triage. When Passchendaele was taken, the only casualties treated were those brought in on stretchers. Anyone who, aware of the shortage of stretcher-bearers, had managed to reach the aid post under his own steam, even on his hands and knees, no matter how much pain and effort it had cost him, was turned away. The

105 Barbusse, *Le Feu*, 300–320; *Under Fire*, 257–70
106 Barbusse, *Le Feu*, 311–12; *Under Fire*, 263
107 Macdonald, *1914–1918*, 248

hope was that these men would still have enough strength to get all the way to the hospitals.[108] On other occasions men who had expended the last of their energy in reaching an aid post were told they could not be helped because the order to retreat had just been received, an order that doctors and nurses had to obey along with everyone else.[109]

The dying were laid on one side. Other casualties struggled further back, after receiving morphine injections and tetanus inoculations, wearing labels signed by a medical officer or with crosses in indelible ink on their foreheads. These warned of dosages given and confirmed to the hospital that they really were sick or wounded, a measure designed to prevent malingering. Renn tells the story of a captain who reported sick at a base hospital but was not admitted because he had no certificate from the dressing station.[110]

It was not always possible for a man to be moved to the next link in the chain. During major offensives especially, about which military medical services were not always informed in advance, the system became overloaded. The aid posts were full and so were the hospitals behind the lines and the base hospitals. There had been too few beds from the start. In early August 1914, for example, 235,000 beds were reserved for French soldiers, but by the end of October there were 275,000 wounded. In late November there were 360,000 beds for almost 500,000 wounded. There were also far too few ambulances, and until March 1915 they were not equipped with autoclaves for sterilizing equipment. This meant that aid posts might become overcrowded while surgeons in hospitals further back down the line had time on their hands. No ambulances would arrive at the forward trenches if the road was being fired at or shelled, as was often the case. If they did arrive, it was sometimes to bring casualties back rather than to take them away, because the field hospitals had become too full to cope.[111] Despite this, French ambulances alone transported an average of 7,000 wounded a day.[112]

There was little opportunity to take seriously wounded men further back behind the lines. The roads to the better equipped dressing stations were always rough and often impassable. A ride in an ambulance was barely any more comfortable than a journey on a stretcher. Many men who had survived the trip from battlefield to aid post, and the not always mild-mannered attentions of overworked doctors, died because they failed to reach hospital, or arrived too late, or because the journey cost them the last of their strength.[113] Sergeant F.M. Packham vividly remembered 10 September 1914: 'That night some of us were taken by lorry to a rear field

108 Macdonald, *Passchendaele*, 228

109 Macdonald, *1915*, 223, 235

110 Renn, *Krieg*, 237

111 Macdonald, *1915*, 309; Eckart & Gradmann, *Die Medizin*, 346–7

112 Winter, *Death's Men*, 194; Wilson, *Myriad Faces*, 326; Whalen, *Bitter Wounds*, 54; Renn, *Krieg*, 229; Barbusse, *Le Feu*, 107

113 Barbusse, *Le Feu*, 315; Jünger, *In Stahlgewittern*, 247; Horne, *Price of Glory*, 66

hospital. It was a very rough journey. One of the men had a stomach wound and had to lay on the hard floor of the lorry. He died just as we arrived at the hospital.'[114] Some did not even make it to the ambulance. Dearden noted in his diary:

> It was an awful job getting our fellows onto stretchers. One knew them all so well and under a bright sun it looked too horrible. The poor lad with his two feet off was quite unconscious and obviously dying. I patched him up and got him onto a stretcher, gave him a cigarette and left him, when he called me back. He said something I couldn't catch, for his lips were very cut about and bleeding. So I wiped his mouth and he said quietly and clearly, 'Shall I live, sir?' 'Live?' I said. 'Good lord yes. You'll be as right as rain when you're properly dressed and looked after.' 'Thank you, sir', he said and went on smoking his cigarette. He died as they were getting him onto the ambulance.[115]

Not everyone could be taken further by motorized transport. Gürtler described the walk from an aid post to a field hospital at Passchendaele:

> [Then came the scene that follows every battle,] medical orderlies in long lines with their stretchers, trying to get to the assembly point, large and small groups of lightly wounded, with their field dressings. Some whimper and complain so much that it rings in your ears for the rest of the day and puts you off eating, and some continue on their way silently, apathetically along the filthy, churned up road, with their heavy low boots that are nothing but lumps of mud, while others are cheerful, since now they will be able to have a good long rest.[116]

Vehicles were in any case vulnerable. On the first day of Passchendaele, Jim Annan was able to carry Jock Gellatly, whose arm had been blown off by a shell, to an ambulance that was already full of wounded men. He went back thinking that at least Gellatly was out of the whole business, when he heard a shell go over. He turned and saw nothing but a cloud of smoke and dust where the ambulance had been.[117] It was not the only time that casualties who had thought themselves safe were killed in an ambulance. Corporal O.W. Flowers was on his way to Bois Delville during the Battle of the Somme.

> What a bombardment there was! There were ever so many ambulances knocked out. … Quite a few ambulances had had a direct hit and we couldn't do much about those, but some of the others had been pretty well splintered with shrapnel and the wounded men they'd put inside had been wounded again after they'd been put in the ambulance. When you looked inside you got the shock of your

114 Macdonald, *1914*, 297
115 Winter, *Death's Men*, 205
116 Witkop, *Kriegsbriefe*, 327–8
117 Macdonald, *Passchendaele*, 99

> life! All we could do was load them into the lorry, try and get them back as quick as you can, because this shelling's going on all the time. When we got back there were five dead in the lorry and the lorry floor was swimming with blood. We made six runs that night towing in ambulances and taking these poor wounded chaps out of the ones we couldn't shift. When I got back from the last run, my mates in the advanced workshop, said, 'What's the matter with you? You look like a ghost!' I simply couldn't speak. It was a long time before I could speak, I was so terrified. Once we'd handed the wounded over I just crawled into the lorry and lay on the floor and went to sleep. The following morning my uniform was soaked in blood, sodden with it. They had to give me a new one. I looked at it and I can remember thinking, 'If the British people could see what I've seen and experience what I experienced last night, this war would stop. They wouldn't have it!'[118]

Often those who survived the journey were horrified to discover they would have to have one or more limbs amputated, although that had not seemed necessary when they were at the aid post. Too much time had passed between wounding and treatment for an arm or leg to be saved.[119] At least, that was the reason usually given. The pages that follow will show that it was not the full explanation.

## The field hospital

When war broke out, Owen was living in Bordeaux. He visited a field hospital as a civilian, just as a large batch of casualties was arriving. The hospital proved quite unprepared for so many patients, with insufficient clean water and no facilities at all for performing surgery under anaesthetic. In a letter to his brother Harold dated 23 September 1914 he wrote: 'One poor devil had his shin-bone crushed by a gun-carriage wheel, and the doctor had to twist it about and push it like a piston to get out the pus. … I deliberately tell you all this to educate you to the actualities of war.' Nurse Alice Slythe said resignedly at the time of the Battle of the Somme: 'You must muddle along with what you can get.'[120] There were certainly some improvements as the war went on, but the flood of wounded only grew, so on balance the picture changed little. Casualties sometimes arrived in such numbers that many were not only unable to find beds in hospitals behind the lines but could not even be taken inside. They had to sleep on the ground nearby, wrapped in blankets and rubber sheets.[121]

---

118 Macdonald, *Somme*, 216

119 Macdonald, *Passchendaele*, 126–7

120 Day Lewis, *Collected Poems*, 20; Brants & Brants, *Velden van weleer*, 124; Liddle, *The 1916 Battle of the Somme*, 89.

121 Liddle, *Passchendaele in Perspective*, 183; Panke-Kochinke & Schaidhammer-Placke, *Frontschwestern*, 137–9, 142–4

When the wounded finally arrived at a hospital, anyone judged to be in need of surgery was operated upon. At the same time, the hospital added one more complication to the life of a soldier, already under enormous strain in such constant close proximity to death. To the tension between soldier and civilian, sick and healthy, front-line service and safety, low and high rank, was added the tension between the wounded and their nurses, or between men and women, which was not made any easier by the image of a nurse as someone who handed out pills and asked: 'How are we feeling today?' Unrealistic though this may have been – nurses rarely had time for such personal attention – it was a pervasive image, and the 'hero' saw himself as a sick child.[122] Many were hoping to put off their return to the front for as long as possible and this might mean resisting medical therapies whenever they could. There were no mutinies or major rebellions in the hospitals, but non-cooperation that might best be described as passive resistance was fairly common.[123]

Officers and their men were treated in separate tents – officers had coloured blankets, other ranks white – and there was usually a tent set apart for abdominal wounds, for example, or for chest wounds, or patients with gas gangrene. Enemy wounded were – if possible – kept away from the rest, of course. None of the armies had more than a limited range of medical instruments: knives, surgical saws, bandages and morphine, and one or all of these might be unavailable if supplies failed to get through. Renn wrote that the shortage or inadequacy of equipment was often the reason a casualty died. It was certainly the reason why a wounded man who had been forced to wait several days might not receive treatment when his turn finally came. Even bandages and splints sometimes ran out.[124]

As the war went on, the percentage of men who died during or immediately after surgery fell, as did the percentage of wounded limbs that had to be amputated. Soldiers had an understandable horror of amputation,[125] but this does not alter the fact that it saved many lives. In the German army, an average of 12.5 per cent of leg wounds led to amputation, a low figure compared to the Allies, but the death rate from these operations was high, at seventy per cent. The Americans amputated no less than 41.4 per cent of leg wounds, but the death rate was only just over one in four. If we consider this in the light of a mortality rate from thigh wounds of 42.5 per cent among Germans and 24 per cent among Americans, then it appears that prompt amputation was a sensible measure from a medical point of view. German soldiers often complained that all doctors did was to saw off legs,

122 Whalen, *Bitter Wounds*, 49

123 Whalen, *Bitter Wounds*, 112

124 Winter, *Death's Men*, 197; Gilbert, *First World War*, 293; Renn, *Krieg*, 85; Macdonald, *Somme*, 326

125 See for instance: Lintier, *Ons Kanon*, 176–7

but we should consider the dispiriting conclusion that German doctors did not do so often or quickly enough.[126]

Percentages do not tell the whole story, of course, and the numbers they relate to were vast. It was the sheer numbers that made a field hospital such a dismal place, which is not to say that aid posts further back were much better. After he was wounded at Ypres on 20 September 1917, New Zealander General Bernard Freyberg vividly remembered seeing a long line of men waiting at a field hospital for their turn to be anaesthetized for surgery.[127] Even there a wounded man could not be offered the tranquillity he craved. Sustained artillery fire would mean everyone had to be evacuated, and field hospitals were regularly shelled. They were places for which the soldier had little affection, run by men and women in once-white coats who were themselves far from popular. Indeed, some soldiers claimed the letters RAMC stood not for Royal Army Medical Corps but for Rob All My Comrades.[128] Nurses were not simply the object of universal praise as courageous Madonnas who somehow existed outside the turmoil of battle, or 'roses of no man's land'.[129] They were sometimes verbally abused, occasionally accused of being whores who were more eager to please doctors than to care for patients. The *Feldpuffordnung* (field brothel regulations) drawn up by German soldiers themselves, which Magnus Hirschfeld describes as the most grassroots expression of front-line eroticism, stated that there was no need to set up brothels in the vicinity of hospitals where Red Cross nurses worked. Even when nurses cared for the troops in precisely the way expected of them, many men believed they were only doing so because of the sexual overtones.[130] Any expression of female sexuality was regarded as reprehensible by the men, although this did not prevent the wounded and sick from making eyes at nurses.

It was a reputation that could make a nurse like De Launoy extremely agitated, but which cannot be dismissed as pure slander and delusion. Her own diary illustrates this on several occasions.[131] Nurses had of course been drawn to the front by a desire to help the sick and wounded, although they were rarely employed at aid posts in the direct vicinity of the front line. The *Frontschwester*, the front-line nurse, celebrated in books like *Frontschwestern – Ein Deutsches Ehrenbuch* (Front-Line Nurses – A German Tribute), published in 1936, is largely a mythical figure. Riemann's *Schwester der Vierten Armee*, for instance, can be

---

126 Verdoorn, *Arts en Oorlog*, 258; Gabriel & Metz, *A History of Military Medicine*, 240–41; Lanz, *De Oorlogswinst*, 8

127 Gilbert, *First World War*, 359

128 Graves, *Goodbye*, 185; Bourke, *Dismembering the Male*, 150; *Van den Grooten oorlog*, 208; Meire, *De Stilte van de Salient*, 78

129 Mosse, *Fallen Soldiers*, 61; see also: 'De Dames van het Roode Kruis', passim

130 Hirschfeld, *Sittengeschichte*, 130–32 (incl. *Ergänzungsheft*, 17); Riemann, *Schwester der Vierten Armee*, 172, 190

131 De Launoy, *Oorlogsverpleegster*, 67, 97–8, 192, 198, 267–70; see also: Thomas, *Die Katrin wird Soldat*, 295

read as an account of her sustained but ultimately futile efforts to be allowed to work close to Ypres and the Yser. Wanting to help the sick and wounded did not preclude other, more human and down-to-earth motives, such as a desire to take part in the war in the only truly feminine way permitted, a longing to serve one's country and prove oneself a worthy citizen, an urge for adventure, or a yearning for male company in women whose menfolk had left for the war. Suddenly they were seeing men in ways they had seldom if ever seen them before. Abruptly coming into contact with large numbers of naked men undoubtedly aroused sexual excitement in completely unprepared nurses, something that Bagnold's *A Diary Without Dates*, for example, makes unambiguously clear. Mary Borden's denial that this applied in her case only serves to confirm the general picture. She wrote that the men she nursed could hardly be called men any longer, 'so why should I be a woman?' As a nurse she was interested in the wounded as patients, not as men, but the fact that she mentions sexual tension so explicitly suggests she was an exception in this respect. Duwez depicts the field hospital as a place where doctors and nurses could have mildly erotic, adventurous encounters with each other. Aside from his rather indelicate way of expressing it, there may therefore be a degree of truth in what Dr Emil Flusser said after the war about some of the nurses, describing them as 'petit bourgeois girls, or ladies from the upper middle classes or aristocratic circles' who wore 'flattering uniforms' that gave them access to hospitals 'because they wanted to nurse the wounded' or in other words 'to see blood, to see bodies naked and tormented by pain'.[132]

It was Vera Brittain who described this aspect of nursing work most frankly. She had not seen a boy without his clothes since she was three or four and had never laid eyes on a naked man. Neither she nor her patients felt the nervousness and shame that would normally have been expected, and, apart from actually having shared a bed with one of the wounded, in her four years as a war nurse she had no choice but to carry out practically every intimate act imaginable. There were not many things for which she was grateful to the war, but she was glad that it had liberated her from much of the sexual reticence instilled by her Victorian upbringing.[133]

This kind of tension has been familiar to army leaders in all eras. It was one of the reasons why many of them believed wounded soldiers should be cared

132 Bagnold, *Diary Without Dates*, 68–73; Borden, 'Forbidden Zone', 95, 102; De Schaepdrijver, *Taferelen uit het Burgerleven*, 93; Flusser, *Oorlog als Ziekte*, 73; Renn, *Krieg*, 125; Liddle, *The 1916 Battle of the Somme*, 92; De Weerdt, *De Vrouwen van de Eerste Wereldoorlog*, 128–9, 134–5; Panke-Kochinke & Schaidhammer-Placke, *Frontschwestern*, 11, 88, 102, 107–8, 112; Riemann, *Schwester der Vierten Armee*, 19, 84, 93, 116, 140, 144–6, 148, 210, 215, 217, 221–3, 235–6, 243, 304; Pflugk-Harttung, *Frontschwestern*, passim; Steiner, 'Selbstdeutungen und Missdeutungen von Frauen an der Front', passim

133 Brittain, *Testament of Youth*, 167–8; Shepard, *War of Nerves*, 148

for by male nurses alone. This touched a sore spot with M.A. St Clair Bofart, who had set up the Women's Sick and Wounded Convoy Corps during the Balkan War of 1912–13 and worked for the St John's Ambulance Association during the Great War. Her fierce objection to the notion was based not on humanitarian principles but in part on a belief that only women could create the comforting atmosphere essential to a quick recovery and the knowledge that it was important to employ female nurses 'in order to set men free for the fighting-line'.[134]

Another factor that contributed to the poor reputation of field hospitals was the shortage of doctors. Their numbers were tiny in proportion to the task they faced and their knowledge inadequate for effective treatment of the wounds the men presented. Even the most skilful of surgeons tended to feel the ground give way under his feet as he witnessed the massive influx of soldiers with terrible, filthy, suppurating wounds. Young and recently qualified doctors simply stared into space, apathetic, paralysed, overwhelmed and aghast, mesmerized by the ceaseless stream of patients.[135] They were arranged into teams that relieved each other according to a strict timetable, carrying out surgery as if on a conveyor belt. This way of organizing medical care seems remarkably appropriate to the industrial war machine, but what a field hospital could offer in medical terms was limited. It was this that prompted the British to replace the term casualty clearing hospital, used for their field hospitals until early 1915, with casualty clearing station, or CCS. The word 'hospital' might arouse unrealistic expectations.[136]

In Stanhope Walker's CCS in Corbie during the Somme offensive, six surgeons, three other doctors, a dentist and eight professional nurses, along with a handful of volunteer staff, were sometimes called upon to care for over one and a half thousand new cases a day. The death rate exceeded fifty per cent, but surgeons who had gone without sleep night after night were obliged to continue operating. Stanhope Walker's diary describes the condition of the wounded, the stink of gangrene and unburied corpses on the battlefield, and the moans of German casualties who were not treated until all the British had either been dealt with or died. He describes making secret nocturnal forays with morphine injections to ease and hasten the inevitable end of some men, even though it went against his religious convictions. For all the changes and improvements as the war went on, field hospitals remained nightmarish places for both the wounded and their doctors.[137]

> *1 July*. … All day long cars of dying and wounded. … They are literally piled up – beds gone, lucky to get space on floor of tent, hut or ward, and though the surgeons work like Trojans many must die for lack of operations. All the CCSs are overflowing. … We have 1,500 in and still they come, 3–4,000 officers, it is a sight – chaps with fearful wounds lying in agony, many so patient, some make

134 Cardinal, *Women's Writing*, 94, 96, 101
135 Eckart & Gradmann, *Die Medizin*, 185
136 Liddle & Cecil, *Facing Armageddon*, 455; Van Raamsdonk, 'De secretaris', 126
137 Moynihan, *People at War*, 69, 71, 73; Brants & Brants, *Velden van weleer*, 147

a noise, one goes to a stretcher, lays one's hand on the forehand, it is cold, strike a match, he is dead – here a Communion, there an absolution, there a drink, there a madman, there a hot water bottle and so on – one madman was swearing and kicking, I gave him a drink, he tried to bite my hand and squirted the water from his mouth into my face – well, it is an experience beside which all previous experience pales. …

*2 July*. What a day, I had no corner in the hospital even for Holy Communion. … I buried thirty-seven but have some left over till tomorrow. …

*3 July*. Now I know something of the horrors of war, the staff is redoubled but what of that, imagine 1,000 badly wounded per diem. The surgeons are beginning to sleep, because after working night and day they realise we may be at this for some months, as at Verdun. …

*9 July*. … We get a lot of frightful wounds, loads of abdominal, chests and heads. No one can imagine what it is unless they come and see it. Will one ever be able to think of anything but mutilated dying men again? …

*16 July.* Still they come and still they die. …

*18 July*. … A good many gassed men came in, a new and very deadly gas, some died, already they look very bad, blue and their mouths full of froth. An officer described it to me, for five hours a stream of shells came whistling over in the dark – on striking the ground the gas was turned on, they were in fact gas cylinders, so there was silence but for the hissing of the cylinders flying over to do their deadly dirty work.

*19 July*. … The great quad of the factory is choked with [cars] and then the shattered bleeding wrecks are taken out, four stretchers from each. …

*21 July.* The wards look packed with a very bad lot. It is a good thing not to be too squeamish, the smell of septic limbs and heads is enough to bowl one over. As usual a good many deaths, one had the back of his head off, another from the nose downwards completely gone. But it is the multiple wounds that appear worst, men almost in pieces, the number intensifies the horror, we get so few slight cases. …

*17 August*. … A good many died today with my hand on their heads. Of course one is so much accustomed that it does not affect one's nerves or anything of that sort, but it keeps coming over one like a wave, the madness and folly of it all. Will the day come when men of all nations refuse military service, leaving the Rt Hon Gents to scratch each other's eyes out?[138]

Duhamel noted:

The waiting-room seemed to have been transformed into a museum of misery: there were blind men, legless and armless men, paralysed men, their faces ravaged by fire and powder. ... On a bench sat fifteen or twenty men with about a dozen legs between them. ... Tricot had suffered greatly; only some fragments

138 Moynihan, *People at War*, 71–80; Ellis, *Eye-Deep*, 114

> of his hands remained; but, above all, he had a great opening in his side, a kind of fetid mouth, through which the will to live seemed to evaporate. ... Here is Bourreau, with the brutal name and the gentle nature, who never utters a complaint, and whom a single bullet has deprived of sight for ever. Here is Bride, whom we fear to touch, so covered is he with bandages, but who looks at us with touching, liquid eyes, his mind already wandering. Here is Lerouet, who will not see next morning dawn over the pine-trees, and who has a gangrened wound near his heart. And the others, all of whom I know by their individual misfortunes. How difficult it is to realise what they were, all these men who a year ago were walking in streets, tilling the land, or writing in an office.[139]

Dorothy Field of the Voluntary Aid Detachment kept a diary that speaks volumes. She worked in a casualty clearing station during the Somme. Even before the battle started, in the last few days of June, convoys of lorries and ambulances arrived one after the other. Each convoy brought 120 to 130 wounded. She seems to have had a fairly quiet night on Saturday 1 July.

> 2 Sun. Convoy came in at 4 a.m. – about 170 and another as we were coming off duty. Two evacuations during day and another convoy in about 8 p.m. Ambulances and trains full of sitting cases running all night. Another convoy in about 4 a.m.
>
> 3 Mon. Waked up about 5 p.m. by band heading endless column of drafts marching we imagine to station en route for the Front. Convoys coming in almost all night. They say we had 11,000 in 24 hours – dying on floor on biscuits in 4 tents and YMCA hut. …
>
> 5 Wed. Spent most of night specialling in D.1. with two awful head cases or in A.1. with 7 amputations – 5 done yesterday. A perfect nightmare and my feet hardly bearable. Convoy in after we left – about 9 a.m. …

It was 11 July before Nurse Field decided there might finally be a chance to take a break. She went off duty that morning, spent the whole night in bed and was told she could take the next day off. It was not to be. '12 Wed. Waked at 7.10 and told to get up and go on duty in Medical Hut!!! Poor Sgt Bromey there – very bad – g.g.w. [gas-gangrene wound, LvB] in chest, he died about 5.30 p.m.' She was given a day off on 13 July, but then too her rest ended abruptly when a large group of German wounded was brought in. In his book *Somme*, Malcolm Brown writes simply: 'The work would continue indefinitely.'[140]

In October 1918, German Red Cross nurse Käthe Russner complained of a splitting headache. She felt as if her head was about to explode, but she needed to stay awake, and she had yet to discover an attic crowded with wounded men left

139 Duhamel, *Vie des Martyrs*, 51–2, 71–2, 221–2

140 Brown, *Somme*, 111–13; see also: Crofton, *Royaumont*, 73; Rompkey & Riggs, *Your Daughter Fanny*, 146–7

to fend for themselves, casualties who had not been able to get into the hospital and whom no one had told her about. In despair she asked in a letter to her father whether this could really be God's will. There were certainly periods of rest, if not always particularly welcome, but as in the wartime letters of Canadian VAD nurse Frances Cluett, the endless work and constant, nerve-wracking exhaustion is a theme that runs all through De Launoy's diary. To judge by an entry for January 1916, the nurses were even more exhausted than the doctors, since nurses had to 'run back and forth incessantly, whereas they stay in one place. We have to arrange everything; they clear off as soon as their mediation is over.' Exhaustion from constant hard labour was made worse by unrelieved stress and emotion, which De Launoy believed affected the quality of her work. At the same time there were repeated evacuations of the building, ordered by higher-ups, and in the early days of the war and during the final offensive especially she had to work alongside untrained and often ill-disciplined volunteers of every description, all of which added to the strain on her constitution. Nursing was a profession that demanded hard work, skill and obedience, and far from everyone was capable of performing it unprepared. In her diary De Launoy took to task a general who believed that all a nurse had to do was to be 'lovable'. 'Unfortunately we have never been able to save anyone by geniality', she wrote. She felt the tiredness was not superficial; it had become integral to her body and mind. This was the kind of exhaustion that would not be relieved by a good night's sleep or even several weeks' rest. In early July 1917 she noted: 'The tiredness goes deep and it will take months if not years to build up resistance again.'[141] She would have agreed with the German front-line doctor who wrote in 1918 that the war had not made him any younger. 'Those four years, which are already behind us, have made demands of our bodies and our mental resilience of which no outsider can have any conception.'[142]

From all this it is clear that the wounded suffered terribly. Jünger, who called the hospital a 'place of piled up misery', remembered a fellow patient in his ward.

> On my left, a very young ensign was on a diet of claret and egg yolks; he was in the very last stages of emaciation. When the sister wanted to make his bed, she picked him up like a feather; through his skin, you could see all the bones in his body. When the sister asked him at night whether he wouldn't like to write his parents a nice letter, I guessed it was all up with him, and, indeed, later that night, his bed too was rolled through the dark door to the dying ward.[143]

---

141 De Launoy, *Oorlogsverpleegster*, 40, 107, 110, 134, 140–41, 166, 182, 201–2, 213, 235, 237, 279, 283, 287, 323, 326; Rompkey & Riggs, op. cit., 77–8, 128, 146, 148; Higonnet, *Lines of Fire*, 226, 228; Mierisch, *Kamerad Schwester*, 78–9; Riemann, *Schwester der Vierten Armee*, 60, 96, 116, 135, 225; Panke-Kochinke & Schaidhammer-Placke, *Frontschwestern*, 83–4, 153

142 Eckart & Gradmann, *Die Medizin*, 20

143 Brants, *Plasje bloed*, 112; Jünger, *Storm of Steel*, 106–7

Jünger wrote that all the horrors of the war came together in the operating theatre.[144] Remarque spoke of a 'chopping-block'[145] and Frank – who asked one doctor to estimate the total number of amputated arms, legs, feet and hands in the war and received the answer five million – called the room where operations took place 'the butcher's kitchen'. 'The sawn off hands, arms, feet, legs swim in blood, cotton-wool and pus in a metre high, two metres wide, moveable tub, which stands near the door in a corner and is emptied every evening.'[146] Emiel Selschotter, the local teacher in Alveringem, a small Belgian village behind the Yser front, took his son to a nearby war hospital in November 1914 because the boy was wondering whether or not to enlist. He did so 'not to scare him off but to show him the insanity of the war'. A man who later became his son-in-law and successor was in complete agreement with him. It was 'the wounded, maimed, damaged' who 'made the insanity of the war clearer to me than all the military operations'. When their compatriot Frans Smits wrote a story about the earlier mentioned large war hospital in De Panne called Océan, he chose as his title 'Het Huis der Smart' (The House of Affliction).[147] Riemann wrote that the nurses saw soldiers who had gone to the front fit and healthy return clinging to 'the remnants of their lives'. De Launoy wrote in her diary about the horrors she witnessed, and Stanhope Walker had similar tales to tell. His stay in hospital was a time he would never be able to forget. He felt that the meaning of war got through to a person more strongly in a CCS than anywhere else, even the battlefield itself, since in the hospitals the results of the conflict could be seen 'in broken humanity'. 'I don't think there is any part of the human body I have not seen wounded, frequently blown to pieces.'[148]

As suggested by the use of either white or coloured blankets, there was a difference in treatment between officers and other ranks. It can be summed up as follows: the men were to be returned to the front and officers must be made comfortable and content. It was far easier for wounded or sick officers to have themselves transferred home, and near the front they received better treatment from the army medical service, in some cases far better. After he was wounded on the Somme, B. Latham told an RAMC sergeant in Boulogne that he was an officer. The sergeant immediately stood to attention and arranged for Latham to be taken by ambulance to the Duchess of Westminster Hospital in Le Touquet. Two days later Latham was asked whether he might like to return to Britain. U. Burke described the many hundreds lying waiting for treatment at a CCS near Ypres and added that it was a problem he had not experienced. He was, after all, an officer.

144 Jünger, *In Stahlgewittern*, 86, 87

145 Remarque, *Im Westen*, 170

146 Frank, *Der Mensch ist Gut*, 146, 160; see also: Rompkey & Riggs, op.cit., 82, 83, 111, 146, 150; Thomas, *Die Katrin wird Soldat*, 290

147 Ureel, *De Kleine Mens*, 50, 60, 235–6; Smits, 'Het huis der smart', passim

148 De Launoy, *Oorlogsverpleegster*, 133; Riemann, *Schwester der Vierten Armee*, 97–8; Moynihan, *People at War*, 69; Mierisch, *Kamerad Schwester*, 118

General J. Jack caught a cold in 1916 and was treated to champagne and port at a field hospital, then given his own bath with plenty of hot water.[149]

Doctors stood ready to be of service even to healthy officers. La Motte described how hospitals were required to respond when a general came to visit, usually on days when they were extremely busy with no time for delays of any sort. All activity stopped and all instruments were laid down. The surgeons worked even harder than usual beforehand, but if they could not get finished they had to stop and carry on only when the visit was over. They might have to leave dressings unchanged while they walked respectfully behind the general, no matter who he might be, even if the visit took all day. 'And it usually took at least two hours, the visits of the Generals.'[150]

At regular intervals, if not quite so regularly as aid posts, hospitals even some way behind the lines were shelled. A hospital set up in a church in Beselare near Ypres in late 1914 was filled with German wounded. A first lieutenant in the reserve described what happened.

> A wounded man has just been bandaged by a doctor when a shell finds its way through the open church door. The head of the wounded man sinks back; the shot has penetrated his forehead and killed him. ... Then suddenly there is a deafening uproar. The walls fall down upon the wounded men. Fragments of shells come whistling down. ... Shrieking and groaning is heard. ... There is a hopeless tangle of men, débris and mattresses. ... The lightly wounded crawl out of the chaos on all fours; the severely wounded are brought into the open air by people belonging to the Medical Corps. Some of the dead are recovered. ... The Church of Beselare is left lonely and abandoned, a picture of devastation.[151]

Even without a direct hit, shelling could have serious or even fatal consequences for the wounded in their weakened state. During the bombardment of Ypres in November 1914, the sisters of Notre Dame Hospital withdrew to Poperinghe. Fifty-six German wounded remained behind in the care of four padres.[152] Duhamel wrote: 'The wounded were moaning, shrouded in acrid smoke. They were lying so close to the ground that they had been struck only by plaster and splinters of glass; but the shock had been so great that nearly all of them died within the following hour.'[153] La Motte wrote about caring for dying men.

> There are three dying in the ward today. It will be better when they die. The German shells have made them ludicrous, repulsive. We see them in this awful

149 Winter, *Death's Men*, 68; *Van den Grooten oorlog*, 156–7; March, *Company K*, 37–8

150 La Motte, *Backwash of War*, 81; Sassoon, *Complete Memoirs*, 550

151 *J'accuse*, 299

152 Macdonald, *1914*, 410

153 Duhamel, *Vie des Martyrs*, 122–3

> interval, between life and death. This interval when they are gross, absurd, fantastic. Life is clean and death is clean, but this interval between the two is gross, absurd, fantastic. … [In one case] meningitis has set in and it won't be long now, before we'll have another empty bed. Yellow foam flows down his nose, thick yellow foam, bubbles of it, bursting, bubbling yellow foam. It humps up under his nose, up and up, in bubbles, and the bubbles burst and run in turgid streams down upon his shaggy beard.[154]

Duhamel described a small separate room for those who were unable to die quietly or without soiling themselves.

> The little room adjoining the closet where I sleep has been set apart for those whose cries or effluvia make them intolerable to the rest. As it is small and encumbered, it will only admit a single stretcher, and men are brought in there to die in turn. ... Madelan was the first we put there. He was raving in such a brutal and disturbing manner, in spite of the immobility of his long, paralysed limbs, that his companions implored us to remove him. ... For four days and four nights, he never ceased talking vehemently. ... For four nights I heard him shouting incoherent, elusive things, which seemed to be replies to some mysterious interlocutor. ... He died, and was at once replaced by the man with his skull battered in, of whom we knew nothing, because when he came to us he could neither see nor speak. ... This man spent only one night in the room, filling the silence with painful eructations, and thumping on the partition which separated him from my bed. ... Then we had as our neighbour the hospital orderly, Sergeant Gidel, who was nearing his end, and whose cruel hiccough we had been unable to alleviate for a week past. This man knew his business, he knew the meaning of probe, of fever, of hardened abdomen. ... He stayed barely two days in the room.[155]

## The base hospital

From the field hospitals, ambulance trains left with appalling regularity for hospitals further away from the front, or for homeland or harbour. They generally did not have the best of reputations.[156] A British nurse described the tumult that always surrounded a train about to depart. She watched as thousands of wounded men 'swarmed about a long ambulance train standing in a field'.

> They crowded the carriages, leaned out of the windows with their bandaged heads and arms, shouting at friends they saw in the other crowds. … There were other

154 La Motte, *Backwash of War*, 86–8

155 Duhamel, *Vie des Martyrs*, 211–15

156 De Launoy, *Oorlogsverpleegster*, 43; Thomas, *Die Katrin wird Soldat*, 187, 230

> wounded men from whom no laughter came, nor any sound. They were carried on to the train on stretchers, laid down awhile on the wooden platforms, covered with blankets up to their chins. … I saw one young Londoner so smashed about the face that only his eyes were uncovered between layers of bandages, and they were glazed with the first film of death. Another had his jaw clean blown away, so the doctor told me. … Outside a square brick building … the 'bad' cases were unloaded: men with chunks of steel in their lungs and bowels were vomiting great gobs of blood, men with arms and legs torn from their trunks, men without noses, and their brains throbbing through opened scalps, men without faces.[157]

The British alone needed ten trains a day during the Somme offensive. Seven were designed to take 400 serious casualties each and the other three had room for a thousand lightly wounded, selected as being able to bear the journey sitting up. Some of the wounded were transported by barge, mainly those with broken bones. The lurching trains would have caused them too much pain.[158]

The same German trains used in the summer of 1914 to transport singing young heroes to the field of honour were soon carrying silent wrecks home. These trains bore no resemblance at all, Stefan Zweig says, to the polished, snow-white carriages with freshly starched sheets in which nurses dressed as princesses had their pictures taken for posterity. They were goods wagons without windows, with only a hatch for air, lit by oil lamps, and they were full to bursting with the moaning wounded, who gasped for breath amid the stink of faeces and iodine. The overtired nurses lurched from one man to the next. From time to time a casualty was found to have died.[159] Frank explains that this was the reason the last carriage of each German train was left empty. It would fill up during the journey. In his view the ambulance train was the central metaphor of the conflict, since it literally brought home the horrors of the war.[160] This did not apply only to German trains, of course. At the start of the war the French used cattle trucks to move the wounded further away from the front; some men were infected with tetanus as a result. Little improved as the years went on. Decades later, an inhabitant of that part of Flanders not under enemy occupation, the Westhoek (literally the western corner), who was very young at the time, could still remember a train 'packed with wounded'.

> Goods wagons were coupled to passenger carriages and nowhere was there a single empty seat. Hundreds of wounded sat or lay piled up against one another. It was a terrible sight, especially since not a sound, not a sob, not a howl came

157 Liddle & Cecil, *Facing Armageddon*, 491

158 Brants & Brants, *Velden van weleer*, 146–7

159 Zweig, *Die Welt von Gestern*, 183; see also: Thomas, *Die Katrin wird Soldat*, 184; Riemann, *Schwester der Vierten Armee*, 27, 47–8

160 Frank, *Der Mensch ist Gut*, 166; Whalen, *Bitter Wounds*, 95; Kammelar et al., *De Eerste Wereldoorlog*, 126–8; Thomas, *Die Katrin wird Soldat*, 230, 245–50, 255–8

> from that hulk. All you could see was bandaged misery, and the train was overflowing with it.[161]

British soldier John Bagot Glubb claims British trains were at least well maintained. His wrath was reserved for the inadequately manned hospital ships that came next,[162] anger that De Launoy, who travelled to Britain by boat at the start of the war, would have understood all too well. She wrote that the misery began immediately on boarding at Dunkirk.

> Stretchers were brought on and laid down; whole groups slept under nothing but their own torn greatcoats. Others lay down on the hay for the horses or slept under tarpaulins. Below decks, where the seriously wounded are laid, it's terrible. Stretchers serve as beds. On the bare planks we bundle a bit of hay together to support suffering heads or wounded limbs. ... Where in normal times robust, experienced sailors sleep they have deposited the most gravely wounded in three layers of what look like boxes, almost like coffins stacked up. You hear them sighing and moaning; it's impossible to change soaked, stinking bandages in there, the most you can do is to give one or two men a bit of temporary relief with a morphine injection. I'll never be able to forget those hours.

The crossing with some 1,500 wounded had yet to begin. They set off without any food.

> There's food only for the fifteen crew, plus rations for three or four officers. The British share out some dry bread. ... The wounded lie ... with empty stomachs and blinking, feverish eyes, shivering under the cloudless heavens. Below decks they continue to cry out for help, wounded men sighing and moaning, and I'm unsteady with exhaustion. Under a magnificent starry sky the ship glides through the night with its perhaps unprecedented load of suffering. When will this road to Calvary end?[163]

Of all the wounded brought by train to British base hospitals, almost 40 per cent were discharged within 2 weeks. Another 40 per cent were in hospital for up to 3 months and the rest for longer. But statistics tell us little. Bernard Gallagher, a US army doctor based in Southampton, wrote on 7 October 1917:

> Went to the station a few nights ago to meet the hospital train load of wounded soldiers for this place, 170 of them. Wounds of every description – legs, arms and eyes gone and bodies peppered with shrapnel. This mournful procession has been going on now for three years here and whereas early in the war the coming

161 Horne, *Price of Glory*, 66; Ureel, *De Kleine Mens*, 182
162 Liddle & Cecil, *Facing Armageddon*, 493–4
163 De Launoy, *Oorlogsverpleegster*, 43–5

> of a convoy of wounded soldiers meant the turning out at the station of the whole town, now the natives of the city hardly turn their heads.[164]

In his book *A Frenchman in Khaki*, Paul Maze described a time when he was the only lightly wounded man in a ward full of serious casualties.

> They have been here some days and I have watched them with the eye of a man who observes but cannot feel – I can feel no more. … I see how nervous they become, those whom the nurses must prepare for the surgeon's visit. They have a horror of the pain which daily they have to endure as a long, sharp needle is inserted in their back and the fluid inside their lungs has to be drawn out by an instrument like a bicycle pump. … Some have to be anaesthetized to have their wounds dressed. … There is a man with gangrene who has to be carried out every second day to have a bit more of his leg off. One boy has both his legs cut off and the nurses watch over him constantly – he smells terribly of decomposition, poor fellow, and infects the ward. I notice the nurse put a screen round his bed and attend him as if she were making him comfortable. I have not understood that he has died until I see a stretcher slip out of the side door, a blanket covering his pitiably short body.[165]

In charge of Hospital Océan was surgeon Antoine Depage, who had acquired the relevant experience during the Balkan Wars. At first he ran the hospital along with his wife Marie, but she visited the United States, and the ship on which she sailed back was the Lusitania. The Depages had set up their hospital in a recently built hotel, converted for the purpose, with the support of Queen Elisabeth of the Belgians. The queen visited quite often, sometimes accompanied by her husband. At first there were 200 beds, but before long the capacity had grown to 1,000 and when necessary it was capable of expanding to accommodate 1,200 to 1,500. During the final Allied offensive of 1918, De Launoy took the royal couple on a guided tour of a shortly to be evacuated ward containing 85 seriously ill or wounded men, for whom she was entirely responsible, helped only by one inexperienced volunteer.

> During our conversation one of the heads in front of us falls to one side; a sick man dies. I pull a sheet over his face. The king is touched. The tour goes on, from bed to bed: brains bulging out into skilfully crossed pressure bandages, meningitis cases with convulsively darting eyeballs and delirium ... muteness, epilepsy, paralysis caused by spinal cord injury or pressure on the bone marrow, paralysis to the left or right side of the body, or to the upper or lower body, as a result of brain damage or skull fracture, wounds to the spine, cuts to the airway below the vocal cords, men with mutilated faces drinking one drop at a time or

164 Macdonald, *1914–1918*, 248
165 Winter, *Death's Men*, 199–200

> being fed through the nose, serious chest wounds (officers), victims of chlorine or phosgene gas (officers) etc. etc. etc., ending up at the broken backs, some of whom will need to be evacuated in contraptions that look like sarcophagi for mummies.[166]

De Launoy anticipated Remarque's famous phrase when she wrote in late 1916 that people were saying everything was quiet on the Belgian front. It was indeed quiet, apart from 'a serious abdominal operation: smashed spleen, perforated stomach wall and intestines... The man dies on the operating table. What does a human life amount to? "All quiet on the Belgian front!"'[167] It was scenes like these that caused Remarque – who may have had some knowledge of books by, for instance, Duhamel – to observe that 'only a military hospital can really show you what war is'.

> On the floor below us there are men with stomach and spinal wounds, men with head wounds and men with both legs or arms amputated. In the right-hand wing are men with wounds in the jaw, men who have been gassed and men wounded in the nose, ears or throat. In the left-hand wing are those who have been blinded and men who have been hit in the lungs or in the pelvis, in one of the joints, in the kidneys, in the testicles or in the stomach. It is only here that you realize all the different places where a man can be hit.
>
> Two men die of tetanus. Their skin becomes pale, their limbs stiffen, and at the end only their eyes remain alive – for a long time. With many of the wounded, the damaged limb has been hoisted up into the air on a kind of gallows; underneath the wound itself there is a dish for the pus to drip into. The basins are emptied every two or three hours. … I see wounds in the gut which are permanently full of matter. The doctor's clerk shows me X-rays of hips, knees and shoulders that have been shattered completely.
>
> It is impossible to grasp the fact that there are human faces above these torn bodies, faces in which life goes on from day to day. And on top of it all, this is just one single military hospital, just one – there are hundreds of thousands of them in Germany, hundreds of thousands of them in France, hundreds of thousands of them in Russia. How pointless all human thoughts, words and deeds must be, if things like this are possible! Everything must have been fraudulent and pointless if thousands of years of civilization weren't even able to prevent this river of blood, couldn't stop these torture chambers existing in their hundreds of thousands.[168]

166 De Launoy, *Oorlogsverpleegster*, 304; De Backer, 'Longinus', 25; De Weerdt, *De Vrouwen van de Eerste Wereldoorlog*, 103, 108–11

167 De Launoy, *Oorlogsverpleegster*, 167

168 Remarque, *Im Westen*, 183–4; Frey, *Pflasterkästen*, 305

There is really only one observation to make here. If there really had been several hundreds of thousands of places like this, Remarque's sketch of this one hospital would have been quite different. Patients would have had more space, doctors and nurses more time and less stress.

The diversity of wounds and diseases to be treated demanded specialization. Germany had a hospital for the blind in Berlin, for instance, run by Dr Silex. Then there was Emil Kraepelin's psychiatric hospital in Munich, where Toller was eventually taken, and a hospital for facial injuries in Düsseldorf. In Britain there were twenty specialist hospitals by 1918 for the treatment of war neurosis alone.[169]

Although a wounded man's chances of survival increased the further along the chain of care he went, death rates remained high in the base hospitals, despite their specialist approach. Triage took place here too, as efforts were made to distinguish between those who would die anyway, those who might survive if operated upon but could no longer contribute to the war effort, and those who, after surgery, might be able to return to the front or at least work in a munitions factory. The doctors focused their attention accordingly, concentrating primarily on the third group. This had inevitable consequences. Although there are examples of wounded men who were written off, or even thought to have died, who survived nonetheless, assignment to the first group generally amounted to a self-fulfilling prophesy. The doctors said a particular soldier would die, so the treatment he needed was denied him and he did indeed die. The survival of men in other categories was anything but assured, since pressure of time meant surgical procedures were often crude.[170] Magnus Hirschfeld, who was to become a celebrated sexologist between the wars, described a German base hospital in his *Sittengeschichte des Weltkrieges* (*The Sexual History of the World War*), one of the first books to be thrown onto the Nazi pyres by German youth in 1933, although the adolescents are said to have taken a quick look at the photographs and drawings of unclothed women first. He hit the nail on the head.

> The entire hospital ... with all its fabled romanticism and its all too real distress was overshadowed by death. The way out led in most cases, either directly or via a detour to the trenches, to the heroes' cemetery. The great war factory known as a hospital normally gave people back to life only after they had left parts of their limbs or what little health they had behind its walls.[171]

169 Whalen, *Bitter Wounds*, 54; Higonnet, *Behind the Lines*, 63
170 Horne, *Price of Glory*, 66
171 Hirschfeld, *Sittengeschichte*, 366

## Too many wounded, too little help

Many died who would have lived had it been possible to treat them in time. Gangrene and other complications arose not only because of the filthy soil that entered wounds but as a result of inadequate medical aid, in many cases no aid at all. There were too few doctors, nurses, hospitals, operating theatres, drugs and instruments, and too many sick and wounded. At certain times and places medical treatment was practically impossible, no matter how much planning went into the provision of medical services as time went on and however well prepared the armies became for large numbers of wounded. As we have seen, it was impossible to treat every casualty after a major battle, despite the willingness of doctors and nurses to work without a break.[172]

Even the largest and best organized of the military medical services, that of the German army, was forced to acknowledge within months that it was no match for this war, and the situation quickly deteriorated towards the end because of the blockade and the priority given to the production of munitions. By the spring of 1918, German doctors were being forced to use paper dressings instead of proper bandages and cotton wadding. Then came the scourge of influenza, which not only made many soldiers sick but depleted the medical staff even further.[173] Richard Holmes writes:

> For most wounded the ancient aspects of the war – painful journeys on stretchers or across a comrade's back, confusing waits in crowded aid posts or dressing stations, and the unspoken competition for the attentions of an exhausted doctor – were more apparent than the modern.[174]

The exhaustion of doctors and nurses caused by staff shortage was not without its dangers. Nurse L. Mitchell of the 24th Field Ambulance at Neuve Chapelle wrote in the spring of 1915:

> Our division … had the heaviest casualties of any of the divisions that took part in the attack and it was an appalling affair. For three days we never stopped dressing the wounded men as they were brought in, and at the end of those three days we still had something like sixty or seventy stretcher cases outside. We just didn't know what to do with them. The Major I was with dropped on the floor exhausted and I had to give an anaesthetic for the removal of an arm and I had never given an anaesthetic in my life.[175]

---

172 Brants & Brants, *Velden van weleer*, 196; Macdonald, *1915*, 233; Moorehead, *Dunant's Dream*, 211

173 Verdoorn, *Arts en Oorlog*, 334; Simkins, *World War I*, 158–9; Higonnet, *Lines of Fire*, 226, 242–3

174 Holmes, *Riding the Retreat*, 69

175 Macdonald, *1915*, 309

We have already touched upon the fact that in many cases a soldier lost his struggle for medical attention at the stage when staff attempted to separate those who were to be given immediate treatment from those who would have to wait or even go untreated. Triage took place at every medical facility, from the first-aid post to the base hospital, but the main decision was taken at the start of the chain. The French described the process as: *triage, transport, traitement*. It involved making as reliable an assessment of a man's wounds as possible and judging their degree of urgency. On this basis a decision was made as to whether or not to transport him further back and if so at which medical unit he would be treated. This process of elimination, selection and sorting was of great importance because the rest of the chain of medical facilities could not function without it. The main purpose of triage was to prevent aid posts from becoming overwhelmed, since if the medical service broke down at that stage it would be impossible to treat anyone at all. To ensure a flow of wounded and avoid reducing their survival chances unnecessarily it was best to prepare for travel all those who could not be sent on immediately and were not destined to be laid aside to die. Whether the journey could actually begin depended on the availability of transport and staff to go with it, and the extent to which the fighting made it dangerous to move. Since the doctor responsible for selection had to take account of all these factors, he could not work according to fixed rules. Circumstances changed continually, so a doctor's decision was based on different premises each time.[176] Selection according to sound criteria was a barely attainable ideal at the best of times, and the profusion of wounded and shortage of staff often stood in its way.

Triage therefore degenerated from medical assessment into guesswork. This had to be kept from the wounded as far as possible, of course, but doctors had few illusions. They knew they could not really tell who would be able to walk to the next aid post or dressing station. They knew they could not really be sure who would benefit from treatment and who, under the circumstances, ought to be left to die. They knew too that this latter group expanded or contracted according to the nature and length of an offensive, rather than for medical reasons, but they continued to select and categorize, since they had no other option.[177]

An orderly in a British field hospital, Harry Streets, brother of casualty John Streets mentioned earlier, described the arrival of a stream of wounded on 1 July 1916. Wounds were bandaged and men were made ready for evacuation. Those who were not expected to live were laid aside and left unattended. 'It was very hard to ignore their cries for help', Streets wrote. 'But we had to concentrate on those who might live.'[178]

Often no more than one in ten of the wounded could be treated inside a dressing station. The rest lay outside, sometimes without blankets and sometimes under

176 Verdoorn, *Arts en Oorlog*, 340–41; Bleker & Schmiedebach, *Medizin und Krieg*, 211

177 Keegan, *Face of Battle*, 267

178 Gilbert, *First World War*, 261–2

fire. Nevertheless, as Lyn Macdonald remarks, terrible though this was they were relatively lucky – not so fortunate as those who escaped uninjured but certainly a good deal better off than 'the wounded men who still lay painfully out in front, with little hope of rescue'.[179] John Keegan agrees. Even the wounded who ended up in what were tacitly known as 'moribund wards' were lucky compared to men abandoned on the battlefield. They would not die alone and they generally suffered less pain. They were washed, sedated, and comforted as far as possible, occasionally even by female nurses.[180]

The shortage of medical personnel was chronic in all the armies, but it was worst among the French. The French military medical service had been set up on the basis of a 1910 assessment of the number of doctors and nurses and the quantity of drugs and other medical supplies that would be needed, estimates that were not adjusted when it emerged that modern warfare produced far more casualties than the military planners had calculated. It was impossible in practice to move doctors, nurses, stretcher-bearers and drugs to the places where casualties were most numerous. There was nothing medical staff could do to adjust their ways of working to the realities of this war. The army high command was in charge of military medicine and any change to its organization had to be approved at the highest level. Such approval was rarely granted, probably because the high command did not regard medical services as a priority.

A typical example is the offensive at the Chemin des Dames on 16 April 1917. After nearly three years of fighting, the high command estimated on the basis of previous experience that there would be 10,000 casualties, the same number as the British had been expecting on the Somme. The French military medical service added another 5,000 to this estimate to be on the safe side. Within a few days the number had exceeded 100,000. Many arrived at a hospital that had 3,500 beds but only four thermometers.[181] It is hardly surprising that France had the largest death toll, both as an absolute number and in percentage terms, of all the armies on the Western Front.[182]

A wounded man at Verdun could regard himself as lucky if he received preliminary treatment within 24 hours, even if he was found straight away. In July 1916 the wounded of the fighting around Fort Souville had to wait six days for attention, lying in filthy, infection-ridden corridors where faeces piled up and many men died. Throughout the war the number of casualties outstripped the capacities of the French medical service, and during the Battle of Verdun the system more than once threatened to collapse completely, or perhaps did collapse, depending exactly what this is taken to mean. A cynic might say there was no

179 Macdonald, *Somme*, 124, 153

180 Keegan, *Face of Battle*, 267; see also: Riemann, *Schwester der Vierten Armee*, 197–200

181 Horne, *Price of Glory*, 322

182 Gabriel & Metz, *A History of Military Medicine*, 245–6; Horne, *Price of Glory*, 65–6

collapse, since nothing very substantial existed in the first place. There were never enough surgeons, never enough ambulances, often no drugs, not even chloroform, only the wounded, in vast numbers.

Duhamel was one of the doctors who worked at Verdun. On his arrival at his primitive field hospital at the start of the battle he remarked that there was work enough for a month. At that stage there were already men who had been waiting several days for treatment. Their greatest fear was of being laid aside to die not because they were dying anyhow but because their wounds were seen as too complicated for the available doctors to treat. Treatment would take too much time, at the expense of men whose needs were more straightforward, so they were laid outside where the bitter cold and German shelling resolved the issue. Nevertheless, the number of wounded remained too great. Even the British and American ambulances that eventually came to their aid could do nothing to alter this. Doctors and nurses worked and worked, but if they made any impact on the enormity of the task then it was imperceptible to them. Although doctors were not generally expected to carry out surgery in field hospitals, they did so on a regular basis. When staff were frantically busy, with no end in sight, there was neither the time nor the personnel to undress and wash the wounded before laying them on the operating table. Surgery was performed despite the mud smeared everywhere and the lice that crawled all over the operating theatre. It may have been no coincidence that Ernest Hood's book on hygiene, littered with military metaphors, called *Fighting Dirt: the world's greatest warfare* was published in London in 1916. A despairing Duhamel wrote:

> Doctors and orderlies, their faces haggard from a night of frantic toil, came and went, choosing among the heaps of wounded, and tended two while twenty more poured in. ... As we explored further, the scene became more terrible; in the back rooms and in the upper building a number of severely wounded men had been placed, who began to howl as soon as we entered. Many of them had been there for several days. The brutality of circumstances, the relief of units, the enormous sum of work, all combined to create one of those situations which dislocate and overwhelm the most willing service. We opened a door, and the men who were lying within began to scream at the top of their voices. Some, lying on their stretchers on the floor, seized us by the legs as we passed, imploring us to attend to them. A few bewildered orderlies hurried hither and thither, powerless to meet the needs of this mass of suffering. Every moment I felt my coat seized, and heard a voice saying: 'I have been here four days. Dress my wounds, for God's sake.' And when I answered that I would come back again immediately, the poor fellow began to cry. 'They all say they will come back, but they never do.'[183]

183 Duhamel, *Vie des Martyrs*, 121–3, 131–2; Horne, *Price of Glory*, 183–4; Lupton, *Medicine as Culture*, 66. Mierisch, *Kamerad Schwester*, 64

As already noted, it was almost impossible for doctors to find an opportunity to sleep, even during their rare periods of rest. Duhamel stretched out on his bed, 'overcome by a fatigue that verged on stupefaction; but the perpetual clatter of sabots and shoes in the passage kept the mind alert and the eyes open'. It was not the sound of footsteps alone that kept medical staff awake.

> There were always in the adjoining wards some dozen men wounded in the head, and suffering from meningitis, which provoked a kind of monotonous howling; there were men wounded in the abdomen, and crying out for the drink that was denied them; there were the men wounded in the chest, and racked by a low cough choked with blood ... and all the rest who lay moaning, hoping for an impossible repose. Then I would get up and go back to work, haunted by the terrible fear that excess of fatigue might have made my eye less keen, my hand less steady than imperious duty required.[184]

One article in *L'Écho du boqueteau* of 12 March 1917 was entirely composed of the shrieks of men in field hospitals, their moans, their sighs, their curses.[185]

After a while the pressure of work shifted from aid posts to field hospitals. The beds were pushed closer and closer together until nurses barely had space to walk between them. When beds ran out, stretchers were brought in to fill the remaining passageways, and the staff had to step over them. The lightly wounded, who would otherwise have been treated in field hospitals and after a week or so returned to the front, were sent further back down the line, since at least they would survive the journey. The misfortune of many thus meant good fortune for a few,[186] but this only contributed to the fact that even the base hospitals could not cope with the influx of wounded. During Verdun, the Somme and Third Ypres, the existing base hospitals proved insufficient and all sorts of buildings – schools, churches, country houses – were hurriedly converted into auxiliary hospitals.[187]

## Complications

Despite acute shortages of medical staff, drugs and instruments, by the time a wounded or sick soldier arrived at a hospital he had a reasonable chance of survival, at least if no complications arose. But blood poisoning, shock, tetanus and especially gas gangrene were all extremely common in hospitals on the Western Front.[188] In his novella *Die Pfeiferstube* (*The Whistlers' Room*), Paul Alverdes tells the story of Pointner, a farmer's son from Bavaria whose jaw and larynx had been

184 Duhamel, *Vie des Martyrs*, 131–2
185 Brants & Brants, *Velden van weleer*, 192
186 Macdonald, *Somme*, 154
187 Macdonald, *Somme*, 177
188 De Launoy, *Oorlogsverpleegster*, 78

crushed by a shell fragment. The wound was serious, but he would have lived had blood poisoning not set in. He was one of three *Frontschweine* and one Tommy who were known as *Pfeifers*, whistlers, because their wounds caused an audible whistling in their throats as they breathed.

> Slowly, almost imperceptibly, the poison irrevocably affected his blood. Often he could not get out of bed, was choosy about the little he ate and had a fever. ... One early morning when everyone was still lying in bed, the whistlers heard him become restless. He shook his bedside table fiercely; a glass fell to the floor and smashed with a tinkling sound. They turned on the light and saw Pointner sitting bolt upright in bed. ... Harry leapt over to him in his nightshirt, barefoot, to give him some support, but Pointner had already fallen slowly backwards and was looking up at the ceiling and no longer moving.[189]

Another of the complications that might set in was shock. Substantial loss of blood and the force of a projectile penetrating the body had a powerful impact on the nervous and vascular systems in general, such that blood pressure could drop dramatically, reducing circulation. The result was circulatory shock. This in turn meant that the organs responsible for maintaining the circulation might be seriously damaged, causing the blood to flow even more slowly. It was the start of a fatal vicious circle. The patient turned pale, became cold and sweaty, then died.

The likelihood of shock was particularly great in the case of wounds to the hip or pelvis. When the casualty was moved, broken pieces of bone rubbed together, causing such immense pain that the patient fell into a coma. Men with chest or abdominal wounds often fell prey to shock, but it could also affect men with minor wounds. This was traumatic or neurogenic shock. The conditions to which soldiers were exposed between the moment they were wounded and the moment they arrived at an aid post, with or without the help of stretcher-bearers, had a considerable impact on their chances of going into shock. Straightforward fear compounded their problems, since it too reduced circulation. Fear could therefore be fatal. The psychological state known as shell shock was capable of producing physical shock. Unlike those who went into shock as a result of blood loss, most patients suffering traumatic shock remained conscious. If they were promptly rested, helped to drink water, kept warm and given blood transfusions if necessary, it was by no means inevitable they would die,[190] but the circumstances often made it impossible to offer such help quickly enough. Its traumatic variant probably explains why shock was most often seen among inexperienced young recruits rather than seasoned veterans, despite the fact that significant blood loss as a result

189 Alverdes, *Die Pfeiferstube*, 17, 81–2; Brants, *Plasje bloed*, 127, 132

190 Verdoorn, *Arts en Oorlog*, 361–2; Whalen, *Bitter Wounds*, 52; Keegan, *Face of Battle*, 268

of serious wounding, leading to circulatory shock, was no more common in either group.[191]

The pre-war expectation that few wounds would become infected, based partly on the experiences of the Boer War, proved entirely incorrect. Artillery fire in an area where the soil, and therefore everyone's clothing, teemed with bacteria meant that the distinction between 'sick' and 'wounded' lost much of its significance. Anyone who was wounded became sick.[192] Within a few months Sir Alfred Keogh, head of the RAMC, was saying despondently that doctors and soldiers had been thrown back into the dark, septic days of the Middle Ages.[193] In the early months of the war, German doctors Marwedel and Mehrig worked at a hospital not far behind the lines in Aachen. They reported that whereas in August 1914 only 29 per cent of wounds turned septic, the rate of infection had risen to 69 per cent only 2 months later. The severity of this type of infection increased as well. Experiments by a British doctor called Dudgeon and Frenchmen Policard and Phélip, who almost certainly knew nothing of the German study, underscored its findings about the seriousness of wound infection. Policard and Phélip concluded that any form of contact between a wound and soil or clothing could lead to infection of a kind that was often so serious that the body's natural immune system proved unable to cope.[194] X-ray machines were rarely available, so it was hard for doctors to locate shards of metal left in the body, which further increased the likelihood of infection.[195] Tetanus claimed many lives, especially early in the war, killing over fifty per cent of men who contracted it, some say more than 75 per cent. This was a problem largely solved by inoculation programmes. The percentage of British casualties who contracted tetanus dropped from 32 in 1914 to 0.1 at the end of the war, although the death rate among those who developed it fell hardly at all. Once again the mortality figures do not tell the full story. Like gas gangrene patients, men suffering from tetanus were a gruesome sight. Riemann therefore had every reason to call tetanus 'the smallest, most horrible and underhand weapon of the war'[196] and De Launoy wrote in early 1916: 'The saliva runs down his cheeks or flies through the air, spattering the nurses. The arms flail. The tongue is trapped between

---

191 Young, *Harmony of Illusions*, 24; Ellis, *Eye-Deep*, 113; Pelis, 'Taking Credit', 252

192 Liddle, *Passchendaele in Perspective*, 191; Horne, *Price of Glory*, 66; Evrard & Mathieu, *Asklepios*, 233. Cooter, Harrison & Sturdy, *Medicine and Modern Warfare*, 165; Cooter, 'War and Epidemics', 298

193 Colebrooke, *Almroth Wright*, 72

194 Winters, *Oorlog en Heelkunde*, 73; Winters, *Staal tegen Staal*, 95–7

195 Winter, *Death's Men*, 203

196 Gabriel & Metz, *A History of Military Medicine*, 242–3; Riemann, *Schwester der Vierten Armee*, 101, see also: 105–6, 123–5, 135–6, 143; Eckart & Gradmann, *Die Medizin*, 310–11; Linton, 'The Obscure Object of Knowledge', 298; De Launoy, *Oorlogsverpleegster*, 78; Dunn, *The War*, 293

locked jaws. The convulsions caused by tetanus are among the most terrible things you can experience.'[197]

Gas gangrene, another consequence of the filth at the front, was curbed only slightly as the war went on. Effective treatment would have required prompt and skilful surgical operations or antibiotics. The latter were not discovered for another decade or more, and competent surgery was often impossible, given the shortage of medical staff and the conditions in which they worked. Moreover, early in the war medical experts clung tenaciously to their conviction that wounds were best left alone and should merely be protected against secondary infection. Sprinkling them with a mild antiseptic – chloride of lime in the form of Dakin's solution, named after a famous biochemist – was a partial remedy at best. A man had a good chance of surviving the amputation of an arm or leg if the wound did not subsequently become infected, but as soon as infection set in his odds fell dramatically.

Wounds caused by shells or bullets were almost always contaminated with scraps of clothing or traces of fertile soil. A clean wound was rare. Gangrene commonly set in, and it often took the form of gas-filled bubbles under the skin around the wound. The severity of the latter was recognized by the soldier. In his eyes normal or dry gangrene *could* mean death, wet or gas gangrene *was* death. Again the statistics are inconsistent, partly because different definitions of gas gangrene were applied, partly because not all medical staff defined an infection as gangrene at the same stage of seriousness, and partly as a result of more general differences in diagnostic practice. A German study from 1917, for example, says that gas gangrene was found in under 1 per cent of wounds in the first 3 months of 1917, whereas a French study reports a rate of 13 per cent. The British recorded a rate of just over 1 per cent. Aside from the question of exactly when an infection can be said to have reached the stage of gas gangrene, on the German side almost 45 per cent of bullet wounds were found to be infected in some way, more than 20 per cent seriously. Almost all wounds caused by mines became infected, seriously in 60 per cent of cases. We should take into account that these figures relate only to immediate primary infection. Secondary infections arose as a result of the huge population of germs. A major aim, perhaps the main aim, of the first-aid posts was to combat infection, and up to a point they succeeded.[198]

If disinfection failed the results were often fatal. As with tetanus, doctors were practically powerless in the face of gas gangrene.[199] Once a wound began to smell, amputation, or further amputation, was the only way to give a man a chance, although in the short term amputation only increased his likelihood of dying. Of all American soldiers who contracted gas gangrene, some 44

---

197 De Launoy, *Oorlogsverpleegster*, 78

198 Verdoorn, *Arts en Oorlog*, 354–5; Liddle & Cecil, *Facing Armageddon*, 453; Bourke, *Dismembering the Male*, 34; Linton, 'The Obscure Object', 299; Lanz, *De oorlogswinst*, 7; Payne, 'British medical casualties', 27–8

199 Brown, *Somme*, 112

per cent died, and among the Germans too the mortality rate was close to 50 per cent.[200] The famous British bacteriologist Almroth Wright saw his first case of gas gangrene shortly after arriving in France in October 1914, in a man wounded two days earlier whose condition had suddenly worsened. His face was grey, he was vomiting and he had an irregular pulse. The wound to his side was icy cold and very swollen, and when it was opened up a terrible smell was released. Much of the exposed muscle tissue was clearly dead. A surgeon cut away the infected flesh, but the man died a few hours later.[201] Australian lieutenant Bert Crowle was wounded on 21 August 1916. Stretcher-bearers had to carry him more than six kilometres, a seemingly endless journey. Three days later Crowle wrote to his wife and son that his days were numbered. 'Had I been brought in at once I had a hope. Now gas gangrene has set in and it is so bad that the doctor could not save it by taking it off as it had gone too far and the only hope is that the salts they have put on may drain the gangrene out otherwise there is no hope.' He died a few agonizing hours later.[202]

Duhamel gathered evidence that proved gas gangrene was a complication specific to the front line. Among two hundred civilians wounded a short distance behind the lines he found not a single case of gangrene. At the front it was a very different story. He described the five-month-long death agonies of a *poilu* who had contracted gangrene after receiving a non-life-threatening wound to the thigh. '[Carré] had one sound leg. Now it is stiff and swollen. He had healthy, vigorous arms. Now one of them is covered with abscesses. The joy of breathing no longer exists for Carré, for his cough shakes him savagely in his bed.'[203] Agnes Howard of the Voluntary Aid Detachment was sent to Dover Military Hospital in December 1915.

> There we received the worst of the wounded from the hospital ships – the boys who were suffering from gangrene or perhaps were likely to haemorrhage but couldn't be sent on to other hospitals because they were too ill. I remember one South African boy in particular who had already lost one leg, which had been amputated in France. We did the best we could for him, but eventually the surgeon decided that there was no alternative but to remove the other leg. He knew he was going to have the operation and he was terribly worried about how he would manage without any legs at all, but it was a very bad case of gangrene and there was no choice. He talked to me about it and I tried to comfort him and cheer him up. He was really very brave. When they were ready for him and the orderlies had put him on the trolley to wheel him to the theatre, he took hold of my hand and said, 'Now for the great adventure!' They brought him back

200 Winter, *Death's Men*, 117; Verdoorn, *Arts en Oorlog*, 357; Eckart & Gradmann, *Die Medizin*, 311; Bourke, *Dismembering the Male*, 34; Linton, 'The Obscure Object', 306–7

201 Colebrooke, *Almroth Wright*, 88

202 Gilbert, *First World War*, 281

203 Duhamel, *Vie des Martyrs*, 41; Winters, *Oorlog en Heelkunde*, 95

> from the theatre but he never regained consciousness after the operation. He just slipped away. Even the surgeon wept.[204]

La Motte noted in her diary:

> Rochard died today. He had gas gangrene. His thigh, from knee to buttock, was torn out by a piece of German shell. It was an interesting case, because the infection had developed so quickly. He had been placed under treatment immediately too, reaching the hospital from the trenches about six hours after he had been wounded. To have a thigh torn off, and to reach first-class surgical care within six hours, is practically immediately. Still gas gangrene had developed, which showed that the Germans were using very poisonous shells. … The various students came forward and timidly pressed the upper part of the thigh, the remaining part, all that remained of it, with their fingers, and little crackling noises came forth, like bubbles. Gas gangrene. Very easy to diagnose. … [It can] be recognized by the crackling noises and the smell, and the fact that the patient, as a rule, died pretty soon.[205]

And De Launoy wrote: 'The body looks yellow with black patches. One foot has been torn off. Poor, poor lad! Rotting alive! Anyone who has not seen this does not know the worst of human suffering.'[206]

When the environment, as at Verdun, was more polluted still, with innumerable uncollected corpses lying everywhere, the doctors found themselves in an even more hopeless situation. The slightest wound could be fatal. In April 1916 one French regiment had thirty-two wounded officers of whom nineteen died of infection, in most cases gangrene. After the war it was estimated that between 21 February and the end of June 1916, 23,000 Frenchmen died of wounds received at Verdun which later became infected. These statistics include only soldiers who managed to reach a hospital.[207] We will never know how many died of infection of various kinds as they waited in vain for help, for days on end, in wet, muddy shell-holes.

Although the presence of gas in a wound did not always mean a patient had gangrene, and in other cases the infection lay so deep in the body that it was not immediately noticeable, most gas gangrene patients were indeed easy to diagnose, as La Motte pointed out, not just by their external symptoms but by the smell. Captain Arthur Osburn, medical officer with the 4th Dragoon Guards and author of *Unwilling Passenger*, remembered that the stench of gangrene could hang around a

204 Macdonald, *Roses of No Man's Land*, 144–5
205 La Motte, *Backwash of War*, 49, 51
206 De Launoy, *Oorlogsverpleegster*, 193
207 Horne, *Price of Glory*, 185

hospital train for days, even after it had been disinfected. He and the nurses would find themselves vomiting repeatedly.[208] La Motte noted in her war memoir:

> In a field hospital, some ten kilometres behind the lines, Marius lay dying. For three days he had been dying and it was disturbing to the other patients. The stench of his wounds filled the air, his curses filled the ward. ... For he had gas gangrene, the odour of which is abominable. Marius had been taken to the *Salle* of the abdominal wounds, and on one side of him lay a man with a faecal fistula, which smelled atrociously. The man with the fistula, however, had got used to himself, so he complained mightily of Marius. On the other side lay a man who had been shot through the bladder, and the smell of urine was heavy in the air round about. Yet this man had also got used to himself, and he too complained of Marius, and the awful smell of Marius. For Marius had gas gangrene, and gangrene is death, and it was the smell of death that the others complained of.[209]

During the war many ways of treating gas gangrene other than amputation were invented, some preventative, others curative. Various interventions had their uses,[210] but it was not until a few weeks before the armistice that certain methods were confirmed as effective, to some degree.[211]

## Is survival a blessing?

In the German hospital where Theodor Lessing worked as a doctor, an Irish soldier was successfully treated in one of the quieter periods. That is to say, he was kept alive. In Lessing's view, given the nature of his wounds it would have been kinder to have administered an overdose of morphine.[212] Lessing was not the only one to think this way. Some wounds were so appalling that doctors, nurses and even fellow soldiers concluded it would be better to let a man die. On the first day of Passchendaele an eighteen-year-old boy was hit by an explosive bullet that blew away the whole of his left cheek. His tongue stuck out from a great hole in his face and he pleaded incessantly for water, which he could not drink because it ran straight out again through the hole.[213] Such cases raised questions as to how best to respond. Should a man be left to die in fear and agony, or should his end be hastened and made more bearable? In Neuve Chapelle in the spring of 1915,

208 Linton, 'The Obscure Object', 302–4; Winter, *Death's Men*, 203

209 La Motte, *Backwash of War*, 22–3

210 Winters, *Oorlog en Heelkunde*, 96

211 Liddle, *Passchendaele in Perspective*, 192; Horne, *Price of Glory*, 185; Crofton, *Royaumont*, 335–9

212 Lessing, 'Das Lazarett', 362–3

213 Macdonald, *Passchendaele*, 111–12

for instance, a soldier was brought in whose wounds defied description. His face was swathed in bandages. The dressing was removed to reveal a face without eyes, nose, chin or mouth. The doctor on duty knew there was no chance the man would survive. He knew what he ought to do, but he could not bring himself to administer the necessary dose of morphine. He ordered the nurse to do it, which achieved the desired result.[214] The same nurse later found herself in exactly the same situation a second time. The casualty was a man with a large shell fragment through the centre of his chest. Once again the medical officer did not have the courage to administer a fatal dose of morphine. 'The Officer tells you to do it and you do it – but you don't forget!'[215]

Many of the horribly mutilated died because it was impossible for them to survive their wounds or because blood poisoning or gangrene set in, but many others survived. Dearden wrote: 'Some of the wounds are perfectly appalling. I have never conceived anything could be so smashed up and yet live.'[216] C.R.M.F. Cruttwell too could barely fathom it. 'The extent to which a human body can be mangled by the splinters of a bomb or shell, without being deprived of consciousness, must be seen to be believed.'[217] It was in cases like these that staff might ask themselves whether survival would be a blessing or not. Bagnold wrote of having to nurse a man called Ryan at the hospital where she worked in England. He lay on five or six pillows, tied down with bandages that ran under his arms and were secured to the bars of the bed. 'He lay with his profile to me – only he has no profile, as we know a man's. Like an ape, he has only his bumpy forehead and his protruding lips – the nose, the left eye, gone.' Then there was a man without nostrils, struggling to breathe through two rubber tubes. 'It gave him a more horrible look to his face than I have ever seen.' Bagnold believed the medical orderly was convinced he would not survive and she asked herself whether the soldier in question might actually prefer that to the prospect of living.[218] Frank told of a wounded man whose spine had been hit and who would never fully recover. He would have to go through the rest of his life jack-knifed, since his torso and legs were permanently fixed at an angle of ninety degrees.[219] In hospital Renn saw a man whose face had been torn apart. His nose and mouth were little more than a bloody lump. He wondered how someone like that could still be alive, even able to stand up. Would he not die of starvation? It must be impossible for him to eat.[220] In his book *Vie des Martyrs* (*The New Book of Martyrs*), Duhamel describes soldiers with dozens of wounds. Others had body parts torn off and yet they lived. Whether they might ever be glad to be alive, however, he could not

214 Macdonald, *1915*, 309; Babington, *Shell-Shock*, 51
215 Macdonald, *1915*, 309–10
216 Dearden, *Medicine and Duty*, 39; Frey, *Pflasterkästen*, 296
217 Wilson, *Myriad Faces*, 127
218 Bagnold, *Diary Without Dates*, 7, 13; Brants, *Plasje bloed*, 133
219 Frank, *Der Mensch ist Gut*, 167
220 Renn, *Krieg*, 374–5

say.[221] In *Civilisation* (*Civilization 1914–1917*) he painted a terrible picture of a war hospital, in which men were patched up sufficiently to stay alive – but what kind of life would they have? There was a man called Sandrap, for instance, 'who relieved himself through a hole in his side'.[222]

Even if the doctors did not feel a casualty would be better off dead, the man himself might well come to that conclusion. Hoffman wrote:

> The more pitifully wounded did not wish to live. They constantly begged doctors and nurses, sometimes at the top of their voices, to put an end to them. Some made attempts to end their lives with a knife or fork. ... One of the orderlies told me that a blinded man who was suffering greatly and did not wish to live had killed himself at one time with a fork. It was hard to drive it deep enough through his chest to end his life, and he kept hitting it with his clenched fist to drive it deeper.[223]

After the war, thousands of maimed survivors needed constant nursing. They included what the French called the *gueules cassées*, the men without faces. Some estimates suggest that around four per cent of all casualties had severe wounds to the face. Since seven million or more men were wounded on the Western Front alone, this would mean 280,000 faces were mutilated. Not all ended up horribly disfigured, but serious cases were often appalling to look at. Worst of all, they found their own appearance ghastly. They avoided mirrors. French nurse Henriëtte Rémi visited a man without a face in the spring of 1918.

> He has only one leg; his right arm is covered by bandages. His mouth is completely distorted by an ugly scar which descends below his chin. All that is left of his nose are two enormous nostrils, two black holes which trap our gaze, and make us wonder for what this man has suffered? ... All that is left of his face are his eyes, covered by a veil; his eyes seem to see.[224]

## Medical experiments

Joe Bonham, the central character in Dalton Trumbo's novel *Johnny Got His Gun*, is modelled on horrendously maimed patients of this kind. Trumbo ascribes the following thoughts to Joe, in the third person because the man lying in bed sees himself as Joe Bonham only in name. He is no longer the Joe Bonham who left for the trenches as a boy.

---

221 Duhamel, *Vie des Martyrs*, 137
222 Duhamel, *Civilisation*, 15; Horne, *Price of Glory*, 66
223 Fussell, *Bloody Game*, 170–71
224 Winter & Baggett, *1914–18*, 364; Winter & Sivan, *War and Remembrance*, 49

> How could a guy lose his arms and legs and ears and eyes and nose and mouth and still be alive? … The doctors were getting pretty smart especially now that they had three or four years in the army with plenty of raw material to experiment on. If they got to you quickly enough so you didn't bleed to death they could save you from almost any kind of injury. Evidently they had got to him quickly enough. … The shell had simply scooped out his whole face and the doctors had got to him soon enough to keep him from bleeding to death. … Things had been pretty quiet for a while just before he got this. That meant the doctors in back of the lines had more time to play with him than during an offensive when guys were being brought in by the truckload. That must be it. They had picked him up quickly and had hauled him back to a base hospital and all of them had rolled up their sleeves and rubbed their hands together and said well boys here's a very interesting problem let's see what we can do. After all they'd only carved up ten thousand guys back there learning how. Now they had come upon something that was a challenge and they had plenty of time so they fixed him up. … There weren't many like him. There weren't many guys the doctors could point at and say here is the last word here is our triumph here is the greatest thing we ever did and we did plenty. Here is a man without legs or arms or ears or nose or mouth who breathes and eats and is just as alive as you or me. The war had been a wonderful thing for the doctors and he was the lucky guy who had profited by everything they learned.[225]

Remarque had seen the true face of the war in a hospital; Bonham saw it within himself.

> He would be an educational exhibit. People wouldn't learn much about anatomy from him but they would learn all there was to know about war. That would be a great thing to concentrate war in one stump of a body and to show it to people so they could see the difference between a war that's in newspaper headlines and liberty loan drives and a war that is fought out lonesomely in the mud somewhere a war between a man and a high explosive shell.[226]

Joe Bonham is a fictional character, but there were many like him. The surgery carried out on mutilated casualties often saved their lives, but some cases raise doubts as to whether the patient was happy to undergo life-saving operations. The Austrian writer and soldier Andreas Latzko has one of his characters in *Menschen im Krieg* (*Men in War*) ask himself whether he still looks human. Through one eye he sees his crumpled face in a mirror, his twisted mouth, his left cheek of swollen raw flesh, his scars like the furrows dug by a plough. He looks at the hollow where his cheek bone used to be and asks himself whether surgeons should be allowed to maul a man like that. His face has changed, certainly, but has it actually improved

225 Trumbo, *Johnny Got His Gun*, 76–80
226 Trumbo, *Johnny Got His Gun*, 205–6

since it was first disfigured by a shell? Is this the result of the seventeen operations he has endured in his many months in hospital, each accompanied by intolerable pain?[227]

In a chapter entitled 'A Surgical Triumph', La Motte tells the story of a barber's son who was gravely wounded. After several operations he was able to return to his father, who fortunately was not short of money. He was alive, but not fit and well – as his father Antoine, crippled by polio as a child and therefore not eligible for military service, had already begun to suspect in the long period between hearing his son had been wounded and his return home.

> He learned that his son was wounded, and then followed many long weeks while the boy lay in hospital, during which time many kind-hearted Red Cross ladies wrote to Antoine, telling him to be of brave heart and of good courage. And Antoine … took quite large sums of money out of the bank from time to time, and sent them to the Red Cross ladies, to buy for his son whatever might be necessary for his recovery. He heard … that artificial legs were costly. Thus he steeled himself to the fact that his son would be more hideously lame than he himself. There was some further consultation about artificial arms, rather vague, but Antoine was troubled. Then he learned that a marvellous operation had been performed upon the boy, known as plastic surgery, that is to say, the rebuilding, out of other parts of the body, of certain features of the face that are missing. All this while he heard nothing directly from the lad himself, and in every letter from the Red Cross ladies, dictated to them, the boy begged that neither his father nor his mother would make any attempt to visit him … till he was ready.
>
> Finally, the lad was 'ready'. He had been four or five months in hospital, and the best surgeons of the country had done for him the best they knew. They had not only saved his life, but, thanks to his father's money, he had been fitted out with certain artificial aids to the human body which would go far towards making life supportable. In fact, they expressed themselves as extremely gratified with what they had been able to do for the poor young man, nay, they were even proud of him. He was a surgical triumph, and as such they were returning him to Paris. …
>
> In a little room back of the hairdressing shop, Antoine looked down upon the surgical triumph. This triumph was his son. The two were pretty well mixed up. A passion of love and a passion of furious resentment filled the breast of the little hairdresser. Two very expensive, very good artificial legs lay on the sofa beside the boy. … From the same firm it would also be possible to obtain two very nice artificial arms, light, easily adjustable, well hinged. A hideous flabby heap, called a nose, fashioned by unique skill out of the flesh of his breast, replaced the little snub nose that Antoine remembered. The mouth they had done little with. All the front teeth were gone, but these could doubtless be replaced, in time, by others. Across the lad's forehead was a black silk bandage, which could be

227 Latzko, *Menschen im Krieg*, 172–3

> removed later, and in his pocket there was an address from which artificial eyes might be purchased. … Antoine looked down upon this wreck of his son that lay before him, and the wreck, not appreciating that he was a surgical triumph, kept sobbing, kept weeping out of his sightless eyes, kept jerking his four stumps in supplication, kept begging in agony: 'Kill me Papa!' However, Antoine couldn't do this, for he was civilized.[228]

Around the same time, La Motte had to deal with a seriously wounded soldier called Grammont and a doctor who went about the hospital with the wildest of career plans and made various attempts if not to save then at least to extend Grammont's life, which in the natural course of things would have ended quickly. Grammont's suffering was therefore prolonged. The doctor did all in his power, trying everything he could think of. Whenever he thought of something he could use, he went straight to the *Directrice*, who had it fetched from Paris right away. While the surgeon made assiduous notes about the precise circumstances in which Grammont could be saved and about the treatment methods that could be tried should his condition change, Grammont lay in bed in agony. On arrival at the hospital, Grammont had a hole in his stomach that was about two to three centimetres wide. After a month's treatment the hole was some thirty centimetres long and rubber tubes stuck out of it everywhere. It had become much deeper as well. His chances of recovery were minuscule. 'But Grammont had a good constitution, and the surgeon worked hard over him, for if he got well, it would be a wonderful case, and the surgeon's reputation would benefit.' Needless to say, Grammont did not survive.[229]

This suggests doctors did not shrink from experimentation. The physical, mental and social horrors, with wounds never seen before, inspired them to try out new ideas. Wax was injected under newly grafted skin on the face in the hope it would create some semblance of a cheek.[230] Major-General August Bier (Med.) of the Germany navy, seconded at his own request to the 18th Army Corps in Belgium, used a magnetic apparatus to remove pieces of metal from the body. It was not a success, but his experiments prompted him to call for the urgent introduction of the steel helmet, appeals that bore fruit, despite opposition from some army commanders who regarded 'creeping away' under a helmet as contravening the Prussian principles of courage and heroism. Bier argued that if a man lit a cigarette at the edge of a trench and was killed by a sniper, heroism and courage had little to do with it.[231]

Artificial arms, legs and eyes, even face masks, all provided free of charge to officers, were manufactured at the Ecole Joffre in Lyon, for instance, built shortly after war broke out as a training centre and workshop for disabled ex-servicemen.

---

228 La Motte, *Backwash of War*, 151–5

229 La Motte, *Backwash of War*, 168–9

230 Macdonald, *Roses of No Man's Land*, 149

231 Van' t Riet, *August Bier*, 5, 25–6; Koch, *Menschenversuche*, 202–4

They were supplied to hospitals in unprecedented numbers and fitted there. In a hospital at Roehampton, tens of thousands of Allied soldiers were fitted with one or more artificial limbs. By the end of the war, German orthopaedists had developed dozens of different types of arms and legs, all tailored to the economic function the disabled man was expected to fulfil. The orthopaedists, like their psychiatric colleagues, as we shall see, were hoping to reduce the financial burden to the state – and so gain its support – by helping workers wherever possible to resume their former occupations. This would benefit them as well as being good for the nation. The handicapped soldier was therefore more than simply a patient. He was a metaphor for the wounded state. The state must recover, and so must the disabled man. Many doctors claimed that recovery was always possible, with the help of artificial limbs, unless a disabled soldier, suffering from 'pension neurosis', did not really want to get well.[232]

No matter how many limbs were manufactured in the combatant countries, there were never enough, if only because half were rejected by the body.[233] This was kept from the men, as was the fact that the artificial limbs the body did accept were far from perfect. Dearden, who always, even when he knew better, told soldiers who asked him whether they would survive that they would, tried to convince the gravely wounded that the damage to their bodies would not hamper them in later life. 'I don't think he heard many of the lies I told him about men who could do everything with an artificial leg that they could ever do before, but there is really nothing else you can say.'[234] Stefan Zweig wrote of doctors who praised their prostheses so extravagantly that you almost felt like opting for voluntary amputation, to have a healthy leg replaced with an artificial one.[235]

Worse even than the loss of an arm or a leg was the damage that could be done to a man's face by shrapnel and shell fragments. It was often so severe that a man could indeed be said to have lost his face. Although facial wounds were fatal in almost 50 per cent of cases, thousands of men were left permanently disfigured,[236] men like John Bagot Glubb, who was chatting with a comrade when he suddenly thought he could hear an incoming shell. He was right.

> For an instant I appeared to rise slowly into the air and then slowly to fall again. … I could feel something lying loosely in my left cheek, as though I had a chicken bone in my mouth. It was in reality half my jaw, which had been broken off, teeth and all, and was floating about in my mouth.[237]

---

232 Perry, 'Re-Arming the Disabled Veteran', 76, 81–4, 87–93, 97; Sassoon, *Complete Memoirs*, 379; Macdonald, *Roses of No Man's Land*, 147; Whalen, *Bitter Wounds*, 61; Lerner, *Hysterical Men* (2003), 160; Voorbeijtel, *Van Veerkracht en Heldenmoed*, 114–15

233 Winter, *Death's Men*, 253

234 Dearden, *Medicine and Duty*, 31–2, 152

235 Zweig, *Die Welt von Gestern*, 170; Riemann, *Schwester der Vierten Armee*, 205

236 Gabriel & Metz, *A History of Military Medicine*, 242

237 Liddle & Cecil, *Facing Armageddon*, 493

For men like Glubb there was no ready-made solution to hand and the answer had to be sought through experimentation. Dutchman Johannes Esser, active in Vienna, Budapest and Berlin, became increasingly famous in Germany and Austria-Hungary. He is known to the Dutch as the father of plastic surgery for his work in war hospitals.[238] When the facilities at the military hospital in Aldershot proved insufficient, the British decided to open a specialist hospital for plastic surgery, Queen's Hospital in Sidcup, Kent. From 1917 to 1925, thousands of soldiers and veterans were treated there by its team of surgeons, which was led by ear, nose and throat specialist Harold D. Gillies, the father of plastic surgery to the English-speaking medical world. In July 1916, when the Somme offensive began, it had quickly become clear that the two hundred beds at the Cambridge Military Hospital reserved for the facially wounded were grossly inadequate, but it was another year before Queen's, with its thousand beds, was up and running.[239]

Queen's was among the best known of the many specialist hospitals. By 1920 Britain had 113 centres where specific types of operation could be carried out. One hospital that specialized in removing metal fragments treated 771 officers and 22,461 men between April 1919 and March 1925. There was no end to the demand. Legs or arms that had initially continued to function to some degree later became useless. Men poisoned by gas continued to lose their sight. Year after year, treatment went on: in 1928 more than 5,000 artificial legs, some 1,100 arms and almost 4,600 artificial eyes were fitted.[240] The specialist hospitals tried to restore each man as far as possible to his previous vigour so that he could function in society again. In his introduction to the report of a Franco-British conference about care for disabled ex-servicemen, author John Galsworthy wrote: 'The flesh torn away, the lost sight, the broken ear-drum, the destroyed nerve, it is true we cannot give back; but we shall so re-create and fortify the rest of him that he shall leave hospital ready for a new career.' In other words, by repairing his body as far as possible and then restoring a man's self-confidence and personal pride, he could be turned back into a healthy individual, a physically strong male breadwinner and a productive citizen.[241]

Nurses at the special hospitals for facial wounds had a complicated task, since this kind of nursing, as Orderly Corporal Ward Muir pointed out, involved an additional problem.

> [The hospital worker] finds that he must fraternise with his fellow-men at whom he cannot look without the grievous risk of betraying, by his expression, how awful is their appearance. Myself, I confess that this discovery came as a surprise. I had not known before how usual and necessary a thing it is … to gaze straight

---

238 238: Neelissen, *Het Tomeloze Leven*, 70–133; Haeseker, *Dr. J.F.S. Esser*, 37–65

239 Liddle & Cecil, *Facing Armageddon*, 494–5; Bamji, *Queen's Hospital*, 1, 3; Neelissen, *Het tomeloze leven*, 93–5

240 Winter, *Death's Men*, 251–2

241 Reznick, 'Work Therapy', 185–6

> at anybody to whom one is speaking, and to gaze with no embarrassment. … [The patient] is aware of just what he looks like: therefore you feel intensely that he is aware you are aware, and that some unguarded glance of yours may cause him hurt. This, then, is the patient at whom you are afraid to gaze unflinchingly, not afraid for yourself but afraid for *him*.[242]

'Hideous' was the only word Muir could come up with to describe such shattered faces. He could never have imagined what moist, empty eye sockets, smashed or missing jaws, and noses partly or entirely blown away could do to a person's appearance, but now he knew, and it often turned his stomach.[243] Patients had every reason to thank their plastic surgeons. Generally speaking their faces looked significantly better after multiple operations than before. 'Better' was a relative term, however, and Muir was aware of this.

> And yet—! Surgery has at last washed its hands of him; and in his mirror he is greeted by a gargoyle. Suppose he is married, or engaged to be married… Could any woman come near that gargoyle without repugnance? His children… Why, a child would run screaming from such a sight. To be fled from by children! That must be a heavy cross for some souls to bear.[244]

It was. One of the men nursed by Henriette Rémi was a former teacher called Lazé. Recovering, but permanently blinded, he said he was ready to visit his wife and son. As he walked home, accompanied by Rémi, a child asked its mother what was wrong with that gentleman, and Lazé answered: 'Have a good look, little one, and don't ever forget that this is war, this and nothing else.' He had no idea how apposite his words were. He thought the child was referring to his blindness, since no one had told him anything about the rest of his face. He realized how disfigured he was only when his son exclaimed, 'That's not Papa!' and no one could persuade the boy otherwise. Back in hospital, convinced he had been transformed from a man into a monster, Lazé committed suicide.[245]

Meanwhile, plastic surgeons at hospitals like Queen's were working overtime. Sometimes patching up a single case demanded the skills of half a dozen specialists and as many operations. Breathing without nostrils, eating without a gullet, speaking despite a ruined palate, these were all unprecedented challenges and new solutions were sought and often found. New, for example, was the reconstruction of a smashed jaw and the cleaning of empty eye-sockets so that artificial eyes

242 Liddle & Cecil, *Facing Armageddon*, 496; Bamji, *Queen's Hospital*, 4–5

243 Bamji, *Queen's Hospital*, 4–5; see also: March, *Company K*, 156–7

244 Liddle & Cecil, *Facing Armageddon*, 496; Bamji, *Queen's Hospital*, 5

245 Winter & Baggett, *1914–18*, 368–9; Winter & Sivan, *War and Remembrance*, 49–50

could be fitted. The surgeons became increasingly inventive, but they were often happier with the results than their patients were.[246]

Many patients became depressed or aggressive. Many isolated themselves. Others were exaggeratedly cheerful, during the stay in hospital at least, which was much easier for the nurses to cope with but no less abnormal. Some opted to stay in hospital for the rest of their lives rather than attempting to return to society, and quite a few became institutionalized because despite all their operations they still looked too hideous to be seen by the outside world. Some, as Hoffman already pointed out in the previous chapter, were in such a terrible state – physically or mentally, or mentally because physically – that it was considered better to keep them in closed residential homes than to return them to their relatives. Their families were told they had died.[247] In 1936 a Dutch newspaper published the following article.

> What Few People Know
> Secret victims of the Great War
> One of the most frightful legacies of the World War has come to light, after 18 years, in Vienna. In an isolated area of the grounds of Vienna's large Franz Josef Hospital stands a small building. Strangers are not allowed anywhere near, former nurses at the hospital who know its secret stay away voluntarily. The few who are not refused access are six carefully selected doctors and around 25 nurses. In this building live 80 'dead men', casualties of the Great War. The world believes them dead; even family members have received formal notification that they are among the fallen. Their names are on the official lists of the dead; they are included among those who 'fell on the field of honour'. Yet they still live!
>
> The reason for their secret isolation is their hideous appearance and their mutilation, caused by explosives and poisonous gases. Each of these 80 wrecks, who were once men, is now completely paralysed, blind, deaf and dumb. These men can do nothing, their carers say, but breathe and eat. No one knows and no one will ever know what they are thinking, if they are still capable of thinking, or what torments they endure. For no complaint ever passes their lips.[248]

In some cases, to enable a man to return to his family and friends, face masks were constructed. The masks were modelled as far as possible on the man's old face, but in some cases even this was no remedy. Men felt like Notre Dame gargoyles turned into Phantoms of the Opera. Some committed suicide, although hospital directors never admitted this; others lost the will to live and slowly but surely slid towards deliverance in death. The masks were unquestionably products of genuine artistry, but while they might make it possible for a man to step outside

246 Macdonald, *Roses of No Man's Land*, 148

247 Liddle & Cecil, *Facing Armageddon*, 499; Bamji, *Queen's Hospital*, 6; Macdonald, *Roses of No Man's Land*, 149

248 Heijster, *Ieper*, 158

the hospital doors, they could not alter the ghastly truth, only conceal it. Beneath the mask was the real, ravaged face and no doctor in the world could repair it. A man's appearance might be improved – temporarily, since no mask lasted for ever – but the psychological wounds remained.[249]

Most experiments were unsuccessful, and failure often had calamitous consequences for the patient. Along with the huge difference between normal peacetime medical services and military medicine – the lack of supplies, the pressure of time, the sheer number of wounded and the types of wounds – the failure rate is further reason to question the usefulness of wartime experiences for medical care in civilian life. As we shall see, there were practical and ethical constraints that made wartime experiments inadmissible in peacetime. New medical expertise was often far less relevant in other contexts than we might suppose, and it was gained at inordinate cost.[250] Many treatments available prior to 1914 that are often assumed to have been placed at the service of civilians only because of their development and use during the war were not actually used by army doctors, who preferred to stick to methods they had been using for years. Certain techniques were widely applied only later, when it became clear that the few patients who had benefited from them during the war had done better than men given more traditional treatments. At Charing Cross Hospital leeches were still commonly used, and mosquitoes were deployed to fight syphilis. Chloroform was administered so amateurishly that liver damage was common. J. Charteris, Professor of Medicine at Glasgow University, was still advocating rhubarb as a purgative against stomach typhus, and calomel fumes in conjunction with wine and bed rest as a treatment for syphilis. Denis Winter sighs: 'Looking back today on the treatment received at the various stages of the process, one can only wonder at the high rate of success.'[251]

As the stories of Antoine and Grammont make clear, we should not assume that all doctors performed experiments purely for the benefit of their patients, although of course many did. The lack of supervision and the availability of enormous quantities of 'interesting material' meant that the war offered an opportunity to carry out experiments that would otherwise have taken place only in doctors' minds or in their notebooks, or might perhaps have been performed on rats or mice. Soldiers have always been 'easy prey', as medical historian Roger Cooter puts it,[252] being a distinct group, often far from home and unused to saying no, but the First World War provided human guinea pigs in unprecedented numbers. Some doctors were tempted astray by the prospect of eternal renown. Experimental operations were

249 Macdonald, *Roses of No Man's Land*, 151, 154

250 For the alleged usefulness of experiments see for instance: Van Bergen, 'The Value of War for Medicine', passim; Cooter, 'War and Modern Medicine', passim; Kater, *Doctors under Hitler*, 225; Van Bergen, 'The Value of War for Medicine', passim; or: Lanz, *De oorlogswinst*, passim

251 Winter, *Death's Men*, 202–3

252 Cooter, 'War and Modern Medicine', 1553

sometimes performed for their own sake, the chances of success being so remote that an attempt to cure the patient cannot have been even a secondary motivation. In many cases an experiment was no more than a test, a trial. If it helped, well and good, if not – and the chances of that were a good deal greater – then it was simply a pity. If the patient died as a result, that was no disaster. So many soldiers were dying that medical practitioners became inured to the fate of individuals. Hoffman wrote in *I Remember the Last War*:

> There were many good surgeons in the war, but there were others who found in it an opportunity to try experiments, theories of their own, on sorely wounded men – men who did not have strength enough to argue back. Some worthy work of plastic surgery was done, but most of them, when the operation was ended, were no better looking than Frankenstein. There were doctors there who thought they could cure flat feet. They tried their experiments on any men who would submit, and certainly they didn't do them any good, but did harm to many. There was considerable faulty setting of bones and rebreaking of these bones, in an endeavour to do a better job of setting them the next time.

Hoffman had himself been wounded in the cheek. Infection set in and he feared the worst, but it turned out to be less serious than at first thought. 'You can be sure I was pleased', Hoffman wrote, 'when I saw what the doctor was doing to other men around me.'[253]

A cynical La Motte wrote about the enthusiasm with which the gravely wounded, the *grands blessés*, were greeted, and the time-consuming, meticulous, mind-numbing drudgery that was essential in caring for the lightly wounded and the sick. Although the rounds of the wards full of men suffering from diseases or minor wounds were regarded as tiresome, no effort was spared. After all, La Motte writes, with a flash of venom, here lay not just sick and wounded men who must be returned to fight for their country but soldiers who, in the near future, could be welcomed back as seriously wounded.[254]

Lessing, a German doctor, philosopher, socialist, pacifist and Jew who was murdered by the SA in 1933, would have concurred with Hoffman and La Motte, to judge by the memoirs he wrote about his service at a war hospital, published in 1928. He described the loss of faith in humanity and human values experienced by many of his colleagues, who sooner or later came to share Lessing's loathing for the war. Doctors including Gottfried Benn (who wholeheartedly endorsed Nazism in 1933), Alfred Döblin, Wilhelm Klemm, Ernst Weiß (author of *Ich: der Augenzeuge*, published in English as *The Eyewitness*, the story of a physician who cures a certain Adolf H. of blindness in 1918), and Martin Gumpert (who in his later years published a biography of Dunant that includes one of the earliest denunciations of the blurring of the distinction between militarism and

253 Fussell, *Bloody Game*, 169–70, 173
254 La Motte, *Backwash of War*, 132–4

humanitarianism) wrote stories and poems that express doubts as to whether the salvation of the world is still possible after such a war.[255]

Like many doctors, Lessing, who opposed the war from the start, worked at a military hospital, but in his case war service had little to do with patriotism. The guns of August seemed to have blotted out the world he had envisioned for a long time, a world peopled by individuals of equal value. It motivated him to write his most important work, *Geschichte als Sinngebung des Sinnlosen* (History as Giving Meaning to the Meaningless), in 1916, publication of which was delayed by censorship until 1919. The hospital was the only place where he could still see something of his ideal, since in death all men are equal, yet at the same time each is distinctly different.[256] He had no illusions about the nature of medical treatment during a war. Around the same time, Mary Borden compared the wounding, patching up, sending back, wounding, patching up and sending back with the repeated darning of socks until they were utterly worn out.[257] Lessing had a similar notion: 'It was all madness. People shot others down only to patch them up again. People saved others, even at the cost of their own lives, purely so that those they had saved could later be killed.'[258]

War, Lessing wrote, was nothing but one great experiment in natural science for the benefit of politicians, army chiefs and doctors, who reasoned that war would be good not only for medicine but for the mental and physical condition of the soldier. This was a notion that persisted even when the war proved far bloodier than had been hoped, and lengthier than anyone had expected. 'About what,' Lessing wrote, 'do the doctors speak to the nursing staff? About daring operations, unprecedented tests, new medicines, bold physiological trials. And what was a person and what was a soul? Material.' It was an experiment involving a wealth of encounters with bacteria and unhygienic conditions rare in peacetime.[259]

This was confirmed, if unintentionally, by Sauerbruch, who volunteered for service as soon as war broke out and was assigned to the Fifth Corps. In 1916, amid the turmoil of battle, he invented the so-called Sauerbruch arm, a prosthesis that made use of residual muscles to enable an amputee to move an artificial hand. In his autobiography *Das war mein Leben* (*A Surgeon's Life*), he wrote that for a surgeon, work immediately behind the front lines was terrible, certainly, but at the same time 'an exciting and unprecedentedly instructive experience'. To underline this he called the chapter in which he writes of his experiences in 1914–18 'War, the Bloody Instructor'. Because a surgeon did not share the repugnance felt by an

---

255 Eckart & Gradmann, *Die Medizin*, 63–4; Eckart, *Eiskalt mit Würgen und Schlucken*, 10–13

256 Lessing, 'Das Lazarett', 360, 374

257 De Launoy, *Oorlogsverpleegster*, 289

258 Lessing, 'Das Lazarett', 364

259 Lessing, 'Das Lazarett', 371; Lerner, *Hysterical Men* (2003), 41–52; Eckart & Gradmann, *Die Medizin*, 13, 212; Ruprecht & Jenssen, *Äskulap oder Mars*, 161; Lemercier, *Lettres*, 146; Kaufmann, 'Science as Cultural Practice', 127

ordinary civilian at the sight of 'blood, wounds, pain in his fellow man – where would we be if he did? – he could, with fire in his heart and a cool head, make observations he would never otherwise have been able to make'. In Sauerbruch's view the extensive experience acquired by doctors in the First World War was, even at the time of writing in 1951, 'the foundation of our surgical capabilities'.[260]

## Medical aid and military necessity

> Not for us the attacking
> 'Mid the bursting shell,
> Smashing, slashing, hacking,
> Giving Germans hell.
>
> It is rather sad we
> Never can be fighters,
> And however bad we
> Want to pot the blighters,
>
> We must never change a
> Stretcher for a gun;
> We get all the danger
> Don't have half the fun.
>
> 'The Rifle Splint'(Royal Army Medical Corps Magazine), 12 February 1915

The enthusiasm with which many doctors, including Sauerbruch, greeted the war brings us to the relationship between military and medical aims. Even more than by the desire of the sick and wounded to get well, even more than by the urge to experiment, medical treatment was driven by military necessity. The medical services were an integral part of their countries' armed forces and like all other army units they had to respond to the demands of warfare. Duhamel in particular, with his book *Civilisation* and especially the chapter 'Discipline', emphasized the point that the primary task of medicine was to maintain fighting strength rather than to care for individual casualties. Hippocrates was not impartial: he served Mars.[261] Many of the difficulties in providing medical care were caused by this order of priority rather than by the vast number of wounded alone. The chain of care was geared accordingly, so a war hospital can be regarded as a prime example of the *Umwertung aller Werte* (reassessment of all values) that always accompanies a war. In peacetime a hospital is seen as an institution that with a bit

260 Sauerbruch, *Das war mein Leben*, 224, 226; Schrep, 'Gebrochen an Leib und Seele', 60

261 Duhamel, *Civilisation*, 235–6; Liddle, *Passchendaele in Perspective*, 175; see also: Riemann, *Schwester der Vierten Armee*, 48–9, 277

of luck a person will never need, with doctors and nurses who aim to discharge their patients as soon as they can in the best possible state of health. To a sick or wounded soldier, by contrast, a war hospital is a route out of misery, a haven of peace. Barthas wrote about a fellow French infantryman with dreadful eczema. In peacetime they would have pitied him; now everyone was jealous, since from time to time his ailment allowed him to enter hospital and then go on leave to recover. Bagnold compared the attitudes of soldiers with those of prisoners. They too, she has heard, seek out hospitals 'as one seeks after one's heaven'.[262] Hospitals were staffed, as ever, by doctors and nurses who wanted to make patients better as quickly as possible, but 'better' no longer meant ready to be discharged healthy, it meant being fit enough for front-line service. The staff had to treat as many wounded as possible as quickly as possible as close to the front as possible, so that they could be sent back up the line. This is illustrated by the title of a memorandum written in 1915 by Almroth Wright, who had serious concerns about the way the RAMC was organized: 'On the Necessity of Creating at the War Office a Medical Intelligence and Investigation Department to get the best possible treatment for the Wounded; diminish Invaliding; and return the men to the Ranks in the shortest time.' It is also illustrated by the story of William Pressey who was sent to Ripon Camp in Yorkshire after being treated at a base hospital for gas poisoning. In Ripon the decision was taken as to which men could be made fit enough for front-line service. Pressey wrote that it was like being sent from heaven to hell, a hell run by devils whose task was apparently either to heal or to kill. The preoccupation with sending men back only served to complicate their treatment.[263]

The war, the huge number of wounded, and the demands imposed by military objectives presented the doctors time and again with problems arising from military rather than medical concerns, which had to be solved on military rather than medical grounds. This is the first paradox of medical aid in wartime. If a doctor wants to help the wounded, which his Hippocratic oath obliges him to do, then he must comply with the wishes of the military high command, otherwise he will not even be allowed into the areas where the wounded are treated. Once there he will often be forced to take decisions that are against the best interests of his patients. In other words, in order to act in a humane fashion he often has to implement inhumane measures.[264] Examples are legion.

At the beginning of the war the RAMC was forbidden to use motorized transport. The roads were crammed with more important traffic.[265] British stretcher-bearers were told that if they came upon two wounded men when they could only carry

---

262 Barthas, *Carnets*, 494; Bagnold, *Diary Without Dates*, 104; Sassoon, *Complete Memoirs*, 364, 366; Andriessen, *De oorlogsbrieven van Unteroffizier Carl Heller*, 35, 142; Mierisch, *Kamerad Schwester*, 91, 103

263 Liddle, *Passchendaele in Perspective*, 188; Colebrook, *Almroth Wright*, 98–9; Moynihan, *People at War*, 141–2; Riemann, *Schwester der Vierten Armee*, 172

264 Bleker & Schmiedebach, *Medizin und Krieg*, 211–12, 220

265 Gabriel & Metz, *A History of Military Medicine*, 247

one, they must take the one they felt had the best chance of eventually being fit enough for active service. Magnus Hirschfeld denounced this policy: 'The one who needed help most, because he was the more severely wounded, was punished by being left there, perhaps to die. After all he was no longer usable "material", merely human scrap.'[266] Keegan's description of the wounded in the moribund ward as lucky compared to men fated to die on the battlefield is therefore accurate only in its own specific context. Those given merely palliative care were mostly wounded men who had not made it through triage because the doctors treating them – or rather not treating them – had decided that any effort to keep them alive would require so much time and energy as to endanger the lives of those who could more easily be helped and might recover sufficiently to play an important part in the war effort once more. In other words, they were lucky not to be condemned to perish on the battlefield, but unlucky in that they were too severely wounded to be saved in a war situation, whereas in other circumstances some at least would have survived. After a while, appeals were heard for more men to be kept alive, including those who would undoubtedly have been left to their fate earlier in the war. This was not based on any sense of contrition. The change of attitude that led, for example, to the establishment of recovery rooms for patients suffering from shock was inspired by purely military considerations. The war was lasting longer than expected and it was clearer than ever that the number of men available for conscription was finite.[267]

The roads to Verdun were congested with vehicles delivering fresh troops and munitions and ferrying away the dead and wounded. Deliveries took priority. The dead and wounded were the *déchets*, the has-beens, the waste. They took second place, as an American volunteer in the ambulance service commented bitterly.[268] For example, ambulances were not allowed to use the wider and still relatively passable roads, since they had to be kept clear for military traffic. There was a war on, after all. Men in charge of medical convoys had to use their initiative in making their way to or from the front line. Duhamel wrote in *Vie des Martyrs*:

> We could see on the hillsides, crawling like a clan of migrating ants, stretcher-bearers and their dogs drawing handcarts for the wounded, then the columns of orderlies, muddy and exhausted, then the ambulances, which every week of war loads a little more heavily, dragged along by horses in a steam of sweat. ... From time to time, the whole train halted at some cross-road, and the ambulances allowed more urgent things to pass in front of them – things designed to kill.[269]

266 Hirschfeld, *Sittengeschichte*, 446

267 Pelis, 'Taking Credit', 249, 253, 270

268 Macdonald, *Roses of No Man's Land*, 134; Brants & Brants, *Velden van weleer*, 212

269 Duhamel, *Vie des Martyrs*, 114–15

The village of Laffaux was in German hands throughout the French offensive at Neuve Chapelle in the spring of 1917. Thousands of Frenchmen wore themselves to pieces there. Duhamel was in charge of a front-line field hospital and in his shabby little building the wounded were admitted in 'groups of one hundred'. Those apparently in the worst condition – who were not necessarily the most gravely wounded – received the best treatment available under the circumstances, but any soldier who was even slightly mobile was patched up immediately so he could be returned to active service as quickly as possible. This was known as *conservation des effectifs* (conservation of the effective).[270]

On 31 July 1917 at Hill 62 near Ypres, in the pouring rain, the British began an attack on the Germans hidden in woods nearby. The first German line was taken, but British units became completely bogged down. Corporal J. Pincombe tried in vain to reach his stranded battalion with food, water and rum.

> We spent about two hours going here and going there and getting into wrong positions to come back again. We had about half a dozen horses that were very badly wounded indeed, and the Transport Officer was very concerned, because horses are highly valued. It cost ten pounds for a horse, only a shilling a day for a man. He said: 'The horses are tired and a lot of them are wounded and we must get them back for treatment if we possibly can, so we'll dump the rations, and Pincombe and Reuter will stay here and sit on them, until dawn. Will you do that?' So the Company Quartermaster Sergeant and myself said, 'Yes sir.' 'Very well,' said the Major, 'and when it gets light you'll be able to find the battalion and distribute the rations in your own time as you find things.' Then he went off. 'Goodnight,' said the Major, 'and the best of good fortune to you both.'[271]

As we saw in an earlier chapter, a large proportion of men with abdominal wounds died. Even if surgery was performed within a reasonably short time – eight to ten hours – they needed a minimum of three weeks' complete rest if they were to have a reasonable chance of surviving. There was no likelihood of that, especially when the trench war turned into a war of movement again. Wounded men who were in no condition to be moved could not be left where they lay if military orders dictated otherwise, for example in the case of a general withdrawal, since the welfare of one man, wounded or not, must never be allowed to jeopardize the strength of the army.[272]

Of the many millions of wounded, around 90 per cent returned to the trenches; of the sick, as many as 95 per cent. They were declared fit, but we may wonder how fit they really were. Victims of trench foot were sent back even after losing several toes. In the spring of 1918 all British soldiers with scabies were ordered to return to the front. In 1917 a doctor observed that lately even men with tuberculosis were

270 Duhamel, *Civilisation*, 259–60

271 Brants & Brants, *Velden van weleer*, 91; Macdonald, *Passchendaele*, 136–7

272 Bleker & Schmiedebach, *Medizin und Krieg*, 219–20; Graves, *Goodbye*, 183

being sent back: 'Unless the "Power" can *spot* it, a man has nothing serious the matter with him.'[273] But even a commanding officer could hardly ignore the fact that a man had lost a foot, as J. Bell had. Yet Bell was sent to the front again, by RAMC doctors, to serve in the Labour Corps.[274]

Bell was far from the only man who ought to have been sent home but was declared fit to play a further part in the war effort. The deployment of semi-invalids in support roles meant that more-or-less healthy men could be reserved for front-line service. Soldiers everywhere were convinced that the doctors were in league with the generals, trying to get as many men as possible back up to the line or into the factories, even those who had not yet fully recovered.[275] Shortly before the war ended, in a hospital in Bucharest, Dr Theodor Brugsch heard from the doctor in charge that the number of men declared *kriegsverwendungsfähig* (fit for front-line duty) must be increased forthwith. Brugsch told him he would not be surprised if the results of such efforts proved minimal, since the men, some of whom had been in the army since August 1914, had absolutely no desire to travel across to the Western Front. They would claim to be sick for as long as they possible could. The doctor was furious. Brugsch sighed: 'He had expected every last one of them "to answer the call of the Fatherland in this hour of need".' That was now out of the question. 'It was a resistance that even disciplinary measures could not repress.'[276]

In late July 1918, Zuckmayer was blown off the top of a twelve-metre colliery tower by the force of an explosion. He was admitted to a field hospital unconscious, with a cut to his face and severe concussion. After eight days he was returned to the front by the doctor who treated him. 'You have a headache? Feel dizzy? Vomiting? No reason to go off in a swoon. You're fit enough to die, and that's what we need young officers for now.' Zuckmayer reported for duty but was sent home immediately by his commanding officer, where he collapsed. His war was over, although only, Zuckmayer added, because he was lucky enough on his return to Germany to fall into the hands of a doctor who had not lost his sense of compassion completely in all those years of war, rather than into the clutches of the infamous Captain Herzog (Med.), for example, who would undoubtedly have reached the same verdict as his afore-mentioned colleague.[277]

It was this attitude that made Oskar Maria Graf explode with rage when a doctor assured him he was only a man, just like him, and that he wanted nothing other than to cure him. No, Graf exclaimed, the doctor was not a man like him.

> You're the greatest criminal! You only heal so that there's someone left to kill! ... The generals, the emperor, all those commanders-in-chief act just as they've

273 Ellis, *Eye-Deep*, 116
274 Winter, *Death's Men*, 197
275 Whalen, *Bitter Wounds*, 112
276 Whalen, *Bitter Wounds*, 112–13
277 Zuckmayer, *Als wär's ein Stück von mir*, 254

> been taught to act, but *you* – you've learned something different but you let yourself be used for the most shameful ignominy. You bring soldiers worn to death back to life so they can be killed again, torn to pieces again! You're a pimp, you're a whore![278]

Graf's reaction will not have been typical, but it does indicate the second paradox of medical aid in wartime. It was not simply subordinate to military necessity; it was itself a military necessity. In his book *Hysterical Men* (whose readers may start to wonder whether the title refers to the people who were diagnosed as hysterical or those who made the diagnosis) Paul Lerner describes the work of German neurologist Kurt Singer, who wrote in early 1915 that a strong nervous system was the key to military success. Strong nerves were indispensable to military discipline, since they enabled a man to obey. This meant that psychiatry had a major role to play in warfare, alongside other important areas of medical activity such as surgery, internal medicine and hygiene.[279] Whatever Singer may have been hoping to achieve by saying this, in essence he was undoubtedly right. Given that of the millions of physically or mentally ill and wounded around ninety percent were sent back up the line, it is clear that whether or not doctors saw it as their primary aim, medical aid was essential in maintaining the size and strength of the armies. Without medical services the armed forces on both sides would have suffered shortages of manpower on a far greater scale, and at a much earlier stage, a conclusion reached many years later by historian Johanna Bleker, with regret, and shortly after the war by one of the most senior officers in the German army, to his great satisfaction. Their view is apparently shared by Anne Summers, who gives as one of her reasons for writing a book about British military nurses, *Angels and Citizens*, 'Why … [the war] broke out came to seem less important than why it went on for so long.'[280] In this sense wartime medicine not only saved lives but probably cost lives. It was because the medical services had supported the war and thereby prolonged it that one American nurse sent back her Croix de Guerre ten years after the armistice. It was for this reason too that in 1926 German medical officer Karl Kassowitz said war was a sickness all doctors had a duty to try to prevent. Dutch nurse Jeanne van Lanschot Hubrecht, and twenty years after the armistice British doctor John A. Ryle, a Cambridge professor, asked themselves whether it would not be a good idea to refuse to give any medical assistance during a war or the preparations for war. Would that not ultimately be more in accord with

278 Graf, *Wir sind Gefangene*, 197; Vondung, *Kriegserlebnis*, 105; Ruprecht & Jenssen, *Äskulap oder Mars*, 41

279 Lerner, *Hysterical Men* (2003), 41; see also: Riemann, *Schwester der Vierten Armee*, 214

280 Riedesser & Verderber, *Aufrüstung der Seelen*, 19, 128; Bleker & Schmiedebach, *Medizin und Krieg*, 17; Summers, *Angels and Citizens*, 1; Kater, *Doctors under Hitler*, 29

the Hippocratic oath and medical ethics than a willingness to provide medical aid?[281]

Of course many doctors complained about having to submit to the demands of the military, but the reactions we have looked at so far leave the impression that at least as many were happy to accept this kind of subordination, if they were aware of it at all. Many refused to believe that medical work had been subordinated to military work, claiming there was no discrepancy between the two. Even a self-declared opponent of the war, Georg Friedrich Nicolai, a physiologist and internist who had been prosecuted for compiling a book with pacifist leanings called *Aufruf an die Europäer* (Manifesto to the Europeans) in late 1914, refused throughout to believe that medical work to treat casualties raised an ethical dilemma. He was a doctor and therefore one of the lucky ones who 'after the outbreak of war did not have to retrain. We doctors simply go on healing the sick and patching up broken bodies. According to the laws that prevail, the enemy to us is not even an enemy but only part of our job of care. For a doctor there is no war, or at least there need be no war.'[282]

The afterthought is not without significance. In hospitals safely out of artillery range, doctors tended to adopt a military bearing that many of their colleagues closer to the front line had quickly abandoned. Medical historian Heinz-Peter Schmiedebach and medical officer Helmut Busse both concluded – again: the former with regret, the latter with pride – that few doctors resisted being seized with enthusiasm for the war, whether they were civilians or professional army medical staff.[283] Indeed, most doctors seem to have responded with cheers to the declaration of war in August 1914. Although both Schmiedebach and Busse were referring only to German doctors – from 1914 onwards, incidentally, there was no longer any difference in rank in the German army between doctors and their non-medical comrades, so that doctors too could climb the military hierarchy[284] – this should be taken as reflecting the general picture. Writing about American doctors, all of whom, whether clinicians or medical scientists, were forced to report to the army in 1917, historian John M. Barry claimed that compulsion made little difference. They would have volunteered for duty anyhow. Most wanted nothing better than to take part in this new crusade against evil. Clearly German and Allied doctors had similar attitudes; Dearden admitted that most were intent on proving nothing was wrong with the people they were treating. We should note that he observed this attitude primarily among doctors who were working near the front

281 Jenssen, 'Medicine Against War', 16; 'Why I Returned my Croix de Guerre', passim; Joules, *The Doctor's View*, 7–8; Lanschot Hubrecht, 'Burgerdienstplicht', 408

282 Ruprecht & Jenssen, *Äskulap oder Mars*, 41, 161–3; Whitehead, *Doctors*, 156–7; Jenssen, 'Medicine Against War', 14–16

283 Bleker & Schmiedebach, *Medizin und Krieg*, 93; Busse, *Soldaten ohne Waffen*, 55

284 Ruprecht & Jenssen, *Äskulap oder Mars*, 40

line, which suggests that proximity to the fighting did not make doctors any more likely to help a man gain exemption from service on medical grounds.[285]

Barthas was particularly unhappy about one doctor he worked with in the early years of the war, a certain Torrès, who quickly became known as *tortionnaire*, torturer. Barthas claims he could not have had any medical training, since he did not recognise an illness until the patient was on the point of death. If it turned out that a man was genuinely sick and not malingering, his answer would be along the lines of: 'Come on, dying is what war is for. What does it matter to you whether you're killed by a bullet or by a disease?' Or: 'You claim you have trouble with your heart, that it's pounding too hard? You'll only be in a bad way if it stops beating at all.' Torrès refused to pay any attention to serious casualties. He swore at stretcher-bearers who brought in gravely wounded men, saying there was nothing he could do for a corpse. When he was promoted, everyone heaved a sigh of relief, although they did have some sympathy with the casualties at the base hospital who would find themselves in his charge. His successor, Major Colombiès (Med.), turned out to be cast in the same mould.[286]

Dearden was one of those doctors who never lost sight of military imperatives, even though in the preface to his diary, published ten years after the war, he expresses criticism of the very nature of medical work in wartime. In retrospect he compared caring for the wounded so that they could be sent back up the line with caring for horses at a bull-ring. The poor beasts were patched up close to a cheering and screaming crowd, so that they could be prodded back into the arena to resume an unequal fight that would end only with their deaths. It made little difference that 'the patching up was better, the prodding more subtle' in the case of wounded soldiers; at best this turned an illogical business into an insane one.[287]

Some wartime doctors regarded the destruction of human life on such a scale with pure horror, but Dearden was not one of them. Ten years later he still regarded his years as a military doctor as the happiest period of his life. Dearden the patriot, gloating over reports of German deaths, especially if they resulted from friendly fire, enjoyed war and everything that went with it. He referred to a day spent treating severely wounded and gassed men as 'very interesting', although he did briefly contemplate the 'quaint' place Britain would be after the war, with such a large number of armless or legless men.[288]

This is not to say that he was filled with enthusiasm for the war in general. All things considered, war was simply 'a thoroughly boring affair which has got some moments of thrill to make it bearable'. Nor was he always enthusiastic about his own part in the conflict. From time to time he envied the men. They had 'at least something to kill with and get excited over'. He resigned himself to his work because medical aid was a military necessity.

---

285 Babington, *Shell-Shock*, 70; Barry, *The Great Influenza*, 140

286 Barthas, *Carnets*, 104–5, 118, 131, 224

287 Dearden, *Medicine and Duty*, vii–viii

288 Dearden, *Medicine and Duty*, xi, 7, 15, 47, 51, 205; Whitehead, *Doctors*, 193–4

The story Dearden tells of a German prisoner of war who asked him for help, saying he could not walk, demonstrates that his patriotism and enthusiasm for combat occasionally stood in the way of his medical work. He had the impression the man's wounds were not particularly serious, so he demanded he be set to work as a stretcher-bearer. The German refused. Furious, Dearden hit him. It then became obvious why the man had asked for help. The blow made him take his hands off his stomach and his intestines poured out. Dearden, embarrassed, administered morphine. The man died.[289]

There were some medical officers who took their role as non-combatants seriously and believed they should not touch weapons, but Dearden was far from the only doctor to struggle with his non-combatant status. In many cases the resulting frustration produced an urge to work as close to the front line as possible, even among those whose specialist knowledge might have been put to better use in hospitals further back, where the work was more challenging from a medical point of view. The majority were satisfied simply to be in the forward line, and most found it a sobering experience, but in some cases front-line service had the opposite effect. Instead of accepting their role as non-combatants, doctors might become frustrated at the sight of friends and acquaintances being killed and express their desire to take up a revolver or rifle themselves, and not only in self-defence. Motivated by hatred, vengeance, shame, or a deeply rooted craving, several doctors exchanged the Red Cross armbands for a gun, as did a number of stretcher-bearers and nurses, both male and female.[290]

One consequence of all this was that doctors began to see themselves as weak, as traitors or cowards, the moment they started feeling compassion for the men in their care, especially if this became noticeable in any way.[291] They were supposed to concern themselves with the strength of the army as a whole rather than the health of individuals, so they could not allow themselves to dwell too deeply on the sickness or injury of a specific patient. Whatever they did to help a man, they always had to bear in mind the interests of his comrades. In giving evidence before the Shell Shock Committee, Dunn, for example, said that he was guided in his work by the conviction that the first duty of a regimental doctor was 'to maintain the discipline and morale of his unit'. He admitted that to achieve this 'the health of individuals may have to be sacrificed temporarily, even permanently'. In 1917, the American magazine *The Military Surgeon* told its readers that the preservation of human life must take second place. The army doctor was obliged to pay more attention to the general good than to the welfare of the individual. Procedures aimed at healing wounded bodies were less important than measures that served a greater cause. 'The whole object of the medical service in war is to provide men

---

289 Dearden, *Medicine and Duty*, 175, 185–6, 222–4

290 De Backer, 'Longinus', 23; Liddle & Cecil, *Facing Armageddon*, 467; Bourke, *Intimate History*, 306; Whitehead, *Doctors*, 186; De Bruyne, *We zullen ze krijgen!*, 144–5, 148

291 Bleker & Schmiedebach, *Medizin und Krieg*, 128

for the fighting line, to keep them fit, and, if sick or wounded, to make them fit and ready for further fighting as soon as possible.'[292] Patients sometimes complained about the inhumane, hard-hearted, patronising treatment they received, especially the sick. In *Diary of a Dead Officer* A. West wrote:

> Brutal injections. Regulation quantity given to every man regardless of his condition. Eye wash for inspections. Dying men made to sit up and smile. Doctors looked on every man as a skrimshanker. Brutality in treatment of patients when they were unwilling to undergo a particular cure. Men wounded and minus an arm insisted on not being put on electric treatment. Was knocked down and held on the bed by two orderlies.[293]

German soldier H. Wandt wrote that a patient being treated for venereal disease would be 'taught to toe the line by the injection needle. Daily, good and proper, so that he could hear the angels singing in heaven.'[294] Men with lung problems, possibly caused by gas, were forced to run and to drill at speed. Protests were quickly silenced. 'Any bloody lip from any of yer and I'll whip him straight off to the guard room.' Denis Winter writes that 'duty back in the front line became almost a release from frustration'.[295]

Indeed, sick men were treated with less respect than the wounded, but we should remember that the normal distinction between sick and wounded did not apply in military hospitals. A wounded man had by definition ended up in hospital as a result of enemy action, whether he had been hit by a bullet, a shell fragment or gas. Anyone who was admitted for any other reason was sick, even if he had shot himself in the foot or hand while cleaning his rifle or been injured by a shell that exploded prematurely. He remained in the same category no matter what happened to him in hospital. He might be wounded and later die of pneumonia, but the official report would still say that he had 'died of wounds'. If he was brought in with frostbitten feet and died after amputation, he would be listed as having died 'from illness'. Anyone who became sick would do all he could to prove it was as a result of the conditions of warfare (which made him 'wounded'), an argument mostly contradicted by stating that there were plenty of diseases that could be contracted behind the lines or on leave. This all had to do with money, with the allocation of pensions, since the 'wounded' were eligible and the 'sick' were not. Doctors decided whether a man was sick or wounded and what his treatment should be, so it was they who were responsible for determining whether his sickness or wounds were war-related and therefore whether or not he had a right to a pension.

---

292 Liddle & Cecil, *Facing Armageddon*, 505; Barry, *The Great Influenza*, 144; Dolev, *Allenby's Military Medicine*, 5; see also: Bourke, *Dismembering the Male*, 92; Bourke, *Intimate History*, 262; Busse, *Soldaten ohne Waffen*, 59

293 Winter, *Death's Men*, 201–2

294 Hirschfeld, *Sittengeschichte*, 185

295 Winter, *Death's Men*, 202

In Britain in 1916, even some disabled servicemen were refused pensions unless they could prove they had lost an arm or a leg while performing a truly heroic deed.[296] We will return to this point shortly in the context of military psychiatry.

Time and again, the evidence suggests that doctors were not motivated primarily by a desire to heal patients but by the need to return sick and wounded men to the front, or at least to a munitions factory.[297] Toller left for Verdun an enthusiastic volunteer, became sick, was declared *kriegsuntauglich*, unfit for duty, and became a pacifist and socialist. As an active opponent of the war he was held in a military prison, where he again became sick. The doctor treating him was not exactly filled with compassion. 'He says all pacifists should be stood against a wall and shot, then he prescribes aspirin and refuses the feverish patient a second blanket.' Toller was sent to the hospital wing, where life was no better.

> The prison sick-room is big enough for two, but there are six of us. Deserters, thieves, mutineers, 'traitors'. Two lie in beds, four on sacks of straw on the floor, the window is bolted and barred, the air pestilential; one chamber-pot serves all six of us and it is emptied only twice a day, at half past six in the morning and five in the afternoon. The man next to me is suffering from an infection of the bladder. His sodden bed stinks like a sewer. He lies near the door. When the food is handed in through the hatch he seizes the bowl with hands soaked and cracked like a washerwoman's. It makes me sick and I don't touch the food.

Toller had a poetry book on his bedside table. The medical officer, a major, stood next to his bed and read aloud from it. '"Anyone who reads such bilge shouldn't be surprised to fetch up in prison", he announces. … The medical officer bows, the assistant doctor clicks his heels, the junior doctor springs to attention and bows deeply. The visit is over.'[298] Given such attitudes it is no surprise to discover that at one stage all male members of the German Peace League, in which Toller was a leading figure, were summoned by the regional high command. Even those previously declared physically unsuitable for war duties were suddenly re-examined, declared fit and sent to the barracks.[299]

These attitudes also made it extremely improbable that, even had there been enough doctors, nurses, hospitals, drugs and medical equipment, patients would have received the individual attention they were hoping for to help them recover. Remarque wrote:

> As long as they haven't amputated anything, sooner or later you'll fall into the hands of one of those staff doctors with a war service ribbon on his chest who

296 Macdonald, *Roses of No Man's Land*, 187; Whalen, *Bitter Wounds*, 65; Bourke, *Dismembering the Male*, 59, 62

297 Hirschfeld, *Sittengeschichte*, 180

298 Toller, *Jugend in Deutschland*, 72–3

299 Toller, *Jugend in Deutschland*, 61; Brants, *Plasje bloed*, 181

> says, 'What's this? One leg a bit on the short side? You won't need to run at the front if you've got any guts. Passed fit for service! Dismiss!'
>
> Kat tells a story that has done the rounds all along the front, from Flanders to the Vosges, about the staff doctor who reads out the names of the men who come up for medical inspection, and, when the man appears, doesn't even look up, but says, 'Passed fit for service, we need soldiers at the front.' A man with a wooden leg comes up before him, the doctor passes him fit for service again – 'And then,' Kat raises his voice, 'the man says to him, "I've already got a wooden leg; but if I go up the line now and they shoot my head off, I'll have a wooden head made, and then I'll become a staff doctor."' We all think that's a really good one.
>
> There may be good doctors – many of them are; but with the hundreds of examinations he has, every soldier will at some time or other get into the clutches of one of the hero-makers, and there are lots of them, whose aim is to turn as many of those on their lists who have only been passed for work detail or garrison duty into class A-1, fit for active service.[300]

The reference to 'good doctors' indicates once again that medical officers did not all act alike, nor were they all content with the way their colleagues performed. Some adopted a strict policy but felt troubled as a result. This, along with the almost unremitting pressure of work, the ghastly wounds they confronted every day and the fear that they too might be killed or maimed[301] caused some doctors to suffer psychiatric collapse. Charles Huxtable, a regimental medical officer, regarded the requirement to take a firm line as the worst part of his job. He remembered a case in which a soldier with painful legs was forced to take part in an attack. It made him feel rotten, but giving in would have produced 'a flood of others' with the same symptoms and would therefore have been militarily irresponsible. In other words, alongside cases of inhumane harshness were instances of severity dictated by military necessity. The line between the two was thin and regularly crossed.[302]

The presence of doctors like Lessing, and even Huxtable to some degree, demonstrates that the tough attitude of many medical men cannot be explained exclusively in terms of the priority given to the interests of the army as a whole as opposed to the individual. Every doctor had to take account of the collective interest, and since the emergence in the late nineteenth century of theories such as social Darwinism, eugenics and racial hygiene, many doctors had been predisposed to subordinate the individual welfare of a sick patient to what they regarded as higher causes. In wartime national imperatives took even greater precedence over the individual, so the war presented them with the opportunity to give practical application to their theories. These were circumstances in which doctors who had previously had doubts could be won over. 'The nation comes first' became the

300 Remarque, *Im Westen*, 195–6
301 Liddle & Cecil, *Facing Armageddon*, 511
302 Liddle & Cecil, *Facing Armageddon*, 470–71

dominant principle, and few tried to distance themselves from it or to resist its demands.[303]

The extreme right-winger Professor Max von Gruber, for example, was a fervent adherent of the theory of racial hygiene. In his view it was not important that 'we imperfect beings' should survive but rather 'that the German actualized himself, came forth, engaged and lived on'. Von Gruber was one of many doctors who saw war – a triumphant war, that is, but he was always convinced the Germans would ultimately emerge victorious – as the most effective way to raise the German people as a whole to a new level. True, many of the best sons of the fatherland were being killed, but the demographic hole that resulted could easily be filled again, as long as a well thought out programme of reproduction was developed and then practiced by the healthiest specimens of the German race. A kindred spirit was Dr Schmidt-Gibichenfels, who declared as early as 1912 that war should not be seen as a destroyer but as a great healer. War was not just an excellent circumstance for doctors to work in, it was itself a doctor, since it would make a clean sweep of the degeneration that Schmidt-Gibichenfels detected on all sides, including the Allied countries, and give back to his own people, nation and race a power lost through its decadence. This was an attitude that many felt had been justified when they heard during the war that front-line soldiers were less troubled by neurosis than men serving behind the lines. The newspapers described Schmidt's ideas as a 'masterpiece of the ethic of war.'[304]

Von Gruber and Schmidt-Gibichenfels may have been extremists – others did see degenerative disadvantages to the loss of the strongest offspring of the German race – but they were by no means alone. An ethic that gave a central place to the welfare of 'the whole, the nation, the people' was widely accepted. The nation's welfare depended on victory, so a doctor's task, both military and medical, was to contribute to that victory. This meant that the war as a cause of suffering had to be pushed into the background as far as possible. A typical example can be found in a passage from *Weyl's Handbuch der Hygiene* (Weyl's Handbook of Hygiene), published in 1918. Although at the beginning of the war several German doctors had warned of the spectre of trench warfare because of the serious medical consequences they believed it would entail, the handbook did not point to dirt, bullets, rain, cold, in other words to war as a major cause of disease but instead to the presence of other sick soldiers.[305]

This suggests another possible reason why doctors acted so harshly. We should bear in mind that the army doctor, apart from being a man of a nationalistic and militaristic disposition, of whom there were many in wartime, was also a policeman, judge and warder rolled into one. The doctor–patient relationship, in

---

303 Bleker & Schmiedebach, *Medizin und Krieg*, 127

304 Bleker & Schmiedebach, *Medizin und Krieg*, 100–102, 123; Glover, *Humanity*, 196; Eckart & Gradmann, 'Medizin', 217; Lerner, 'Psychiatry and casualties of War in Germany, 1914–18', 27.

305 Whalen, *Bitter Wounds*, 59, 65–6

other words, was mixed up with the relationship between officers and other ranks, one result being that the sick and wounded were deprived of their basic right to treatment by consent. Franz de Backer recalled a man who had arrived sick at an aid post but was sent away. A little later there was a bang followed by a shout and the man came in again, 'his hand burned black and stripped of its flesh: the small bones red as a flower from dislocation'. The doctors bandaged his hand and pinned a label to his chest that said *mutilation voluntaire*. Céline claimed that generally speaking the troops were not badly treated, and yet:

> We felt we were being watched every minute of the day by the staff of silent male nurses endowed with enormous ears. After a varying period of observation, we'd be quietly sent away and assigned to an insane asylum, the front, or, not infrequently, the firing squad. ... We saw our doctors every morning. They questioned us amiably enough, but we never knew exactly what they were thinking. Under their affable smiles as they walked among us, they carried our death sentences.[306]

This is not to say that Magnus Hirschfeld was justified in writing in his *Sittengeschichte des Weltkrieges* that medical officers no longer paid any heed to the Hippocratic oath.[307] Many doctors gave a great deal of thought to that oath, but it was interpreted differently during the war, indeed they had no option but to interpret it differently, since it was never intended for men involved in a war, with any number of other responsibilities to consider. However, the fact that Hirschfeld and many others believed that the Hippocratic oath had been forgotten shows they were aware of an inherent conflict between medicine as such and medical practice in wartime, under military command. In their view this was a matter of principle and ultimately impossible to resolve. If doctors in wartime wished to cling to the idea that they were practising medicine, then they had no choice but to deny there was any conflict between medical work and military duty. No compromise position was available.

The military importance of medical treatment inevitably eroded the neutrality of aid posts and hospitals, and indeed the non-combatant status of army medical personnel. Whenever doctors adapt, voluntarily or otherwise, to the needs of an army, hospitals arguably become legitimate military targets. Hospitals were shelled, even though this was explicitly forbidden under the Geneva Convention, and in the light of the above it may seem less scandalous than at first sight. Of the 1,318 doctors in the French professional army, 125 were killed. A bomb dropped on a hospital from a plane produced America's first fatal casualty after the United States declared war on Germany, Lieutenant William T. Fitzsimmons

306 De Backer, 'Longinus', 20; Céline, *Voyage*, 62–3; Dorgelès, *Croix de bois*, 33–4 Eckart & Gradmann, 'Medizin', 210

307 Hirschfeld, *Sittengeschichte*, 186

of the Medical Corps. Over 200 American medical officers would share his fate.[308] Nevertheless, no one has ever proven beyond doubt that hospitals were deliberately shelled and hospital ships deliberately torpedoed; mistakes and miscalculations and the presence of munitions dumps in the near vicinity of hospitals are all part of the picture. Noyes thought that so many munitions depots or machine-gun nests were located close to hospitals that this could not be dismissed as a coincidence. Sometimes the bombing of hospitals might simply be unavoidable. The former mental institution 't Heilig Hart (The Sacred Heart), converted into a hospital for wounded soldiers by the Quakers, was hit in late December 1914 during the bombardment of Ypres. It would have been impossible to bomb Ypres without hitting the hospital.[309]

As with the 'live and let live system', the fact that it is impossible to prove hospitals were deliberately targeted does not mean that armies hesitated to shell them because of humanitarian considerations or respect for international law. Justifiable though the bombing of hospitals might seem from a military point of view – and if there had been any clear military advantage to be gained by it, it would have been done – it would not be without consequences for whichever side was responsible. If one side deliberately targeted hospitals, so would the other. Lying in hospital sick or wounded under bombardment has a terrible effect on morale. This brings us to the care of the mentally ill and psychologically wounded, in other words to military psychiatry. It is there that we find the most detailed and powerful evidence of all for the urge to experiment and for the subordination of medical aid to military imperatives. Psychiatrists developed endless theories, asked countless questions and suggested innumerable answers on subjects like the nature of sickness and health, the difference between insanity and normality, exactly what therapies should involve, and what the results ought to be. A broken leg is straightforward, a wounded mind is not.

## Military psychiatry

Wilfred Owen and Siegfried Sassoon were treated by psychiatrists who advocated humane methods, based on conversations with patients. Owen's doctor, A. Brock, urged him to write a poem on the classical theme of Antaeus, the malicious giant, son of Mother Earth, who derives his strength from contact with his mother. He even arranged for Owen to give readings at a local school. Brock always did his

308 Verdoorn, *Arts en Oorlog*, 256; Garrison, *History of Military Medicine*, 197, 200; Gabriel & Metz, *A History of Military Medicine*, 249; Barbusse, *Le Feu*, 317–19; Dunn, *The War*, 439

309 Liddle, *Passchendaele in Perspective*, 187; Brants & Brants, *Velden van weleer*, 79–80; De Launoy, *Oorlogsverspleegster*, 164, 254–5, 267; Noyes, *Stretcher-Bearers*, 88; Audoin-Rouzeau & Becker, *'14–'18*, 120; Panke-Kochinke & Schaidhammer-Placke, *Frontschwestern*, 100

best to ensure that his patients were as actively involved as possible in the local community, since he regarded it as useful therapy.[310] Not everyone was as lucky as Owen, however, and ordinary soldiers were treated very differently indeed.

*War and madness*

In the early months of the war doctors had no idea what to do with psychiatric patients. The following remark by Moran is telling:

> At Armentières, one day in 1914, when the 1st battalion of the Royal Fusiliers was in billets, Wickham, who commanded D company, told me that one of his sergeants was out of sorts. I found him sitting staring into the fire. He had not shaved and his trousers were half open. He seemed a morose fellow; I could get nothing out of him. Wickham did not want to send him sick, away from the battalion; besides, he did not appear to be ill. We agreed to give him a rest, to let him stay in his billet till the battalion came out of the trenches. But next day when everyone had gone up the line he blew his head off. I thought little of this at the time; it seemed a silly thing to do. I knew nothing of the tricks war can play with men's minds.[311]

Moran later began to appreciate that war could lead to psychiatric problems, but he always had a low opinion of psychiatrists and, during the war at any rate, he regarded the term 'shell shock' as a pleasant sounding euphemism for fear.[312]

This initial ignorance is attributable in part to a neglect of the knowledge gained by Russian doctors during the 1904–1905 Russo-Japanese War and in part to the fact that in 1914 the medical profession had little interest in the psychiatric impact of traumatic experiences. The effects of this lack of interest made themselves felt in the early years of the First World War and led to a good deal of quackery. In 1915 British newspapers were still advertising *Dr. Muller's Nerve Nutrient*, adding – presumably for the same reasons that prompted Sassoon to omit his first name when signing his anti-war article – 'guaranteed not German'.[313]

In 1916 an angry letter appeared in the British medical journal *The Lancet*. The author was a senior doctor at a medical facility. He attacked colleagues who were still insisting that the number of psychiatric patients would be reduced if drunkenness and syphilis could be combated successfully, asking whether fellow doctors had been asleep since 1914. Many psychiatric patients had no history

---

310 Day Lewis, *Collected Poems*, 164; Brants & Brants, *Velden van weleer*, 321; Howorth, *Shell-Shock*, 6

311 Bamji, *Queen's Hospital*, 1

312 Shepard, *War of Nerves*, 194; Shepard, 'Shell-Shock', 37

313 Myers, *Shell Shock*, 85, 88–9; Winter, *Death's Men*, 130; Brants & Brants, *Velden van weleer*, 321; Young, *Harmony of Illusions*, 40; Lengwiler, *Zwischen Klinik und Kaserne*, 186–9; Shepard, *War of Nerves*, 109; Jones & Wessely, *From Shell Shock to PTSD*, 16–17

of mental problems and did not show any signs of either syphilis or alcoholism. There was another cause: the war. Unless their problems were correctly diagnosed at an early stage – by which the author of the letter did not mean the all too easy conclusion that these particular soldiers had not proven mentally robust enough for combat or that they came from psychologically inferior groups in the population – they would inevitably spend the remainder of their lives in insane asylums.[314]

His comments come close to saying that the war was mad rather than the patients. It was a notion particularly prevalent in the Dada movement but it can be found elsewhere too, in Céline's novel *Voyage au Bout de la Nuit* for example.[315] Ernst Friedrich's Anti-War Museum in Berlin grew out of the conviction that in 1914 the whole world had shown itself to be a madhouse. Friedrich decided to document this ubiquitous mental illness in the hope that his efforts might contribute to its reduction or even disappearance. Wilhelm Lamszus called the second volume of one of his books, written before the war but published only after it, *Menschenschlachthaus. Visionen vom Krieg*: *Das Irrenhaus* (the madhouse), and the pacifist and future Nobel Peace Prize winner Carl von Ossietzky wrote in the foreword that 'we have meanwhile experienced the madhouse ourselves'. Stefan Zweig spoke of enthusiasm for the war as evidence of mass psychosis, insanity and hate-hysteria, and Theodor Lessing remarked: 'It is certainly valid and legitimate to speak of the great world war and the self-laceration of the white race in the occident as a symptom of the madness of humanity.'[316] This same insight would lead to the publication in 1932 of a book by Emil Flusser, with an introduction by Albert Einstein, entitled *Krieg als Krankheit* (War as Illness), which concluded that doctors, especially psychiatrists and psychologists, had a role to play in combating the mental illness known as war.[317]

Nowadays the 'madness' and 'absurdity' of the Great War are familiar concepts, and a large part of the literature, eye-witness accounts and films produced in the 1920s appear to point in that direction. While the war raged, however, the vast majority emphasized its 'purpose' and truly believed it had one. Fighting a war was in no way at variance with what most people felt to be right, in fact soldiers and civilians alike were generally in complete agreement with their countries' rationales and war aims. Most of those who regarded the war as insane believed that the entire world and all those who lived in it had gone mad, and that by some twist of fate this was more clearly visible in some than in others. Those who moved in the same circles as Toller and Grosz, on the other hand, believed not that

---

314 Withuis, 'Het oplappen', 85

315 Céline, *Voyage*, 62–71, 85–110; see also: Audoin-Rouzeau & Becker, *'14–'18*, 128

316 Vondung, *Kriegserlebnis*, 92–3, 106, 113; Zweig, *Die Welt von Gestern*, 166, 170, 172, 175; Heyman, *World War I*, 180; Sassoon, *Complete Memoirs*, 510; Van Bergen, 'De oorlog als spiegel', 3–5

317 Flusser, *Oorlog als Ziekte*, 80–100

the soldiers had gone mad but that the politicians and generals who wanted war had long been insane. This kind of anti-war stance meant inverting commonly held notions about what was mad and what was mentally sound, even asking whether the doctors who administered so-called treatments were quite sane themselves. In the eyes of Toller, Graf and their like, something odd was going on in military psychiatry and in the minds of doctors responsible for treating men driven mad by the war. After all, if the Great War was madness, what was the appropriate word for the soldiers whose minds were unable to cope with its insanity? Is a man driven mad by madness mad? Is he cured once he can handle the madness once more? Toller and others asked what kind of mental health care military psychiatry could hope to provide, if it meant making sure that men who quite understandably could no longer tolerate the insanity of this war were made able to return to it. Surely that made it a service whose doctors ensured healthy people were driven crazy once more. A psychiatrist was not a patient's ally but his adversary, not an opponent of insanity but its accomplice.

Oskar Maria Graf was sent to a psychiatric hospital after he refused an order to bone a horse that had been killed and was now frozen, his punishment for a minor offence. He was there for a full year and a half. Between the lines of his *Wir sind Gefangene* (*Prisoners All*) he tells his readers that he and his fellow patients were not mad. The doctors who tried to cure them were mad, since it was their job to incite people to kill on a massive scale and to ensure those who had at some point refused to kill were brought to the stage where they would be able and willing to kill again.[318] Leonhard Frank takes a similar stance in his *Der Mensch ist Gut*. A soldier who in Frank's eyes had become a human being again by refusing to shoot his fellow man would be declared insane. He could be healed. That is to say, it was possible to persuade him to take up a gun again. Whereas in peacetime the role of the psychiatrist was to keep aggression under control, in wartime his task was precisely the opposite.[319]

This was Toller's view of the matter as well, and to some extent he was right.[320] Having discovered that the 'enemy' was a man of flesh and blood, Toller became, as we have seen, an active opponent of the war. Like Sassoon he escaped court martial only because his family helped to arrange for him to be committed to a psychiatric institution. He too could sometimes no longer tell who the true madmen were. He was treated by the famous psychiatrist Kraepelin, who in 1883 had developed a comprehensive classification of mental disorders. His distinction between two types of psychosis, schizophrenia and manic depression, has stood the test of time. He advocated a somatic-biological approach; the social factors involved in mental illness did not concern him. The key word was 'degeneration', a popular diagnosis from the late nineteenth century onwards. It referred mainly

318 Whalen, *Bitter Wounds*, 63–4; Vondung, *Kriegserlebnis*, 102, 105; Audoin-Rouzeau & Becker, *'14–'18*, 128, 219

319 Frank, *Der Mensch ist Gut*, 84

320 Bourke, *Intimate History*, 267

to the damaging influence of modern maladies such as alcoholism and venereal disease, which endangered the future of the nation. Race-based explanations of illness had a place in Kraepelin's thinking as well. He concentrated his efforts on tackling prostitution, sexually transmitted disease and alcoholism, and he was active in the eugenics movement. When the war started he set up the extreme nationalist *Bund zur Niederkämpfung Englands* (Movement to Overpower England) in a Munich *Bierkeller*. All this points to a significant difference between the ways he and Toller perceived the war, made explicit by Kraepelin's stated belief that unfortunately the conflict was plucking the finest flowers of the nation while appearing to spare the egotists and malingerers.[321]

Kraepelin was part of a select group of psychiatrists who had published research on soldiers and the problems of military psychiatry even before the war. Prior to 1914 Kraepelin identified not the life of the soldier as pathogenic but war itself. Chronic tiredness and a relentless stream of horrific events inevitably led to psychiatric problems. In this sense he was quite unlike most other German psychiatrists, who saw neither soldiering nor war as the source of mental illness but rather, if anything, as contributory factors, the trigger rather than the underlying cause.[322] The subtleties of Kraepelin's interpretation did not survive the nationalism stirred up by August 1914, however, which made Toller's stay in the hospital he ran all the more unpleasant. Kraepelin berated him. His face red with indignation, he asked how he could have taken it into his head to question Germany's perfectly justified war aims. Toller and people like him were responsible for the failure to capture Paris. This led Toller to the conclusion that there were two types of mentally ill people: those who posed no danger, who were locked up and labelled 'insane', and those who were dangerous and had the power to lock away the harmless ones in hospitals or prisons.[323]

Toller and those Germans who agreed with him were not alone. Dr Bloch, a Frenchman who had been a law tutor at the Sorbonne, shared his views on psychiatry. Bloch was nursed in the German hospital where Lessing worked and there he acted as an interpreter between French casualties and German doctors who were often hostile towards them. His internationalist and pacifist convictions led him to see the hospital as a place where the mentally healthy were locked up to be nursed by the mentally ill.[324]

It all depends, of course, on how the word 'mad' is defined. In the view of many psychiatrists, men like Toller, Grosz, Graf and others were undoubtedly mentally disturbed, because they were not like other people. They deviated from

321 Eckart & Gradmann, *Die Medizin*, 100; Kaufmann, 'Science as Cultural Practice', 130, 132; Gijswijt-Hofstra & Porter, *Cultures of Neurasthenia*, 11–12, 187–8; Lerner, *Hysterical Men* (2003), 22

322 322 Lengwiler, *Zwischen Klinik und Kaserne*, 68–9, 183, 215–16, 262–4

323 Toller, *Jugend in Deutschland*, 78; Whalen, *Bitter Wounds*, 64; Vondung, *Kriegserlebnis*, 105; Riemann, *Schwester der Vierten Armee*, 115

324 Lessing, 'Das Lazarett', 358–9

the norm. It was the psychiatrists' task to heal them, in other words to make them embrace 'normal' values once again.[325] All this applied to war neurotics in general. Like others often named in the same breath, including pacifists, socialists, Jews, gypsies and homosexuals, they were regarded by many psychiatrists as belonging to an 'abnormal' group. War neurotics, or all those seen as such, were soldiers with a 'deviant attitude to life' impossible to correct by disciplinary means. It was the job of the military psychiatrist to protect the army against them. By today's standards they would not be described as mentally ill, but the military high command and a large majority of doctors firmly believed that their presence in the armed forces constituted a threat to the proper functioning of the army as the instrument of sanctioned violence. Renn describes the case of a soldier who tried to kiss a sergeant. He was sent to a mental institution. Homoerotic feelings were certainly present in the trenches, but explicit expressions of homosexuality were a sign of mental illness.[326]

Of all these groups it was assumed, rightly or wrongly, that they did not wish to comply with the norms and values accepted by the social elite. They undermined the society their countries' elites regarded as desirable and even blurred the clear-cut distinction between masculinity and femininity. Their inability to cope with the conditions of war was a rebellion against the very things society was founded upon: strong nerves, willpower and gender differences. There were certain ways in which a man had to be a man. A neurotic soldier was by definition refusing to comply, so his will would have to be broken. It was perfectly legitimate for the medical profession to be engaged in efforts to bring this about.[327]

Setting all this aside for a moment, it would have been hard for Toller or Graf to claim there was nothing wrong with most of their fellow sufferers. The phobias that afflicted them were often extremely debilitating, and many did not improve when they were evacuated to safety. It would be difficult if not impossible for them to function normally in civilian life. These men clearly needed psychiatric help, but in many cases the treatment they received did not even touch upon what Toller and others regarded as the cause of their sufferings: the war. Moreover, as is evident time and again, the aim of military medicine and therefore of military psychiatry was not to cure the patient but to help sustain the armed forces. The state must be saved as far as possible from the obligation to pay war pensions, and soldiers must either be returned to the front or sent to work in munitions factories. However, men like Toller, Graf and Sassoon may have held deviant political opinions, but they showed no signs of mental deviance. The diagnosis most often produced in the face of the resulting dilemma was 'lack of willpower'.[328] Psychiatrists saw opponents of the war as men too weak-willed to transform a reluctance to kill,

325 Bourke, *Moral Economy*, 7

326 Renn, *Krieg*, 168–9; Bourke, *Dismembering the Male*, 24–5

327 Young, *Harmony of Illusions*, 67–8; Howorth, *Shell-Shock*, 6; Mosse, *Shell Shock*, 2, 5–6

328 Whalen, *Bitter Wounds*, 64

normal in peacetime, into a desire to kill, advantageous in wartime. This was typical of military psychiatry in general, in that it allowed communal, military and national imperatives to take precedence over individual medical needs. Treatments were developed that were appropriate to the military mentality and that reflected the brutality of the war.

Many people, both victims and historians, would later label this attitude inhumane.[329] More and more patients resisted treatment and accused their doctors of cruelty, and when revolution broke out in Germany in 1918, some military psychiatrists took to their heels, afraid of what might happen to them if the revolution succeeded, a revolution that Berlin psychiatrist Karl Bonhoeffer described as a 'dictatorship of the psychopaths'.[330] One of those who fled was Max Nonne, in the light of which it seems rather curious that he was one of the two German doctors called to Moscow only five years later to help the dying Vladimir Ilyich Ulyanov, otherwise known as Lenin, in his hour of need.[331]

In Austria in 1920, six psychiatrists were taken to court by former patients. One of the six was Julius Wagner Ritter von Jauregg, a Vienna-based rival to psychotherapist Sigmund Freud. He believed there was little distinction between hysteria and malingering. Until the allegations were made, he was a member of a commission set up that same year to look into alleged abuses by the army and by military doctors, which in practice soon became an investigation into the methods used by army psychiatrists. A lieutenant in the Austro-Hungarian army accused Wagner-Jauregg of excessive use of electrotherapy. The officer felt his honour had been impugned, since in his view electrical treatment, known as faradization or galvanization, ought to be reserved for malingerers and hysterics, in other words for ordinary soldiers. The lieutenant had not been treated by the eminent psychiatrist himself but by his assistant Kozlowski, described by historian Ben Shepard as a sadist. As head of department, however, Wagner-Jauregg was the doctor responsible, and Kozlowski was back in his native Poland by 1920, so Wagner-Jauregg was the man called to account. They had subjected him to the 'Kaufmann cure' – so named after the psychiatrist Fritz Kaufmann, of whom more later – but this was not the only treatment tried out by Wagner-Jauregg and his colleagues during the war. He had noticed that psychotic patients occasionally showed some degree of improvement after a serious fever, so in 1917, convinced that a series of attacks of fever could drive out war neurosis, he started infecting soldiers with malaria. None improved, some died, partly because Wagner-Jauregg began treating the malaria itself only after the first dozen attacks. He did discover that the cure had some apparent success in combating *dementia paralytica*, a combination of psychological and organic disorders that was most commonly a

329 Bleker & Schmiedebach, *Medizin und Krieg*, 122

330 Shepard, *War of Nerves*, 132–3; Lerner, *Hysterical Men* (2003), 162, 215

331 Koch, *Menschenversuche*, 38; Lerner, *Hysterical Men* (2003), 94, 213, 219–20

result of infection with syphilis. As a result, in 1927 he became the only psychiatrist ever to be awarded a Nobel Prize.[332]

The trial, the *Wagner-Jauregg Prozeß*, became famous for Freud's much-discussed testimony. In 1915, in his *Zeitgemässes über Krieg und Tot* (*Reflections on War and Death*), Freud had expressed his revulsion at the extreme violence of total war and his disappointment at civilized Europe's relapse into barbarism and the loss of scientific neutrality even among psychiatrists, but in subsequent years Freud had said little about war neurosis. He first addressed the subject in a speech given in Budapest in September 1918 and he devoted part of his *Jenseits des Lustprinzips* (*Beyond the Pleasure Principle*) of 1920 to the subject. He regarded war neurosis as a conflict within the ego, a battle between the old peace-loving self and the new self in its soldierly role. Neurosis could sometimes rise to the surface as soon as the *Friedens-ich* or 'peace-self' became aware of the risks run by its martial alter ego.[333]

Freud, who according to Robert Jay Lifton had fallen prey to a brief enthusiasm for war in August 1914, had not treated any war neurotics himself, so his knowledge was derived entirely from accounts by Austrian and German colleagues such as Ernst Simmel, a psychoanalyst who specialized in disorders suffered by soldiers who had been buried alive, a condition known to the Germans as *Verschüttungsneurose* or burial neurosis. Simmel used a method called psychocatharsis, which combined analysis with hypnosis. Patients had to give their consent before being hypnotized, which indicates the considerable difference between this and the aggressive hypnotherapy practiced by Nonne (a treatment not used on officers), which was intended to produce results after a single session. Simmel believed that the psychiatrists now being accused of abuses had made the treatment sheer torture so that patients would 'flee into health'.[334] During the trial the fact that his information was second-hand did not prevent Freud from reproaching military psychiatrists – with the exception of the psychoanalysts among them – for having acted not as physicians but as 'machine-guns aimed at [soldiers]' behind the lines. It seemed to him that the task had been not to cure patients but to drive them back into front-line service. 'Medicine was serving purposes foreign to its essence.' This had forced every army psychiatrist to seek a compromise where none was possible: 'The insoluble conflict between the claims of humanity, which normally carry decisive weight for a physician, and the demands of a national war, was bound to confuse his activity.' In Freud's view the various methods of treatment had failed, or had succeeded only in the short term and from a military

332 Klee, *Auschwitz*, 116; Binneveld, *Om de geest*, 100; Kaufmann, 'Science as Cultural Practice', 141; Shepard, *War of Nerves*, 135–6; Lerner, 'Psychiatry and Casualties of War', 22; Lerner, *Hysterical Men* (2003), 138, 219–20

333 Kaufmann, 'Science as Cultural Practice', 135–6; Shepard, *War of Nerves*, 107; Audoin-Rouzeau & Becker, *'14–'18*, 193, 244

334 Leed, *No Man's Land*, 176; Kaufmann, 'Science as Cultural Practice', 141; Lifton, *Nazi Doctors*, 469; Lerner, *Hysterical Men* (2003), 101, 137–8, 171–5

point of view, and he believed this was inevitable, since they were based on a false premise. In contrast to the assumptions of most of his military colleagues, Freud saw war neurotics neither as cowards nor as malingerers.[335] Psychoanalyst Fritz Wittel, in his novel *Zacharias Pamperl*, published in 1923, supported this verdict wholeheartedly.

> These gentlemen used machines generating electrical currents, such as are used in America against armed robbers who kill, and they tickled the defenders of the fatherland until no option was left to them but suicide or a return to the gunfire. They injected them with emetics, so that they spewed up their very souls and preferred death for the fatherland to going on living like that. Maria Theresa had abolished torture; the nerve doctors reintroduced it during this war.[336]

People like Freud and Wittel felt that psychiatrists had behaved like military men rather than doctors. They claimed their colleagues had placed their knowledge of psychiatry at the service of the armed forces, as illustrated by their acceptance that each course of treatment must end, if at all possible, with the words 'Restored to fitness for front-line service'. Clearly Freud disagreed with many of Wagner-Jauregg's methods and with most of his defence during the trial. Freud was among those who said that Wagner-Jauregg should not be absolved of responsibility simply because it was Kozlowski who had actually administered the treatment. It is striking, however, that despite his tough statements about military psychiatry in general, Freud was generous towards Wagner-Jauregg during the investigation, playing down the severity of the methods he had used. It is conceivable that he was hoping this would gain him more respect among non-psychoanalysts, thereby placing psychoanalysis on a firmer footing within psychiatry. If that was indeed Freud's intention, then he failed miserably, since when he did not appear in court the following day, Wagner-Jauregg's supporters launched a fierce verbal attack on psychoanalysis. Such a hope on Freud's part would however help to explain why after the trial, at the end of which Wagner-Jauregg was thoroughly rehabilitated, Freud declared that he had never had more than a 'scientific difference of opinion' with him.[337]

Differences of outlook between psychoanalysts and people like Wagner-Jauregg were indeed fairly slight. Most psychoanalysts agreed that the distinction between hysteria and fakery was only one of degree. The war gave them an excellent opportunity to demonstrate the truth of their convictions, not just to fellow psychiatrists and neurologists who had either been sceptical or rejected

---

335 Ruprecht & Jenssen, *Äskulap oder Mars*, 220–21; Bleker & Schmiedebach, *Medizin und Krieg*, 122; Winter & Baggett, *1914–18*, 217; Babington, *Shell-Shock*, 65–6, 109; Young, *Harmony of Illusions*, 7, 78, 81; Jenssen, 'Medicine against war', 16

336 Hirschfeld, *Sittengeschichte*, 360

337 Taipale, 'German Physicians against War since 1870', 273; Kaufmann, 'Science as Cultural Practice', 142. Shepard, *War of Nerves*, 137–8

their theories completely but to the army and the state. Psychoanalysts too had been trying to make men fit to return to war, and it was no coincidence that several prominent figures among them had run their own military hospitals. These included the Berlin psychiatrist Karl Abraham. Like Kaufmann, Nonne and others, Abraham believed that the war meant each individual must sacrifice his interests to those of the community, to national affairs, and denied that the cause of neurosis could sometimes lie in traumatic wartime experiences. He was convinced the cause lay in the patients themselves, who must have been unstable even before the war.[338]

The trial of Wagner-Jauregg was no isolated case. France too had its criminal proceedings. In his article 'A Patient Fights Back', Marc Roudebush looks at the case of Baptiste Deschamps, who in 1916, during his trial for aggressive behaviour towards his physician, accused psychiatrist Clovis Vincent of torture by electrical current. The case dragged on, ultimately to the detriment of Vincent rather than the accused. It did not persuade psychiatrists to stop using galvanization machines, but it certainly had repercussions for the way French war neurotics were treated by their physicians, who had up to then been subjecting them to a psychiatric version of *l'attaque à outrance*. The trial undoubtedly influenced the reaction of the French high command to the mutiny several months later, which was generally moderate.

Deschamps had a whole medical odyssey behind him by the time he found himself a patient of Vincent at the Lycée Descartes in Tours. There was only one thing he wanted: to be declared unfit and allocated a war pension. In the two days before his treatment was due to begin he heard so many terrifying stories from fellow patients that he had no desire at all to receive therapy. After a short – some witnesses said cursory – examination, Vincent concluded that Deschamps' symptoms were not serious and that he could cure him. This did not mean merely rectifying the soldier's condition and returning him to the front line, it meant restoring 'the real man' by methods that might be tough but would produce instant results. A real man was a man of action who did not show his feelings, who did his duty and knew what honour and glory were all about. Vincent saw Deschamps as the opposite of such a man in every respect. He had been unable to cope with trench warfare and therefore with the ultimate test of his manhood: the willingness to fight and die for his fatherland. He did not even have any desire to be cured. During the trial Vincent gave his own side of the story.

> [Deschamps] had been proposed for a discharge, he had glimpsed the prospect of returning home, and of the pension that was waiting for him. He may not have wanted to be cured. Some have said: 'You do not have the right to impose pain upon a man.' … But I believe that when pain cures it is not a bad thing. It is all very well to proclaim the rights of the individual, but we must think also of the

338 Lerner, *Hysterical Men* (2003), 163–89

> duty of the soldier. What would be the indignation of the heroes of Verdun if we showed them their comrades who were able but not willing to recover?[339]

At first public opinion was on Vincent's side, prompted to a great degree by the conservative press. The newspapers said cowards like Deschamps should not be exempted from military service to live out the rest of their lives on a pension while the heroes of the nation fought and suffered at the front to save their people and fatherland from rule by the Hun. Newspaper stories were reinforced by testimony from a number of former patients, who spoke in Vincent's favour. Lucien Chaissaigne, for example, (who admitted that the electrotherapy he had received was milder than Deschamps') confessed that although, to say the least, the treatment had been far from pleasant, it had certainly helped him, and he went on to claim that 'the *poilus* who at the front suffered without complaining about the real *torpilles* – those of the *Boches* – will not be frightened by those of the Lycée Descartes.' Dr André Gilles explained that the name Vincent had given to his electrotherapy, the terrifying '*torpillage*', from *torpille*, a general term for a bullet, shell, grenade or torpedo, was used purely for effect and should not be taken literally. The impact of the word was part of the treatment. Gilles testified that apparent paralysis of the legs, arms, or vocal cords was merely a failure of the will, and it was the job of the doctor to restore a patient's will, in the man's own interests. Vincent's method, he said, was an extremely appropriate means of achieving this.

All to no avail. Slowly public opinion began to change, especially after testimony from Dr Doyen, a champion of patients' rights. Far more powerfully than Freud a few years later, Doyen railed against military medicine or 'medical militarism'. He spoke of incompetent surgeons who had recklessly performed operations on patients without their consent. In his view the tasks of doctor and soldier were diametrically opposed and any combination of the two was a contradiction in terms. He declared before the court that 'as soon as a man is wounded … he ceases to be a soldier … and recovers all of his rights'. Doyen said it was not Deschamps who should be called to account but Vincent. While Doyen was giving evidence, the courtroom grew rowdy, and when he finished speaking the judge was forced to clear part of the court. The prosecutor protested loudly, as did a number of military doctors, while many in the public gallery shouted their agreement.

In the end Vincent and his supporters failed to convince the French people that a doctor had the right to save a patient from himself by restoring his 'manliness', his personal honour and courage, with the aid of an entire medical armoury. The majority of the public actually believed it was Deschamps who had defended the

339 Roudebush, 'A Patient Fights Back', 6–7; see also: Myers, *Shell Shock*, 103, 108–9; Micale & Lerner, *Traumatic Pasts*, 270

honour and pride of the ordinary soldier against exploitation by a hypocritical elite, which patently included members of the medical profession.[340]

The example of Clovis Vincent indicates that the harsh treatment of war neurotics by army psychiatrists can largely be explained by the task those psychiatrists imposed upon themselves, which stemmed from their military function. Although they could not deny there were some neurotics who had endured the horrors for years before finally suffering psychological collapse, the view that prevailed among army psychiatrists, psychologists and neurologists was that neurotics with their so-called abnormalities had failed a Darwinian test, one that reflected the doctors' own interpretation of the theory of the survival of the fittest. In their view, war was the ultimate test of the will to be healthy and the will to survive, in both the nation and the individual.[341] They believed it was not just their military duty but their medical purpose to return a patient to the front, or at least to get him into a munitions factory.

This interpretation of their role meant that one of the jobs that fell to psychiatrists and neurologists was to identify malingerers, fakers, lead-swingers, just like their colleagues who treated physical diseases and wounds. An apparent headache, feigned blindness, and deafness or muteness with no detectable physical cause were among the many tricks soldiers used to avoid active service. There were several methods by which appendicitis, for example, could be faked. Corrupt or sympathetic nurses were prepared to make a man sick rather than better and there were even a few doctors who had done this sort of thing, whether to soldiers or to themselves. Simulated insanity was popular too. One German soldier shaved a cross into his hair, saying it would protect him from bombs dropped by aircraft. Another put a frog on a lead and took it with him to his commanding officer to ask for permission to bring his bear along.[342] Psychiatrists tried to prove that these cases and many others were examples of calculated deception and that there was absolutely nothing wrong with the men concerned. They could not rely on much support from a man's fellow soldiers, incidentally. The chances of a malingerer being unmasked by his comrades were minimal, which indicates that pretending to be sick was regarded to some extent as acceptable practice.[343]

Doctors paid special attention to regiments that had been put together quickly, since they would have had little time for rigorous discipline. One even claimed he was more detective than doctor. Disciplinary problems increased as the war went on – the British, for instance, had seen a professional army replaced by a

340 Roudebush, 'A Patient Fights Back', passim; Micale & Lerner, *Traumatic Pasts*, 268–9, 272–3; Winter & Baggett, *1914–18*, 217; Mosse, *Shell Shock*, 1–2; Shepard, *War of Nerves*, 103, 131

341 Leed, *No Man's Land*, 171–2

342 Riedesser & Verderber, *Aufrüstung der Seelen*, 12; Bourke, *Dismembering the Male*, 84–5; Mierisch, *Kamerad Schwester*, 114; Riemann, *Schwester der Vierten Armee*, 134–5, 151

343 Bourke, *Dismembering the Male*, 86

volunteer army that in turn gave way to a conscript army – and the number of cases of simulated illness rose as a result, or so doctors believed. The real picture may have been quite different. Although we can be confident that some men feigned sickness, and descriptions by soldiers of popular ways of doing so have been found, lead-swinging was probably similar to desertion in the sense that it never became a major military obstacle. Of course the scale of the phenomenon is hard to gauge, since those with a real talent for acting will never have been found out.[344]

Real or not, the problem of mental illness was energetically addressed. Like many senior officers, some psychiatrists believed that any acknowledgement that such a thing as war neurosis existed made fear respectable and therefore encouraged 'weaklings' to make a nuisance of themselves. One officer, and he was certainly not alone in his way of thinking, said to psychiatrist and neurologist H.W. Hills that if a man let his comrades down he should be executed, and 'if he's a loony, so much the better'. Many army doctors assumed that a soldier apparently suffering from neurosis was a malingerer unless proven otherwise, or even that the only difference between real and fake neurotics was that the former were feigning their disorders unconsciously. They were fooling themselves rather than their doctors, but unconscious fakery was fakery all the same. This was another reason why war neurotics were branded hysterics. Neurasthenics were not completely absolved of suspicion, but it was hysteria that was seen as virtually synonymous with feigned madness. The *Report of the War Office Committee into Shell Shock* described the dividing line between simulation and hysteria as extremely tenuous and claimed that many cases of shell shock were hysterical in nature. The compilers of the report had good reason to draw attention to this point. They noted that even at the time of writing, four years after the end of the war, many doctors were still refusing to accept the existence of shell shock and were extremely sceptical as to the veracity of many of the symptoms. Lieutenant-Colonel Scott-Jackson, for example, declared that in 1915 there had been not a single case of shell shock in his battalion, since he had refused to accept such a thing existed. After the symptoms became generally known, however, there had been no end to it, even among new recruits. In *Shell Shock in France 1914–1918*, after summing up various complaints from the army about cases of men taking advantage of what he calls the 'war neurosis epidemic', Myers fully endorsed what Scott-Jackson had said: 'I also had seen too many men at Base Hospital and at casualty clearing stations boasting that they were "suffering from 'shell shock', Sir", when there was nothing appreciably amiss with them save "funk".' Complaints like this boiled down to a belief that men seemed to have trouble with their nerves only after they had been informed about the existence of something called shell shock. The harshness of the methods used to treat them should be seen in this context, since

344 Bourke, *Dismembering the Male*, 89; Frey, *Pflasterkästen*, 231–3

they were intended to dissuade soldiers from feigning psychiatric problems in future.[345]

A wide range of books appeared on the market with advice on how to tell a true neurotic from a malingerer. Doctors were told they must pretend to show sympathy in order to win a man's trust, but the actual treatments recommended were often harsh. In a book first published in 1913 and rewritten during the war, *Malingering and Feigning Sickness*, John Collie, later Chairman of the Special Pension Board on Neurasthenics, wrote that it was striking how quickly some shell-shock patients recovered if electricity was administered repeatedly.[346] Other methods designed to make suspected malingerers change tack – methods very much in line with those to which acknowledged neurotics were subjected – included submerging the head in a basin of water, lumbar puncture,[347] extremely strict diets with aspirin to induce sweating, doses of powdered quinine, flushing of the stomach several times a day with a litre of warm water, enemas of soap and glycerine, and wrapping of the entire body in cloths soaked in cold water. Medical historians Riedesser and Verderber write with some cynicism in their book *Aufrüstung der Seelen* (Mobilization of Souls) that there were some brave men who endured all this and had themselves carried to the graveyard in small coffins. 'But there were also faint-hearted people who, once they got to the enemas, declared that they already felt much better and wanted nothing other than to leave for the front with the next battalion.'[348]

This will certainly have had consequences for the frequency with which faking occurred. The result of pretence or exaggeration being so uncertain, men probably quickly moved on to deliberately contracting some form of disease or getting themselves wounded. Another possibility was to refuse an operation, which was everyone's right even in wartime. Although the numbers of times this route was taken should be anything but overestimated, this led to great unease among some doctors, who wanted this basic right suspended for the duration. They considered it wrong that a man could be court-martialled for self-wounding but not for refusing surgery, even though the motive was exactly the same in both cases – to get away from the front. Hirschfeld claims there were a number of occasions on which surgery was carried out on casualties, especially ordinary soldiers, against their will. In the view of army doctors, the rights of the state took precedence over the rights of the individual.[349]

345 Myers, *Shell Shock*, 52, 59, 95–6, 120–21; Babington, *Shell-Shock*, 104–5; Binneveld, 'Herstel op bevel', 74; Winter, *Death's Men*, 136; Bourke, *Dismembering the Male*, 109–10, 112, 116; Bourke, *Intimate History*, 252–3; Shepard, *War of Nerves*, 71

346 Withuis, 'Het oplappen', 88, 91; Riedesser & Verderber, *Aufrüstung der Seelen*, 110–11; Bleker & Schmiedebach, *Medizin und Krieg*, 122; Young, *Harmony of Illusions*, 58; Bourke, *Dismembering the Male*, 84, 91–2

347 Winter, *Death's Men*, 136

348 Riedesser & Verderber, *Aufrüstung der Seelen*, 111

349 Hirschfeld, *Sittengeschichte*, 362–3

To return to the psychiatrists, they needed to legitimize warfare in an ethical sense. Of course there were some who saw the many neuroses as a logical consequence of the way the war was being fought, but a substantial number had other ideas. They refused to believe that a modern, industrialized war of vast magnitude, fought by immense conscript armies, had become too much for the human psyche to deal with. This was a war like all others, only perhaps on a somewhat larger scale. The soldier who went mad was not a victim of the circumstances; he was a man who had let his comrades down and failed a test that his comrades had passed.[350]

Finally, but no less importantly, the psychiatrist, like every other military doctor, was an insurance broker. He had to do his best to prevent soldiers from making successful claims for war pensions. This was actually one of the reasons why in all the belligerent countries the state began paying so much attention to psychiatric services so quickly after the start of the war; the cost of psychiatric care was negligible compared to the sums their work could save in pensions. Many of the psychiatrists, psychologists and neurologists who worked in the army medical services therefore refused to recognize neurosis as a mental war wound. Myers complained that because of the often unprofessional treatment given to war neurotics, a large number had been granted pensions unnecessarily. He also pointed to the therapeutic benefits of not allocating a pension too readily. The prospect of a pension stood in the way of a cure.[351] In 1917 psychologist Myers, who was generally regarded as 'soft' despite such views, was replaced by the tough neurologist Gordon Holmes, which suggests that attitudes actually hardened as the war went on. More than ever, the doctors' long-term policy, focused on individual welfare, was replaced by a short-term policy focused on fighting strength.[352]

Attempts to prove that most neurotics were fakes did not end with the armistice. This was a feature of Germany in particular, but British ex-servicemen too had to pull out all the stops if they were to prove their mental troubles were a result of their wartime experiences. The desperate financial state of the Weimar Republic, faced with demands for huge reparations payments, exacerbated the problem. The psychiatrically wounded would represent an enormous burden to the impoverished country if they were all to be paid a war pension, so doctors continued to 'expose' men as malingerers, or found other causes for problems that were undeniable, causes unrelated to the war, such as hereditary defects. A genetic predisposition to schizophrenia was a popular diagnosis. Doctors could find no convincing reason why this particular predisposition had manifested itself on such a huge scale during the war, but they refused to accept that any external cause could lie behind the problem of war neurosis. After all, had war been a cause of psychiatric illness, then everyone would have gone mad: all soldiers to a man, the aristocracy,

350 Leed, *No Man's Land*, 180

351 Riedesser & Verderber, *Aufrüstung der Seelen*, 12, 19; Whalen, *Bitter Wounds*, 59; Myers, *Shell Shock*, 111–12, 139

352 Shepard, *War of Nerves*, 46–51

the politicians, the generals. During the war and afterwards, it was a conclusion that simply could not be entertained. Most doctors genuinely believed it was nonsense to give a psychiatrically wounded man the same financial settlement as a physically wounded man, who might have to live without an arm or a leg. The loss of a limb was surely worse, and an amputee had clearly incurred his misfortune while rendering a service to his people and his country. Doctors believed that psychiatrically disturbed men would be easy to cure, were it not that many had declined help or obstructed their own treatment after 1918 as Deschamps had done during the war, so that they could continue to collect pensions.[353]

The story Weldon Whalen tells about postman Wilhelm S. represents a typical case of a man denied a pension on the grounds that a hereditary defect lay at the root of his problems. Before 1914 there had been nothing wrong with the hard-working Wilhelm. Then he was called up and after serving in the army for two years he began to exhibit strange behaviour. He had a range of physical aches and pains and a habit of reciting poetry and biblical passages at the most inappropriate moments, warning over and over again that the Last Judgement was nigh. He became impossible to handle, at which point the army discharged him and he went back to his old job. His behaviour did not improve, however, and he hindered other postmen in their work. Eventually S. ended up in a mental institution and was declared insane. After the war his family applied for a pension for him, but the medical examiner refused. He saw no justification for complying with the wishes of the family, since S. was clearly suffering from schizophrenia and there was evidence that it was hereditary. His sister, the doctor said, exhibited strange behaviour too.[354]

It is arguable that, like other military medical men, the army psychiatrist was not just a doctor and a soldier but a policeman and judge at the same time. This indicates another reason for the frequent use of harsh methods. The choice of treatment was no longer simply a matter of sickness and recovery but of crime and punishment, guilt and atonement. In fact treatment was a form of punishment. This helps to explain why doctors did not regard their therapies as unnecessarily severe.[355]

A further explanation for the debatable history of military psychiatry from a medical and humanitarian point of view is that psychiatrists had an even harder time in the army than other doctors. Generally speaking, medical officers were regarded by army commanders as odd men out. Warfare is extremely physical in character, so it is normal in military circles to venerate the well-built, healthy body. Doctors are seen at best as a necessary evil, and in the early twentieth century their social status was lower than that of other officers, if not in rank then certainly in perception. Those who did not concern themselves with visible wounds but with

---

353 Werth, *Verdun*, 265–6; Micale & Lerner, *Traumatic Pasts*, 140; Lerner, 'Psychiatry and Casualties of War', 24–6; Barham, *Forgotten Lunatics*, 195–6

354 Whalen, *Bitter Wounds*, 63

355 Leed, *No Man's Land*, 175; Céline, *Voyage*, 89

something as vague as mental illness were regarded with particular distrust.[356] Military psychiatrists had to do even more than other doctors to prove that they had iron in their souls and thereby gain some minimal acceptance from their non-medical brothers in arms. In 1918, when Hills, after four years of experience with soldiers who had collapsed under the strain of combat, reported to the headquarters of the British Fourth Army and explained the job he had come to do, he was met with roars of laughter.[357] In an attempt to gain acceptance from other officers, psychiatrists made their hospitals as much like barracks as they could, to an even more radical degree than most other doctors. Drill, discipline and orders were essential aspects of the apparatus available to the average army psychiatrist. Many thought the war would be decided according to which side had the strongest nerves, so they fought their own analogous battle of wills. This meant that much military psychiatric treatment might more accurately be labelled 're-education' than 'healing', although that is not how the doctors would have seen it.[358]

Hostile behaviour towards patients, hostile in intent as well as method, to which we shall return shortly, lead Riedesser and Verderber to the unflattering conclusion that the psychiatrists were 'not the medical advocates' of war neurotics who were facing up to their fear of death and their objections to being compelled to kill. Rather they were 'conscious helpers of a military leadership that demanded the smooth functioning of the soldier and where necessary his rapid return to combat readiness'.[359]

### *Kaufmann and colleagues*

Who exactly were the psychiatrists and what were their methods? Turning first to Germany, the story begins with Fritz Kaufmann, who was attached to the military hospital in Ludwigshafen. He offered German psychiatry, which was gradually being overwhelmed by the huge influx of war neurotics, a way out of medical trouble. Clarence Neymann, a young American psychiatrist working in Germany as a psychiatrist who reported for duty to the German Red Cross as soon as war was declared, claimed that right from the start, hardly any convoys of casualties arrived without some psychiatric cases. They were delivered to ordinary military hospitals, where they were generally ignored and regarded as a nuisance. They were eventually sent on to nursing homes further back behind the lines from where, after a period of rest, they were returned to the front. On arrival in the trenches they quickly relapsed into war neurosis, their symptoms often worse than before. Once every military hospital had been sent a psychiatrist, the situation improved

356 Binneveld, *Om de geest*, 138–9; Liddle & Cecil, *Facing Armageddon*, 503; Shepard, *War of Nerves*, 26. De Bruyne, *We zullen ze krijgen!*, 186

357 Babington, *Shell-Shock*, 105; Shepard, *War of Nerves*, xvii

358 Binneveld, *Om de geest*, 140–56; Binneveld, 'Herstel op bevel', 67–8; Withuis, 'Het oplappen', 88; Lerner, *Hysterical Men* (2003), 104

359 Riedesser & Verderber, *Aufrüstung der Seelen*, 19

considerably, but it was Kaufmann who pointed to the real solution, at least from a military point of view.[360]

It is important to bear in mind that not only the military high command but army doctors too regarded war neurosis as a violation of military discipline. A German medical officer made it known in 1915 that he believed some 50 per cent of the men in his care had symptoms of neurosis. Most such soldiers, especially if they were relatively mature in years, did not want to recover, he said, since that meant they would be returned to the front. Harsh measures were therefore needed if the fatherland was to continue to benefit from the services of these men. Not long after this recommendation was made, Kaufmann presented his cure. It serves as a prime example of the approach of the military psychiatrist to his professional work: quick, systematic, harsh and occasionally ruthless.[361] The therapy would reveal of its own accord whether a man was malingering, since no lead-swinger could endure it for long. He would swiftly comply with the demands of the therapist, who was determined to make painfully clear what the consequences of neurosis involved, in an effort to persuade the patient to resume his function in society as a soldier, a worker, a man. It was the therapist's task to convince the patient that not his own wishes but the interests of the state defined his social role.[362]

Kaufmann's main concern was to spare the state as many pension payments as possible, which meant that patients must be made to recover by whatever means it took. The end result Kaufmann had in mind was therefore not necessarily the restoration of a man's fitness for war service. If anything that was a higher level of recovery. He was certainly in favour of initial attempts to 'cure' men as close as possible to the front – which was still regarded as having a curative effect – and of keeping them as far away as possible from their homeland, where they would be embraced by their wives and families and have their perception of themselves as ill reinforced. A return to front-line service was therefore the primary aim, but once a soldier had been taken further back behind the lines to the point where Kaufmann would treat him, efforts would have to be concentrated on making him fit to re-enter society. He must recover sufficiently to be able to support the war effort as a factory worker. It was of course unfortunate that most patients preferred this solution to a return to the front, but nothing could be done about that.[363]

The 'Kaufmann cure', which he called the *Überrumpelungsmethode* or 'surprise attack method', amounted to a single series of applications of an electric current not quite powerful enough to make the patient lose consciousness and therefore no longer feel pain. In between 'electric massages' the order 'You will heal' was

---

360 Babington, *Shell-Shock*, 47–8; Kaufmann, 'Science as Cultural Practice', 138; Shepard, *War of Nerves*, 100

361 Babington, *Shell-Shock*, 65; Binneveld, 'Herstel op bevel', 66; Lerner, *Hysterical Men* (2003), 102–11

362 Leed, *No Man's Land*, 171, 175

363 Eckart & Gradmann, *Die Medizin*, 106; Binneveld, *Om de geest*, 141–2, 144; Lerner, *Hysterical Men* (2003), 155–9

repeated endlessly, and the treatment lasted just long enough for the patient to opt for 'healing' rather than sickness and an extended stay in hospital – if he had not died in the meantime. Parts of the body that had not been working properly were treated with electricity for several minutes, after which the soldier was ordered to exercise them. He was then wired up to the faradization machine again. It was made very clear to him that the horrendously painful treatment would not stop until he was able to leave hospital 'healthy'. In other words the soldier was given not just a physical shock but a mental shock as well, enabling the doctor, to put it mildly, to gain more influence over him. An additional advantage of this method, at least from the doctor's point of view, was that the man could not withdraw from it, as he could from hypnosis or other more humane treatments.[364]

Kaufmann's 'cure' and other harsh therapies intended to produce immediate results began a triumphal march through the German and Austrian military psychiatric hospitals, although there were individuals like Kurt Goldstein who consistently opposed such methods. At the start of the war neurosis was still seen as an organic disorder. Within a few years, after a period in which the blame fell on mental anguish as a result of observing the horrors of war, especially the sight of corpses and disfiguring wounds, German doctors began increasingly to emphasize pathological causes of neurosis. One of the symptoms of pathology was a desire to be discharged from service and the hope of being allocated a pension. It was factors like these that were now brought to public attention. Much was made of the fact that men who had not even experienced active service were known to have became neurotic, so there must have been something wrong with them mentally even before the war.[365]

Methods known as active treatments were adapted to this way of thinking. According to the most senior German military physician, Otto von Schjerning, active treatments transformed mentally ill men back into human beings and made them capable of working, in other words of living what the doctors and the state regarded as useful lives. Special hospitals were set up to administer the new treatments, based on the doctors' own ideas about German manliness, which boiled down to a sense of duty, obedience, and above all economic productivity. This approach was due in part, incidentally, to the fear that if neurotics were returned to the front they would only help to produce more neurotics.[366]

Men like Robert Gaupp, who worked with Kraepelin in Munich for many years and from 1906 onwards headed the psychiatric institution in Tübingen, naturally felt no reluctance to use electrotherapy to make the 'war tremblers' they so despised productive again. Even those who were initially critical of active

364 Binneveld, *Om de geest*, 142–3; Binneveld, 'Herstel op bevel', 67; Hirschfeld, *Sittengeschichte*, 359–60. Leed, *No Man's Land*, 174; Lerner, *Hysterical Men* (2003), 126

365 Lerner, *Hysterical Men* (1998), 1; Bleker & Jachertz, *Medizin im 'Dritten Reich'*, 100

366 Lerner, *Hysterical Men* (1998), 6–7; Lerner, 'Psychiatry and Casualties of War', 20–21; Lerner, *Hysterical Men* (2003), 128–9

treatments, such as Kurt Mendel, who believed that even in wartime there was a difference between a hospital and a barracks, were won over. Otto Schulze, like Mendel, had at first employed more humane methods, but he admitted that although there were dubious aspects to the cure, Kaufmann's method was worth emulating. Success had its price – it was as simple as that. Schulze pointed out that the pain a patient had to endure when he underwent the Kaufmann treatment was only of the same order as the sufferings of a woman in labour. Surely that should not present any difficulty to a soldier.

Shortly before the war ended, Kaufmann was forced to admit that his method had not achieved the effect he had hoped for and indeed expected. He adopted the line already taken by some of his early followers, who had discovered that the same results could be achieved without electricity. Many had turned instead to hypnosis, since it placed the doctor in the position of lord and master, which turned out to be just as effective a medical weapon as placing the patient in the position of a submissive creature by means of the 'Kaufmann cure'. In other words, although electricity was no longer used, the thinking and intention behind the treatment remained the same. Practitioners continued to be known as 'miracle doctors', since they guaranteed success by the use of a single method, by whichever variant of active treatment they preferred. The fact that they had abandoned electrotherapy did not imply any acknowledgment that the handful of experts who criticized them, such as Hermann Oppenheim, of whom more later, were right. Their critics claimed that although many of the symptoms did disappear, temporarily, the underlying problem had not been addressed. Such criticism was aimed not only at Kaufmann's approach but at Nonne's even more successful hypnosis therapy.[367]

Schulze was right, more so than he realized. Success indeed had its price. This is the most obvious deduction to make from a letter written in March 1918, still to be found among the records of the medical department of the War Ministry in Bavaria. It advocates a degree of caution in applying the Kaufmann cure, saying that a number of fatal accidents have occurred – an estimated twenty or thereabouts – quite apart from the many suicides that have followed treatment. Six months later this letter was followed by another in which it was impressed upon doctors that they should be careful to avoid any suggestion that they were concerned only about state finances and did not care in the least about the welfare of soldiers. These letters tend to support Riedesser and Verderber's conclusion that German military psychiatrists were able to do as they liked with seriously disturbed *Frontschweine*, and that they were not worried at all about subordinating the interests of the patient to the higher interests of the nation and its armed forces. It is important to emphasize, however, that the doctors at whom the criticism implied by these letters was directed did not feel it was justified. This amounts to further evidence that the war widened the gulf between doctor and patient. Psychiatrists

367 Binneveld, *Om de geest*, 179; Lengwiler, *Zwischen Klinik und Kaserne*, 66; Shepard, *War of Nerves*, 101; Lerner, 'Psychiatry and Casualties of War', 21; Lerner, *Hysterical Men* (2003), 90, 98–102, 106, 109, 114, 149

claimed that problems had arisen with only a tiny minority of those treated and that meanwhile the vast majority had been enabled to function normally again, whereas they would otherwise have remained mentally ill for the rest of their lives. Gaupp argued that this meant the Kaufmann method was not harsh at all but humane. Moreover, it was horribly gruelling for the doctors themselves, and rather more attention might profitably be paid to this fact.[368]

As we have seen, the Kaufmann cure was not the only disciplinary method of treatment, quite apart from the fact that at certain times men clearly suffering from war neurosis were deliberately ordered to advance towards the enemy, since this would be of 'great prophylactic value' to them.[369] Other methods were: immersion in icy water; extensive punishment drill; long periods of solitary confinement, sometimes in pitch darkness; being wrapped from head to toe in damp cloths or placed in a bath for many hours at a time, with assurances that there would be no release without healing; exposure to X-rays in dark rooms; lumbar puncture and faked operations under ether; the refusal of leave; being induced to cry out in fear; and simulated suffocation. As with men suspected of malingering, the patient was to be made more afraid of the hospital than of his life as a soldier. It was crucial that he should not experience the hospital as a pleasant place to be, since ideally he was to be persuaded to return to front-line service voluntarily. This was one of the reasons why no women were allowed to work as nurses in any of the clinics run by Kaufmann, Nonne, or those administering similar treatments. It was felt that only men had the willpower necessary to apply active treatments, and the mere presence of women would make a stay at the hospital more pleasant. Whenever a patient was sent to work in a munitions factory, or indeed returned to the front, the words 'treatment successful' were entered in his records.[370]

Graf provides a revealing description of immersion in a long bath, which indicates that such treatment was not always successful, in either the medical or the military sense of the word.

> We were defenceless, lying stark naked in a bath of hot water at 104 degrees Fahrenheit. The room was full of steam and wet and slippery. Three attendants walked to and fro at the window. If one of us tried to get out of the bath, they simply pushed him in again. So we just had to lie still, to lie and wait. We were given our dinner in the bath, but we were not hungry. We grew weary and then

368 Binneveld, *Om de geest*, 144–5; Bleker & Schmiedebach, *Medizin und Krieg*, 17; Babington, *Shell-Shock*, 66; Kaufmann, *Science as Cultural Practice*, 139; Shepard, 'Shell-Shock', 36; Lerner, *Hysterical Men* (2003), 106–8

369 Riedesser & Verderber, *Aufrüstung der Seelen*, 18

370 Bleker & Schmiedebach, *Medizin und Krieg*, 122; Riedesser & Verderber, *Aufrüstung der Seelen*, 13; Eckart & Gradmann, *Die Medizin*, 105; Lerner, 'Psychiatry and Casualties of War', 21, 27; Lerner, *Hysterical Men* (2003), 147

> weak, unutterably weak. … It was not till the third day that I was taken out of the bath, utterly exhausted, and put to bed.[371]

Another man besides Nonne who proved that psychiatric treatment could be made to serve the war machine even without electrotherapy was Ferdinand Adalbert Kehrer, senior psychiatric doctor at the university clinic in Freiburg. He combined hypnosis with compulsory drill. Psychotherapy was administered with the tone and bearing of an army officer.[372] Although he did not use the Kaufmann method himself, Kehrer had no objection to the harshness of such treatments. He had been one of the doctors who welcomed the war, since it provided an opportunity to apply to a large number of men all kinds of methods and techniques that would have been unworkable or even unthinkable in peacetime. In 1917 he wrote that it was not in keeping with the spirit of the times to advance ethical or moral objections to a treatment already in use. The doctor had a single task and should have a single aim in mind: to make as many 'war hysterics' as possible fit for active service as quickly as possible. Any method that contributed to this was a good method, and even aside from that, any conceivable method must be tried. It was the only way to eliminate the outdated and improve the old-fashioned.[373] Kehrer denounced the stance of the War Ministry, which wanted dangerous methods to be applied only with the patient's consent. He could see no military or medical reason at all to ask for a man's permission. There was no basis for the argument that psychiatric patients should be exempted from 'the duty of obedience'.[374]

*The Allies*

As suggested by the court case in France, we should not be tempted to assume that these treatment methods were used by the Germans alone. The pre-war battle between neurological and psychological methodology continued in wartime France and the neurologists won. French psychiatrists and neurologists were far less surprised by the psychological consequences of the war than their British allies, with their tendency towards biological explanations. This was one of the reasons why the French felt little need to create new descriptive terms to suit the occasion. They recognized that wartime psychiatry faced many problems, but they regarded few of them, if any, as new. Psychologists Jules-Joseph Déjerine and E. Gauckler described their experiences in an article entitled '*Le Traitement par l'Isolement et la Psychothérapie des Militaire Atteints de Trouble Fonctionnels*

371 Graf, *Wir sind Gefangene*, 201; Lerner, *Hysterical Men* (2003), 119

372 Bleker & Schmiedebach, *Medizin und Krieg*, 193; Riedesser & Verderber, *Aufrüstung der Seelen*, 14; Lerner, *Hysterical Men* (2003), 150–51

373 Riedesser & Verderber, *Aufrüstung der Seelen*, 12; Cooter, 'War and Modern Medicine', 1553; Lerner, *Hysterical Men* (2003), 43

374 Riedesser & Verderber, *Aufrüstung der Seelen*, 13

*du Système Nerveux*' (Treatment by Isolation and Psychotherapy of Soldiers with Functional Disorders of the Nervous System).

This approach meant that the patient's progress would be carefully monitored. Improvements were rewarded and resistance punished, for example with solitary confinement (as indicated by the name of the treatment) or denial of visiting rights. Clearly *la traitement par l'isolement* was no holiday. Like advocates of even harsher therapies, Déjerine and Gauckler tackled the symptoms only. They argued in favour of 'disciplinary psychiatry', which held the patient responsible for his own recovery. If he failed to heal, the patient must be resisting, so he must be punished, as any healthy soldier would be. Nevertheless, there was a significant difference between the methods they used and defended and the treatments men were subjected to by other French psychiatrists and neurologists. Déjerine had trained as a psychotherapist, although he was convinced psychotherapy could be successful only if the patient trusted the doctor completely. He regarded neurasthenia, for example, as having an entirely mental and emotional origin. His sympathies lay with Freud and Pierre Janet – although he had removed Janet from the Hôpital de la Salpêtrière when he took over there in 1910 – and he was opposed to the *traitement brusqué* that Joseph Babinski had deployed against hysterics as early as 1900, a practice Babinski naturally continued to promote during the war and on which Vincent's intensive re-education treatments, for example, were based. Déjerine continued to protest against the 'brusque' approach until his death in 1916, but increasingly he was a voice crying in the wilderness. Tough times called for tough measures. It is rather sad, therefore, that the Centre for Psychoneuroses, set up in the spirit of Déjerine to treat soldiers by less harsh methods, began to use suggestion and electrotherapy as well. It did so out of a perceived need, which Déjerine also recognized, for therapeutic authority, in other words for medical power over patients.[375]

In France too, therefore, where hospital conditions for psychiatric patients were appalling, hysterical, mute, paralysed and neurotic patients were subjected to faradization. Unlike many German psychiatrists, French doctors were motivated exclusively by a desire to return patients to the front. They did not regard a job in a munitions factory as an acceptable alternative. The conditions of war made it extremely important to come up with a simple and patriotic definition of hysteria, and from August 1914 onwards Babinski's conviction that there was no more than a theoretical distinction between hysteria and faking or malingering was adopted wholesale. Quite a few psychiatrists dropped even the theoretical distinction. Babinski had originally said that a neurosis was a result of suggestion, rather than of a difficult life, and now he believed that war neurosis originated not in the war but in either an idea unintentionally put into a man's head by doctors or relatives, or a form of auto-suggestion by the patient himself. As with malingerers,

---

375 Shepard, *War of Nerves*, 12, 98, 104; Gijswijt-Hofstra & Porter, *Cultures of Neurasthenia*, 377; Binneveld, 'Shell Shock Versus Trouble Nerveux', 57; Binneveld, 'Beter worden op bevel', 32–3

harsh, authoritarian methods could reverse the process. Like Kaufmann, Babinski admitted after the war that this way of thinking had been too simplistic. There was no denying that some soldiers had been genuinely ill. One man never tired of pointing out the difference between permissible commotional disturbances on the one hand and mental, emotional and therefore reprehensible problems on the other. This was Professor Andre Léri, who worked at a psychiatric centre attached to the French Second Army. He claimed he had succeeded in returning ninety-one per cent of his patients to the trenches in the period July to October 1916. He had no ethical difficulty with this. A neurotic should be regarded as a 'moral invalid'. He was an *embusqué*, a coward and profiteer, who must be turned into a *poilu*, the personification of the honest and cheerful French soldier. The need for such a transformation formed the background to the harsh treatment methods used by Vincent and others.[376]

The quick and from a military point of view effective treatment was aimed above all at reducing to an absolute minimum any chance that other men might become 'infected', and the patient must be prevented from becoming fixated on his symptoms. Discussion among French psychiatrists and neurologists primarily concerned measures that might prevent malingering. The policy was threefold: isolation, surveillance and therapy. The psychosomatic sequence of 'shock, emotion, suggestion, exaggeration, simulation and progression' had to be cut short. Céline wrote in *Voyage au Bout de la Nuit*:

> Professor Bestombes, our medical major with the beautiful eyes, had installed a complicated assortment of gleaming electrical contraptions which periodically pumped us full of shocks. He claimed they had a tonic effect. ... 'That, Bardamu, is how I mean to treat my patients, electricity for the body, and for the mind massive doses of patriotic ethics, injections as it were of invigorating morality!'[377]

The refusal by a large majority of French psychiatrists in 1916 to accept a proposal by Babinski (who could hardly be accused of oversensitivity) that at least that small group of war neurotics who had failed to respond to therapy of any kind should be given the status of 'war invalids' follows naturally from this line of argument.[378] The fact that French soldiers with mental problems had no right to a disability pension, and on similar grounds could not be dismissed from the army, certainly seemed to put a brake on the number of soldiers presenting with mental illness.[379] Not that they had been malingerers before, but the threshold to admitting

376 Babington, *Shell-Shock*, 99; Leed, *No Man's Land*, 170–71; Shepard, *War of Nerves*, 102; Shepard, 'Shell-Shock', 34; Micale & Lerner, *Traumatic Pasts*, 260–61, 263–5; Binneveld, op. cit. 31

377 Céline, *Voyage*, 89, 94

378 Hermans & Schmidt, 'De traumatische neurose', 537

379 Binneveld, 'Herstel op bevel', 71

to any kind of mental disorder was raised. Perhaps men subconsciously tried to keep going until a physical wound provided them with a period of rest that would alleviate their psychological difficulties. Perhaps they transformed their mental problems into physical sufferings in order to become eligible for discharge and a pension.

Evacuation was a slow process, so the French set up several hospitals immediately behind the front line. As a result, French psychiatrists discovered that treatment close to the front was conducive to recovery.[380] We should not forget that they still believed war had a positive effect on male health. A return to the battlefield was clearly simpler if a soldier had not spent too much time in safer areas, and French psychiatrists soon realized that from a military point of view the best results were obtained when the responsibility for recovery was laid entirely at the door of the patient. If a man did not accept this responsibility with good grace, then harsher methods would be tried, such as prolonged solitary confinement. For the French too, a stay in hospital was designed to be extremely unpleasant and each man was made aware at all times that he had not become a patient but was still a soldier.[381]

It may seem natural, therefore, that for the really tough cases French psychiatrists reserved a truly extreme form of treatment: the 'front cure'. The patient was taken to a shelter near a section of the front line that was being systematically shelled by the Germans and there he was given a painful subcutaneous injection of ether. Doctors claimed these men were always cured, although they do not mention exactly how such a 'cure' manifested itself, nor how long their patients remained 'healthy'.[382]

The success of the French principle of proximity – the first in what would later become the accepted threesome of proximity to the front, immediacy of treatment and expectation of returning to front-line service – led the British too to set up special hospitals near the front, largely at the prompting of Myers, who saw returning soldiers to front-line duty as the doctor's ultimate task.[383] Anyone who resisted treatment would be forced to carry out highly unpopular chores such as the cleaning of latrines. A rich philanthropist set up four specialist hospitals for officers, mainly so they would not have to be treated in mainstream psychiatric hospitals.[384] In the early months of the war Britain had no specialist hospitals on the continent for psychiatric patients. In 1915 Myers established a mental ward in Boulogne, although it was nothing more than a poorly maintained, draughty and cramped attic in a building originally intended as a hotel. The overcrowded

380 Binneveld, 'Herstel op bevel', 71

381 Binneveld, 'Herstel op bevel', 71

382 Leed, *No Man's Land*, 173. Some German army units are said to have sent their neurotics to areas that were under heavy shelling. Even Nonne regarded this as ethically dubious. Lerner, *Hysterical Men* (2003), 156

383 Myers, *Shell Shock*, 55–6; Howorth, *Shell-Shock*, 5; Leed, *No Man's Land*, 173

384 Babington, *Shell-Shock*, 54; Dean, *Shook Over Hell*, 31–2

conditions were partly a result of the fact that the army medical authorities sent it not only shell-shock cases but epileptics, prisoners and the 'simply mad', who tended to be muddled up with war neurotics even at the best of times. Myers protested above all against the use of his attic to house prisoners, whether or not they were awaiting mental health assessment and were themselves therefore victims of 'the stress of war'. It was highly undesirable, Myers said, 'that innocent men who had mentally broken down under the strain of warfare should be so closely associated with those accused and convicted of such offences as murder, attempted suicide, theft or desertion'.[385]

Serious cases, around ten per cent of the total, were still sent to Britain, and they too ran the chance of having to endure electrotherapy, despite the fact that the British described the Kaufmann cure as indicative of German inhumanity. Gordon Holmes believed the application of electricity was the best way of getting neurotics walking and talking again, and doctors in most clinics reached the same conclusion.[386] Among them was Lewis Yealland, made famous by Pat Barker's novel *Regeneration*, a neurologist at the National Hospital for the Paralysed and Epileptic, where he treated British soldiers and a small number of Belgians brought across the channel on the *Stad Antwerpen* to be nursed at King Albert's Hospital. Along with his colleague E.A. Adrian, he developed a rapid cure that was no less harsh than the Kaufmann method. Yealland claimed it never failed. The men – officers were never subjected to his treatment – were invariably 'healed'. This alone is enough to indicate that he paid little attention to the problems that gave rise to their symptoms, which did indeed usually disappear. The case of A1 is the best known.

A1 was a twenty-four-year-old soldier who had taken part in nine major battles on the Western Front before being transferred to Thessalonica. There he experienced mental problems for the first time. Overwhelmed by heat exhaustion one day, he was unconscious for five hours. When he woke he was trembling all over and could no longer speak. After nine fruitless months of fairly harsh therapy designed to produce a quick cure, he was transferred to the National Hospital. In a separate room with the door shut and the blinds drawn, he was connected to the faradization machine, at which point Yealland – who took his lead primarily from Babinski – told him he would not be allowed to leave the room until he could talk as well as ever. The treatment was successful.[387] The case of A1 also serves to remind us that we should not exaggerate the number of neurotics who were forced to undergo electrotherapy and other unpleasant and painful treatments, either on the German or the Allied side. People like Yealland, who was a civilian rather than

385 Myers, *Shell Shock*, 76–9, 82; Babington, *Shell-Shock*, 53, 90

386 Shepard, *War of Nerves*, 59, 101; Barker, *Regeneration*, passim

387 Young, *Harmony of Illusions*, 69–70; Binneveld, *Om de geest*, 145–8; Binneveld, 'Herstel op bevel', 67. Binneveld, 'Shell Shock Versus Trouble Nerveux', 69; Leed, *No Man's Land*, 174–5; Shepard, *War of Nerves*, 76–8; Jones & Wessely, *From Shell Shock to PTSD*, 38–9

an army doctor, treated only those cases that were the most challenging from a military and medical point of view.[388] One difference between him and Kaufmann was that the Germans were aware of one limitation of such therapies, namely that they could be used only between the declaration of war and the armistice. Yealland, by contrast, thought that his treatment could equally well be applied to civilians in peacetime.[389] In this respect, Rotterdam Professor of History Hans Binneveld, author of *Om de Geest van Jan Soldaat. Beknopte geschiedenis van de militaire psychiatrie* (*From Shell Shock to Combat Stress. A comparative history of military psychiatry*), takes Kaufmann's side. In all but a few exceptional cases, he says, military psychiatry, like many other branches of military medicine, has proven of little value to civilian health care.[390]

The British, who always spoke of neurological problems, incidentally, rather than psychiatry,[391] had other treatment methods in their armoury, and sometimes two or more were combined. They included extinguishing a lighted cigarette on a man's skin or tongue; pressing a hot metal plate to the back of his mouth; injecting ether under his skin; and holding a tube filled with uranium to his head, which in retrospect does not sound like an entirely safe method for the doctor either.[392] Some British doctors asked themselves whether inflicting pain on a patient was a permissible means of restoring him to health. William Bailey, like Vincent, concluded it was, on condition that it happened during a war fought to preserve and defend civilization, as was manifestly the present circumstance.[393]

One might nevertheless ask – and not merely with hindsight – what the point of such treatments can have been, in the long term especially. Even the doctors who carried out these experiments were by no means always convinced they benefited patients. The best outcome was for a soldier to return to the front or go to work in a munitions factory voluntarily, and this result was frequently achieved. Among ordinary soldiers, that is. Bailey acknowledged and attempted to justify the fact that these disciplinary methods were not applied to officers. Apart from pointing out that the nature of their problems often made them unsuitable for treatment by electrotherapy, he claimed their better education, superior intelligence and other qualities attributed to their social class meant that the treatment of neurosis in officers was often more difficult. It therefore required more time and patience.[394]

388 Young, *Harmony of Illusions*, 72

389 Binneveld, *Om de geest*, 148

390 Binneveld, *Om de geest*, 139–40; Binneveld, 'Herstel op bevel', 66

391 Young, *Harmony of Illusions*, 61

392 Interview with Pat Barker, *NOVA* (Dutch television), 28-3-1996; Bourke, *Dismembering the Male*, 116; Shepard, *War of Nerves*, 77

393 Leed, *No Man's Land*, 169

394 Leed, *No Man's Land*, 169

*Discipline versus analysis*

All this is not to say that every psychiatrist engaged in caring for nervous wrecks in uniform in the years 1914–18 endorsed such harsh methods. Following advice based on the experiences of American psychiatrist Weir Mitchell, who had treated 'nostalgia' patients during the American Civil War, a month of bed rest on a dairy-based diet was quite regularly prescribed, sometimes combined with hypnosis, although this might mean solitary confinement as well.[395] Throughout the war, Rivers stuck firmly to his humane methods, based on conversations with patients, who were of course always officers. Like Myers and others, he assumed that shell shock was above all an emotional trauma, but whereas Myers thought it led to disintegration of the personality, Rivers was more inclined to think there was a connection with some kind of struggle between the instinct for self-preservation and culturally determined tendencies such as the refusal to show fear. He drew upon Freudian thinking about repression, although he regarded the war as proving that repression did not necessarily have sexual origins.[396] He and others based their ideas on an analytical form of therapy, which involved trying to help the patient sort out mental conflicts, usually taking place in the unconscious, between individual needs and harsh reality. A great deal of attention was paid to the patient's past.

It is certainly the case that psychiatrists, neurologists and psychologists who showed 'too much' compassion for the individual soldier were not making life any easier for themselves. Lieutenant Kirkwood examined the 11th Border Regiment 97th Infantry Battalion one week after the start of the Battle of the Somme and concluded that a large proportion of the men were not fit for duty because they were suffering from shell shock of one form or another. He was relieved of his position.[397] Hills acquired a reputation for being too kind-hearted and received an order from higher up not to send so many patients to the base hospitals. He had to be reminded that, given the shortage of manpower, it was not his task to heal his patients but to get them back to the battlefield as quickly as possible.[398]

The behaviour of these compassionate psychiatrists is in striking contrast to the approach of men like Yealland or Kaufmann, who adhered to a disciplinary form of therapy based on methods and techniques that originated in animal training. Yealland, Kaufmann and their like believed that a patient was not, or not only, a sick soldier who needed help but a recalcitrant figure who must be forced to toe the line. They were conscious of their dual role and endorsed it. They must rein in the disease on the one hand and the patient on the other, and the patient's past was significant only in the sense that they impressed upon him that he would be able to endure in the future what he had endured in the past. They adhered to the theory

395 Howorth, *Shell-Shock*, 6

396 Howorth, *Shell-Shock*, 4; Shepard, 'Shell-Shock', 36

397 Babington, *Shell-Shock*, 78–81; Bourke, *Dismembering the Male*, 93; Shepard, *War of Nerves*, 42–3; Wessely, 'The Life and Death of Private Harry Farr', 442–3

398 Babington, *Shell-Shock*, 105

that suggestion was both the cause of the disease and its cure. A man had got hold of the idea he was sick (or rather, that sickness was better than health) and the doctor needed to convince him of the opposite. Healing became a battle of wills.

Disciplinary therapy was intended to break the will of the patient, who wanted to remain sick. The doctor must be confident of the possibility of healing and radiate this confidence; whatever happened, he must not give up until healing was achieved. Partly because of the military setting, this meant that the doctor took on the role of a commanding officer. Disciplinarian doctors repeatedly reminded their patients that willpower was the key to recovery. Any man could get back to work if his will was strong enough; conversely, any man incapable of working lacked willpower. Despite this constant emphasis on the individual will of the soldier, the patient had to listen to the doctor and follow his orders at all times. 'Will' did not mean having ideas of your own, and certainly not being so bold as to assert your own opinions against those of the medical profession. Indeed, opposition to the doctor, characteristic of Toller's behaviour, demonstrated a lack of will. 'Will', as defined by the doctor, meant that the patient submitted to the prescribed regime without complaint.[399]

Gaupp was reflecting the official position of psychiatrists and other medical professionals when he claimed that it was not the method that mattered but the doctor. The element of suggestion was more important than the means used.[400] Why then did so many doctors adopt the Kaufmann method, and why were some treatments regarded as suitable for officers, others for the men? The answer would have been that while the choice of a particular approach made little difference, in terms of final recovery certain methods achieved the same results more quickly and cheaply, a crucial requirement of medical services in wartime, with its shortages of everything except patients. Some treatments may have been harsh, but, their advocates and practitioners claimed, they achieved in a few hours what would have taken days, weeks, even years using talking therapies. This is the main reason, along with a re-evaluation of psychoanalysis, for the further increase in harsh methodology in the later stages of the war, especially on the German side. To the horror of many psychiatrists, more soldiers than ever were refusing to cooperate with the recovery programmes laid out for them. They no longer wished to be healed so that they could be deployed in a war they had already lost, a conflict they no longer recognized as their own.[401]

It was in Germany above all that 'the will' played a dominant role, not only in the way soldiers were treated but in the definition of mental illness. Even more than in France and Britain, it was the relationship between the individual and the state that shaped attitudes to psychiatric problems. As Paul Lerner explains in his 'Ein Sieg Deutschen Willens' (A Victory of German Will), the readiness of a man to

399 Whalen, *Bitter Wounds*, 64–5

400 Eckart & Gradmann, *Die Medizin*, 105; Lerner, 'Psychiatry and Casualties of War', 21; Lerner, *Hysterical Men* (2003), 86, 114

401 Eckart & Gradmann, *Die Medizin*, 104; Lerner, *Hysterical Men* (2003), 163–4

make sacrifices and to conform to the demands made upon him by his superiors in the interests of his nation and its armed forces became the yardstick of his mental health. Individual willpower meant subordination to the will of the community. As the Germans saw it, willpower determined how a person would react in a given set of circumstances. If the will was strong enough, a man could deal with any situation. The regime prescribed by the doctor was inseparable from a conviction that submitting to the requirements of the nation was the highest goal of mankind. The purpose of human life was made manifest in the will to obey the demands of the state. In neurotics this will had been lost, and they were healed when it was restored.[402] Psychiatrist Willy Hellpach wrote in 1915 that the art of medicine was to save a threatened life, but this became truly an art only if the person saved could then be persuaded to venture his life again. Two years later Gaupp added that to achieve such a result, all available means were permissible. By enduring 'a little pain' these 'inferior beings' with 'ethical defects', these 'egotists', could earn back their health.[403]

There was a second sense in which Germany distinguished itself from France and Britain. In Germany too hysteria was seen as a primarily female affliction. Nonne was initially convinced hysteria was something that would typically affect French men and he was not alone in his astonishment at the *hysteria virilis* (male hysteria) that emerged within a few months of the outbreak of war. It put an end to a notion common among neurologists and psychiatrists, namely that the war would automatically resolve the mental crisis of the German people.[404] This is odd, because it was the Germans who had for some time questioned the idea that male hysteria was a contradiction in terms. In the late nineteenth century, for example, in Germany as in other countries, the phenomenon of hysteria after railway accidents had been recorded on several occasions, an effect the Americans called 'railway spine'. It had also been noted that workers could be traumatized by conditions in modern factories. Hermann Oppenheim pointed to the experience of harsh circumstances as a cause of the traumatic neuroses he diagnosed, but most of his professional colleagues rejected this conclusion as dangerous and unpatriotic. His theory was scientifically flawed, they said, and detrimental to the health of the patient, who would become trapped in his illness. Above all perhaps, it threatened the economic interests of the state. It was not the war that made a soldier sick; combat was actually good for a man. If he were to recover, the patient must not be hospitalized but get back to work as quickly as possible.

It is impossible to separate this fierce criticism of Oppenheim from the fact that he was a Jew. Anti-Semitism was far from rare at the turn of the twentieth century, certainly in the nationalist circles in which many doctors moved.

---

402 Eckart & Gradmann, *Die Medizin*, 6, 85, 87, 91

403 Eckart & Gradmann, *Die Medizin*, 86, 105; Kaufmann, 'Science as Cultural Practice', 137

404 Eckart & Gradmann, *Die Medizin*, 94; Shepard, *War of Nerves*, 99; Lerner, 'Psychiatry and Casualties of War', 13; Lerner, *Hysterical Men* (2003), 1, 15, 48–58

It was not the main motivation for opposition to Oppenheim's ideas, however. Indeed, Kaufmann too was Jewish. The controversy can in part be traced back to the difference between Oppenheim, a practising psychiatrist, and the mainly university-based theoreticians who rejected his theory of traumatic neurosis. In fact the critics had a point. They did not all deny there was a connection of some sort between horrific experiences and the development of mental problems, but even those who recognized the link claimed the two were less directly connected than Oppenheim seemed to be insisting. After all, only a tiny minority actually went crazy. Why not the majority? Why not all? Why did so many men who had not even seen active service become insane and why did madness not occur, or at any rate far less frequently, among prisoners of war? According to Oppenheim's critics, most of whose views occupied the opposite extreme, the cause of neurosis should not be sought outside the patient but within him, a possibility by the way that Oppenheim had never completely rejected.

War neurotics as a group were economically significant, and their treatment reflected this. In France and Britain, theories about the origins of hysteria were largely gender-based, whereas in Germany they were mainly, though not entirely, bound up with social factors. The male hysteria found in factory workers was explained as part of the desire of a work-shy class for sickness benefits. Soldiers who could not, or could no longer, cope with the conditions of war were work-shy labourers who had no wish to carry out their allotted task and lacked the will to do what was expected of them in the interests of the state. Just as the work-shy class represented a threat to the economy, the work-shy soldier represented a threat to Germany's military aims. Critics of Oppenheim claimed that war neurosis had little to do with the war, not least because neurotics were men who had serious mental defects even before the war started. Neuroses were hysterical psychological reactions seen in fearful, weak, lazy men, just like the problems suffered by psychiatric patients in normal times; wartime traumas were in essence the same as peacetime traumas. German theorists accepted that there was a relationship between circumstances and hysteria, but most psychiatrists and neurologists said there was no difference in principle between harsh conditions in peacetime and in wartime. A bombardment was not significantly different from an industrial accident, they claimed, or only in degree. Just as the factory must not be labelled the cause of mental illness, so the war must not now be blamed. If it were, that would amount to an attack on the nation's military and economic well-being, and a threat to a generation of doctors who wanted above all to do their bit for what they regarded as the national interest.

This meant that the first duty of the psychiatrist was to restore the soldier's will to work. Like a worker, he was the product of an environment he regarded as hostile and dangerous. The worker's environment was the impersonal factory and the soldier's the trench war, in which, holding his spade and rifle, he was a human cog in a thoroughly technologized world, one that Jünger extolled and cultural critics like Grosz ridiculed. The doctors wanted to create 'a generation of fit and dutiful men', as Gaupp put it. Although Nonne had once said that it was impossible for any German soldier to suffer from hysteria, it was a diagnosis that came in useful. Oppenheim's critics were well aware that traumatic neurosis meant a lifelong pension, whereas hysteria was curable, so state benefits could be discontinued after a while and the soldier made ready to serve his fatherland again. Here lies the main motivation behind criticism of Oppenheim. His diagnosis of 'traumatic neurosis' represented a threat to the nation's economic strength and the war effort, and therefore to the nation's health. A true patriot was bound to oppose it.[405]

It was this same Gaupp who suggested at the special War Congress of the German Association for Psychiatry in September 1916 in Munich, which was attended by around three hundred German and Habsburg psychiatrists and neurologists, that there was no place in the social insurance system for war neurosis. This allowed the government to tighten the already quite stringent administrative guidelines governing the payment of social security benefits.[406] Gaupp and others like him did not regard hysteria as a form of malingering. They saw it as a genuine illness, but it was one in which soldiers had taken refuge, prompted by the prospect of a war pension. Men who received pensions, those 'worthless parasites' in Gaupp's words, lived at the community's expense. The troops must be denied the prospect of a pension. The number of cases of mental illness would then fall dramatically of its own accord.[407]

The War Congress of 1916 was the highpoint of the discussion between supporters and opponents of Oppenheim's ideas, and his opponents won hands down. The theory that neurosis resulted from a lack of willpower – which in their view was confirmed by cases of simulation, since that too was a sign of a weakness of character – had triumphed over the theory of traumatic external experience.[408] Oppenheim was flabbergasted. He could not believe that 'doctors trained in neurology and psychiatry could disregard to such an extent the effect of the war's violent mental and psychical traumas, and assume that they left only a fleeting impression on the nervous system'.[409]

405 Micale & Lerner, *Traumatic Pasts*, 142, 157, 160, 162, 170–71; Lerner, *Hysterical Men* (2003), 63, 67–71, 102; Lerner, *Hysterical Men* (1998), 2–3; Lerner, 'Psychiatry and Casualties of War', 13, 16–17, 27; Eckart & Gradmann, *Die Medizin*, 93–4; Shepard, 'Shell-Shock', 34; Jones, Wessely, *From Shell Shock to PTSD*, 14–15

406 Hermans & Schmidt, 'De traumatische neurose', 538; Micale & Lerner, *Traumatic Pasts*, 163

407 Eckart & Gradmann, *Die Medizin*, 96, 106; Kaufmann, *Science as Cultural Practice*, 138; Lerner, *Hysterical Men* (2003), 1, 64

408 Eckart & Gradmann, *Die Medizin*, 95–6; Eckart & Gradmann, 'Medizin', 216; Kaufmann, 'Science as Cultural Practice', 133–4; Micale & Lerner, *Traumatic Pasts*, 157; Cocks, *Psychotherapy in the Third Reich*, 32; for the War Congress see: Lerner, *Hysterical Men* (2003), 74–85

409 Kaufmann, 'Science as Cultural Practice', 134; Lerner, 'Psychiatry and Casualties of War', 17; Lerner, *Hysterical Men* (2003), 77

We should not overlook the fact that many German psychiatrists regarded a lack of willpower as something that typically affected women and children. The difference between socially-based theories and those founded to a greater degree on notions of masculinity and femininity is far less clear-cut than it may seem. In Germany too, many psychiatrists were convinced of the essentially female nature of hysteria.[410] The hysterical worker was an effeminate worker and the hysterical soldier an effeminate soldier. Among German psychiatrists, however, attitudes to hysteria were not governed by ideas about allegedly sexually-determined characteristics of the mind so much as by beliefs about the relationship between the individual and the state. The neurotic soldier was not described primarily in terms of femininity – nor, as was so common in Britain, homosexuality – but in terms of egotism, parasitic behaviour and an absence of the willpower a man needed to subordinate himself to a larger whole. Hysterics were suffering from a lack of patriotism and therefore, according to Gaupp, 'the correct disposition with regard to the war', a war he revered as 'the master of all things'.[411]

In Germany the war and the factory were consistently spoken of in the same breath, which helps to explain why German psychiatrists were usually satisfied if a soldier could at least be put to work, whereas the British and French, whose aim was to restore an effeminate soldier's manhood, were more concerned to return him to the forward trenches. The Germans saw the front and the factory as one and the same. It was no accident that their special psychiatric clinics were located close to munitions factories. War-related work was good for the patients, who would be less likely to relapse into neurosis; it was good for the psychiatrists, who would not have to treat the same patients again and again; it was good for the economy, since former patients could help to resolve the shortage of workers, and therefore it was good for the German war effort. Work on the home front that benefited the war effort was part of what was known as active therapy, of which active treatment was merely the first stage. Work was both part of the German psychiatric strategy and its goal.[412]

One difficulty with all this was that most soldiers had never been factory workers. The majority were farm labourers. Although it was generally accepted that city boys – clever but weak – were more likely to break down than country lads – strong but stupid – one of the causes of mental problems on such a huge scale may well have been that a modern, mechanical, technical war was fought by predominantly pre-modern soldiers. Factory workers had joined the army, the object of their hatred for so many years past, largely out of a desire to escape their infernal industrial environment.[413] They will not have been pleased to find

410 Kaufmann, 'Science as Cultural Practice', 130

411 Eckart & Gradmann, *Die Medizin*, 99, 101–2; Lerner, *Hysterical Men* (2003), 44

412 Eckart & Gradmann, *Die Medizin*, 104; Lerner, *Hysterical Men* (1998), 3–4; Van Heeckeren, '"Die Vorstellung ist alles"', 80–90.

413 Leed, *No Man's Land*, 30, 63

themselves in another industrial environment, one in which they were far worse off than before.

Gaupp, who found it hard to accept that his task was to remove weak men from the front line so that their stronger compatriots were even more likely to be killed,[414] was one of a number of German psychiatrists who believed that the defeat and revolution of 1918 had happened because the army was stabbed in the back, and that the German policy of sending neurotics back to the fatherland had made a significant contribution to this. Those who agreed, including Gaupp's assistant Otfrid Foerster, gained the upper hand in 1933. Partly as a result, neurosis in the German army would not be seen as a medical matter at all during the Second World War but as a disciplinary problem.[415] Nevertheless, the Kaufmann method and Gaupp's ideas do not mean that German military psychiatry during the First World War should be seen as a forerunner of Nazi 'medicine'. The all too common tendency to see the medical history of Germany, indeed Germany's entire history, primarily in the light of 1933–45 is a mistake. The treatments used in the years that led up to the Third Reich were not determined by future events, they were a product of circumstances and ideas that prevailed at the time. Indeed, the methods of countries that were 'on the right side' in the Second World War rivalled anything done by Kaufmann and his supporters. Since generally speaking his destination was the factory rather than the front, the German worker-patient – the sick equivalent of Jünger's worker-soldier – had less to fear from psychiatric treatment than the British or French man-patient, however harsh German methods of 'healing' may have been. The way German military psychiatrists acted in 1914–18 was the result of dilemmas about the role of psychiatry in an emerging modern, industrial state, a state that was also at war. It arose out of preconceived notions, and out of the specific circumstances of their time and place, rather than from the shadow of events to come. Moreover, the notion of 'race' played only a minor role, despite the popularity of eugenics in the entire Western world at the time and the presence in the Germany military-medical corps of men like Fritz Lenz and Eugen Fischer, who in 1921 jointly published the book *Menschliche Erblichkeitslehre und Rassenhygiene* (Principles of Human Heredity and Race-Hygiene) and later became leading ideologists of Nazi racism.

Vehement ethical arguments used against disciplinary psychiatry by psychiatrists who practised psychoanalysis, such as Simmel and Rivers (attacks that differed little from today's expressions of outrage at such methods) were ineffective. They were based on a conviction that healing and discipline were at odds with each other, which was not at all the way Kaufmann and others saw it. Far from the two

---

414 Kaufmann, 'Science as Cultural Practice', 137; Lerner, *Hysterical Men* (2003), 202

415 Koch, *Menschenversuche*, 39–41, 68; Shepard, 'Shell-Shock', 40; Lerner, *Hysterical Men* (2003), 213

being incompatible, healing meant discipline and discipline meant healing.[416] By the same token, we cannot simply condemn the declarations of insanity passed on dissidents like Toller, Grosz and Sassoon as abuses of political power. In their cases too, the doctors concerned saw deviant political convictions as signs of mental disorder – anti-war neurosis – and therefore regarded healing through discipline as permissible medical treatment. For the military authorities this had the advantage that an often tricky legal problem could be resolved by medical means.[417]

It is important to note that although treatment by hypnosis – which was banned in the French army, incidentally, because of its unscientific basis and the aura of mysticism that surrounded it – may have been less damaging physically, in experienced hands it was hardly any less authoritarian, coercive and behaviour-modifying than electrotherapy and, certainly when carried out by Nonne, no more humane in its effects or intentions. This is true to some degree even of psychoanalysis. Simmel and men like him recommended psychoanalysis not simply because they believed it was more effective in the long term than the Kaufmann method or other harsh treatments, nor because they wished to spare their patients a humiliating and painful experience, but because it would best serve the interests of the armed forces. Psychoanalysis was not merely aimed at tackling a patient's symptoms, like the various active treatments; it was intended to heal the entire person. So while the treatment itself may have been more humane, the patient's ultimate destination was not the factory but the front.[418]

The aftermath of the war appeared to prove Gaupp and his colleagues right, despite the fact that with the armistice and the revolution, active treatments suddenly seemed to lose a great deal of their efficacy. The military setting lost its impact and therefore the doctor lost his dominant position, but this did not matter a great deal in practice, since the changed circumstances seemed to bring about healing to an extent comparable with the most successful of cures. Symptoms of neurosis melted away like snow in summer, although they returned in full force when the revolution failed and economic disaster struck. Although psychoanalysts, along with psychiatrists and neurologists who had practised active treatments, saw this as incontrovertible proof that Oppenheim's theories were wrong, they did not draw the conclusion that hysteria and simulation were one and the same; it was simply that the revolution and the armistice had obviated the need for a 'flight into hysteria'.[419]

As will be clear by now, although the battle of wills was a concept recognized by the British, theories held by the Allies were generally tailored more to alleged psychological differences between the sexes. The man who could not cope with

416 Lerner, *Hysterical Men* (2003), 4, 10, 161; Lerner, *Hysterical Men* (1998), 7; Lerner, *Psychiatry and Casualties of War*, 23

417 Leed, *No Man's Land*, 168–9

418 Leed, *No Man's Land*, 177; Kaufmann, 'Science as Cultural Practice', 140; Micale & Lerner, *Traumatic Pasts*, 278; Lerner, *Hysterical Men* (2003), 174

419 Lerner, *Hysterical Men* (2003), 194, 211, 226–7

the stress of war had become a 'woman', and in most cases his symptoms had been detectable before he joined up. In his book *War Neuroses*, published in 1918, John T. MacCurdy noted that in one case a twenty-year-old soldier who had never displayed any neurotic symptoms before the war nevertheless 'showed a tendency to abnormality in his make-up'. The evidence amounted to the fact that he was 'rather tender-hearted'.

> [He] never liked to see animals killed. Socially, he was rather self-conscious, inclined to keep to himself, and he had not been a perfectly normal, mischievous boy, but was rather more virtuous than his companions. He had always been shy with girls and had never thought of getting married.

In other words, as Joanna Bourke comments, a normal man was capable of killing, did not mind seeing animals killed, was lively and naughty in childhood and actively heterosexual later. Such a man could handle the conditions of war. Anyone who could not was obviously not a real man. It was a verdict many of those suffering from neurosis accepted, heads bowed.[420]

In this context it is striking that in nineteenth-century France, hysteria was by no means seen as the preserve of upper-class women. The disorder had been more widespread in France than anywhere else in Europe, and it seemed to heed no social or sexual boundaries, despite the fact that the well-known French psychiatrist Jean Martin Charcot, former director of the famous mental institution La Salpêtrière, had called hysteria *la grande simulation*.[421] This same Charcot, who nevertheless believed there was a relationship between hysteria and invisible damage to the central nervous system, was accused of causing the epidemic of hysteria. After his death in 1893, Déjerine taking his place at La Salpêtrière, it became generally accepted, mainly because of the zealotry of his adversary Babinski of La Pitié Hospital, that Charcot had not simply carried out scientific research into hysteria but had given it status. People had started to suffer from hysteria not because they were sick but because they thought they were. As Babinski would claim during the war, it was not a question of simulation but of suggestion. His personal solution to this was a powerful counter-attack, the brusque treatment already described, which aimed to turn the psychological process around, making use among other things of electrical massage. The number of cases of hysteria did indeed fall quickly after this 'unmasking' and by the eve of war, hysteria had virtually disappeared.[422] Perhaps this explains why in France too the experts reverted to the theory of feminization.

420 Bourke, *Intimate History*, 253–4; Bourke, *Moral Economy*, 6; Bourke, *Dismembering the Male*, 117–18; Bourke, 'Effeminacy, ethnicity and the end of trauma', 59

421 Young, *Harmony of Illusions*, 57; Bourke, *Moral Economy*, 6

422 Binneveld, *Om de geest*, 98–9; Binneveld, 'Nederland en de oorlogsneurosen', 38; Kaufmann, 'Science as Cultural Practice', 129; Shepard, *War of Nerves*, 12; Gijswijt-Hofstra & Porter, *Cultures of Neurasthenia*, 1

## In summary: the character of military medicine

The examples of Rivers, Brock, Kirkwood, Goldstein and others do not alter the fact that what Remarque said of military medicine in general applies to military psychiatry in particular. In fact their cases tend to confirm it. As with slavery, it was not a matter of individuals but of the system, and that system was wrong in the eyes of many soldiers and therefore in the eyes of patients. The image of the doctor as torturer and the soldier as the victim of torture is an oversimplification, since many doctors and nurses undoubtedly took the patient's side. Yet there was a very good chance that sooner or later a patient would come up against a doctor who was more concerned about military imperatives than about medical needs, or more interested in intriguing experiments than in the welfare of his patients. Such doctors regarded the thoroughly practical approach of some officers at the front who, whenever they could, left behind in the trench any soldier who at that moment was clearly incapable of fulfilling his duty to attack, as 'mawkish humanitarianism', in the words of an RAMC officer during Third Ypres.[423] Their main concern was to achieve their 'quota of declarations of fitness' and to make sure that, whatever it took, around ninety per cent of the sick and wounded could be returned to active service. This was the success rate claimed by men like Kaufmann and Nonne, for example, and it led Hirschfeld to make the cynical remark that it would be nice to be able to attribute it entirely to their medical capabilities.[424]

It is important not to exaggerate the differences between doctors, whether patient-friendly versus army-friendly or analytical versus disciplinary. The fact that the methods used by disciplinary psychiatrists were based on animal experimentation is sufficient to indicate that the use of electricity was not new. The school in which harsh, painful methods were employed had existed for some time, in civilian as well as military medicine. Kaufmann, for example, had adopted his method from Wilhelm Erb, his teacher at Heidelberg where he worked in the 1900s. Like Nonne's hypnosis, the treatment had simply fallen into disuse and the war made its revival possible. The hysterical women of the late nineteenth century had been regarded with hostility and contempt, so why should the 'effeminate' or 'weak-willed' neurotic soldier be treated any differently?[425] If criticism in hindsight is justified, then it should not be targeted primarily at the methods used, as it was immediately after the war. Nor should it be restricted to the group represented by Kaufmann and Yealland. For all the differences between disciplinary and analytical psychiatrists, both applied their treatments mainly for military, political and economic reasons rather than on medical and humanitarian grounds. Rivers

423 Dunn, *The War*, 410; Keegan, *Face of Battle*, 270–71; Bourke, *Dismembering the Male*, 92; Sassoon, *Complete Memoirs*, 459–60

424 Hirschfeld, *Sittengeschichte*, 359; Whalen, *Bitter Wounds*, 95; Kaufmann, 'Science as Cultural Practice', 127; Lerner, *Hysterical Men* (2003), 89, 110

425 Young, *Harmony of Illusions*, 70; Leed, *No Man's Land*, 173; Higonnet, *Behind the Lines*, 65; Lerner, *Hysterical Men* (2003), 103–5

and men of his ilk knew that treatment was supposed to end with a signature under the words 'fit for front-line service', and in most cases they too had this in mind as the desired result.[426]

Kirkwood's story suggests that we should ask how free doctors were to choose their own path. Once we question whether, under the circumstances, the doctors could have acted in fundamentally different ways than they did, we begin to see how little choice they had. Even had they wanted to, there was a limit to the degree to which they could have treated their patients sympathetically. During his service as a military doctor, the famous psychologist Alfred Adler was all too well aware of the consequences of declaring a soldier healthy, in fact he was haunted by nightmares about soldiers he had returned to the front. But he could not have acted any differently. His function as a doctor in wartime, in the service of the War Ministry, did not allow him to act in any other way.[427] Belgian doctor Armand Colard came to the same conclusion. He regretted for the rest of his life every occasion on which he had handed over to the military court a soldier who was simulating illness, but there had been no other option open to him.[428] The medical profession was not in any sense independent. Anyone who was too 'lenient' would be removed from his post. One of the officers responsible in Kirkwood's case, for example, said:

> Sympathy for sick and wounded men under his treatment is a good attribute for a doctor but it is not for an M.O. [medical officer] to inform a C.O. [commanding officer] that his men are not in a fit state to carry out a military operation. The men being in the front line should be proof that they are fit for any duty called for.[429]

We should not forget that financial support for research and therapy was firmly linked to the desirability of the results from a military point of view. This is one reason why we should not become too fixated on those military-medical films in which unsparing use is made of electrical currents, after which the lame walk and the dumb speak. The films were made at least in part as propaganda, to convince the military high command that money was being well spent and more funds should be made available.[430]

These are chiefly theoretical notes in the margin. The main point is that like the majority of doctors and nurses, the bulk of psychiatrists, psychologists and neurologists neither saw nor felt there was any conflict between their medical and military tasks. Mentally or physically wounded soldiers had to be healed, and

426 Binneveld, *Om de geest*, 150–51

427 Vondung, *Kriegserlebnis*, 105–6

428 Evrard & Mathieu, *Asklepios*, 263

429 Bourke, *Dismembering the Male*, 94; Bourke, *Intimate History*, 263; Bourke, *Moral Economy*, 9; Shepard, *War of Nerves*, 43

430 Lerner, *Hysterical Men* (2003), 86–7

healing meant they had to be made fit for active service. Many people undoubtedly objected to this, on grounds of medical ethics, but there were just as many whose aims were entirely in accord with those of the high command, among them, although by no means exclusively, those who had worked as army doctors before the war. They regarded not the sick and wounded but their commanding officers as their clients, and their medical procedures were guided by the wishes of the high command.[431] It was because of this feature of medical care in wartime that several thousand British Quakers not only refused active service but, as one of them put it, 'did not wish to embark for the quiet waters of the auxiliary ambulance service'.[432] They preferred prison, with the high possibility of mistreatment that went with it, to service in the Friends' Ambulance Unit.

John Ellis believes the fact that various military offensives, although comparable in magnitude, casualty rate and horror, produced vastly different numbers of psychiatric casualties indicates that doctors were primarily concerned with returning men to the front. Were the soldiers of Third Ypres – with officially just over 7,000 British shell-shock cases – so much more capable of standing up to the strain than those who had served a year earlier on the Somme, in a battle that produced more than 16,000 such patients? Obviously not. If anything the reverse. But the definition of shell shock had been adjusted, in order, Ellis claims, to keep the number of men who would have to be removed from active service in the trenches within bounds.[433]

It has to be said that Ellis' comments are slightly simplistic. It was the complexity of the symptoms that made diagnosing neurosis so difficult in the short term. As we have seen, some doctors started to apply the term 'shell-shocked (wounded)' to every case they encountered. This meant that if more thorough examination indicated there was nothing seriously wrong with the man concerned and he was ordered to return to active service after a few days, he might well resist. He had been diagnosed as shell-shocked (wounded), and so he believed he was. He felt he had the right to be treated in a specialist hospital back home. Without any overt intention of malingering, a man would start to develop symptoms previously absent. The disease followed the diagnosis. This was one reason for the introduction in June 1917 of the term 'Not Yet Diagnosed (Nervous)'. Premature diagnosis had to be avoided. NYD(N) was intended as a provisional diagnosis, but in practice it often became the only one. At the same time, psychiatric clinics were established close to the front, so that (the flight) into shell shock no longer automatically meant a trip across the English Channel.[434] The new terminology – in which the word 'proximity' was increasingly important – and the reorganization of the chain of aid stations and hospitals that accompanied it were not simply intended to limit

431 Bourke, *Intimate History*, 262; Bourke, *Moral Economy*, 9

432 Heering, *Zondeval*, 102; Haas, *Oorlogsjammer*, 15; Sassoon, *Complete Memoirs*, 511

433 Ellis, *Eye-Deep*, 119; Shepard, 'Shell-Shock', 40

434 Young, *Harmony of Illusions*, 52–3; Shepard, 'Shell-Shock', 40

the number of cases of shell shock, to return neurotic soldiers to the front line more quickly, or to obstruct claims for war pensions. They at least also were an attempt at a medical answer to a real medical problem.[435]

Yet even when the diagnosis NYD(N) was introduced, after years of experience with the psychological effects of war, neurotics were still regarded with suspicion, especially in the higher circles of military medicine. This too gave rise to change. Rivers told Sassoon that the local Director of Medical Services said he had never recognized shell shock and never would recognize it.[436] In 1918 Rivers expressed indignation at the fact that many psychiatrists still assumed the war had at most been a spark that caused a latent insanity to erupt, that all the conditions for madness had already been present in the shell-shocked patient before the war.[437]

It was therefore not for medical reasons alone that the new system – a month's observation a short distance behind the front line during which it would become clear who was genuinely sick or wounded and who was not – led to fewer than one in five soldiers being moved on for further treatment. More than half did not even stay the full month, and many were sent back to active service almost immediately.[438] This was due at least in part to the refusal of many army officers, medical officers among them, to see the emotional problems known as neuroses as either sicknesses or wounds. Although the Battle of the Somme had demonstrated that special medical care was necessary, many continued to believe that shell shock indicated either malingering or weakness of character. The attitude of doctors is illustrated by the fact that even the new system was regarded by many medical officers as too lenient towards soldiers with mental problems. They felt that the opening of specialist hospitals close to the front meant a welcome refuge was being established, an invitation to the men to report sick.[439]

If we interpret Ellis to mean that the term NYD(N) and treatment close to the front were not a purely medical answer to a purely medical problem then he is right. The proximity of treatment did have an apparently beneficial effect on psychiatric patients, but the military setting in which it took place left little room for doubt as to the aim that lay behind it: return to active service, which proximity would make possible all the quicker.

Of the well over 5,000 mental cases admitted to Casualty Clearing Station no. 62 during the Third Battle of Ypres, only 16 per cent were transferred to base hospitals and only ten per cent shipped back to Britain. The organic way of thinking contained in the term shell shock allowed soldiers to see their psychological problems as symptoms of wounding rather than of illness. Mental problems too, therefore, must surely entitle them to medals or pensions. From the point of view

435 Liddle, *Passchendaele in Perspective*, 193; Macdonald, *Roses of No Man's Land*, 218–19

436 Babington, *Shell-Shock*, 96, 104

437 Hermans & Schmidt, 'De traumatische neurose', 536

438 Chielens, 'Bekrachtigd, genoteerd, uitgevoerd', 8

439 Liddle, *Passchendaele in Perspective*, 193–4

of the state, the abandonment of the organic way of thinking and with it terms such as shell shock would have the positive effect of considerably reducing the number of successful pension applications. Many commentators go so far as to insist that the need to control a significant medical problem was not the real reason behind the change of direction that took place during the war, away from the identification of physical causes of neurosis and towards a focus on its psychological and pre-war origins, as indicated for example by changes in medical terminology. For all the qualifications they place upon the claim, the true motivation, many argue, alongside the need to sustain a given level of manpower, was the desire to minimize the financial burden of future war pensions.[440]

440 Bleker & Schmiedebach, *Medizin und Krieg*, 218; Liddle, *Passchendaele in Perspective*, 194; Hermans & Schmidt, 'De traumatische neurose', 536; Bourke, *Dismembering the Male*, 118; Shepard, *War of Nerves*, 151

# Chapter 5
# Death

I used to think, 'It is awful to die,'
But who knows what compliance the years will bring?
What is awful is to die young.

Enid Bagnold, *A Diary Without Dates*

## Introduction

War is about strategy and tactics, about politics, technology and culture, about class and sex; war is about everything, but above all it is about killing and being killed. This chapter focuses on physical death, in other words not the metaphorical death of the old pre-war world, whether its passing was mourned or not, nor the symbolic death that flowed from defeat, as described by Alfred Hoche, for example, a German nationalist professor of psychiatry and one of Hermann Oppenheim's earliest and fiercest opponents, who would become famous several years later as one of the authors of *Die Freigabe der Vernichtung lebensunwerten Lebens* (Allowing the Destruction of Life Unworthy of Life). In a talk entitled 'Vom Sterben' (On Dying), which he gave shortly before the war ended, Hoche argued that only with the approaching defeat would German soldiers killed in the war truly die. He claimed that to die at that moment would mean a different kind of death, a more terrible death, than in the advance of summer 1914.[1] The obvious question here is whether the reverse also applies. Was the death of a French or British soldier in the final months of the war a death more glorious, a death with a smile on the lips, compared to an ignominious death in August and September 1914?

There is one fundamental problem in studying physical death. We have plenty of descriptions to enable us to form an image of death in the Great War, but everything ever written about death suffers from the major shortcoming that it tells us only about the experiences of survivors. We can only guess at the tribulations, the final thoughts and emotions of those who were killed. Did they feel hatred towards the survivors? Did they resign themselves to their fate? Did they resist to their last breath? Did they curse the war? Did they speak to God with every ounce of strength that remained to them? We have only second-hand evidence. Unless

1 Hoche, *Vom Sterben*, 1, 21–2; Micale & Lerner, *Traumatic Pasts*, 150–51; Lerner, 'Psychiatry and Casualties of War', 15; Schmidt, *Karl Brandt: The Nazi Doctor*, 33–7

we accept séances as a source of scientifically valid evidence, these are questions we can never resolve.

As we saw in the first chapter of this book, death in the trenches and on the battlefield was rarely a matter of personal choice even to the degree it had been in earlier wars, and still was in that anachronism of the First World War, the desert battle. Technology had defeated human will and courage. A man was rarely killed because he faced a mentally and physically superior opponent. Death did not come from close by but from far away. A man did not look death in the eye; it was a great unknown far beyond the horizon. You could hardly ever choose death. It chose you. Death had become impersonal,[2] and hideous. Around half the men who died were mutilated beyond recognition.[3]

Even more than conditions in the trenches, it was the considerable likelihood of being killed that made soldiers feel there was a huge gulf between them and people working in safety behind the lines. The ubiquitous presence of death led them to describe the front as an island with its own volcanic eruptions, surrounded by a sea of peace. This image, although understandable, is not quite accurate. With the constant stream of men marching up to the front line or stumbling away from it, a better metaphor might be that of a peninsula. The many letters home meant that despite all the censorship, civilians who chose not to close their eyes could gain a clear impression of the horrors played out at the front, although there was always a considerable difference between knowledge and experience, between hearing and understanding. It is important to note that for all the estrangement he may have felt, 'home' remained a soldier's paradise and he wanted to be informed about it constantly. Stéphane Audoin-Rouzeau and Annette Becker point out that some men even ran their professional and family affairs from a distance, which indicates that life in the vacuum of norms and values at the front was not incompatible with engagement with the old system of norms from the days before August 1914.[4]

Despite all the technology and all the hatred, the chances of surviving even the bloodiest battles – aside from a few exceptional engagements within them – were always greater than the chances of dying. In some particularly ferocious confrontations up to 30 per cent died, but the figure was generally far lower.[5] It goes without saying that the chances of being killed rose the more time a man spent in the trenches. He might survive many battles, but few survived the whole war. Very few indeed shared the happy fate of Barthas, who served at the front throughout the war and came through with barely a scratch. When he was admitted to hospital in the spring of 1918 it was for deathly exhaustion after 4 years of almost continual front-line service. This cumulative effect led to a final death toll of around 15 per

---

2 Hynes, *Soldiers' Tale*, 70

3 Chickering, *Imperial Germany*, 101; Keegan, *First World War*, 451

4 Liddle & Cecil, *Facing Armageddon*, 223, 225–6; Bourke, *Dismembering the Male*, 21–2; Holmes, *Firing Line*, 276; Andriessen, *De oorlogsbrieven van Unteroffizier Carl Heller*, 77, 91; Audoin-Rouzeau & Becker, *'14–'18*, 55–6

5 Ellis, *Eye-Deep*, 106, 116; Whalen, *Bitter Wounds*, 40

cent of those mobilized and almost 20 per cent of men who had ever served in the front line. The death rate among British males in the war years was 7 to 8 times higher than normal and in France up to 10 times higher. In Germany almost 13 per cent of the 15.6 million men born between 1870 and 1899 died in the 4 years and 3.5 months of the war. This is an astonishingly high percentage, but even more remarkable is the fact that of German males born between 1892 and 1895, who were aged between 19 and 22 in 1914, some 35 to 37 per cent did not live to see 11 November 1918.[6]

Many died slow painful deaths, but most were dead before they realized they had been hit.[7] Large numbers were simply assumed dead, because it was considered impossible that they could have survived wounds they were known to have received, or because someone thought he had seen them dead. Cases of mistaken identity were common. Graves was once declared dead erroneously, Feilding no fewer than four times.[8] Their families were informed in error. Other families had to live with uncertainty for months, after which they were frequently told that a son, brother or husband had been killed, but not where, when or how.[9]

Most messages sent to inform the next of kin of the fate of loved ones who were in hospital were form letters. They gave little if any details as to the nature and seriousness of wounds, and letters or telegrams informing families of a death were not exactly models of clarity either. An official missive would tell of a noble soldier or officer who, in fulfilling his duty to the fatherland on the field of honour, had died a quick, painless and above all heroic death, and who while he lived had been a shining example to others by his high spirits and courage.[10] The truth, it was felt, would only make the loss harder to bear. A family's grief would be terrible enough without all the distressing details.

These letters were unlikely to mention that, for example, far from dying a heroic death on the battlefield, a man had been shot by a sniper while using the latrine. Only rarely would relatives read of the harsh reality, like Bernard Pitt's widow. He had been killed in an explosion. 'We have been unable to find a trace of him since.' Most officers reasoned the way Arthur Agius did when called upon to tell Harold Scarlett's widow about a similar fate five months after her wedding. He wrote that Scarlett had been killed doing his duty and had been buried at the spot where he died.[11] We may wonder whether such reticence did in fact help, not least because people on the home front quickly learned to see through the standard

---

6 Whalen, *Bitter Wounds*, 40–41; Keegan, *First World War*, 452–3

7 Winter, *Death's Men*, 204–5

8 Winter, *Death's Men*, 247

9 De Schaepdrijver, *De Groote Oorlog*, 117

10 See for instance: *Kriegsbriefe gefallener Deutscher Juden*, 84–5; March, *Company K*, 63–4

11 Gilbert, *First World War*, 240; Macdonald, *Somme*, 259–60; Winter, *Sites of Memory*, 29

phrases. Eugène Lemercier wrote the usual letter to one Madame L., but he still feared it would come as a blow from which she would never recover.[12]

Letters written in reply by the bereaved reinforce doubts about the standard approach. Ethel Bath had been married for three weeks when her husband was killed. Bath had been sent to the front and was killed there. 'It is a small comfort to know he gave his life in a successful attack. … I am very proud of my boy but at the same time it grieves me dreadfully to think those boys are given such a small chance to show their true grit.'[13] Florence Scarlett too wrote back.

> I wish to take this opportunity of thanking you for your kind letter of sympathy, and for the few details you were able to give me concerning my dear husband's death. The sad news was a terrible shock to me, and, up till now, I have felt too ill to write to you, although I have been eager to do so.'[14]

Parents wrote letters begging to have their only remaining son withdrawn from the front line. There was Private Stream's mother, for example, driven almost insane by the loss of two of her three sons. His commanding officer promised he would be sent into the back area the next time his unit came out of the line. It was impossible to fulfil her request immediately. A few days later he became the only fatality of that tour of duty.[15] Edmund Knoellinger's mother wrote to the German War Ministry asking to have him, the last of her three boys, withdrawn from front-line combat. The ministry agreed to her request, but Edmund himself refused. 'My brothers went to their deaths as heroes – and I am to seek shelter? Never!' By mid-October 1917 Frau Knoellinger had no sons left.[16]

The news was brought by a variety of means. Families could often read on the postman's face the nature of the message he was about to deliver. In small villages in France the mayor himself was often charged with this difficult task; elsewhere there were the black-clad ladies of the *Commission du Devoir*. In Britain the news came by letter in the case of an ordinary soldier and by telegram if the deceased had been an officer. Occasionally the family was given the bad news by telephone. In a few cases an open letter was published in a local newspaper because the number of casualties from a single area, as a result of the Pals Battalions system, was too great for everyone to be informed personally at the same time. In Australia a man of the cloth came to visit. Sometimes he simply had a letter with him, sent by a man's parents or wife, on which the word 'deceased' had been written. Sometimes word came not long after the man was killed, but often it took some time, and there might even be several years of uncertainty as to which of various contradictory messages was true and therefore whether a loved one was among the

12 Lemercier, *Lettres*, 151
13 Macdonald, *Somme*, 291–2
14 Macdonald, *Somme*, 292
15 Winter, *Death's Men*, 131; Fussell, *Great War*, 45
16 Witkop, *Kriegsbriefe*, 333–4

missing, the captured, or the dead. In some cases the uncertainty lasted until long after the armistice.

Organizations were set up to help family members and it was clear from the start that little could be expected from the army or the government, although in Germany 'mourning centres' were established with state funds. The bereaved found their own ways of coping and supported others in the same situation. If they were lucky they might receive help from bodies that could mediate between the individual and the state, the nascent Red Cross being the most obvious example. It is striking that in contrast to most official letters, those from Red Cross organizations usually called a spade a spade. If there was any room for doubt, this was conveyed to the family; if there was none, the family was told the truth. If a relative had died a terrible death, the Red Cross did not conceal the fact under layers of euphemism.[17]

The chances of dying were higher than in any previous war, but it was the unpredictability of death that assured the First World War a distinctive place in military history. Nowhere was a man safe, at any time. Good and bad luck determined who lived and who died. Although the chances of survival were higher than the chances of dying, courage, stamina and skill made less difference than ever. Westman left his company for a moment to relieve himself. A shell exploded amongst his comrades. The pack on which he had been resting his head was pierced by a shell fragment.[18] An officer serving with Moran survived the Battle of Hooge in August 1915 but was beheaded by a splinter from a stray shell, the only one to have landed anywhere in the vicinity for several days.[19] Historian Denis Winter's father saw a man shot in the abdomen miles behind the front line. A bullet had ignited in the heat of a brazier used to burn waste. Dearden saw a man whose stomach had been blown out as he was chopping down a tree. He had missed the tree and hit a buried hand grenade. A British cook made a fire directly above a dud shell that had sunk into the mud of the Ypres salient. He was taken to an aid post gravely wounded and there was little chance he would live.[20]

Even though more men survived than died, even though more were wounded than killed, the fact that pure chance determined who lived and who died, along with the sheer numbers, meant that the front was synonymous with death. Louis Mairet wrote on 10 March 1917, shortly before his own demise:

> Death! that word which booms like the echo of sea caverns, striking and restriking in dark and unseen depths. Between this war and the last, we did not die: we ended. Neatly, in the shelter of a room, in the warmth of a bed. Now we

---

17 Winter, *Sites of Memory*, 31–44; Winter & Baggett, *1914–18*, 15, 187; Whalen, *Bitter Wounds*, 74; 'Jahrhundert der Kriege', 108

18 Holmes, *Firing Line*, 193

19 Holmes, *Riding the Retreat*, 191; Winter, *Death's Men*, 131

20 Macdonald, *Passchendaele*, 218

> die. It is the wet death, the muddy death, death dripping with blood, death by drowning, death by sucking under, death in the slaughterhouse.[21]

Jack Brown felt infuriated when a padre at a dressing station during the Battle of the Somme asked whether they had seen anyone killed. 'See anybody get killed! I should say we did!'[22]

It is not just the more-or-less objectively quantifiable deaths that determine our image of the war, not merely the deaths recorded in casualty lists, medical reports and statistics but the experience of living amid death. It was death with a capital D, Death whom men saw wandering the battlefield with a scythe in his hands, a constantly present, tangible, visible, all-pervasive, stinking, dispiriting Death. Death would permeate the area for all time. Death held the living too in his clutches, since a man might confront him at any moment, even if he did not fall victim himself.[23]

## Death outside of battle

### *'Ordinary' losses*

It was clear from the start that death would not be confined to the battlefield. Because the enemy was invisible, Dorgelès called even dying in battle 'death without combat'. In so-called lulls in the fighting, periods when it was 'all quiet on the Western Front', the casualty figures were so high that those of today's battles seem negligible by comparison.[24] British GHQ estimated that in 6 months of major offensives they could reckon on more than 500,000 casualties and in 6 months of 'ordinary' trench warfare 300,000.[25] Whole companies were virtually wiped out in periods when they were required merely to hold the line, with no significant fighting at all.[26] At Ypres alone on such days the British might suffer 300 deaths.[27] Augustin Cochin, a French officer, spent five days in the trenches at the Mort Homme in April 1916, of which 'the last two days soaked in icy mud, under terrible bombardment, without any shelter other than the narrowness of the trench.' He had arrived there with 175 men; he left with 34, 'several half mad … not replying any more when I spoke to them'.[28]

---

21 Eksteins, *Rites of Spring*, 153
22 Macdonald, *Somme*, 150
23 Whalen, *Bitter Wounds*, 37
24 Dorgelès, *Croix de bois*, 221; Eksteins, *Rites of Spring*, 155
25 Ellis, *Eye-Deep*, 61
26 Winter, *Death's Men*, 90
27 Keegan, *Face of Battle*, 208
28 Keegan, *First World War*, 305–6

This enabled the high command to gloss over the casualty figures while their offensives lasted. In July 1916 on the Somme and in October 1917 at Ypres, 150,000 and 110,000 British soldiers respectively lost either their lives, their limbs or their minds. Still, the high command and the war cabinet argued, even in an average month 35,000 men were carried either to the grave or to hospital and therefore the true losses were 'only' 115,000 and 75,000, which could not be regarded as excessive.[29] They were referring to 'normal wastage', men killed or wounded because they happened to be standing at the spot where a shell landed, because they lit a cigarette and were spotted by a sniper, because they were buried alive and unable to wriggle out, or because a rifle went off while they were cleaning it.[30] The high command and the politicians neglected to mention that casualty figures featured a much higher proportion of wounded to killed in normal wastage than during a battle.[31] As we have seen, it made little difference from a military point of view whether a man was sick, wounded or dead.

### *Accidents and snipers*

A considerable proportion of normal wastage was attributable to accidents. With so many shells and grenades stored in confined spaces there were many dangers besides the deliberate firing of rifles and artillery pieces. In the German army alone more than 55,000 men were accidentally killed.[32] Fatal accidents were usually the result of spontaneous explosions.[33] The products that poured out of the munitions factories were by no means always reliable. Barthas claimed that the French automatic pistol may have killed more Frenchmen than Germans.[34] In his essay '*Als Ich Blind Geschossen War...*' (When I was Blinded by a Shot), Hans Henning Freiherr Grote described what happened when he tried out a new kind of star shell.

> The instant I fired it, I was surrounded by a ghastly flaming hell, a deafening boom filled my ears, some kind of immense fist grabbed me by the chest and flung me from my fire-step deep into the clay at the bottom of the trench. I knew for certain that my body had been cleaved in two and my conscious mind floated numbly somewhere above the ruptured remains, about to disappear completely at any moment.

29 Prior & Wilson, *Passchendaele*, 186; Macdonald, *Somme*, 178
30 Horne, *Price of Glory*, 61; Winter, *Death's Men*, 149
31 Macdonald, *Somme*, 179
32 Whalen, *Bitter Wounds*, 42
33 Winter, *Death's Men*, 111
34 Barthas, *Carnets*, 522

Grote was lucky. He was only temporarily blinded and unable to speak. He heard later that others had been killed or seriously wounded.[35]

Blunden described an accident at Étaples in the spring of 1916 in which an instructor and several others were killed when a rifle grenade exploded prematurely. It was a case of pride coming before a fall. The instructor had told the men a moment earlier that he had been in Étaples since the beginning of the war and nothing had ever gone wrong.[36]

Not all munitions came from factories. All manner of explosive devices were assembled at the front. In the early months of the war, British trench mortars were extremely amateurish improvisations, little more than jam tins filled with high explosives that were quite likely to go off prematurely.[37] Lieutenant Rory MacLeod told of a demonstration with trench mortars at Neuve Chapelle in the winter of 1915. The British had no factory-made trench mortars as yet but the Germans did, so it was felt advisable to practise by testing the effectiveness of some self-made products. The fourth device exploded in the bore. Fourteen men were killed and forty wounded.[38]

The frequency of accidents was partly a result of the unrelieved stress of life in the trenches, stress rarely punctuated by the excitement of battle but exacerbated by long periods of inactivity and boredom. Men knew they had to be vigilant at all times, but no one could remain alert for days, weeks, months on end.[39] The unremitting tension, along with the continual handling of explosives that made the hazards seem ordinary, led to carelessness in place of caution.[40] Graves writes of a man who threw a percussion bomb but aimed too low. The bomb hit the edge of the breastwork instead of going over it, blasted back and killed him.[41] A sergeant decided to demonstrate how dangerous a percussion grenade could be, a demonstration that could not have been more vivid. He rapped the edge of a table with it, killing himself and the man standing next to him instantly. Twelve others were wounded, several seriously.[42]

A major accident took place at Verdun. On 4 September 1916 a munitions depot exploded in a railway tunnel and more than five hundred French troops living there were blown to pieces or burned alive. One of the few survivors described how 'a shattered body flew into me, or rather poured over me. I saw, three metres away, men twisting in the flames without being able to render them any help. Legs,

35 Jünger, *Antlitz*, 220–21
36 Blunden, *Undertones of War*, 18
37 Simkins, *World War I*, 88–9
38 Macdonald, *1914–1918*, 64
39 Winter, *Death's Men*, 89
40 Jünger, *In Stahlgewittern*, 38
41 Graves, *Goodbye*, 84
42 Graves, *Goodbye*, 159

arms, flew in the air amid the explosion of the grenades which went off without cease.'[43]

This was not even the most devastating accident of the war. Several months earlier, on 8 May 1916, hundreds of German soldiers had died in an explosion at Fort Douamont. Westman was there and described what he saw.

> I could feel how the whole fort shook when a particularly heavy shell, most probably with a delayed action fuse, landed and exploded. … Afterwards I strolled through the fort, with its many dug-outs and casements. The entrance to one of them was bricked up and someone had fixed a plaque, with the inscription, 'Here rest 1052 German soldiers' – a whole battalion, who were sleeping in that casemate. Apparently one of them had smoked, and barrels of fuel for flame-throwers, which were stored there, had exploded, and not a single soul had survived.[44]

Most of the casualties of this incident were burned alive, but some died when hand grenades were thrown at them by fellow soldiers who thought they were under attack from black French colonial troops. By the time they realized the men were fellow Germans with their faces scorched black it was too late – the grenades had set off further stores of munitions, this time shells, some containing gas, which raised the death toll considerably. There is no way of knowing whether the figure of 1,052 is accurate. Other sources speak of 700 casualties and inside the fort a notice currently gives the number as 650. Ultimately it makes little difference. They were many. In the wide passageways Dr Hallauer saw

> young infantrymen sitting on the ground sunk in apathy next to the wounded and others evidently mentally disturbed. In the tunnels down to the bunkers lay bodies and body parts: torsos, arms, legs, all black and covered in dust. ... In the corner they lay piled up three or four high, some seeming to be stuck to the wall.[45]

Death from sniper fire was certainly no accident. The best marksmen on both sides were concealed at strategic places along the front, lying in wait until someone put his head above the parapet, if only by a couple of inches. Their accuracy was terrifying, their patience angelic. Jünger spoke of a soldier hit in the centre of his forehead. It was the only shot heard in several hours. Lieutenant Fenton of the Cameronians made the mistake of looking over the parapet of a trench twice in the same place and was hit the second time by two snipers at once. Marksman Turner was hit by his German counterpart in his aiming eye, the one he used to

43 Gilbert, *First World War*, 284–5

44 Winter & Baggett, *1914–1918*, 163

45 Brants & Brants, *Velden van weleer*, 220; Werth, *Verdun*, 286–90; Johannsen, *Vier von der Infanterie*, 57–8; Runia, *Waterloo Verdun Auschwitz*, 142

peer through the sights to target his next victim. Turner's colleague MacBride kept a diary, and it demonstrates yet again that men were not always reluctant to take human life: 'December 9th, 1915. Hazy. Cool. One leaning against tree. *Tué*. One fifty yards right. Fell across log. Shot three successive helpers. … December 16th, 1916. Clear. Fine. Good hunting. Sixteen good shots. Seven known hits and feel sure of four more.'[46]

Of course the number of casualties as a result of this kind of patient, individual killing pales into insignificance beside the total, but snipers rarely missed and they were present always and everywhere. In December 1915, 3,285 British soldiers were wounded in fourteen days and about a quarter had wounds to the head and neck. More than likely many of them had been hit by sniper fire. Snipers usually worked from nests behind the front line, but some wore camouflage and took up positions in no man's land. They were like gas in the sense that their psychological effect was many times greater than might be assumed from the number of casualties caused. The constant mortal fear felt by the troops was disproportionately attributable to them. As a result they were targeted in much the same way as flame-throwing sections were. The discovery of a sniper did not meet with a flexible response but with massive retaliation,[47] so they were hated not only by the enemy but by their own side. As with gas, therefore, the number of casualties caused indirectly by snipers is a good deal higher than the number of direct hits. Sniper Billy Howell admitted that no one liked them.

> The men loathed us, and the officers hated us. They could not order us out of their sector. The trouble was, we would watch through a loophole for hours, and when we were absolutely sure of a target, we would fire. No other firing went on without an order, and Jerry knew it was a sniper, and he would let everything he had loose on that section. Of course we hightailed it out, as fast as our legs would carry us, and poor old Tommy had to take it.[48]

### *Prisoners of war*

We have already noted that prisoners of war cannot generally be regarded as casualties. Many soldiers did not want to be captured, or felt ashamed at being caught and tried to escape, like the man who would later become the most famous of all First World War prisoners, Charles de Gaulle. Whatever else it might bring, captivity meant hardship and the loss of freedom. The latter in particular was often experienced as a great psychological burden and could even lead to what was sometimes called 'barbed-wire neurosis'. Osburn wrote with enormous resentment

---

46 Winter, *Death's Men*, 91

47 Ellis, *Eye-Deep*, 68–70; Binneveld, *Om de geest*, 65; Winter, *Death's Men*, 90, 205; Jünger, *In Stahlgewittern*, 94; Macdonald, *Passchendaele*, 207

48 Richter, *Chemical Soldiers*, 222; Bourke, *Intimate History*, 67

about British soldiers who allowed themselves to be taken prisoner during the retreat in the opening months of the war.

> Once taken prisoner under circumstances for which they could not very strictly be blamed, they would naturally think themselves safe; at least safe from being roused at three o'clock in the morning; safe from forced marches with an eighty-pound pack on their backs; safe from any more pitched battles with the possibility of death and mutilation. … Suddenly released from all discipline, with no adjutant or sergeant-major to shout or threaten … they could hurl their burdensome packs into the nearest ditch and wait until the German advance patrols … arrive[d] and they could comfortably surrender.[49]

As the war went on, Osburn began to have far more sympathy with men who chose this course of action. He became an opponent of the war, not unlike Siegfried Sassoon, and he gave the term 'prisoner of war' a different interpretation, as did Barthas, Latzko and others: not those who had surrendered but those still on active service at the front line were prisoners, Osburn said. They were 'prisoners of the war'.[50] In a conversation with Stefan Zweig, Rainer Maria Rilke went even further. The war itself was a prison. It kept everyone within its walls, soldiers and civilians alike.[51] Few will have given much thought to these alternative meanings of the term, but the fact remains that there were many, if always a minority, to whom the idea of safety in a prisoner of war camp seemed inviting. The notion of 'voluntary capture' is a myth, and one that made many prisoners of war furious, but it is a myth with some basis in truth. Soldiers preferred to be prisoners of war than to fight on in the face of almost certain death. Unless they were convinced they would be mistreated or executed on the spot, surrender represented an alternative to futile combat. When the conflict became a war of movement again, many put their hands up after offering only token resistance, first on the Allied side, later in even larger numbers among German troops.[52]

In general, soldiers who surrendered were treated well and had little to fear (unless they were tank crews or snipers, or members of gas or flame-throwing sections).[53] They had endured the same sufferings as their captors, who might meet the same fate any day. Sympathetic treatment can be attributed to self-interest rather than altruism. Poor treatment of those who surrendered would have

---

49 Holmes, *Riding the Retreat*, 196–7; Audoin-Rouzeau & Becker, *'14–'18*, 111–12, 116

50 Latzko, *Friedensgericht*, 258–9; March, *Company K*, 84; Winter & Baggett, *1914–18*, 246

51 Zweig, *Die Welt von Gestern*, 174–5

52 Holmes, *Firing Line*, 324; Barthas, *Carnets*, 404; Johannsen, *Vier von der Infanterie*, 49; *Van den Grooten oorlog*, 183; Audoin-Rouzeau & Becker, *'14–'18*, 115, 117; De Bruyne, *We zullen ze krijgen!*, 203

53 Holmes, *Firing Line*, 386–7; Keegan, *First World War*, 390; Dunn, *The War*, 407

rebounded, so fate was usually well-disposed towards them, especially if they quickly transformed themselves from soldiers into men by removing their tin hats or gas masks and holding up crucifixes or photos of wives and children. There was no absolute guarantee, however.[54] It was important to surrender immediately and to signal the fact unambiguously. If there was any doubt about a man's intentions – 'he … asked for mercy but his eyes said murder' – his opponent would take no chances.[55] An order from British GHQ during the Battle of the Somme stated that all troops had a duty to use their weapons against the enemy,

> until it is beyond all doubt that these have not only ceased all resistance, but … that they have definitely and finally abandoned all hope or intention of resisting further. In the case of apparent surrender, it lies with the enemy to prove his intention beyond the possibility of misunderstanding, before the surrender can be accepted as genuine.

The fear of a failed surrender was further nourished by naturally rather sad stories told by returned prisoners of war. Together with the existence of so-called 'mopping up parties' – soldiers who, often having volunteered to do so, finished off any men who had survived in captured enemy trenches – they suggest that for all the benevolence they were often shown, First World War prisoners could be described as men fortunate enough to have survived their surrender.[56]

This indicates that in most cases life as a prisoner of war did not begin with a free choice but as the only option left to a man who wanted to save his own skin. On 29 September 1916 on the Somme, Fritz Heinemann suddenly noticed 'as far as we could see' British soldiers moving towards him and his comrades at a trot.

> Our front line must have been completely torn up by the frightful shelling for we had not heard any rifle or machine-gun fire. Facing the oncoming wave, we could not think of getting up to run to the rear. We would have been shot down like rabbits. And staying to defend the place was as good as committing suicide.[57]

By the time his company had been marched off into captivity, only two officers and twelve men were left out of several hundred troops.[58]

Once captured they were still far from safe. First of all they might be taken for enemy soldiers by a second wave. Next came the hazard of shells fired from their own side, which fell behind enemy lines across a wide area; it was not uncommon

54 Holmes, *Firing Line*, 381–3

55 Zuckmayer, *Als wär's ein Stück von mir*, 230; Winter, *Death's Men*, 213–14

56 March, *Company K*, 79–86, 145, 154; Holmes, *Firing Line*, 384; Macdonald, *Somme*, 288–9; Audoin-Rouzeau & Becker, *'14–'18*, 60, 117

57 Macdonald, *1914–1918*, 171

58 Macdonald, *1914–1918*, 173

for prisoners to be killed by their own artillery fire, along with their escorts.[59] Thirdly they might become the victims of revenge for an act their own armed forces had committed. The Canadians, for example, killed their German prisoners after the first gas attack at Ypres on 22 April 1915.[60] Behind enemy lines, prisoners relied on medical services that would always give priority to the home side. Barthas once had to go looking for a doctor because a German prisoner was seriously ill. The doctor refused 'to go out of his way for a Boche. If he "snuffed it" they'd simply have to carry the carcass off to the dump.'[61] This attitude, which was usually not the result of unwillingness, as here, but of the appalling shortage of medical staff, must go some way to explaining the deaths of more than 50,000 German prisoners of war. The supply of food was so poor that starvation, sometimes in combination with cold, ended more than one prisoner's life. This applied mainly to those held by the Germans, who became victims of their own blockade.[62] Nevertheless, the chances of survival at the front line were far smaller.

From time to time there were exchanges of German and British prisoners of war, men so badly wounded that it was clear they could never be returned to active service. These exchanges took place via the neutral and strategically located Netherlands, which also declared itself willing, in an agreement signed on 2 July 1917, to intern 16,000 less seriously wounded soldiers, although this quota was never filled. The exchanges did not always go smoothly. The chaos during one embarkation at Rotterdam in early January 1918 was described as scandalous both in the Netherlands and internationally. Organizational failures were the main cause, although both British and Germans had supplied inaccurate information and should therefore bear part of the blame.[63]

Aside from their physical discomforts, prisoners were relatively lucky. Attitudes towards those who wanted to surrender were benevolent in the main, but many did not survive the moment of casting down their weapons, whether or not they were members of the most hated sections. Callous, indeed murderous behaviour towards soldiers who tried to surrender increased as the war went on, and it had not been entirely absent even in the early days of the conflict.[64] One experienced soldier, hardened by more than two years of war, broke down after escorting a number of German prisoners back behind the lines only to see them promptly shot by an officer who happened to notice them. This kind of outcome will usually have

59 Fussell, *Bloody Game*, 110; Keegan, *Face of Battle*, 278; Brown, *Somme*, 71; Johannsen, *Vier von der Infanterie*, 49

60 Wilson, *Myriad Faces*, 127

61 Barthas, *Carnets*, 32

62 Macdonald, *To the Last Man*, 358

63 De Roodt, 'Britse en Duitse krijgsgevangenen in Nederland', passim; Leclerq, *Het informatiebureau*, 125–7

64 Holmes, *Riding the Retreat*, 189–90, 218; Barbusse, *Le Feu*, 279; Macdonald, *Somme*, 281; Audoin-Rouzeau & Becker, *'14–'18*, 191

been a result of specific circumstances at the time. Jünger described the case of two British soldiers, food carriers, who had got lost.

> They approached perfectly serenely; one of them was carrying a large round container of food, the other a longish tea kettle. They were shot down at point-blank range; one of them landing with his upper body in the defile, while his legs remained on the slope. It was hardly possible to take prisoners in this inferno, and how could we have brought them back through the barrage in any case?[65]

Many soldiers had no opportunity to surrender. They were shot before they could make their intentions known. No one was about to look inside a bunker without throwing a hand grenade in first. The nature of the fighting made the taking of prisoners an uninviting prospect, which leads Holmes to comment that the amazing thing about the German army's Michael Offensive was not how many British soldiers were killed trying to surrender but how few.[66]

This was not due to the conditions alone, however. Soldiers were often too charged up to switch from intense concentration on killing to the idea of letting a man live. It is a problem integral to the nature of combat.[67] Men who had spent hours repeatedly emptying their rifles into attacking forces could not expect to be left in peace once their trenches were overwhelmed. The attackers wanted to kill them. They thought of nothing else and showed no mercy towards men who surrendered purely because they had not been able to kill everyone on the attacking side before their own positions were reached. Now it was their turn. Jünger went so far as to say that in such circumstances a soldier had no moral right to be shown mercy.[68]

The diary of Private Gallwey of the 27th Battalion, 4th Australian Division, illustrates the problem. Deployed frequently during Third Ypres, the mood of Gallwey and his comrades was none too cheerful towards the end of that battle. They came under sustained fire from the Germans as they waited for the order to attack. When they were finally given the signal to advance they faced heavy machine-gun fire from a bunker. The machine-gun was knocked out and Gallwey and his comrades forced their way into a block house where several German soldiers had crawled into a corner together.

> No time was lost here however and [our] … men fired point blank into the group. There was a noise as though pigs were being killed. They squealed and made guttural noises which gave place to groans after which all was silent. The bodies

---

65 Jünger, *In Stahlgewittern*, 75; *Storm of Steel*, 101; Brants, *Plasje bloed*, 107; Shepard, 'The Nerve Doctors', 16

66 Holmes, *Firing Line*, 382

67 Holmes, *Riding the Retreat*, 114

68 Holmes, *Riding the Retreat*, 218; Holmes, *Firing Line*, 381; Jünger, *In Stahlgewittern*, 203–4; Andriessen, *De oorlogsbrieven van Unteroffizier Carl Heller*, 211

> were all thrown in a heap outside the block house to make sure all were dead. There were five of them altogether. It was a good thing this hornets nest had been cleaned out so easily. Nearly all were young men.
>
> It is an impossibility to leave wounded germans [*sic*] behind us because they are so treacherous. They all have to be killed. Too often after an advance, our men have been shot in the back by the wounded they left on the field. Now to obviate such a thing, we have what is called a 'mopping up party'. This consists of a small number of troops and [they] despatch any of the enemy who might have been passed over in the first rush. Sometimes in our hurry we leave a wounded man and then the duty of the mopping up party is to finish him. Their work would be light today for we are determined to kill every german we come across.[69]

Machine-gunner Private J. Parkinson was taken prisoner by a German officer. He was amazed. He knew well enough what he would have done had he managed to enter a German machine-gun post uninjured with a revolver in his hand.[70] And Major John Stewart of the 9th Battalion of the Black Watch made abundantly clear in a letter to his wife that at Loos the Black Watch had taken '*very* few prisoners'.[71]

Personal revenge all too frequently explains the fatal shooting of unarmed opponents. W.H.A. Groom watched a group of Germans surrender only for a British soldier to shoot them in cold blood. 'That's for my brother.'[72] The desire for vengeance meant that earlier attitudes did not serve as a benchmark for later decisions. P.G. Bourne prevented fellow soldiers from killing a batch of German captives. Shortly afterwards one of his best friends was killed. The next time his own side advanced he was again confronted by German soldiers who wanted to lay down their arms, but this time Bourke had no mercy. Grief had turned to hatred, which expressed itself in a desire to kill.[73] Whether or not a man was still battle-fit was irrelevant. If someone felt a need to take revenge, a wounded enemy soldier had no chance. Men might even go looking for the wounded to finish them off.[74] Under cover of darkness they had an excellent chance of success. Graves tells of a German officer who walked across the battlefield shooting British casualties and of a British soldier who bayoneted a wounded German shouting 'In, out, on guard!', as if the wounded man were a sandbag during an exercise.[75]

---

69 Prior & Wilson, *Passchendaele*, 63–4

70 Keegan, *First World War*, 428

71 Liddle & Cecil, *Facing Armageddon*, 326

72 Holmes, *Firing Line*, 386

73 Wilson, *Myriad Faces*, 682–3

74 Graves, *Goodbye*, 112; see also the chapter 'Settling a Score' in: Sandstrom, *Comrades-in-Arms*, 146–53, esp. 152

75 Graves, *Goodbye*, 175

Sometimes soldiers who were taken prisoner discovered that their escort was not well disposed towards them. Graves claimed everyone had stories to tell of prisoners being killed on the way back behind the lines. He said the walk back offered the only opportunity to perpetrate atrocities against prisoners, which he felt were a quite different matter from atrocities committed in the heat of battle. They might be prompted by a longing for revenge, by fear, dissatisfaction with the job in hand, excessive soldierly enthusiasm, or by jealousy towards men who were being taken to a comfortable place far from the filth and the guns. It is rarely if ever possible to substantiate these stories. If prisoners failed to reach their destination they were invariably recorded as 'killed by artillery fire' and everyone was content.[76]

Graves wrote of a Canadian who, on the principle 'No good Fritzes but dead 'uns', had a group of German prisoners he was moving back covered with the pistol the officer among them had been carrying while he put a Mills bomb in each of their pockets, with the pin out. He also recounts a story told by an Australian who ordered German prisoners to hand over their valuables, then sent them down into a bunker and blew it up. 'We weren't taking prisoners that day.'[77] Richards spoke to a man who had been ordered to accompany a group of six German prisoners back down the line but was not in agreement with the plan, partly because of the heavy artillery fire and partly because a friend of his had just been killed who was worth as much as 'these six Jerries put together'. He was determined to rid himself of the prisoners as quickly as possible and he came back a short time later, smiling with satisfaction. He had not even needed to do it himself, since two bombs had got there before him – or so he said. Before he had gone another twenty yards he was hit by a shell fragment.[78]

Conditions like these meant that quite often a stray shot fired by someone who did not realize that his comrades had given up might be attributed to men who had already surrendered. The prisoners would then be killed immediately, before the full facts became clear. Sometimes a shot was fired by someone who was well aware of his comrades' plans, with the same result. It was not uncommon for a group of soldiers to disagree on whether to surrender or not. Those who wanted to go on fighting could settle the matter by firing just one round.[79]

We should bear in mind that prisoners had no military value. Most survived because people felt sorry for them, and because otherwise no one on either side could be confident of decent treatment if forced to surrender. To the Allies the Germans who surrendered were 'only Germans' and to the Germans the Allies were 'only Englishmen, only Frenchmen',[80] and soldiers would have to be sent to escort and guard prisoners, at the cost of manpower at the front. Captives consumed

76 Graves, *Goodbye*, 153–4
77 Graves, *Goodbye*, 154
78 Fussell, *Bloody Game*, 110
79 Keegan, *Face of Battle*, 48–9; Holmes, *Firing Line*, 383–4
80 Keegan, *Face of Battle*, 278; Macdonald, *Somme*, 289

valuable rations as well, which Graves saw as the reason the Germans, whose food shortages were far more acute than those of the Allies, had a greater tendency to kill prisoners than the British and French.[81] It followed quite naturally that prior to attacks agreements were sometimes made that no prisoners would be taken, not because the hatred was so great but because life was already hard enough without prisoners to deal with, or because having to take enemy soldiers back behind the lines through a barrage meant putting your own life in the balance unnecessarily. In the winter of 1917, L.M. Baldwin was among a group of stretcher-bearers who found a wounded German. He was saved only because Baldwin intervened. The other stretcher-bearers wanted to finish him off, since they felt it was too dangerous to carry him back under shellfire. They were willing to take that risk only for their own wounded.[82]

It was of course a different story if there was any hope that a captured soldier might be able to provide valuable information about enemy manoeuvres, troop concentrations and so forth, although even that did not necessarily mean he would be taken alive. If it was considered too dangerous to get wounded enemy soldiers back to the rear for interrogation, then attempts were made to gather information about the regiment and division to which they belonged to by cutting the badges off their uniforms. This could naturally be done more quickly and quietly if the casualty was dead. Graves thought this was one of the reasons why enemy wounded were killed almost as often as they were taken prisoner.[83]

Behaviour of this kind was understood by everyone, general or private, friend or foe. Allen recalled an event that took place during the Allied advance near the end of the war. A wounded German officer assured the British that there were no Germans left in a particular village. They gathered in the square in front of the church and were mown down by machine-gun fire. A corporal ran back to the German officer, who seemed to be expecting him, and 'his face did not flinch as the bayonet descended'.[84]

The killing of prisoners was not only universally understood but often sanctioned. Indeed the willingness to kill captives was seen as one of the characteristics of a good soldier, and not only in the 1914–18 war. Men who had experienced combat approved, and those who had never fought were perhaps even more likely to understand. Dearden sometimes read letters found among the clothes and belongings of dead soldiers. One included the passage: 'When we jumped into their trench, mother, they all held up their hands and shouted "Camerad, Camerad", and that means "I give in" in their langwidge. But they ad

81 Graves, *Goodbye*, 153–4
82 Holmes, *Firing Line*, 384; Macdonald, *1914–1918*, 192
83 Graves, *Goodbye*, 111–12
84 Winter, *Death's Men*, 214

to have it, mother.' Non-combatant Dearden commented: '"They ad to have it." just delights me.'[85]

The fact that everyone understood why prisoners, officers included, were sometimes killed indicates that it often more or less amounted to following orders. The order might even be explicit, as when officers made it known that they did not want to deploy men as prisoner escorts, but more often it was implied. Which is not to say much was left to the men's imaginations. Reg Lawrence was told by his colonel that he should remember he had a bayonet on his rifle and use it accordingly.[86] Barthas was ordered to hand out butcher's knives to the men in his squad. No one had any doubts about what they were for.[87] The regulations issued by British GHQ quoted earlier in this section were interpreted by many, probably with good reason, as indicating that no one should be allowed to surrender; after all, when could you know for certain that an enemy had 'abandoned all hope and intention of resisting further'? Many soldiers began to believe that they were not supposed to take prisoners under any circumstances, and that the General Staff would be far from pleased if they did.[88]

Acts of retribution were the inevitable result. Advancing troops who had seen what happened to comrades who tried to surrender during a less successful phase of the battle showed no mercy when their turn came. Barthas tells of one such incident during a German attack. At an aid post the attackers killed everybody they found, 'the medical officer, the orderlies, the wounded, in some cases by beating them to death with rifle butts'.[89]

As Baldwin, for one, reported, not all soldiers could come to terms with orders like these. In her book *An Intimate History of Killing*, Joanna Bourke describes the case of Arthur Hubbard who on 7 July 1916 tried to explain in a letter to his mother why he was no longer at the front. He had been admitted to one of the British specialist hospitals for war neurotics. He attributes his breakdown to a single event 'I shall never forget as long as I live'.

> We had strict orders not to take prisoners, no matter if wounded[. M]y first job was … to empty my magazine on 3 Germans that came out of one of their deep dugouts, bleeding badly, and put them out of their misery. They cried for mercy, but I had my orders, they had no feeling whatever for us poor chaps. … It makes my head jump to think about it.[90]

---

85 Dearden, *Medicine and Duty*, 42; Holmes, *Firing Line*, 382; Bourke, *Intimate History*, 182

86 Macdonald, *1914–1918*, 200; Ferguson, *The Pity of War*, 373

87 Barthas, *Carnets*, 165

88 Macdonald, *Somme*, 289

89 Barthas, *Carnets*, 298

90 Bourke, *Intimate History*, 242; Bourke, *Moral Economy*, 1; Bourke, 'Effeminacy, ethnicity and the end of trauma', 57

Hubbard was an experienced front-line soldier. He had seen a considerable amount of fighting and watched Germans being killed from close up; he had been buried alive and seen friends and comrades die. There can be no doubt that his earlier experiences contributed to his mental collapse, but it is striking that the only reason he gives is the guilt he felt about following orders to kill men who were trying to surrender. It is also worth noting that in his previous letters he had always described the men he killed as 'the Huns', whereas now he refers to them as 'Germans'.[91]

Should the killing of the wounded, or of unarmed men with their hands in the air, be called murder? From a strictly judicial point of view it certainly should, since it was clearly against the rules of the Hague conventions of 1899 and 1907. But as becomes obvious time and again, war has its own rules, one of which is: the victor finishes off the vanquished.[92] Richard Holmes comments:

> To expect respect for the letter of the law from a man who has passed through the beaten zone of his enemy's fire, seen a popular officer have his brains blown out, and watched men who have apparently surrendered become combatants once more, is to hope for more than flesh and blood can deliver.[93]

### *Friendly fire*

The fate of prisoners of war who were hit by their own artillery fire on the way back behind enemy lines points to another cause of death outside of battle. This was so-called friendly fire. It has been estimated, for example, that in the French army alone, around 75,000 men were killed by fire from their own infantry or, even more likely, artillery. Barthas believed that the French gunners rarely succeeded in 'firing accurately and caused casualties among us almost daily'.[94] This was sometimes the result of chaotic circumstances or of barrels worn by intensive firing, but it was also blamed on the hasty and substandard training of the gunners. Simply put, their aim was poor. Jean Girandoux wrote to Paul Morand in a cynical mood that he belonged to the French regiment that had killed the largest number of British troops.

It was not only the French who killed their own allies or indeed their own men. Both Graves and Blunden regularly mention incidents of friendly fire. Graves even describes one engagement in which more British soldiers were killed by the British army than by the Germans. The German 49th Field Artillery Regiment was commonly referred to as the 48.5th because other regiments said that the

---

91 Bourke, *Intimate History*, 243–4; Bourke, *Moral Economy*, 2
92 Holmes, *Riding the Retreat*, 144
93 Holmes, *Riding the Retreat*, 218
94 Barthas, *Carnets*, 300

shells they fired more often than not fell short.[95] Jünger and his comrades once found themselves under fire from German artillery whose range was set short. The gunners did not stop firing despite being quickly informed and before long the trench looked like a butcher's shop, with bloodstains everywhere, and pieces of brain and flesh on which swarms of flies settled.[96]

Advancing troops were the most likely to become casualties of friendly fire. Few gunners were skilful enough to adjust the creeping barrage, introduced at the Battle of the Somme, to the pace of troops marching, or rather trudging, through mud. The aim was to create a hail of shells that would land just ahead of the advancing infantry, but the barrage intended to protect them often either moved forward too fast, so that it no longer had any defensive effect, or fell short so that shells landed on friendly troops. At Passchendaele, for instance, the New Zealand Reinforcements suffered disastrous losses this way. Sometimes the attack might move ahead more quickly than anticipated for a change, or the timing might go awry and the barrage begin only after the men had begun to advance. The barrage might move back more quickly than troops in retreat, so that they were overtaken by their own shellfire. Sometimes the barrage began only at the stage when the wounded were attempting to make their way back, as happened during one British attack on the Somme. The 13th Rifle Brigade had suffered heavy losses during the advance, but Macdonald writes that it was shellfire from their own side as they withdrew that virtually wiped out the entire brigade. At roll call at the end of the day, an 'M' for missing was written next to most of the hundreds of names.[97]

The most regrettable form of friendly fire came from troops who were involved in an engagement only to discover later that they had been targeting their own troops. Sections, platoons, even whole companies sometimes became completely lost as they advanced, partly because of the confusion that accompanies any battle and partly because it was hard to maintain a sense of direction in the blasted landscape. They inevitably thought that any body of men coming towards them must be enemy troops, which was not always the case.[98]

The chaos of the battlefield or the muddle of a hasty retreat often meant rifle fire was no longer well-aimed, orderly and disciplined. As 1914 came to an end and the British and Germans engaged each other at Ypres, exhaustion among the British infantry resulted in rifle fire so uncoordinated that some say the much feared British rapid fire hit as many British as Germans.[99]

95 Brants & Brants, *Velden van weleer*, 219; Ellis, *Eye-Deep*, 61–2; Holmes, *Firing Line*, 227; Macdonald, *1914–1918*, 45; Jünger, *In Stahlgewittern*, 134; Graves, *Goodbye*, 121; Blunden, *Undertones of War*, 33, 35; Sassoon, *Complete Memoirs*, 330–31

96 Jünger, *In Stahlgewittern*, 231–2

97 Macdonald, *Somme*, 82–3, 123–5, 238, 311; Macdonald, *Passchendaele*, 173; Macdonald, *1914–1918*, 244; Prior & Wilson, *Passchendaele*, 62

98 Winter, *Death's Men*, 179; Holmes, *Riding the Retreat*, 169; Macdonald, *Somme*, 210; Blunden, *Undertones of War*, 74–5

99 Macdonald, *1914*, 269

British tanks, first deployed in mid-September 1916 on the Somme, were another source of friendly fire, mostly attributable to the fact that their crews found it hard to see what was going on. The third of the first three tanks ever deployed fired on a trench full of British soldiers. Another tank crew made the same mistake only a few hours later, except that this time the casualties were New Zealanders.[100]

Similar errors often occurred while troops were returning to their own lines after scouting out no man's land or after raids on enemy trenches. Happy to have survived participation in a raid, they were greeted with machine-gun fire from their own side.[101] Jünger described one such event. Elsewhere he wrote about a soldier who was shot because he failed to give the password. He turned out to have a stutter.[102] Graves told of a British officer who was checking the barbed-wire entanglements and was shot by a sentry who mistook him for a German.[103]

Particularly tragic cases of friendly fire were those in which the casualty was the man firing the round. This was usually the result of faulty weaponry or ammunition, or of some other kind of accident, but not always. Walter Ambroselli, killed on 12 May 1916, wrote in a letter dated 19 January 1915 about a fellow German who had crept close to a trench full of French troops. He pulled the plug out of the fuse on a hand grenade and was about to throw it into the trench when suddenly German soldiers appeared in front of the target. There was no way he could throw the grenade without doing more damage to his comrades than to the enemy. So he simply held it until it exploded.[104]

The killing of comrades was occasionally deliberate. Officers might sometimes fire on their own troops for disciplinary reasons. One German general addressed his men, who had just returned from the Battle of the Mort Homme, a bloody conflict for both sides, with the words 'I give you, and above all the young leaders of companies and platoons, express permission to intervene as strongly as possible if your men do not wish to go on. Blow to oblivion anyone you find to have displayed cowardice. There must be no mercy on this point!'[105]

In all armies men were sometimes shot by their own officers either because they had lost the will to fight or because they were no longer psychologically capable of climbing up over the parapet and marching towards enemy machine-guns.[106] In April 1918 Hutchison ordered his machine-gunners to open fire on a small group of British soldiers who were attempting to surrender. This would quickly become known throughout the army and dissuade others from laying down their arms.[107]

---

100 Macdonald, *Somme*, 276, 284; Marix Evans, *Battles of the Somme*, 47
101 Jünger, *In Stahlgewittern*, 130
102 Jünger, *In Stahlgewittern*, 44
103 Graves, *Goodbye*, 196
104 Witkop, *Kriegsbriefe*, 148
105 Brants & Brants, *Velden van weleer*, 237; Werth, *Verdun*, 412
106 Holmes, *Riding the Retreat*, 202
107 Holmes, *Firing Line*, 339

There was a fairly widespread belief that a soldier ought to be more afraid of his own officers than of enemy fire, since otherwise he would refuse to fight. The assumption was that a soldier could be kept at his post only by the knowledge that he would be killed if he left it.[108] One French divisional commander ordered his artillery to open fire on any divisions that failed to leave the trenches, but the gunners refused to obey unless the order was put in writing. This brings us to the unarmed colonial workers of the French Labour Corps who, shortly before the mutiny in September 1917, were shot at Étaples. They had downed tools in protest at inhumane working conditions. Twenty-three died, twenty-four were wounded.

Sometimes this kind of heavy-handed action by officers against their own men was necessary, not just from a military point of view but to avoid an even larger number of casualties. John Baynes tells of a wounded soldier in a field ambulance who panicked when a German attack started. He began yelling hysterically 'Get out! Get out! We're all going to be killed'. A sergeant split his skull open with a shovel. His shouts could easily have provoked panic and the rest of the men might have been slaughtered in the resulting confusion.[109] Carnage as a result of panic was not always caused directly by enemy shelling. The Americans came under sustained artillery fire at Cantigny and several of the men, exhausted after three days of combat, were driven mad by the guns. One, a lieutenant, started shooting wildly at his own troops, until he was killed by a German shell.[110]

Despite instances such as that described by Baynes, in which one man was shot for the good of all, the vast majority of 'shots in the back' were part of a military strategy. A revolver in the ribs and its legal counterpart the court martial – along with a sense of comradeship, solidarity, and a fear of showing the slightest reticence – may sometimes have been necessary to persuade a man to walk out into no man's land rather than run like a hare in the opposite direction, towards relative safety. Most went forward. This gave them some chance of surviving or, if it came to that, dying in battle and being remembered as heroes rather than cowards. If a whole platoon refused to advance, a few well-aimed shots would ensure they did so, if in slightly smaller numbers.[111] Keegan refers to this in his article 'Towards a Theory of Combat Motivation' by saying that to the army rule 'kill or be killed' might usefully be added 'risk being killed by the enemy or else risk being killed by your own provost marshal'.[112]

Incidents of this kind again throw a fresh light on the concept of courage. A mortally wounded Frenchman in hospital was given a medal for valour in the face of the enemy. Shortly before he died he admitted: 'I was mobilized against my inclination. Now I have won the *Médaillon Militaire*. My Captain won it for me. He made me

108 Holmes, *Firing Line*, 338–9

109 Holmes, *Firing Line*, 227; Dallas & Gill, *Unknown Army*, 85–6

110 Gilbert, *First World War*, 426

111 Holmes, *Firing Line*, 44; Winter, *Death's Men*, 179; Macdonald, *1914–1918*, 160; Macdonald, *Somme*, 118, 157; Eksteins, *Rites of Spring*, 171; Glover, *Humanity*, 157

112 Addison & Calder, *Time to Kill*, 6

brave. He had a revolver in his hand.'[113] Far from all soldiers would have described as cowards those of their comrades who, exhausted, underfed and plastered with mud, refused to attack even when threatened with death or court martial.

It is but a short step to our next subject: murder. This was certainly not the order of the day, but neither was it a sporadic occurrence. The German army stopped counting once the total reached 294, or an average of 1 murder every 5 days.[114] This is merely the official total. Who can say how many men were murdered and listed as killed or missing in action? Moreover, there is a problem of definition. It was mostly a case of soldiers shooting officers they hated. This was always defined as murder. If an officer shot one or more of his men it might well be defined as 'duty arising from military necessity'.

The conditions of war presented the perfect opportunity for murder. The chances of anyone discovering that a man had been murdered rather than killed by the enemy were negligible, so men regularly took opportunities to wreak revenge. A bullying British NCO had a bomb with the pin extracted 'placed between his shirt and trousers' and a sergeant-major was bayoneted in the ribs. A French officer who refused to surrender in a situation his men regarded as hopeless was murdered, and his troops then laid down their arms. Graves tells the story of two young soldiers who turned themselves in after murdering their company sergeant-major. When asked how it had happened, they answered that it had been an accident. 'We mistook him for our platoon sergeant.' It almost goes without saying that both were executed.[115]

### *Death by execution*

Not every case of capital punishment was as clear-cut as the above example. The authors of the book *Shot at Dawn*, Julian Putkowski and Julian Sykes, have good reason to concur with lawyer Anthony Babington, author of *For the Sake of Example*, in pointing out that for the accused 'army procedures had seriously jeopardised the prospects of a fair trial'. Nor could a man expect fair treatment once convicted. Putkowski and Sykes, again following the line taken by Babington, note the absence of proper medical assessments. This reduced even further the chances that a mentally disturbed soldier would receive justice.[116] Putkowski and Sykes, like Babington, look exclusively at executions on the British side. This is understandable given that they are themselves British, but it is also true that in percentage terms the British military authorities dealing with men on active service on the Western Front imposed and implemented the largest number of death

113 La Motte, *Backwash of War*, 125

114 Whalen, *Bitter Wounds*, 42

115 Holmes, *Firing Line*, 331, 344; Graves, *Goodbye*, 93–4; Eksteins, *Rites of Spring*, 108; Barthas, *Carnets*, 389

116 Putkowski & Sykes, *Shot at Dawn*, 6; See also the report of the conference on WWI executions at http://www.inflandersfields.be:archief.Synopnl.doc

sentences. 3,080 British soldiers were condemned to death and approximately 340 executed between August 1914 and April 1920. About 30 were shot for crimes such as murder, but most were guilty of military offences. 'For desertion 268 were shot, for cowardice: 18, leaving post: 7, disobedience: 5, hitting a superior officer: 5, mutiny: 4, sleeping on duty: 2, throwing down arms: 2, and violence: 1.'[117] Of all the men executed, only three were officers. They included Lieutenant Edwin Dyett, who was probably the model for Harry Penrose, the central character in A.P. Herbert's *The Secret Battle*, a book that makes short work of the charge of cowardice.[118]

The figures for executions in the various armies diverge quite markedly. Australia declined to introduce the death penalty for volunteers who were fighting far from home, no matter how hard the British tried to persuade them it was necessary. More than a hundred Australians were condemned to death by British courts martial, but they could not be executed without the permission of the Australian government and this was refused in all cases. In the Canadian army around 25 men were executed, all for crimes punishable in civilian life. The same goes for the five New Zealand soldiers who were shot at dawn on the orders of their superiors. The American army too executed a relatively small number of men, 35 in Europe and 25 back in the US, and again they were mostly found guilty of crimes.[119] In the vast German army, the opportunities to impose severe punishments were minimal, although several senior officers wished this were otherwise. Officially at least, 'only' 48 German soldiers were shot. Some historians explain the all but absence of such drastic measures by pointing out that Germany tended to define 'cowardice' as an illness rather than as a disciplinary and military offence. This again could help to explain why German therapies for mentally ill soldiers were often harsh. They not only had a disciplinary function, but were an alternative to the death penalty, or the threat of it. Of course, the problem with this theory is that neurotics were not exactly treated with kid gloves by the Allies either. Whatever the case may be, reluctance to impose the death penalty resulted partly from the fact that German doctors were ordered to investigate whether an accused man was fit to be held responsible for his crimes. This was not a standard regulation in any of the other armies on the Western Front. Doctors' findings were taken extremely

117 Even the numbers of those executed differ in the different sources. Putkowski & Sykes talk about 349 but in a recent article in *Stand To!*, the author mentions the number as 332. The main difference is in the number of criminal offences: 37 against 23. Putkowski & Sykes, *Shot at Dawn*, 8, 16; Chielens, 'Bekrachtigd, genoteerd, uitgevoerd', 7, Tattersfield, 'Discipline in the BEF', 12.

118 Putkowski & Sykes, *Shot at Dawn*, 16; Winter, *Death's Men*, 68; Holmes, *Firing Line*, 337; Herbert, *The Secret Battle*; Oltheten, 'Voorwoord', 11–12

119 Putkowski & Sykes, *Shot at Dawn*, 17–18; Brants & Brants, *Velden van weleer*, 126; Chielens, 'De normen van de tijd', 235

seriously by the German army.[120] As we shall see, this was certainly not the case across the board.

In the Belgian armed forces, tiny in comparison to the German, at least thirteen soldiers were executed. It is important to note that all the Belgian soldiers whose death sentences for 'desertion in the face of the enemy' were implemented faced the firing squad within a year of the outbreak of war. Belgian firing squads were composed of gendarmes, and initially executions took place out of sight of fellow soldiers. Before long a man's comrades were being made to watch, in the hope this would have a more profound impact on discipline, which clearly indicates one motive for carrying out executions. Condemned men were to serve as an example to others. Their trials were hardly proper court proceedings at all, and there was no opportunity to appeal against the sentence. Even after June 1915, many were condemned to death for desertion, but because of a special dispensation (King Albert is said to have had a hand in it, although this is far from certain), no further executions took place, although this did not apply to anyone convicted of a criminal act such as murder. In May 1915 a punishment corps called the *Corps Spécial* was established in Belgium, charged with ensuring that 'undesirable elements' were removed from the mainstream army for a time. After serving terms of imprisonment, they would be assigned to penal companies and later to special companies in which they could earn back their honour. Anyone who went through the full process without causing any further trouble could take his place in the army once more, his honour fully restored. Nowhere was it officially stated that this system obviated the need for further use of the death penalty, but that was the result in practice.[121]

In all armies other than the British and French, most death sentences were imposed for criminal activities such as murder, rather than for 'cowardliness in the face of the enemy' or other military offences. In this sense it made a great deal of difference in which army a man served,[122] an exception to the general rule that the war as such was the primary cause of suffering. The war did not make executions inevitable. Individuals imposed death sentences and ordered them to be carried out.

No one has ever been able to explain to universal satisfaction why the British courts martial – and to a slightly lesser extent the French – handed out much harsher punishments than their counterparts in other national armies. It must have something to do with the extremely hierarchical character of the British and French armies compared to the German army, for example, and especially the Australian army. The Germans paid more attention to other methods of sustaining morale and

120 Kaufmann, 'Science as Cultural Practice', 132; Eckart & Gradmann, 'Medizin', 215

121 Addison & Calder, *Time to Kill*, 374; De Schaepdrijver, *De Groote Oorlog*, 209; Holmes, *Firing Line*, 338; De Backer, 'Longinus', 39; television documentary 'Soldatenverhalen: In het aanschijn van de vijand', BRT 2, 10-11-98

122 Putkowski & Sykes, *Shot at Dawn*, 18

the fighting spirit. The considerable amount of responsibility placed on the lower echelons indicates one aspect of the German approach. Another relevant factor is surely that the British and French armies were even more independent of political control than most, and that a fairly high proportion of their troops were volunteers from urban, proletarian backgrounds, while the army high command in both cases was drawn from the landowning classes.

Despite the militaristic reputation of the German Reich, the German military code of 1872 was mild compared to those of many other countries. Furthermore, the respect shown in Germany towards the law and the legal system ensured that an accused man could count on a fair trial. Twice, in 1916 and 1918, the German parliament voted almost unanimously, against the wishes of the army high command, for a reduction in minimum sentences. Parliament believed this would have no appreciable effect on discipline. There were, however, special measures designed to deal with groups that were suspected of innate disloyalty, including men from Alsace or Lorraine. In many cases disloyalty was precisely the result.

Official French statistics suggest that 133 French soldiers were executed during the war, more than a third as a result of the mutiny of 1917. Richard Holmes endorses the view of Putkowski and Sykes that we should treat this figure with caution.[123] French historian Nicolas Offenstadt claims around 600 men were executed, fewer than 10 per cent of them for participation in the mutiny. Belgian historian Piet Chielens writes of 550 executions in the French army, 350 in the first year of the war and 'only' two hundred in the years that followed, despite the mutiny. Whatever the case may be, it is clear that the French realized more quickly than the British – among whom the number of executions began to fall only in 1918 – that the death penalty had hardly any deterrent effect. As with the British and the Germans, we should assume that summary executions took place in the French army, leaving little or no trace.

In September 1914 special *Conseils de Guerre* were established to try soldiers for dereliction of duty. Early in the war in particular, French courts martial took a robust line, with another burst of activity during the mutiny of 1917. Horne claims that death by execution was the sentence usually passed on those found guilty. The death penalty was often commuted, but those executed were in most cases shot within twenty-four hours of their trial. This is sufficient to indicate that the judicial system gave a man no opportunity to appeal against his sentence.[124]

Aside from the mutiny, most death sentences were passed after failed offensives. They were intended to set an example, and the scapegoats were soldiers or NCOs selected at random. Hence the well-known phrase: *pour encourager les autres* (to encourage the others). Their fate was decided by drawing lots. This was known as 'decimation'. Those selected had no hope of a fair judicial process. Show trials awaited them.[125] In November 1915, for instance, an entire battalion was court-

123 Putkowski & Sykes, *Shot at Dawn*, 16–17

124 Horne, *Price of Glory*, 63–4; Chielens, 'Normen van de tijd', 234

125 Horne, *Price of Glory*, 64

martialled for refusing to attack and one man from each company was shot.[126] Officers and NCOs at the front were held responsible for the behaviour of their men. On 17 March 1915, at Souain, four corporals lost their lives because their units were said to have shown insufficient attacking spirit.[127] Barbusse described how an execution was carried out in the French army. 'They gave it the full works, ... the whole ceremony from A to Z, the colonel on horseback, the stripping of rank. Then they tied him to that little post, something you'd tie an animal to. He must have been forced to kneel or sit on the ground with a stake like that.'[128]

Sidney Chaplin, who was a military policeman at the time, sitting on horseback on a nearby hill, gave an impression of how the British executed their soldiers.

> I saw the man brought out to the post and the firing squad march into position, turn right and take up stand. I heard the report as they fired and saw the smoke from their rifles. Then they turned and marched off. The officer, with revolver in hand, inspected the body, then turned away. The dead man was then taken away in a blanket and buried in the small cemetery in the next field. It was over. I came down, but it did not seem real.
>
> The next one followed the same pattern, except the APM [Assistant Provost Marshal, LvB] said, 'Cowardice' – and the man said, 'Never!'[129]

They were shot by men from their own units, in front of comrades forced to attend, only a few hours after they had been told their sentences would not be commuted. Twelve men were chosen, by drawing lots, to form a firing squad. Each was given a rifle, some loaded only with blanks so that any one of the twelve could convince himself if he so wished that he had not been responsible for the death of his brother in arms.[130] Death sentences were proclaimed in writing and read out to the entire British army to demonstrate that the assurance given before every battle that the severest military law would apply was no empty threat. Most Australians are said to have been horrified by this, and they were not alone. In his *With a Machine-Gun to Cambrai*, G. Coppard writes that he felt stupefied when, only a few minutes before the start of an offensive, a long list of executed men was read out: names, ranks, offences, dates and times of execution.[131]

In the House of Commons the British government hotly denied that any soldiers had been executed, in response to questions from one of the few MPs to cast doubt on the way the war was being conducted. Instead of making any attempt to rein in military rigour in this respect, the ministers responsible simply misled their own

126 Ellis, *Eye-Deep*, 181

127 Brants & Brants, *Velden van weleer*, 197

128 Barbusse, *Le Feu*, 141; *Under Fire*, 119; see also: Dorgelès, *Croix de bois*, 179–81

129 Macdonald, *1914–1918*, 185

130 Babington, *For the Sake of Example*, ix–x; Winter, *Death's Men*, 43

131 Winter, *Death's Men*, 171; Dallas & Gill, *Unknown Army*, 43

parliament and the executions went on.[132] Government ministers believed it was good for army discipline that men were occasionally shot at dawn, but what was good for the army was not necessarily good for morale at home, so denial and deception became standard policy. Civilians were told the executed men had died in the fighting,[133] but of course eventually the truth had to come out.

The first British soldier to be put through this ritual after the General Routine Order was promulgated was T.J. Highgate, born in 1895. He was accused of desertion, a charge that was not uncommon, since a huge number of men went missing during the Great Retreat. The charge was often unjustified, although not in Highgate's case. He had fought at Mons and Le Cateau before disappearing during the Battle of the Marne and changing into civilian clothes. He lost his way and asked a gamekeeper for directions. The gamekeeper turned out to be an Englishman, who immediately handed Highgate over to the military authorities. He was executed on 8 September 1914, two days after what Putkowski and Sykes claim was one of the quickest sentences of the war. This indicates that the authorities wanted to nip any weakening of discipline in the bud, whatever it took.[134]

It is an impression reinforced by the story of the second man executed, George Ward. After three days on active service he fled the battlefield on 16 September 1914, telling his commanding officer that, like two of his friends, he had been wounded. Six days later he retraced his steps and reported to his battalion, but when it became clear he had not been wounded he was court-martialled and sentenced to death. Once again the army high command had felt it necessary to make an example of one of its men.[135]

On 8 August 1916 the Germans released gas in the Ypres salient. Nineteen-year-old John Bennett panicked and fled. Six hours later he was back. He discovered that six soldiers had not survived the gas attack and forty-six others were close to death. He was arrested. An officer intimated during his trial that Bennett, who had enlisted six weeks before the outbreak of war, had gone to pieces under shellfire, and as a result a brigadier-general afterwards recommended that his death sentence should be commuted. The corps commander, however, said that cowardice represented a serious threat to the war effort and pointed out that the death penalty existed to make a soldier more afraid of his superiors than of enemy fire. Bennett was executed.[136]

The doubts these stories raise about the grounds for harsh verdicts – and indeed about the accusation itself, 'cowardice in the face of the enemy' – are reinforced

132 Graves, *Goodbye*, 198; Babington, *For the Sake of Example*, x; Babington, *Shell-Shock*, 114–15

133 Winter, *Death's Men*, 43; Graves, *Goodbye*, 213; Sassoon, *Complete Memoirs*, 402–3

134 Putkowski & Sykes, *Shot at Dawn*, 8; Holmes, *Riding the Retreat*, 283; Gilbert, *First World War*, 72

135 Gilbert, *First World War*, 82, 83 (note 1)

136 Gilbert, *First World War*, 275

by the last two British executions to be carried out before the war ended, both of which took place four days before the armistice (as indicated at the start of this section, the executions did not cease on 11 November 1918). One of the condemned men was 23 years old. He had volunteered in March 1915 but failed his medical examination. After medical standards were lowered, he was called up in April 1916. The other man was 32 and suffered from various hereditary mental disorders. In both cases, medical reports were consulted when the decision was made to proceed with execution.[137] Clearly these men were casualties of a system that placed discipline above all else, a military-judicial system that favoured harsh punishment, and a military-medical system that would not stand in the way in difficult times. As we shall see, hereditary susceptibilities, whether real or presumed, tended if anything to work to the disadvantage of the accused.

Like the French, those sentenced to death by British courts martial, among them a relatively large number of Irishmen and colonial troops, could not appeal against their sentences no matter how minor their offences: a moment of weakness after days under bombardment, for example, or a refusal to obey an absurd order issued miles from the front. In some cases death sentences were commuted after convictions for murder, which indicates just how arbitrary the system was. In fact there was no consistency at all in the way the various penalties available were imposed. Often the severity of the punishment was decided by an unfortunate remark at the wrong moment. Then there was the question of whether a man was able to call upon influential friends. His sentence might well be decided by the date on which the offence took place. In difficult times, during the Battle of the Somme for example, the maintenance of discipline was seen as particularly important and the chances of a mild sentence were smaller than usual.

Obviously these trials did not exactly show the British judicial system at its best. A fifth of those condemned to death were under 21, the age of majority, and their average age was just over 25. One in ten had no legal assistance, some were illiterate, many had very little education. They were subjected to intimidating interrogations during which they often made statements that completely contradicted their own earlier accounts.[138] Courts Martial Officer Arthur Page described a typical session: 'Dim light of a few sputtering candles … the tired and drawn faces of the witnesses under their tin helmets; and the accused himself, [with] apparently only a languid interest in the evidence as it accumulates against him.'[139]

This approach points to the fact that judges and prosecutors were not primarily concerned with giving a man a fair trial but rather with obtaining a conviction, as can also be deduced from the amount of time they took. No fewer than 90 per cent of the accused were found guilty as charged in trials lasting barely 20

137 Putkowski & Sykes, *Shot at Dawn*, 8

138 Putkowski & Sykes, *Shot at Dawn*, 13, 16; Dallas & Gill, *Unknown Army*, 38, 40, 43; Macdonald, *Passchendaele*, 140; Chielens, 'Bekrachtigd', 7; Chielens, 'Normen van de tijd', 227–9

139 Liddle, *Passchendaele in Perspective*, 356

minutes. Once again it is clear that as far as the military authorities were concerned the execution of individuals was not so much an end in itself as a means to an end: discipline. In the British army as in the French, executed men were often scapegoats, selected more or less at random to serve as a warning to others. The same offences – even those undoubtedly worthy of the name – would have had very different consequences at other times and in other places. The trials smacked of class-based justice. The judges and prosecutors were all members of the upper classes and ninety-nine per cent of the accused were from the lower ranks of the British class system. Given the nature of British society at the time, it is perfectly understandable that trials would be organized and run by the highest social class, but the number of accused of lowly social origins was disproportionate in the extreme.[140] The arbitrariness inherent in the system is evident again in the way pardons were handed out. A man might be pardoned because he was popular. He might be refused a pardon because the general responsible for the decision believed it was time to crack the whip. Personal relationships within the courts of justice might prove decisive; if a particular officer was in favour of issuing a pardon, others would automatically oppose clemency, or vice versa. An officer once said at a trial that two pages of the dossier had been removed and he would like to know by whom. It emerged that another officer, one rank above him, had stuck two pages together. The man admitted this straight out but added: 'What were you intending to do about it?'[141]

The courts martial system led Noyes to make one of his rare, and therefore all the more striking, complaints against the business of war. Across the street from the Flemish school building where his hospital had been set up was a hall in which the British army court-martialled its men. Some of the scenes on view there 'left us stunned with horror and sickened with disgust'. The Canadian doctor and his colleagues were in complete agreement that before condemning a soldier, the judges ought to spend a good stretch of time in the trenches, experiencing all that the soldiers were put through and seeing the kinds of things the men had seen. They were convinced they would judge them less harshly if they did. How could you condemn a man to death when he had probably volunteered, fought many battles valiantly and then had one moment of perfectly understandable weakness? This was not justice, it was murder, caused 'by the Prussianism in our own army'.[142] Noyes would have been amazed at the low rate of execution in the German armed forces.

Only a small percentage of those prosecuted ultimately faced a firing squad. 170,000 suspects were brought before the British courts martial and almost 90 per cent were found guilty. Many were tried by their own commanding officers, but only for minor offences. (Whether or not an offence was minor was decided on

140 Putkowski & Sykes, *Shot at Dawn*, 14
141 Chielens, 'Bekrachtigd', 8–9
142 Noyes, *Stretcher-Bearers*, 112–13

the spot, and not always consistently.)[143] Any man who appeared before a Field General Court Martial was suspected of acting, or failing to act, in such a way that his behaviour was detrimental to 'the efficiency of a man in his character of a soldier', an offence that the Army Act stated must be severely punished. It might be a matter of desertion or insubordination, but drunkenness and the like fell into this same category.[144] Before the trial began, many accused men, although not all, were offered the help of a 'prisoner's friend', an officer who acted as a lawyer. He rarely provided any real legal input. The 'lawyer' was permitted to cross-examine witnesses after they had given evidence, but he rarely did so, and even if he did it hardly ever brought any benefit to the defendant. Up to a point this explains why some men refused their help, although in practice such a refusal will not have done their defence any good. In fact it has been estimated that around ten per cent of those executed, thirty-one men to be precise, had no legal support of any kind. Twenty-six of those thirty-one were under twenty-one years old.[145]

Crucial evidence that might have proven a suspect's innocence was rarely investigated by the court. An accused man's background was not taken into account, nor, in many cases, were any mitigating factors considered.[146] Young officers responsible for passing judgement were keen to prove how decisive they could be and knew it would not be good for their future careers to show too much leniency. They were expected to be harsh, so they generally were. Those who stood firm and refused to give their assent to a tough verdict often faced a dressing-down from their superiors.[147]

If an accused man was lucky he might be given corporal punishment. Relatively lucky, that is. Corporal punishment existed in all the armies on the Western Front, but it was used most often and most harshly by the British, whose sentences were known as Field Punishment no. 1 (FP1) and Field Punishment no. 2 (FP2). These involved unrelenting hard labour and the binding of feet or hands, lasting for a specified period, usually about 3 weeks, in a few cases up to 60 days. The condemned man might have to run back and forth for hours at the double with full kit, under the eyes of the military police. A man condemned to FP1 might, to humiliate him, be tied to a fixed object of some kind on several occasions, usually for a number of hours a day on three out of every four days. The object was usually a wagon wheel, to which he was bound with his legs and arms spread. FP1 was therefore commonly referred to as crucifixion. All financial

143 Winter, *Death's Men*, 43; Ellis, *Eye-Deep*, 185

144 Liddle, *Passchendaele in Perspective*, 349–50; Ellis, *Eye-Deep*, 185

145 Babington, *For the Sake of Example*, ix; Putkowski & Sykes, *Shot at Dawn*, 12–13, 19

146 Babington, *For the Sake of Example*, ix–x

147 Putkowski & Sykes, *Shot at Dawn*, 14; Babington, *For the Sake of Example*, 279

aid to his wife and children would be stopped.[148] Nevertheless, this was one of the few contexts in which a man might feel fortunate to have been born at the end of the nineteenth century rather than the eighteenth. In Wellington's army FP1 had involved whipping as well, sometimes as many as 800 lashes, in which case it was little more than a euphemism for capital punishment.[149] FP1 produced some far from elevating scenes. Frank Maxwell, who was in favour of the death penalty, abolished FP1 in his unit in June 1916.[150] When Rowarth was sentenced to five days of FP1 he was pleased. Surely anything was better than front-line duty. Later he had to admit he had been wrong, 'as usual'.[151] Surfleet wrote: 'I don't think I have ever seen anything which so disgusted me in my life and I know the feelings amongst our boys was very near to mutiny at such inhuman punishment. … I'd like to see the devils who devised it having an hour or two lashed up like that.' William Pressey agreed. On a bitterly cold winter's day he helped carry out such a punishment, imposed by a major 'with a very sour nature'. They put some warm clothes on the man but were ordered to remove them. No one was allowed to speak to him at any stage during the punishment, which lasted four and a half hours. Afterwards Pressey and two others removed him from the wheel, virtually frozen. He could move neither arms or legs because of the cold and because the major had ordered the men to tie the ropes extra tight, so they had to help him. 'As no officers were around, we carried him to the cookhouse. Plenty of pain, for as we loosened him and rubbed him, tears flowed from his eyes. And unprintable words from his mouth.'[152]

As the examples given earlier demonstrate, some of the accused – although certainly not all as is sometimes suggested – were really only guilty of one thing: they were no longer psychologically capable of taking part in the war. They were not cowards and they had not deserted. They were suffering from shell shock.[153] Many had fought in several battles and reached their limit. Quite a few had been grabbed by the scruff of the neck somewhere behind the lines, completely dazed and unable to say how they came to be there.[154] They often threw medical officers hopeful glances, if there were any medical officers around, while knowing in their hearts it would do them no good. Regimental Medical Officer Captain James Dunn, for instance, believed in severe punishment. He saw a direct connection

---

148 Putkowski & Sykes, *Shot at Dawn*, 14; Macdonald, *Passschendaele*, 81; Graves, *Goodbye*, 147; Dallas & Gill, *Unknown Army*, 44; Liddle, *Passchendaele in Perspective*, 356

149 Hynes, *Soldiers' Tale*, 18; *Van den Grooten oorlog*, 202–3

150 Liddle & Cecil, *Facing Armageddon*, 307

151 Bourke, *Dismembering the Male*, 99

152 Wilson, *Myriad Faces*, 358; Moynihan, *People at War*, 137–8

153 Babington, *Shell-Shock*, 55–6

154 Addison & Calder, *Time to Kill*, 374; Macdonald, *Passchendaele*, 139; Binneveld, *Om de geest*, 15

between demoralization and the refusal to execute deserters and shirkers.[155] Babington concludes: 'The army doctors as a whole seem to have set themselves up as an extra branch of the provost corps, intent on securing the extreme penalty for such offenders wherever possible.'[156] Accused men confirmed to be suffering from shell shock, or in whom it was suspected, were often kept under observation for a period. The reproach sometimes heard that the military courts refused to recognize psychiatric problems is therefore unfounded, but there is no indication that such considerations had much effect on the outcome. Many victims of shell shock were condemned to death and around ten per cent were executed, which is no different from the overall figure.[157] By no means all were even seen by a doctor. Contrary to claims by the British government at the time, only a tiny proportion of executed men had been medically examined. In the 1930s, Dr H. Joules would write that the 'monstrous injustice of war' could be looked at from many different perspectives.

> But it is a specially horrible thought to consider that it was the merest accident, depending sometimes on the whim of an unpleasant superior officer, whether the man was labelled 'shell-shock' and sent to a hospital, or whether he had to face a court-martial and a firing squad for cowardice.[158]

The question remains as to why the death sentence was commuted in nine out of ten cases, or rather why it was carried out in the remaining one in ten. It is impossible to determine the reason in every case, but medical historian and psychiatrist Simon Wessely has looked into the story of Harry Farr who, along with hundreds of others, was pardoned in 2006 on the grounds that he was mentally ill. Farr, who came from a military family, volunteered for service in the early days of the war. In 1915 he was diagnosed with shell shock and spent several months in hospital. In April 1916 and again in July that year he was briefly treated for psychiatric problems. On 17 September, during the Battle of the Somme, he refused to fight. He said he could not take any more. The doctor, however, must either have said there was nothing wrong with him or simply refused to see him because he had no physical injury. Farr repeatedly refused orders to move up to the trenches and fiercely resisted efforts to force him to do so. He was arrested on the morning of 18 September on a charge of 'misbehaving before the enemy in such a manner as to show cowardice'. The dossier consists of seven small, sparsely written pages. It cannot have taken more than twenty or thirty minutes to compile. The prosecutor was able to call four witnesses, each of whom spoke against Farr. He had no witnesses of his own, partly because the doctor who treated him had since

155 Liddle & Cecil, *Facing Armageddon*, 515; Manning, *Her Privates We*, 224

156 Babington, *For the Sake of Example*, x; Babington, *Shell-Shock*, 56; Liddle & Cecil, *Facing Armageddon*, 515

157 Winter, *Death's Men*, 140

158 Joules, *The Doctor's View*, 54

been wounded. He had no counsel either. He chose to defend himself and his plea was that he felt better 'away from the shellfire'. He was executed on 16 October 1916 at Carnoy. The clemency shown to the vast majority – where the charge was cowardice it exceeded 95 per cent – was withheld. It is useful to examine why.

First of all, in the late summer of 1916 the outcome of the Battle of the Somme was still uncertain and the British army was increasingly composed of Kitchener's men. The military high command did not think much of them, so greater importance than ever was ascribed to discipline. Old hands like Farr were expected to set an example. Secondly, his declaration that he felt better away from the guns was seen as proof that his psychiatric problems could not be genuine. Thirdly it was clear to everyone, including Farr, that very shortly, probably the next day, his unit would go over the top. The guns that sparked his terror were those of his own side, firing the preparatory barrage. For refusing to serve at that particular moment he was seen as letting his comrades down. The possibility that soldiers might develop psychiatric problems because of the conditions in which they were fighting was recognized, even by the military high command and the courts martial, but anyone who was truly courageous and of strong character would recover from shell shock and not have regular relapses. Therefore his condition did not indicate an understandable and forgivable psychiatric collapse as a result of the sufferings of war but rather an unforgivable weakness of character. Farr's previous episodes of psychiatric illness worked to his disadvantage, as did the fact that he had dug in his heels on the eve of battle, when everyone was expecting great loss of life, predictions that were soon realized. In the eyes of the court and the military high command – and as far as the timing went, many of his comrades as well – these were signs not of illness but of deep-rooted cowardice. This explains why no one spoke up for him. In other words it is not entirely clear whether Farr was suffering from shell shock at the time of his desertion. There are simply no indications either way. In fact his condition was described during the trial as 'satisfactory', although we can have no idea what was meant by the word. It would be reasonable to assume that according to today's understanding of psychiatry there was definitely something wrong with him and a degree of prudence and further examination would have been appropriate. The truth of the matter is that his refusal to serve came at precisely the wrong moment.[159]

While it is not completely clear whether or not Farr was suffering from shell shock at the time he committed his offence, in the case of Private Frederick Butcher there can be little doubt. Butcher had volunteered in October 1915. He was executed in August 1918 after nearly three years on active service. Observations made about him in a newspaper article by an RAMC doctor (who writes 'I shall call him Jim') indicate that his presumed cowardice was caused by shell shock.

159 Wessely, 'The Life and Death', passim; Babington, *Shell-Shock*, 83–4; Gilbert, *First World War*, 288; Chielens, 'Bekrachtigd', 8; Shepard, *War of Nerves*, 67–8; Ferguson, *The Pity of War*, 347

After functioning like any other soldier for three years, he suddenly stood stock still and refused to accompany his comrades any further on their trench raid.

> In an instant he became a marked man. His comrades could not quite determine whether it was bravery or idiocy. Perhaps some string had snapped. … He was exceedingly nervous, but such a breach of discipline was in itself sufficient to account for that. By the time he stood on the mat before the Court he had partly regained his normal composure, but the seriousness of the situation had washed away the colour from his face, and there was a dull leaden look in his blue eyes.
>
> His record saved him. … The Court gave him a chance. He made no excuse whatever, but when asked the question, he promised that it would not occur again.

But it did occur again, naturally, and after only a week. The firing squad was largely composed of friends, none of whom regarded him as a coward. The doctor wrote: 'From what the CO and Jim's pals told me I am fully persuaded that Jim died as a martyr for discipline.'[160]

In contrast to Farr's dossier, Second-Lieutenant Eric Skeffington Poole's was exceptionally thick. In November 1916 he became the first of three British officers to be executed. He was also one of the few for whom an official medical dossier was compiled. This was seen as necessary because doctors at hospitals he had visited previously had diagnosed shell shock, after he was knocked unconscious by a clod of earth in July 1916. Moreover, a military policeman had declared that Poole was extremely confused at the time of his arrest. The battalion medical officer made it known that his return to the front had 'probably' caused Poole to suffer a relapse. No attention was paid to these last two statements, and the deposition concerning shell shock was contradicted by a new medical team hastily drummed up by the court: a gynaecologist, a paediatrician and a general practitioner. Skeffington Poole was executed on 10 December 1916.[161]

Dearden was one of the doctors who sometimes had to confirm that soldiers facing court martial were cowards rather than sick. One of the accused, who must have held out little hope after Dearden's initial description of him as a 'pitiful degenerate' and 'obviously of no use to anyone', was such a pathetic creature that the doctor put in a word for him, and successfully too, even though on the way to the courtroom he had been 'determined to give him no help of any sort, for I detest his type'. Above all the thought that 'so many good fellows go out during the night's shelling' made him determined not to offer any support in such cases. When the man deserted again his fate was sealed. Dearden examined him and thought it was ridiculous to kill someone because he was a coward. Cowardice could surely

160 Putkowski & Sykes, *Shot at Dawn*, 291–2
161 Babington, *Shell-Shock*, 84–5; Chielens, 'Bekrachtigd', 8

not be regarded as a crime. And yet 'one has seen so many splendid fellows lay down their lives so bravely that one can find no pity for such as he'.[162]

Even when it was clear that a man should never have been passed fit for military service, a doctor might well decline to help. Slack saw a 'poor little' man approaching.

> He was a half-wit. … He ran away, and he was caught and ran away again, deserted, and he was court-martialled to be shot, and I had to pick, together with my Sergeant-Major, ten men to shoot him, which we did, and one of my Subalterns had to be in charge of the party with a revolver, and he was shot.[163]

In an epilogue to Babington's *For the Sake of Example*, army doctor Frank Richardson asked himself whether it would have made much difference if medical officers had spoken out against the death penalty for soldiers who were not so much cowardly as ill. Probably not, he concluded, since even pleas from commanding officers who had been directly involved with a condemned man had little or no influence on the verdict. A twenty-year-old soldier with the Black Watch disappeared from the front line in January 1916. Ten days later he was sentenced to death. Two medical officers testified that he was suffering from severe neurasthenia. Their testimony did not help. He was executed in a Belgian abattoir.[164] Courageous behaviour on previous occasions, extreme youth, or anything else that was brought forward in mitigation made little impact on the judges.[165] Nevertheless, the relevant question here is not: Would anything doctors said have made any difference? It is unlikely to have occurred to a medical officer to think: 'Will my evidence help? If not, then I'd better go along with whatever the court decides.' Most of them genuinely agreed with the court. Had they felt they ought to object, then there could have been no excuse for not doing so, even if they were convinced it was a lost cause – and Dearden's account suggests that doctors certainly did have influence. If they believed execution would be unjust, they had a moral obligation to try to prevent it, no matter how negligible their chance of success.

Dearden wrote that cowardice should not really be a reason to shoot a man. Richardson on the other hand maintained that cowards put the lives of others in danger.[166] But, as with heroism resulting from a revolver in the back, the term 'cowardice' requires further examination. Were those who deserted, who refused to go over the top again, truly cowards, even if they were not suffering from shell shock? Might not the refusal to walk into a hail of bullets be more accurately

162 Dearden, *Medicine and Duty*, 154–7, 170–71; Liddle & Cecil, *Facing Armageddon*, 515–16

163 Macdonald, *1914–1918*, 183

164 Babington, *Shell-Shock*, 56–7

165 Babington, *For the Sake of Example*, 279

166 Babington, *For the Sake of Example*, 279

described as a sign of common sense? Was Barthas wrong to say that courage meant refusing to obey an order from a superior instead of following it blindly, if it was an order that meant the senseless sacrifice of human lives?[167]

The word 'coward' did not mean what it usually meant. Conscientious objectors were labelled 'cowardly', although as Sassoon pointed out it took a good deal of courage to refuse to don a uniform year after year, in the face of public pressure, women handing out white feathers,[168] and all the social consequences that would follow. The word acquired a new meaning at the front as well. Graves was asked to assist at a trial in which a man was accused of cowardice after taking to his heels during a heavy bombardment. The only sentence available was death, but Graves asked himself how he could put his name to such a sentence when he might well have acted in precisely the same way in similar circumstances.[169] Barthas wrote that a soldier would sacrifice himself 'so as not to seem more of a chicken than the next man'. After hearing his regiment fulsomely praised for its courage, he remarked that these 'brave men' had no other choice. If they were not brave, court martial awaited them.[170] Eric Partridge described an encounter with what he regarded as cowardice. During the Battle of the Somme he thought more than once of deserting and planned his means of escape, but when the time came to make his move he carried on fighting. He was 'too cowardly' to desert. Johannsen had one of his central characters in *Vier von der Infanterie* comment that 'if we weren't such cowards' he and the men would refuse to move up into position. In other words they only went up the line because they were too cowardly to move back. In *Die Pflasterkästen*, Frey has his protagonist declare that he too is a coward, for not daring to say 'no' to military service.[171]

Even in its original sense, the word 'coward' no longer conferred any stigma as far as the troops were concerned. As we have seen, any man could reach breaking point, the stage at which he could not go on, and every soldier knew this. Private James Smith had been a professional soldier since 1910. He had fought at Gallipoli and was sent to the Western Front in 1916, where he was buried alive by a German shell. After breaching military discipline a number of times, he deserted in August 1917. Smith was arrested and sentenced to death. Among those ordered to shoot him was a friend of his, Private Richard Blundell. After the firing squad had done its work, it became clear that Smith was still alive. Someone would have to give

---

167 Barthas, *Carnets*, 122

168 British men of military age who appeared in public in civilian clothes were handed white feathers by women outraged by their apparent failure to enlist. Sometimes they were indeed conscientious objectors, but often they had failed their medical examinations. Occasionally they were men on leave who had not felt like going everywhere in uniform.

169 Sassoon, *Complete Memoirs*, 403; Graves, *Goodbye*, 198; Cummings, *Enormous Room*, XII; Higonnet, *Behind the Lines*, 209; Glover, *Humanity*, 163

170 Barthas, *Carnets*, 320, 376

171 Hynes, *Soldiers' Tale*, 60, 62; Johannsen, *Vier von der Infanterie*, 15; Frey, *Die Pflasterkästen*, 226

him the *coup de grâce*. The officer in charge could not go through with it, so he handed his revolver to Blundell and ordered him to shoot Smith in the head at close range. Blundell obeyed orders. As a reward he was granted ten days' leave. On his deathbed, 72 years later, he repeated over and over: 'What a way to get leave, what a way to get leave.'[172]

Blundell protested inwardly against the task he had been assigned. Like many others, he condemned the harshness of the way justice was meted out, but instances of open criticism were rare. They were not unknown. Barbusse described how the troops sided with one condemned man, probably because they had known him at other times and not only in his moment of weakness, and because they could imagine themselves in his place. He had 'tried to get out of the trenches'. The execution post was covered in angry scrawls and protest slogans.[173] Men ordered to shoot seventeen-year-old Joseph Byers on 6 June 1915 fired into the air twice before carrying out the sentence, and when William Smith was shot at Reningelst on 14 November 1917, Padre Achiel Van Walleghem from the nearby village of Dikkebus noted of the firing squad: 'It's a man's own mates who are appointed to do it. Many soldiers have already declared how painful it is for them. There are some who shriek with remorse.'[174]

Despite such protests, there was never an occasion on which an execution had to be abandoned. Stephen Graham saw a firing squad at Neuve Chapelle refuse to shoot a deserter who they said was clearly suffering from shell shock. The next day the men were lined up again and this time the prisoner was shot without hesitation. Graham wrote: 'Our mutiny was only in the heart, such was the power of discipline.'[175]

Did all this have the intended effect? Did discipline indeed improve? Was execution effective in sustaining fighting strength and did fewer soldiers in the French and especially the British army attempt to flee the conflict as a result? According to Peter Scott in his *Law and Orders: Discipline and morale in the British armies in France, 1917*, the death penalty had no effect at all, just as the death penalty appears not to work as a deterrent to murder in civilian life.[176] There is certainly plenty of reason to doubt whether the threat of execution made men any less likely to show 'cowardice in the face of the enemy'. There was no death penalty in the Australian army and whatever else may be said about the Australians, they were certainly no more cowardly on average than the British. In fact executions do not even seem to have had much influence on the behaviour of condemned men whose sentences were commuted. In one case a British soldier was sentenced to death on three separate occasions before he was actually shot. Perhaps he wanted to die. We have noted that malingerers were rarely betrayed

172 Gilbert, *First World War*, 359
173 Barbusse, *Le Feu*, 140–41; *Under Fire*, 119
174 Chielens, 'Bekrachtigd', 9
175 Winter, *Death's Men*, 44
176 Liddle, *Passchendaele in Perspective*, 356

by their comrades. Similarly, the likelihood of execution made soldiers extremely reluctant to inform on deserters and shirkers. It is a small step to the ultimate question: Did cowardly soldiers in fact put their comrades in danger? After all, traumatized or not, soldiers were most likely to bolt when they heard an attack was coming up, not moments before it began.[177]

In this connection it is interesting to look at the degree to which the various armies were susceptible to collapse. The British did not flinch anywhere near as badly in the spring of 1918 as the Germans did in the autumn of that year. Hew Strachan points to the stronger 'negative' discipline among the British as a partial explanation for this; discipline by a revolver in the back and by the death penalty. For comparison he looks at the German armies that fought to the bitter end in 1945. In 1914–18 fewer than 50 German soldiers were executed, whereas in the Second World War the total was around 15,000.[178] The fact that the British army executed only four men in the Second World War, however, does not seem to have had any adverse effect on its discipline and stamina.[179] Strachan's attempt at a partial explanation therefore seems to make sense only in relation to specific times and circumstances.

If the death penalty had any effect at all during a battle then it was probably not the effect intended. No matter how deeply the men detested executions, a comrade convicted of cowardice brought shame on the entire company and regiment. In 1915 a company swore to erase the shame of the execution of one of its number as quickly as possible by refusing to surrender. In the next attack, forty of the company's eighty men were killed.[180]

After the war, the executions that had taken place certainly had an effect on the British, but again not in the way the military high command had hoped. In 1930 the death penalty was abolished for breaches of military law. 'Desertion' and 'cowardice in the face of the enemy' were no longer capital offences.[181] This was the result of public disquiet about whether justice had been done, a question that arose of its own accord when the truth about the executions could no longer be concealed, even though it was another seventy years before books by Babington and by Putkowski and Sykes brought the full facts to light. Of course the numbers were negligible compared to the total death toll in the war, but death by execution was not 'random and abrupt, on the field of battle', as Babington wrote. Instead 'it came with measured tread as the calculated climax of an archaic and macabre ritual carried out, supposedly, in the interests of discipline and morale'.[182] Concern for

---

177 Chielens, 'Bekrachtigd', 9; Bourke, *Dismembering the Male*, 95–6

178 Addison, *Time to Kill*, 374

179 Putkowski & Sykes, *Shot at Dawn*, 309; Babington, *For the Sake of Example*, 275

180 Winter, *Death's Men*, 209; Bourke, *Dismembering the Male*, 97–8

181 Babington, *Shell-Shock*, 137; Holmes, *Firing Line*, 337–8

182 Babington, *Shell-Shock*, ix

discipline and morale lies uneasily with the administration of justice irrespective of the cost to individuals.

## Death in battle

### *Bayonet and barbed wire*

Before the war many people – although not all – thought the bayonet would again be a significant battlefield weapon. As we have seen, it was not. According to Denis Winter the bayonet was 'simply an anachronism, useful as a toasting fork, biscuit slicer or intimidator of prisoners'. This was partly a consequence of the development of the hand grenade, which took the place of the bayonet in attacks on enemy trenches. Many Germans made such frequent use of grenades that they found the bayonets on the ends of their rifles heavy and awkward and generally left them off.[183] A second and more important reason why the bayonet had largely lost its relevance lies in the nature of the fighting. Only rarely did a man have a chance to use a blade. There was little in the way of single combat.

The statistics for men killed or wounded by bayonets are not reliable, however. They differ, but hardly any of the generally accepted figures are above a few hundredths of one per cent. There are even those who say no one at all was killed with a bayonet in the Great War 'unless he had his hands up first'.[184] Once again we face the impossibility of saying anything with certainty about the causes of death on the battlefield. The figures for death by bayoneting relate to men who were wounded, brought in for medical attention, and then died. With the exception perhaps of a few who were found with rifles sticking out of their chests, men killed with bayonets who were left on the battlefield will not have been included, and bayoneting must usually have been fatal. Bodies brought in for burial that clearly had bayonet wounds were not necessarily recognized as falling into a separate category, since cuts and stab wounds might well have been inflicted after death. It is not unusual in warfare for enemy corpses to be mutilated. Dead enemy soldiers were often stripped of their medals, epaulets, helmets and other items suitable as souvenirs to be shown off back home as proof of active service, and pieces of clothing were not alone in serving this purpose. To judge by the absence of any reference to it in memoirs, the removal of body parts was not such a common feature of the First World War as it was of wars between whites and 'inferior' races (the genocide of the North American Indians, colonial wars, the wars between Nazi Germany and Eastern European nations, or the war in Vietnam, for example), but Ian Rashan wrote that his bayoneting instructor had said he wanted to see not

183 Ellis, *Eye-Deep*, 78; Winter, *Death's Men*, 110

184 Ellis, *Eye-Deep*, 78; Winter, *Death's Men*, 40; Keegan, *Face of Battle*, 264; Whalen, *Bitter Wounds*, 42

German medals but German 'ears and other things', which suggests mutilation was not unknown.[185]

In other words, little can be said with certainty about the use and effectiveness of the bayonet in the years 1914–18, although it was probably deployed more often than the statistics suggest, especially at night, in fog, in forests, or in other situations where visibility was poor and the chances of encountering the enemy in person higher than usual. French and British colonial troops in particular seem to have used cold steel quite regularly, and Bert Chaney writes of a group of Australians who crept out into no man's land in the dead of night armed only with bayonets. A few hours later they returned and cleaned their weapons on sandbags, smiling broadly.[186] Moreover, as with gas, we should bear in mind that the bayonet often claimed its victims indirectly. One of the reasons why bayoneting was such a prominent feature of training, despite the lack of opportunities to use the weapon as originally intended, was that it nourished the spirit of attack. With bayonets fixed, troops were more inclined to attack than to seek cover. Most soldiers seem to have been aware of this. They were keen to fix bayonets because doing so symbolized what they felt war ought to be: a personal encounter with an opponent, from which, after a fair fight, the stronger man emerged victorious. The bayonet also had powerful sexual connotations. It was a sword, pointing forwards, that could penetrate a body and then be withdrawn, dripping. Fixing bayonets reinforced the urge to move forward and in this sense too the bayonet cost lives.[187]

Although it may have had little effect overall and although it was rarely used in battle, there are a number of known cases in which the weapon came into its own,[188] especially in the first few weeks of the war. In a diary entry dated 28 August 1914, Lintier described a conversation he had with a French soldier during fighting near the Meuse. The Frenchman's unit attacked a German brigade that had already crossed the river. French bayonets awaited them.

> Oh, you've no idea what it's like, you lot, the charge! It's terrible... There's nothing like it... If hell exists, then I'm sure they're forever fighting with bayonets there... I'm not joking. You pitch in... You roar... A few fall... A whole load of them fall... The fewer there are left, the harder you have to roar to keep the whole thing going. And then, when you've really got them, then you go crazy... You thrust, you thrust... The first time you feel a bayonet like that go into a stomach, though, that's quite something... It's pulpy, you just stab right through... But then

185 Holmes, *Firing Line*, 378; Ellis, *Eye-Deep*, 79; Simkins, *World War I*, 86–7; Keegan, *Face of Battle*, 264; Bourke, *Intimate History*, 38, 42

186 Winter, *Death's Men*, 110; Manning, *Her Privates We*, 245; Moynihan, *People at War*, 130; Marix Evans, *1918*, 29; *Van den Grooten oorlog*, 216; Kammelar et al., *De Eerste Wereldoorlog*, 77

187 Bourke, *Intimate History*, 92; see also: March, *Company K*, 172–3; Moynihan, *People at War*, 130; Marix Evans, *1918*, 29; *Van den Grooten oorlog*, 216

188 Lemercier, *Lettres*, 57–8

> you have to get the thing out again!... I'd got ... one pinned to the ground, a pot-bellied lad with a red beard. I couldn't get my bayonet out and I had to put my foot on his stomach. I felt him wriggling under my foot. Hey, look at that...
>
> He has produced his bayonet, red to the hilt. As he walks away he yanks up a handful of grass to clean it.[189]

One British brigade used its bayonets during First Ypres, at Nonnenbosse, against inexperienced German teenagers. Corporal J. Cole said: 'We went into [them] stabbing. "*Cold remorseless steel.*" The heat soon went out of them.'[190]

Those few sources that mention the use of the bayonet in anger make it clear that however happy soldiers may have been to fix bayonets, they often found their actual use frightful. It is certainly true that many experienced the act, the killing of a man face to face, as 'glorious'. It was a welcome change from distant and impersonal killing by machine-gun or gas, shelling or sniper fire. But others reacted with horror. During the Battle of the Somme, R.H. Stewart bayoneted a German. It was the first time he had ever killed a man at close quarters. He was not even able to see him clearly, but he heard him all the better for that. On the way back he 'started to shake' and then 'shook like a leaf on a tree for the rest of the night'.[191]

It would generally be fair, nevertheless, to describe the bayonet as an anachronism. The opposite applies to another non-explosive piece of equipment. Unlike the bayonet it was neither a weapon nor of use in the attack, but it was inextricably bound up with defensive strategies in trench warfare: barbed wire. Along with the machine-gun and heavy artillery, it helped to make the bayonet almost useless on the battlefield, since a man could no longer reach the enemy trench. A line in one of the best known of the many songs of the war goes, 'If you want to find the old battalion, I know where they are: They're hanging on the old barbed wire.'[192] There are innumerable stories of soldiers caught in barbed-wire entanglements being shot to pieces by machine-gun fire. Ypres, the Somme, Verdun: everywhere men became ensnared in the many coils of wire, ripping their flesh to shreds in hopeless attempts to free themselves, efforts that often served only to entangle them further. Gaps a few metres deep blasted into the wire were no answer. They were a fatal trap.[193]

---

189 Lintier, *Ma pièce*, 134

190 Macdonald, *1914*, 370; Riemann, *Schwester der Vierten Armee*, 20

191 Bourke, *Intimate History*, 60–61, 222

192 Fussell, *Bloody Game*, 84–5

193 Brants & Brants, *Velden van weleer*, 94; Winter, *Death's Men*, 207; Holmes, *Firing Line*, 179; Macdonald, *1914–1918*, 245; Wilson, *Myriad Faces*, 325

*The trench raid*

The trench raid was the ideal way for soldiers to commit suicide without ever being found out, since anyone who volunteered to take part had a good chance of not coming back. Jünger writes of a raid in which only four out of fourteen men survived.[194] For anyone who wanted to end it all but did not dare kill himself, or felt it would be wrong to do so, a raid was the ideal alternative, especially since he would be honoured rather than derided after his death. The whole phenomenon of the trench raid was a great source of misery to officers, who might at any moment be ordered to mount one and have to call for volunteers. Blunden states this repeatedly in his book.

> The word 'raid' may be defined as the one in the whole vocabulary of the war which instantly caused a sinking feeling in the stomach of ordinary mortals. … I do not know what opinion prevailed among other battalions, but I can say that our greatest distress at this period was due to that short and dry word 'raid'.[195]

Although it is usually taken to be a Canadian invention of 1915, the first trench raid seems to have taken place in November 1914 at Ypres. It was carried out by members of the Indian Corps, men hoping to experience something that resembled traditional Indian frontier fighting. British and Dominion troops were the first to adopt the method, later followed by the Germans. Raids were often carried out by groups of fewer than twenty men, but sometimes they were mounted by whole platoons or even companies. The initial intention was to gather information about enemy troop movements by bringing back as many shoulder flashes as possible, with or without their owners. If new regiments were discovered, this might indicate plans to attack; if not, there was a good chance the enemy was concentrating purely on holding the line. The fact that in the first half of 1916, among the British alone, almost 6,000 soldiers were killed in trench raids and around 120,000 wounded shows how dangerous these 'minor' operations could be. Many said they were a good training school, but naturally only the survivors would benefit.[196]

The fatality rate was extremely high even when raids were carefully planned and prepared, and sometimes there was little or no preparation. Cloete remembered a raid under a harvest moon, and Feilding writes of similar dicing with death. In mid-February 1917 almost 200 British troops, without any preliminary bombardment, 'made a wild dash' across no man's land at a quarter past seven one morning and into the barbed wire. The Germans emerged from their trenches and rifle fire from both sides began. 'After two hours' firing, all was quiet.'[197]

---

194 Jünger, *In Stahlgewittern*, 154

195 Blunden, *Undertones of War*, 44, 162; Glover, *Humanity*, 163

196 Winter, *Death's Men*, 92; Keegan, *First World War*, 198; Bourke, *Intimate History*, 118

197 Winter, *Death's Men*, 93

Good preparation could bring remarkable success. E. Herd joined a raiding party that took several prisoners including two German officers. Even food and drink were seized. They were rewarded with six days' home leave, an incentive often used to encourage men to volunteer for such an enterprise. If a raid was unsuccessful, there would be no reward. Sometimes no men were left to be rewarded. The raid carried out by Herd and his party was certainly successful, but only 194 of the 650 men who took part returned safely.[198]

On even the best prepared raids innumerable things could go wrong. A British operation at Hamel on 8 June 1916 that had been planned down to the finest detail was given away when the machine-guns opened up fifteen seconds too soon. In the chaos that followed, two eighteen-pounders fired short, hitting their own men. Another attack failed because a subaltern failed to distinguish between magnetic north and true north, so that the raiding party arrived at unbroken barbed wire. In his *A Schoolmaster at War*, Major R.T. Rees describes a raid at Hooge shortly before the start of Third Ypres. He had noticed the Germans firing on their own forward trenches and believed there could be only one reason for this. They must have withdrawn because they knew an attack was imminent. He contacted headquarters, but the order came back to carry out the raid anyhow. It was too late to change plans; the creeping barrage could not be cancelled at this stage, and it would be a shame to fire a barrage if there were no men following up behind. The number of deaths that resulted is unknown, but nothing was achieved. The divisional history for that day states: 'there were no incidents of special importance on the divisional front.'[199]

### *Artillery, the great destroyer*

Every offensive was preceded by an intense artillery barrage that could last for days or even weeks, but when no offensive was planned, shells and mortars continued to fly back and forth, and this kind of unheralded artillery fire was treacherous. It was often impossible to take cover in time.[200]

Even at night there was no safety from the guns, since searchlights were available. Around the turn of 1915 a night-time bombardment aided by searchlights cost one British regiment half its men. Ironically, searchlights had originally been brought in to help the Red Cross search for bodies after sundown. Thereafter they were mainly used so that the fighting could continue into the night.[201]

Huge shells churned the earth, uprooting trees and throwing them into the air along with mud, chunks of rock and human corpses. Some craters were as big as swimming pools. A medical officer with the 2nd Royal Welch Fusiliers gave a vivid description of the power of shellfire: 'Two men suddenly rose into the air

198 Winter, *Death's Men*, 94

199 Winter, *Death's Men*, 95

200 Binneveld, *Om de geest*, 65

201 Winter, *Death's Men*, 26; Hutchinson, *Champions of Charity*, 166–8

vertically, fifteen feet perhaps, amid a spout of soil 150 yards ahead. They rose and fell with the easy, graceful poise of acrobats. A rifle, revolving slowly, rose high above them before, still revolving, it fell.'[202]

High explosives were fired by gunners from positions well behind the front line. They were targeted by the enemy with particular animosity. In fact artillerymen were another group disliked even by their own side. This was partly because of frequent cases of 'friendly fire', but above all it was because they caused massive casualties while apparently too far back to be in any danger themselves. They aroused feelings of repugnance as well as jealousy, but although the infantry certainly paid the highest price, the notion that the gunners were safe was a myth, as Lintier's diary, for example, demonstrates.[203] This became increasingly clear as the war went on. War reporter Philip Gibbs described the ordeal of those who fired shells at Third Ypres and came under heavy fire themselves: 'I saw the enemy's shells searching for them.'[204] The gunners were subjected to both shelling and gas, but their sufferings were invisible to the foot soldiers in the forward trenches.[205]

Estimates of the average number of shells and mortars the infantry needed to fire to kill one man – not including those aimed at earthworks and barbed wire rather than into the trenches or at strongpoints and advancing troops – range from several dozen to hundreds, even over a thousand. No matter which figure is the more accurate, the fact that the majority of the millions killed were victims of artillery fire is a reminder of the enormous quantity of explosives fired between August 1914 and November 1918.[206] A single shell did not usually kill a large number of men, but collectively they did, mostly in a gruesome manner, occasionally very cleanly indeed. Frank Richards penetrated a machine-gun nest and found eighteen dead Germans, all without a scratch. A shell had burst directly above them and they had been killed by the blast. Explosives could cause death by concussion up to ten metres away,[207] which is not to say that in all cases the displacement of air left no trace. *Im Westen Nichts Neues* includes a scene in which a soldier is stripped of all his clothes, except for his helmet, by the blast from a trench mortar.[208] Remarque's soldier was not killed by concussion alone, however. He was torn in two by a fragment of mortar casing. The usual effects of mortars and shellfire were ghastly, sometimes even without the explosives being triggered. Lieutenant Phelps Harding of the American Expeditionary Force told of a huge dud that landed right on top of a man and smashed his leg. He bled to death.[209] Of course shells that did explode caused far greater carnage. Barbusse wrote:

---

202 Keegan, *Face of Battle*, 164; Eksteins, *Rites of Spring*, 140
203 Lintier, *Ma pièce*, passim
204 Wilson, *Myriad Faces*, 476
205 Winter, *Death's Men*, 120
206 Holmes, *Firing Line*, 170; Winter & Baggett, *1914–18*, 166
207 Fussell, *Bloody Game*, 106; Winter, *Death's Men*, 117
208 Whalen, *Bitter Wounds*, 51
209 Macdonald, *1914–1918*, 305; Bourke, *Dismembering the Male*, 212–14

> '[Barbiers] had the top of his back taken off by a shell,' Marchal says, 'as if it had been cut with a razor. Besse had a piece of shrapnel through his belly and his stomach. Barthélemy and Baubex were hit in the head and neck. We spent the night racing backwards and forwards along the trench, avoiding the gunfire. You remember little Godefroy? The middle of his body was blown right away. He was emptied of blood on the spot, in an instant, like turning over a pail. … Gougnard had his legs blown off by shrapnel. ... I'd been on guard with them, but when the shell fell, I'd gone back to the trench to ask the time. I found my rifle, which I'd left behind, bent in two as though someone had done it with his bare hands, the barrel like a corkscrew and half the stock shredded to sawdust. ... Did they tell you about Franco, who was next to Mondain? The roof falling in broke his spine. ... Vigile was with them, too. His body was untouched, but his head was completely flattened, like a pancake, and huge, as wide as this.'[210]

Jünger wrote of twenty blackened corpses, all unrecognisable. Some had lost any form of identification and had to be listed as missing.[211] In May 1916 *Le Poilu du 37* told its readers: 'The storm passed, we found nothing in the red tide but a head, a few remains of limbs at the bottom of the shell-hole and some unidentifiable fragments plastered over the parapet. That is all that remained here of our poor friend.'[212]

*The offensive*

A barrage was the prelude to battle proper, the bombastic opening bars to what was often called a symphony of death. Several days before being ordered out across no man's land, the men were moved up to the front-line trenches. Deathly tiring preparations began under enemy fire. Yates arrived in a forward trench with 33 men on 27 August 1916; a week later only 13 were left to mount the attack with him. The remainder were either dead, wounded, or too sick with fatigue to be of any use.[213] A week later Captain Thomas Kettle of the Royal Dublin Fusiliers wrote to his wife:

> We are moving up tonight into the battle of the Somme. The bombardment, destruction and bloodshed are beyond all imagination, nor did I ever think the valour of simple men could be quite as beautiful as that of my Dublin Fusiliers. I have had two chances of leaving them – one on sick leave and the other on a staff job. I have chosen to stay with my comrades. I am calm and happy but desperately anxious to live.[214]

---

210 Barbusse, *Le Feu*, 53–4; *Under Fire*, 46

211 Jünger, *In Stahlgewittern*, 192

212 Audoin-Rouzeau, *Men at War*, 78

213 Macdonald, *Somme*, 243

214 Holmes, *Firing Line*, 290–91

Men prayed, they pooled their money so it could be shared out among the survivors, they exchanged addresses so that relatives could if necessary be notified by one of their own instead of by an official letter. Rum rations were issued. Then came the order to prepare for the attack. One foot was placed up against the side of the trench, bayonets were fixed and rifles held at the ready. Men waited for the signal to clamber up over the parapet and run forward, or walk, or stumble. The tension rose. Many carried what might be their last letter home in their uniform pockets, so that it could be sent posthumously if need be. The barrage became even heavier. Everyone knew he would be exposing his entire body to machine-gun fire. Sweat broke out. Hands shook. It was almost impossible to keep one's nerve. Men felt sick, but often they had nothing in their stomachs to bring up, partly because nerves had given them diarrhoea. Their heartbeats seemed to keep pace with the rattle of the machine-guns. They could feel their blood race. No one knew how far he would get before being hit.[215]

A whistle was blown and the men climbed out of the trench, one long line as far as the eye could see, followed by another line and another, as if driven by an invisible force, a will beyond their own. One man described that first step as like jumping into a cold bath. The sensation took your breath away. The tension of waiting evaporated and the shaking that accompanied sitting still under shellfire ceased, but a new tension took its place, caused by chaos, by greater danger than ever, by loneliness and a torrent of impressions that included the sight of wounded or dead comrades falling.[216] Barbusse wrote: 'I have trouble recognizing those that I know, as if all the rest of life had suddenly become very far away. Something is working inside them and changing them; a frenzy has taken hold of them all and lifted them out of themselves.'[217]

In front of the line of men – if everything was going to plan – the shells of their own creeping barrage were bursting. The curtain of smoke and dust offered some protection, but it also prevented them from seeing where they were going. The barrage moved forward by 100 metres every 3 minutes, irrespective of whether the men were able to keep pace, or whether they happened to be advancing faster than expected.[218] The troops found themselves amid deafening scenes with no way of telling where the noise was coming from. The enemy, however much weaponry he fired, was invisible too. Denis Winter writes that when a British soldier attacked 10,000 Germans, he might see perhaps 10 of them.[219] German Captain Walter Bloem of the 12th Brandenburg Grenadiers asked himself during the opening days

---

215 Winter, *Death's Men*, 177; Macdonald, *Roses of No Man's Land*, 219; Witkop, *Kriegsbriefe*, 191; Audoin-Rouzeau & Becker, *'14–'18*, 64; Meire, *De Stilte van de Salient*, p. 56

216 Holmes, *Firing Line*, 174–5; Kammelar et al., *De Eerste Wereldoorlog*, 77

217 Barbusse, *Le Feu*, 275; *Under Fire*, 233

218 Winter, *Death's Men*, 177

219 Winter, *Death's Men*, 178

of the war where the enemy had got to; he was nowhere to be seen while the bullets whistled over, around and into his own men.[220]

In *Le Feu* Barbusse described an advance.

> One can see, one can feel the chunks of shrapnel whizzing past one's head with the sound of red-hot iron hitting the water. At one point my hands are so burnt by the blast from an explosion that I drop my rifle. I pick it up, swaying on my feet, and set off again through the storm with its savage lights, through the crushing rain of molten things, stung by jets of dust and soot. The screeching of the fragments going past makes your ears hurt, hits you in the nape of your neck and bangs at your temples; it is impossible to keep from crying out. You feel sick, your stomach turned by the smell of sulphur. The blast of death pushes us, carries us onward, rocks us this way and that. We leap on, without knowing where we are going. ... Now we are almost running. You can see some men falling like logs, head first, while others drop, humbly, as though sitting down on the ground. You step suddenly this way or that to avoid the dead, prone, stiff and well behaved, or else rearing upwards, and also, more dangerous snares, wounded men struggling and clinging on to you.[221]

In March 1915 Lemercier had 'seen officers die, the ranks of my regiment thinned. For those in the midst of the firestorm all human hope is lost.'[222] *L'Écho de tranchées-ville* of 28 October 1915 published the following account:

> The guns were crackling away ahead of us, the machine-guns spitting out their ribbons of death. Tack, tack, tack, tack. We caught up with our friends but – to our horror – we met a barbed-wire barrier that was still intact and more than 30 metres deep. And all this time the enemy machine-guns went on, tack, tack, tack, tack, while we could see our friends on our left, falling, covering the ground with their blue uniforms, red with blood where they were hit.[223]

Alexander Aitken wrote of an advance during the Battle of the Somme:

> In an attack such as this, under deadly fire, one is powerless as a man gripping strongly charged electrodes, powerless to do anything but go mechanically on; the final shield from death removed, the will is fixed like the last thought taken into an anaesthetic, which is the first thought taken out of it. Only safety, or the shock of a wound will destroy such auto-hypnosis. At the same time all normal emotion is numbed entirely.[224]

---

220 Holmes, *Riding the Retreat*, 127–8
221 Barbusse, *Le Feu*, 266–8; *Under Fire*, 226–7
222 Lemercier, *Lettres*, 148
223 Audoin-Rouzeau, *Men at War*, 70
224 Eksteins, *Rites of Spring*, 172

Campion Vaughan and his men staggered through the mud of Passchendaele.

> Shells bursting around us. A man stopped dead in front of me, and exasperated I cursed him and butted him with my knee. Very gently he said, 'I'm blind, Sir,' and turned to show me his eyes and nose torn away by a piece of shell. 'Oh God! I'm sorry, sonny,' I said. 'Keep going on the hard part,' and left him staggering back in his darkness. … A tank had churned its way slowly behind Springfield and opened fire; a moment later I looked and nothing remained of it but a crumpled heap of iron; it had been hit by a large shell. It was now almost dark and there was no firing from the enemy; ploughing across the final stretch of mud, I saw grenades bursting around the pillbox and a party of British rushed in from the other side. As we all closed in, the Boche garrison ran out with their hands up. … We sent the 16 prisoners back across the open but they had only gone a hundred yards when a German machine-gun mowed them down.[225]

Maze felt the earth shake beneath him:

> The ground seemed to quake under me and everything appeared to be moving along with me, figures popping up and down on every side over the convulsing ground and I felt the rush of others coming on behind. The waves in front were merged in smoke, moving like animated figures projected on a glaring screen. Flashes made everything wobble and vacillate. I felt stunned and hardly conscious of anything. … The noise was deafening.[226]

Karl Feick, who was killed on 9 April 1917, described how, after a barrage lasting seventy hours, the French came storming towards them on the morning of 25 September 1916 during the French offensive in Champagne, thousands of blue figures, bayonets at the ready.

> [They were] all completely confident they would find us already dead, so that they could storm right over our corpses and finally bring freedom to their fatherland. A few minutes later almost all of them were lying in front of our trench, horribly mutilated corpses, and the unfortunately very small remnant, all the more courageously for that, opened a hellish volley into our tightly packed columns of assault troops.[227]

By contrast, another German, Arthur Goldstein, had his work cut out for him, but the eventual result was no different.

---

225 Campion Vaughan, *Some Desperate Glory*, 224–5; Keegan, *First World War*, 389

226 Winter, *Death's Men*, 178

227 Witkop, *Kriegsbriefe*, 272–3

> As soon as it got light, the enemy approached in tight columns, one after the other. We fired in desperation. But no matter how much their ranks are thinned, a dispiritingly superior force emerges from the trench and overpowers the right wing. ... Those were moments of great and troubling tension, and, when the troops that had broken out closed behind our back in a tight line, of deep despondency.

Fortunately for Goldstein, the German artillery was alerted and its shelling tore apart the new French line.

> Our courage restored, we fired into the withdrawing columns. In the trench, in the valley, the entire area occupied by the enemy was cleared with hand grenades. Several more columns of enemy troops were thrown into the battle but in vain. The great enemy attack has been beaten back, mainly thanks to the infantry that held its ground. ... Enemy losses are immense. The fields around us are littered with the dead...[228]

Captain Thomas Kettle of the Royal Dublin Fusiliers, whom we met at the start of this section, did not survive his leap into the unknown. He had not been made captain for nothing. Kettle was a writer, Professor of Economics at the University of Dublin, and the Member of Parliament for East Tyrone from 1906 to 1910. A prominent Irish nationalist, he wrote shortly before his death of the Irishmen executed in 1916 for their part in the Easter Rising that they would go down in history 'as heroes and martyrs and I will go down – if I go down at all – as a bloody British officer'. In the letter to his wife quoted earlier, he wrote that should he survive the war he would dedicate the rest of his life to creating and maintaining peace. 'I have seen war, and faced modern artillery, and know what an outrage it is against simple men.'[229]

No matter how many shared Kettle's fate, no matter how many died outright rather than later of their wounds, during every battle the wounded could eventually be seen struggling back. Henry Williamson wrote:

> Men, single and in couples, … answering no questions, … men without rifles, haggard, bloodshot-eyed, slouching past in loose file, slouching on anywhere, anyhow, staggering under rifles and equipment, some with jaws sagging, puttees coiled mud-boiled around ankles, feet in shapeless mud boots, swelled beyond feeling, men slouching on beyond fatigue and hope, on and on and on … Stretcher-bearers plodding desperate-faced. Men slavering and rolling their

228 *Kriegsbriefe gefallener Deutscher Juden*, 53–4

229 Marix Evans, *Battles of the Somme*, 45; Liddle & Cecil, *Facing Armageddon*, 256

> bare-teethed heads, slobbering and blowing, blasting brightness behind their eyeballs, supported by listless cripples.[230]

At the end of each day a roll call would be taken. Manning remembered the evening of 1 July 1916. His 2nd Middlesex had gone over the top with 24 officers and 650 men. Fifty reported present when their names were called.

> 'Redmain', was the name called out; and at first there was no reply. It was repeated. 'Has anyone seen anything of Redmain?' 'Yes, sir,' cried Pike with sullen anger in his voice. 'The poor bastard's dead, sir.' 'Are you sure of that, Pike?' Captain Malet asked him quietly, ignoring everything but the question of fact. 'I mean are you sure that the man you saw was Redmain?' 'I saw 'im, sir; 'e was just blown to buggery,' said Pike, with a feeling that was almost brutal in its directness. ''e were a chum o' mine sir, an' I seen 'im blown to fuckin' bits.'[231]

The survivors felt half dead themselves. After five days of fighting in France in September 1916, 'perhaps the worst hours that I have been through thus far', Joachim Friedrich Beutler wrote that those days had naturally not been without their effects on his body.

> You become nervous, you barely feel like eating. Five days without a warm bite to eat, enormous thirst, along with rain, so that you lose your boots and have to plod barefoot through the old mud. You sink to your thighs, underpants and trousers are plastered with thick crusts of mud. And incessant shells, shrapnel, terrible 100-pound mines, that bury men alive or fling them high into the air, hand grenades – that is the battlefield here. Dead and wounded, carcasses of horses, characterize the abominable hand of Mars.

Men who survived battles like these, men not been embraced by Death, had certainly looked him in the eye. Beutler's turn to be carried off by Death came later. On 17 November 1917 he wrote in a letter home from Flanders that he was leaving for the front line 'hopefully for the last time'. It would indeed be the last time. He died the next day.[232]

---

230 Ellis, *Eye-Deep*, 119–21

231 Manning, *Her Privates We*, 21; Winter, *Death's Men*, 186; Liddle & Cecil, *Facing Armageddon*, 805–6

232 *Kriegsbriefe gefallener Deutscher Juden*, 30, 31–2

## Meetings with Death

*Individuals*

Death's work could be seen everywhere, and in some sense he became visible himself; he sat next to you in the trench and walked beside you on the battlefield. He lay next to you in hospital. He was such an overwhelming presence that the boundary between death and life faded. Sassoon saw the dead and living next to each other in the trenches and could no longer tell which was which, 'for death was in all our hearts'.[233] The inability to distinguish between the two was a consequence of the sheer numbers of dead. Corporal Jack Beament would never forget the things he saw as he and his men marched forward during the Battle of the Somme. A corpse without a head, a hand sticking out of the ground. Human remains wherever you looked.[234] The massive numbers meant that from time to time the living had to walk over the bodies of the dead. During night marches up to the line, dead men lying in the way were kicked aside, the wounded trampled to death. Soldiers trod on heads, the wheels of gun carriages crushed chests.[235] The trenches themselves sometimes seemed paved with cobble-stones of flesh. With every step men took in the mud of Passchendaele or the Somme, there was a chance they might discover they were treading on dead men, even their faces.[236] Private Charlie Miles of the 10th Battalion, Royal Fusiliers found the sucking sound of mud underfoot terrible enough, but it was even worse if you did not hear it, since then you knew you had trodden on a corpse. 'It was terrifying. You'd tread on one on the stomach, perhaps, and it would grunt all the air out of its body. It made your hair stand on end. The smell could make you vomit.'[237]

Men usually trod on dead bodies only when they had no alternative. A few weeks before his death, August Hopp had to walk with fellow soldiers along a trench in which German and French corpses were piled up together, constantly blocking their way, 'so that you had to clamber over the piles of bodies and in so doing come into contact with the cold hands and faces and those terrible, bloody wounds. Mud and blood clung to our boots, clothes and hands.'[238] Towards the end of the fighting at Passchendaele, Corporal D.R. Macfie had no choice but to step on a body in order to move forward. He could not help noticing that the clothes had been worn off the man's back by the many mules that had gone ahead of him.[239] In 1915 Ambroselli had to walk along a French trench beneath which a mine had just exploded. Mutilated French corpses lay piled up together with many

233 Fussell, *Bloody Game*, 67
234 Macdonald, *Somme*, 140
235 Horne, *Price of Glory*, 175; Macdonald, *Passchendaele*, 37
236 Macdonald, *Somme*, 286, 314
237 Macdonald, *Passchendaele*, 186–7; Wilson, *Myriad Faces*, 473
238 Witkop, *Kriegsbriefe*, 37–8
239 Macdonald, *Passchendaele*, 213

wounded between them who could not move or be moved, moaning and crying and pleading. 'It was impossible to climb out of the trench to avoid this mound. Our hearts sank as we climbed over them in our hobnailed boots, but we had no choice.'[240]

Sometimes it happened without anyone noticing. M. Evans was sent out one evening to dig an improvised trench.

> The men, expert with spade and pick, seemed to have trouble in getting started. Their tools would not respond. A Verey light went up and we went down on our hands and found them touching cold, jelly-like swollen faces. We slithered and rocked and lost our balance on wobbling, bloated bellies. It was a jerry graveyard. The stench was indescribable.[241]

The vast death toll was not always the result of a long and bloody battle. Sometimes huge numbers were killed without warning. A single heavy shell could wipe out a whole platoon almost instantly. Osburn witnessed one such event at the beginning of the war.

> Fragments of stone, manure, pieces of clothing and hair came falling about me as I ran through an archway into the yard and beheld one of the most heartrending sights I have ever seen, even in war. The detachment of 9th Lancers had almost completely disappeared. In the centre of the yard where I had seen them but a moment before, there was now a mound four or five feet high of dead men and horses. … Around this central heap of dead men the wounded lay on all sides. Some had been blown to the other end the yard, their backs broken. One sat up dazed and whimpering, his back against a wall, holding part of his intestines in his hand.[242]

John Lucy had only just spotted a large number of casualties, and was feeling envious of those with slight wounds because for them the fighting was over, when he heard an enormous bang behind him. The place that had been full of the fortunate wounded was now scattered with the unfortunate dead.[243]

The loss of the ability to tell the dead from the living was also a result of Death's thousand faces, which often looked just like those of men still alive. Barbusse saw a man on whom death had bestowed 'the look and gestures of a grotesque'.

> With his hair flopping down over his eyes, his moustache drooping in his mouth and his face swollen, he is laughing. One eye is wide open, the other shut and he is sticking his tongue out. His arms are extended in the shape of a cross, with

240 Witkop, *Kriegsbriefe*, 148–9
241 Winter, *Death's Men*, 183
242 Holmes, *Riding the Retreat*, 51–2
243 Macdonald, *1914–1918*, 35

> open hands and fingers stretched. His right leg is reaching to one side while the left, which was broken by a piece of shrapnel, causing the haemorrhage that killed him, is completely turned round, dislocated, soft, with nothing to support it. A sad irony made the last twitches of his dying agony look like the gesticulations of a clown.[244]

John Glubb saw a body at Ypres. A man had been killed as he climbed a steep slope. He had raised a foot and stretched out a hand to pull himself up. 'By some miracle he remained in the same identical position. Except for the green colour of his face and hand, one would never have believed that he was dead.'[245] Ludwig Finke, who was killed on 9 May 1915, was serving at the front near Roeselare on 23 December 1914 when he was ordered to fetch rations. When he got back he saw that a shell had burst exactly at the spot where he had been sheltering a short time before. 'My mate Henn, up to his hips in rainwater, was dead; his skull was broken and he had a shell fragment in his back. He was still sitting exactly as he had been fifteen minutes earlier, when I left him, his rifle under his arm.'[246] In June 1915 during the Battle of Lorette, Barthas saw a young German soldier at the entrance to a trench who seemed to be asleep, leaning on the parapet. 'No sign of a wound, but death had brushed him with its wings, respecting the smile that still hovered about his youthful face.' On the Somme he spotted, or rather smelled, six German corpses. They were lying 'in positions so natural you might have thought they were still alive'.[247]

It was sometimes necessary to look twice to make sure a man was dead. Barbusse wrote: '"And what's that?" A milestone? No, it isn't a milestone. It's a head, a black head, tanned and waxed. The mouth is askew and you can see the moustache bristling on either side: a large, scorched cat's head. The body, a German one, is underneath, buried upright.'[248] During the offensive that followed the detonation of the mines along the Messines Ridge, Private Victor Fagence of the Queen's Royal West Surrey Regiment saw a soldier sitting on the parapet of a trench with his back to the enemy. He sat there calm and composed while others rushed about trying to dodge the shells bursting all around. Curious, Fagence zigzagged back.

> I saw that his face was very pale, and as I got up to the trench I could see why. The poor fellow was stone dead. His right leg had been completely severed between the knee and the thigh by a large shell splinter. It was lying there, all

244 Barbusse, *Le Feu*, 291–2; *Under Fire*, 246–7
245 Holmes, *Firing Line*, 179
246 Witkop, *Kriegsbriefe*, 66
247 Barthas, *Carnets*, 126, 381
248 Barbusse, *Le Feu*, 163; *Under Fire*, 139

> jagged, in the bottom of the trench and all his blood had poured out from the stump of his leg over it.[249]

Several months later Captain P. Coltman spotted one of his men in a shell-hole, on one knee, ready to leap out and rush towards German positions. The moment arrived. 'I shook him on the shoulder and shouted, "Come on!" As I shook him his tin hat fell off and half his head with it. He had been scalped as he waited.'[250] Something very similar happened to Blunden at Thiepval. He too saw a soldier on one knee, facing east. It was scarcely credible that the man could be dead. 'Death could not kneel so, I thought, and approaching I ascertained with a sudden shrivelling of spirit that Death could and did.'[251]

Tricks of the light were fairly common. Barbusse wrote in *Le Feu*:

> Someone shouted: 'His face is all black!' Another voice panted: 'What kind of a face is that?' ... 'His face? It's not his face!' Instead of a face, there was hair. It was then that we realized that the body, which had seemed to be seated, was in fact twisted, and broken backwards. In dreadful silence we looked at this vertical back facing us from the dislocated remains, these hanging arms, bent backwards, and the two extended legs lying on the soft earth with their toes dug into it.[252]

Death played games; he was an artist of sorts. Frey described dead men who were so unblemished and apparently ready for action that they were more like figures in a waxworks than dead men. On 15 August 1916 *L'Argonnaute* published the story of a French soldier who had seen five bodies in the bottom of a shell-hole in perfect symmetry, heads towards the outside, feet in the middle, laid out in a ring. A shell must have landed right in the middle of them and blown each of the five in a different direction. German NCO Carl Heller witnessed a similar sight. In a shell-hole lay five blackened soldiers 'as if they were at a game of cards. They had been killed instantly by concussion from a heavy explosion, yet remained in position.'[253] On the first day of Third Ypres, Jim Annan saw a Scotsman sliced in half by a shell fragment.

> He dropped his rifle and bayonet and threw his arms up in the air, and the top part of his torso fell back on the ground. The unbelievable thing was that the legs and the kilt went on running, just like a chicken with his head chopped off. One

---

249 Macdonald, *Passchendaele*, 54

250 Macdonald, *Passchendaele*, 178

251 Blunden, *Undertones of War*, 130

252 Barbusse, *Le Feu*, 366; *Under Fire*, 309

253 Frey, *Pflasterkästen*, 255–6; Audoin-Rouzeau, *Men at War*, 78; Andriessen, *De oorlogsbrieven van Unteroffizier Carl Heller*, 107; Eckart, *Eiskalt mit Würgen und Schlucken*, 8

> of my boys – I think it was his special pal – went rushing after him. He had some mad idea of picking up the upper part of the torso and chasing the legs to join him up. I shouted him back and he was wild with me because he wanted to help his pal. He couldn't realise that he was beyond help.[254]

Death was impartial, in small things as well as large. Graves came upon the corpses of two men who had bayoneted each other simultaneously.[255] It was not the only time such a sight was recorded. Ambroselli reported seeing two soldiers who had bayoneted each other at the same moment. 'The weapon of each was still sticking out of his opponent's body.'[256]

This indicates that one death might make a greater impression than another. In fact the way in which Death put in an appearance and the time and place he chose could make a huge difference. Blunden looked into his store dugout and was shocked to find that it was being used as a collection point for bodies recovered from the field, most of them horribly mangled, which would be left until there was enough time to bury them.[257] Denis Winter's father would never forget an officer who was shot 'leading the company into the attack by driving a golf ball with a club in front of him.'[258] Boy soldier Thomas Hope told of a limbless corpse with a torso so swollen that the uniform fitted like a glove. 'He may have wanted a tunic to fit him like that all his life – he gets it in death.'[259] Campana took a photograph of one of his dead comrades, 'laid open from the shoulders to the haunches like a quartered carcass of meat in a butcher's window'. It served as proof of how lucky he was himself.[260] Toller never forgot the corpse he had seen on his first day at the front. Many ex-servicemen could still vividly remember their first dead man,[261] no matter how many more they saw after that and later forgot, or even failed to notice at the time.

> I get up before daybreak. I wander about the village, past the blackened walls of shattered houses, stumbling into the shell-holes that pit the streets. A church door is open and I go in. The dawn shows greyly through the shattered windows and my heavy boots resound on the flagstones. A soldier is lying before the altar. When I bend down over him I see that he is dead. His head is broken open in the middle, the two sides gape apart like a giant egg-shell, the pulpy brain bulges out.[262]

---

254 Macdonald, *Passchendaele*, 99–100; see also: *De Vlaamsche Ziel*, 82
255 Graves, *Goodbye*, 175
256 Witkop, *Kriegsbriefe*, 149
257 Blunden, *Undertones of War*, 108
258 Winter, *Death's Men*, 60
259 Winter, *Death's Men*, 132
260 Horne, *Price of Glory*, 187; Brants & Brants, *Velden van weleer*, 237
261 Barthas, *Carnets*, 53; Macdonald, *Passchendaele*, 187
262 Toller, *Jugend in Deutschland*, 43

Men killed moments earlier left an indelible impression. Gladden wrote:

> The dead man lay amidst earth and broken timber. It seemed like a sacrilege to step over him but there was no evading the issue. Never before had I seen a man who had just been killed. A glance was enough. His face and body were terribly gashed as though some terrific force had pressed him down, and blood flowed from a dozen fearful wounds. The smell of blood mixed with the fumes of the shell filled me with nausea. Only a great effort saved my limbs from giving way beneath me. I could see from the sick grey faces of the file that these feelings were generally shared. A voice seemed to whisper with unchallengeable logic, 'Why shouldn't you be the next?'[263]

Above all, though, it was the mutilated corpses that stayed with you. Hoffman wrote of a group of men who were sent out to report on a section of the front line and were immediately faced with the job of trying to bury men who had been lying there since an engagement two weeks earlier.

> I knew all of these men intimately and it was indeed painful to learn of their condition. Some had apparently lived for some time; had tried to dress their own wounds, or their comrades had dressed them; but later they had died there. … Many of the men had been pumped full of machine gun bullets – shot almost beyond recognition. A hundred or so bullets, even in a dead man's body, is not a pretty sight. One of our men was lying with a German bayonet through him – not unlike a pin through a large beetle. Bayonets are hard to remove when once they have been caught between the ribs, especially the saw-tooth bayonets many of the Germans carried. To dislodge them it is usually necessary to shoot once or more to loosen the bayonet. This German had not waited but had left his gun and passed on. The little Italian boy was still lying on the barbed wire, his eyes open and his helmet hanging back on his head. There had been much shrapnel and some of the bodies were torn almost beyond recognition.[264]

Some time later a man called Vaugn was shot in the head right next to Hoffman. His head was blown away above the ears and eyes. Hoffman wrote that this suggested a dumdum bullet had been used, with a groove in the lead that caused it to spin and make a huge wound. Even an ordinary bullet could cause massive damage like this, however, if the skull was hit at a certain angle, causing the head to explode.[265] Whatever the precise cause, the effect was terrible. 'His brains ran out there in front of me like soup from a pot. … Vaugn lay there for a couple of days; finally

---

263 Winter, *Death's Men*, 133
264 Fussell, *Bloody Game*, 179–80
265 Holmes, *Firing Line*, 179

he was carried down and stored in the room where we had the other dead piled up like logs of wood; but he had to have his own place in the corner.'[266]

However mangled a dead man was, his comrades knew he had once been as much alive as they were, which emphasized the point that they too could be killed and mutilated at any moment, although it was a truth they immediately rejected. Manning wrote:

> Death, of course, like chastity, admits of no degree; a man is dead or not dead, and a man is just as dead by one means as by another; but it is infinitely more horrible and revolting to see a man shattered and eviscerated, than to see him shot. And one sees such things; and one suffers vicariously, with the inalienable sympathy of man for man. One forgets quickly. The mind is averted as well as the eyes. It reassures itself after the first despairing cry: 'It is I!'
>
> 'No it is not I. I shall not be like that.'
>
> And one moves on, leaving the mauled and bloody thing behind, gambling in fact on that implicit assurance each one of us has in his own immortality.[267]

Even more than shells and bullets, fire left its mark on the dead – if it left anything other than soot and ash. George Worsley described the effects of a fire that raged after a shell hit a munitions depot at Guillemont in August 1916.

> There was a young officer staggering round blinded and screaming and, as we ran, I saw our cook – just his head sticking out of the earth where he'd been buried, and he was screaming too. Not that you could hear anything in the terrible roaring of all these explosives, but you could see by the men's faces if they were screaming. And you could see that this man had gone stark staring mad by the frenzy in his face.

By dawn the fire had burned itself out and a few sleepless, shocked and pale survivors began stumbling back towards the guns. There was nothing left, except for a few bits of twisted metal and some smouldering rubble, no sign of the cook, nor of the blinded officer, nor of a single survivor among the many mangled bodies.[268] These corpses were at least visible. Sometimes the entire battlefield might be set alight by shelling. The bodies would be incinerated, the wounded burned alive.[269]

Naturally death had a greater impact in the case of friends or relatives. Toller saw two boys, one of whom had his cap over his face so that it was not immediately obvious he was dead.

266 Fussell, *Bloody Game*, 182–3
267 Manning, *Her Privates We*, 11; Winter, *Death's Men*, 132–3
268 Macdonald, *Somme*, 218–19
269 Jünger, *In Stahlgewittern*, 208

> Blond locks fall in a tangle over his vaulted forehead, the eyes in his narrow, angular face are closed, his mouth, his chin … nothing but a bloody mess. The boy is dead. 'He was my friend,' the other boy says. 'We went to the same school, were in the same class. He was a year younger than me, not yet seventeen. I joined up as a volunteer, but he wasn't allowed to. His mother wouldn't let him. He was her only son. He was ashamed, and we both begged her until at last she gave in. We got to the front a week ago and now he's dead. What should I write to his mother?'[270]

A man might meet Death in the form of innumerable corpses of friends, in other words when his work was done, but he might also meet Death in action. A soldier in hospital once said, 'You may get used to seeing wounded men, but not to seeing men wounded'. The same went for seeing men killed; it was an experience few could forget.[271] Quigley remembered a man who, laden with ammunition, had decided to act the hero. He ran forward and the last that was seen of him were 'two arms straining madly at the ground, blood pouring from his mouth while legs and body sank into a shellhole filled with water'.[272] Charles Carrington saw Corporal Matthews shot right before his eyes.

> I was looking straight at him as the bullet struck him and was profoundly affected by the remembrance of his face, though at the time I hardly thought of it. He was alive, and then he was dead, and there was nothing human left in him. He fell with a neat round hole in his forehead and the back of his head blown out.[273]

Private R. Le Brun of the 16th Canadian Machine-Gun Company saw his friend Private Tombs, the only other survivor of his section, hit in the head by a burst of machine-gun fire. It was not a tidy death. Bits of Tombs were spattered all over Le Brun's uniform and gas mask. 'I stood there trying to get the bits off. It was a terrible feeling to be the only one left.'[274]

The following report appeared in *On progresse* of 1 July 1917:

> I can see those men who were two living beings just a moment ago and now one is nothing but a mass of mud and blood, the other is just this long stiff body, burnt, with a blackened face and three holes, in the face, stomach and thighs, and his two fists held up in self-defence, two fists asking for mercy and trying to ward off his death. The awfulness of this body! It would mean nothing now

270 Toller, *Jugend in Deutschland*, 53; Brants, *Plasje bloed*, 177
271 Bourke, *Dismembering the Male*, 137
272 Winter, *Death's Men*, 180
273 Holmes, *Firing Line*, 176
274 Holmes, *Firing Line*, 178

to any of those who were fond of him, for human feelings no longer exist in the corpses that war has crushed.[275]

The process of dying invariably left its mark on survivors. Patrick MacGill came upon a friend lying up against the barbed wire, 'one arm round it as if in embrace'. He had been mortally wounded in his side by a shell fragment.

'In much pain, chummy?' I asked. 'Ah, Christ, yes, Pat. Wife and two kiddies too. Are we getting the best of it?' 'Winning all along.' 'That's good. Any hope for me?' 'Of course there is,' I lied. 'You have two morphia tablets and lie quietly. You'll be back in England in two or three days' time.' I placed the morphia under his tongue and he closed his eyes as if going to sleep. Then with an effort he tried to get up and gripped the wire. His legs shot out from under him and, muttering something about rations being fit for pigs and not for men, he fell back and died.[276]

Graves suddenly saw a group bending over a man lying in the bottom of the trench.

He was making a snoring noise mixed with animal groans. At my feet lay the cap he had worn, splashed with his brains, I had never seen human brains before; I somehow regarded them as a poetical figment. One can joke with a badly-wounded man and congratulate him on being out of it. One can disregard a dead man. But even a miner can't make a joke that sounds like a joke over a man who takes three hours to die, after the top of his head has been taken off by a bullet fired at twenty yards' range.[277]

Charles Delvert meticulously recorded the death of fellow French soldier Jégoud.

The death of Jégoud was atrocious. He was on the first steps of the dugout when a shell … burst. His face was burned; one splinter entered his skull behind the ear; another slit open his stomach, broke his spine, and in the bloody mess one saw his spinal cord gliding about. His right leg was completely crushed above the knee. The most hideous part of it all was that he continued to live for four or five minutes.[278]

On 17 August 1916 Stanhope Walker noted in his diary:

---

275 Audoin-Rouzeau, *14–18. Les combattants*, 85
276 Winter, *Death's Men*, 181–2
277 Graves, *Goodbye*, 98
278 Eksteins, *Rites of Spring*, 152–3

> Officer said 'No padre, I am not as bad as that, I am not dying' – 'well, old chap, I did not say you were, but you never know how these wounds turn out.' 'I shall recover, I feel I shall not die, but oh why can't I enjoy a rest now I am here, why do I feel no interest in the things round me? Yes, I will recover and enjoy life again – gasp – are they attacking again? – now sergeant major – gasp –' (silence whilst I pronounce the committal) – two or three gasps – I call up the sister, his pockets are emptied and his body carried out.[279]

Killing a man meant a direct and intimate encounter with death. Descriptions of man-to-man fighting are rare in diaries, letter and memoirs, but the opposite is true of novels. Of course it is never completely clear which passages are autobiographical. The paucity of accounts of personal acts of killing is partly a reflection of the fact that it was indeed quite rare. As we have seen, most casualties died anonymous deaths as far as their enemies were concerned, killed from a long way away. Another reason, however, must be that those who wrote war memoirs were not ordinary soldiers. Their generally middle-class upbringing and above average education produced a tendency to self-censorship when it came to reporting on killing at first hand. Many will have felt a reluctance to admit frankly in public that they had driven a bayonet into a man's stomach. Samuel Hynes regards a story told by Eric Partridge in his *Frank Honeywood, Private* as typical. He shot a German soldier, but, he writes, he suspected at the moment he fired that the man was already dead. Since his target hardly moved when he was hit, Partridge knew this for certain. So the only man he was ever aware of having shot was already dead. He had hit a corpse.[280] Had the artillery already done his work for him? Or another infantryman perhaps? Did Partridge try to talk himself out of the notion of having killed a man because killing was against his nature? Did he censor his account afterwards? Did he really have this thought while he was firing the shot or was it an idea that arose while he was writing his book, which then became projected onto the past?

German Lance-Corporal Westman was one of the few to admit killing a man at close quarters. During an attack on a strong French position he suddenly saw a French corporal standing in front of him. Both Westman and the Frenchman held their bayonets at the ready, 'he to kill me, I to kill him'. In his youth in Freiburg, Westman had fought duels with the sabre, so he was the quicker of the two and managed to stab his opponent through the chest. 'He dropped his rifle and fell, and the blood shot out of his mouth. I stood over him for a few seconds and then I gave him the *coup de grâce*. After we had taken the enemy position, I felt giddy, my knees shook, and I was actually sick.' The dead Frenchman would haunt Westman's dreams for many nights to come.[281]

---

279 Moynihan, *People at War*, 80
280 Hynes, *Soldiers' Tale*, 66–7
281 Holmes, *Firing Line*, 378–9

Men often repressed thoughts of their encounters with death, so that they re-emerged as part of a neurosis of some kind or, as in Westman's case, nightmares. Occasionally, however, they could lead to a profound change of attitude. One day Toller was standing in a trench, hacking at the earth with a pick.

> The steel point sticks, I yank and pull it out with a jerk. Hanging from it is a slimy knot and whichever way I look at it, I see human entrails. A dead man is buried here.
>
> A – dead – man.
>
> What makes me pause? Why do these words force me to stand still, why do they press upon my brain like a vice, why do they close up my throat and freeze my heart? Three words like any other three.
>
> A dead man – ultimately I want to forget these three words. What is it about these words? Why do they overpower and overwhelm me?
>
> A – dead – man.
>
> And suddenly, like darkness splitting itself from light, the word splits from its meaning and I grasp the simple truth of Man, which I had forgotten, which was buried and covered over; the oneness, the unity, the uniting.
>
> A dead man.
>
> Not: a dead Frenchman.
>
> Not: a dead German.
>
> A dead man.
>
> All these dead are men, all these corpses have breathed as I do, all these dead had a father, a mother, wives whom they loved, a piece of land where they put down roots, faces that told of their joys and sufferings, eyes that saw the light and the sky.

From that moment on Toller could 'never pass a dead man again without stopping to contemplate his face' and wonder: 'Who were you? ... Where did you come from? Who is mourning for you?'[282] Toller signed up for the air force to escape the impersonal life of the mechanized masses on the ground, but before he could take to the skies he was declared medically unfit, with stomach and heart ailments. The way was open for him to take an active role in the battle against the war.

### *The battlefield*

The aftermath of a battle was a desolate, deathly sight. Hoffman described it as the most pitiful place on earth.[283] To Stanhope Walker, the landscape after a battle was an 'absolute scene of destruction, miles and miles of country battered beyond all possible recognition', demonstrating the enormity of contemporary warfare. Blunden spoke of the Schwaben Redoubt as a web of trenches in which 'mud,

282 Toller, *Jugend in Deutschland*, 52; Brants, *Plasje bloed*, 176

283 Fussell, *Bloody Game*, 180

and death, and life were much the same thing'. Seeing dead men strewn all about him, he concluded 'the whole zone was a corpse'.[284] Death had done his work and could take a rest; he had wreaked havoc on the field of honour and the field now belonged to him, or perhaps more accurately, as Blunden suggested, death and the battlefield had become one. Barbusse described a battlefield that had been swept by slaughter the day before and compared it to a cemetery with the top layer of earth scraped away. Alongside the remains of the recently killed were older corpses, some of which had lain there for months. 'Even in their scattered remains, spread around by the weather and already almost dust and ashes, one can detect the ravages made by the machine-guns which killed them, holing their backs and sides, cutting them in half.'[285] On 6 April 1915 Herbert Weißer wrote:

> Yesterday I was in the trenches. There I finally got to see the real war. Everything is played out on a very narrow (although endlessly long) strip of land that seems far, far too cramped for its immense significance. And this strip of land also sustains green grass, colourful flowers, trees and friendly little houses. ... But do you know what else there is to see in the meadows? There lie the Marburger Jäger: students and professors, the hope and future of the German people. One beside the next they lie stretched across the meadow. Yes, there lay such a fresh young man, right at the front, perhaps the furthest forward as they struck. Forgetting everything around him, he stormed ahead into the hail of bullets. 'One more leap and I'm in the enemy trench' – but he could not even think that thought through to the end. Three metres in front of the trench he sank into a heap, maybe he had time to see that all was in vain, that the attack would not succeed, maybe he lived another day and slowly starved, because there between the trenches no one could help him.[286]

When the fighting ended, the battlefield was an unreal place. A French pilot, looking down on Verdun, described the landscape as 'the humid skin of a monstrous toad'[287]. A Belgian soldier looked at the landscape around the Yser and saw 'a swamp, but with varying heights and depths'. On that swamp lay, or floated, bodies in the most bizarre poses or – worse – parts of bodies: arms, heads, torsos, or boots with feet still in them. In mid-October 1915, several weeks before his death, German NCO Karl Neumann described the pockmarked French meadows the pilots saw from above. There were fields where each shell-hole touched the next, craters several metres deep and more than five metres across.[288] Years later Dix described the battlefield he had seen on his arrival in Champagne in the autumn of 1915: 'Endless and abandoned, rising and falling, interrupted by nothing but a few

284 Moynihan, *People at War*, 81; Blunden, *Undertones of War*, 130–31
285 Barbusse, *Le Feu*, 278–9; *Under Fire*, 244
286 Witkop, *Kriegsbriefe*, 82–3
287 Eksteins, *Rites of Spring*, 147
288 *De Vlaamsche ziel*, 81–2; *Kriegsbriefe gefallener Deutscher Juden*, 98–9

blackened pines, a white, greyish yellow landscape of death stretches out before me.' The battle zone filled men with a sense of nihilism. The war turned cultivated land into a prehistoric landscape and soil into a kind of bubbling primeval slime from which it was impossible for a human being to escape. To this the armies had added a labyrinthine network of trenches and dugouts, which only served to increase the sense of unreality, since there was no life to be seen at all.[289] Dix's compatriot Lieutenant Heinrich Koch felt a sense of unreality creep over him when he noticed in February 1915, for the first time, the amazing beauty of the stretch of landscape to which 'an absurd war' had brought 'indescribable misery' – beautiful, but nonetheless carpeted by death. After the war, farmers would 'bump up against the bones of the dead with every step' as they ploughed their fields.[290] As early as September 1914, Lieutenant Gottfried Sender described the battlefield as a place where corpses and mass graves stared at you and 'where ruined fields, gardens and villages told of the horrors of recent battles'.[291]

Jünger walked about in a daze when he saw his first battlefield. 'We looked at all these dead with dislocated limbs, distorted faces, and the hideous colours of decay, as though we walked in a dream through a garden of strange plants, and we could not realize at first what we had all round us.'[292] Jünger also described what gas did to a battlefield; mustard gas in particular transformed it from a dead landscape into a deadly one. 'A large proportion of the plants had withered, snails and moles lay dead, and the horses that were stabled in Monchy for use by the messengers had watering eyes and muzzles. The shells and ammunition splinters that lay all over the place had a fetching green patina.'[293]

Hans Forster, who was killed on 29 November 1916, wrote on 1 July that year about the battlefield of the Somme emerging before him, saying there were no colours any longer 'besides brown, grey and black' and no shapes 'apart from shell-holes'[294] Even when, as in the accounts by Jünger and Weißer, other colours were visible, they only made the scene seem more unreal. Hayward remembered the violent contrast between the hot sun, larks singing, and the broken bodies of the men whose red blood stood out so starkly against the bright blue of the cornflowers.[295]

Hynes remarks that war memoirs, letters and soldiers' diaries, although they made the war vivid by telling what happened where, and what it all meant for the men who experienced it, did not make the war familiar. Some may even have felt an urge to write precisely in order to show how unfamiliar war was, how totally

289 Conzelmann, *Der andere Dix*, 78, 91, 97; Sassoon, *Complete Memoirs*, 624

290 *Kriegsbriefe gefallener Deutscher Juden*, 72

291 *Kriegsbriefe gefallener Deutscher Juden*, 106

292 Holmes, *Firing Line*, 177

293 Jünger, *Storm of Steel*, 82; Eckart & Gradmann, *Die Medizin*, 154; see also: Ureel, *De Kleine Mens*, 115

294 Witkop, *Kriegsbriefe*, 261

295 Winter, *Death's Men*, 249

alien to everything generally regarded as normal, even to everything most people had in mind when they thought about war. A battle zone was not landscape, it was anti-landscape. Binding wrote of the Somme:

> I can still find no word nor image to express the awfulness of that waste. There is nothing like it on earth, nor can be. A desert is always a desert; but a desert which tells you all the time that it used not to be a desert is appalling. That is the tale which is told by the dumb, black stumps of the shattered trees which still stick up where there used to be villages.[296]

Masefield had never in his life seen such mud, nor such a sight as at the Leipzig Redoubt near Thiepval.

> Other places are bad and full of death, but this was deep in mud as well, a kind of chaos of deep running holes & broken ground & filthy chasms, and pools & stands & marshes of iron-coloured water, & yellow snow & bedevilment. Old rags of wet uniform were everywhere, & bones & legs & feet & heads were sticking out of the ground, & in one place were all the tools of a squad just as they had laid them down; in order, & then all the squad, where they had been killed, & the skull of one of them in a pool, &, nearby, the grave of half a German, & then a German overcoat with ribs inside it, & rifles & bombs & shells literally in heaps. … Such a hell of a desolation all round as no words can describe.[297]

Jünger's brother wrote of the area around Ypres, in one of its rare quiet moments:

> Out of the hideously scarred soil of Flanders rose black, splintered trunks of trees, all that was left of what had once been a large forest. Vast swathes of smoke hung around, and dimmed the evening with their heavy, gloomy clouds. Over the naked earth, which had been so pitilessly and repeatedly ripped open, hovered choking yellow or brown gases that drifted sluggishly about.[298]

Paul Nash described the same landscape, which as a soldier in the Ypres salient he had helped to create and which he would immortalize on paper when, after being invalided home, he returned to the continent as a war artist.

> Sunset and sunrise are blasphemous. … Only the black rain out of the bruised and swollen clouds … is fit atmosphere in such a land. The rain drives on, the stinking mud becomes more evilly yellow, the shell-holes fill up with green-white water, the roads and tracks are covered in inches of slime, the black dying

296 Hynes, *Soldiers' Tale*, 6–7
297 Marix Evans, *Battles of the Somme*, 54
298 Jünger, *In Stahlgewittern*, 142; *Storm of Steel*, 175

> trees ooze and sweat and the shells never cease, … they plunge into the grave which is this land. … It is unspeakable, godless, hopeless.[299]

The landscape was desolate, dismal, depressing. No wonder that during the spring offensive of 1918 Binding could not sleep the night before the German Third Army was due to leave the old battle region. Of course the cold alone made sleep almost impossible, and Binding felt the excitement of the hunt. With all his heart he longed to take part in a real advance again, finally, after all those years of sitting waiting. But it was also the prospect of advancing across a landscape that was still more or less intact that excited him, a landscape of occupied farms and villages, with green trees. Where he was now the villages and towns were nothing but names, and even the ruins had been pounded repeatedly.[300]

Because the battlefield was at such variance with everything the men knew, it was impossible for people at home to gain a clear impression of the reality. They heard about it but could not know it. If those who had never been to the front thought about the battlefields and trenches at all, they saw neat, inviting, deep, broad, spacious passageways, where soldiers smoked their pipes or cigars contentedly as they played cards. They might retain this impression even after men on leave, or sick, or wounded had told them again and again that the truth was very different from the propaganda, quite apart from the fact that not every returning soldier told them anything of the sort. The innumerable unfamiliar experiences men carried with them from the trenches could rarely be shared with those who had remained at home, and there were many men who believed they should not even be mentioned. This was one reason why people back home continued to take propaganda seriously. Even those who did listen to the stories, believed them, and knew they reflected the real state of affairs were often incapable of really knowing the truth, of letting it sink in. In June 1916 T.S. Eliot sent the *Nation* magazine a letter he had received from a young officer, eighteen years old, who had gone straight from public school to the trenches. The author was a young man angry with the outside world, which refused to look reality in the face and was happy to have dust thrown in its eyes. He had decided to lay out one more time all the horrors of the trenches, no man's land and the battlefield. He tells of a 'leprous earth, scattered with the swollen and blackened corpses of hundreds of young men'. His description goes on:

> The appalling stench of rotting carrion. ... Mud like porridge, trenches like shallow and sloping cracks in the porridge – porridge that stinks in the sun. Swarms of flies and bluebottles clustering on pits of offal. Wounded men lying in the shell holes among the decaying corpses: helpless under the scorching sun and bitter nights, under repeated shelling. Men with bowels dropping out, lungs shot away, with blinded, smashed faces, or limbs blown into space. Men

299 Eksteins, *Rites of Spring*, 146–7

300 Macdonald, *To the Last Man*, 257; Frey, *Pflasterkästen*, 269–70, 293

screaming and gibbering. Wounded men hanging in agony on the barbed wire, until a friendly spout of liquid fire shrivels them up like a fly in a candle. ... But these are only words and probably convey only a fraction of their meaning to the hearers. They shudder, and it is forgotten.[301]

Could the reader of this passage have reacted any differently? The conditions of war are impossible for anyone who has not experienced them at first hand to comprehend. War is too strange, too much a reversal of what is seen as normal in civilian life. Barbusse was one of those who complained that people on the home front understood nothing about it,[302] but if Barbusse had not been a *poilu*, he too would have failed to understand the stories and feelings of the troops. It is telling that Robert Graves' wife remained convinced that the sufferings inflicted on working-class married women in British society in the early twentieth century were even worse than what the soldiers in the trenches had been put through.[303]

The battlefield was an unreal playground of death from the start and would remain so throughout the war. In late September 1914 there was heavy fighting in the Bois de St Rémy. The French wanted to prevent German units from breaking out northwards. In his book *Ceux de 14*, Maurice Genevoix described the fighting that followed and the scene that resulted, a scene that played itself out in a single icy night and was dominated by the cries of the wounded left behind in the wood.

And those heartrending cries and moans are a torment to anyone who hears them, a cruel torment, especially for the soldiers who have had strict orders not to leave their posts, who would like to run to their gasping comrades, to care for them, to comfort them, and who cannot... 'Water! – Are you going to leave me here to die? – Stretcher-bearers! – Water!... – God I don't want to die here!...' A German (he's lying no more than twenty metres away) makes the same appeal to us, incessantly: 'Kamerad Franzose! Kamerad! Kamerad Franzose!' And then more softly, imploringly: 'Hilfe! Hilfe!'[304]

Exactly four years later, in Belgium, Robert W. Wilson looked out across no man's land and saw a vast ruined landscape marked by years of trench warfare.

As far as the eye can see truly a piteous spectacle. Trees standing dead, stark and bare, the remains of woods, shell-holes innumerable, pill-boxes rent by shell-fire, … debris of all sorts, munitions, rifles, equipment, bodies alas of Germans horribly battered, and of our Belgian allies.[305]

---

301 Fussell, *Bloody Game*, 36; Gilbert, *First World War*, 337–8; Andriessen, *De oorlogsbrieven van Unteroffizier Carl Heller*, 184

302 Barbusse, *Le Feu*, 324–5

303 Graves, *Goodbye*, 237

304 Brants & Brants, *Velden van weleer*, 251

305 Richter, *Chemical Soldiers*, 209

The battlefield was seldom truly peaceful and quiet. Along with the wounded crying out in pain and begging for help there was almost always the sound of gunfire from a nearby battle or bombardment. Even the dead might not be silent. Jünger walked utterly alone into an abandoned no man's land, 'that eerie cratered landscape', where he heard a 'stifled, unpleasant sound; with a degree of calm that astonished me, I registered that it came from a bloated disintegrating corpse'.[306]

There were nevertheless some battlegrounds silent as the grave, with no fighting in the vicinity, the wounded either removed or expired, the corpses no longer making the slightest noise. Barbusse said such fields were not asleep but dead. The battlefield itself had been killed and drowned and the dead who lay there were terrible: swollen, formless, colourless, pulpy and wrinkled.[307] A British gunner wrote of Passchendaele:

> Figure to yourself a desolate wilderness of water-filled shell craters, and crater after crater whose lips form narrow peninsulas along which one can at best pick but a slow and precarious way. Here a shattered tree trunk, there a wrecked 'pill box' sole remaining evidence that this was once a human and inhabited land. Dante would never have condemned lost souls to wander in so terrible a purgatory. … Even the birds and rats have forsaken so unnatural a spot.[308]

Sassoon noted in his diary on 30 March 1916:

> There are still pools in the craters; they reflect the stars like any lovely water, but nothing grows near them; snags of iron jut from their banks, tin cans and coils of wire, and other trench-refuse. If you search carefully, you may find a skull, eyeless, grotesquely matted with what was once hair; eyes once looked from these detestable holes, they made the fabric of a passionate life, they appealed for justice, they were lit with triumph, and beautiful with pity.[309]

Jünger described the land around a country road at Guillemont, where the Germans had held back advancing British troops during the Battle of the Somme.

> The defile proved to be little more than a series of enormous craters full of pieces of uniform, weapons and dead bodies; the country around, so far as the eye could see, had been ploughed by heavy shells. ... The defile and the land behind was strewn with German dead, the field ahead with British. Arms and legs and heads stuck out of the slopes; in front of our holes were severed limbs and bodies, some of which had had coats or tarpaulins thrown over them, to save us the

306 Brants, *Plasje bloed*, 104
307 Barbusse, *Le Feu*, 350, 352
308 Prior & Wilson, *Passchendaele*, 178
309 Fussell, *Bloody Game*, 53

> sight of the disfigured faces. In spite of the heat, no one thought of covering the bodies with earth.[310]

This is a mournful description from a man famous for describing war as a grand affair, but not so out of character as it may seem. There were two distinct kinds of German war literature, just as in France there were Barthas and Barbusse on the one hand and Lécluse on the other, and in Britain Sassoon and Owen as opposed to Brooke. In Germany the writers who denounced the war included Frank, Toller, Frey, Johannsen and Remarque, while those literary authors who described war as the greatest of moments, as the only time in which a man could live life to the full, included Jünger and Friedrich Lehmann.[311] But the distinction between the two does not emerge particularly strongly in their descriptions of warfare or of the things they witnessed personally, nor even in the language they used to express what they saw. The difference between the two types of war literature lies above all in the interpretation of the things portrayed, in the connotations ascribed and conclusions drawn. To Barthas and Toller, men had died for nothing, whereas to De Lécluse and Jünger they were heroes and martyrs who had given their lives for victory, yet Lécluse's description of mutilated corpses could equally well have come from *Le Feu*. Both Remarque's and Johannsen's appraisals of comradeship find echoes in Lehmann's work, and Lehmann's account of the battlefield would not have been out of place in theirs:

> A field of the dead. ... Not a trace of life is left, the tree stumps are dead, the grass has been burned away, the soil has been churned to a depth of four metres, ploughed open, desecrated, martyred, ashen and dead, just like the many, friend or enemy, who still lie around unburied. Here a skeletal hand sticks out of the ground, there a half-rotten skull under a German steel helmet.[312]

It is striking how often descriptions of the battlefield make no mention of houses or villages, even though they may feature other traces of lives once lived there. This too makes the zone an unreal anti-landscape, especially when we consider that the lands of the Western Front belong to one of Europe's most densely populated regions. Masefield described the area around the Somme as 'skinned, gouged, flayed and slaughtered, and the villages smashed to powder, so that no man could ever say there had been a village there within the memory of man'. In mid-March 1918, Heller was ordered to pass on the news that Zonnebeke had been taken. He asked in amazement where on earth Zonnebeke was. He turned out to be standing in it. Most towns and villages on the Western Front that were bombarded to a pulp were rebuilt, usually at the same spot. Ypres is the best known example; Passchendaele and Albert too rose from the ashes. But many of the original

---

310 Jünger, *In Stahlgewittern*, 72; *Storm of Steel*, 97–8; Brants, *Plasje bloed*, 104–5

311 Boterman, *Oorlog als bron*, 255–6

312 Sandstrom, *Comrades-in-Arms*, 85–6; Werth, *Verdun*, 271

inhabitants would never return to the lands around Verdun. No mention is ever made of Fleury or Cumières any longer except in relation to the war. They were wiped off the map for ever in 1914–18.[313]

Never absent from descriptions of battlefields are the corpses, scattered, covered in flies, lying next to each other, on top of each other, in sun and rain, putrefying, gnawed at by rats, wind-blown and devoured by the mud. Those not recovered remained there, and those not yet dead were killed by renewed shelling or machine-gun fire, by loss of blood or by drowning, by starvation, thirst or exhaustion. Even the lightly wounded must often have met such an end. Hellish gunfire made it impossible for them to stand up and walk back. By the time the firing abated they had grown weak. Their suffering might last several days, even weeks before death brought deliverance.[314] Many described them, the dead men between the trenches, 'already half sunk into the ground'. Frank wrote in *Der Mensch ist Gut*:

> The dead. Really little more than scraps of uniform. Their faces and hands had already become one with the ground. A second layer of earth, made of corpses. ... [One of the dead] could not be brought back, even though he was only two metres away. Because if just one head was raised, ten rifles would be raised instantly. That dead man had been lying in front of the trench for six weeks, staring and stinking.[315]

Thomas Hope saw three wounded men who had drowned, their heads still poking up out of the water. It looked as if they had used the last of their strength to keep their faces above the rising surface. In another small pool only a hand could be seen, holding a rifle, and in the next pool a steel helmet with half a head in it. The eyes seemed to be staring icily at the green slime floating on the surface.[316]

Jünger could see no sense in covering the dead with sand or lime, or throwing a tarpaulin over them, 'in order to escape their black, bloated faces'.

> There were too many. Everywhere, shovels struck something buried. All the secrets of the grave lay open in a grotesquerie worse than the most lunatic dream. Hair fell in clumps from skulls like rotting leaves from autumn trees. Some decayed into a green fish-flesh, which gleamed at night through the torn uniforms. If you stepped on one of these, you left behind phosphorous foot-prints. Others dried into lime-covered mummies. Elsewhere, flesh fell from bones like a reddish-brown gelatin. In humid nights, the swollen cadavers awoke to a ghastly

313 Dyer, *Missing*, 120–21; Andriessen, *De oorlogsbrieven van Unteroffizier Carl Heller*, 220; Audoin-Rouzeau & Becker, *'14–'18*, 225

314 Keegan, *History of Warfare*, 362; Witkop, *Kriegsbriefe*, 178–9; Wilson, *Myriad Faces*, 471

315 Frank, *Der Mensch ist Gut*, 80–81

316 Brants & Brants, *Velden van weleer*, 90

> life, as gas, sputtering and whispering, escaped from the wounds. The worst was the bubbling mass of countless worms which oozed from the corpses.[317]

R. Naegelen described rain pouring down unceasingly onto corpses in September 1918, 'and the bullets smashed their bleached bones. ... [One dead man] showed his grinning, fleshless head, the skull naked, the eyes eaten away. A set of false teeth slid onto the faded shirt and from the wide open mouth leapt a repulsive creature.'[318] Three weeks after the slaughter of 1 July 1916, Gerald Brenan crossed the battlefield to visit a friend. He reported on what he had seen. 'The wounded, who could not be brought in, had crawled into shell holes, wrapped their waterproof sheets round them, taken out their Bibles, and died like that.'[319]

For surviving soldiers the part of the battle zone that was constantly within their field of vision was the most mentally taxing of all. At Arras, Hugo Müller was continually faced by the sight of bodies shot to pieces, hanging on the barbed wire. 'In front of the trench there lay until recently a human hand with a ring, and a few metres from it a forearm of which eventually only the bones remained.'[320] Barbusse had looked out upon a similar scene:

> Ahead of us, some ten metres away at most, there were motionless, outstretched bodies, one beside another, a row of soldiers, mown down; and, from every direction, clouds of bullets and shells were riddling this row of dead men with holes. The bullets ... were holing and battering the bodies rigidly pinned to the ground, breaking the stiffened limbs, pounding into pale, empty faces, bursting liquefied eyeballs. ...
>
> [*later*] Then I turn and look at the dead who are gradually being exhumed from the night, showing their stiffened, spattered forms. There are four of them. They are our companions, Lamuse, Barque, Biquet and little Eudore. They are decomposing there, right beside us, half obstructing the wide, twisting, muddy furrow that the living still care to defend.
>
> [*later again*] That was four nights ago and now I can see the shapes of the bodies appearing in the dawn, which has come once again to wash over this hell on earth. Barque is rigid and seems extended. His arms are stuck to his sides, his chest has collapsed, his belly has sunk into a bowl. With his head raised on a pile of mud he watches over the top of his feet those who approach from the left, with his darkened face, smudged by the viscous stain of hair that has fallen across it, thickly encrusted with black blood, and his scalded eyes, looking bloodshot and as though cooked. ... A pestilential cloud is starting to hang around the remains of these creatures with whom we lived so closely and suffered for so long. When

317 Whalen, *Bitter Wounds*, 43
318 Brants & Brants, *Velden van weleer*, 195
319 Keegan, *Face of Battle*, 269
320 Witkop, *Kriegsbriefe*, 241

> we see them, we say: 'All four of them are dead.' But they are too misshapen for us to really think: 'This is them.'[321]

Owen sighed in the bleak winter months of 1916–17 that he could live with the cold and fatigue and danger as well as any man but not with the ubiquitous and depressing '*Ugliness*'. The landscape was hideous, the noises vile, the language – even his own – foul. And then there were the frozen bodies, broken and blasted like everything else and impossible to bury in the frosted ground. '[They] sit outside the dug-outs all day, all night, the most execrable sights on earth. … And a week later to come back and find them still sitting there in motionless groups, THAT is what saps the "soldierly spirit".'[322]

Graves noted that many of the craters contained the corpses of wounded men who had crawled into them to die. Some had been reduced to skeletons, picked clean by rats.[323] This demonstrates, incidentally, that even the most appalling phenomena could have their advantages. Captain J.M. McQueen of the RAMC condemned the practice of spraying bodies with disinfectants like chloride of lime or quicklime as recommended in the pamphlet *Treatment of Bodies Exposed in the Open which cannot be Buried or Cremated.* It was 'the height of folly', he said, and not only because they had nowhere near enough disinfectant to make a proper job of it. If corpses could not be buried, then rats and bacterial decay should be given the chance to reduce them to heaps of bleached bones as quickly as possible.[324]

However much scenes like these depressed the spirit and eroded morale, it was the audible process of dying that affected the nerves most of all. Toller wrote:

> One night we hear cries, as if someone is in excruciating pain; then all is quiet. A man must have been killed, we think. After an hour the cries begin again. This time they do not stop. Not this night. Not the next night. Naked and wordless, the cries moan on. We cannot tell whether they come from the throat of a German or a Frenchman. The cries exist in their own right, an indictment of heaven and earth. We press our fists to our ears to block out the moaning; it does not help: the cries cut into our heads like a circular saw, stretching minutes into hours, hours into years. We whither and grow old from sound to sound.
>
> We have discovered who is crying out; one of ours, hanging on the barbed wire. Nobody can save him. Two have tried and were shot. Some mother's son is hopelessly trying to fight off death. Hell, he's making so much fuss, if he goes on much longer we'll go mad. On the third day death silences him.[325]

321 Barbusse, *Le Feu*, 237, 244–8, *Under Fire*, 201, 207 & 209–10
322 Day Lewis, *Collected Poems*, 162
323 Graves, *Goodbye*, 117
324 Macdonald, *1914–1918*, 204; Fussell, *Bloody Game*, 32
325 Toller, *Jugend in Deutschland*, 51–2

But perhaps even this kind of experience was less horrific than the most direct, physical encounter with Death: the burial of innumerable, often half-decomposed corpses. It was a mark of respect that, as will be clear by now, was not granted to every dead man.

## Burial in wartime

> What passing-bells for these who die as cattle?
> Only the monstrous anger of the guns.
> Only the stuttering rifles' rapid rattle
> Can patter out their hasty orisons.
> No mockeries now for them; no prayers nor bells,
> Nor any voice of mourning save the choirs, –
> The shrill, demented choirs of wailing shells;
> And bugles calling for them from sad shires.
>
> What candles may be held to speed them all?
> Not in the hands of boys, but in their eyes
> Shall shine the holy glimmers of good-byes.
> The pallor of girls' brows shall be their pall;
> Their flowers the tenderness of patient minds,
> And each slow dusk a drawing-down of blinds.
>
> Wilfred Owen, 'Anthem for Doomed Youth'

In war films the dead never seem to be buried. But war films are fictional. Burial is an extremely common wartime task. Indeed it is essential, both from a military point of view, since bodies attract pests and other sources of disease, and for humanitarian and psychological reasons. A reasonably civilized funeral is as important for soldiers and their families in wartime as for civilians in peacetime. It provides a crucial opportunity to reflect and remember.[326] It is doubtful, however, whether a civilized funeral can ever be offered in wartime, certainly in circumstances like those of 1914–18.

### *Bodies in hospital*

Men died not only in battle or under artillery fire but in hospital, and if there was a chance of a proper funeral anywhere, then it was here. In the base hospitals most of the dead will have been given some form of ceremony. Bagnold watched a stretcher being carried into a ward. She knew all too well what that meant and what was going on behind the curtains around the bed. 'I hear the shuffle of feet as

326 Holmes, *Firing Line*, 200

the men stand to attention, and the orderlies come out again, and the folds of the flag have ballooned up to receive and embrace a man's body.'[327]

Descriptions of hospitals and casualty clearing stations near the front line are couched in quite different terms. Stanhope Walker had to bury 900 men in three months at his own CCS alone. Little wonder that he regarded the 'moribund ward' as the most depressing place he knew. 'Two large tents laced together packed with dying officers and men, here they lie given up as hopeless, of course they do not know it.' Duhamel would have recognized the scene had he read Stanhope Walker's account. He wrote in similar terms about the hospital outbuildings, often more than one, that were used as mortuaries. The dead lay there 'side by side, their feet together, their hands crossed on their breasts, when indeed they still possessed hands and feet'. Sometimes, despite the heavy medical workload, there was time to give a man a fairly decent funeral, although the ceremony was never lengthy. 'The burial-ground is near. About a dozen of us follow the lantern, slipping in the mud, and stumbling over the graves. Here we are at the wall, and here is the long ditch, always open, which every day is prolonged a little to the right, and filled in a little to the left.' This in turn would have sounded familiar to Stanhope Walker. On 2 July 1916 he wrote of the dead that 'of course' they were buried in the 'trench we had prepared in a field adjoining'.[328]

Although Noyes writes rather cynically that with so many shell-holes around there was no need to dig burial pits, it was common practice for the dead at field hospitals to be buried in a single large grave in an improvised mass ceremony. Barthas more than once witnessed this kind of funeral.

> It was quickly done, quickly expedited, like a tiresome chore. The territorial troops ... dug a communal pit and then, to save space, they laid the coffins right next to each other, with a bit of earth to cover them, a small cross on top with a name and number, and that was it. And the team of territorial gravediggers worked on and on in a pit where the sun and a threatening storm made the air oppressive, since they had to make room for those who tomorrow, the day after, or the days after that would end up in this ominous ditch. ... Not far from our quarters three graveyards on the hillside displayed their long rows of little crosses. Every morning several unfortunates who had died at aid posts in neighbouring sectors were brought there. Nothing made for a sadder sight than an emaciated hag pulling an old cart with two, three, four bodies juddering on it, simply wrapped in muddy tarpaulins, legs in puttees and spattered boots sticking out the back, since the cart was too short. A padre in his greatcoat, accompanied by a soldier-seminarist, were following behind and constituted the only escort, along with three or four old territorials, pick and shovel over their shoulders,

327 Bagnold, *Diary Without Dates*, 25

328 Moynihan, *People at War*, 69, 72; Duhamel, *Vie des Martyrs*, 143, 226; Thomas, *Die Kartrin wird Soldat*, 290–91; Mierisch, *Kamerad Schwester*, 57

> transformed into gravediggers. This is how those whose fate is enviable, as we sing, are brought to the field of honour.[329]

Macdonald writes that this degenerated into a sickening, constantly repeated and monotonous ritual, especially during major battles. Several British padres were disinclined to comply with the clearly expressed wishes of the high command that they should always stress in their sermons that the British were fighting for the good of all humanity.[330]

Individual deaths passed unmarked. Shortly after New Year's Day 1915, Ernst Günther Schallert wrote to his parents in Germany that they had only two sons left. He had gone to visit his brother Helmuth in hospital, but the bed was empty and spread with clean sheets. He was told that his brother must be lying somewhere in the hospital cemetery, but no one knew where. Four months later, incidentally, Schallert's mother and father had only one son left.[331] If nothing else, the ceremonies that approximated funerals made clear that the distinction between officers and other ranks outlasted death. The coffins in which officers were laid to rest were made of seasoned timber rather than green, unseasoned wood.[332]

*Burial parties*

At the front line there was no opportunity, especially during an offensive, to go looking for good quality seasoned timber. The conditions of war meant that no individual attention could be given to burials. Men had to be buried nevertheless, so burial parties were put together to ensure that the corpses lying about, or the remains that passed for corpses,[333] were cleared away. If it could not be put off any longer, this was sometimes accomplished while battle raged, or it might take place months later, or during the night, after the signal 'all quiet' had been given. First the bodies were collected together. Barbusse saw the dead lined up 'on a patch of wasteland, dirty and sick, where the dried grass is mired with black mud'.

> They are brought here when the trenches and no man's land are emptied during the night. They are waiting – some have done so for a long time – until they are transported, again by night, to the cemeteries in the rear. ... A little further on a corpse has been brought in in such a state that, to avoid losing it on the way, they had to pile it on a wire rack which was afterwards fixed to the two ends of a stake. He was brought here in this metal hammock and left. You can't tell the top

329 Barthas, *Carnets*, 102, 237–41; Noyes, *Stretcher-Bearers*, 178
330 Macdonald, *Somme*, 85
331 Witkop, *Kriegsbriefe*, 74
332 Winter, *Death's Men*, 68–9
333 Holmes, *Riding the Retreat*, 58

> of this corpse from the bottom; all that can be recognized in the pile is a gaping trouser pocket.[334]

Some men brushed all this off, but few members of burial parties accepted their task with complete equanimity. The sights they saw and the things they were called upon to do could be gruesome in the extreme. As a cause of psychological problems, the work of burial parties was on a par with going into battle.[335] Barthas and his men were ordered to remove the oval disk that identified each corpse.

> Some wore it on their wrists, others round their necks, or it might be in their pockets. What a job! Groping, feeling the bodies and taking a knife or wire-cutters to cut the string or chain with the identification tag attached. It seemed like defilement and we spoke softly, as if we were afraid of waking them.[336]

After the war Ferdinand Bringolf committed his memories of burial parties to paper under the title *Das Grauen* (The Horror). Bringolf and several other young German soldiers had to clear the market square at Wytschaete near Ypres at midnight after the battle fought there in November 1914. In despair he dug pit after pit while his comrades dragged corpse after corpse towards him. Always two of them, one dead and one living, and Bringolf did not know 'who felt colder'.

> And always the first spadeful of earth fell onto the disfigured, once human face, always the second onto the clenched hands, until gradually what had once been a human being disappeared under lumps of earth – it was November after all. They brought a young, handsome captain with soft feminine hands as if made of wax, and with a Henry IV beard on his interesting pale face – what a shame that he'd lost the top half of his skull somewhere![337]

Graves called his war memoirs *Goodbye to All That*. Burials were one of the things he was glad to put behind him, although he had found the lugging of heavy gas cylinders just that bit more dreadful still.[338]

> Every night we went out to fetch in the dead of the other battalions. … After the first day or two the corpses swelled and stank. I vomited more than once while superintending the carrying. Those we could not get in from the German wire continued to swell until the wall of the stomach collapsed, either naturally or when punctured by a bullet; a disgusting smell would float across. The colour

334 Barbusse, *Le Feu*, 160–61; *Under Fire*, 136
335 Hyams, 'War Syndromes', 399
336 Barthas, *Carnets*, 184
337 Jünger, *Antlitz*, 13
338 Richter, *Chemical Soldiers*, 50

> of the dead faces changed from white to yellow-grey, to red, to purple, to green, to black, to slimy.[339]

Jünger too painted a sorry picture of the work of burial parties. On one occasion he and his comrades had to recover bodies from a bunker that had collapsed under shelling.

> We seized hold of the limbs sticking out from the wreckage, and pulled out the corpses. One man had lost his head, and the end of his torso was like a great sponge of blood. Splintered bones stuck out of the arm stump of the second, and his uniform was drenched with blood from a great wound in his chest. The intestines of the third were spilling out of his opened belly. As we pulled him out, a splintered piece of board caught in the wound with a hideous noise.[340]

Often the teams had to bury men who had been dead for some time. As if this were not disturbing enough, their bodies had usually been hit by artillery fire from both sides. As Horne says in his *Price of Glory*, the dead were 'quartered and re-quartered'. Some who saw the battlefield described it as strewn not with corpses but with body parts.[341] Lieutenant Paddy King said of his task shortly before the end of Third Ypres:

> It was an appalling job. Some had been lying there for months and the bodies were in an advanced state of decomposition; and some were so shattered that there was not much left. We did have occasions where you almost buried a man twice. In fact we must have done just that several times. There was one officer whose body we buried and then shortly after we found an arm with the same name on the back of a watch on the wrist. … If they had any identity discs, then we marked the grave – just put the remains in a sandbag, dug a small grave and buried him. … Where the bodies were so broken up or decomposed that we couldn't find an identity we just buried the man and put 'Unknown British Soldier' on the list. It was a terrible job. The smell was appalling and it was deeply depressing for the men. … [The battlefield] was utter desolation. There was nothing at all except huge craters, half the size of a room. They were full of water and the corpses were floating in them. Some with no heads. Some with no legs. They were very hard to identify. We managed about four in every ten. There were Germans among them. We didn't bury them. We hadn't been told to.[342]

---

339 Graves, *Goodbye*, 137

340 Jünger, *In Stahlgewittern*, 101; *Storm of Steel*, 136; Eksteins, *Rites of Spring*, 152

341 Horne, *Price of Glory*, 175; Andriessen, *De oorlogsbrieven van Unteroffizier Carl Heller*, 67

342 Macdonald, *Passchendaele*, 210–11

Cloete too had to clear away bodies that had lain in no man's land for a long time, at Serre on the Somme battlefield, for instance, after an attack 'by green, badly led troops who had had too big a rum ration, … against a strong position where the wire was still uncut'.

> As you lifted a body by its arms and legs, they detached themselves from the torso, and this was not the worst thing. Each body was covered inches deep with a black fur of flies, which flew up into your face, into your mouth, eyes and nostrils as you approached. The bodies crawled with maggots. There had been a disaster here. … [The soldiers] hung like washing on the barbs, like scarecrows who scared no crows since they were edible. The birds disputed the bodies with us. This was an awful job for all ranks. No one could expect the men to handle these bodies unless the officers did their share. We stopped every now and then to vomit. … The bodies had the consistency of Camembert cheese. I once fell and put my hand through the belly of a man. It was days before I got the smell out of my hands.[343]

The stench of corpses offered one important advantage: it was never hard for burial parties to find them at night.[344]

Of all those who put into words the revulsion they felt at the work of burial parties, which everyone regarded as essential, it is perhaps Hoffman whose account makes the deepest impression. In the summer of 1918 his regiment was sent to bury bodies that had lain in the July sun for three weeks. Worse, his men had been ordered to remove the identification tags from German dead who had been buried still wearing them. Having to dig up bodies made the work literally sickening, but the rules of war meant there was no alternative. The rules did not take account of the fact that fighting might be going on at the same time, Hoffman says. A cloud of gas came over and because of the stench of corpses no one noticed. The men were sweating from the hard labour in hot sunshine, which provided optimal conditions for mustard gas to do its work. Almost half the men in the company were poisoned so badly that they had to go to hospital. He writes that many died.[345]

First, however, they buried the decomposing bodies, a job that was not made any easier by the fact that they had stiffened as they decayed. The dead horses had to be buried too, and many of them had swollen to twice their already considerable size. Hoffman and his comrades got the job done as quickly as possible. 'Germans, French and Americans alike. Get them out of sight, but not out of memory. I can remember hundreds and hundreds of dead men. I would know them if I were to meet them in a hereafter.'[346]

---

343 Winter, *Death's Men*, 207–8
344 Audoin-Rouzeau, *Men at War*, 79
345 Fussell, *Bloody Game*, 178–9
346 Fussell, *Bloody Game*, 180

Unfortunately there were places where the composition of the ground made it extremely hard to dig a suitably deep hole. This plus *rigor mortis* might mean that a compromise solution had to be found. Sometimes it was impossible to straighten out a man who had died in a sitting position. Standing on the torso made the legs stick up in the air, and pushing down on the legs made the rest of the body sit up. There was no way to dig a grave deep enough to bury a body like that, so the legs would be left poking out of the ground. They could be used to make a cross. Sometimes a large man had to be buried in a small grave. The burial party would press on his belly or stand on it until he was squashed into a shape that would fit the hole.[347] Even Hoffman got used to this to some extent. At first he was terrified of the dead and hated having to touch them. Before long, however, he was able to bury 78 men in a morning and then eat his lunch without even washing his hands, although he could have done so had he wished.[348]

*No peace, no rest*

We may have good reason to feel sorry for those who had to bury the corpses, but those they buried will have imagined their funerals very differently. Under the circumstances there was no chance they might 'rest in peace', in fact they were not even allocated a 'final resting place'. For one thing, most of the graves were inevitably too shallow. This had some bizarre consequences. Toller wrote:

> Spring comes again. Grass grows on the soldiers' graves in the clearing in the wood. The graves were shallow, too shallow. Rain has washed away thc thin covering of earth from the feet of one dead soldier so that two coarse leather boots show above the soil in horrifying nakedness.'[349]

Rainfall sometimes caused sections of trench wall to collapse, revealing rows of dead from earlier battles,[350] or piles of bodies that had been used to raise the breastwork. On the Yser front the level of the groundwater made it almost impossible to bury anyone, so bodies were placed inside mounds of earth.[351] In other areas a trench occasionally had to be dug or a road laid across a patch of ground where men had been interred.[352]

Worst of all was the effect of artillery. It was impossible to make graves deep enough to prevent the bodies being dug up again by shelling, and men in shallow graves were all too likely to be exposed or worse. They might be buried, dug up

347 Fussell, *Bloody Game*, 182
348 Fussell, *Bloody Game*, 180–81
349 Toller, *Jugend in Deutschland*, 53
350 Jünger, *In Stahlgewittern*, 33
351 De Schaepdrijver, *De Groote Oorlog*, 176
352 Dearden, *Medicine and Duty*, 58

by artillery fire, reburied and dug up again several times over.[353] Often troops discovered at first light that the place where they had buried someone the previous day was now a shell-hole.[354]

Gürtler writes that a battlefield was little more than an enormous cemetery. Aside from shell-holes, torn clumps of trees and smashed farmhouses, there was nothing to be seen but countless little white crosses, 'in front of us, behind us, left and right', English and German, 'friend next to friend, enemy next to enemy'. He was irritated by lines in the newspapers such as: 'Peacefully they rest at the spot where they have bled and suffered ... and the guns thunder over their graves, avenging their heroic deaths.' It seemed the journalists could not get it into their heads that enemy guns also thundered, that shells landed among the graves, and that therefore the bones of the dead 'are mingled with the filth which they scatter to the four winds and that after a few weeks the muddy ground closes over the last resting-place of the soldier'.[355]

Lance-Corporal Ken Lovell lay in hospital troubled by his promise to tell a man's parents exactly how he had died. He particularly dreaded them asking him where their son was buried. 'We'd buried him all right, a few yards behind our position in the wood, with a rifle plunged into the earth to mark the grave and his tin hat on top of it. But by the next morning it had entirely disappeared.' Heller remembered a neatly maintained German cemetery. When he visited it again at the end of the war 'it was recognizable only by a few splintered crosses and bleached bones sticking half out of the ground here and there'.[356]

James Smith of the Cyclist Corps was ordered to bury his best friend Ernie Gays, and he described it as the hardest thing he had to do in the whole war. He remembered 'feeling a bit upset'. He had grown callous after seeing so much, but it was different when you had to bury a friend. The hole was only four feet deep and the area was continually churned up by shellfire, so he knew Ernie would probably not lie there for long. Indeed, Ernie Gays' grave does not merit the name of 'final resting place'. If his body was ever found, then it was not identified. His is among the tens of thousands of names of missing men engraved in marble at Tyne Cot cemetery near Ypres.[357]

This was no exception; it was the general rule. Herbert Jahn, who died at Verdun, wrote in a letter about a grave he had noticed with a simple wooden cross. The inscription was illegible, so no one could any longer tell who had been buried there. Had the man been a friend or foe? Did his family know where he lay? Did

353 Horne, *Price of Glory*, 175–6; Renn, *Krieg*, 327

354 Macdonald, *Somme*, 269

355 Witkop, *Kriegsbriefe*, 328–9; Macdonald, *1914–18*, 255

356 Macdonald, *Somme*, 297; Andriessen, *De oorlogsbrieven van Unteroffizier Carl Heller*, 220

357 Macdonald, *Passchendaele*, 161, 169

they even know he was dead? Soon no trace of the grave would be left and the dead man would have vanished for ever.[358]

Soldiers were not alone in being buried by men and dug up by shellfire. The old cemeteries of the villages and towns near the battlefields were no longer places of rest. In the late 1970s one Belgian woman, Pulcherie Demeulenaere, still remembered vividly that her mother had been buried only two hours before she and her coffin were blown into the air. German impressionist Max Beckman, who served as a nurse during the war, wrote to his first wife Minna:

> Yesterday we came through a cemetery which was completely ruined by shellfire. The tombs were ripped open, and the coffins lay around in awkward positions. The indiscreet shells had exposed the ladies and gentlemen to the light – bones, hair and clothing peeked out from the coffins.[359]

Soldiers found the violation of graves by industrial warfare distressing. The spiritual importance of a final resting place is clear from their reactions. On 19 February 1915 Gotthold von Rohden wrote: 'In the churchyard the crosses and gravestones are broken, even the dead have no peace under the earth; the graves are churned open to a great depth – at such places the entire misery of the war takes hold of you.'[360]

*Too many dead*

Those for whom someone at least tried to provide a burial, if only a temporary one, were in some sense lucky. The reality of war meant there was often no chance of a funeral. The dead might be unreachable, or there was no time to fetch them in, let alone to bury them. If we are to believe Lécluse, enemy dead were sometimes deliberately left on the battlefield as a warning to their comrades. If they were buried at all, then the bodies were thrown into hastily dug mass graves with crude wooden crosses on top.[361] The survivors had their hands full bringing in the wounded and could not make time for even a rapid, provisional burial.[362] The bodies that lay on the battlefield for days, weeks, even months, were yet another visible sign that the image of a romantic war so many soldiers had in mind at the start of the conflict bore no relation to the reality. Jünger admitted he had never imagined 'that in this war the dead would be left month after month to the mercy of wind and weather, as once the bodies on the gallows were'.[363]

358 Witkop, *Kriegsbriefe*, 140

359 *Van den Grooten Oorlog*, 35; Winter, *Sites of Memory*, 164–5

360 Witkop, *Kriegsbriefe*, 120; Eckart & Gradmann, *Die Medizin*, 177

361 Dyer, *Missing*, 12; Witkop, *Kriegsbriefe*, 191; Sandstrom, *Comrades-in-Arms*, 58; Rompkey & Riggs, *Your Daughter Fanny*, 120

362 Macdonald, *1914*, 381–2; Macdonald, *Somme*, 71

363 Hynes, *Soldiers' Tale*, 67

The sheer number of dead made it essential to improvise. On 22 October 1914, Flemish soldier Emiel Selschotter wrote in his diary that 'between the cedars in the graveyard' the dead had been laid in mass graves. From time to time use had been made of a large shell-hole or an abandoned trench. Lime was scattered over 'each layer'. German soldier Alfons Ankenbrand witnessed a 'parade of the dead' in Lens in March 1915, a month before he was granted his own improvised funeral. The dead were laid in a mass grave to the accompaniment of loud singing and cheers. At the front it was more usual for the dead to be flung out of the trenches, where they would lie exposed or gradually be covered in earth and liquid mud by the impact of shells.[364] Years after the war one man remembered seeing soldiers cursorily buried where they fell at Loos, many in the bottom of trenches. It had been impossible to do a proper job. Earth was simply laid on top of them and most of it had washed off again in the rain.

> You'd go along the trenches and you'd see a boot and puttee sticking out, or an arm or hand, sometimes faces. Not only would you see them, but you'd be walking on them, slipping and sliding. ... The stench was terrible because of all that rotting flesh.[365]

The impossibility of burying men promptly and properly meant that soldiers were continually confronted with putrefying bodies. Jünger was once walking around a stretch of land recently taken from the French when he suddenly found himself looking at a crouching corpse.

> Flesh like mouldering fish gleamed greenishly through splits in the shredded uniform. Turning round, I took a step back in horror: next to me a figure was crouched against a tree. It still had gleaming French leather harness, and on its back was a fully packed haversack, topped by a round mess-tin. Empty eye-sockets and a few strands of hair on the bluish-black skull indicated that the man was not among the living. There was another sitting down, slumped forward towards his feet, as though he had just collapsed. All around were dozens more, rotted, dried, stiffened to mummies, frozen in an eerie dance of death. The French must have spent months in the proximity of their fallen comrades, without burying them.[366]

Never were there so many unburied, decomposing corpses as after the First Battle of Ypres. Almost three years later, men fighting the Third Battle of Ypres still saw their remains, consisting mainly of boots, not yet rotten fragments of gold-braided

---

364 Ureel, *De Kleine Mens*, 47; Witkop, *Kriegsbriefe*, 54–5; Middlebrook, *First Day*, 249

365 Babington, *Shell-Shock*, 62; Bourke, *Dismembering the Male*, 215

366 Jünger, *In Stahlgewittern*, 16; *Storm of Steel*, 25

uniforms and 'broken fancy-dress helmets'.[367] Many of those not recovered had disappeared into the muddy soil or been hit so often by the continual shellfire that they had literally disappeared.

At Verdun the stench of putrefying bodies was one of the first things that struck each batch of fresh troops. It made them gasp for breath. One anonymous commentator said it even gave a kind of charm to the smell of gas. The British, who had always prided themselves on taking better care of dead comrades than their French allies did, were forced to admit that at Verdun it was not a question of failing to take the trouble to bury everyone but of being unable to. As with attempts to rescue the wounded from no man's land, it was fairly common for attempts at burying comrades to result simply in a greater number of corpses awaiting burial. A safer option was usually found. The dead might be wrapped in ground-sheets and rolled over the parapet of the trench into a nearby shell-hole. Horne writes that there were few craters 'in which did not float some ghastly, stinking fragment of humanity'.[368]

Sergeant Jack Cross explained that when there was a chance to bury the dead on the Somme, the men would be allocated different tasks. Some, and he was one, were detailed to collect the identification tags, others were responsible for collecting rifles and others the rest of the men's equipment, 'and then there was a band of stretcher-bearers who picked up these dead gentlemen and took them to the edge of this crater and tipped them over, rolled them down and they buried themselves in the chalk before they got to the bottom.'[369] Acting Corporal Ruper Wecber was one of those who took part in this kind of 'funeral'. There was no other way of doing it, he said.

> As far as you could see there were all these bodies lying out there – literally thousands of them, just where they'd been caught on the First of July. Some were without legs, some were legs without bodies, arms without bodies. A terrible sight. They'd been churned up by shells even after they were killed. We were just dumping them into the crater – just filling them over.[370]

After a while this same process of burial would start all over again. The bodies slowly sank, by the weight of their numbers, into the crumbling chalk.[371]

Weeks after the slaughter of 1 July 1916 the dead, many already partially decomposed, still lay on the battlefield, some covered by the bodies of men who had advanced behind them. Eventually an entire battalion was sent out as a burial

---

367 Macdonald, *Passchendaele*, 229; Holmes, *Firing Line*, 179
368 Horne, *Price of Glory*, 175
369 Macdonald, *Somme*, 113; Jünger, *In Stahlgewittern*, 127
370 Macdonald, *Somme*, 114
371 Macdonald, *Somme*, 114

party, and some of its members were killed as they worked.[372] The word 'burial' barely seems appropriate. Corporal Joe Hoyles described the experience.

> There was a terrific smell. It was so awful it nearly poisoned you. A smell of rotten flesh. The old German front line was covered with bodies – they were seven and eight deep and they had all gone black. The smell! ... Colonel Pinney got hold of some stretchers and our job was to put the bodies on them and, with a man at each end, we *threw* them into the crater. There must have been over a thousand bodies there. I don't know how many we buried. I'll never forget that sight. Bodies all over the place. I'll never forget it. I was only eighteen, but I thought, 'There's something wrong here!'[373]

Bodies had weight and volume, and the advantages of this did not pass unnoticed. Corpses were used to repair the walls of trenches damaged by shelling; they even served to fill holes in roads essential for military traffic. During Third Ypres, driver J. McPherson admitted there was nothing to be done about the dead,

> and there were so many bodies about that you got callous about it. All that time, before the push in September, I was up and down the Menin Road, up and down, up and down, taking ammunition on the backs of horses and mules up to the dump. They had to keep the Menin Road open, because it was the only way you could get up to that sector with horses and limbers, and it was shelled day and night. ... They filled [the shell-holes] up with anything. If a limber got a shell and was blown to pieces they just shovelled everything into the crater and covered it over, dead horses, dead bodies, bits of limber – anything to fill it up and cover it over and keep the traffic going.[374]

The problem with such improvised burial methods was that the military authorities later had to try to identify the bodies, if they could find them at all. It was a difficult and unpleasant job. In mid-November 1914, Lord Killanin was part of a group charged with identifying the dead of early September. The months that had elapsed meant the men could no longer be identified even by their hair or teeth. The conditions to which they had been exposed made it a grim and hopeless task. 'The faces were quite unrecognisable, often smashed, and were all thickly coated with clay and blood.'[375]

Cremation was an option, of course, at least for enemy dead. Philip Gibbs walked across the battlefield of the Marne in the autumn of 1914 accompanied by a member of a burial party and spotted several funeral pyres close to piles of

---

372 Macdonald, *Somme*, 110–14
373 Macdonald, *Somme*, 113
374 Macdonald, *Passchendaele*, 169
375 Holmes, *Riding the Retreat*, 268

German dead. '"See there", he said, "they take some time to burn." He spoke in a matter of fact way, like a gardener pointing to a bonfire of autumn leaves.'[376]

There were some bodies that could not be either buried or burned, since they had been blasted into inaccessible places. General Frank Crozier met a soldier holding a leg. When he asked whose it was, the man answered laconically, 'Rifleman Broderick's, Sir.' When he asked where Rifleman Broderick was, he was told: 'Up there, Sir' The man pointed to the top of a tree. 'There sure enough is the torn trunk of a man fixed securely in the branches of a shell-stripped oak. A high-explosive shell has recently shot him up to the sky and landed him in mid-air above and out of the reach of his comrades.'[377]

After the war a considerable amount of time passed before the dead were truly given a chance to 'rest in peace'. The French in particular were troubled by the question of what to do with the bodies. The British contemplated the problem of transporting hundreds of thousands of corpses across the channel. They decided instead to lay them to rest close to where they had died. The Germans made the same decision, or rather the decision was taken for them by the victors. The French simply could not make up their minds. Burial close to the battleground? Exhumation for burial at home? And where was home? Should they be returned to wives or girlfriends if they had them, or to their parents? This did not always amount to the same thing. After several years a decision was finally made: repatriation on request, in which case the remains would be returned to the parents, while the rest of the dead would be collected and interred in communal cemeteries. This huge task was accompanied by persistent rumours about scandalous conduct. Bodies were said to have been dragged hither and thither before being dumped unceremoniously in mass graves, others were said to have been robbed. There were even rumours about contractors who had received payment for corpses they had never laid eyes on, let alone moved.[378]

The British dead were laid in intensively maintained cemeteries, below interminable rows of white gravestones. German soldiers received rather less careful treatment. Wooden crosses compulsorily smeared with tar – to represent the 'blackness' of the German soul – marked the places where the dead were thrown together. When the French government offered several years later to replace the crosses with white tombstones, the German War Graves Commission, which had been allowed to take over the task of caring for German war cemeteries in 1926, withheld permission. It had come to realize that the tarred crosses the enemy had vindictively obliged it to use actually gave the cemeteries the sober and subdued character appropriate to places intended to evoke quiet remembrance.[379]

In short, the dead were a problem that had to be solved, from both a humanitarian and a military point of view, but for which no obvious solution existed. From time

376 Winter & Baggett, *1914–18*, 85
377 Terraine, 'Inferno', 185
378 Whalen, *Bitter Wounds*, 185
379 Heijster, *Ieper*, 162–3; Audoin-Rouzeau & Becker, *'14–'18*, 256

to time the problem had been anticipated. During the Battle of the Somme, prior to a renewed attack in November 1916, Surfleet came upon freshly dug graves. They were intended for the men who would inevitably fall. 'If that is not callous, I don't know what is.'[380]

380 Wilson, *Myriad Faces*, 360; Bourke, *Dismembering the Male*, 214; see also: Dorgelès, *Croix de bois*, 279–82

# Afterword

After weapons were laid down, the dead could finally be counted and properly interred, a job that was still unfinished at the end of the 1920s, with the French continuing to hand over to the British an average of 40 bodies a week.[1] All sides were still taking stock of the living. Some 20 million soldiers were seriously wounded in the war and around 8 million had returned home disabled for life.

Roughly 6,000,000 children never saw their fathers again, while about 3,000,000 more watched them come home only to die.[2] In Britain in 1929, 2,414,000 men were in receipt of some form of war pension or allowance, 40 per cent of all those who had served. They included over 25,000 rheumatics, 65,000 hospitalized neurotics and almost 10,000 men who had lost an arm. The vast majority had 'ailments of indeterminate nature and origin'. Innumerable other long-term casualties had either been refused pensions or had declined to apply. This was not entirely the fault of a parsimonious government. Many men were unable to prove to sometimes absurdly rigid or frankly unfair doctors, trained and paid by the authorities to examine them, that their physical or mental problems were connected with the war, while others declared themselves fit and healthy simply so they could leave the army and the war behind them.[3]

Strict policies of this kind – France for example made no payments at all to the mentally ill – were due not to thrift and rigidity alone but at least in part to financial constraints. Germany, needing somehow to make reparations payments, was particularly hard up and developed a highly regulated pensions policy as a result. (The Germans were forced to relinquish control of the Bayer chemicals firm, for instance, along with the company's patent on acetylsalicylic acid and the trade name used to market it: Aspirin.) Here too the neurotics, known as *Kriegszitterer* or 'war tremblers', were worst off, finding it almost impossible to get pensions. In 1926 they were declared ineligible. Several doctors claimed this had a beneficial effect on them, and some categorized neurotics as perpetrators rather than victims by speaking of them in the same breath as Jews, Marxists and Anarchists, whose 'stab in the back' was blamed for the German defeat. Nevertheless, war pensions cost the Weimar Republic billions of marks. Almost ten per cent of German society was reliant on pensions and at least a third of the financial resources of the Weimar government were tied up in pension funds. The insoluble problem of war pensions is undoubtedly one of the factors at the root of the tragic history of Weimar, from

1 Winter & Baggett, *1914–18*, 364; Brants & Brants, *Velden van weleer*, 28–30

2 Cohen, 'Will to Work', 295

3 Winter, *Death's Men*, 252; Whalen, *Bitter Wounds*, 55–6, 136, 163–5; Bourke, 'Effeminacy, ethnicity and the end of trauma', 63

which one party in particular benefited. Many war invalids cheered the Führer in 1933. The Nazi regime certainly succeeded in bringing pensions expenditure under control, although it would have fallen at almost the same rate had events been left to run their natural course, and six years after taking power the regime began adding to the problem again. Moreover, although the Nazi movement showcased its war invalids before the *Machtsübernahme*, calling them pearls of the fatherland, it cut back on their share of the budget considerably after January 1933. Once again war neurotics bore the brunt. Those who were in receipt of financial support saw their allowances reduced. Some even became victims of the sterilization programme.[4]

Tragically, the driving force behind Germany's National Association of Disabled Soldiers and Veterans was a Social Democrat, Erich Kuttner. He was forced to flee the country in 1933, after the new regime was brought to power with the help of men whose struggles he had supported for so many years. He moved to the Netherlands, where he was arrested during the Nazi occupation. He was taken to a concentration camp and executed in 1942.[5] Another tragic aspect was that the Weimar Republic, compared to Britain for example, had done a great deal for disabled soldiers, despite all its financial problems, yet most German war veterans turned their backs on the republic, whereas British ex-servicemen expressed little hostility towards their government. Ironically, this was because in Germany, unlike Britain, the care of disabled veterans was seen as the job of the state. In the second half of the 1920s the Weimar Republic paid out around twenty per cent of its gross domestic product in war pensions. In Britain payments amounted to about seven per cent of GDP. As Deborah Cohen has shown, rather than expressing the anger they felt towards the government of the republic directly, disabled German veterans focused their resentment on their healthy fellow citizens, who appeared not to care about them, showed no respect for what they had done for the fatherland, and had even started to envy the 'privileged' position given to war invalids by a range of state policies. The British tended instead to regard support for the casualties of war as a task for charitable institutions. Care provided and financed by benevolent citizens helped ensure that no widespread anger was directed at the government by British ex-servicemen.[6]

In late 1918 the whole of Europe was in mourning. There were some parts of the continent where, relatively speaking, the losses were less severe, but whole regions found themselves with barely any men in their twenties. In Britain the hard-hit Pals Battalions left huge demographic gaps. In early 1916 German soldier Friedel Dehme noted that of his class at secondary school, eight had already been

4 Whalen, *Bitter Wounds*, 16–17, 104–5, 132, 141, 143, 148–9, 156, 168, 178–9; Shepard, *War of Nerves*, 152; Lerner, 'Psychiatry and Casualties of War', 28; Neuner, *State Insurance*, 12–13

5 Whalen, *Bitter Wounds*, 121–4, 191

6 Cohen, 'Will to Work', passim; Cohen, *The War Come Home*, passim, esp.: 3, 7–9, 12

killed. At least one more would follow.[7] Historian Arnold Toynbee had photographs on his mantelpiece showing six young men in uniform. They had been his best friends at university in 1914. None had survived the war.

In the belligerent countries there was hardly a single family that did not have at least one loss to mourn, and it was at the level of the family and of personal relationships that the pain was hardest to bear. Of course there were parents who had lost none of their sons, but there were others who had lost all or almost all. For them the war would never end. The well-to-do Cawleys, for instance, found themselves with only one of four sons left by the time the war was over. The famous Goodyear family from Newfoundland lost three sons as well, and the two who remained were seriously wounded. Vera Brittain lost her fiancé and her brother, while Arthur Conan Doyle lost his son, brother and brother-in-law.

All those named here with the exception of Dehme were lucky in their way. Either they had the talent required to express their grief in words or they were famous enough for their sufferings to be chronicled by others. The death of Wilfred Owen remained in the thoughts of the nation while the individual deaths of millions of other young men did not, and the post-war sufferings of workers and farmers were soon forgotten, although no one would suggest they were any less terrible than those of the Goodyears and Conan Doyles. There was the misery of 630,000 French widows, for instance, many of them young, and a million fatherless French children, a substantial number born after their fathers left for the front, and the sufferings of millions like them in the other belligerent nations. If they received a pension at all then it was a mere pittance, and it was not adjusted when prices rose, a particular problem in Germany with its hyperinflation. In fact German inflation was inextricably linked to the problem of war pensions. Mental institutions were flooded with people unable to overcome their grief. In Britain, Kate Claydon, mother of two children, failed to recover from her husband's death in 1918. Shortly after the war she suffered a nervous breakdown. She died in an asylum 56 years later.[8]

Men too continued to suffer after 11 November 1918. Some found it impossible to settle back into the lives they had left years before. German ex-servicemen returned to a bankrupt society, so it was even harder for them than for their French and British counterparts to find their feet as civilians. Invalids were everywhere, many abandoned to their fate. Honoured in parades, they were soon forgotten in everyday life, times being hard even for the fit and untroubled. Many died of wounds inflicted during the war, or of health problems arising from them.

7 Witkop, *Kriegsbriefe*, 246; Winter & Baggett, *1914–18*, 175–8; Wilson, *Myriad Faces*, 327

8 Winter, *Death's Men*, 255, 259, 263; Holmes, *Riding the Retreat*, 258; Simkins, *World War I*, 217; Gilbert, *First World War*, xvi–xvii; Winter & Baggett, *1914–18*, 10, 15, 127, 382–5; Wilson, *Myriad Faces*, 677; Winter, *Sites of Memory*, 2, 46–7, 58; Winter & Sivan, *War and Remembrance*, 44–6; Whalen, *Bitter Wounds*, 74–6, 95, 105; Keegan, *First World War*, 343; Runia, *Waterloo Verdun Auschwitz*, 134; Shepard, *War of Nerves*, 152

Kathleen Gibbs' fiancé, for instance, suffered lung damage in a gas attack. He died of tuberculosis in 1922.[9] She was no exception. Hundreds of thousands of parents, wives, sons, daughters, friends and girlfriends watched helplessly as the men they loved lost their battle with physical wounds.[10] Others succumbed to psychological afflictions brought home from the war, often exacerbated by their long separation from those dear to them, and committed suicide.[11]

Post-war suffering is not represented in the many cemeteries, some on a monumental scale, that are scattered across the countryside of Belgium and France, but these places have successfully immortalized the sorrows of the war itself. For British fatalities alone there are 1,665 graveyards in France and 385 in Belgium. Chiselled into the Menin Gate at Ypres are the names of 54,896 officers and men who vanished for ever in the surrounding area in the years up to 15 August 1917. When the Germans occupied Ypres in 1940, the monument was only just nearing completion. In Tyne Cot cemetery are the names of 34,888 officers and other ranks who went missing near Ypres between 15 August 1917 and Armistice Day. At Thiepval stands a vast monument to the 73,412 British soldiers who went over the top on the Somme and of whom no identifiable trace was ever found.[12]

In one graveyard, however, post-war suffering, civilian suffering, is starkly evident. In Germany after the war, a small group of leftwing intellectuals fiercely opposed the soldier cult, with its veneration of youth and glorification of death. Toller and others set out to 'deheroicize' death. They campaigned against the idea that death was something a man should long for on the grounds that the death of an individual meant the community would live, saying that sacrifice on the 'altar of the fatherland' was not heroic, it was senseless. Käthe Kollwitz, whose eighteen-year-old son Peter had been killed in the Battle of the Yser at the beginning of the war, was receptive to their protest. In those early months she had still been in thrall to the glorification of youth and was therefore quite unlike the anti-war militant she later became. Yet even before her son was killed she had begun to have doubts that verged on abhorrence. Her personal loss increased those doubts: 'There is in our lives a wound which will never heal. Nor should it.'

Her sorrow and rebellion inspired a sculpture of a man and a woman that was erected at the Roggenveld cemetery in Esen, where her son was buried. It portrays a grieving father and mother, with no image of a soldier to accompany them – although that had been her original intention when she began the work in the early stages of grief – let alone an image of martial glory. The sculpture was the product of great inner torment, of her search for a way to express all she felt, of her struggles with a sense that her ripening pacifist convictions amounted to a betrayal of her dead son and his ideals, and of a belief that had slowly grown within her that

9 Macdonald, *1914–1918*, 332; Winter, *Sites of Memory*, 45–6; Whalen, *Bitter Wounds*, 113

10 Gilbert, *First World War*, 541

11 Winter & Baggett, *1914–18*, 371

12 Simkins, *World War I*, 219; Gilbert, *First World War*, xvii

only through a work of art could his death and those of so many others like him be given any meaning. His loss had not been a sacrifice; he had died for nothing. She became convinced that it was not she who had betrayed her son and all those other young men who had been killed, and with them the ideals they had held and that she regarded as misplaced, no, they had been betrayed by the people who put those ideals into their heads in the first place. It was a painful process, but when it was over she was able to visualize the form into which she would pour all her grief, and by 1932 it was finished: two parents, on their knees, begging their son's forgiveness for failing to hold back the madness called war, which had cost him his life. Ten years later, in 1942, she produced another major work with a similar anti-war message, a drawing of a despairing mother embracing her children, entitled *Saatfrüchte sollen nicht vermahlen werden*, Seed Corn Must Not Be Ground.

A year after Kollwitz completed her sculpture, which would be moved from Esen to Vladslo in 1956 along with all the graves, a regime came to power in her country that would revive the soldier cult in a more virulent form than ever. Her 1942 drawing can be interpreted as a scream uttered in the face of cold, invincible power. By then the new great *Vermahlen* had been underway for several years, and her drawing was inspired by the fact that it had claimed the life of another Peter Kollwitz, this time her grandson.[13]

13 Winter & Baggett, *1914–18*, 9, 387–91; Winter & Sivan, *War and Remembrance*, 56–9; Vondung, *Kriegserlebnis*, 266–70; Holmes & De Vos, *Langs de Velden van Eer*, 105; Cardinal, *Women's Writing*, 123–5

# Bibliography

**Primary literature (memoirs, diaries, novels, published sources)**


Alverdes, Paul, *Die Pfeiferstube*, Postdam 1940 (orig. 1929)

Andriessen, J.H.J. (ed.), *De oorlogsbrieven van Unteroffizier Carl Heller. Geschreven tijdens de Eerste Wereldoorlog*, Soesterberg 2003

Backer, Franz de, 'Longinus', in: A.G. Chistiaens (ed.), *De Grote Oorlog. Novellen over 1914–1918*, Louvain 1994 (3) (orig. 1934), pp. 7–52

Bagnold, Enid, *A Diary Without Dates*, London 1978 (orig. 1918)

Barbusse, Henri, *Le Feu. Journal d'une escouade*, Paris 1916

Barthas, Louis, *Les carnets de guerre de Louis Barthas, tonnelier 1914–1918*, Paris 1983

Binding, Rudolf G., *Aus dem Kriege*, Frankfurt aM 1925

Bloch, Johann von, (Ivan), *Die Unmöglichkeit, den Verwundeten auf dem Schlachtfelde Hilfe zu bringen. Nach Angaben des russischen Werkes: Der Krieg*, Berlin 1899

Blunden, Edmund, *Undertones of War*, London 1982 (3)

Borden, Mary, 'The Forbidden Zone', in: Margaret R. Higonnet (ed.), *Nurses at the Front. Writing the wounds of the Great War*, Boston 2001, pp. 79–161

Brants, Chrisje (ed.), *Een plasje bloed in het zand. Literaire getuigenissen van de Grote Oorlog*, Amsterdam 1995

Brittain, Vera, *Testament of Youth*, Glasgow 1978 (6)

——, *Chronicle of Youth*, London 2000

Bruyne, Inge De, (ed.), *We zullen ze krijgen! Brancardiers aan het IJzerfront. 1914–1918*, Louvain 2007

Campion Vaughan, Edwin, *Some Desperate Glory*, London/Edinburgh 1982 (2)

Cardinal, Agnès, Dorothy Goldman & Judith Hattaway, *Women's Writing on the First World War*, Oxford 2002

Céline, Louis-Ferdinand, *Voyage au bout de la nuit. Suivi de: Mort à crédit*, Paris 1962

Collingwood, R.G., *An Autobiography*, Oxford 1978 (orig. 1939)

Cummings, E.E., *The Enormous Room*, New York 1970 (orig. 1922) introd.: Robert Graves

'Dames van het Roode Kruis. De', *Tijdschrift voor Ziekenverpleging*, 1916, pp. 328–9

Day Lewis, C., *The Collected Poems of Wilfred Owen. With a memoir by Edmund Blunden*, London 1963

Dearden, Harold, *Medicine and Duty. A war diary*, London 1928

Dieren, E. van, *Over den Oorlog*, Amsterdam 1915

Dorgelès, Roland, *Les croix de bois*, Paris 1919

Duhamel, Georges, *Vie des Martyrs*, Paris 1922 (orig. 1917)

——, *Civilisation 1914–1917*, Paris 1929 (73rd edn)

[Dunn, J.C.], *The War the Infantry Knew 1914–1919. A chronicle of service in France*, London 1993 (orig. 1938)

Erzberger, M., *Erlebnisse im Weltkrieg*, Berlin 1920

Fitzgerald, F. Scott, *Tender is the Night*, New York 1962 (orig. 1933)

Flusser, Emil, *Oorlog als Ziekte*, Amsterdam 1938

Frank, Leonhard, *Der Mensch ist Gut*, Zürich 1918 (6–15 thousand)

Frey, A.M., *Die Pflasterkästen*, Berlin 1929

Fussell, Paul (ed.), *The Bloody Game. An anthology of modern warfare*, London 1992 (2)

Graf, Oskar Maria, *Wir sind Gefangene*, Munich 1978 (orig. 1926)

Graves, Robert, *Goodbye to All That*, London 1960 (orig. 1929)

Guéno, Jean-Pierre, & Yves Laplume (eds), *Paroles de Poilus. Lettres et carnets du front 1914–1918*, Paris 2004

Haas, M. (ed.), *Van Oorlogsjammer en Vredeszegen. Bloemlezing*, Bolsward n.d. (approx. 1930)

Haffner, Sebastian, *Geschichte eines Deutschen. Die Erinnerungen 1914–1933*, Munich, 2002 (orig. 2000)

Heering, G.J., *De zondeval van het Christendom. Een studie over christendom, staat en oorlog*, Arnhem 1933 (3)

Herbert, A.P., *The Secret Battle*, Oxford 1982 (1919)

Higonnet, *Lines of Fire. Women writers of World War I*, London 1999

Hoche, A., *Vom Sterben. Kriegsvortrag gehalten in der Universität am 6. November 1918*, Jena 1919

Innes, T.A. & Ivor Castle, *Covenants with Death*, London 1934

*J'accuse. Von einem Deutschen*, Lausanne 1915

Johannsen, Ernst, *Vier von der Infanterie. Ihre letzten Tage an der Westfront 1918*, Hamburg 1929

Joules, H., *The Doctor's View of War*, London 1938

Jünger, Ernst, *In Stahlgewittern. Aus dem Tagebuch eines Stoßtruppenführers*, Berlin 1922 (4)

—— (ed.), *Das Antlitz des Weltkrieges. Fronterlebnisse deutscher Soldaten*, Berlin 1930

Kammelar, Rob, Jacques Sicking & Menno Wielinga, *De Eerste Wereldoorlog door Nederlandse ogen. Getuigenissen – verhalen – betogen*, Amsterdam 2007

Köppen, Edlef, *Heeresbericht*, Berlin 1930

*Kriegsbriefe gefallener Deutscher Juden*, Stuttgart 1961 (orig. 1935)

Kuiper, Taco, 'Voordracht over zenuwverwondingen in den oorlog', in: *Militair Geneeskundig Tijdschrift*, 1916, pp. 91–105

Lanschot Hubrecht, Jeanne C. van, 'Burgerdienstplicht', in: *Nosokómos*, 26–6–1918, pp. 406–9

Lanz, Otto, *De Oorlogswinst der Heelkunde. Rede uitgesproken op de Dies Natalis der Universiteit van Amsterdam 8 januari 1925 door den rector magnificus*, n.p., n.d.
Latzko, Andreas, *Friedensgericht*, Zurich 1918
——, *Menschen im Krieg*, Zurich 1918
Launoy, Jane de, *Oorlogsverpleegster in Bevolen Dienst*, Gent 2000
[Lemercier, Eugène E.], *Lettres d'un soldat*, Paris 1918
Lessing, Theodor, 'Das Lazarett', in: Idem, *Ich warf eine Flaschenpost im Eismeer der Geschichte*, Darmstadt 1986, pp. 354–86
Lintier, Paul, *Ons Kanon. Herinneringen van een artillerist 1914*, Amsterdam z.d.
——, *Ma pièce. Avec une Batterie de 75. Souvenirs d'un canonnier 1914*, Paris 1916
——, *Le tube 1233. Souvenirs d'un chef de pièce 1915–1916*, Paris 1917
Manning, Frederic, *Her Privates We*, London 1986 (orig. 1929)
Marc, Franz, *Brieven van het Front*, Zeist 1987
March, William, *Company K*, New York 1975 (orig. 1930)
Mierisch, Helene, *Kamerad Schwester 1914–1918*, Leipzig 1934
Motte, Ellen N. La, *The Backwash of War. The human wreckage of the battlefield as witnessed by an American hospital nurse*, London 1916
Moynihan, Michael (ed.), *People at War 1914–1918. Their own account of the conflict in the trenches, in the air and at the sea*, Devon 1973
Myers, Charles M., *Shell Shock in France 1914–18. Based on a war diary*, Cambridge 1940
Noyes, Frederick W., *Stretcher-Bearers ... At the Double! History of the Fifth Canadian Field Ambulance which served overseas during the Great War 1914–1918*, n.p., n.d. [1935]
Overbeek, H.J., 'Oorlogspsychosen en verwondingen van het zenuwstelsel', in: *Militair Geneeskundig Tijdschrift*, 1915, pp. 209–16
Panke-Kochinke, Birgit, & Monika Schaidhammer-Placke, *Frontschwestern und Friedensengeln. Kriegskrankenpflege im Ersten und Zweiten Weltkrieg. Ein Quellen- und Fotoband*, Frankfurt am Main 2002
Pflugk-Harttung, Elfriede (ed.), *Frontschwestern – Ein deutsches Ehrenbuch*, Berlin 1936
Remarque, Erich Maria, *Im Westen nichts neues*, Frankfurt a/M 1983 (orig. 1929)
Renn, Ludwig, *Krieg*, Frankfurt a/M, 1929 (61.–80.000)
Riemann, Henriette, *Schwester der Vierten Armee*, Berlin 1930
Rompkey, Bill & Bert Riggs (eds), *Your Daughter Fanny. The war letters of Frances Cluett, VAD*, St. John's 2006
Sandstrom, Roy E. (ed.), *Comrades-in-Arms. The World War I memoir of Captain Henry de Lécluse, the Count of Trévöedal*, Kent (Ohio)/London 1998
Sassoon, Siegfried, *The Complete Memoirs of George Sherston*, London/Boston 1972
Sauerbruch, Ferdinand, *Das war mein Leben*, Bad Würishofen 1951

Schaepdrijver, Karel de & Julius Charpentier, *Vlaanderens Weezang aan den IJzer*, n.p., n.d. [approx. 1918]
Smits, Frans, 'Het huis der smart', in: A.G. Chistiaens (ed.), *De Grote Oorlog. Novellen over 1914–1918*, Louvain 1994 (3) (orig. 1920), pp. 229–58
Soesman, F.J., *Oorlogspsychose*, The Hague 1915
Stuiveling, Garmt (ed.), *Het Vraagstuk van de Vrede*, Baarn 1930
Thomas, Adrienne, *Die Katrin wird Soldat. Ein Roman aus Elsass-Lotharingen*, Amsterdam 1938
Tienhoven, A. van, *De Gruwelen van den Oorlog in Servië*, Rotterdam 1915
Toller, Ernst, *Jugend in Deutschland*, Reinbek 1984 (orig. 1933)
Trumbo, Dalton, *Johnny Got His Gun*, London 1999 (orig. 1939)
Ureel, Lut (ed.), *De Kleine Mens in de Grote Oorlog. Getuigenissen van twee generaties dorpsonderwijzers uit de frontstreek*, Tielt/Weesp 1984
*Van den Grooten oorlog*. Volksboek, Kemmel n.d. (1978)
*Vlaamsche Ziel. Brieven van het Yser-front, De*, Amsterdam 1918
Voorbeijtel, M.C.M., *Van Veerkracht en Heldenmoed aan en achter het Fransche Front*, Amsterdam n.d.
'Why I Returned my Croix de Guerre', in: *The World Tomorrow*, November 1928, pp. 440–43
Witkop, Philipp (ed.), *Kriegsbriefe gefallener Studenten*, Munich 1933 (2)
Zuckmayer, Carl, *Als wär's ein Stück von mir. Horen der Freundschaft*, Vienna 1967 (2)
Zweig, Stefan, *Die Welt von Gestern. Erinnerungen eines Europäers*, Frankfurt a/M 1974 (orig. 1944)

**Quotations from literary works in translation have been taken from the following:**

Barbusse, Henri, *Under Fire* (*Le Feu*), translated by Robin Buss, Penguin Books, London, 2003 (2). Reproduced by permission of Penguin Books Ltd.
Céline, Louis-Ferdinand, *Journey to the End of the Night (Voyage au bout de la Nuit)*, translated by Ralph Manheim, Calder Publications Ltd, London 2004 (3)
Duhamel, Georges, *The New Book of Martyrs* (*Vie des Martyrs*), translated by Florence Simmonds, George H. Doran Company, New York 1918
——, *Civilisation 1914–1917* (*Civilisation 1914–1917*), translated by E.S. Brooks, The Century Company, New York, 1919
[Grelling, Richard], *J'Accuse. By a German* (*J'accuse. Von einem Deutschen*), translated by Alexander Gray, Hodder and Stoughton, London 1915
Jünger, Ernst, *Storm of Steel (In Stahlgewittern)*, translated by Michael Hofmann, Penguin Books, London, 2004 (1) (First published by Allen Lane 2003). Reproduced by permission of Penguin Books Ltd.

Remarque, Erich Maria, *All Quiet on the Western Front (Im Westen nichts Neues)*, translated by Brian Murdoch, Vintage, London 1996 (First published by Jonathan Cape Ltd, 1994)

## Secondary literature

Addison, Paul & Angus Calder (eds), *Time to Kill. The soldier's experience of War in the West 1939–1945*, London 1997

Ashworth, Tony, *Trench Warfare 1914–1918. The live and let live-system*, London 1980

Audoin-Rouzeau, Stéphane, *Men at War 1914–1918. National sentiment and trench journalism in France during the First World War*, Oxford 1992

——, *Les combattants des tranchées 14–18*, Paris, 1986

—— & Annette Becker, *14–'18. De Grote Oorlog opnieuw bezien*, Amsterdam 2004

Babington, Anthony, *For the Sake of Example. Capital courts martial 1914–18*, London 1985 (2)

——, *Shell-Shock. A history of the changing attitudes to war neurosis*, London 1997

Bamji, Andrew, *The Queen's Hospital, Sidcup: Physical and psychological rehabilitation after facial injury, 1917–1925*, Sidcup 1998 (unpubl. ms.)

Barham, Peter, *Forgotten Lunatics of the Great War*, London 2004

Barker, Pat, *Regeneration*, London 1992

Barry, John M., *The Great Influenza. The epic story of the deadliest plague in history*, London 2004

Bastier, J., 'België tijdens de Eerste Wereldoorlog', in: *Algemene Geschiedenis der Nederlanden*, Gouda 1958, Deel XII, pp. 1–52

Bartov, Omer, 'Industrial killing: World War I, the Holocaust, and representation', http://www.anti-rev.org/textes/Bartov97a/

Bergen, Leo van, *'Zo bezien mag men toch niet van een mislukking spreken'. Hoe in Nederland en Indonesië de geweldloze bevrijdingsstrijd van M.K. Gandhi beoordeeld werd, tussen 1920 en 1965*, Zwolle 1987

——, *Waarde Generaal: Voelt u zich wel goed? Geneeskunde, leger, oorlog en vrede*, Nijmegen 1991

——, *De Zwaargewonden Eerst? Het Nederlandsche Roode Kruis en het vraagstuk van oorlog en vrede 1867–1945*, Rotterdam 1994

——, 'De oorlog als spiegel. Militaire psychiatrie en oorlog als gekte', in: *'t Kan Anders*, April/May 1996, pp. 3–5

——, 'Met te weinig riemen in een gammel bootje. Militaire geneeskunde en de beide wereldoorlogen', in: *Geschiedenis der Geneeskunde*, 5, nr. 3 (Jan 1999), pp. 192–200

——, 'The Value of War for Medicine: questions and considerations concerning an often endorsed proposition', in: *Medicine, Conflict and Survival*, 23, nr. 3 (Aug 2007), pp. 189–97

——, '"Blijdschap op het slagveld!" De militarisering van de medische zorg en van het Rode Kruis', in: Patrick Dassen & Petra Groen, *Van de Barricaden naar de Loopgraven. Oorlog en samenleving in Europa 1789–1918*, Amsterdam 2008, pp. 167–98

——, '80,000 British shell shock victims, a rarely questioned number', in: http://www.wereldoorlog1418.nl/shell-shock/index.html

Billstein, Heinrich, 'Gashölle Ypern', in: Christine Beil et al., *Der Erste Weltkrieg*, Hamburg 2006, pp. 97–129

Binneveld, Hans, *Om de geest van Jan Soldaat. Beknopte geschiedenis van de militaire psychiatrie*, Rotterdam 1995

——, 'Herstel op bevel. Beknopte geschiedenis van de militaire psychiatrie', in: H.M. van der Ploeg & J.M.P. Weerts (eds), *Veteranen in Nederland*, Lisse 1995, pp. 63–76

——, 'Nederland en de oorlogsneurosen', in: Hans Binneveld et al. (eds), *Leven naast de catastrofe. Nederland tijdens de Eerste Wereldoorlog*, Hilversum 2001, pp. 37–49

——, 'Shell Shock Versus Trouble Nerveux', in: Hans Andriessen et al. (eds), *De Grote Oorlog. Kroniek 1914–1918*, deel 3, Soesterberg 2003, pp. 54–71

——, 'Beter worden op bevel. De psychisch gewonde soldaat en het ontstaan van de militaire psychiatrie', in: *Kleio*, 2007, 8 (Dec 2007), pp. 30–33

Bleker, Johanna & Heinz-Peter Schmiedebach (eds), *Medizin und Krieg. Vom Dilemma der Heilberufe 1865 bis 1985*, Frankfurt a/M 1987

—— & Norbert Jachertz (eds), *Medizin im 'Dritten Reich'*, Keulen 1993 (2)

Boterman, Frits, 'Oorlog als bron van zuiverheid. Ernst Jünger's conservatieve revolutie', in: Rob van der Laarse et al. (eds), *De Hang naar Zuiverheid*, Amsterdam 1998, pp. 251–83

Bourke, Joanna, *Dismembering the Male. Men's bodies, Britain and the Great War*, London 1996

——, *The Moral Economy of Guilt: pain, pleasure and trauma in the narratives of British servicemen, 1914–1918*, London 1998 (unpubl. ms.)

——, *An Intimate History of Killing. Face-to-face killing in twentieth-century warfare*, London 1999

——, 'Effeminacy, ethnicity, and the end of trauma: the sufferings of "shell-shocked" men in Great Britain and Ireland, 1914–39', in: *Journal of Contemporary History*, vol. 35, nr. 1 (Jan 2000), pp. 57–69

——, *Fear. A cultural history*, London 2005

Brants, Chrisje & Kees Brants, 'Inleiding', in: *De Oorlogsdagboeken van Louis Barthas [tonnenmaker] 1914–1918*, Amsterdam 1988

——, *Velden van weleer*, Amsterdam 1995 (4)

Brown, Malcolm, *Somme*, London 1996

Browning, Christopher R., *Doodgewone mannen. Een vergeten hoofdstuk uit de jodenvervolging*, Amsterdam 1993

Brusse, Peter, 'De grootste plaag sinds de pest', in: *de Volkskrant*, 19–1–1998, p. 6

Busfield, Joan, 'Class and Gender in Twentieth-Century British psychiatry: shell-shock and psychopathic disorder', in: Jonathan Andrews & Ann Digby (eds), *Sex and Seclusion, Class and Custody*, Amsterdam/New York 2003, pp. 295–322

Busse, Helmut, *Soldaten ohne Waffen. Zur Geschichte des Sanitätswesens*, Berg am See 1990

Byerly, Carol R., *Fever of War. The influenza epidemic in the U.S. army during World War I*, New York/London 2005

Chickering, Roger, *Imperial Germany and the Great War, 1914–1918*, Cambridge 1998

Chielens, Piet, 'Bekrachtigd, genoteerd, uitgevoerd. "Shot at dawn": Britse executies tijdens WOI', in: *DS Magazine*, 12-11-1993, pp. 7–9

——, 'De normen van de tijd. Over de appreciatie van executies en "lafaards" in de Eerste Wereldoorlog', in: Hans Andriessen et al. (eds), *De Grote Oorlog. Kroniek 1914–1918*. deel 2, Soesterberg 2003, pp. 218–37

Cocks, Geoffrey, *Psychotherapy in the Third Reich. The Göring Institute*, Oxford 1985

Cohen, Deborah, 'Will to Work: Disabled Veterans in Britain and Germany after the First World War', in: David A. Gerber (ed.), *Disabled Veterans in History*, Michigan 2000, pp. 295–321

——, *The War Come Home. Disabled veterans in Britain and Germany, 1914–1939*, Los Angeles/London 2001

Conzelmann, Otto, *Der andere Dix*, Stuttgart 1983

Cooter, Roger, 'War and Modern Medicine', in: W. Bynum & R. Porter (eds), *Companion Encyclopedia of the History of Medicine*, London 1993, pp. 1536–72

——, 'Of War and Epidemics: unnatural couplings, problematic conceptions', in: *Social History of Medicine*, 16 (2003), nr. 2, pp. 283–302

Cooter, Roger, Mark Harrison & Steve Sturdy (eds), *War, Medicine and Modernity*, Phoenix Mill 1999

——, *Medicine and Modern Warfare*, Amsterdam/Atlanta 1999

Crofton, Eileen, *The Women of Royaumont. A Scottish women's hospital on the western front*, East Lothian 1999

Dallas, Gloden & Douglas Gill, *The Unknown Army. Mutinies in the British army in World War I*, London 1985

Dassen, Patrick, 'Radicalisering, polarisatie en totale oorlog. De Eerste Wereldoorlog als splijtzwam voor Duitsland', in: Patrick Dassen & Petra Groen (eds), *Van de barricaden naar de loopgraven. Oorlog en samenleving in Europa, 1789–1918*, Amsterdam 2008, pp. 237–84

Davidson, Roger & Lesley A. Hall (eds), *Sex, Sin and Suffering. Venereal disease and European society since 1870*, London/New York 2001

Dean, Eric T. Jr, *Shook over Hell. Post Traumatic Stress, Vietnam, and the Civil War*, London 1999

Dolev, Eran, *Allenby's Military Medicine. Life and death in World War I Palestine*, London/New York 2007

Dunk, H.W. von der, *Voorbij de Verboden Drempel. De shoah in ons geschiedbeeld*, Amsterdam 1999 (5)

Dunning, A.J., 'Het soldatenhart', in: Idem, *Uitersten. Beschouwingen over menselijk gedrag*, Amsterdam 1990, pp. 46–58

Dyer, Geoff, *The Missing of the Somme*, London 1994

Eckart, Wolfgang U., 'Kriegsgewalt und Psychotrauma im Ersten Weltkrieg', in: Günter Seidler & Wolfgang U. Eckart, *Verletzte Seelen. Möglichkeiten und Perspektiven einer historischen Traumaforschung*, Giessen 2005, pp. 85–105

——, 'Eiskalt mit Würgen und Schlucken. Körperliches und seelisches Trauma in der deutschen Kriegsliteratur, 1914–1939. Eine Übersicht', in: *Trauma & Gewalt*, 3, 2007, pp. 2–15

—— & Christoph Gradmann (eds), *Die Medizin und der Erste Weltkrieg*, Pfaffenweiler 1996

—— & Christoph Gradmann, 'Medizin', in: Gerhard Hirschfeld, Gerd Krumeich & Irina Renz (eds), *Enzyklopädie Erster Weltkrieg*, Paderborn/Munich/Vienna/Zürich 2003, pp. 210–19

Eijkelboom, J., *De War Poets. Engelstalige gedichten over de Eerste en Tweede Wereldoorlog*, Sliedrecht 2002

Eksteins, Modris, *Rites of Spring. The Great War and the birth of the modern age*, New York/London 1989

Ellis, John, *Eye-Deep in Hell. Trench warfare in World War I*, Baltimore 1976

——, *The Social History of the Machine Gun*, London 1976

Evrard, E., J. Mathieu et al., *Asklepios onder de Wapenen. 500 jaar militaire geneeskunde in België*, Brussels 1997

Fabi, Lucio, 'Der alltägliche Krieg', in: Idem, (ed.), *La Guerra in Salotto/Der Krieg im Salon*, Udine 1999, pp. 78–88

Farrar-Hockley, A.H., *The Somme*, London 1964

Feenstra, Gerbrand, 'Spaanse griep kwam eigenlijk uit het Oosten', in: *de Volkskrant*, 24-4-1999, Wetenschap, p. 1

Ferguson, Niall, *The Pity of War*, London 1999

Fussell, Paul, *The Great War and Modern Memory*, Oxford 1977

Friedländer, Saul, *Nazi-Duitsland en de Joden. Deel 1: De jaren van vervolging 1933–1939*, Utrecht 1998

Gabriel, Richard A. & Karen S. Metz, *A History of Military Medicine*, London 1992, part II: From the Renaissance through modern times

Gammage, Bill, *The Broken Years*, Victoria 1975 (6) (orig. 1974)

Garrison, Fielding H., *Notes on the History of Military Medicine*, New York 1970 (2)

Gersons, Berthold, 'Posttraumatische stressstoornis: de geschiedenis van een recent begrip', in: *Maandblad Geestelijke Volksgezondheid*, 45 (1990), nr. 9, pp. 891–909

Gevaert, F. & F. Hubrechtsen, *Oostende 14–18. Deel 2*, Koksijde 1996

Gibelli, Antonio, *Schell Shock et Grande Guerre: l'experience des combatants*, n.p. 1998 (unpubl. ms.)

Gijswijt-Hofstra, Marijke & Roy Porter, *Cultures of Neurasthenia. From Beard to the First World War*, Amsterdam/New York 2001

Gilbert, Martin, *First World War*, London 1994

Gillespie, R.D., *Psychological Effects of War on Citizen and Soldier*, New York 1942

Gooijer, A.C. de, *De Spaanse Griep van '18. De epidemie die meer dan 20.000.000 levens eiste*, Amsterdam 1978

Glover, Jonathan, *Humanity. A moral history of the twentieth century*, London 2001

Haeseker, Barend, *Dr. J.F.S. Esser and his Contributions to Plastic and Reconstructive Surgery*, Rotterdam 1983

Hardy, Anne, '"Straight Back to Barbarism": Antityphoid inoculation and the Great War, 1914', in: *Bulletin for the History of Medicine*, 74 (2000), pp. 265–90

Harrison, Mark, 'The Medicalization of War – The Militarization of Medicine. Review article', in: *Social History of Medicine*, 1996, pp. 267–76

Heeckeren, Pauline van, '"Die Vorstellung ist alles". Psychiatrische behandeling van Duitse soldaten met oorlogsneurose, 1914–1918', in: Hans Andriessen et al. (red.), *De Grote Oorlog. Kroniek 1914–1918. 6*, Soesterberg 2004, pp. 9–111

Heijster, Richard, *Ieper 14/18*, Tielt 1998

Hendryckx, Michiel, 'In het spoor van de Grote Oorlog. Beelden van Nieuwpoort tot Compiègne', in: *DS Magazine*, 12-11-1993, pp. 2–6

Hermans, Hubertien & Sonja Schmidt, 'De traumatische neurose. Een sociaal-historische verkenning', in: *Amsterdams Sociologisch Tijdschrift*, 23, nr. 3 (Dec 1996), pp. 525–50

Herrman, David G., *The Arming of Europe and the Making of the First World War*, Princeton 1996

Heyman, Neil M., *World War I*, London 1997

Higonnet, Margaret Randolph, 'Introduction', in: Margaret R. Higonnet (ed.), *Nurses at the Front. Writing the wounds of the Great War*, Boston 2001, pp. vii–xxxviii

Higonnet, Margaret Randolph et al. (eds), *Behind the Lines. Gender and the two world wars*, New Haven/London 1987

Hirschfeld, Gerhard, 'Let op, Levensgevaar', in: *Spiegel Special 1. Über den 1. Weltkrieg und die Folgen*, 2004, pp. 64–5

Hirschfeld, Hans Magnus, *Sittengeschichte des 1. Weltkrieges*, Hanau n.d. (1978. Reprint second, rewritten, edition 1965)

——, *Sittengeschichte des Weltkrieges. Ergänzungsheft*, Vienna 1931

Hofman, Jaap, 'Oorlog aan het thuisfront', in: Hans Andriessen et al. (eds), *De Grote Oorlog. Kroniek 1914–1918. Deel 1: Essays over de Eerste Wereldoorlog*, Soesterberg 2002, pp. 362–70
Holmes, Richard, *Firing Line*, London 1994 (2)
——, *Riding the Retreat. Mons to the Marne – 1914 revisited*, London 1996 (2)
——, *War Walks. From Agincourt to Normandy*, London 1997 (2)
—— & Luc de Vos, *Langs de Velden van Eer. Wandelingen langs slagvelden*, Weert/Antwerp 1998
Horne, Alistair, *The Price of Glory. Verdun 1916*, London 1993 (3)
Howorth, P., *Shell-Shock and Psychiatry*, n.p. 1998 (unpubl. ms.)
Hulst, Wim van de & Koen Koch, *Ooggetuigen van de Eerste Wereldoorlog*, Amsterdam 2004
Hutchinson, John F., *Champions of Charity. War and the rise of the Red Cross*, Oxford/Boulder 1996
Hyams, Kenneth C. et al., 'War Syndromes and their Evaluation: From the U.S. Civil War to the Persian Gulf War', in: *Annals of Internal Medicine*, 125, nr. 5 (1–9–1996), pp. 398–405
Hynes, Samuel, *The Soldiers' Tale. Bearing witness to modern war*, London 1997
'Jahrhundert der Kriege, Das: Der Erste Weltkrieg', in: *Der Spiegel*, 1999, nr. 3, pp. 101–21
Jenssen, Christian, 'Medicine Against War', in: Ilkka Taipale et al. (eds), *War or Health? A reader*, London et al. 2002, pp. 8–29
Johnson, Nuala C., 'The Spectacle of Memory: Ireland's remembrance of the Great War, 1919', in: *Journal of Historical Geography*, 25, nr. 1 (Jan. 1999), pp. 36–56
Johnson, Niall P.A.S. & Juergen Mueller, 'Updating the Accounts: Global mortality of the 1918–1920 "Spanish" Influenza pandemic', in: *Bulletin of the History of Medicine*, jrg, 76 (2002), pp. 105–15
Jones, Edgar & Simon Wessely, 'War Syndromes: the impact on medically unexplained symptoms', in: *Medical History*, jrg. 49 (2005), pp. 55–78
——, *Shell Shock to PTSD: military psychiatry from 1900 to the Gulf War*, New York 2005
Kater, Michael H., *Doctors under Hitler*, Chapel Hill/London 1989
Kaufmann, Doris, 'Science as Cultural Practice: psychiatry in the First World War and Weimar Germany', in: *Journal of Contemporary History*, vol. 34, 1 (Jan 1999), pp. 125–44
Keegan, John, *The Face of Battle. A study of Agincourt, Waterloo and the Somme*, London 1992 (3)
——, *A History of Warfare*, London 1993
——, *The First World War*, London 1998
Kester, Bernadette, 'Het (on)gewapend oog', in: *Tijdschrift voor Mediageschiedenis*, 1 (1998), nr. 0, pp. 5–25
Kielich, Wolf, 'De grote schande', in: *Revue*, 25–7–1964, pp. 20–32

Klee, Ernst, *Auschwitz, die NS-Medizin und ihre Opfer*, Frankfurt a/M. 1997

Koch, Koen, 'Het begin van de barbarij', in: *de Volkskrant*, 22–6–1996, Het Vervolg, p. 7

——, 'Einde aan de onschuld', in: *De Groene Amsterdammer*, 24 May 2003, http://www.groene.nl/2003/0321/kk_essay.html, pp. 1–7

Koch, Peter-Ferdinand, *Menschenversuche. Die tödliche Experimente deutscher Aerzte*, Munich 1996

Kolata, Gina, *Griep. Het verhaal van de grote influenza epidemie van 1918 en de zoektocht naar het dodelijke virus*, Amsterdam 2000

Langford, Christopher, 'The Age Pattern of Mortality in the 1918–19 Influenza Pandemic: an attempted explanation based on data for England and Wales', in: *Medical History*, 46, nr. 1 (Jan 2002), pp. 1–20

Lebrook, Leonard, *Almroth Wright. Provocative doctor and thinker*, London 1954

Leclerq, Th.H.L., *Het informatiebureau van het Nederlandsche Roode Kruis en zijne werkzaamheden in verband met den oorlog 1914–1918*, The Hague 1924

Leed, Eric, *No Man's Land. Combat & identity in World War I*, Cambridge 1979

——, *Shell Shock*, n.p. 1998 (unpubl. ms.)

——, 'Fateful Memories: Industrialized War and Traumatic Neuroses', in: *Journal of Contemporary History*, Vol. 35, No. 1, Special Issue: Shell-Shock. (Jan 2000), pp. 85–100

Lefebvre, Jacques-Henri, *Die Hölle von Verdun. Nach den berichten von Frontkämpfern*, Verdun 1997

Lengwiler, Martin, *Zwischen Klinik und Kaserne. Die Geschichte der Militärpsychiatrie in Deutschland und der Schweiz 1870–1914*, Zurich 2000

Lerner, Paul, *Hysterical Men: War, memory and German mental medicine, 1914–1926*, n.p. 1998 (unpubl. ms.)

——, 'Psychiatry and Casualties of War in Germany, 1914–18', in: *Journal of Contemporary History*, vol. 35, nr. 1 (Jan 2000), pp. 13–28

——, *Hysterical Men. War, psychiatry, and the politics of trauma in Germany, 1890–1930*, London 2003

Levy, Howard, 'The Military Medicinemen', in: John Ehrenreich (ed.), *The Cultural Crisis of Modern Medicine*, London 1978, pp. 287–300

Lichtenstein, Heiner, *Angepaßt und treu ergeben. Das Rote Kreuz im 'Dritten Reich'*, Cologne 1988

Liddle, Peter, *The 1916 Battle of the Somme*, Ware 2001

—— (ed.), *Passchendaele in Perspective: the 3rd battle of Ypres*, Barnsley 1997

—— & Hugh Cecil (eds), *Facing Armageddon. The First World War experienced*, London 1996

——, *At the Eleventh Hour. Reflections, hopes and anxieties at the closing of the Great War*, London 1998

Lifton, Robert Jay, *The Nazi Doctors. Medical killing and the psychology of genocide*, New York 1986

Linton, Derek S., 'The Obscure Object of Knowledge: German Military Medicine confronts Gas Gangrene during World War I', in: *Bulletin for the History of Medicine*, 74 (2000), pp. 291–316

——, 'Was Typhoid Inoculation Safe and Effective during World War I? Debates within German Military Medicine', in: *Journal of the History of Medicine and allied sciences*, 55, 2 (April 2000), pp. 101–33

Löffler, Fritz, *Otto Dix 1891–1969. Oeuvre der Gemälde*, Recklinghausen 1981

Lupton, Deborah, *Medicine as Culture: illness, disease and the body in Western societies*, London 2003

Macdonald, Lyn, 1914. *The Days of Hope*, London 1989 (2)

——, 1915. *The Death of Innocence*, London 1994 (2)

——, *Somme*, London 1993 (2)

——, *They Called it Passchendaele*, London 1978

——, *To the Last Man. Spring 1918*, London 1998

——, *The Roses of No Man's Land*, London 1984

——, *1914–1918. Voices and Images of the Great War*, London 1988

Marix Evans, Martin, *The Battles of the Somme*, London 1996

——, *1918. The Year of Victories*, London 2002

Meire, Johan, *De Stilte van de Salient. De herinnering aan de Eerste Wereldoorlog rond Ieper*, Tielt 2003

Micale, Mark S. & Paul Lerner (eds), *Traumatic Pasts. History, psychiatry, and trauma in the modern age, 1870–1930*, Cambridge 2001

Middlebrook, Martin, *The First Day on the Somme*, London 2001

Moeyes, Paul, *Siegfried Sassoon: scorched glory. A critical study*, Amsterdam 1993

——, *Buiten Schot 1914–1918. Nederland tijdens de Eerste Wereldoorlog*, Amsterdam/Antwerp 2001

Moorehead, Caroline, *Dunant's Dream. War, Switzerland and the history of the Red Cross*, London 1998

Mosse, George L., *Fallen Soldiers. Reshaping the memory of the world wars*, New York 1990

——, *Shell Shock as a social disease¸lecture Peronne 3 July 1998* (unpubl. Man.)

Munck, Luc de, *De Grote Moeder in de Grote Oorlog. De hulpverlening van het Rode Kruis tijdens de Eerste Wereldoorlog*, Ypres n.d. (2001)

Murray, Williamson A., 'The West at war', in: Geoffrey Parker (ed.), *The Cambridge Illustrated History of Warfare*, Cambridge 1995, pp. 266–97

Neelissen, Ton, *Het Tomeloze Leven van Johannes Esser. Grondlegger van de plastische chirurgie*, n.p. 2002

Neuner, Stephanie, *State Insurance and Welfare Policy for "War Neurotics" of WWI. Politics and psychiatry in Germany, c. 1920–1939*, n.p. 2006 (unpubl. ms.)

Nys, Liesbeth, 'De grote school van de natie. Legerartsen over drankmisbruik en geslachtsziekten in het Belgisch leger (circa 1850–1950)', in: *Bijdragen en Mededelingen Geschiedenis der Nederlanden*, 115 (2000), pp. 392–425

Oltheten, Fons, 'Voorwoord', in: A.P. Herbert, *De Verborgen Strijd*, Bodegraven 2006, p. 7–15

Otterspeer, Willem, 'Wetenschap en wereldvrede', in: Idem, *Utopieën van een Onvermoeibaar Mens*, Amsterdam 1996, pp. 92–110

Payne, David, 'British medical casualties on the Western Front in the Great War. Part 1: Dealing with wound related trauma', in: *Stand To!*, nr. 82 (Aug–Sep 2008), pp. 25–30

Pelis, Kim, 'Taking Credit: The Canadian Army Medical Corps and the British conversion to blood transfusion in WWI', in: *Journal of the History of Medicine and allied sciences*, 56 (2001), pp. 238–77

Perry, Heather R., 'Re-Arming the Disabled Veteran', in: Katherine Ott, David Serlin & Stephen Mihm (eds), *Artificial Parts, Practical Lives. Modern histories of prosthetics*, New York/London 2003, pp. 75–101

Petri, Stefan J., *Eignungsprüfung, Characteranalyse, Soldatentum. Veränderung der Wissenschafts- und Methodenauffassung in der Militärpsychologie des Deutschen Reiches, Großbritanniens und der USA 1914 bis 1945*, Groningen 2004

Preston, Paul, 'The Great Civil War. European Politics 1914–1945', in: T.C.W. Blanning (ed.), *The Oxford Illustrated History of Modern Europe*, Oxford 1996, pp. 148–81

Prior, Robin & Trevor Wilson, *Passchendaele. The untold story*, London 1996

Putkowski, Julian & Julian Sykes, *Shot at Dawn*, London 1989

Raamsdonk, Wouter van, 'De secretaris van de soldaten. Georges Duhamel en de Grote Oorlog', in: *Streven*, Feb 2004, pp. 123–32

——, 'Nawoord', in: Georges Duhamel, *Civilisatie 1914–1917. Arts aan het front van WOI*, Amsterdam 2007, pp. 191–203

Reznick, Jeffrey S., 'Work Therapy and the Disabled British Soldier in Great Britain in the First World War: The Case of Shepherd's Bush Military Hospital', in: David A. Gerber (ed.), *Disabled Veterans in History*, Michigan 2000, pp. 185–203

Richter, Donald, *Chemical Soldiers. British gas warfare in World War One*, London 1997

Riedesser, Peter & Axel Verderber, *Aufrüstung der Seelen. Militärpsychologie und Militärpsychiatrie in Deutschland und Amerika*, Freiburg 1985

Riesenberger, Dieter, *Für Humanität in Krieg und Frieden. Das Internationale Rote Kreuz 1863–1977*, Göttingen 1992

Riet, A. van 't, *August Bier en de homeopathie*, Eindhoven 1978

Roodt, E. de, 'Britse en Duitse krijgsgevangenen in Nederland. Uitwisseling en internering tijdens de Eerste Wereldoorlog', in: *Militaire Spectator*, 168, nr. 1 (Jan 1999), pp. 40–53

——, *Onsterfelijke Fronten. Duitse schrijvers in de loopgraven van de Eerste Wereldoorlog*, Soesterberg 2005

'Rotz und Milzbrand', in: *Der Spiegel*, 1998, nr. 30 (20 July), p. 55

Roudebush, Marc, 'A Patient Fights Back: Neurology in the court of public opinion', in: *Journal of Contemporary History*, vol. 35, nr. 1 (Jan 2000), pp. 29–38

Runia, Eelco, *Waterloo Verdun Auschwitz. De liquidatie van het verleden*, Amsterdam 1999

Ruprecht, T.M. & C. Jenssen (eds), *Äskulap oder Mars? Aerzte gegen den Krieg*, Bremen 1991

Russell, E., *War and Nature. Fighting humans and insects with chemicals from World War I to Silent Spring*, Cambridge 2001

Schaepdrijver, Sophie de, *De Groote Oorlog. Het Koninkrijk België tijdens de Eerste Wereldoorlog*, Antwerp/Amsterdam 1997

——, *Taferelen uit het Burgerleven*, Antwerp/Amsterdam 2002

Sauerteig, Lutz, 'Etische Richtlinien, Patientenrechte und ärztliches Verhalten bei der Arzneimittelerprobung', in: *Medizin Historisches Journal*, 35 (2000), pp. 303–34

Schepens, L., 'België in de Eerste Wereldoorlog', in: *Algemene Geschiedenis der Nederlanden*, Haarlem 1979, part 14: Nederland en België 1914–1940, pp. 19–39

Schmidt, Ulf, *Karl Brandt: The Nazi Doctor. Medicine and power in the Third Reich*, London/New York 2008

Schrep, Bruno, 'Gebrochen an Leib und Seele', in: *Spiegel Special 1. Über den 1. Weltkrieg und die Folgen*, 2004, pp. 58–60

Shepard, Ben, 'The Early Treatment of Mental Disorders', in: G. Berrios & H. Freeman (eds), *150 Years of British Psychiatry, 1841–1991* (Vol. 2), London 1996, pp. 434–64

——, 'Shell-Shock', in: H. Freeman (ed.), *A Century of Psychiatry*, London 1999, pp. 33–40

——, *A War of Nerves. Soldiers and psychiatrists 1914–1994*, London 2000

——, 'The Nerve Doctors', in: *Oxford Today*, July 2000, pp. 16–17

Shortridge, Kennedy F., 'The 1918 "Spanish" flu: pearls from swine?', in: *Nature Medicine*, 5, nr. 4 (April 1999), pp. 384–5

Simkins, Peter, *World War I – The Western Front*, Godalming 1991

Smith, Leonard V., Stéphane Audoin-Rouzeau & Annette Becker, *France and the Great War, 1914–1918*, Cambridge 2003

Spoor, Ronald, 'Tegen de Hollandse kleingeestigheid. De brieven van Alexander Cohen', in: *Historisch Nieuwsblad*, Sept. 1996, pp. 28–31

Steiner, Petra, 'Selbstdeutungen und Missdeutungen von Frauen an der Front. Literatur von und über Krankenschwestern im Ersten Weltkrieg', http://www.kritische-ausgabe.de/hefte/krieg/steiner.pdf

Strachan, Hew, 'Military Modernization 1789–1918', in: T.C.W. Blanning (ed.), *The Oxford Illustrated History of Modern Europe*, Oxford 1996, pp. 69–93

Summers, Anne, *Angels and Citizens*, London 1988

Taipale, Ilkka, 'German Physicians against War since 1870', in: *Medicine and War*, 6 (1990), pp. 269–74

Tattersfield, David, 'Discipline in the BEF. An analysis of executions in British Divisions 1914–1918', in: *Stand To!*, nr. 82 (Aug.–Sept. 2008), pp. 12–16

Terraine, John A., 'The Inferno: 1914–18', in: Theo Barker (ed.), *The Long March of Everyman*, Middlesex 1978 (2), pp. 167–99

Townshend, Charles (ed.), *The Oxford Illustrated History of Modern War*, Oxford 1997

Tuchman, Barbara, *The Guns of August*, New York, 1994 (orig. 1962)

Tucker, Spencer C., *The European Powers in the First World War. An encyclopedia*, New York/London 1996

Verdoorn, J.A., *Arts en Oorlog. Medische en sociale zorg voor militaire oorlogsslachtoffers in de geschiedenis van Europa*, Rotterdam 1995 (2)

Verhey, Jeffrey, *The Spirit of 1914. Militarism, myth and mobilization in Germany*, Cambridge 2000

*Vluchten voor de Groote Oorlog. Belgen in Nederland 1914–1918*, Amsterdam 1988

Vondung, Klaus, (ed.), *Kriegserlebnis. Der Erste Weltkrieg in der literarischen Gestaltung und symbolischen Deutung der Nationen*, Göttingen 1980

Vos, Luc de, *De Eerste Wereldoorlog*, Louvain n.d. (3)

——, et al., *Van Gifgas tot Penicilline. Vooruitgang door oorlog?*, Louvain 1995

Vugs, Reinout, *In veel huizen wordt gerouwd. De Spaanse griep in Nederland*, Soesterberg 2002

Weerdt, Denise de, *De Vrouwen van de Eerste Wereldoorlog*, Gent n.d.

Weindling, Paul, *Health, Race and German Politics between national unification and Nazism 1870–1945*, Cambridge 1991 (2)

Weltman, John J., *World Politics and the Evolution of War*, London 1995

Werth, German, *Verdun. Die Schlacht und der Mythos*, Bergisch Gladbach 1982

Wesseling, H.L., *Soldaat en Krijger. Franse opvattingen over leger en oorlog aan de vooravond van de Eerste Wereldoorlog*, Amsterdam 1988

Wessely, Simon, 'The Life and Death of Private Harry Farr', in: *Journal of the Royal Society of Medicine*, Sept. 2006, 440–43

Whalen, Robert Weldon, *Bitter Wounds. German victims of the Great War, 1914–1939*, London 1984

Whitehead, Ian R., *Doctors in the Great War*, London 1999

Wilbrink, Maurice, '"Moeder, geen enkele jongen uit Grosvenor leeft nog". De verschrikkingen van de Eerste Wereldoorlog begonnen 75 jaar geleden', in: *Leeuwarder Courant*, 12-8-1989, Zaterdagse bijlage S&S, p. 7

Wilson, Trevor, *The Myriad Faces of War. Britain and the Great War 1914–1918*, Oxford 1986

Winter, Denis, *Death's Men. Soldiers of the Great War*, London 1979 (2)

Winter, Jay, *Sites of Memory, Sites of Mourning. The Great War in European cultural history*, Cambridge 1997 (2)

——, 'Shell-Shock and the Cultural History of the Great War', in: *Journal of Contemporary History*, vol. 35, nr. 1 (Jan. 2000), pp. 7–11

—— & Blaine Baggett, *1914–18. The Great War and the shaping of the 20th century*, London 1996

—— & Emmanuel Sivan (eds), *War and Remembrance in the Twentieth Century*, Cambridge 2000

Winters, V.M.E., *Oorlog en Heelkunde. Bijdrage tot de kennis der oorlogschirurgie*, Amsterdam 1931

——, *Staal tegen Staal. De oorlogs-chirurgie van de oudste tijden tot heden*, Utrecht 1939

Withuis, Jolande, 'Het oplappen van soldaten. De Eerste Wereldoorlog en de veranderende opvattingen aangaande de behandeling van oorlogstraumata', in: *ICODO-Info*, 1997, 2, pp. 85–93

Young, Allan, *The Harmony of Illusions. Inventing post-traumatic stress disorder*, Princeton 1995

# Index